LANGUAGE ARTS
PROCESS, PRODUCT, AND ASSESSMENT

SECOND EDITION

Pamela J. Farris
Northern Illinois University

Brown & Benchmark
PUBLISHERS

Madison, WI Dubuque Guilford, CT Chicago Toronto London
Mexico City Caracas Buenos Aires Madrid Bogotá Sydney

Book Team

Executive Publisher *Edgar J. Laube*
Managing Editor *Sue Pulvermacher-Alt*
Developmental Editor *Suzanne M. Guinn*
Production Editor *Terry Routley*
Designer *Jamie O'Neal*
Proofreading Coordinator *Carrie Barker*
Art Processor *Miriam Hoffman*
Photo Editor *Rose Deluhery*
Visual Editor *Rachel Imsland*
Production Manager *Beth Kundert*
Production/Costing Manager *Sherry Padden*
Production/Imaging and Media Development Manager *Linda Meehan Avenarius*
Visuals/Design Freelance Specialist *Mary L. Christianson*
Marketing Manager *Amy Halloran*
Copywriter *Jennifer Smith*
Proofreader *Mary Svetlik Anderson*

Basal Text *10/12 Garamond Book*
Display Type *Garamond Bold Italic*
Typesetting System *FrameMaker*
Paper Stock *45# Restorecote*

Brown & Benchmark
P U B L I S H E R S

Executive Vice President and General Manager *Bob McLaughlin*
Vice President, Business Manager *Russ Domeyer*
Vice President of Production and New Media Development *Victoria Putman*
National Sales Manager *Phil Rudder*
National Telesales Director *John Finn*

A Times Mirror Company

Cover design by Lesiak/Crampton Design, Inc.

Cover photograph © Tony Freeman/PhotoEdit

Copyedited by Erin Falligant; proofread by Ann M. Kelly

Library of Congress Catalog Card Number: 95-83394

ISBN 0-697-24135-1

Printed in the United States of America by Times Mirror Higher Education Group, Inc.
2460 Kerper Boulevard, Dubuque, IA 52001

10 9 8 7 6 5 4 3 2 1

D e d i c a t i o n

To Dick and Kurtis,

who provided encouragement, support, patience, and love

Contents

Preface xiii

Chapter 1 *Children and Teachers in the Classroom 1*
Introduction   2
Children and Their Teachers 3
Children and Their World 6
Effective Teaching 8
   Summary 19
   Questions 19
   Activities 19
   For Further Reading 20
   References 20

Chapter 2 *Teaching the Language Arts 21*
Introduction   22
**Historical Overview of the Teaching
   of the Language Arts 24**
The Language Arts 27
      Speaking 27
      Writing 27
      Listening 29
      Reading 30
Interdisciplinary Instruction 31
Assessing the Language Arts 32
Multicultural Considerations 35
Meeting the Learning Needs of Every Student 38
   Summary 40
   Questions 41
   Activities 41
   For Further Reading 41
   References 41

Chapter 3 *Strategies for Processing Language 43*
Introduction   44
Thinking and Language 46
      Egocentric and Socialized Behavior 46
      Information Processing 47

The Nature of Intelligence: Multiple Intelligences 48
   The Educational Implications of Seven
     Intelligences 49
Teaching Models for Language Arts Instruction 50
   Advance Organizers 51
   Nondirective Teaching/Constructivism 52
   Cooperative Learning 53
Literature Circles 58
   Organizing Literature Circles 61
   Suggestions for Initiating Literature Circles 65
Developing Higher-Level Thinking Skills 67
   Summary 70
   Questions 70
   Activities 70
   For Further Reading 71
   References 71
   Children's Books 72

Chapter **4** *Children's Literature: Opening Windows to New Worlds 73*
   Introduction 74
The Selection of Literature 75
   Characterization 75
   Plot 78
   Setting 80
   Theme 80
   Style 81
   Illustrations 82
   Literary Elements and the Sharing of
     Literature 82
Genre 83
   Picture Books 83
   Traditional Literature 85
   Modern Fantasy 86
   Contemporary Realistic Fiction 86
   Historical Fiction 88
   Biography and Autobiography 88
   Informational Books 89
   Poetry 90
Multicultural Literature 94
   Criteria for Selecting Multicultural Literature 95
Thematic Units 99

Literature Response Journals 118

Summary 119

Questions 119

Activities 120

For Further Reading 120

References 120

Children's Books 121

Chapter

5 *Oral Language: Developing the Base of Expression 125*

Introduction 126

The Development of English 126

Coinages of English Words 130

Aspects of Language 132

Phonology 132

Morphology 132

Syntax 133

Semantics 133

Children's Language Acquisition 133

Babbling 135

Semantic Development 135

Telegraphic Speech 136

Overgeneralization 137

The Functions of Language 138

Language in the Classroom 139

Children with Special Needs 142

Dialects 142

Multicultural Considerations About Language 143

Black English 144

Spanish-Influenced English 145

Asian-Influenced English 147

Native American Languages 148

Evaluating Language Development 150

Summary 151

Questions 151

Activities 151

For Further Reading 151

References 151

Chapter

6 *Speaking: The Oral Expression of Thoughts 155*

Introduction 156

Speaking and the Other Language Arts 156
Language Settings 158
   Conversational Skills 159
   Conversation in the Classroom 159
Intonation 160
Oral Interpretation of Poetry and Prose 161
   Choral Speaking and Reading 162
   Reader's Theater 163
   Storytelling 165
Discussions as Small Group Activities 169
   Brainstorming 171
   Panel Discussions and Debates 172
Media and Oral Language 172
Drama as Creative Play 174
   Drama as a Process 175
   *Language Expansion and Extension in
     Drama 175*
   Types of Drama 176
   Summary 181
   Questions 182
   Activities 182
   For Further Reading 182
   References 183
   Children's Books 184

Chapter   **7** *Listening: A Receptive Skill 185*
   Introduction 186
Factors in Effective Listening 188
   The Teacher as Listener 190
Levels of Listening 190
   Marginal Listening 190
   Appreciative Listening 191
   Attentive Listening 195
   Critical Listening 198
Guidelines for Developing Listening Strategies 199
Instructional Approaches 201
   Directed Listening Activity 204
   Directed Listening-Thinking Activity 205
   Summary 209
   Questions 209
   Activities 209
   For Further Reading 210
   References 210

Chapter **8** *Writing: A Multidimensional Process 213*

Introduction 214

Initial Attempts at Writing 215

The Writing Process 216

    Prewriting 216

    Writing 217

    Rewriting 217

    Publishing 218

Writing Considerations: Audience and Voice 220

    Audience 220

    Voice 221

The Development of Children's Writing 224

    Kindergarten 225

    First Grade 226

    Second Grade 231

    Third Grade 233

    Fourth Grade 235

    Fifth and Sixth Grades 238

    Seventh and Eighth Grades 240

The Teacher's Role in the Writing Process 241

    The Teacher as a Writing Model 242

    Conferencing with Students 244

    Summary 247

    Questions 248

    Activities 248

    For Further Reading 248

    References 248

Chapter **9** *Writing: Personal and Practical 251*

Introduction 252

Personal Writing 253

    Dialogues 253

    Journals 255

    Letters 257

    Autobiographies 260

    Poetry 261

Practical Writing 277

    Academic Learning Logs 277

    Biographies 278

    Note Taking 279

Technology and Writing 282

    Word Processing and Writing 283

Evaluating Student Writing 288

   Portfolios 288

   Responding to Children's Writing 299

   Anecdotal Records and Checklists 299

   Holistic Evaluation 302

   Summary 304

   Questions 305

   Activities 305

   For Further Reading 305

   References 305

   Children's Books 307

   Internet Sites 307

C h a p t e r **10** *Grammar 309*

   Introduction 310

Standard and Nonstandard English 311

Systems of Grammar 311

   Traditional Grammar 312

   Structural Grammar 312

   Transformational Generative Grammar 313

Grammar Instruction 314

   Teaching Punctuation 315

   Teaching Grammar 318

Grammar for Second-Language Students 321

The Revision Process 322

   Proofreading 323

   Editing 323

   Summary 324

   Questions 324

   Activities 325

   For Further Reading 325

   References 325

C h a p t e r **11** *Supportive Writing Skills: Spelling and Handwriting 327*

   Introduction 328

Stages of Spelling Development 329

Instruction in Spelling 333

   Spelling Errors 336

   Assisting Children with Spelling 337

   Students with Special Needs 338

Spelling Generalizations 339

Dictionary Skills 340
Handwriting 342
Children's Handwriting Development 344
Instruction in Handwriting 344
   Writing Instruments 348
   Gripping the Pencil 348
Manuscript Handwriting 348
   Letter Reversals 349
Cursive Handwriting 352
Legibility 352
Left-Handed Children 353
Special Problems 356
Evaluating Handwriting 356
   Summary 357
   Questions 358
   Activities 358
   For Further Reading 358
   References 358

C h a p t e r **12** *Reading: Interaction Between Text and Reader 361*

Introduction 362

Approaches to the Teaching of Reading 363
   Transactional View of Reading 364
   Basal Reading Program 365
   Whole Language Approach 366
Instructional Practices for Emergent and Beginning Readers 369
   Emergent Reading 369
   Instruction for Children as They Begin to Read 374
Instructional Methods for Primary and Middle Childhood Readers 381
   Graphic Organizers 381
   Questioning 383
   Book Clubs 390
   Directed Reading Activity 391
   Directed Reading-Thinking Activity 391
Content Area Reading 397
   Study Skills 397
   SQ3R 397

Response 397
Reciprocal Teaching 400
*Instructional Approaches for High-Risk, Bilingual,
    and Special Needs Students 401*
High-Risk Students 401
Bilingual Students 402
Special Needs Students 404
Computers and Reading 404
Evaluating Reading 404
Formal Evaluation Measures 405
Informal Evaluation Measures 406
Anecdotal Records 406
Summary 408
Questions 408
Activities 408
For Further Reading 408
References 409
Children's Books 412

C h a p t e r   **13** *Extending the Language Arts
                          Curriculum 413*
Introduction 414
Family Literacy 414
Classroom Volunteers 417
The World 421
Summary 423
Questions 423
Activities 423
For Further Reading 424
References 424

Appendix 425
Books for the Teacher's Library 425
Professional Journals 427
Caldecott Medal and Honor Books (1996–1970) 428
Newbery Medal and Honor Books (1996–1970) 430
Multicultural Literature for Children 432
Trucker Buddy Program 436

Subject Index 437

Children's Literature and Author Index 446

Preface

S hortly after the turn of the century, John Dewey extolled the values of allowing children to be active participants in their learning. Dewey referred to this as "learning by doing." Now as we approach the twenty-first century, Dewey's premise still holds true. By emphasizing the learning process, teachers can serve as facilitators in the classroom as children enthusiastically engage in relevant language arts activities in which they are interested. Self-motivation drives students to pursue new knowledge and to challenge themselves.

This book stresses the teaching of the language arts via an integrated curriculum. As such, it presents both the product/content-oriented view of learning and the process approach so that readers may compare and contrast the two educational views. While many school districts have adopted the process approach (nontraditional whole language and literature-based instruction), a number of school districts still maintain a product/content, traditional focus. Thus, readers of this book need a clear understanding of both the traditional and nontraditional approaches.

For those readers who believe in a process approach to learning and in assessing the child's development in the language arts, this book offers a plethora of activity suggestions, references to quality children's literature, and listening, speaking, and writing ideas. For those who favor the product approach, direct instruction ideas are included as well. Most readers will adopt aspects of each approach to meet their teaching needs.

Throughout, the text provides assistance to both the novice and the experienced classroom teacher. "Focus Boxes" give brief explanations and descriptions of various concepts. "In the Classroom Mini Lessons" and "In the Classroom Teaching Hints" offer examples of language arts activities that can be easily adopted for classroom use. Assessment suggestions are offered throughout the text. At the back of the book are a series of sections entitled "Fingertip References," which include lists of key reference books for teacher use, prominent journals in the area of language arts, Caldecott and Newbery Award winners and honor books from 1970 through 1996, and multicultural children's books. The inserts depicting children, teachers, and current classroom practices help make the text come alive.

The accompanying instructor's manual contains chapter goals and objectives. A suggested portfolio for preservice teachers, as well as additional class readings, are included. Questions may either be used for group or class discussion or as essay test items. Several recently produced videos that complement the various chapters are described. In addition, transparency masters are available.

The test items at the back of the instructor's manual, as well as those in the Test Bank, have been used in the examinations of undergraduate students as part of their language arts methods. Each test item is rated according to its level of difficulty as obtained through actual testing conditions.

This text is part of the Brown & Benchmark Methods Series. This means that you can choose the chapters you want, in the order you want them, to create your own course-specific black and whilte language arts text. You can combine these chapters with chapters from *Elementary & Middle School Social Studies: A Whole Language Approach,* Second Edition, by Farris and Cooper and *Reading for Success in Elementary Schools,* by Cheek, Flippo, and Lindsey, or even add your own material to create the custom text that best meets your needs. Talk to your Brown & Benchmark sales representative for more information on custom text option.

In writing this book, I observed and taught in numerous elementary classrooms. I watched several outstanding teachers and hundreds upon hundreds of energized, highly motivated children actively engaged in listening, speaking, reading, writing, and thinking throughout the entire school day, across the entire school curriculum. Many teachers shared a wealth of ideas, concerns, problems, and suggestions with me. An untold number of stories, reports, books, and poems written by children were also shared with me. To those teachers and children, I owe a great debt of thanks.

In turn, I must thank my former and current teachers, including my elementary, secondary, and college teachers as well as my own students. My current and former students, elementary, undergraduate, masters, and doctoral, all helped me formulate the ideas and suggestions contained in this book. I continue to learn from them. Likewise, I wish to thank the students and their teachers in the many classrooms I visit each year. They, too, teach me new ways of thinking and learning.

This book was critiqued by several reviewers whose suggestions proved to be helpful. Their comments were appreciated. I want to extend particular appreciation to the following individuals for their in-depth reviews of the manuscript:

Mary Ann Wham, Ed.D. University of Wisconsin—Whitewater	Jean Strait Augsburg College
Rebecca Brent East Carolina University	Barrie Ann Brancato Clarion University of PA
Nancy R. Williams University of Houston	Dr. Mary Theresa McVicar Mercy College
Eugenia Blake Campbell University	Wendy C. Kasten, Ph.D. Kent State University
Constance L. Hoag, Ed.D. University of South Dakota	Jeanne Peck Harding University

My deep appreciation goes to Sue Pulvermacher-Alt, Managing Editor, Suzanne Guinn, Developmental Editor, and Terry Routley, Production Editor, for all their assistance and guidance.

My hope is that every reader of this book will come away with new insights and ideas that he or she will carry back to an elementary classroom to light up the eyes of enthusiastic children. Then all the time and effort put forth in writing this book will have been worthwhile.

I teach because it is what I enjoy. Teaching is what I do best. And, most of all, teaching is what I love. Being in a classroom teaching is an electrifying experience for me as I see students turn a glimmer of knowledge into a roaring flame. This happens day after day, year after year. What more exciting profession is there?

Pamela J. Farris
Presidential Teaching Professor
Northern Illinois University

Children and Teachers in the Classroom

©James L. Shaffer

Live a balanced life—learn some and think
some and draw and paint and sing and dance
and play and work every day some.
—**Robert Fulghum**
All I Really Needed to Know I Learned in
Kindergarten

Introduction

*T*he school doors open at 8:15 A.M. for yet another day of learning. Kim McNamara's fourth graders scurry into the classroom. Two girls offer their services to Miss McNamara to unpack the paperback book order that has just arrived. Other students quickly hang up their jackets and book bags and then head to one of the activity tables Miss McNamara has set up in the back of the classroom—a writing center on parodies, a table filled with humor and joke books, a computer with math games, and a science center with the materials necessary to make a homemade camera. Two students who were previously assigned the responsibility of feeding the classroom pets are carefully measuring the appropriate amounts of food for the two gerbils and an aquarium of guppies. Next, the two students will give the box turtle the house flies they caught before school.

A few students go to a box labeled "Concerns" to scribble a brief note about a problem that they are struggling to overcome—for example, the death of a family cat or a lost necklace. Having changed their "concerns" from mental worries to tangible notes, they deposit their "concerns" for the day into the box; they will pick up the notes when school is over and they can try to resolve their problems without interfering with their learning.

It is only the fifth week of the school year, but all the children appear to be confident and at ease as they pursue the many different opportunities available to them. Electricity permeates the air as the children excitedly immerse themselves in the day's activities that Miss McNamara has carefully planned.

The classroom itself is enticing. Two bulletin boards offer variety and color, containing timely themes that coincide with a learning goal of the class or of the school. The bulletin boards, which are changed biweekly, typically are working bulletin boards that the students can manipulate. One of the bulletin boards has parodies written by the students and Miss McNamara. The other is an action bulletin board with questions about photography, the current science topic.

Looking around the classroom, one observes library books prominently displayed on chalk rails and tables and colorful posters of popular sports and movie heroes and heroines. Three simple rules describing acceptable classroom behavior are listed above the chalkboard. Mobiles hanging overhead depict the students' favorite characters in recently read books. Clearly, students' attitudes and interests have been considered in the creation of the classroom environment.

A bell rings, signaling the official beginning of the school day. What was a silent classroom when Kim McNamara arrived at 7:30 A.M. has now become one marked by low murmuring voices, an occasional giggle followed by laughter, the rattling of papers and books as the students take their seats—the sounds of children readying themselves for a day of learning.

Only one year ago, Kim McNamara had been studying methods of teaching—learning techniques of instruction in language arts, reading, mathematics, science, and social studies, among other subjects—to elementary students. As she was learning theories about teaching, she was able to observe and participate with elementary students as part of her preservice teacher education program. Kim is now *the teacher.* She must put theory into practice, making decisions that could affect her students for the rest of their lives. How well she is prepared, how much time she has devoted to the planning of the lessons, and how enthusiastic she is about each lesson are reflected in the learning of her students.

Kim has discovered that as a teacher she is also a "student," learning something new about children and teaching every day. She has students with different cultural and ethnic backgrounds and a wide range of abilities and interests. According to Kim, "Teaching has proved to be a major challenge, the greatest I've ever encountered. But I've found that I love every minute of it!"

Kim has made a special attempt to communicate with each of her fourth graders. Prior to the beginning of school, she wrote a letter to each of her students introducing herself. She described her hobbies of playing golf and swimming as well as her interest in reading mysteries. Kim also asked what the students enjoyed doing after school. She asked each one to think of something he or she wanted to learn more about, promising to try to include it some time during the school year. Kim has continued the open communication pattern by regularly writing achievement notes to parents and students. Each student has a mailbox encouraging rather than discouraging "note passing." "My goal is to be supportive of literacy (reading and writing). If a student writes a note and the recipient reads it, literacy has been reinforced and promoted," Kim states. "Communication has taken place between an author (the note writer) and the reader (the note's recipient)."

Kim closely monitors the pulse of her class as she meets the academic needs of her students in ways they find stimulating. Kim McNamara is aware that students have many needs and concerns. This chapter discusses children and their teachers, as well as classroom organization and management.

Children and Their Teachers

Children possess a natural curiosity and desire to learn that is coupled with their wanting to be accepted by others. To kindergartners and primary-grade children, their teacher is nothing short of a god. Young children are amazed to see their teacher, dressed in jeans and a sweatshirt, shopping in the local supermarket or eating at McDonald's. For them, it is difficult to conceive that their teacher is but a mere mortal.

The enthusiasm and energy that children have when they enter school must be nurtured by understanding teachers who set realistic but challenging goals. Teaching is not an easy profession, but it is a rewarding one in that teachers help others to better their lives. Such satisfaction accompanies very few other career

Children possess a natural curiosity and desire to learn. Using technology capitalizes on that curiosity.

Photo courtesy of Rockford Register Star

choices. To quote a saying found on a coffee mug in a teachers' lounge, " Those who can, teach. Those who can't, go into some lesser profession."

The inner need one human being has to help another is the essence of teaching. Some refer to this as an idealistic call to teaching, a conviction deeply rooted in one's soul to work to make life better for the generations that follow. Qualified, caring, and dedicated teachers are needed more than ever before in our nation's schools. Living in a complex, technological society, today's children encounter more problems and demands than any previous generation ever did. Yet children are resilient; given all their problems, as a group, they are survivors.

Schools are challenged to provide education and training that will prepare today's students to live full and productive lives in an ever-changing world. Students must become accustomed to life within a technological world requiring critical thinking and problem-solving skills. According to Frank Smith (1988, p. 55), author and theorist within the field of literacy, "Children learn when they have opportunities and reason to use language and critical thinking personally. . . . Children learn from what is demonstrated to them, from what they see others doing." Being able to analyze, organize, and synthesize information will be essential to them in applying their knowledge to newly encountered situations. Many will be employed only to discover later that their labor skills or careers have become obsolete, necessitating the return to school for more education. Lifelong learning will become a necessity.

How do children and teachers adapt to the challenges? What makes an effective teacher of language arts? These questions are examined next.

In the Classroom Teaching Hint

Using Online Computer Services to Obtain Lesson Plans in Language Arts

*T*eachers who have access to a computer with a modem can obtain literally hundreds of lesson plans for teaching language arts. There are also lesson plans that integrate language arts, social studies, science, and math. In addition, electronic versions of CNN Newsroom Classroom Guides and Discovery Education Online are available. These are all part of the AskERIC Virtual Library. To obtain access to the library, use the following address:

gopher ericir.syr.edu
or use
telnet ericir.syr.edu

Be sure to log in as "gopher."

Internet Resources

> *Links to Education Resources*
> http://tiger.coe.missouri.edu/Resource.html

> *NCREL (North Central Regional Educational Laboratory)*
> http://www.ncrel.org/school_house

> *Education Related LISTSERVs*
> http://www.clark.net/pub/listserv/lsedu1.html

> *Education Related Information—YAHOO*
> http://www.yahoo.com/Education

> *Search Engines*
> http://www.yahoo.com/computers_and_Internet/Internet/World_Wide_Web

> *Library of Congress*
> http://www.yahoo.com/Government/Agencies/Library_of_congress

> *WWW Meta-Indexes and Search Tools (lists all WWW servers)*
> http://lcweb.loc.gov/global/metaindex.html

> *Internet Resources Meta-Index*
> http://www.ncsa.uiuc.edu/SDG/Software/Mosaic/MetaIndex.html

> *AskERIC*
> http://ericir.syr.edu

Children and Their World

Children learn best when they are interested in the topic and are allowed to include their own previously gained knowledge as part of the learning setting (Calkins & Harwayne, 1991; Goodman, 1986). Keeping these points in mind, Marcia Beymer worked diligently on a unit on *Clifford the Big Red Dog* by Norman Bridwell (1986) for her second graders. Most of the students read the entire classroom collection of the "Clifford" series of books, more than 16 different books in all. The class discussed and laughed at Clifford and his various escapades, including his life as a puppy, his good deeds, and his friends. Each morning Mrs. Beymer shared a Clifford riddle with the class. The children thoroughly enjoyed the hilarious adventures of the less-than-perfect giant pet dog.

Mrs. Beymer rewarded children who displayed good work habits or achieved a goal by having them put their names on pieces of paper and dropping them into Clifford's dish. At the end of each day, one name was drawn from Clifford's dish. The child selected received a small duffle bag containing a stuffed Clifford, a journal to record the classroom activities Clifford "did" with the students, and a Clifford book to read. Each child took the Clifford bag home overnight until all the students had taken the bag home once.

After the class spent more than 2 weeks reading and talking about Clifford, Mrs. Beymer assigned students to work in groups of three as the class wrote its own book, Celebrate with Clifford. A Clifford poster purchased through a paperback book club was laminated on a large piece of tagboard. Each group selected a different holiday to celebrate: Valentine's Day, St. Patrick's Day, Memorial Day, Arbor Day, the Fourth of July, Labor Day, Halloween, Thanksgiving, and Christmas. One group even elected to "Celebrate summer with Clifford! Take swimming lessons!" Each group made a picture of Clifford for their portion of the book. Each student wrote a sentence or paragraph on the tagboard before all the members of the group drew pictures to depict their holidays. Using a paper punch and three metal rings, Mrs. Beymer put the book together for the class.

To celebrate the writing of the book, Mrs. Beymer's class held a Clifford party. Borrowing a large bowl and spoon from the school's cafeteria, the class made "Puppy Chow." Mrs. Beymer gave each student a brown lunch bag. The students then used their red crayons to draw the famous checkerboard square design on their bags, leaving room in the middle of the bag to print the words "Puppy Chow." At recess, Mrs. Beymer melted two sticks of margarine and two cups of peanut butter in a bowl in the microwave oven in the faculty lounge. When class resumed, she mixed the melted margarine and peanut butter along with two boxes of Crispix cereal. Next, she placed a pound of powdered sugar in each of two large, paper grocery bags. After pouring half of the margarine, peanut butter, and cereal mixture into each bag, Mrs. Beymer had two students fold the bags' tops down and shake the bags. Two other students served the "Puppy Chow" to their classmates by placing a cupful in each student's "Puppy Chow" bag. The class then reviewed the steps in making "Puppy Chow."

By focusing on a well-loved book character such as Clifford, the Big Red Dog, Mrs. Beymer was able to keep her students motivated and eager to learn new reading and writing strategies.

Mrs. Beymer had organized her entire curriculum around Clifford, including not only reading and writing but also math as the students worked Clifford story problems, science as they discussed the care and feeding of pets, and even social studies in their discussion of how Clifford related to his neighbors and his family. This took considerable planning on Mrs. Beymer's part, but it proved worthwhile because the students were excited about the lessons.

Children prefer learning about what is relevant to themselves. They also differ in their abilities and interests. For instance, in the United States and Canada, a 6-year-old child is usually considered to be a first grader; however, society cannot dictate readiness. Many children attend preschool before entering kindergarten and have had opportunities to engage in social and oftentimes academic activities. For such children, the structure and demands of kindergarten and first grade are usually taken in stride. For children who lack the maturity needed to cope in school, this is not the case. "When children enter school before they are developmentally ready to cope with it, their chances for failure increase dramatically" (Uphoff & Gilmore, 1986, p. 11).

Children who are younger than their classmates, often the children with summer birthdays, are at a disadvantage in the classroom. Research indicates that older children in a grade are much more likely to score in the above-average range on achievement tests, whereas younger children in a grade are far more likely to fail at least one grade (Uphoff, 1985). Retaining, or failing, a child increases the risk by 40 to 50 percent that the student will drop out of school later (Riley, 1986).

Children's differences make the classroom interesting and teaching challenging. Consider Charles, a 6-year-old who was driven to school by his mother on the first day of the school year. Charles held his mother's hand tightly while she talked to his teacher, Marilyn Wright. When Mrs. Wright asked Charles a question, Charles's mother would answer. When his mother began looking around the room for a place to sit, it was clear to Mrs. Wright that the mother intended to stay for the entire day. Upon informing Charles's mother that parents needed to complete paperwork in the principal's office, Mrs. Wright took Charles by the hand and led him to his desk. He sat quietly until time for the morning milk break. Charles held up the line because he couldn't decide whether he wanted chocolate or white milk. When asked, he volunteered that he *really* liked chocolate milk, but his mom didn't let him have it because if it spilled on his clothes it made a mess. As Charles reached for a carton of chocolate milk, Mrs. Wright winked at him and said, "Chocolate is my favorite, too." Charles shyly grinned and handed her the carton of chocolate milk before picking up another one for himself.

Over the next few years, it was apparent that Charles had had few opportunities to make choices. Little things, like getting mustard on his shirt or tearing a hole in the ever-so-thin first-grade writing paper, would upset him.

The same year Charles was in Mrs. Wright's first-grade classroom, Emily was too. The children had gone home at the close of the first day of school, and Mrs. Wright had kicked off her shoes to ease the pressure on her feet when Emily appeared in the classroom doorway. Wearing a dress that was inside out and socks that did not match, Emily burst into the classroom with a barrage of questions. She said, "Hi! My name is Emily. What's yours? Are you my teacher? Will you teach me how to read? I don't know how, so somebody has to teach me." When she finally stopped to catch her breath, Mrs. Wright managed to recover enough from this abrupt appearance of an apparent whirlwind to respond, "Well, Emily, I don't know if I'll be your teacher or Mrs. Johnson will be. But I do know that you'll learn to read. And you'll find that reading is a fun thing to do."

Mrs. Wright considered Charles her "toe tester," willing to stick his toe in the water but always being somewhat reluctant to do so, while Emily was her "plunger," willing to dive headfirst into anything. Shy Charles delighted in finding a library book on his desk that Mrs. Wright thought he might like, while boisterous Emily discovered that writing was a great outlet for expressing one's feelings. Emily enjoyed doing a "you write to me, I'll write to you" dialogue journal with Mrs. Wright throughout the year. Both children met with success because they had a responsive teacher.

Effective Teaching

"The act of teaching is always a dynamic interaction of individuals (teachers and teachers, teachers and learners, and learners and learners)" (Orlich et al., 1990, p. 3). As such, teaching is an exciting profession; every day in the classroom is unique. School is a place where children learn from the teacher, children learn from each other, the teacher learns from the children, and the teacher learns from other teachers. Learning is contagious!

Effective teachers are many things. One of the qualities that makes for a good teacher is the underlying determination to be a success within the classroom despite any obstacles that may arise.

Teachers must be experienced readers, writers, and thinkers. "An experienced teacher can, at a strategic moment and with one question or observation, move a class discussion into an entirely different dimension. There is no way to become more experienced at doing this except by doing it" (Rosenthal, 1995, p. 118).

Effective teachers have perseverance. Rather than avoiding lessons that can be risky in lieu of the safety of convergent questions or work sheets, effective teachers tend to attempt to stretch their students—and their own teaching abilities as well. This requires a sense of optimism that they convey to the students and to fellow teachers. Mistakes are not highlighted in the classroom; everyone makes mistakes. Often mistakes lead to future successes. Thus, learning from one's mistakes becomes important.

Rosenthal and Jacobsen's classic (1968) study points out the need for teachers to have high expectations of their students. When teachers assume, sometimes even prior to meeting with their students, that they have a good class of "capable learners," the children tend to perform according to such corresponding teachers' expectations. Rosenthal and Jacobsen referred to this as the self-fulfilling prophecy.

In addition to possessing the above qualities, effective teachers are aware of learning theories and their application. Two views of learning are prevalent today. The first, a direct approach to learning, tends to be quite organized and highly structured. The other view is the nontraditional view, which states that learning is "continuous, spontaneous, and effortless; . . . learning occurs in all kinds of situations" (Smith, 1992, p. 432). Thus, the nontraditional view deems learning to be holistic in nature. In addition, the nontraditional view of learning considers it to be social rather than solitary, or as Smith writes, "we learn from the company we keep." Inspired, successful teachers tend to "analyze their particular situation and create instruction to meet the needs of that situation" (Duffy, 1992, p. 442). Thus, the best of both views of learning are adopted when needed and appropriate.

Teachers must be careful not to get caught up in instructional methods and forget about the children. Bill Talbot, a teacher in Alberta, Canada, writes that "we also need to realize that the magic in teaching lies less in the strategies and methodology than it does in the rapport we have with our students" (1990, p. 56).

When the school day is geared toward providing students with maximum learning opportunities, teachers find that they themselves are more satisfied with their own teaching. This means that the teacher must create a classroom that has a warm environment that fosters learning, follow a curriculum that teaches important content and skills, and have high standards and expectations of students in the class (Lewis, 1986).

In the Classroom Teaching Hint

Organizing the School Day

Organizing the school day is one of a teacher's most important tasks. The classroom itself needs to be neat and orderly, but also enticing to students. Books and activities must be accessible and easily stored.

Below are examples of two daily schedules.

First-Grade Classroom's Daily Schedule

8:15	Children arrive, put away coats, and take a rest room break. Papers and lunch money are collected. Lunch count and attendance are taken. Pledge to the flag.
8:20	Read aloud—The teacher reads a book to the class, stopping to ask questions from time to time. The class may discuss the book after each chapter and at the end. (Most read alouds in first grade are picture books.)
8:30	Mini lesson—Short language arts lesson (listening, speaking, reading, and writing).
8:45	Big Books—Teacher reads on Monday and Tuesday with children reading along orally the second time through. On Wednesday, the class reads the book together. On Thursday, students take turns reading the book in pairs. On Friday, students take turns reading the book.
9:00	Activity centers—In groups of five, the students rotate through the five activity centers (reading and writing, math, science, social studies, and computer center). Groups rotate between activity centers every 20 minutes.
9:30	Rest room break.
9:40	Recess.
10:05	Activity centers continued.
11:20	Preparation for lunch.
11:25	Lunch and recess.
12:15	Rest room break.
12:25	Book sharing by students and teacher (art on Monday; library on Wednesday).
12:45	Math.
1:15	Social studies (physical education on Tuesday and Thursday).
1:45	Rest room break.
1:55	Science (computer lab on Wednesday).
2:30	Sustained silent reading (Monday, Wednesday, and Friday). Journal writing (Tuesday and Thursday).
2:45	Review of what was learned during the day.
2:55	Preparation for dismissal.
3:00	Dismissal.

Fifth-Grade Classroom's Daily Schedule

8:15   Children arrive, put away coats, and take a rest room break. Papers and lunch money collected. Lunch count and attendance are taken. Teacher talks briefly with students who were absent the day before to catch them up.
Pledge to the flag.

8:30   Mini lesson—Short language arts lesson (listening, speaking, reading, and writing).

8:45   Reading and writing (individual and group activities).

10:00   Rest room break.

10:10   Reading and writing continued (physical education on Monday; library on Thursday).

10:45   Sustained silent reading (art on Wednesday).

11:05   Social studies (music on Tuesday).

11:45   Preparation for lunch. Rest room break.

11:55   Lunch and recess.

12:45   Rest room break.

12:55   Math.

1:40   Read aloud—The teacher reads a book, such as a picture book or a portion of a novel, to the class and stops to ask questions or to discuss points along the way.

1:55   Rest room break.

2:05   Science (computer lab on Monday and Wednesday).

2:45   Review of what was learned during the day.

2:55   Journal writing.

3:00   Preparation for dismissal.

3:05   Dismissal.

Whenever possible, these teachers use an interdisciplinary approach. For instance, while studying the Revolutionary War, Civil War, and World War II, the fifth-grade teacher may devote the entire day to social studies. The morning might involve reading, writing, listening, and speaking activities using historical novels, literature response journals, poetry, and songs of the era. The usual social studies period may be devoted to research time using the social studies textbook and library materials. Science might take into consideration the scientific developments of the period being studied (i.e., battlefield nurses, submarines, carbine rifles, and problems of poor sanitation during the Civil War). Math might involve calculation of supplies and troops, and economic considerations (i.e., the cost of funding the Revolutionary War and the use of script instead of money).

During elementary school, children receive instruction in many subject areas: language arts, mathematics, science, and social studies. These content areas are usually given the most time and are typically taught daily. While art, health, music, and physical education are not taught as often, they are still important parts of the elementary curriculum.

Typically in early childhood education, particularly during kindergarten through Grade 3, the major portion of the school day—often the entire morning—is devoted to language arts instruction. This includes the teaching of speaking, listening, reading, and writing. Language arts receives smaller time allotments in middle childhood education, but it still receives more attention than any other subject area.

Trying to fit all of the subjects into one school day is by no means easy. As Sue Sunberg, a student teacher, remarked, "It took me 3 weeks to figure out how to schedule everything. And then there are always unexpected interruptions—school pictures, a special convocation, a child who must leave for a dental appointment. If anything, a teacher must be flexible!" Sue adapted to the hectic world of the classroom by creating a "filler pack" as part of what she called her "teaching survival kit." She scoured professional journals for learning activities that took only a few minutes to do and used them to "fill" short time lapses between lessons or before lunch and recess.

Presenting new material and skills may occasionally require extra time. Sometimes students become so involved in a lesson, additional time is needed. Ron Lindberg found it difficult to predict how long a lesson would take, especially when he first began teaching. "Sometimes I would plan for a 30-minute lesson only to find that the kids could complete it in 10 minutes. Over the years, I've adopted the whole language approach. This has enabled me to teach by bringing things that interest my sixth graders into the classroom. Rather than having several short lessons, I have large blocks of time for each subject area. Language arts is usually a 2-hour segment in which we read, write, act out, share, react, discuss, reflect, and appreciate. We start out with a short review of material, discuss and explain new skills, work on the task at hand, and close the period with sharing and more review."

Ron went on: "It's not unusual for us to spend a few days on a social studies unit that includes reading, writing, and discussing so we cover both social studies and language arts. For example, we were discussing immigration in social studies and talked about the waves of immigrants that came from Europe in the 1800s and 1900s. Because there had been recent changes in the United States immigration laws, we talked about the economic and social impacts that immigration has on the United States today. Since my sixth graders love the work of Gary Paulsen, the class read *The Crossing* (1987). The book is about a Mexican orphan who illegally crosses the border into the United States, where he meets an alcoholic Vietnam veteran. The result was a discussion of illegal immigration, the economic and social problems of Latin American countries, and the role of the United States as a keeper of world peace. Language arts and social studies fit together perfectly in this instance."

Mr. Lindberg had high expectations of his students because The Crossing is a book that challenged their abilities. A few students found the book difficult to read, but their love of Paulsen's depictive writing style in his adventure books and the high interest maintained by their classmates gave them the motivation to continue through the book. Mr. Lindberg believed that, given the opportunity, the students would succeed in reading the book and gaining from the vicarious experiences they encountered. The students' interactions with their classmates made the classroom an exciting environment. Students asked and responded to questions and sought out additional information about the cultural and geographical aspects of Latin America. They brought in newspaper clippings for a bulletin board display, shared television news reports, and debated the reporters' speculations. Learning took on an active role for every student in the class as well as for Mr. Lindberg.

In order for his students to better understand immigration and its effects on the economic environment as well as on society, Mr. Lindberg asked both convergent and divergent questions. He asked convergent questions, or those with a right answer, at the beginning of class discussions to help put the students at ease and set the stage for probing more deeply into the topic. When Mr. Lindberg began the initial discussion about immigration, he asked several convergent questions. What is immigration? Did any of the students want to share a story about a relative who immigrated to the United States? Did anyone know about contributions immigrants had made to this country? And so on. The students joined in the

Pairing students to work together on projects, read together, practice choral reading, or share their writing pieces is a common practice. Unfortunately, it takes a great deal of time each day to match up students to work together. Beth Kovalenko, a second-grade teacher, solved the problem by making a class grid in which all of the students were paired. Since Beth had 18 students, she had 17 pairs created on her grid.

Instead of using a color code, alphabet system, or some other approach to label sets of pairs, Beth elected to use time slots since her second graders were learning the concept of telling time. She called the time during which partners worked together "appointments." Thus, Beth would say, "Today we're going to work together on writing our spider poems. Pretend that it is 9:25 A.M. Meet with your 9:25 A.M. appointment." The students would then check their appointment schedule on top of their desks and find their colleague to coauthor a spider poem.

8:00	8:20	9:05	9:25	9:45	10:10	10:35	11:15	11:38	12:02	12:36	12:55	1:15	1:40	2:12	2:34	3:08		
2	3	6	5	7	4	8	9	10	15	12	13	14	11	16	17	18	1	Izabela
1	4	3	6	10	8	5	7	9	12	11	14	13	18	15	16	17	2	Kevin
4	1	2	9	5	10	15	6	8	7	13	11	16	17	12	18	14	3	Lora
3	2	9	7	8	1	18	17	16	14	15	10	11	12	13	5	6	4	Mike
6	7	18	1	3	16	2	11	12	13	17	9	8	10	14	4	15	5	Gianna
5	8	1	2	13	12	11	3	18	17	9	16	7	14	10	15	4	6	David
8	5	15	4	1	9	10	2	13	3	14	17	6	16	18	12	11	7	Kathryn
7	6	14	18	4	2	1	16	3	9	10	15	5	13	17	11	12	8	Eddie
10	18	4	3	17	7	14	1	2	8	6	5	12	15	11	13	16	9	Brian
9	12	11	15	2	3	7	18	1	16	8	4	17	5	6	14	13	10	Joey L.
12	13	10	14	16	15	6	5	17	18	2	3	4	1	9	8	7	11	Chris
11	10	17	16	15	6	13	14	5	2	1	18	9	4	3	7	8	12	John
14	11	16	17	6	18	12	15	7	5	3	1	2	8	4	9	10	13	Sarah R.
13	16	8	11	18	17	9	12	15	4	7	2	1	6	5	10	3	14	Vince
16	17	7	10	12	11	3	13	14	1	4	8	18	9	2	6	5	15	Victor
15	14	13	12	11	5	17	8	4	10	18	6	3	7	1	2	9	16	Joe V.
18	15	12	13	9	14	16	4	11	6	5	7	10	3	8	1	2	17	Joanna
17	9	5	8	14	13	4	10	6	11	16	12	15	2	7	3	1	18	Sarah Z.

Here is an example of a master appointment schedule for an entire class. This enables the teacher to know precisely which students are meeting to work together.

Below are the appointment schedules of two students.

Kathryn's Appointment Schedule			
A.M. Appointments	Name	P.M. Appointments	Name
8:00 A.M.	Eddie	12:02 P.M.	Lora
8:20 A.M.	Gianna	12:26 P.M.	Vince
9:05 A.M.	Victor	12:55 P.M.	Joanna
9:25 A.M.	Mike	1:15 P.M.	David
9:45 A.M.	Izabela	1:40 P.M.	Joe V.
10:10 A.M.	Brian	2:12 P.M.	Sarah Z.
10:35 A.M.	Joey L.	2:34 P.M.	John
11:15 A.M.	Kevin	3:08 P.M.	Chris
11:38 A.M.	Sarah R.		

Brian's Appointment Schedule			
A.M. Appointments	Name	P.M. Appointments	Name
8:00 A.M.	Joey L.	12:02 P.M.	Eddie
8:20 A.M.	Sarah Z.	12:26 P.M.	David
9:05 A.M.	Mike	12:55 P.M.	Gianna
9:25 A.M.	Lora	1:15 P.M.	John
9:45 A.M.	Joanna	1:40 P.M.	Victor
10:10 A.M.	Kathryn	2:12 P.M.	Chris
10:35 A.M.	Vince	2:34 P.M.	Sarah R.
11:15 A.M.	Izabela	3:08 P.M.	Joe V.
11:38 A.M.	Kevin		

These are examples of individual students' appointment schedules. For instance, if the teacher said to the class, "Meet with your 10:35 A.M. appointment now," Kathryn would meet with Joey and Brian would meet with Vince.

*S*ometimes it is helpful to have students work in groups of various sizes. For instance, some activities lend themselves to work in pairs while other activities may work best with three or four participants. By using 4″ by 6″ colored index cards, a variety of combinations can be used to control students.

For kindergartners and beginning first graders, use stickers placed in the four corners of the index cards. For instance, use the upper left-hand corner to have students get into pairs. The sticker on each student's index card would match the sticker on only one other card; the two students with a Tasmanian Devil sticker, for instance, would work together. Shuffle the cards well before making another combination so that the cards can be used for a variety of grouping patterns. Use the upper right-hand corner to have students get into groups of three. Thus, the sticker on each student's index card would match the stickers on two other students' cards. Numerals in the bottom left-hand corner could be used for forming groups of four and colored stickers in the lower right-hand corner could be used for forming groups of five.

Second and third graders can read and do simple math. Students might match an author in the upper left-hand corner of the card with his/her book in order to form pairs (i.e., the student with the Eric Carle card would try to locate the student with *The Very Hungry Caterpillar* card; the student with the Steven Kellogg card would try to locate the student with the *Johnny Appleseed* card; the student with the Peggy Parish card would try to locate the student with the *Amelia Bedelia* card; and vice versa). The upper right-hand corner could list notable threes (Nina, Pinta, and Santa Maria; George Washington, John Adams, and Thomas Jefferson; and Curly, Larry, and Moe). The lower left-hand corner could present a simple math problem, and four cards could have problems with the same answer. The lower right-hand corner could show clockface and digital readings of time to help students form pairs and also to reinforce the telling of time.

Middle childhood and middle school students could have similar matchings, using authors and titles of books for pairs; notable threes; and math problems using addition, subtraction, multiplication, and division. In addition, one corner of the card could include five aspects of a familiar book: author, title, main character, setting, and theme (i.e., E. B. White, *Charlotte's Web,* Wilbur the pig, farm/fairgrounds, and friendship).

Laminating the cards will insure their durability throughout the school year. Also, using colored index cards that have been shuffled makes the cards more appealing.

Sample card for middle first grade/second grade:

<u>Frog</u> and <u>Toad</u> <u>Are</u> <u>Friends</u>   Huey

4 + 8 =   8:15

Sample card for middle childhood student:

Roald Dahl   Lions

5 x 7 =   <u>Bridge</u> <u>to</u> <u>Terabithia</u>

These are sample cards for grouping students in a variety of ways (i.e., in pairs, in threes, or in fours).

discussion. One student had a great-great-grandfather who made harnesses for horses, while another had a relative who opened a hotdog stand in Chicago at the turn of the century. Someone recalled that her great-grandmother took in other people's laundry to earn money to buy food for her family. The students enjoyed sharing stories about their families. Later they talked of discoveries that were made and buildings that were built by immigrants.

After asking several convergent questions, Mr. Lindberg began to interject divergent, open-ended questions into the discussion. He pointed out that the United States has a large population and has problems taking care of its own citizens, including the need for better health care and fulfilling the needs of the homeless. Limited resources and concern for the environment because of increased waste were mentioned as other examples.

The class decided that thousands of people each year try to immigrate to the United States because of the freedom and opportunities it offers. Should the United States shut its gates to new immigrants? Or does the United States have an obligation to take care of those people who want to live as we do? Students pointed out that their own community was becoming crowded. Jobs were still plentiful but many were low paying. Several students had noticed workers or shoppers in the area who didn't speak English. Was a new type of "slavery" being created, with the slaves being immigrants and migrant workers? The students took over the discussion completely as they began to address questions to the entire class. How do the workers who don't speak English understand their jobs and know what to do? Isn't it dangerous for them? Perhaps it is dangerous for others, too, if they make a mistake with chemicals, for example. Where do they live? How do they shop when products are packaged in English? Today many immigrants work in service industries as nannies, taxi drivers, or landscapers. Their work is hard to do. And what about athletes who immigrate to America? Several have scholarships to play basketball, run track, or participate in some other sport. If they are "real" good, they go pro and play in the NBA or NFL, taking a spot on a team that would otherwise go to an American athlete who would make millions of dollars. Is that right?

As the students continued their initial discussion, they soon realized that immigration is a complex issue. The students decided to divide into groups and gather more information on the topic before their next discussion. Mr. Lindberg helped them select different aspects of immigration that were then assigned to the groups. Each group was to report back to the class. Mr. Lindberg also sought out materials to use as references and monitored each group's progress.

By giving his students the opportunity to have frequent open-ended discussions about various topics, Mr. Lindberg encouraged them to develop their creative and critical thinking skills. By searching for information and analyzing it together in groups, the students discovered the importance of gathering data before coming to a conclusion.

Effective teachers like those described in this chapter instruct at levels that students can understand. They communicate by using clear, concise language to facilitate the learning process. By moving about and interacting with their students, teachers see to it that the classroom becomes an exciting environment.

By asking and responding to questions as well as seeking additional information that the students provide, teachers can ensure that learning involves active participation by everyone in the classroom. Not only do effective teachers expect students to achieve, but such teachers develop activities and units of study that provide plenty of opportunities for students to succeed.

S u m m a r y

Children possess a variety of interests and have gathered a great deal of knowledge that needs to be tapped in the learning setting. By interacting with other students and their classroom teacher, students acquire new knowledge, incorporating it into their own knowledge bank. By probing to seek the answers to relevant questions about the world in which they live, children develop the ability to summarize, analyze, and evaluate. They adopt new learning strategies and begin to rely on their creative and critical thinking skills.

Effective teachers respect their students. They also run a well-organized classroom. By learning within an atmosphere of warmth and trust, children possess a sense of security and of belonging. They can't wait to get to school, to be a part of class activities, to share ideas, and to learn new things. The classroom is student centered, with the teacher serving as a facilitator of the learning process.

Questions

1. What types of experience have you had that you could share with students to enrich their lives?
2. How will you encourage students to work together and respect each other?
3. How can you check yourself to see that you are objective in working with students?
4. How will you deal with the diverse backgrounds and needs of your students?
5. What will a typical day be like in your classroom?
6. What kinds of activities can you do outside the classroom to better prepare yourself as a teacher?

Activities

1. Observe a primary and an intermediate classroom. Note how the children are alike and how they differ culturally, emotionally, physically, and intellectually.
2. Interview an experienced teacher and ask what changes have occurred in education during the past 10 to 15 years.
3. Read two articles concerning methodologies and strategies for teaching multicultural education. React to the articles in terms of your own beliefs about teaching.
4. Plan a field trip to a nearby historical landmark. Try to integrate activities that include the language arts (listening, speaking, reading, and writing) with other curricular areas (math, music, science, and social studies).
5. Develop a set of classroom rules that are brief, clear, and positive.
6. Read an article about children with special needs and share it with your classmates.
7. Create a way to introduce yourself to your students before the opening day of school.
8. Describe and illustrate how your classroom will look on the first day of school.

For Further Reading

Dreher, M.A. (1989). The teacher's role in students' success. *The Reading Teacher, 42* (8), 612–617.

Duffy, G. (1992). Let's free teachers to be inspired. *Phi Delta Kappan, 73* (6), 442–447.

Farnan, N. (1996). Connecting adolescents and reading: Goals at the middle level. *Journal of Adolescent and Adult Literacy, 39* (6), 436–445.

Goodman, G. (1989). Worlds within worlds: Reflections on an encounter with parents. *Language Arts, 66* (1), 14–20.

Strickland, D. (1995). Reinventing our literacy programs: Books, basics, balance. *The Reading Teacher, 48* (4), 294–302.

References

Bridwell, N. (1986). *Clifford, the big red dog.* New York: Scholastic.

Calkins, L., & Harwayne, S. (1991). *Living between the lines.* Portsmouth, NH: Heinemann.

Duffy, G. (1992). Let's free teachers to be inspired. *Phi Delta Kappan, 73* (6), 442–447.

Goodman, K. (1986). *What's whole in whole language.* Portsmouth, NH: Heinemann.

Lewis, A.C. (1986). The search continues for effective schools. *Phi Delta Kappan, 68* (4), 187–188.

Orlich, D.C., Kauchak, D.P., Harder, R.J., Pendergrass, R.A., Callahan, R.C., Keogh, A.J., & Gibson, H. (1990). *Teaching strategies: A guide to better instruction* (3rd ed.). Lexington, MA: Heath.

Paulsen, G. (1987). *The crossing.* New York: Orchard.

Riley, R. W. (1986). Can we reduce the risk of failure? *Phi Delta Kappan, 68* (4), 214–219.

Rosenthal, I. (1995). Educating through literature: Flying lessons from *Maniac Magee. Language Arts, 72* (2), 113–119.

Rosenthal, R., & Jacobsen, L. (1968). *Pygmalion in the classroom.* New York: Holt, Rinehart & Winston.

Smith, F. (1988). *Joining the literacy club: Further essays into education.* Portsmouth, NH: Heinemann.

Smith, F. (1992). Learning to read: The never-ending debate. *Phi Delta Kappan, 73* (6), 432–441.

Talbot, B. (1990). Writing for learning in school: Is it possible? *Language Arts, 67* (1), 47–56.

Uphoff, J. K. (1985). Pupil chronological age as a factor in school failure. Paper presented at the annual conference of the Association for Supervision and Curriculum Development, Chicago.

Uphoff, J. K., and Gilmore, J. (1986). Pupil age at school entrance—How many are ready for success? *Young Children, 41* (2), 11–16.

*T*eaching *the* Language Arts

Copyright 1995 by the National Council of Teachers of English. Used with permission.

As adults we must keep in mind the wonder of
childhood—the magic, the mystery, and the
miraculous.
—Lee Bennett Hopkins
Let Them Be Themselves

Introduction

*T*he language arts consist of listening, speaking, reading, and writing. To some extent, the language arts are paired together: listening and speaking, reading and writing. While such pairings are evident, the language arts are interwoven. As a child develops skills in one of the language arts, the others are also enhanced. Thus, the development of listening, speaking, reading, and writing is concurrent and interrelated. Such development, however, is not sequential or linear in nature.

By the time a child reaches the age of 2, many different classification systems have been developed, modified, and eliminated as the youngster seeks to bring order to his or her world. This order, or structure, greatly influences the child's perceptions of and reactions to the environment. For instance, the child learns that cats and dogs may be kept in the house while cows and horses must live in barns. The child also learns that he or she can, to some extent, structure the environment. For example, Kurtis, at age 20 months, discovered that he could not only select but also control which books his mother would read to him. He only had to first sort out the books that he wanted read and then carry them to his mother. Then Kurtis learned he could stack the books in the order he wanted them to be read. He would hand his mother a book to read and upon its completion, clap his hands. Then he would give her the next book in the stack and say, "Read it." Like teenagers or adults who program their CD players in order to listen to songs in their own chosen order, Kurtis developed a similar preferred order to his listening pleasure, "programming" his mother rather than a CD player.

The thinking process is not only aided by the classification of information, but it is also facilitated by children's natural tendency to be curious. By capitalizing on this innate ability to experiment playfully—be it through manipulation of toy cars or Playdoh, exploring a neighbor's backyard, pretending to be a superhero, or testing simple hypotheses by floating sailboats down a stream—thinking can be enhanced. When adults and other children interact with a child, such whimsical acts by the child can be further developed into observing, comparing, classifying, organizing, hypothesizing, applying, and summarizing (Strickland, 1977).

Children gain understanding of the printed word through their personal interactions with others. For example, 3- and 4-year-olds can identify places where their family frequently shops: Sears, Toys 'R' Us, and those fast-food restaurants they love, Burger King and McDonald's. They know these words, and others, because Mom or Dad tells them that is where they are going to shop or eat. Children obtain additional knowledge through their observations of adults and other children, as well as their own oral and written experiences with language. Children, like adults, try to make sense of the world around them. They do so by moving from global generalities to specifics, using knowledge they have previously acquired (Farris & Kaczmarski, 1988).

Children increase their ability to listen, speak, read, and write by becoming involved with language that is somewhat more mature than what they currently use (Johnson & Louis, 1987). In addition, the learning environment should provide ample opportunities for meaningful use of the language arts (Templeton, 1991). To paraphrase Jim Trelease (1989, p. 202), an authority on reading aloud to children, "The more you do it, the better you get at it; the better you get at it, the more you like it; and the more you like it, the more you do it." Children need to use language in different settings and in different ways to develop their communicative skills to the fullest. And they need to know that language can be fun to use.

In teaching the language arts to children, teachers may follow a traditional or a nontraditional mode of instruction or attempt to select the best of both philosophies in an eclectic approach. In the traditional approach, the language arts are generally taught as separate subjects with skills being introduced as small parts of larger units—the underlying premise being that once the parts are learned, the whole is learned. This is called direct instruction. In the nontraditional approach, also called the whole language approach, the student is taught from whole to part. As Goodman (1986, p. 19) puts it, "Language is actually learned from whole to part. We first use whole utterances in familiar situations. Then later we see and develop parts, and begin to experiment with their relationship to each other and to the meaning of the whole." This is an inquiry approach.

According to Dixie Lee Spiegel (1992, p. 39), a leader in literacy research, "One of the most important benefits of whole language is that we are at last becoming *literacy* educators, not just reading teachers and occasionally writing teachers. Writing is increasingly viewed from the perspective of a process of communication, not as a set of mechanics to be mastered and then applied. Even very young children are being perceived as both writers and readers. . . ."

The language arts are best taught as integrated language modes; however, teachers need to understand fully each of the language arts. The integrated language arts curriculum is described by Searfoss (1989, p. 1) as follows:

> In an integrated language arts curriculum, reading instruction is nestled among instruction in writing and oral language, resulting in greater command of all these language tools than is possible when they are taught in isolation. . . . Children must *read* about what they hear and talk about; they must *write* about what they read and hear and talk about; they must *talk* about what they read and write and hear.

As a means of closely scrutinizing the language arts, this book presents each one separately. Sample lesson plans are included to demonstrate different methods used to integrate the language arts throughout the curriculum, thereby making instruction more efficient and effective.

The language arts and their history are introduced in the following section.

Historical Overview of the Teaching of the Language Arts

Historically, the teaching of the language arts in the United States began with an emphasis on oral language. In the 1700s, children learned the letters of the alphabet from hornbooks, which were shaped like Ping-Pong paddles and made of wood or cardboard. Today few hornbooks are left because children used them to hit paper wads or small rocks back and forth to each other. When stories were shared, they were read or told orally as family and friends gathered together in the evening. In those days, children learned to read primarily from the Bible or *The New England Primer,* a book filled with didacticism based on the religious ideas of that period.

Next to *The New England Primer,* Noah Webster's *The Elementary Spelling Book* was the most important textbook of the colonial period. More commonly referred to as the "Blue Back Speller," this book was handed down within families from sibling to sibling and generation to generation. Initially, children were instructed in single letter recognition. This was later combined with letter-sound correspondence, such as *ab* and *ac.* Word parts, such as *bab* and *bat,* were introduced next, and whole words, such as *babble* and *battle,* were presented as the last step before sentences. Thus, learning was from part to whole.

During this period, listening and speaking were not stressed. The primary listening skill was to "pay attention." Speaking was to occur only when the student was asked to recite or respond to the teacher's questioning.

In the mid-1800s, William Holmes McGuffey created a graded reading series based on a controlled repetition of letters, sentence length, and vocabulary. Since copyright laws were less rigorous in those days, McGuffey borrowed pieces of literature from all over the English-speaking world to include in his readers. Noted authors such as William Shakespeare and Henry Ward Beecher had stories, parables, or poetry that fit McGuffey's didactic theme for the *McGuffey Eclectic Readers.* The texts more than hinted that if a child disobeyed his or her elders, fate would intervene and severe punishment would be dealt to the evildoer. Handwriting and, to a limited extent, spelling and writing were included in the lessons. Even though McGuffey only earned a total of $500 for his books, his work was the pioneering effort of what is known today as the basal reading series.

Although early writing instruction emphasized the correctness of the written product, no attempt was made to consider the writing process. Essays were common assignments for children in the upper-elementary grades.

Toward the end of the 1800s, reading instruction changed after a phonetics method was introduced. However, the emphasis on word analysis rather than comprehension resulted in teachers becoming dissatisfied and seeking another method for teaching reading. The phonetics approach was replaced by the "look-say" method, which required a child to learn words as "sight" words. In other words, children memorized the words so they could recall the words on sight.

During the early 1900s, reading continued to dominate language arts instruction. Technology was advancing and affecting society in general—indoor plumbing, electricity, the telephone, and the radio were advances that touched the masses. Reading, too, advanced as "scientific instruments" were used to evaluate the effectiveness of reading materials and methods. The introduction of standardized reading tests led to a multitude of research studies. Even today, standardized reading tests prevail in many school districts.

During this period, particularly around 1920, the emphasis on oral reading changed to that of silent reading. Later, during World War II, reading methodologies underwent careful analysis when it was discovered that many of the men drafted into the armed forces were illiterate. As a result, reading became a national concern at the end of World War II. The baby boom and the trend toward conservatism in the 1950s led to the very successful basal readers published by Scott, Foresman, which centered on the middle-class lives of the mythical Dick and Jane and their pets, Spot and Puff. Children were usually divided into three reading groups, high, average, or low ability, in which they took turns listening to each other read short passages out loud as they followed the life-styles of Dick and Jane and middle-class America.

The basal reader program included a reader and a teacher's manual. Later, a student workbook was added. Stories in the basal reader were written with a controlled vocabulary. Some publishers even attempted to present sentence patterns that paralleled children's oral language development. Around the middle of the 1950s, reading instruction again returned to a focus on phonics.

During the 1970s, the trend was toward humanism, with the key educational terms being *individualization* and *integration*. Children progressed at their own rates, not at a rate determined by their teacher. The language arts were taught as integrated subjects. For the first time, listening and speaking skills took the lead in early childhood grades as children were taught poetry and songs to share and enjoy. The language experience approach promoted by Roach Van Allen (1976), among others, emphasized individualization and integration of language arts instruction. "Personal language," or the language of the child, was the key to teaching language arts. The child would dictate a story to the teacher, who wrote it down word for word and read it back to the child. The child would read it again, thereby relating his or her own orally spoken words to the printed words on the paper.

In the 1980s, writing gained increased interest as researchers began to consider the relationship between reading and writing development. Rather than the end product, the process of writing was viewed as being of primary importance. Children were encouraged to share their writing with classmates who listened and commented on their reactions. Once again, listening and speaking grew in importance. The process approach contends that a hierarchy of subskills does not exist in the development of the language arts.

A major publication appeared in 1984, entitled *Becoming a Nation of Readers: The Report of the Commission on Reading* by Richard C. Anderson, Elfrieda H. Hiebert, Judith A. Scott, and Ian A. G. Wilkinson. The recommendations in the report included the need for parents to read to preschoolers and to support school-age children's interest in reading. In addition, teachers were encouraged to allow children more time for writing and independent reading. Phonics instruction, according to the report, was necessary for beginning reading.

In the 1980s and 1990s, the whole language approach came into vogue as the child was encouraged to "take control" of his or her own learning. Children's literature and writing were moved to the forefront. Basal reader publishers took note of the holism-constructivism of whole language and began to change their materials from their previous behavioristic bent. According to Fuhler (1990, p. 312), new basal reading series

> reflect a concerted effort to include recognized children's authors, a variety of literary genre, excerpts, and complete stories from award winning books to entice children to read. Depending on the publisher, there is increased emphasis on process writing, thought-provoking questions, and techniques to teach effective reading strategies as well as a decreased emphasis on skills in the middle to upper grades.

In the late 1980s, leaders in language arts still could not agree on how beginning reading should be taught—a phonics or a whole language approach. Because of the intensity of the controversy, the U.S. Department of Education funded a study by Marilyn Adams (1990) entitled *Beginning to Read: Thinking and Learning about Print* to examine the merits of both approaches. The summary concluded that beginning reading "programs for all children, good and poor readers alike, should strive to maintain an appropriate balance between phonics activities and the reading and appreciation of informative and engaging texts" (p. 125).

Current practices vary between the traditional approach, with its reliance on textbooks and skills, and the nontraditional whole language approach, which emphasizes learning processes and more choice and flexibility in instruction, but provides less structure and direction for the classroom teacher. The whole language approach has resulted in basal readers that emphasize process rather than product and acquisition of learning strategies rather than skills. Increasingly, children's literature is being used to teach reading and content area subjects such as science and social studies. According to Strickland (1995, p. 295), "Textbooks continue to be important classroom resources, but they are no longer the dominant materials for literacy or learning in the content areas." However, as recently as 1989, Shannon (1989) estimated that 90 percent of elementary classroom reading programs were organized around a commercially prepared basal reading series.

Many classroom teachers have continued to rely on the basal reader as the predominant approach in the teaching of reading. Most teachers, however, have adopted what they consider to be the best of the traditional and nontraditional approaches—an integrated process approach to language arts instruction, incorporating reading, writing, listening, and speaking. Combination of traditional and nontraditional approaches has a distinct advantage in that skills and strategies are learned in a relevant, real-life context (Duffy, 1992).

The Language Arts

Speaking

By the time children enter kindergarten, they have two expansive vocabularies, listening and speaking. Their listening vocabulary greatly exceeds their speaking vocabulary; however, they are easily able to carry on an adultlike conversation. These vocabularies have been shaped to a large extent by the children's experiential backgrounds. Early and frequent exposure to books; opportunities to visit stimulating places of interest such as zoos, museums, and libraries; involvement in discussions with family members; and conversations about the television programs they watch are all important in the development of vocabulary and speaking skills.

In the classroom, speaking needs to be encouraged rather than discouraged. Research suggests that children will not benefit from being told about language and how it should be used; rather, they must be active users of language to master it (Fisher & Terry, 1990). Language play is a part of childhood, and children need to have many opportunities to experiment with it. For instance, Kurt, a 5-year-old, described his reversible down vest as his "switcher vest" because he could wear it to school as a red vest, "switch" it, and wear it home as a blue vest.

All children need to interact with the teacher and their peers, but this is especially critical for children who are bilingual, language delayed, learning disabled, or mentally challenged. According to Hennings (1990, p. 496), such children need a "language-rich environment." Whole language activities that capitalize on these children's oral language skills are beneficial (Ford & Ohlhausen, 1988).

Writing

Writing, like reading, is acquired early by children, perhaps even before reading. Two-year-olds make pencil or crayon marks on paper, marks that are meaningful to them even though they are meaningless scribbles to most adults.

Writing is the most difficult language art to acquire because years of development are needed before this skill is mastered. In fact, some professional writers assert that it takes between 20 and 30 *years* to learn to write because of the complexity of writing. Whereas the reading process requires one to take symbols from the printed page and extract meaning from them, the writing process is more complicated. It incorporates a large number of skills: grammar, handwriting, and spelling. Not only must a child initiate an idea, but the idea must be developed and expanded upon, modified or deleted, and organized so that it makes sense to the reader; moreover, correct grammar and spelling must be included and the handwriting must be legible. These are high expectations for children to accomplish! Indeed, when Frank Smith (1988) began observing children to better understand how they go about the process of writing, he said, "The first time I explored in detail how children learn to write, I was tempted to conclude that it was, like the flight of bumblebees, a theoretical impossibility" (p. 17).

In the Classroom Mini Lesson
Biographical Poetry

*I*n an attempt to become acquainted with students, the teacher may have them write a biographical poem at the beginning of the school year. For the teacher, this is also an opportunity for sharing some information about himself or herself so that, in turn, the students get better acquainted with their teacher. The format for a biographical poem (Danielson, 1989, pp. 65–68) follows.

Title: First and last name
Line 1:   First name
Line 2:   Four traits that describe you
Line 3:   Brother/sister of . . . (May substitute Son/daughter of)
Line 4:   Lover of . . . (Gives names of three people or ideas)
Line 5:   Who feels . . . (Gives three feelings)
Line 6:   Who fears . . . (Give three items)
Line 7:   Who would like to see . . . (Give three items)
Line 8:   Resident of . . . (Give city and state)
Line 9:   Last name only

Michael Pedersen

Michael
Smart, athletic, funny, musical
Brother of Pat and Phil
Lover of baseball, singing, and my dog
Who feels excited when the Mets win, happy when I go to Florida,
    and sad when it rains
Who fears high places, power blackouts, and black widow spiders
Who would like to see the movie *Batman,* a New York Knicks game,
    and Disneyland
Resident of Rochester, New York
PEDERSEN
    —Michael Pedersen, Grade 4

Because of writing's many aspects, researchers have discovered that the writing process entails not only inventing and choosing ideas but also writing the first draft, editing and rewriting the draft, and finally, sharing the finished product with others.

Children enjoy writing, and they really want to write down their ideas and thoughts. However, when preschoolers and kindergartners begin to write, they lack spelling proficiency. This does not deter them in their eagerness to communicate with the world. If they don't know how to spell a word, they simply invent their own spelling. For instance, Paul, a kindergartner, wrote "I WT TWO A FDHS" for "I went to a friend's house." Other examples of this type of spelling include "ET" for "eat" and "LF" for "laugh." From the outset, children use invented spelling as a way to convey meaning, the most important part of the writing product. Through their invented spellings, they share imaginative stories and personal experiences.

A classroom teacher must be an advocate of writing and a master of the craft. Donald Graves (1983), a leader in the teaching of writing as a process, refers to the teacher as a craftsperson, "a master follower, observer, listener, waiting to catch the shape of the information" (p. 6). In essence, the teacher assists children in discovering their strengths and in learning from their failures. Teachers gently push and form children into writers, each with a unique style. The end results are children who are in control of their own writing—confident, self-assured writers who write for the love of writing.

Listening

Listening is the first language art that children acquire. As mentioned earlier, the ability to hear and recognize sounds is actually a prenatal development. Amazingly, within 2 weeks after birth, a baby can distinguish its mother's voice from the voices of other adults.

Listening is often considered the neglected language art because it receives less instructional attention in the classroom than do the other language arts. Yet children are required to spend most of the school day listening. They must listen to the teacher to understand newly introduced concepts or directions for an assignment, to classmates during group and class discussions, to the librarian at story time, to announcements broadcast over the school's intercom, and so on. More time is spent listening than in any other language art, including reading.

Listening enables young children to develop a wide vocabulary, establish sentence patterns, and follow directions—all essential for developing speaking, reading, and writing skills. One aspect of listening, auditory discrimination or the ability to distinguish the difference between sounds, aids spelling and reading proficiency.

Both external and internal factors affect children's listening. For example, a sixth-grade class in Indiana had a teacher who had been born and reared in Connecticut. It took the students nearly 6 weeks before they could fully understand his dialect as well as keep up with his fast New England style of speech. In the meantime, the scores on their weekly spelling tests suffered. Schools located near airports or construction areas may have lots of background noise that drowns out speakers from time to time—another external hindrance.

In terms of internal factors, attitude, experiential background, vocabulary, ability to relate new knowledge to previously learned knowledge, and intelligence all play a role in listening. Moreover, emotional or physical problems may hinder listening.

Lessons in listening need to involve children as active listeners; for instance, discussing a book they've read gives children a purpose for listening (Hennings, 1992). Such instruction requires the teacher to eliminate external hindrances to the listening process. The teacher must speak with clarity, adjust delivery speed to that which is comfortable for the majority of the class, carefully examine any dialect differences, present material in an orderly manner, and reduce classroom noise.

Focus Box 2.1

Underlying Assumptions of Direct and Whole Language Instruction

Direct Instruction	versus	Whole Language
1. Children are expected to be passive participants in the learning process.		1. Children are expected to be active participants in the learning process.
2. The product is the most important part of learning.		2. The process is the most important part of learning.
3. Part to whole is stressed.		3. Whole to part is stressed.
4. Learning is based on a sequence of skills.		4. Learning is based on relevant, real experiences.
5. Motivation to learn is extrinsic (material rewards such as stickers are given out).		5. Motivation to learn is intrinsic (child learns because of desire to learn).
6. Children are placed in groups according to ability (low, average, and high).		6. Children are grouped by interests and regrouped as topics change.
7. Competition is encouraged.		7. Cooperation is encouraged.
8. The teacher makes the decisions as to what will be taught and how it will be presented to students.		8. Children make choices as to what and how they will learn.
9. The teacher directly guides instruction, serving as a leader.		9. The teacher indirectly guides instruction, serving as a facilitator.
10. Textbooks serve as the materials for teaching		10. Children's literature and children's own writing serve as the materials for teaching.
11. Multiple choice, true/false, and essay tests are used for evaluation.		11. Samples of the children's own work are used for evaluation.
12. The classroom is book centered (the child must fit the book).		12. The classroom is child centered (the book must fit the child).

Reading

Ask a 4-year-old what he or she wants to learn to do in school and the answer will most likely be to "learn how to read." Children consider reading a grown-up, "big stuff" activity. Reading is a major step in learning, for it opens up a vast new world to youngsters and gives them independence as learners.

Reading and writing are interrelated and develop concurrently, secondary to listening and speaking which are the two primary language skills. The development of these two language skills in young children is called *emergent literacy,* meaning that there is in fact a continual emergence or recognition of the printed word. Homes that provide ample opportunities for young children to look at picture books and to hear the books read out loud by their parents or grandparents, to watch Mom and Dad read the local newspaper for items of interest or add an item to the weekly grocery list, and to explore literacy on their own by playing store and school are homes that foster literacy.

Research by Cochran-Smith (1984) and Taylor (1983) has shown that when such literacy surrounds the child, learning usually occurs. Adults should reinforce children by "praising what they have written and read" (Danielson, 1992, p. 279). Indeed, many children from home environments that foster literacy become readers and writers before entering kindergarten.

Having many firsthand and vicarious experiences greatly aids children in learning to read because reading is actually the processing of

When reading with a child, a parent should ask the child to predict what will happen next. Questions about characters and their actions may be included, as well as having the child note details in the illustrations.

Photo courtesy of Rockford Register Star

meaning from the printed page. Thus, children who have had a wide experiential background are better able to relate to and are more likely to be familiar with many reading topics. Smith (1978, 1992) claims that the child's world knowledge actually enriches a passage of text because less is required to identify a word or meaning from the text itself. Take for example, Timmy, a 4-year-old. The word *Crest* on a tube of toothpaste was pointed out and Timmy was asked to read the word out loud. He looked at the word but didn't respond. Then Timmy was asked what kind of toothpaste it was, and he beamed and said, "Crest." Young children can "read" by recognizing commonly used household items, but they often fail to understand that such identification is reading. As children become competent, the reading process becomes progressively more automatic.

Reading can be so personal that it is almost as though the author wrote the words solely for the reader. It is not unusual for a child to laugh out loud at the antics in Mike Thaler's (1993) *The Principal from the Black Lagoon* and to ride a roller coaster of emotions while reading Karen Cushman's (1995) *The Midwife's Apprentice*. Whether the message is broad or narrow, happy or sad, informational or sublime, the reader can relate to the message intellectually and emotionally.

Interdisciplinary Instruction

Increasingly, schools are moving toward interdisciplinary instruction in which all content areas are taught in one thematic unit. This makes for more relevant learning experiences, often more "personal, authentic, and inquiry-driven" (Whitin & Whitin, 1996, p. 84) than relying solely upon science or social studies textbooks.

There are many successful elementary and middle school programs throughout the country that use an interdisciplinary approach to language arts instruction. For instance, Pope Elementary School in Pope, North Carolina, was recently recognized for its exemplary language arts program. Emily Kyser Ramey (1995, p. 418), principal of Pope Elementary, described her school as follows:

> "Language arts instruction is built on the research-based position that children learn to read by reading and being read to and that children learn to write by writing and reading the writing of others. Daily instruction integrates reading, writing, listening, and speaking activities with content area subjects. . . .
>
> Daily time is provided for students to read silently from self-selected materials, to write in journals, and to read aloud to classmates. Learning logs, for subject areas such as science, math, and social studies, allow students to comprehend and summarize new information for themselves and provide additional text for individual and class reading."

Ramey (1995, p. 419) is careful to point out that teachers alone cannot make an outstanding language arts program, that there must be a

> "combined effort of parents, teachers, and administrators committed to a quality language arts program for all students. . . . Pope School strives to provide an integrated language arts program that promotes critical thinking, builds literacy, and helps to develop a lifetime love of reading."

Lafayette Township School in rural New Jersey, also recognized for its outstanding language arts program, views reading, writing, listening, and speaking as integral to the content areas—math, science, and social studies. Students at Lafayette Township have a portion of the school day set aside for silent reading and are read to regularly by their teachers. Writing is often combined with reading (Mahler, 1995).

Assessing the Language Arts

Listening, speaking, reading, and writing require that the classroom teacher rely on a variety of assessment measures. Checklists that specify what precisely has or has not been accomplished are helpful. Some teachers use a rubric to let students know what is expected for an assignment. "In the Classroom Mini Lesson—Biography Assignment Presentations" describes an assignment that has four rubrics or requirements. Two activities are optional.

Anecdotal records are also helpful measures. These may be notes recorded throughout the school day in a daily log, perhaps using a notebook or a clipboard. Interests, behaviors, academic work and so on can all be included in anecdotal records. At the end of each day, the teacher may organize the notes by individual students and convert the notes to a computer disk. A quick and efficient means of organization is to use $4'' \times 6''$ index cards taped inside a photo album in a layered fashion as described in "In the Classroom—Anecdotal Record Keeping." After filling a student's card, it may be placed in a portfolio.

In the Classroom Mini Lesson

Biography Assignment Presentations: March 3

Name _____

Description: For this assignment, you will need to read a biography or an autobiography about a person of your choice. Be sure to check your person with Mrs. Towner. Your final presentation must give the class important and interesting information about the person. To present the information, you may read from a paper or you may memorize it and act it out for the class. You may wish to bring in some artifacts to share with the class. These may be a picture of the person and/or examples of the person's work (a picture painted or a song composed). For this final presentation, you must dress up as the person.

Rubrics:

_____ I checked with Mrs. Towner about the person I want to report about.

_____ I read a biography or autobiography.

_____ I have written a few paragraphs about the person to read to the class.

_____ I have a costume to wear that is typical for my person to have worn.

Optional:

_____ I memorized my presentation and will act it out for the class.

_____ I have artifacts to share with the class.

Biography Presentation Rubric

Student's Name: _____

Famous Person: _____

	Yes	No
I checked my book with Mrs. Towner.		
I wore a costume that would be typical for my person to have worn.		
My presentation consisted of some interesting facts about my person.		
Optional—I brought some artifacts pertaining to my person.		
Optional—I acted out my presentation.		
Comments		

In the Classroom Teaching Hint
Anecdotal Record Keeping

The classroom teacher must stay abreast of students' reactions to activities and materials, their development of learning strategies, and their basic interests and dislikes. The development of self-discipline, an important life skill, should also be noted. In addition, it is important to maintain a record of students' physical well-being. Such information is useful to the teacher in that certain patterns tend to evolve; such patterns influence each child's development in the language arts as well as other curricular areas. These patterns may be shared with the parents during a parent-teacher conference. For instance, if a note indicates that Rod fell asleep in class three times in 2 weeks, the teacher should make a phone call to Rod's parents. Perhaps Rod stays up too late at night or has a medical problem.

A simple record-keeping device is a photo album designed to hold 4″ × 6″ photos in plastic flip sheets. When the album is opened, one set of flip sheets lies on each side. The teacher writes the child's name on the bottom left-hand side of a 4″ × 6″ index card and tapes it to a flip sheet. The students' names are placed in alphabetical order so that when the teacher wants to write a note about a particular child, the other cards are quickly flipped up and that student's card is ready for the teacher's note taking. When a card is filled, the tape is removed and the card is placed inside the plastic photo cover for future reference. Later the cards may be placed in a student's portfolio. A flip record book and student card are shown in figure 2.1.

Lisa A.	Hector L.
Adam A.	Jimmy N.
Mark B.	Ty P.
Jose B.	Carole P.
Roberta B.	Leon P.
Melinda C.	Eric R.
Gary C.	Roberto S.
Glenda D.	Susan S.
Ivan F.	Harry J.
Melissa H.	Jason J.
Terry H.	Julie J.
Jenny K.	Linda W.
Linda L.	

9/5 Brought her new public library card
9/6 Wrote a poem for social studies
9/14 Had trouble deciding which group to join

Lisa A.

Student Cards

9/5 Very happy about being back in school
9/6 Forgot homework
9/7 Brought homework from yesterday; worked well with Hector on writing project
9/8 Brought in a box turtle he found on way home from school
9/14 Requested to work with Hector and Eric on science project; Joked
9/16 Late to school
9/21 The science coop project turned out great; Mark complimented Hector and Eric on their work

Mark B.

9/6 Worked well with Ivan on writing up science experiment
9/8 Has trouble with writing topic sentences
9/13 Lost his library book
9/14 Found   "   "   "   in his locker
    Wrote a nice letter to Jason who was out ill.

Hector L.

Figure 2.1
Example of a flip record book and a student card.

FOCUS BOX 2.2

Alternative Assessment Methods

Assessment Methods	Paper and Pencil	Performance (Process and Product)	Personal Communication (Teacher and Student)
Objective Scoring	Multiple choice True/False Matching Fill-in-the-blank	Checklist or rubric of specific attributes present or absent in behaviors or products	Questions with right/wrong answers
Subjective Scoring	Essay	Rating scale reflecting degrees of quality in behaviors or products	Interviews Portfolios Conferences

While standardized achievement tests continue to be used in most school districts, portfolios have also become popular ongoing assessment measures. Standardized achievement tests are given once a year to evaluate how a group performs. Standardized achievement tests are summative measures and can be compared to a onetime photo that may or may not turn out to the individual's satisfaction. On the other hand, portfolios offer a series of photos, or pictures of the child's achievement, over a period of time—a type of formative assessment during the year that becomes summative at semester or year end and throughout a child's school career. Portfolios can contain writing samples, from first draft through the final product, lists of books read independently and as part of classroom assignments, and videos and audio tapes of the student presenting a dramatic piece or reading poetry or a favorite passage from a children's book. Each item in the portfolio is dated.

Some schools require that each item in a portfolio have an attached index card describing why it is in the portfolio. The student and/or the teacher must then defend the piece. For instance a student may decide to put in a narrative writing selection because she had a well-developed character, or a science fair project about the human body including an illustration of the human digestive system that she drew.

It is best to use a wide variety of assessment measures that are integral to the instruction process, not added on (see "Focus Box 2.2—Alternative Assessment Methods").

Multicultural Considerations

In teaching language arts, the teacher should be sensitive to the needs of multicultural students. In addition, the teacher must help the other students in the class develop a familiarity with and respect for different cultures. As Walker-Dalhouse (1992, p. 416) writes,

FOCUS BOX 2.3

Portfolio Interest Inventory

Name:	Grade:

I like to do:
1. _____
2. _____
3. _____

I like books about:
1. _____
2. _____
3. _____

My favorite books are:
1. _____
2. _____

My favorite authors are:
1. _____
2. _____

Titles of books I'd like to read:
1. _____
2. _____
3. _____

I've written about:
1. _____
2. _____
3. _____

I want to write about:
1. _____
2. _____
3. _____

I'd like to know more about:
1. _____
2. _____
3. _____

I'd like to see videos about:
1. _____
2. _____
3. _____

The multicultural and multiethnic composition of our society today necessitates instruction that addresses the literacy needs of all of its people. Instruction must promote cultural awareness and a valuing of parallel cultures. Parallel culture is used here to denote equality in value and respect for the contributions of cultures co-existing within an area.

James Banks (1992, p. 32), a leading black educator, says "As the ethnic texture of the nation deepens, problems related to diversity will intensify rather than diminish." Banks (1993) suggests that teachers use literature to have students identify problems related to cultural differences and then take actions to solve those problems. Multicultural education requires that *both* teachers and students be committed to improving human relations (Rasinski & Padak, 1990).

According to Sleeter and Grant (1988), there are five primary approaches to teaching children about different cultures and about people with special needs.

The first approach is that of "teaching the exceptional and culturally different." Teachers focus on culturally different or exceptional children and attempt to apply teaching strategies that remediate deficiencies. Cultural

In presenting his report for Women's History Month, this fifth grader is describing how he conducted his research study and compiled his results.

Photo courtesy of Rockford Register Star

background, language, learning style, and/or learning ability are believed to hinder these students in fitting into the mainstream of American society.

The second approach is one of "human relations." Teachers attempt to develop self-confidence in all students. The idea of a melting pot is promoted as students are encouraged to acquire tolerance toward other cultures and toward groups with special needs. Like the first approach, this one promotes assimilation into the mainstream of American society.

The third approach is that of "single-group studies." One group is selected and studied by the class. For example, African Americans might be studied during Black History Month (February). Supporters of this approach hope to reduce social stratification and thereby raise the status of the group being studied.

The fourth approach is one of "multicultural education" and has five goals (Gollnick, 1980);

1. To promote the strength and value of cultural diversity
2. To promote human rights and respect for those who are different from oneself
3. To promote alternative life choices for people
4. To promote social justice and equal opportunity for all people
5. To promote equity in the distribution of power among groups

This approach supports structural equality and cultural pluralism. Rather than being a melting pot, American society is more reflective of a tossed salad in that each ingredient is individual and distinct.

The fifth approach is that of "education that is multicultural and social reconstructionist." Undoubtedly, this approach deals most directly with oppression and social structural inequality in the areas of disability, gender, race, and social class (Sleeter & Grant, 1988). With this approach, teachers attempt to make the entire curriculum multicultural. Discussions and units can revolve around current social issues and life experiences of the students themselves. For instance, why are so few buses accessible to people with disabilities? Why does the price of gasoline in predominately African-American neighborhoods tend to be higher than in predominately white areas?

One of these approaches may be adopted as part of the elementary curriculum. In teaching language arts, the classroom teacher will be asked to implement the approach, thus requiring a familiarity with different cultures and those with special needs.

Meeting the Learning Needs of Every Student

Children vary greatly in their learning needs. Thus every class has students with differing interests, abilities, and weaknesses. To help each student develop to the fullest, the classroom teacher must plan in advance how to approach the student's strengths and weaknesses. There has been much debate among educators about inclusion of severe learning disabled or physically challenged students in the regular classroom.

Physically challenged students may or may not have greater difficulty with language arts than other children. It may depend upon the child's particular disability. For instance, Melissa who was severely injured in an auto accident and suffered head and leg injuries had trouble with language in all forms—speaking, listening, reading, and writing. Dave was injured in an accident and lost his right arm. His language skills were fine, but he had to learn to write with his left hand. Children with cerebral palsy usually have difficulty speaking, but their thinking is not impaired.

Students who are mentally challenged due to retardation tend to learn more slowly and need lots of opportunities to practice skills. Repetition and structure are very important. Such children need to learn the basic skills of listening, speaking, reading, and writing in order to communicate effectively with others. Concrete, hands-on activities should be stressed. Activities that they can relate to are important so that interest in learning is maintained. Pairing these students who work on projects with other students in the class benefits all of the students.

Students with one or more specific learning disabilities may have trouble with listening, speaking, reading, writing, and/or math. They may have trouble conversing with others, reading fluently, organizing their writing, and spelling. Their handwriting tends to be slow and often illegible to anyone but themselves. If a computer is available, it can help speed up a learning disabled child's writing. Like mentally challenged students, it is important to structure the learning experiences for learning disabled students.

Structure is also important for behaviorally challenged students, who often display inappropriate behavior both inside and outside the classroom. They may be overly assertive, aggressive, or disruptive—frequently or perhaps only occasionally. Often they are unhappy or depressed children. It is

Focus Box 2.4

Incorporating Ethnic/Multicultural
Content into the Curricula

*B*anks (1989) believes there are four curricular models for incorporating ethnic/ multicultural content into the curricula. The levels are described below.

First Level: Contributions Approach. The focus is the highlights, heroes, and holidays of a particular culture. A lesson may depict a particular cultural trait. In the study of the Jewish culture, students might read *Mr. Blue Jeans, A Story About Levi Strauss* (Weidt, 1990), who left the Bavarian Alps to live in America where he invented the ever-popular blue jeans. In addition to reading about famous Jewish people, students would also learn about Jewish holidays such as Hanukkah and Passover.

Second Level: Additive Approach. This is similar to the contributions approach in that the basic curriculum remains the same; however, content, concepts, and themes that are reflective of other cultures are "added" to the already established curriculum. For instance, *Aunt Martha and the Golden Coin* (Rodriguez, 1993), a picture book that tells of an African-American woman who migrates north during the post-Depression era, might be added to the literature curriculum.

Third Level: Transformation Approach. Students are encouraged to view problems, themes, concerns, and concepts from the perspective of different cultural groups. For instance, a major historical event might be studied in terms of the various cultures involved, such as the completion of the transcontinental railroad as viewed by Native Americans and by Chinese and Irish railroad workers. To determine the different viewpoints, students would do research, including reading such books as Lawrence Yep's (1993) *Dragon's Gate.*

Fourth Level: Decision-Making and Social Action Approach. Students identify social problems and concerns, then make decisions and take steps to help resolve the identified problems and concerns. Typically students take action on a community level to try to improve conditions for a particular cultural/ethnic group. Students may read the local newspaper or tune in to a local radio or television station to identify a cultural or ethnic group that is being treated unfairly.

References

Banks, J. (1989). Integrating the curriculum with ethnic content: Approaches and guidelines. In J.A. Banks & C.A. McGeen Banks (Eds.), Multicultural education: Issues and perspectives (pp. 189–207). Boston: Allyn & Bacon.

Children's Books

Rodriguez, A. (1993). *Aunt Martha and the golden coin.* New York: Clarkston Potter.
Weidt, M.N. (1990). *Mr. Blue Jeans: A story about Levi Straus.* Minneapolis: Carolrhoda.
Yep, L. (1993). *Dragon's gate.* New York: HarperCollins.

important to find learning activities that the child can do successfully. Praise and support from the teacher are essential. Developing such students' communication skills is crucial, particularly if the children recognize the need to communicate in a positive manner, both orally and in writing.

Attention deficit hyperactivity disorder (ADHD) students also need structure as they have difficulty attending to activities and staying on task. The seating arrangement in the classroom should take into consideration the fact that they are very easily distracted. An activity center too near the door may result in the child wandering down the hallway, or a window seat may result in the child staring at a squirrel in a tree. Like behavior disordered children, ADHD students tend to be disruptive and have mood swings. Some ADHD students are given medication to assist them in coping with the demands of the classroom structure, such as sitting quietly and working attentively.

Students who are gifted are academically talented but may not be equally proficient in all areas. A child may be brilliant in math and science but average in writing if he or she isn't as motivated in that area. Spelling may be a problem if the gifted student is interested in getting ideas down on paper but not necessarily in having them spelled correctly. Some gifted students are underachievers because they lack motivation. Others may be outspoken and lack tolerance of other students, which can lead to difficulty in group work. The classroom teacher needs to find activities that challenge the gifted student and enrich his or her learning.

Non-English-speaking students have varying needs. Because Spanish more closely resembles English than do the languages spoken by Native American or Asian American students, Hispanic students have to learn fewer new consonant and vowel sounds. However, there are still major language differences, such as pronouns in English which don't exist in Spanish. In addition to language, non-English-speaking students encounter many cultural differences (as previously discussed.) Teachers need to be supportive of these students, and their families as well. Working in pairs or small groups is beneficial for such students as is providing a structured environment.

Meeting the learning needs of all students becomes increasingly difficult each year and will probably continue to do so. Consider the fact that "crack babies" are in school now, suffering from learning problems caused by their mothers' drug addiction. The same is true for those children whose mothers consumed an excess of alcohol while they were pregnant. The number of single mothers continues to increase; thus, many children lack a father figure. Working parents may not have the time to talk with their children each day, let alone read to them and help them develop their writing skills. Then there is the child who comes from a model home environment but who lacks self-confidence. Meeting the needs of all students will be a continual challenge for every teacher.

S u m m a r y

This chapter has briefly described the language arts: listening, speaking, reading, and writing. The development of the language arts is concurrent and interrelated. Children enter kindergarten with some language arts skills well established. For instance, they can carry on a conversation with adults. They can identify labels that surround them: McDonald's, Sears, and Toys 'R' Us. Many even attempt to write out a scrawling message for others to read.

Today the language arts are taught traditionally, "part to whole," or nontraditionally, "whole to part." Followers of the former theory stress the development of separate skills. Those who have adopted the "whole to part" theory follow the whole language approach, which focuses on the learning process rather than the product and presents the language arts in an integrated curriculum. Most teachers use some portion of both theories in their language arts instruction.

Questions

1. What types of habits possessed by a speaker interfere with the audience's ability to listen?
2. How does the home environment help or hinder the development of emergent literacy?
3. Compare and contrast the traditional teaching of the language arts with current approaches.

Activities

1. Listen to young children as they play in a park or at a daycare center. In what unique or unusual ways do they use words?
2. List several factors, both internal and external, that affect your listening.
3. Research indicates that children fail to benefit from being told about language and grammar. Recall a situation in which a teacher "told" you about usage.

For Further Reading

Madigan, D. (1993). The politics of multicultural literature for children and adolescents: Combining perspectives and conversations. *Language Arts, 70* 168-176.

Sharer, P.L., & Detwiler, D.B. (1992). Changing as teachers: Perils and possibilities of literature-based language arts instruction. *Language Arts, 69* (3), 186-192.

Short, K.G., & Burke, C. (1996). Examining our beliefs and practices through inquiry. *Language Arts, 73* (2), 97-102.

Smith, E.M. (1992). Answering the voices in my head: Students and teachers make a difference. *The Reading Teacher, 45* (6), 424-427.

References

Adams, M.J. (1990). *Beginning to read: Thinking and learning about print.* Urbana, IL: Center for the Study of Reading.

Allen, R.V. (1976). *Language experiences in communication.* Boston: Houghton Mifflin.

Anderson, R.C., Hiebert, E.H., Scott, J.A., & Wilkinson, I.A.G. (1984). *Becoming a nation of readers: The report of the Commission on Reading.* Washington, DC: National Institute of Education.

Banks, J.A. (1989). Integrating the curriculum with ethnic content: Approaches and guidelines. In J.A. Banks & C.A. McGeen Banks (Eds.), *Multicultural education: Issues and perspectives* (pp. 189-207). Boston: Allyn & Bacon.

Banks, J.A. (1992). Multicultural education for freedom's sake. *Educational Leadership, 49,* 32-36.

Banks, J.A. (1993). The canon debate, knowledge construction and multi-cultural education. *Educational Researcher, 47,* 4-14.

Cochran-Smith, M. (1984). *The making of a reader.* Norwood, NJ: Ablex.

Cohn, J. (1987). *I had a friend named Peter* (G. Owen, Illus.). New York: Morrow.

Cushman, K. (1995). *The midwife's apprentice.* New York: Clarion.

Danielson, K.E. (1989). Helping history come alive with literature. *Social Studies, 80* (2), 65-68.

Danielson, K.E. (1992). Learning about early writing from response to literature. *Language Arts, 69* (4), 274–280.

Duffy, G. (1992). Let's free teachers to be inspired. *Phi Delta Kappan, 73* (6), 442–447.

Farris, P.J., & Kaczmarski, D. (1988). Whole language: A closer look. *Contemporary Education, 59* (2), 77–81.

Fisher, C., & Terry, A. (1990). *Children's language and the language arts* (3rd ed.). Boston: Allyn and Bacon.

Ford, M., & Ohlhausen, M. (1988). Tips from reading clinicians for coping with disabled readers in regular classrooms. *The Reading Teacher, 42* (1), 18–22.

Fuhler, C.J. (1990). Let's move toward literature-based reading instruction. *The Reading Teacher, 43* (4), 312–315.

Gollnick, D.M. (1980). Multicultural education. *Viewpoints in Teaching and Learning, 56,* 1–17.

Goodman, K. (1986). *What's whole in whole language: A parent/teacher guide to children's learning.* Portsmouth, NH: Heinemann.

Graves, D. (1983). *Writing: Teachers and children at work.* Portsmouth, NH: Heinemann.

Hennings, D.G. (1990). *Communication in action: Teaching the language arts* (4th ed.). Boston: Houghton Mifflin.

Hennings, D.G. (1992). *Beyond the read aloud.* Bloomington, IN: Phi Delta Kappa.

Johnson, T.D., & Louis, D.R. (1987). *Literacy through literature.* Portsmouth, NH: Heinemann.

Mahler, W.R. (1995). Practice what you preach. *The Reading Teacher, 48* (5), 414–15.

Ramey, E.K. (1995). An integrated approach to language arts instruction. *The Reading Teacher, 48* (5), 418–19.

Rasinski, T. & Padak, N. (1990). Multicultural learning through children's literature. *Language Arts 67,* 576–580.

Searfoss, L. (1989). Integrated language arts: Is it whole language? *California Reader, 22,* 1–5.

Shannon, P. (1989). *Broken promises.* Granby, MA: Bergin & Gavey.

Sleeter, C.E., & Grant, C. (1988). *Making choices for multicultural education: Five approaches to race, class, and gender.* Columbus, OH: Merrill.

Smith, F. (1978). *Comprehension and learning.* New York: Holt, Rinehart, & Winston.

Smith, F. (1988). *Joining the literacy club: Further essays in education.* Portsmouth, NH: Heinemann.

Smith, F. (1992). Learning to read: The never ending debate. *Phi Delta Kappan, 73* (6), 442–447.

Spiegel, D.L. (1992). Blending whole language and systematic instruction. *The Reading Teacher, 46* (1), 38–44.

Strickland, D. (1977). Promoting language and concept development. In B. Cullinan & C. Carmichel (Eds.), *Language and young children.* Urbana, IL: National Council of Teachers of English.

Strickland, D. (1995). Reinventing our literacy programs: Books, basics, balance. *The Reading Teacher, 48,* (4), 294–302.

Taylor, D. (1983). *Family literacy.* Norwood, NJ: Ablex.

Templeton, S. (1991). *Teaching the integrated language arts.* Boston: Houghton Mifflin.

Thaler, M. (1993). *The principal from the Black Lagoon.* New York: Scholastic.

Trelease, J. (1989). Jim Trelease speaks on reading aloud to children. *Reading Teacher, 43* (3), 200–206.

Walker-Dalhouse, D. (1992). Using African-American literature to increase ethnic understanding. *Reading Teacher, 45* (6), 416–423.

Whitin, D.J., & Whitin, P.E. (1996). Inquiry at the window: The year of the birds. *Language Arts, 73* (2), 82–87.

*S*trategies for Processing Language

The child sees everything that has been experienced and learned as a doorway. So does the adult. But what to the child is an entrance is to the adult only a passage.
—**Friedrich Nietzsche**
On the Future of Our Educational Institutions

Introduction

W alking into Paul Carter's fifth-grade classroom, one immediately becomes invigorated. His students have been working in groups of three, with each group having selected a state to study in depth. The success of each group's project requires that all three group members work together cooperatively. In addition, Paul wants to integrate his already crowded curriculum, so each group must respond to at least 7 of 10 questions that the class developed together and put on the chalkboard. The questions range from historical and geographical information to climate to industry and economic status to famous people. Paul also requires that each presentation include something about the humanities, the social sciences, and the sciences. Each group must present its findings to the entire class and make a time capsule for next year's class to open.

Each group was allowed to select any state that had not already been chosen by another group. When two groups wanted the same state, California, they were given 10 minutes to formulate their reasons for wanting to examine that state. Each group presented its reasons to the rest of the class, who served as the jury. After much discussion, the class decided that California was sufficiently large for two reports, one on the northern area and one for the area south of Sacramento. Although Paul was a bit skeptical of how this would work out, he held his concerns in check. After all, this was a democratic process.

Shelly, Edwin, and Max had selected Indiana. Carefully, they prepared their time capsule: a Match Box Indianapolis-style race car, photos of Michael and Janet Jackson, a newspaper clipping of an Amish buggy with a "slow-moving vehicle" sign on the rear, a bottle of prescription drug capsules (empty) from Eli Lilly, a drawing of the political campaign slogan of William Henry Harrison ("Tippecanoe and Tyler Too"), a copy of a poem by James Whitcomb Riley, a cassette recording of Cole Porter's "Anything Goes," and pictures of the boys' and girls' state high school basketball champs. Using a laser disk player connected to a computer with a hypercard, Shelly, Edwin, and Max presented their overview of the state. With actual film clips of a tornado touching down in a rural area, the group explained how tornadoes are formed and pointed out the devastating effects of tornadoes, which are common in Indiana in March and April. A film clip of a recent Indianapolis 500 race enabled the group to emphasize the economic benefits of a race that occurs only once a year. With other film clips, a poster board of pictures of products manufactured or grown in the state, and their written report, the group members shared the information they had concluded would be the most beneficial to the class.

The other groups also had intriguing reports. The groups that selected Kansas and Montana were both stumped as to what existed in the way of the humanities in their states. The Kansas group went to the local art museum and

This baby will develop schemata based on the experiences it has growing up.

discovered that the Cowboy Museum of Art is in Wichita, Kansas. The Montana group learned that Mel Gibson and other movie stars have ranches in the state. Clearly, the integrated, cooperative learning activity Paul had hoped would be successful proved to be an excellent learning activity for the entire class.

Thinking and language are closely related and their development is largely concurrent. Children who can deal effectively with tasks requiring the use of thinking strategies are usually those who are proficient in listening, speaking, reading, and writing. For example, Tompkins (1990, p. 2) found that developmental trends in writing can be observed as children "learn to express more complex thoughts."

This chapter briefly discusses children's thinking processes: how information is gathered, interpreted, encoded, and related. By learning about the thinking processes, teachers can teach the language arts more efficiently. Major criticisms of instruction and instructional materials have been that they ignore recent research on learning and are thus ineffective (Anderson, Hiebert, Scott, & Wilkinson, 1984; Gardner, 1991). By understanding the thinking processes, teachers can help students become effective communicators and independent thinkers as they solve problems and make critical judgments.

├ ─ ─── ─ ─ ── ─ ─ ── ─ ─── ─ ─ ── ─ ─ ── ─ ──├ ─ ─ ── ─ ─ ── ─ ─ ── ─ ─── ─ ── ─ ── ─ ─── ─ ──┤

Innative
(innate factors)

Constructivist
(interaction between
child and environment)

–Cognitive developmental
stages
–Information-processing
strategies

Behaviorist
(stimulus-response
formula)

Figure 3.1
Theories of learning.

Thinking and Language

Egocentric and Socialized Behavior

Children progress through two phases of behavior as they develop thinking and language skills: egocentric and socialized. During the egocentric phase, a young child plays with sounds and words for the sheer joy of it. Beth, a 2-year-old, heard the word "no" from her parents many times, as do all children who reach the "terrible twos." After having yet another encounter with her parents and being told "no," Beth walked up to Herman, the family's basset hound who was lying peacefully in his bed, pointed a chubby finger at his nose, and said, "No! No! No!" Herman, the dog, may have been confused, but Beth probably felt a small tinge of satisfaction in being able to correct the dog's behavior, even if it did not need correcting. Such is egocentric behavior!

A child will engage in other egocentric behavior, such as talking out loud in a monologue. For instance, Kurtis, at 30 months of age, loved to sing in a bathtub filled with toys. He would invent songs by combining various sounds, ending each by throwing back his head and yelling out, "Yee-ooo!" At that point, Kurtis would bow to his audience of toys and say, "Thank you, duck. Thank you, frog"—as if his yellow rubber duck and green plastic frog had given him a standing ovation.

Children may share their thoughts as they describe aloud each action they take in a task or an activity. Five-year-old Cynthia was drawing along with her mother and 9-year-old sister. When her sister announced that she was drawing a house, Cynthia responded by telling everyone, "I'm going to draw a picture of a house." Her sister then mentioned that she was going to draw a pumpkin. Cynthia immediately proclaimed, "I'm going to draw a pumpkin by my house."

Socialized behavior, on the other hand, involves children's desire to share and acquire information. For instance, a child may volunteer to give a friend the directions for making a potato chip sandwich or tell the friend where to buy the most gummy bears for a dollar. Children will also respond to questions asked by others and ask questions themselves, expecting a response in return. Through such independent and assertive actions, they gain new insights and develop new concepts.

Information Processing

The underlying assumption of information-processing theory is that the human memory is an "active, complex organizer, and processor of information" (Bell-Gredler, 1986, p. 160). The thinking process involves gathering, selecting, perceiving, organizing, encoding, storing, retrieving, and relating information. Thus, multiple operations, interpretations, and inferences are made before the brain constructs an entire picture of the exciting and complex reality (Wittrock, Marks, & Doctorow, 1975).

Children, like adults, rely upon organized networks of information structures called *schemata* (singular, *schema*) to relate past experiences and previously gained knowledge to new situations. Schemata also provide the structure or format into which new information must fit in order to be understood and fill gaps or voids in information.

Concepts exist within a hierarchical framework of information that enables one to identify interrelationships among concepts. This framework functions as a type of "on-line" conceptual family tree. For instance, a child's concept of "home" may be part of a larger framework of "houses," which in turn is part of a still larger structure of "buildings." The schemata that children possess influence how they will interpret new information and experiences and, in turn, will ultimately have an impact on the learning process. For instance, a child who has read most of the *Little House* books by Laura Ingalls Wilder will have a much different interpretation of pioneer life than will a classmate who primarily reads mysteries. Likewise, a sixth grader who has grown up in Pennsylvania will have a much different interpretation of the Civil War than a sixth grader reared in South Carolina.

Three major developments have resulted from information-processing research. First, teachers place greater emphasis on how children process information as they are learning. Because each child brings a personal knowledge base to the learning situation, a teacher must take such a knowledge base into consideration. For example, the child who has read several *Little House* books and the child who is not as familiar with life on the prairie may both find Patricia MacLachlan's (1985) *Sarah, Plain and Tall* to be interesting and enjoyable reading. Both children will gain from the book but probably in different ways.

Second, teachers need to instruct children directly in developing problem-solving skills. Children should be taught ways in which they can organize knowledge and how they can correct mistakes in understanding. For example, many children are afraid of thunderstorms. By sharing the book *Thunderstorm* by Mary Szilagyi (1985), young children can develop empathy for the young girl in the story, who is frightened by a sudden summer thunderstorm but is reassured by her mother. The students can discuss what sights and sounds of a thunderstorm frighten them. By using an overhead projector or the chalkboard, the teacher can help students to formulate the problem: fear of thunderstorms. Then they may discuss potential ways of resolving their problem. The teacher may share *Flash, Crash, Rumble, and Roll* by Franklyn Branley (1985), which explains what causes lightning and thunder so that the children better understand the problem and can develop concrete ways to solve it.

The third area of information processing that has been highlighted is the need to use semantic networks in both curriculum organization and the analysis of content. Through integrated instruction, the common concepts taught in more than one subject area are presented (Bell-Gredler, 1986). For instance, in solving the problem of being afraid of thunderstorms, knowledge of the cause of a thunderstorm, a scientific concept, was needed before the problem could be resolved.

Information processing requires the teacher to be aware of students' goals, experiences, and motivation and also to demonstrate and teach problem-solving strategies. Because concepts acquired for language arts are likely to be similar to those for other content areas, the teacher should attempt to integrate the curriculum to develop and extend students' abilities to apply information-processing strategies. Such instruction is important in that recent cognitive research findings suggest that children are capable of higher-level thinking at a relatively young age.

> One of the most significant ideas emerging from recent research on thinking is that the mental processes we have customarily associated with thinking are not restricted to some advanced or "higher order" stage of mental development. Instead, "thinking skills" are intimately involved in successful learning of even elementary levels of reading, mathematics, and other subjects. Cognitive research on children's learning of basic skills such as reading and arithmetic reveals that cultivating key aspects of these thinking processes can and should be an intrinsic part of good instruction from the beginning of school. Thinking, it appears, must pervade the entire school curriculum, for all students, from the earliest grades. (Resnick & Klopfer, 1989, pp. 1–2)

In accordance with the foregoing statement, teachers must recognize that learning should be thinking and meaning centered. In other words, children are not recorders of information and knowledge but builders of knowledge structures (Resnick & Klopfer, 1989).

The Nature of Intelligence: Multiple Intelligences

Howard Gardner states in his theory on multiple intelligences that there is not just one form of intelligence based on verbal and reasoning abilities, but that there are seven different intelligences, each having a unique neurological pattern and course of development. With this expanding view, he redefined the concept of intelligence. According to Gardner, intelligence should be defined as follows:

> An intelligence entails the ability to solve problems or fashion products that are of consequence in a particular cultural setting. The problem-solving skill allows one to approach a situation in which a goal is to be obtained and to locate the appropriate route to that goal. The creation of a cultural product is crucial to capturing and transmitting knowledge or expressing one's views or feelings. The problems to be solved range from creating an end to a story to anticipating a mating move in chess to repairing a quilt. Products range from scientific theories to musical composition to successful political campaigns (Gardner, 1993, pp. 7–8).

The seven intelligences included in his theory are as follows:

1. *Linguistic Intelligence*
   This intelligence involves sensitivity to the meaning of words, their order and syntax, the sounds, rhythms and inflections of language, and the uses of language.
2. *Musical Intelligence*
   This intelligence consists of sensitivities to rhythm, pitch, and timbre. It also has an emotional component. Gardner relates musicians' descriptions of their abilities that emphasize an individual's natural feel for music and not the reasoning or linguistic components of musical ability.
3. *Logical-Mathematical Intelligence*
   This intelligence involves interaction with objects and is often called "scientific thinking." Deductive thinking and reasoning, numbers and recognizing abstract patterns are included.
4. *Spatial Intelligence*
   This intelligence is the capacity to perceive the physical world accurately, to perform transformations and modifications on these perceptions, and to produce or recreate forms.
5. *Body and Kinesthetic Intelligence*
   This intelligence involves the ability to use the body in highly specific and skilled ways, both for expressive and goal-directed purposes.
6. *Intrapersonal Intelligence*
   This intelligence involves the ability to access one's own feelings and to label, discriminate, and symbolize one's range of emotions in order to understand behavior.
7. *Interpersonal Intelligence*
   This intelligence involves the ability to notice and make distinctions about other people's moods, temperaments, motivations, and intentions.

The Educational Implications of Seven Intelligences

According to Gardner, much of the school day favors children who are skilled at reading and writing. It does not address the spatial intelligence skills of a student who could, for instance, operate a film projector after watching the teacher set it up once—the same student who may not be considered intelligent because his/her reading and writing skills are poor. Gardner feels that there are too many children just like this whose educational needs are not being met because educators have too narrow a view with regard to who is intelligent. He feels they need to broaden their definition of intelligence to include all seven of the intelligences and then include each of these when they plan their learning experiences for their students.

Also, Gardner states that "genuine understanding—going beyond repetitive learning and short answers" (1993, p. 27) should be the fundamental goal of education. To promote this understanding he proposes that education systems should increase learning activities that involve individual and group projects, apprenticeships, and hands-on experiences. For, Gardner states, "I often hypothesize that people probably learn more from the few projects they do in school than from hundreds and hundreds of hours of lectures and homework assignments" (Gursky, 1992, p. 28). Also, he believes that schools should help children discover subject areas that interest them instead of just focusing on the learning of basic skills. In doing this he feels that children's senses of adventure, flexibility, creativity and natural enthusiasm for learning will be enhanced instead of suppressed. This then would facilitate the attaining of a genuine understanding of whatever children would be learning and, therefore, would facilitate the transferring of this understanding to situations in everyday life.

Teaching Models for Language Arts Instruction

Learning requires children to rely on information processing as they build structures for making sense of the surrounding world. As stated by Jensen and Roser (1990, p. 10), "readers and writers are thinkers: they analyze and synthesize; they compare and contrast; they assimilate and accommodate; they weigh and refine ideas." The teacher must create a "learning tone" by using methodologies in which students are aware of which learning behaviors are accepted and which are not. The learning tone influences whether students will be active or passive learners.

Children must use what they themselves know about learning and apply that knowledge. As Wells (1990, p. 15) notes, "simply telling students to read more critically or to make their point more effectively in writing will be of no help unless they have developed an understanding of the mental activities involved." To put it more concisely, children must think about thinking.

This knowing about knowing and knowing how to know is called *metacognition*. Teaching children to use metacognition requires that teaching be indirect (Derry & Murphy, 1986). Children become responsible and accountable for their own learning as they monitor their own understanding and comprehension. They must know about knowing: how to know, when to know, and the reasons for knowing. Through opportunities to learn and apply various learning strategies, children can adopt the best study approach for a particular problem. Thus, learning becomes tactical as children are aware of and try to control their efforts to use particular learning strategies and skills (Jones, Palincsar, Ogle, & Carr, 1987).

By capitalizing on children's past experiences and having them relate what they have already learned through observation, experience, and language, teachers will find that learning is facilitated. Through the sharing of such existing knowledge, especially at the beginning of a lesson, children further develop the framework of knowledge as they associate the new learning experience with older and more familiar ones.

In the Classroom Mini Lesson
Inner and Socialized Speech Activities

*C*onsider the suggestions below to promote thinking development through inner and socialized speech.
1. Have children take puppets home as a means by which to retell to family members stories that were read to the class.
2. Set up three or four science experiments in the classroom and have the students tape-record their descriptions of how to conduct the experiments and their reactions to the results.
3. Have young children illustrate the events that took place on a field trip, and then videotape their descriptions of the events as they explain their drawings.
4. Encourage children to reread a difficult passage of text aloud softly to better understand it.
5. Have students rewrite and illustrate the ending of a story they read in their reading group. Afterward, have them try to persuade the group that their ending is better than the author's original version.
6. Have students give impromptu speeches to describe major historical events—for example, Custer's last speech to the U.S. Seventh Cavalry, Franklin's reaction when he invented the lightning rod, Amelia Earhart's last radio dispatch, or Dr. Christian Barnard's first human heart transplant.

Teachers, however, must be cautious in that cultural differences exist, differences that affect literate thinking. For instance, in Western culture one type of text attempts to persuade the reader to take action, to buy a particular product after reading an advertisement about that product. Another type of text conveys factual information, as in reference and do-it-yourself books. A third type of text depends on the emotional engagement between the reader and the author and the previous experience of the reader, as in novels, poetry, and so forth (Wells, 1990).

Some of the teaching models that aid students in their development of learning strategies include advance organizers, nondirective teaching, and cooperative learning. A discussion of these models follows.

Advance Organizers

Advance organizers are organizing ideas that are presented prior to an assigned reading or at the beginning of a lesson. Ausubel (1963) developed the theory of advance organizers on the assumption that students can be assisted with concept development; providing information to students will result in greater understanding and retention on their behalf. In Ausubel's opinion, if a child begins with the right "set" and is presented with material that is understandable, then meaningful learning can occur.

The way the subject matter is to be organized should parallel the way in which students organize knowledge in their own minds. Meaning, therefore, necessitates the connecting of the new information with the existing knowledge of the child. The child must take an active role in the learning process because advance organizers "explain, integrate, and interrelate" the new material of a lesson or assignment with previously learned material (Joyce & Weil,

1986). It has been shown that students who have been exposed to such advance organizer techniques over a long period of time tend to be more adept at organizing ideas and information as a means to anchor content (Joyce, Showers, & Rolheiser-Bennett, 1987).

Typically, a teacher will introduce a lesson, presenting all new concepts before the assigned reading. By using previously learned concepts and terminology as a means to introduce unfamiliar ideas, the teacher makes the acquisition of the new material easier for the students. The initiation of a study dealing with Middle Eastern peoples will require that the concepts of culture and religion be understood. A beginning lesson on reptiles will require that the idea of a reptile be comprehended.

Nondirective Teaching/Constructivism

Creating a classroom where students are self-directed requires that students be both self-motivated and confident learners. A term often used to describe nondirective teaching is constructivism; the goal of nondirective teaching is to facilitate student learning through the establishment of a stimulating classroom environment in which examining, probing, and questioning take place. Inquiry is the focus. Newly gained knowledge may influence the learner to reevaluate previous perceptions. This approach is used in many whole language classrooms because it forces the student to attempt to make sense of the surrounding world.

The teacher's role is that of a facilitator. The teacher accepts all responses, feelings, and beliefs without judgment. As a warm, responsive individual, the teacher must be supportive and sincerely interested in the intellectual growth and welfare of all the students in the classroom. There is a "permissiveness" in the classroom: permission to learn without coercion or pressure from the teacher. Encouragement is offered freely by both the teacher and the student's peers.

Student-centered group discussions play a major role in nondirective teaching. Conferences and interviews are commonplace; divergent thinking and self-evaluation are emphasized inasmuch as learning is highly personalized.

One good example of nondirective teaching took place in a first-grade classroom in a small New Mexico town. The teacher asked her students to hurry and finish their work so they would be on time for lunch. This prompted one of her students to ask, "Who controls time?" The teacher responded with another question: "Who do you think controls time?" The students began looking at each other. No one knew. One boy raised his hand and said, "The mayor controls time." Other students disagreed, each volunteering the name of a person or persons who they thought directed people's comings and goings.

Seizing the opportunity to use an inquiry approach, the teacher suggested that the students write letters to various individuals to find out who controls time. That afternoon, the students wrote to every important person in town: owners of businesses, politicians, religious leaders, municipal employees, and the like. Every one of the letters received a response, which the teacher read to the class before placing it on a "Who Controls Time?" bulletin board. A three-page, single-spaced letter from a judge explained the importance of time and promptness. Other individuals not only wrote letters but either arranged to visit the classroom or to provide a walking field trip through their place of work for the entire class. Paramedics demonstrated how they used medical equipment as quickly and efficiently as possible to save lives. A rancher discussed how cattle grow over a period of several months, while a postal employee explained how time is needed to get mail from different parts of the United States.

The first graders undoubtedly learned more about time from this non-directive teaching episode than they would have from any form of direct instruction. They also gained respect for community members—just as the community leaders gained an understanding of 6-year-olds and how they think.

Cooperative Learning

Teachers have three types of instructional goal structures from which to choose: cooperative, competitive, and individualistic (Johnson & Johnson, 1987). Students can help one another in the learning process by working together in heterogeneous groups in which the success of each member depends on the success of each of the other group members. Such group interaction is more popularly referred to by educators as cooperative learning (Watson & Rangel, 1989).

A competitive goal structure exists when students perceive that they can meet their own goals only if other students fail to meet their goals—for instance, listing the names of students by rank order according to their achievement on a spelling test. An individualistic goal structure exists when the students are able to achieve their learning goal independently of the goal achievement of other students—for example, learning how to correctly form a cursive capital F. Both competitive and individualistic goals structures are a major part of classroom instruction because students need to learn to compete for fun and to work autonomously (Johnson & Johnson, 1978).

Cooperative learning, as already noted, is based on a teamwork philosophy whereby students help one another in the learning process. According to Slavin (1988), the collaboration of children attempting to accomplish a common task or goal is expected to produce a better finished product than would

The success of a cooperative learning activity requires that each participant of the group contribute and fulfill his/her assignment.

© James L. Shaffer

be produced if the students worked individually. Serving as a social model, cooperative learning requires that small groups be formed by the teacher for the purpose of unified investigation of a topic or development of a specific end product. Students may be encouraged to form their own groups without direct teacher influence after they have experienced cooperative learning and understand the associated requirements; however, most cooperative learning groups are formed across ability levels (Meloth, 1991).

Because cooperative learning is the sharing of knowledge among peers and ultimately helping the other members of the group master academic material, divergent thinking is fostered and valued. Through the verbalization of both new ideas and previously acquired information, decision making and the ability to compromise are promoted along with the sharpening of speech and investigative skills. Conducive to activating and stimulating children's prior knowledge (Flood, 1986), cooperative learning enables children to share their thoughts and ideas in a type of group brainstorming. Cooperative learning also contributes to concept attainment (Johnson & Johnson, 1985) because students can introduce new concepts and ideas, explaining and interpreting them for their group colleagues.

If students of different ethnic backgrounds are grouped together, cultural awareness along with the knowledge base is expanded (Slavin, 1983). However, because of the students' diverse backgrounds, the accomplishment of the final goal will probably require additional time. A commonality of beliefs and

Focus Box 3.2

Using Cooperative Learning for Group Investigation

G roup investigation requires students to take an active part in planning what they will study and how. Groups are formed on the basis of interest in a topic. Each group member contributes to the investigation by seeking out needed information. The group gets together to synthesize and summarize the work and presents its findings to the entire class. Group investigation includes the following six stages:

Stage 1: The topic to be investigated is identified, and students are organized into research groups.

Stage 2: The investigation is planned in the groups.

Stage 3: The investigation is carried out by group members.

Stage 4: Each group synthesizes and summarizes information and prepares a final report.

Stage 5: Each group presents its final report to the class.

Stage 6: Each group's investigation, including the process used and its products, are evaluated.

Adapted from Sharan and Sharan, 1989–1990, pp. 17–21.

experiences serves as a type of "shorthand form of communication" whereby each of the group's participants can assume certain responses or agreements without the need for discussion or negotiation (Ouchi, 1981).

Research findings suggest that cooperative learning improves academic performance for all students, enhances ethnic interactions, and increases proficiency in English for second-language students (Watson & Rangel, 1989). Three elementary teachers in Minnesota who have used cooperative learning with their students for a combined 23 years have found that cooperative learning can benefit all students, low ability, mainstreamed, or gifted (Augustine, Gruber, & Hanson, 1989–1990).

Being able to participate within a successful group, despite each individual child's actual performance and contributions, allows for an increased self-perception of ability, satisfaction, and price, as well as increased peer esteem (Ames, 1981). For cooperative learning to be effective, (1) the children must work toward a group goal, and (2) the achievement of the goal must depend on the individual learning of *all* group members (Slavin, 1988). Thus, the group goal must be both challenging and attainable.

In the teaching of language arts, there are numerous opportunities to use the cooperative learning strategy effectively. One good example of cooperative learning in spelling is presented by Augustine et al. (1989–1990). At the beginning of the school year, data that indicate individual spelling abilities are collected for each student. After spending a month teaching in the traditional spelling format in which children are pretested, given the words, given the opportunity to study the words, and tested, the teacher divides the class into groups of three students. Each group has a high, an average, and a below-average speller. The groups, or triads, work together for the remainder of the year. A reward system is used to promote positive interdependence, or a kind of teamwork, "sink or swim" atmosphere. Spelling is taught as follows:

Monday: *Pretest*
Group members take the three pretests together, sharing information. Each student has his/her own list of words. Group members grade the tests together later and point out any difficult or tricky words.

Tuesday: *Spelling Games and Activities*
The group selects from a variety of activities to study the words.

Wednesday: *Practice Test*
Group members devote 5 minutes to coaching each other on the words before taking the three practice tests. Each student takes his or her test individually. The group is reconvened after the test to review missed words and applaud correct papers.

Thursday: *Study Day*
Time is devoted to studying the words. If all three group members had perfect practice tests, the group earns free time and may engage in other activities.

Friday: *Final Test*
Group members spend 5 minutes coaching each other on the words prior to taking the final tests. The students take the tests individually, meeting as a group afterward to discuss and praise each other's work. If all three group members mastered their word lists, the group earns a reward.

Cooperative learning may be based on common interests. For example, a group of students may wish to read the same book, discussing it within the cooperative group on a daily basis until they have completed the book. Mrs. Wells's class of inner-city students had one small group of sixth-grade boys who decided to read *Sounder* (Armstrong, 1969). Although the boys were close friends and inseparable on the playground, their reading skills varied widely. Still, they made up their minds that they were going to read *Sounder* together. Mrs. Wells got multiple copies of the book for the group, but before she gave the boys the books, she had them create some guidelines for studying and discussing it. Together, the boys decided to write down any questions they had as they read the book and to talk about them the next day when they met as a group. Any new words or parts of the book they especially liked, they also jotted down in their notebooks. The group members decided to pace themselves by reading and sharing a chapter a day.

The boys became engrossed in *Sounder* and by far surpassed their daily reading goal. Even though none of the boys had ever been to a farm or even outside the large northern city in which they lived, their interest in southern rural living intensified as they progressed through the book. One of the boys saw an analogy between *Sounder* and *Uncle Tom's Cabin* (Stowe, 1982), which he had seen on television as a late, late movie. Tim, the poorest reader in

In the Classroom Mini Lesson
Sequencing Events

*A*fter reading Mary Ann Hoberman's (1978) *A House is a House for Me,* have the students get into groups of four. Give each group the following materials:

2 green paper plates
a can of chocolate frosting
a package of graham crackers
a plastic knife
8 pieces of red licorice
a variety of colors of small gumdrops
thin, 2-inch pretzels
sentence strips

Have the children make a house for their group. When the houses are complete, have each group write the directions for building their house on sentence strips. Younger children may dictate their directions to the teacher or a parent volunteer.

This is also a good activity to do with reading buddies from another grade level. The older student can assist the younger student in building the house. Then the younger student can give the instructions in the correct sequence to the older child.

The following is an example dictated by a group of first graders:

First we made the floor. Next we used icing to add the walls. Then we put on the ceiling and the roof. Then we made doors and windows and a sidewalk. Last, we made trees and a chimney.

Hoberman, M.A. (1978). *A house is a house for me* (B. Frasier, Illus.). New York: Viking.

the group, was the first to notice that Armstrong did not refer to any of the characters by name except for the dog, Sounder, and individuals outside the described family.

When the group began daily discussions, Mrs. Wells would occasionally join the students. She made a few suggestions, but primarily she listened to their interactions. Later in the class sessions, she would find herself working with other children but still listening to the *Sounder* group's conversation because of the boys' high level of enthusiasm and excitement.

In their discussions and sometimes arguments, the boys' vocabularies grew. They were now using words such as *prejudice, empathy,* and *apathy;* by reading and rereading passages, they were able to make comparisons and interpretations. In using their newly acquired skills, they selected one passage as the most powerful in the book and shared it with the entire class. The passage described the boy now grown, remembering his father and faithful coon dog, Sounder, as they were in the prime of life, a time prior to the tragedies that befell the family and resulted in the deaths of his father and dog. The boy knows that he will forever remember the deep voice of Sounder echoing through the night.

When the boys finished *Sounder,* they were emotionally spent. The lower-ability readers had kept up with the other members of the group in their readings throughout most of the book. Realizing how draining the book had been for the boys and trying again to utilize the advantages of cooperative group interaction, Mrs. Wells suggested that they read another book together. She provided copies of *Be a Perfect Person in Just Three Days!* by Stephen Manes (1984), a humorous book lacking the complex literary merit of *Sounder.* Mane's book enabled the boys to laugh together, and because they were such good friends, they readily shared personal stories of embarrassing situations when they appeared to be "cool" and to have everything under control. The boys later read two other books together as a group.

Drama, storytelling, and writing each lend themselves to cooperative learning. For example, a writing activity may require students in a group to formulate questions for investigation of a particular subject; group members must then conduct research and contribute information for the purpose of uncovering the answers. Each student may write a portion of the final report to be read to the class. Similarly, the *Foxfire* series of books by Eliot Wigginton is based on an experience of secondary students in a small, rural school in Rabun Gap, Georgia. These students worked together in groups to interview individuals and record stories, tales, recipes, and home remedies of those living in the Appalachian Mountains. Wigginton's (1985) *Sometimes a Shining Moment* describes some of the approaches that can be used to teach composition.

The following lesson plan on organizing information reveals a method for making cooperative writing an enjoyable experience as students work together to solve a mystery. (See "In the Classroom Mini Lesson—Organizing Ideas for Writing.")

Literature Circles

Literature circles have become popular with many teachers in that they foster both independent reading and writing as well as collaborative learning (Daniels, 1994; Harste, Short, & Burke, 1988; Kroll, & Paziotopoulos, 1991). Kitagawa (1994) describes literature circles as a hands-on approach that promotes reading as an expressive process. Literature circles are groups of three to nine students who have read the same story, picture book, or novel and who have gathered to talk about their feelings, reactions, and responses, both written and oral, to what they have read. For young students in kindergarten through third grade, the teacher is usually present during the discussion to lend support but not to dominate the discussion. For older students, the teacher is nearby, usually roaming between groups, to provide support or resolve a problem if needed. However, the students lead the discussion since the goal of literature circles is to ensure that students converse with each other rather than talking only to the teacher (Gavan, 1994). The long term goal of literature circles is that children will become lifelong readers and will enjoy sharing their interest in reading with relatives, friends, and colleagues.

The following seven benefits of literature circles are outlined by Scott (1994)

In the Classroom Mini Lesson

Organizing Ideas for Writing

Objective: To stress the importance of organizing information in writing
Subjects: Language arts (writing, listening, speaking, and reading)
Social studies

Prepare different clues and make six copies of each clue. Mix the clues and place three clues in each envelope.

On a piece of colored cardboard, write the following questions:

When did the murder take place?
Where did the murder occur?
How was the victim killed?
What was the killer's motive?
Who killed the victim?

Display the questions for all the students to see. Tell the students they are to play detective and solve the murder by answering all five questions. Then randomly divide the class into groups of five students each. Give each student an envelope containing three clues to the murder. All the groups will attempt to solve the same murder. The groups will have 10 minutes to solve the mystery, trying to answer as many of the questions as possible.

Each group member must read the clues in his or her envelope to the other four members of the group. After all the clues have been read, group members may begin their discussion.

At the end of 10 minutes, ask for answers to the five questions. Unless the clues clearly point out the answers, probably two or fewer responses will be correct and the murder will go unsolved. At this point, ask the students why they did not (or did) solve the murder. What strategy would have helped the group solve the murder? Move from solving the murder mystery to modeling the importance of organizing facts. (Note: Organize the clues. Point out that when a person reads, it helps if the information is organized. This is true for letters, recipes, newspaper accounts of a crime, and so forth.)

On an overhead transparency prepared in advance, show the students 20 different factual statements about the life of George Washington, from his childhood to his farewell address as president. Then have each group organize the facts into categories, labeling each category. The groups should organize the statements and, afterward, share their categories with the class by explaining how and why they selected their categories.

As a final step, have each group tie together the statements in one of the categories and write a paragraph for that category.

In the Classroom Mini Lesson

Leadership and Cooperation

*S*wimmy, by Leo Lionni (1963), is the story of a small fish who is left alone when a large tuna eats his school of fish. Swimmy meets and joins another school of fish. He instructs his new school of fish in how to work together to overcome obstacles. The teacher may read this book to second and third graders and then have the students engage in the following activities:

1. Find poems or other books about fish: for example, "Fish?" and "The Silver Fish" in Shel Silverstein's *Where the Sidewalk Ends* (1974).
2. Continue Swimmy's story and write another adventure for him.
3. In a small group, talk about the food chain in the ocean and draw a picture to illustrate it.
4. Write a riddle about a kind of fish and have the other students guess what kind it is.
5. Make a warning sign for Swimmy to alert him and his school of fish to the dangers of the big fish.
6. Join with five classmates and move as a school of fish. What does it feel like?
7. Observe fish in an aquarium. Describe what they do when they eat, move, and so on.
8. Pretend you are Swimmy. Write a note warning little fish of the dangers of big fish. Tell the little fish how they can protect themselves.
9. Swimmy showed that he was a true leader. Discuss what kinds of things he did that made him a leader.

Lionni, L. (1963). *Swimmy*. New York: Pantheon.
Silverstein, S. (1974). *Where the sidewalks ends*. New York: Harper & Row.

1. Literature circles help students converse about literature.
2. Sharing personal responses to literature is essential for students to understand what they have read.
3. Literature circles use the social nature of the classroom to invite reading, extend thinking, and prolong involvement with text.
4. Since there is no ability-grouping with literature circles, they promote an acceptance of other students' ideas, strengths, and responses.
5. As students participate in literature circles, they can see their own growth as they learn to participate in literature circles.
6. Literature circles support the kind of skills students will need in the future in the workforce and as community leaders.
7. Literature circles help develop reading strategies and proficiency in responding to text in different ways.

A literature circle may last for a day on a picture book or basal reader story or 2 to 3 weeks on a novel. A literature circle can require between 1 to 2 hours of class time each day, depending on the reading level of the material, the reading ability of the students, the degree of experience students have had leading their own discussions without adult supervision, and how well organized the teacher is initially.

Organizing Literature Circles

Implementing literature circles can appear to be overwhelming at first. Thus it is important for the teacher to become organized and to plan out the activity before plunging into the activity with the students. The size of the group itself must be considered. With six or seven students in a group, more topics are covered, but the pace is usually fast and furious with the participants all vying to engage in the discussion. With three or four students, the pace slows down but the context is covered in greater depth. Thus, groups of four to five students tend to be the most popular.

The following are methods of establishing structure and providing guidance for students as they engage in literature circles.

Read Aloud. Each literature circle begins with a read aloud. What is selected to be read aloud by the teacher may differ with each book as well as with each grade level. For instance, the introduction or first chapter of a chapter book or novel may be most appropriate for third graders through eighth graders while a page or two of a picture book may be most appropriate for first or second graders. In some cases, a small portion of the text somewhere in the middle of the book may be the best choice. It largely depends on the book and the ability level of the students. The teacher may decide, for instance, to read the prologue or introduction from Lois Lowry's (1993) *The Giver* or Jerry Spinelli's (1990) *Maniac Magee* to a fifth- or sixth-grade class or Avi's (1994) *The Barn* to a seventh- or eighth-grade class to entice them into the story.

A good picture book to start literature circles with kindergartners or first graders is Denise Fleming's (1993) *In the Small, Small, Pond,* as children enjoy the delightful rhyming that describes the activities of the animals in the pond. Mem Fox's (1988) *Koala Lou* is also a good choice as children at this age may question their mother's love for them. A couple of good picture books that can be used for literature circles with first and second graders are Lynn Cherry's (1990) *The Great Kapok Tree* and Helen Lester's (1994) *Three Cheers for Tacky* (1994). Gail Gibbons (1994) *St. Patrick's Day* is a good nonfiction book for first through third graders, particularly since by March 17, St. Patrick's Day, most first graders can read this book on their own.

Picture books can be used for literature circles from the early childhood grades through middle school. In fact, some teachers prefer to begin with a picture book for introducing literature circles to upper-grade students. Jane Yolen's (1987) classic *Owl Moon* opens with an intriguing first page that makes for a good, albeit brief, read aloud that works well with third and fourth graders. Katherine Paterson's (1994) *Flip Flop Girl,* the story of a girl who moves to a new town, is also appropriate for this age level.

The Fortune-Tellers, by Lloyd Alexander (1992), the story of a carpenter who accidentally becomes a fortune teller and marries a wealthy merchant's daughter in the process, is a great humorous story to use for a literature circle. Other types of picture books lend themselves to literature circles, as well. Allan Say's (1993) *Grandfather's Journey,* the biography of Say's Japanese grandfather's life in Japan and the United States, makes for an interesting discussion of life before and after World War II in both countries. Patricia Polacco's (1994) *Pink and*

Say is the actual Civil War story of Polacco's great grandfather, Say, who had his life saved by an African-American Union Army soldier, Pinkus, and Pinkus's mother, both of whom died in helping Say. *Pink and Say* can be used in literature circles with children from second through eighth grade. Newbery Award winners are often superb choices for fourth- through eighth-grade literature circles.

Response and Reaction. After reading a portion of the text aloud, the teacher divides the students into pairs and lets them spend 2 minutes discussing the material that was read, encouraging them to give open, honest responses and reactions.

Share (Teacher Evaluates). Three or four students share the main focus of the discussions they had with their partners. This enables the teacher to determine to what extent the students are on target with the assignment because information is received from three to four different sets of students.

Form Groups. The teacher divides students into groups of four or five. Consideration needs to be given to students interests, skills, and behavior. A list of the groups and of which students will be assigned to each group should be established *before* starting the read aloud, preferably the night before so changes can be made before school begins in the morning.

Assign Students Roles. The teacher gives each student a role to play in the group. This, too, should be prepared beforehand, as organizing students by group saves time involved in handing out assignment sheets.

Obviously, the size of the group will determine to some extent the roles assigned. For a group of three students in Grade 3 and higher, the role assignments may double. For instance, one student may be both the discussion leader and the passage master, while another student may be the character captain and the summarizer, and the last student may be the connector and the illustrator. The book itself may dictate that certain roles be included while others not be included. Also the teacher may want to change the roles used for different stories or books in order to keep the activity fresh and interesting for students. The roles are as follows:

Discussion Leader. This student is responsible for keeping everyone on task, taking charge of the interchange as the group decides how they will get the tasks accomplished. Later this student monitors each group member's progress and serves as a troubleshooter if a group member needs help. The discussion leader writes a brief summary of what went on in the group.

Character Captain. This student jots down responses about the actions and thoughts of the characters in the story.

Scene Setter. This student tracks and describes the different scenes in the story.

Passage Master. This student notes and shares important passages in the story.

Literary Critic. This student responds to literary questions about the book or book chapter. The student is given a worksheet with the following questions listed at the top:

In what way is this book or book chapter important?

What does it provide in terms of the following:
 —significant ideas or points?
 —character development?
 —plot development?
 —setting (time and/or place)?
 —theme?
 —writer's style?
How does this chapter fit into the book?
If this chapter were to be eliminated from the book, what essential elements would need to be put into other chapters?

Illustrator. This student creates an art project that reflects the content of the material read in the book, for example a major scene in the story or chapter. The art project may be a collage, a comic strip, a drawing, a computer graphic, a clay sculpture, or some other art medium.

Word Reporter. This student finds seven or eight unfamiliar words or words used in an unfamiliar context in each chapter. Each word is jotted down on a sheet of paper along with the page number on which it appeared. The word reporter also writes down the sentence in which it was used. When the group meets to discuss what they have read, the word reporter shares the words. The group then determines which three or four words need to be shared with the entire class.

Connector. This student makes connections between the book and real life.

Summarizer. This student briefly summarizes the key points of the story.

All Students in Group (Optional). All of the students keep a literature response journal to record their reactions and responses as they read. This may be a shared role.

Clarify Student Roles. The teacher selects a student from each group to read aloud the task description for his or her role until all the roles have been shared. After each task description has been read aloud, the teacher invites questions. Each role is clarified before moving on to the next one. Before sending the groups off to read the chapters and then to meet as a group, the teacher emphasizes that the discussion is to involve everyone.

Assign Reading. At this point, students read the assignment, for instance chapters one through three, keeping their role in mind. As they read, they take notes. If students finish reading the material before others in the group (and someone always finishes quite a bit ahead of the remainder of the group), they jot down possible discussion topics for the group or their own reactions to the material they read.

Groups Meet and Share. The groups meet for at least 15 minutes to talk about what they have read and their responses to the material. While the students are meeting in their groups, the teacher drifts from group to group, noting reactions as well as offering assistance when needed.

Reconvene the Class and Debrief. The teacher focuses the initial discussion on the content of the material the students have just read. Then, students are encouraged to share their personal reactions and responses to the book. Finally, students discuss the roles they played in their respective groups (Daniels, 1994).

Extension Activities. The teacher assigns extension activities for each group. The following are examples of creative projects:

- a semantic map of the relationships between characters
- a mural
- a clay sculpture
- a drawing
- a diorama
- an audio tape advertisement to promote the book
- a videotape of a readers' theater based on lines from the book
- a play based on a portion of the book
- a written report (particularly if the book is nonfiction)
- a biography of the author's life
- a panel debate
- letters of correspondence between characters
- a diary of the main character or a supporting character
- a poem based on the events of the book

The timetable below shows how one teacher incorporates literature circles into his class. With older students such as fourth through eighth graders, each group may establish its own timetable to accomplish its goals.

Literature Circle Weekly Timetable

Monday

Read Aloud—Chapter 1	5–10 minutes
Response and Reaction	2 minutes
Share (Teacher Evaluates)	5 minutes
Form Groups	2 minutes
Assign Students Roles	2 minutes
Clarify Student Roles	3 minutes
Assign Reading—Chapters 2–5	1 minute
Reading time	40 minutes

Tuesday

Groups Meet and Share	20 minutes
Reconvene the Class/Debrief	15 minutes

Wednesday

Assign Students Roles	2 minutes
Clarify Student Roles	3 minutes
Assign Reading—Chapter 6–10 (End of book)	1 minute
Reading time	30–45 minutes

Thursday

Groups Meet and Share	20 minutes
Reconvene the Class/Debrief	15 minutes

Friday

Extension Activities	50 minutes

Suggestions for Initiating Literature Circles

Perhaps the easiest way to begin incorporating literature circles in the classroom is to use picture books or short stories. On the first day, the teacher reads aloud and then has the class discuss their reactions to the read aloud. Groups and roles are assigned and each role is carefully explained. The students then are given the short story or picture book reading assignment. As they read, they perform the tasks corresponding to their assigned roles. Then the students meet in groups and share their reactions and responses to what they have read. They also share what they have done to complete the tasks assigned to their roles. The class reconvenes and shares with the teacher, who supervises the final debriefing. The next day, the students stay in the same groups but are given different roles to perform. This process continues until all of the students have had a chance to serve in each of the different roles.

Marianne Kroll and Ann Paziotopoulos (1991) use literature circles with kindergarten and first-grade students. They modify the literature circle by adding a "quiet voice monitor," a child who is given a red circle to place in the middle of his or her group when the discussion becomes too loud. Students start with wordless picture books and record their reactions by drawing pictures in a notebook. With kindergartners and first graders, the teacher remains with the group throughout the literature circle activity. Thus, only one group is engaged in the literature circle activity at a time. The other students are working at other activities, such as math, science, computers, and art.

When Kroll and Paziotopoulos perform a read aloud, they select from one of several bookmarks they have made. For example, they use bookmarks labeled "magic" for *Cinderella*. Later, when the students read in their groups, they put a magic bookmark at the places in the story where the fairy godmother uses magic.

At the kindergarten and first-grade level it is important to assign each group a different book so that children learn about four or five different books during the class sharing and debriefing stage. This helps to keep the attention level high during class discussion time. Copies of all the books shared are available for the children to read or to take home for their parents to read. Some teachers find that recording the books and placing the books and audiotapes in the listening center after the class discussion is an effective way to motivate students to read.

In using literature circles at the middle school level, Jill Scott (1994), a seventh- and eighth-grade teacher in Henry, Illinois, found that to begin with modest hopes is the best route. By starting with short stories and moving gradually to novels, student aren't overwhelmed by the tasks and more willing to become involved in their group's discussion. During the first few attempts, students tend to be somewhat reserved as they attempt to figure out exactly what is expected of them as part of the literature circle activity. After two or three times through literature circles, the students become more confident and take charge of their own learning.

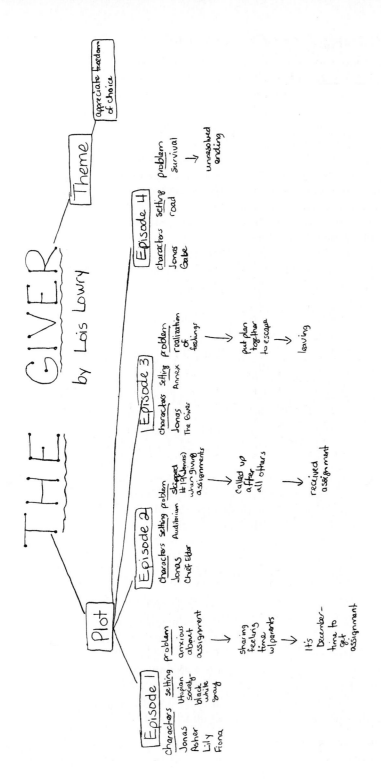

Figure 3.2
This is a semantic web of *The Giver* along with an illustration of a scene from the book. These were part of the culminating project of a literature circle for a group of middle school students.

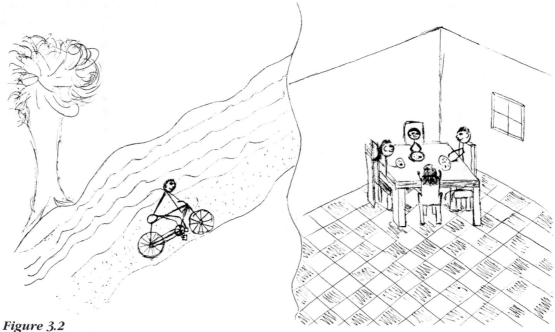

Figure 3.2
(*Continued*)

Developing Higher-Level Thinking Skills

Children process information and utilize it through different levels of thinking. Bloom's (1956) taxonomy of education provides such a hierarchy of thinking processes (see focus box 3.3). The examples provided in focus box 3.3 relate to the use of children's literature in teaching thinking skills.

It is important to realize that the six levels of Bloom's taxonomy can be used to formulate questions for most children's literature, from wordless picture books to adolescent novels. In many instances, it is possible, for example, to use a picture book to question children at both lower levels of thinking (knowledge, comprehension, and application) and higher levels (analysis, synthesis, and evaluation). For example, consider the following use of Jon Scieszka's (1989) classic, *The True Story of the Three Little Pigs:*

Knowledge:	What did the wolf want to borrow?
Comprehension:	Why did the wolf eat the first little pig?
Application:	Why did the wolf become angry with the third little pig?
Analysis:	Why wouldn't the newspaper reporters believe the wolf's story?
Synthesis:	Why do you think the wolf frequently got into trouble?
Evaluation:	Do you think the wolf was clever or dumb? Tell why you think so, giving examples from the book to back up your opinion.

Focus Box 3.3
Bloom's Taxonomy of Education

1. **Knowledge**   *Recalling information*
   Example: Giving the sequence of events in *Spot's First Walk* by Hill (1981)
2. **Comprehension**   *Understanding*
   Example: Making generalizations about Oaf's three gifts in Cunningham's (1986) *Oaf*
3. **Application**   *Abstracting and applying the information*
   Example: Inferring traits of characters in *R, My Name is Rosie* by Cohen (1978)
4. **Analysis**   *Analyzing*
   Example: Predicting the outcome of *The Sign of the Beaver* by Speare (1983) with three chapters still to be read
5. **Synthesis**   *Breaking information down and putting it together in a new way*
   Example: Interpreting the personal conflict of Bright Morning as her Navaho tribe is forced to march 300 miles as prisoners of white men in O'Dells (1970) *Sing Down the Moon*
6. **Evaluation**   *Making judgments*
   Example: In the book *The Wish Giver* by Brittain (1983), a stranger promises to make wishes come true for 50 cents. Considering individuals who rely in their work on making their own predictions come true (astrologers, psychics, and so on), what makes their work appear to be honest and thereby acceptable to society?

Brittain, B. (1983). *The wish giver.* New York: Harper & Row.
Cohen, B. (1978). *R, my name is Rosie.* New York: Lothrop.
Cunningham, J. (1986). *Oaf.* New York: Knopf.
Hill, E. (1981). *Spot's first walk.* New York: Putnam.
O'Dell, S. (1970). *Sing down the moon.* Boston: Houghton Mifflin.
Speare, E.G. (1983). *The sign of the beaver.* Boston: Houghton Mifflin.

Formulating good questions is an art and a science. It requires preparation prior to teaching the lesson itself. Creating and asking the lower-level questions is a rather simple task; an elaborate list can be developed quite quickly. In the case of *Peter Rabbit,* for instance, one might ask: What color was Peter's coat? What did Mrs. Rabbit tell her children before she left to go shopping? Where did Peter go? What did Peter eat in the garden? What did Mr. McGregor hold in his hand as he chased Peter? Where did Peter hide? Who encouraged Peter to get up and run? What did Peter leave in Mr. McGregor's garden? And so on.

Asking such lower-level questions may appear to be almost a waste of time; however, such questions do have value in discussions. By initially answering basic questions, children tend to be more apt to answer higher-level questions. This is because in providing correct responses to the easier questions, students actually become more confident overall. Starting out with higher-level, rigorous questions often intimidates students, especially those who are insecure or shy to respond.

Lower-level questions tend to be closed-ended in that either a right or wrong response exists. For example, the question "What did Peter leave in the

In the Classroom Mini Lesson
Problem Solving

*P*roblem solving can be an effective group thinking activity for children of all grade levels. The books listed below are excellent choices for problem-solving activities. The teacher reads to the point in the text where the problem has been firmly established. The teacher then divides the class into groups of three students and instructs them to resolve the problem. The groups must first brainstorm for ideas and then select one idea that will best solve the problem. Each group then writes its solution down and shares it with the class.

Compton, P.A. (1991). *The terrible eek* (S. Hamanaka, Illus.). New York: Simon & Schuster.
  A wolf overhears a man discussing his fear of a "terrible eek," but the wolf misinterprets it as a fear of a "terrible leak." The wolf searches for the meaning of a "terrible leak."
Goble, P. (1988). *Iktomi and the boulder.* New York: Orchard/Watts.
  This book tells the story of Iktomi, a Plains Indian, who is vain and manipulative. Iktomi gets into trouble when a boulder begins chasing him and won't let him escape. Children in the intermediate grades will enjoy solving this problem.
Johnston, T. (1994). *Amber on the mountain* (R. Duncan, Illus.). New York: Dial.
  Amber becomes friends with Anna, who teaches her to read. When Anna returns to the city, Amber must find a way to communicate with her.
Martin, A.M. (1988). *Ten kids, no pets.* New York: Holiday.
  The mother in this story refuses to yield to a persistent request by her children for a pet. Students in Grades 3 through 5 will enjoy coming up with the perfect pet and the reason why the mother should let the children keep it.
Pfister, M. (1992). *The rainbow fish.* New York: North-South Books.
  The rainbow fish is the most beautiful fish in the ocean but must discover how to be happy.

garden?" was answered by Tim, who said, "his coat and shoes." This was the response the teacher sought. However, Sarah interpreted the closed-ended question in a more open manner when she suggested, "He also left behind his courage"; this was quite a divergent and insightful response for a 6-year-old. Although both Tim and Sarah gave correct responses to the same question, clearly their levels of thinking were markedly different.

Higher-level, open-ended questions require more thought, in relating and interpreting information. Why do you think the author/illustrator included a robin in many of the pictures with Peter? Was Mrs. Rabbit cautious? Why or why not? Do you think Peter visited the garden again on another day? Why or why not? Such questions obviously have more than one correct response and are worthy of discussion time. The question "Was Mrs. Rabbit cautious?" can be answered by both yes and no. Jordan believed Mrs. Rabbit was very conservative in her life-style, asserting, "Yes, she's cautious, because she took an umbrella with her. She also took time to clearly warn her children of the dangers of Mr. McGregor's garden." However, Ginger believed otherwise and said, "No, she would have taken her children with her when she shopped if she was cautious." Which child is correct? Both have valid arguments. Does a right answer exist for this question?

According to Goodlad's study (1984) of over 1,000 observed classrooms, 99 percent of all questions asked by teachers were found to be closed-ended, and only 1 percent were open-ended. While these findings probably would not be replicated today, it is apparent that not only is convergent thinking stressed, but that reasoning and arguing are not promoted by teachers. Inquiry through logic in math, problem solving in science, and critical reading, however, can be used to encourage reflective thinking and deliberation. The actual use of open-ended questions has produced results that teachers describe as "fascinating," being both rich and inventive. Unfortunately, research indicates that even in schools where such questioning is encouraged, only 4 percent of all the questions asked by the teachers over an extended period of time are higher-level open-ended questions (Holt, 1988).

S u m m a r y

Because of the close relationship between language and thinking, instructional procedures should consider the thinking processes in the teaching of language arts. By gaining an understanding of how children think, teachers can help students become more effective and efficient in their learning. Children need to develop strategies for learning that enable them to utilize prior knowledge along with their problem-solving capabilities.

Advance organizers, cooperative learning, and nondirective teaching are teaching models that can be used in language arts instruction at the elementary level to enhance student learning depending on the skill being taught. All three models necessitate much planning by the teacher prior to the presentation of a lesson or the organization of a study group.

The posing of both lower- and higher-level questions can greatly enhance the development of children's thinking skills. Bloom's (1956) taxonomy of education objectives offers a hierarchy of thinking processes that can be used across the curriculum.

Questions

1. How would you incorporate cooperative learning in your classroom?
2. What is an advance organizer? Give an example of an advance organizer in teaching one of the language arts to a fifth-grade class.
3. What is a schema and how does it affect a child's learning?
4. As a teacher, how would you model problem solving?
5. Name the levels of Bloom's taxonomy, and define each level.
6. What is the difference between emphasizing lower-level questions and emphasizing higher-level questions?

Activities

1. Develop questions based on Bloom's taxonomy for a children's book.
2. Prepare three advance organizers for chapter 3.
3. Observe your own learning strategies for a week. Write down the ways in which you use your prior knowledge and problem-solving techniques to study for another class.
4. Pretend you are a famous person and model problem solving from that person's perspective—for example, Kennedy and the Cuban missile crisis; Eisenhower and the D-day invasion of Europe; Martin Luther King and the march in Selma, Alabama; Sandra Day O'Conner and her decision to accept the appointment to become the first woman Supreme Court justice; Elizabeth Taylor and her decision to make public her addiction to painkilling drugs; and President Bill Clinton and his decision to send troops to Bosnia.

For Further Reading

Gardner, H. (1993). *Multiple intelligences.* New York: Basic Books.

Lipman, M. (1988). Critical thinking—What can it be? *Educational Leadership, 46* (1), 38–43.

Madden, L. (1988). Improving reading attitudes of poor readers through cooperative reading teams. *The Reading Teacher, 42* (3), 194–199.

Scott, J. (1994). Literature circles in the middle school. *Middle School Journal,* 26 (2), 37–41.

Shepard, L. A. (1995). Using assessment to improve learning. *Educational Leadership, 52* (5), 38–43.

References

Because of the large number of children's books cited in this chapter, these titles are documented in a separate subsection below.

Ames, C. (1981). Competitive versus cooperative reward structure: The influence of individual and group performance factors on achievement attributions and affect. *American Educational Research Journal, 18* (3), 273–288.

Anderson, R. C., Hiebert, E. H., Scott, J. A., & Wilkinson, I. G. A. (1984). *Becoming a nation of readers: The report of the commission on reading.* Washington, DC: National Institute of Education.

Augustine, D. K., Gruber, K. D., & Hanson, L. R. (1989–1990). Cooperation works! *Educational Leadership, 47* (4), 4-7.

Ausubel, D. (1963). *The psychology of meaningful verbal learning.* New York: Grune & Stratton.

Bell-Gredler, M. E. (1986). *Learning and instruction: Theory into practice.* New York: Macmillan.

Bloom, B. (1956). *Taxonomy of education objectives.* New York: David McKay.

Daniels, H. (1994). *Literature circles: Voices and choice in the student-centered classroom.* York, ME: Stenhouse Publishers.

Derry, S. J., & Murphy, D. A. (1986). Designing systems that train learning ability: From theory to practice. *Review of Educational Research, 56* (1), 1-39.

Flood, J. (1986). The text, the student, and the teacher: Learning from exposition in the middle schools. *The Reading Teacher, 40* (8), 414–418.

Gardner, H. (1991). *The unschooled mind: How children think and how schools should teach.* New York: Basic Books.

Gardner, H. (1993). *Multiple intelligences.* New York: Basic Books.

Gavan, E. M. (1994). Who's in control? Is there enough "empowerment" to go around? *Language Arts, 71,* 192–199.

Goodlad, J. (1984). *A place called school.* New York: McGraw/Hill.

Gursky, D. (1992). The unschooled mind. *The Education Digest, 58,* 27–29.

Harste, J., Short, K., & Burke, C. (1988). *Creating classrooms for authors: The reading-writing connection.* Portsmouth, NH: Heinemann.

Jensen, J. M., & Roser, N. L. (1990). Are there really 3 R's? *Educational Leadership, 47* (7), 7–12.

Johnson, D. W., & Johnson, R. T. (1978). Cooperative, competitive, and individualistic learning. *Journal of Research and Development in Education, 12* (1), 3-15.

Johnson, D. W., & Johnson, R. T. (1987). *Learning together and alone: Cooperative, competitive, and individualistic learning.* Englewood Cliffs, NJ: Prentice-Hall.

Johnson, R. T., & Johnson, D. W. (1985). Student-student interaction ignored but powerful. *Journal of Teacher Education, 36* (1), 22-26.

Jones, B. F., Palincsar, A. S., Ogle, D. S., & Carr, E. G. (1987). *Strategic teaching: Cognitive instruction in the content areas.* Elmhurst, IL: North Central Regional Educational Laboratory.

Joyce, B., Showers, B., & Rolheiser-Bennett, C. (1987). Staff development and student learning: A synthesis of research on models of teaching. *Educational Leadership, 45* (2), 12-23.

Joyce, B., & Weil, M. (Eds.). (1986). *Models of teaching.* Englewood Cliffs, NJ: Prentice-Hall.

Kitagawa, M. (1994). Revisiting Britton, as in James. *Language Arts, 71,* 116-120.

Kroll, M. & Paziotopoulos, A. (1991). *Literature circles: Practical ideas and strategies for responding to literature.* Portsmouth, NH: Heinemann.

Meloth, M. S. (1991). Enhancing literacy through cooperative learning. In E. H. Hiebert (Ed.,), *Literacy for a diverse society* (pp. 172-183). New York: Teachers College Press.

Ouchi, W. (1981). *Theory Z: How American business can meet the Japanese challenge.* Reading, MA: Addison-Wesley.

Resnick, L. B., & Klopfer, L. E. (1989). Toward the thinking curriculum: An overview. In L. B. Resnick & L. E. Klopfer (Eds.), *Toward the thinking curriculum: Current cognitive research.* Arlington, VA: Association for Supervision and Curriculum Development.

Scott, J. (1994). Literature circles in the middle school. *Middle School Journal, 26* (2), 37-41.

Sharan, Y., & Sharan, S. (1989-1990). Group investigation expands cooperative learning. *Educational Leadership, 47* (4), 17-21.

Slavin, R. E. (1983). *Cooperative learning.* New York: Longman.

Slavin, R. E. (1988). Cooperative revolution catches fire. *School Administrator, 45* (1), 9-13.

Tompkins, G. (1990). *Teaching writing: Balancing process and product.* Columbus, OH: Merrill.

Watson, D., & Rangel, L. (1989). Can cooperative learning be evaluated? *School Administrator, 46* (6), 8-11.

Wells, G. (1990). Creating conditions to encourage literate thinking. *Educational Leadership, 47* (6), 13-17.

Wigginton, E. (1985). *Sometimes a shining moment: The Foxfire experience.* Garden City, NY: Anchor Press/Doubleday.

Wittrock, M. C., Marks, C., & Doctorow, M. (1975). Reading as a generating process. *Journal of Educational Psychology, 67* (4), 484-489.

Children's Books

Alexander, L. (1992). *The fortune-tellers.* (T. Hyman, Illus.). New York: Dutton.

Armstrong, W. (1969). *Sounder.* New York: Harper & Row.

Avi. (1994). *The barn.* New York: Orchard/Richard Jackson.

Branley, F. (1985). *Flash, crash, rumble, and roll.* New York: Crowell.

Cherry, L. (1990). *The great kapok tree.* San Diego: Harcourt Brace.

Fleming, D. (1993). *In the small, small pond.* New York: Henry Holt.

Fox, M. (1988). *Koala Lou* (P. Lofts, Illus.). Orlando: Harcourt Brace.

Gibbons, G. (1994). *St. Patrick's Day.* New York: Holiday.

Lester, H. (1994). *Three cheers for Tacky.* Boston: Houghton Mifflin.

Lowry, L. (1993). *The giver.* Boston: Houghton Mifflin.

MacLachlan, P. (1985). *Sarah, plain and tall.* New York: Harper & Row.

Manes, S. (1984). *Be a perfect person in just three days!* New York: Bantam.

Paterson, K. (1994). *Flip flop girl.* New York: HarperCollins.

Polacco, P. (1994). *Pink and Say.* New York: Philomel.

Potter, B. (1982). *The complete works of Peter Rabbit.* New York: Warne.

Say, A. (1993). *Grandfather's journey.* Boston: Houghton Mifflin.

Spinelli, J. (1990). *Maniac Magee.* Boston: Little, Brown.

Stowe, H. B. (1982). *Uncle Tom's cabin.* New York: Viking.

Szilagyi, M. (1985). *Thunderstorm.* New York: Bradbury.

Yolen, J. (1987). *Owl moon.* (J. Schoenherr, Illus.). New York: Philomel.

Children's Literature: Opening Windows to New Worlds

READ TO THEM

Read to them
  Before the time is gone and stillness
  fills the room again.
Read to them.

What if it were meant to be that you
  were the one, the only one, who could
  unlock the doors and share the magic
  with them?
What if others have been daunted by
  scheduling demands, district
  objectives, or one hundred other
  obstacles?

Read to them
Be confident Charlotte has been able to
  teach them about friendship,
and Horton about self-worth;

Be sure the Skin Horse has been able to
  deliver his message.

Read to them
Let them meet Tigger, Homer Price,
  Aslan, and Corduroy;
Take them to Oz, Prydain, and Camazotz;

Show them a Truffula Tree.

Read to them
Laugh with them at Soup and Rob,
and cry with them when the Queen of
  Terabithia is forever lost;

Allow the Meeker Family to turn loyalty,
  injustice, and war into something
  much more than a vocabulary lesson.

What if you are the one, the only one,
  with the chance to do it?
What if this is the critical year for even
  one child?

Read to them
Before the time, before the chance, is
  gone.

————**Steven L. Layne**

Layne, Steven L. (October 1994). Read to Them. *The Reading Teacher, 48* (2). Reprinted with permission of Steven L. Layne and the International Reading Association. All rights reserved.

Introduction

*M*rs. Nesbitt, a kindergarten teacher, shared the book *Leo the Late Bloomer* by Robert Kraus (1971) with her class. Leo, the main character, is a young tiger cub who can't draw, read, or write and who is also a messy eater. Leo doesn't even talk. His parents, especially his father, are concerned about his inability to do the things that the other young animals are able to do. One day Leo finally blooms: He can read, write, draw, eat neatly, and even talk. After reading the book to her class, Mrs. Nesbitt and her students talked about things they each could do as well as the things they were still learning to do. The next day at recess, 5-year-old Sally raced up to Mrs. Nesbitt on the playground and shouted, "It happened! I finally bloomed! I can pump!" Sally had learned how to pump her legs to keep the momentum going and thus keep swinging.

Adults once considered children's literature a form of entertainment, but one that lacked content. Children read basal readers; library or paperback books were read during "free time" and not before. Children's literature was used to entice students to read on their own, without prompting by the teacher. For instance, Smith (1992) believes that "Teachers' culminating responsibility is to hand each child over to authors" (p. 435). But literature has become a part of the reading program for reasons other than merely motivating children to read. As Cullinan (1987, p. 6) points out, "Literature educates the imagination, provides language models, and molds the intellect. The heritage of humankind lies in books; we endow students with the key to their legacy when we teach them to read."

Mrs. Nesbitt's sharing of *Leo the Late Bloomer* introduced her class to a cliché in our culture. In particular, the book provided Sally with some encouragement as she discovered that it is quite all right to be a late bloomer. Learning, whether it be to "pump" while swinging or any other skill, is still exciting.

"The single most important activity for building the knowledge and skills eventually required for reading appears to be reading aloud to children" (Adams, 1990, p. 46). Children make the greatest strides in acquiring such knowledge and skills when the vocabulary and syntax are slightly above the child's own level of language development (Chomsky, 1972). Indeed, research indicates that a single oral reading of a book may result in new word meanings being acquired by young children (Elley, 1989).

Consider, for instance, Nick, age 22 months, who became quite familiar with *Brown Bear, Brown Bear, What Do You See?* by Bill Martin, Jr. (1964/ 1983). While watching television, Nick and his mother observed a new commercial that contained several different colorful scenes; the last of these was a lingering shot of a goldfish in a fishbowl next to a stack of encyclopedias. Nick's mother pointed to the television screen and said, "Fish." Nick looked at the screen, then up at his mother and said, "Goldfish." As far as Nick's mother knew, the only other goldfish with which he was familiar was the one in *Brown Bear, Brown Bear, What Do You See?* Yet he was confident he could correctly categorize the fish as a goldfish.

The content of children's literature can expand a child's knowledge and understanding of the surrounding world. In writing about the California reading initiative, Bill Honig (1988, p. 235), then state superintendent of public instruction in California, stated "our children must be taught about the world and ethical values that are generally considered to be important in our culture, such as the sanctity of human life, justice, integrity, respect for the dignity of the individual, honesty, and the importance of family."

Quality literature should not only be read aloud but read by students themselves. Fisher (1989) emphasizes the need for literature to be the primary focus of the reading program in that students should read it, respond to it, create their own meanings from what they have read, and share their findings and understandings with peers.

Reading should be both educational and enjoyable. In other words, literature can be the central means of teaching reading, or it can be used in conjunction with a basal reading program. According to Huck (1996, p. 30), "Teachers must know literature to help children find the right book for them. And . . . they need an understanding of children's responses to books and ways to help them link books to their own personal experience." This chapter discusses the various aspects of selecting and integrating literature into the elementary curriculum.

The Selection of Literature

In choosing literature for elementary students to read, the classroom teacher must be familiar with five important literary elements: (1) characterization; (2) plot; (3) setting, both time and place; (4) theme; (5) author's style; and (6) for picture books and some informational books, illustrations. While a book typically contains all five of these, one element may be emphasized more than the others. Each literary element is described below.

Characterization

The development of characterization is crucial because children often identify with and have empathy for a character, and that character may not necessarily be a main character. It is important that characters be believable, having both good and bad qualities. Laura Ingalls in the *Little House* books displays honest, humor, and bravery as well as jealousy, unhappiness, and fear. Her behavior is predictable to a large extent in that it is quite normal for a child her age to demonstrate such feelings.

Unlike characters who fail to mature and are considered to be "flat" characters, Laura grows and learns from her successes and failures in life as well as from other characters around her. Because of Laura's humanness, children find it easy to relate to her, often reading several of the books in the *Little House* series as a result of the kinship they develop. Other books that exemplify strong

In the Classroom Mini Lesson

Sharing Previous School Experiences

> When I was Young and in Kindergarden
>
> When I was young in kindergarden the class guiny pig was a big deal. We all brought him lettuce. He was my best friend until I picked him up by his feet. For some reason he didn't like me anymore.
>
> When I was young in kindergarden we had a class play of Peter Rabbit. I wanted to be Cottontail. I even made an extra puffy tail. I was Mopsy I screamed "no fair." I soon learned that things don't work that way.
>
> When I was young in kindergarten, I had a lot to learn.
>
> Michelle
> 3A

A good activity is to have children share their experiences with younger students. For instance, Kim McKenna reads Cynthia Rylant's *When I Was Young in the Mountains* (1982) to her fifth graders. Then she shares her own written reflections of being a fifth grader, including both school and family experiences. After students have the opportunity to discuss their own experiences as kindergartners, each student writes "When I Was Young and in Kindergarten." Afterward, the class goes to the kindergarten classroom where the fifth-grade students are each paired up with a kindergartner. The older students read their remembrances of kindergarten to the younger students.

Since many of the fifth graders attended the same kindergarten in the same school, this activity creates a record of the school's "history." This activity can also include parents and grandparents by inviting them to come to school to share their school experiences. Most are willing to share a humorous story along with some more serious school recollections.

Rylant, C. (1982). *When I was young in the mountains* (D. Goode, Illus.). New York: Dutton.

Michelle shares her kindergarten experiences.

characterization are Mem Fox's (1985) *Wilfrid Gordon McDonald Partridge,* Steven Kellogg's (1986) *Best Friends,* Emily Arnold McCully's (1992) *Mirette on the High Wire,* Lynore Reid Banks's (1980) *The Indian in the Cupboard,* Lois Lowry's (1989) *Number the Stars,* and Mildred Taylor's (1995) *The Well.*

In *Bridge to Terabithia* (Paterson, 1977), children can relate to Jess and Leslie's friendship and empathize with Jess when tragedy strikes Leslie. *Letters*

In the Classroom Mini Lesson
Stories About Pigs

*I*n recent years, pigs have become increasingly popular; in fact, March 1 has been declared "National Pig Day." Perhaps the most favorite pig story of all time is that of the infamous humble pig, Wilbur, in the middle reader *Charlotte's Web* by E.B. White (1952). Below is a sampling of picture books about pigs.

Lowell, S. (1992). *The three little javelinas* (J. Harris, Illus.). New York: Scholastic. (K–3)
> This is the Southwestern U.S. version of the three little pigs in which the pigs are called javelinas (pronounced ha-ve-LEE-nas), the Spanish word for wild pigs, and the culprit is a coyote, not a wolf.

McPhail, D. (1993). *Pigs aplenty, pigs galore!* New York: Dutton (K–1)
> When the narrator of the book investigates sounds of feeding in the kitchen, he finds pigs throughout his house. This book includes lots of rhyming words and repetitive patterns for children to repeat.

Raynor, M. (1993). *Garth pig steals the show.* New York: Dutton (1–3)
> A concert is planned by the pig family, but they need an additional musician. A big hairy sousaphone player with a long pointed nose arrives. Soon Garth Pig and the sousaphone player are missing, but the conductor saves Garth Pig with a startling finale.

Scieszka, J. (1989). *The true story of the tree little pigs! by A. Wolf* (L. Smith, Illus.). New York: Viking. (1–3)
> This is the hilarious version of the three little pigs as told by the much maligned wolf. This is the book that launched Jon Scieszka (rhymes with Fresca) from successful classroom teacher to best-selling children's author.

Teague, M. (1994). *Pigsty.* New York: Scholastic. (1–3)
> Wendell Fultz's bedroom is so messy that it is a real pigsty. But Wendell doesn't mind until pigs start showing up in his room. Then Wendell devises a plan to clean up his room—with his new friends helping along the way.

Trivizas, E. (1993). *The three little wolves and the big bad pig* (H. Oxenbury, Illus.). New York: Maxwell Macmillan (K–3)
> Once upon a time there were three cuddly wolves who were told by their mother to go out and build a house for themselves but to beware of a big bad pig. This is a delightful twist on an old tale.

Waddell, M. (1992). *The pig in the pond.* Boston: Candlewick. (K–2)
> On a hot day, Pig decides to cool off by joining the ducks and geese in the pond. The humorous events that follow will definitely make children laugh.

These picture books are great to share with children in Grades K–2. After reading the books aloud to the class, students can then compare and contrast the characters as well as the story lines in a class discussion.

from Rifka (Hesse, 1992) shares the hardships of leaving behind friends and traveling to a new country.

The author may develop particular character through that character's actions, thoughts, and conversations with other characters; through other characters' thoughts about that character; and/or through narration. By sharing and discussing books that develop characters through one or more of these methods, children can acquire insights into the personalities and beliefs of different characters. Such insights are beneficial for children in that they can use them to understand people in real life.

Children often convince their classmates to read a book which they, themselves, enjoyed.
© Jean-Claude Lejeune

Plot

The plot is what a story is all about. A good plot contains, in some measure, action, conflict, intrigue, and resolution. For example, consider folktales and fairy tales, stories that were handed down orally for generations before they were written down. They contain action, intrigue, and conflict that is resolved at the end of the story. Such tales have been handed down from parent to child for generations, and many are as popular today as when they were first told hundreds of years ago.

For children, the plot needs to begin to unfold early in a book. A good beginning is essential to maintaining children's interest. Typically, the conflict and accompanying intrigue are introduced after the reader has gained some information about the main character(s), and the resolution comes at the end of the book. Since children prefer order and predictability, most children's literature follows chronological order; that is, events are described in the order in which they occur.

In biographies, the plot typically begins with the character at a certain age and then describes events during a specific time in the character's life. Cumulative tales such as "Henny Penny," "The Gingerbread Boy," and "The House That Jack Built" are examples of chronological order in picture books. *Why Mosquitoes Buzz in People's Ears* by Verna Aardema (1975) and *The Book That Jack Wrote* by Jon Scieszka (1994) are cumulative tales that describe the events in chronological order and also review the events as they take place. Madeline

Dunphy's *Here is the Tropical Rainforest* (1994) is a beautifully illustrated science book on ecology told as a cumulative tale complete with lyrical words.

Plot conflict may be of several different types: (1) person against person, (2) person against nature, (3) person against self, and (4) person against society. An example of a picture book that depicts a conflict between two characters is Steven Kellogg's (1986) *Best Friends* in which jealousy nearly destroys the friendship between two girls. Similarly, in Dav Pilkey's (1990) *Twas the Night Before Thanksgiving,* a group of schoolchildren go on a field trip to a turkey farm the day before Thanksgiving. The children become fast friends with the turkeys and manage to smuggle the gobblers home under their coats—safe from Farmer Mack Nuggetts's axe. Thomas J. Dygard's (1978) *Winning Kicker* offers intermediate-grade students a conflict between a football coach and a female placekicker, along with conflicts within the community and school.

Conflict between a character and nature is commonplace in intermediate-level books but rare in books for primary-grade students. One of the best lower-level books is Norma Green's (1974) *The Hole in the Dike,* which tells the legend of the Dutch boy who discovered a hole in the dike and bravely put his finger in the hole until help arrived the next day. Lynn Cherry's (1990) *The Great Kapok Tree* tells of the decline of the Amazon rain forest as a man struggles with the decision to either do his job and cut down a tree or to save it for the animals who need it to live. Scott O'Dell's (1980) *Sarah Bishop,* based on an actual historical event, tells the story of a young girl who fled the horrors of the Revolutionary War to live in a cave in the Connecticut countryside.

A good portrayal of conflict between the main character and himself or herself is Bernard Waber's (1972) *Ira Sleeps Over,* a picture book that describes the inner turmoil caused when a child must decide whether or not to take his teddy bear with him when he goes to spend the night at a friend's house. Kevin Henkes's (1993) *Owen* has a similar problem with his yellow blanket called Fuzzy, but his mother saves the day. *Amazing Grace* (Hoffman, 1991) is the uplifting story of Grace who dreams of portraying Peter Pan in a school play despite being a girl and an African American. Felice Holman's (1986) *Slake's Limbo,* a book that is appropriate for upper-grade students, involves a teenager who becomes lost for 4 months in the New York City subway system. Jean Craighead George's (1989) *Shark Beneath the Reef,* a contemporary story like *Slake's Limbo,* tells of the choice that Toma, a 14-year-old boy, must make between his two loves, school and fishing. He struggles to decide whether to continue his education or to take up his family's occupation of fishing. Older students will enjoy Bruce Brooks's (1984) *The Moves Make the Man* and Walter Dean Myers's (1983) *Hoops,* both novels with basketball themes that pit person against self as the plot.

A thought-provoking example for young children of conflict between character and society is Patricia Beatty's (1981) *Lupita Mañana,* which describes the plight of impoverished illegal immigrants who enter the United States by crossing the Mexican border. In reading Jerry Spinelli's (1991) *There's a Girl in My Hammerlock,* older students will enjoy examining society's influence on what is and what is not proper behavior in a culture.

By reading books with different types of plot conflict, children are encouraged to examine their own strengths and weaknesses and, hopefully, to gain acceptance and understanding of themselves. Moreover, children often mature in their interactions with peers and adults as they acquire increased awareness of cultural and social influences.

Setting

Setting refers to both time and place. The development of characterization and plot can be dependent upon the geographic location and time period in which a story occurs. Multisensory experiences are evoked through careful descriptions that connect time and place with plot and characters. For instance, consider pioneer life in the United States. In *Aurora Means Dawn,* a picture book, Scott Russell Sanders (1989) tells of a family traveling through the Ohio River Valley in the 1800s to settle in Aurora. The setting of time and place are crucial as the author describes the family's hardships, hopes, and dreams. *Who Came Down That Road?* (Lyon, 1992) poses a young child's question to his mother, who responds with answer after answer. The boy's great-great-grandparents, as well as Union soldiers in the Civil War, pioneers, Shawnee and Chippewa Native Americans, buffalo, bear, elk, mastodons, and woolly mammoths all came down that road in Kentucky. In Pam Conrad's (1987) *Prairie Songs,* a novel set in the late 1800s on the Nebraska prairie, the reader encounters the importance of the setting in the book's opening. Conrad describes the prairie as a giant plate and two children as two peas on that plate. The book goes on to describe how some pioneers loved the prairie and the hardships that accompanied life there while others found that the prairie offered only loneliness and despair.

In some instances, a setting may be deliberately vague in terms of location and/or time; the story might have occurred in any location, for example. In such a case, setting obviously contributes little to the plot. However, when the setting is specific, details must be accurate and realistic. This is especially true for biographies and historical fiction.

Theme

The theme of a book is the central idea of the story. In other words, it is the point or meaning the author wants to convey to the reader. For instance, E.B. White (1952) uses friendship as the theme for *Charlotte's Web,* while Jeanette Winter (1988) focuses on the desire for freedom and the Underground Railroad in *Follow the Drinking Gourd.* The importance and value placed on knowing how to read is depicted in Eve Bunting's (1989) *The Wednesday Surprise,* which tells about Anna, who spends every Wednesday evening reading books to her illiterate grandmother. At the end of the book, Anna and her grandmother throw a surprise birthday party for Anna's father; the biggest surprise occurs when Grandma reads to them.

Three moving books about life and death that are appropriate for fifth through eighth graders are Robert Newton Peck's (1972) *A Day No Pigs Would Die,* Gary Paulsen's (1987) *Hatchet,* a story of survival, and Cynthia Rylant's (1993) *Missing May,* a Newbery Award winner.

Dioramas can be made from file folders and construction paper to represent settings from various picture books or novels.

Camille Yarbrough's (1989) *The Shimmershine Queens* tells the story of a black inner-city fifth grader who gets the lead in a school play. Yarbrough uses the themes of confidence and motivation to illustrate how dreams can be achieved despite challenges and problems.

Style

Style refers to the author's word choice and sentence construction. Repetition, for example, is a style often used in writing picture books, such as Nancy White Carlstrom's (1986) *Jesse Bear, What Will You Wear?*. Rhyme is also commonly found in picture books, such as *Quacky, Quack-Quack!* by Ian Whybrow (1991) and Nancy Shaw's (1986) *Sheep in a Jeep.*

Authors of books for students in the intermediate grades sometimes emphasize images through word usage. This may involve the description of characters or setting. A humorous or suspenseful thread may continue throughout a story's plot. In realistic fiction, such as Gary Paulsen's (1987) *Hatchet,* the author needs to use engaging language. Cullinan and Galda (1994, p. 226) suggest that the language for realistic fiction should have a "rhythmic, melodic quality appropriate to the theme, the setting, and the characters." Or as one children's literature editor put it, the language should sing! The style for a biography differs somewhat from that of realistic fiction in that facts are presented; however, the writing still must be engaging. Consider the language of *Abigail Adams: Witness to a Revolution* (Bober, 1995), of *The Wright Brothers: How They Invented the Airplane* (Freedman, 1991), or of *Mother Teresa: Helping the Poor* (Jacobs, 1991). Certainly the style of writing for nonfiction must present information and facts in a refreshing way, such as in Milton Meltzer's (1990) *Brother Can You Spare a Dime?,* a book about the Great Depression, or William Jay Jacobs's (1990) *Ellis Island: New Hope in a New Land.*

Children may become familiar with an author's style and want to read every book the author has written. This is often the case with authors Paul Goble, Virginia Hamilton, Gloria Houston, Steven Kellogg, Lois Lowry, Katherine Paterson, and Gary Paulsen, among others. Classroom teachers can promote an author's works by simply reading a chapter or captivating passage from a selection and providing additional copies of the book (known as text sets) as well as other works by the same author. In essence, this is an attempt by the teachers to broaden their own interests and familiarize themselves with various authors while trying to entice the children to discover new works of literature.

Illustrations

Illustrations in picture books, as well as in informational books, must add to and extend the story and/or concept being presented. Art quality and visual appeal to children are both important when considering illustrations. If the illustrations fail to keep the child interested in the story, they are not appropriate.

Illustrations vary greatly because of the wide variety of media available to artists. Still, each illustrator carves out his or her own characteristic style. For instance, Jan Brett (1990) includes delicate borders in her books, such as in *The Mitten: A Ukranian Folktale,* while Tomie de Paola (1975, 1988) is noted for his folk art as portrayed in *Strega Nona* and *The Legend of the Indian Paintbrush.* Eric Carle uses collage, relying on vividly colored sheets of tissue paper that he tints in his own studio. Good examples of Carle's work are *Brown Bear, Brown Bear, What Do You See?* by Bill Martin, Jr. (1964/1983) and Carle's (1969) own, *The Very Hungry Caterpillar.* Lois Ehlert, like Carle, relies upon vivid colors in her work. Her books include *Eating the Alphabet* (1989), *Color Zoo* (1989), and *Fish Eyes: A Book You Can Count On* (1990).

The softness of watercolors is used by award-wining illustrator Jerry Pinkney in Robert San Souci's (1990) *The Talking Eggs* and Patricia McKissack's (1988) *Mirandy and Brother Wind* both of which were Caldecott honor books. The artwork of Lane Smith accentuates the bizarre antics in author Jon Scieszka's (1989, 1992, 1995) books, *The True Story of the Three Little Pigs, The Stinky Cheese Man: And Other Fairly Stupid Tales,* and *Math Curse.* Certainly the cultural influences on an author's life emerge in the illustrations. For instance, Ed Young (1989, 1992) was born in China, and his art clearly reflects his roots in his books *Lon Po Po* and *Seven Blind Mice.*

Literary Elements and the Sharing of Literature

Like teachers, children need to discover and develop an understanding of literary elements. This can begin as early as kindergarten with a discussion about characterization in *Don't Fidget a Feather* (Silverman, 1994). Five-year-olds are quick to point out the bad qualities of the fox. They are equally adept at noting the positive characteristics of the two young friends, Duck and Goose.

First graders may be introduced to a literary web. Rather than including all literary elements, it is better to focus on one element at a time; this allows students to grasp and understand one element before being introduced to another. For instance, with appropriate books, the teacher can explain theme as a simple literary element to young students. Mary Ann Hoberman's (1978) *A House Is a House for Me* delightfully describes and illustrates different types of houses found in nature. Her book is appropriate for a science lesson with a theme of shelter. After the teacher reads the book to the class, students can discuss the different names and types of homes that were mentioned. The students might also bring in houses made of different objects and create a shelter display in the classroom.

Literary webs for upper-primary and intermediate students should include all of the literary elements. Figure 4.1 presents an example of such a web.

Genre

Genre here refers to the different categories that comprise children's literature. These include picture books, traditional literature, modern fantasy, contemporary realistic fiction, historical fiction, biography and autobiography, informational works, and poetry. Each genre is described below.

Picture Books

Picture books are books in which the pictures are as important as, if not more important than, the accompanying text (Sutherland & Hearne, 1984). In fact, picture books may be just that, books containing only pictures and no accompanying text. Such books are called wordless picture books. The story is told completely through the illustrations. This requires the reader to gather, interpret, and relate information from artwork or photographs. Because only illustrations are included in a wordless picture book, the characters, setting (usually

Figure 4.1
Literary web.

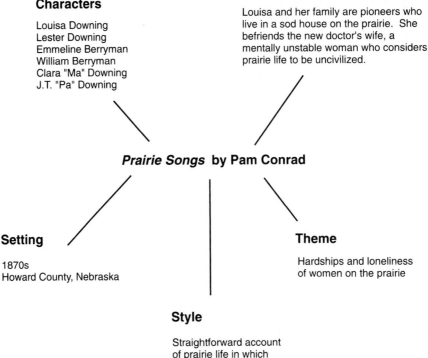

Characters

Louisa Downing
Lester Downing
Emmeline Berryman
William Berryman
Clara "Ma" Downing
J.T. "Pa" Downing

Plot

Louisa and her family are pioneers who live in a sod house on the prairie. She befriends the new doctor's wife, a mentally unstable woman who considers prairie life to be uncivilized.

Prairie Songs by Pam Conrad

Setting

1870s
Howard County, Nebraska

Theme

Hardships and loneliness of women on the prairie

Style

Straightforward account of prairie life in which poetry intertwines the beauty and harsh reality of pioneer life

place rather than time), and plot must all be conveyed through the illustrations. Such books often provide opportunities for children to develop their story-telling skills while at the same time expanding their oral language skills. Mercer Mayer's (1971) *A Boy, a Dog, and a Frog* is a good example of an effective wordless picture book.

Picture books can be excellent sources of information for young children. In *Can You Find Me? A Book About Animal Camouflage* (1989), Jennifer Dewey, a naturalist as well as an author and an illustrator, describes the survival techniques of animals in their use of camouflage to avoid predators. Even seemingly ordinary events of nature can prove to be interesting information. For instance, Betsy C. Maestro's (1989) *Snow Day* describes how a snowstorm may result in a day home from school for children but hard work for the people who must use shovels, snowblowers, and huge snowplows to clear away the snow.

Although picture books are typically associated with preschoolers and students in the primary grades, many picture books are best suited for older students. For example, *Lincoln: A Photobiography* (Freedman, 1987) and *My Hiroshima* (Morimoto, 1990) are appropriate for students in intermediate grades.

Students of all grade levels can analyze and compare picture books. For example, when presented with several versions of a folktale such as "Little Red

Riding Hood" or "The Three Billy Goats Gruff," children can discuss the commonalities of the stories as well as how the authors and illustrators differ in their interpretations. Appropriate stories can also contribute to science and/or social studies discussions. For instance, William T. George's *Box Turtle at Long Pond* (1989) can be part of a discussion of ecology and the life cycle of animals.

An underlying theme, such as trickery and deception, may also emerge. In *The Little Mouse, the Red Ripe Strawberry, and the Big Hungry Bear,* by Don and Audrey Wood (1984), a mouse picks a strawberry only to discover that strawberries are the favorite food of the big hungry bear. The mouse attempts to keep the strawberry by hiding it, locking it up, and disguising it. Finally, the mouse eats half the strawberry giving the unnamed narrator the other half. A folktale with a similar theme is *Tops and Bottoms* by Janet Stevens (1995), in which a lazy bear is tricked by a clever hare who offers to give the bear half of all he grows on the bear's land—either the tops or bottoms of the crop. Such a theme of underlying trickery goes undetected by most kindergarten and first-grade students, and even some intermediate-grade students. Only through discussion and the sharing of similar stories do students discover the underlying theme. Other enjoyable picture books that provide good discussion topics are *Miss Spider's Tea Party* (Kirk, 1994), *Pete's Chicken* (Ziefert, 1994), *The Dumb Bunnies* (Denim, 1994), and *Cinder Edna* (Jackson, 1994).

Picture books offer examples of a wide variety of media. Children's aesthetic development can be enhanced through their exposure to illustrations done in acrylics, block prints, chalk, collage, ink, and water colors. Whether it be the intricate details of the line drawing in David Macaulay's (1981) *Cathedral* or the cut paper illustrations of David Wisniewski's (1991) *Rain Player,* children can discover new ways of examining their world by analyzing the illustrations in picture books.

Research findings suggest that children who were read to at home while they were still preschoolers have an advantage in terms of literary development over their peers who were not read to at home. This is particularly evident in children's early attempts to read and write (Taylor & Dorsey-Gaines, 1988; Teale & Sulzby, 1985). According to Roser, Hoffman, and Farest (1990, p. 554), "children from economically disadvantaged homes enter school with fewer exposures to the tools of literacy and [are] more 'at risk' relative to their literacy acquisition." Because of this, early childhood teachers must become familiar with picture books in order to share a wide variety of topics and create a rich literary environment in the classroom.

Traditional Literature

Traditional literature has its roots in oral stories that were handed down from generation to generation even before writing came into existence. Religion and heroes are common themes. Usually a heroic deed results in overcoming an adversary by cunning or trickery.

Traditional literature includes folktales, such as cumulative tales ("The House that Jack Built"), humorous tales ("The Princess and the Pea"), beast tales ("Beauty and the Beast"), and wonder or magic tales (*Princess Furball*

[1989] retold by Charlotte Huck). Traditional literature also includes fables (Aesop's "The Lion and the Mouse"), myths (Jane Yolen's *Wings*, 1991), and legends (Tomie de Paola's *The Legend of the Indian Paintbrush*, 1988).

Traditional literature allows children to distinguish easily between goodness and evil through the deeds and actions of the characters: Heroes are good through and through, while villains are rotten to the core. Because such literature is based on conflict and its resolution, children can be encouraged to create and develop their own solutions to the problems depicted in the stories.

Sharing traditional literature is an excellent way to enable children to appreciate the contributions of various cultures. For instance, Laurence Yep's (1989) *The Rainbow People*, a collection of Chinese folktales, can enrich children's knowledge of life in another country and the beliefs of the people who live there.

Modern Fantasy

Modern fantasy involves the creation of a time and a place where the unbelievable becomes believable. The plot may be outrageous, yet within the context of the fantasy it becomes imaginable.

Characters in modern fantasy may be real people who have imaginary experiences (C. S. Lewis's *The Lion, the Witch, and the Wardrobe,* 1950), animals who take on human characteristics (Lynne Cherry's *The Great Kapok Tree,* 1990), personified toys (Lynne Reid Banks's *The Indian in the Cupboard,* 1980), lilliputian people (Carol Kendall's *The Gammage Cup,* 1959), or even supernatural beings (Ted Hughes's *The Iron Giant,* 1985; Chris Van Allsburg's *Jumanji,* 1981; and David Wiesner's *Tuesday,* 1991).

The setting of modern fantasy may be in the past, but most often it is in the present or the future. Traveling through time and space is common, as in Chris Van Allsburg's (1985) picture book, *The Polar Express.* The future is the setting of *The Iron Giant,* noted above, a book that describes a giant robot that stalks the earth until an alien creature challenges the robot's rule. *The Giver* (1993) by Lois Lowry is a science fiction novel that describes a futuristic Utopian society.

Contemporary Realistic Fiction

The characters, setting, and plot of contemporary realistic fiction are believable in that they could appear in real life. While the story is invented by the author and is therefore fictitious, it appears to be true.

Contemporary realistic fiction offers children insights into the personal and social values of our culture and permits them to become actively involved in the dilemmas and the triumphs of the characters. Growing up, family life, and friendship are all themes of contemporary realistic fiction. Animal, sports, and humorous stories also fall into this category.

Popular authors of contemporary realistic fiction include Judy Blume (*Are You There God, It's Me Margaret,* 1970; *Deenie,* 1973; and *Tales of a Fourth Grade Nothing,* 1972), Betsy Byars (*The Cybil War,* 1981, and *The Night Swimmers,* 1980), Beverly Cleary (*Ramona the Pest,* 1968), Vera and Bill Cleaver (*I Would Rather Be a Turnip,* 1971, and *Where the Lilies Bloom,* 1969), Jean

Craighead George (*My Side of the Mountain,* 1959, and *River Rats, Inc.,* 1979), Phyllis Reynolds Naylor (*Shiloh,* 1991), Gary Paulsen (*Hatchet,* 1987, and *The Winter Room,* 1989), Jerry Spinelli (*Maniac Magee,* 1990) and Theodore Taylor (*The Cay,* 1969, and *The Trouble with Tuck,* 1981). A child may read a book by one of these or other authors only to follow it by another book by the same author. This may continue until the student has completed all of the author's works contained in the school library.

In some instances an author may write one or more sequels to a book. Beverly Cleary is a prime example with her many books about Ramona growing up. Cleary has also written a sequel to *Dear Mr. Henshaw* (1983), a story about how an author helps a boy, Leigh, overcome problems related to his parents' divorce. The sequel, *Strider* (1991), finds Leigh as an adolescent who adopts an abandoned dog which Leigh names "Strider."

Contemporary realistic fiction often deals with actual problems. For instance, Ann Cameron's (1988) *The Most Beautiful Place in the World,* the story of Juan, an abandoned Guatemalan boy, could actually take place today. The tragedy of the effects of Alzheimer's disease is portrayed in Vaunda Micheaux Nelson's (1988) *Always Grandma.* The turmoil in Hong Kong between ancient ties and modern trends is the subject of Riki Levinson's (1988) *Our Home Is the Sea.* Such books can be tied to current events and provide enrichment for class discussions.

Historical Fiction

In historical fiction, the characterization, setting, plot, and theme must be realistic. The characters must be developed through dialogue, which poses a problem if a real person is included as a major character. For this reason, many authors of historical fiction include famous historical characters as background characters, relying upon fictitious characters to carry the plot.

The setting, both time and place, needs to be authentic in every detail. Such exactness often necessitates considerable research on the part of the author. Descriptions of everyday life must be realistic depictions of the daily routines that existed at that particular time. In *Back Home,* Gloria Pinkney (1992) accurately portrays a rural setting—North Carolina in the 1950s.

The plot of a piece of historical fiction may involve a real historical event or one that could have taken place given detailed information from the period. In *Drylongso,* for example, Virginia Hamilton (1992) portrays a boy who performs "water witching"—finds water with a dowsing rod (a forked stick) during a drought. Plots in this genre frequently center around personal conflicts.

Most works of historical fiction have simple, basic themes that are as relevant for today's children as they were for those who lived in the time period in which the work is set. In stressing the need to use children's literature in social studies, Billig (1977, p. 857) writes, "When a social studies unit arises spontaneously out of honest interest and curiosity, the depth of understanding that develops is immeasurably greater than that resulting from an often irrelevant teacher-imposed assignment." This is due, according to Billig, to the human element that exists in historical fiction but is absent from social studies textbooks.

An example of an informative, historically accurate book for kindergartners through second graders is Kate Waters's (1989) *Sarah Morton's Day: A Day in the Life of a Pilgrim Girl.* The story is based on actual people who lived in Plymouth, Massachusetts, in 1627. Sarah Morton's day begins with the crowing of the rooster and continues with making breakfast, feeding the chickens, and learning verses from the scripture. Sarah also has time for playing, singing, and sharing dreams and secrets with her best friend, Elizabeth.

The Borning Room by Paul Fleischman (1991) is a good middle-childhood-level book which takes place in rural Ohio over a period of several generations, from before the Civil War to the advent of modern medicine and the electrification of rural America. The "borning room" is the room in the family's farmhouse where babies are born and the dead lie. In *Dateline: Troy,* Fleischman (1996) compared today's headlines to life in ancient Troy.

Biography and Autobiography

Biographies should depict their subjects accurately rather than present only the good points of their subjects. As with historical fiction, biographical writing requires much research by the author. A good example of a well-researched biography is *Follow the Dream: The Story of Christopher Columbus* (1991) written and illustrated by Peter Sis, who used fifteenth-century maps as a basis for mapping out Columbus's journey.

Biographies are excellent ways to present history, especially since so many good ones have been written for children. Biographies for children have featured artists, scientists, and sports heroes, among others. Wendy Towle's (1993) *The Real McCoy: The Life of an African-American Inventor* describes the problems encountered by Elijah McCoy, inventor of the automatic oil cup which became standard equipment on locomotives. Because his invention was the best of its kind, engineers referred to it as "the real McCoy."

While biographies are prevalent, autobiographies written for children are in short supply. Jean Fritz is one of the few children's contemporary literature authors who has shared her childhood experiences via her autobiography, *Homesick: My Own Story* (1982). *A Girl from Yamhill* (1988) is the title of Beverly Cleary's autobiography, while Roald Dahl (1984) called his *Boy: Tales of Childhood*. Tomie de Paola's (1989) *The Art lesson* describes the author's own experiences in school as he developed his early artistic skills. In this autobiography, de Paola tells of the first-grade teacher who insisted that he use a box of 8 crayons rather than his box of 64 because the teacher believed it was unfair for de Paola to have a box of 64 crayons when his classmates had boxes of 8. Richard Peck and Laura Ingalls Wilder are two other authors who have shared their childhood experiences through their works. Despite the fact that there are so few autobiographies for children, children delight in writing their own autobiographies. Clearly, this is an area that needs additional publications.

Informational Books

Factual material makes up informational books: the how to, where to, and why books. These books range from directions for making a bird house and caring for pets to how computers are made and what it is like to travel in space. Bruce Brooks (1993), the popular sports novelist, combines humorous and thought provoking essays in *Boys Will Be,* a collection of 12 essays.

Informational books need to be accurate and should not mislead students. A good example of such a book is Sam and Beryl Epstein's (1989) *Bugs for Dinner? The Eating Habits of Neighborhood Creatures,* a zoological book about animal survival in a city neighborhood. In this book, the food-seeking habits of birds, honeybees, ants, squirrels, and other animals are explained in an engaging manner. Likewise, Clare Walker Leslie's (1991) *Nature All Year Long* provides detailed information about hibernation, migration, plants, and weather. This book is presented as a calendar of events which occur in nature. Breathtaking photographs of earth from space are combined with a narrative that describes our environment in *Seeing the Earth from Space* by Patricia Lauber (1990).

Informational books can portray the drama of history without misleading students. Gillian Osband's (1991) *Castles,* a pop-up book, provides students with accurate and fascinating descriptions of how castles were built. The three-dimensional book illustrated by Robert Andrew portrays actual life in castles during medieval times, including the reasons for moats and how catapults worked during battles. This book is of interest for children from early childhood through middle school. Sheila Cowing (1989) gives children an accurate historical overview of the American Southwest in *Searches in the American*

Desert. The book begins with the Spanish explorers seeking the seven cities of gold during the 1500s and continues through the story of Brigham Young and the Mormons and on to current times.

A good example of a book that focuses on a narrow historical period is Rhoda Blumberg's (1989) *The Great American Gold Rush,* which depicts the migration of people to California between 1848 and 1852 as "gold fever" set in. Blumberg presents interesting details and asides about individuals who journeyed to California to become rich, all of which adds to children's historical perspective of the period. In addition Blumberg covers the treatment of minorities during the Gold Rush. Jim Murphy's (1993) *Across America on an Immigrant Train* depicts the true story of Robert Louis Stevenson's trip in 1879 to the West Coast. Students learn from Stevenson's journal entries about the harshness of rail travel during that time.

Children can also gain a better understanding of current events through informational books. Older children will find K. C. Tessendorf's (1989) *Along the Road to Soweto: A Racial History of South Africa* a compelling book. In it, the author traces the history of South Africa from tiny European settlements to Chief Shaka's Zulu war against the Bantu and on to the Boer War and the eventual independence of South Africa. Walter Dean Myers's (1991) *Now is Your Time!: The African-American Struggle for Freedom* goes back to the slave traders and continues on to today's African-American leaders.

Some informational books can be interactive. For instance, a good book for sharing with five- and six-year-olds is *The M&M's Counting Book* (McGrath, 1994). In this book, children learn how to count to 12 and to add. Of course, children delight in subtraction—that's when they get to eat the M&M's! *Ten Sly Piranhas* (Wise, 1993) is a funny counting book that introduces subtraction as the piranhas eat each other—all in rhyme, of course!

In informational works, facts should be clearly distinguishable from theory, and the most recent findings and information should be included. Because of this and because of limited funding for book purchases, school libraries generally have difficulty obtaining informational books that reflect the cutting edge of science and technology.

Poetry

Poetry can be humorous, reflective, insightful, and descriptive. Above all, it offers diversity of themes. The first encounter most young children have with poetry comes through the sharing of Mother Goose rhymes. Later, rhymes and chants of the playground extend the playful, teasing side of poetry to children.

Unlike the other genre described in this chapter, poetry requires that each and every word be accountable for its existence in the poem. This is because a word carries more meaning in the shorter passages of poetry than the same word does in prose.

Based on the use of connotative rather than denotative meanings, poetry is often abused by teachers, particularly at the junior and senior high school levels, who insist that their students dissect poetry to find the poet's intent and "true" meaning. Such analysis usually results in the destruction of the desire to

In the Classroom Mini Lesson

Tracing the Journeys of Explorers

A good geography and cartography lesson for students in Grades 4 through 8 is to trace the journeys of explorers. For land travels, raised relief maps help students to understand the difficulties encountered by the exploration party.

Students also benefit from considering the primitive maps that were available to the explorers, many of which were highly speculative. For instance, Lewis and Clark had heard of the Missouri River, but upon their arrival at the fork of the Missouri and the Platte, they had no idea which fork was the larger Missouri River and which was the smaller Platte River. As a result, the expedition had to temporarily split up into two parties to determine which river to follow, thus costing valuable travel time.

Two good trade books to use for this activity are listed below.

Fritz, J. (1994). *Around the world in 100 years: From Henry the Navigator to Magellan* (A.B. Venti, Illus.). New York: Putnam. (4–8)

> Jean Fritz has written an interesting view of 10 explorers including Diaz, daGama, and Balboa. She places them in the context of the time period in which they lived. The observations and fascinating facts included about each explorer will keep students reading and talking about this book. The illustrations, unfortunately, are a bit lacking.

Roop, P., & Roop, C. (Eds.). (1993). *Off the map: The journals of Lewis and Clark* (T. Tanner, Illus.). New York: Walker. (4–8)

> This book traces, through their own journal entries and excerpts, the journey of William Clark and Meriwether Lewis as they explored the territory of the Louisiana Purchase. At the beginning of the book, the editors include the letter from President Thomas Jefferson authorizing the expedition. An epilogue summarizes the return journey of the expedition and offers intriguing information regarding the fates of the members of the expedition.

Historical novels can also be used in teaching social studies, especially geography. Here is an example:

Van Leeuwen, J. (1995). *Bound for Oregon* (J. Watling, Illus.). New York: Dial. (3–6)

> Nine-year-old Mary Ellen Todd and her family leave their Arkansas home and set out for the Oregon Territory in 1852. The difficulties and excitement they encounter along their journey are recounted in this book. Students can trace the family's trip and note geographical differences along the way.

read and share poetry. Poetry ceases to be enjoyable when the reader is expected to be accountable for the reasons why each word in the poem was selected for use by the poet.

Elementary children delight in the sharing of humorous poetry. They relish the poetry in *Something Big Has Been Here* (1990) and *The New Kid on the Block* (1984), both by Jack Prelutsky. His *The Snopp on the Sidewalk and Other Poems* (1976) and *Poems of A. Nonny Mouse* (1991) are both excellent collections for encouraging children to write their own poetry. Another popular poet is Shel Silverstein and his classic *Where the Sidewalk Ends* (1974). Middle- and upper-level students particularly delight in Judith Viorst's (1981) *If I Were in Charge of the World, and Other Worries* as she describes the commonly shared concerns, joys, and dreams of children. Sports are the emphasis in Arnold Adoff's (1986) *Sports Pages,* a book of poetry boys and girls can enjoy.

In the Classroom Mini Lesson
Poetry Anthologies

*C*hildren love poetry if it is shared in an enjoyable way. Teachers need to include poetry throughout the school day so that children can learn the power of word choice.

The following is a list of poetry anthologies along with suggested grade levels:

Booth, D. (1990). *Voices on the wind* (M. Lemieux, Illus.). New York: Morrow. (K–4)

Carle, E. (1989). *Animals, animals.* New York: Philomel. (K–3)

Carlson, L. M. (1994). *Cool salsa: Bilingual poems on growing up Latino in the United States.* New York: Holt. (6–8)

Cassedy, S. (1993). *Zoomrimes: Poems about things that go* (M. Chessare, Illus.). New York: HarperCollins. (K–2)

Chandra, D. (1993). *Rich Lizard and other poems* (L. Bowman, Illus.). New York: Farrar, Strauss, & Giroux. (K–4)

Colen, K. (1995). *Peas and honey: Recipes for kids (with a pinch of poetry)* (M. Victor, Illus.). Honesdale, PA: Boyds Mills. (3–6)

de Regniers, B.S. (1988). *Sing a song of popcorn.* New York: Scholastic. (1–5)

Fisher, A. (1986). *When it comes to bugs* (C. & B. Degan, Illus.). New York: Harper & Row. (1–4)

Fleischman, P. (1988). *Joyful noise: Poems for two voices* (E. Beddows, Illus.). New York: Harper & Row. (3–8)

Goldstein, B. (1989). *Bear in mind.* New York: Penguin. (K–3)

Greenfield, E. (1988). *Under the Sunday tree.* New York: Harper & Row. (K–3)

Hoberman, M.A. (1991). *Fathers, mothers, sisters, brothers.* Boston: Little, Brown. (K–6)

Hopkins, L.B. (1988). *Side by side poems to read together.* New York: Simon & Schuster. (1–4)

Hopkins, L.B. (1990). *Good books, good times!* New York: Harper & Row. (1–5)

Hopkins, L.B. (1994). *April bubbles chocolate* (B. Root, Illus.). New York: Simon & Schuster. (K–5)

Hughes, L. (1994). *The dream keeper and other poems* (B. Pinkney, Illus.). New York: Knopf. (3–8)

Larrick, N. (1990). *To the moon and back.* New York: Dell. (K–5)

Levy, C. (1994). *A tree place* (R. Sabuda, Illus.). New York: McElderry. (4–8)

Lewis, J. (1994). *July is a mad mosquito* (M.W. Hall, Illus.). New York: Atheneum. (3–8)

Livingston, M.C. (1993). *Roll along: Poems on wheels.* New York: McElderry. (K–3)

Livingston, M.C. (1994). *Riddle-me rhymes* (R. Perry, Illus.). New York: McElderry. (K–2)

McNaughton, C. (1994). *Making friends with Frankenstein: A book of monstrous poems and pictures.* New York: Candlewick. (K–up)

Prelutsky, J. (1983). *Random House book of poetry.* New York: Random House. (K–8)

Prelutsky, J. (1984). *The new kid on the block.* New York: Greenwillow. (2–6)

Prelutsky, J. (1994). *The dragons are singing tonight* (P. Sis, Illus.). New York: Greenwillow. (K–5)

Silverstein, S. (1981). *A light in the attic.* New York: Harper & Row. (K–6)

Silverstein, S. (1996). *Falling up.* New York: HarperCollins. (K–6)

Stevenson, J. (1995). *Sweet corn.* New York: Greenwillow. (3–5)

Walton, R. (1995). *What to do when a bug climbs in your mouth and other poems to drive you buggy* (N. Carlson, Illus.). New York: Lothrop, Lee & Shepard. (K–6)

Feelings and reflections about life are popular poetic themes. Arnold Adoff's (1981) *Outside Inside Poems* and X.J. Kennedy's (1985) *The Forgetful Wishing Well: Poems for Young Children* are poetry collections that share the joys, problems, and turmoil of being a child. *I'm Going to Pet a Worm Today and Other Poems* by Constance Levy (1991) is a collection of fresh, insightful poems about everyday things.

Focus Box 4.2

Genre

Picture book stories:	Picture books are books in which the illustrations are as important to the telling of the story as the written text. In fact, some picture books contain only illustrations.
Traditional literature:	Traditional literature includes folktales, wonder or magic tales, humorous tales, beast tales, fables, myths, and legends.
Modern fantasy:	Modern fantasy consists of stories that rely on the creation of time and place to make the unbelievable become believable.
Contemporary realistic fiction:	Contemporary realistic fiction consists of fictitious works in which the characters, setting, and plot are believable and could actually appear in real life.
Historical fiction:	Historical fiction consists of fictitious works in which the characters, setting, and plot are realistically presented in terms of the historical authenticity of the period being described.
Biography and autobiography:	A biography is a nonfiction account of someone other than the author. An autobiography is an author's account of some or all of his or her own life.
Informational works:	Informational works are nonfiction books. These may include how-to books or reference books.
Poetry:	Poetry books are typically collections of poetry by one or several poets. The poems may have the same or different themes.

Poetry should be included in the various content areas. For instance, a wide variety of poetry is appropriate for inclusion in science lessons, including Paul Fleischman's (1988) Newbery award-winning *Joyful Noise: Poems for Two Voices,* which contains poems that verbally recreate the unique sounds of insects. A delightfully silly poetry book about insects is Rick Walton's (1995) *What to do When a Bug Climbs into Your Mouth.* (The answer is "chew," of course!) Children will delight in sharing Walton's poems about cockroaches, slugs, bumblebees, gnats, and other insects. *Earth Verses and Water Rhymes* by J. Patrick Lewis (1991) contains poetry that celebrates nature. Its simple language, combined with bold, double-page prints, provides rich images of the natural world. Myra Cohn Livingston's (1984) *Sky Songs* tells of the tranquility of a peaceful summer day and the "grumble and growl" of a thunderstorm. Livingston's *Up in the Air* (1989), a collection of poems about flying, contains a poem that describes the snow-covered mountain ranges. Jack Prelutsky's (1988) *Tyrannosaurus Was a Beast* is popular with children who are captivated by prehistoric creatures and is appropriate for introducing this theme in science.

Social studies also lends itself to the sharing of poetry. Virginia Driving Hawk Sneve (1989) collected poetry from American Indian children for her book *Dancing Teepees: Poems of American Indian Youth.* The poetry in this collection covers a variety of topics and includes pieces from the oral tradition and contemporary works.

Multicultural Literature

In the book *Growing up Literate: Learning from Inner-City Families* (Taylor & Dorsey-Gaines, 1988), the authors point out that children from economically disadvantaged homes who were read to by their parents or some other significant adult developed literacy knowledge and skills. The adoption of a literature-based reading program in a Brownsville, Texas, school district in which more than 80 percent of the students were Hispanic resulted in significantly improved student reading scores (on a state test) in five of the six schools in the district (Roser et al., 1990). Clearly, the sharing of literature with children of various cultural backgrounds is essential. As Stotsky (1992, p. 56) writes, "teachers are responsible, in a highly multireligious and multiethnic society, for creating and cultivating common ground through the literature they teach in all its many forms."

Until recently, the overwhelming proportion of children's literature represented white middle-class America. With the number of minority authors increasing, the number and quality of multicultural children's books have greatly increased. With the advent of many new books in this important area, more have found their way into the classroom. A 1991 study of elementary classroom libraries found that multicultural titles constitute up to 38 percent of classroom collections (Hildreth, 1991).

Through the sharing of multicultural literature with all children, different cultures and races can be better understood and the development of stereotypical images avoided. Minority children need to have positive role models and to become more familiar with their own culture (Bishop, 1992). All children need to understand and tolerate differences in cultures and beliefs.

Quality multicultural children's literature should have the same essential ingredients as quality children's literature in general: well-developed characters, strong plots, recognizable settings, and positive themes. Other characteristics may include minority characters who have a good self-concept and plots that are realistic. If the work is a picture book, the illustrations should be representative of the culture.

In selecting children's literature, teachers need to consider the contributions of various racial and ethnic groups. African Americans, Asian Americans, Hispanics, Jewish Americans, and Native Americans have all contributed to children's literature in significant ways (Cullinan & Galda, 1994). "When children are left on their own, they generally choose literature that is familiar and that reflects their own interests and culture. Therefore, it is important for teachers to expose children to literature that reflects many cultures, themes, and views" (Bieger, 1996, p. 309). In poetry, for instance, Lulu Delacre's (1989) *Arroz Con Leche: Popular Songs and Rhymes from Latin America* offers elementary children insight into the cultures of neighboring countries. Julius Lester's (1989) *How Many Spots Does a Leopard Have?* is a collection of African and Jewish folktales that have universal themes to which children can relate: magic, bravery, loyalty, and vanity.

Norton (1990) suggests that upper-elementary and middle-school teachers may want to adopt a five-phase model for studying multicultural literature:

(1)traditional literature of varying genre; (2)traditional tales from one area; (3)autobiographies, biographies, and historical nonfiction; (4)historical fiction; and (5)contemporary fiction and poetry. By starting with traditional literature and moving through the other four phases, the class can become quite familiar with one cultural group. At the conclusion of the fifth phase, another cultural group can be selected and the process repeated.

Criteria for Selecting Multicultural Literature

Selecting multicultural literature for children is not an easy task for teachers. For some ethnic groups, such as African Americans, there is a multitude of children's literature available from which to choose. However, for other cultures, such as Latvian, there are few titles available. The areas of Asian-American and Latino children's literature can be confusing to teachers because these are conglomerates of many cultural groups. For instance, Asian-American children's literature includes not only Chinese and Japanese children's books but also Cambodian, Indonesian, Korean, Laotian, Malaysian, Thai, and Vietnamese, among others. Likewise, Hispanic includes Cuban, Dominican, Mexican, Nicaraguan, and Puerto Rican, as well as the South American countries—all very different cultural groups.

Cullinan and Galda (1994, p. 344) suggest that teachers look for books representing culturally diverse groups that:

1. avoid stereotypes,
2. portray the cultural groups and their values in an authentic way,
3. use language that reflects standards set by local usage,
4. validate children's experience,
5. broaden our vision, and
6. invite reflection.

Through discussing and sharing multicultural literature with other teachers, teachers can become more familiar with appropriate titles to relate to students.

There should be enough books available to give students different perspectives on issues and historical events, such as the Native American view on the European settlement of North America, both on the eastern seaboard and in the Southwest. In addition, books should be available that correct distortions of information (Bishop, 1992), such as the fact that many Native Americans died, not at the hands of pioneers and soldiers, but from illnesses such as small pox, a disease brought to North America by Europeans.

Following is a list of African-American, Asian-American, Hispanic, and Native American multicultural books.

African-American

Adoff, A. (1973). *The poetry of black America: Anthology of the 20th century.* New York: Harper & Row. (K-8)
Adoff, A. (1973). *Black is brown is tan.* New York: Harper & Row. (K-8)
Arkhurst, J. C. (1964). *The adventures of spider: West African folktales.* Boston: Little, Brown. (K-2)
Arkhurst, J. C. (1986). *Lion and the ostrich chicks.* New York: Atheneum. (3-5)

Bryan, A. (1991). *All night, all day: A child's first book of African-American spirituals.* New York: Macmillan/Atheneum. (3-8)

Burchard, P. (1995). *Charlotte Forten: A black teacher in the Civil War.* New York: Crown. (4-7)

Collier, J., & Collier, C. (1981). *Jump ship to freedom.* New York: Delacorte. (5-8)

Cox, C. (1993). *The forgotten heroes: The story of the Buffalo Soldiers.* New York: Scholastic. (5-8)

Farris, P. J. (1996). *Young mouse and elephant: An East African folktale* (V. Gorbachev, Illus.). Boston: Houghton Mifflin.

Golenbeck, P. (1990). *Teammates* (P. Bacon, Illus.). Orlando, FL: Gulliver. (3-8)

Hamilton, V. (1974). *Paul Robeson: The life and times of a free black man.* New York: Harper & Row. (5-8)

Hamilton, V. (1985). *The people could fly: American black folktales* (L. Dillon & D. Dillon, Illus.). New York: Knopf. (3-8)

Hamilton, V. (1991). *The all Jahdu storybook* (B. Moser, Illus.). San Diego: Harcourt Brace. (3-8)

Hamilton, V. (1992). *Drylongso* (J. Pinkney, Illus.). San Diego: Harcourt Brace. (3-6)

Hansen, J. (1986). *Which way freedom?* New York: Walker. (5-8)

Harris, J. C. (1986). *Jump! The adventures of Brer Rabbit.* Orlando, FL: Harcourt Brace Jovanovich. (K-8)

Haskins, J. (1977). *The life and death of Martin Luther King, Jr.* New York: Lothrop, Lee, & Shepard. (4-8)

Haskins, J. (1993). *Get on board: The story of the Underground Railroad.* New York: Scholastic. (5-8)

Hoffman, M. (1991). *Amazing Grace* (C. Birch, Illus.). New York: Dial. (K-3)

Hopkinson, D. (1993). *Sweet Clara and the freedom quilt* (J. Ransome, Illus.). New York: Knopf. (2-5)

Hoyt-Goldsmith, D. (1993). *Celebrating Kwanzaa* (L. Midgale, Illus.). New York: Holiday. (K-8)

Hurmence, B. (1982). *A girl called boy.* Boston: Houghton Mifflin. (4-6)

Isadora, R. (1991). *At the crossroads.* New York: Greenwillow. (3-5)

Kimmel, E. A. (1994). *Anansi and the talking melon* (J. Stevens, Illus.). New York: Holiday. (K-3)

Knutson, B. (1990) *How the guinea fowl got her spots: A Swahili tale of friendship.* New York: Carolrhoda. (K-2)

Lawrence, J. (1993). *The great migration: An American story.* New York: HarperCollins. (3-6)

McKillack, P. (1986). *Jesse Jackson.* New York: Scholastic. (4-6)

Meltzer, M. (1984). *Black Americans: A history in their own words.* New York: HarperCollins/Crowell. (4-8)

Mettger, Z. (1994). *Till victory is won: Black soldiers in the Civil War.* New York: Lodestar. (5-9)

Mollei, T. M. (1995). *Big boy.* (E. B. Lewis, Illus.). New York: Clarion. (K-3)

Myers, W. D. (1988). *Scorpions.* New York: Harper & Row. (5-8)

Myers, W. D. (1991). *Now is your time!: The African American struggle for freedom.* New York: HarperCollins. (4-8)

Petry, A. (1955). *Harriet Tubman: Conductor on the Underground Railroad.* New York: Crowell. (4-6)

Pinkney, A. D. (1993). *Seven candles for Kwanzaa* (B. Pinkney, Illus.). New York: Dial. (K-up)

Ringgold, F. (1991). *Tar beach.* New York: Crown. (1-3)

Ringgold, F. (1992). *Aunt Harriet's Underground Railroad in the sky.* New York: Crown. (1-4)

Yates, E. (1950). *Amos Fortune, free man.* New York: Dutton. (4-6)

Asian-American

Cassedy, S. & Suetake, K. (Trans.). (1992). *Red dragonfly on my shoulder* (M. Bang, Illus.). New York: HarperCollins. (K-3)

Choi, N.S. (1991). *Year of impossible goodbyes.* Boston: Houghton Mifflin. (4-8)

Clark, A.N. (1978). *To stand against the wind.* New York: Viking. (4-8)

Coerr, E. (1993). *Sadako* (E. Young, Illus.). New York: Putnam. (3-8)

Compton, P.A. (1991). *The terrible eek* (S. Hamanaka, Illus.). New York: Simon & Schuster. (1-3)

Conger, D. (1987). *Many lands, many stories: Asian folktales for children.* New York: Tuttle. (3-5)

Dunn, M., & Ardath, M. (1983). *The absolutely perfect horse.* New York: Harper & Row. (3-6)

Hamanaka, S. (1990). *The journey: Japanese Americans, racism, and renewal.* New York: Orchard. (4-7)

Haugaard, E.C. (1995). *The revenge of the forty-seven samurai.* Boston: Houghton Mifflin. (6-8)

Hong, L.T. (1991). *How the ox star fell from heaven.* New York: Albert Whitman. (4-6)

Johnson, R. (1992). *Kenji and the magic geese* (J. Tseng & M. Tseng, Illus.). New York: Simon & Schuster. (K-2)

Lord, B.B. (1984). *In the year of the boar and Jackie Robinson.* New York: Harper & Row. (4-6)

Morris, W. (1992). *The future of Yen-Tzu* (F. Henstra, Illus.). New York: Atheneum. (1-4)

Nhuong, H.Q. (1982). *The land I lost: Adventures of a boy in Vietnam.* New York: Harper & Row. (4-8)

Say, A. (1990). *El chino.* Boston: Houghton Mifflin. (4-8)

Say, A. (1993). *Grandfather's journey.* Boston: Houghton Mifflin. (K-3)

Shea, P.D. (1995). *The whispering cloth* (A. Riggio & Y. Yang, Illus.). Honesdale, PA: Boyds Mills. (K-2)

Siberell, A. (1990). *A journey to Paradise.* New York: Henry Holt. (4-6)

Surat, M.M. (1983). *Angel child, dragon child.* Racine, WI: Carnival/Raintree. (3-5)

Uchida, Y. (1993). *The bracelet* (J. Yardley, Illus.). New York: Philomel. (K-2)

Wallace, I. (1984). *Chin Chiang and the dragon's dance.* New York: Atheneum. (3-7)

Yacowitz, C. (1992). *The jade stone.* (J.H. Chen, Illus.). New York: Holiday. (1-3)

Yee, P. (1990). *Tales from gold mountain: Stories of the Chinese in the new world* (N. Ng, Illus.). New York: Harper & Row. (4-8)

Yee, P. (1991). *Roses sing on new snow* (H. Chan, Illus.). New York: Macmillan. (3-6)

Yep, L., (1989). *The rainbow people* (D. Wiesner, Illus.). New York: HarperCollins. (4-8)

Yep, L. (1993). *Dragon's gate.* New York: HarperCollins. (5-8)

Hispanic

Aardema, V. (1991). *Borreguita and the coyote: Tale from Ayutia, Mexico.* New York: Knopf. (K-3)

Ancona, G. (1994). *The piñata maker/El piñatero.* San Diego: Harcourt. (K-8)

Anzaldua, G. (1993). *Friends from the other side/Amigos del otro lado.* Chicago: Children's Book Press. (1-7)

Bunting, E. (1990). *The wall* (R. Himler, Illus.). New York: Clarion. (3-8)

Cisñeros, S. (1994). *Hairs/Pelitos.* New York: Apple Soup/Knopf. (K-3)

Clark, A.N. (1980). *Secret of the Andes.* New York: Viking. (4-8)

De Gerez, T. (1981). *My song is a piece of jade: Poems of ancient Mexico in English and Spanish.* Boston: Little, Brown. (3-8)

de Paola, T. (1980). *The lady of Guadalupe.* New York: Holiday. (3-6)

Dorros, A. (1991). *Abuela.* New York: Dutton. (4-8)

Ets, M.H., & Labastide, A. (1959). *Nine days to Christmas: A story of Mexico.* New York: Viking. (4-8)

Mohr, N. (1993). *All for the better: The story of El Barrio.* Dallas: Steck-Vaughn. (2–5)

Mora, P. (1995). *The desert is my mother/El desierto es mi madre* (D. Leshon, Illus.). Houston: Piñata.

O'Dell, S. (1981). *Carlota.* Boston: Houghton Mifflin. (5–8)

Palacios, A. (1993). *¡Viva Mexico!: The story of Benito Juarez and Cinco de Mayo.* Cleveland, OH: Modern Curriculum Press. (2–5)

Pitre, F. (1993). *Juan Bobo and the pig: A Puerto Rican folktale* (C. Hale, Illus.). New York: Lodestar.

Rodriguez, G. M. (1994). *Green corn tamales/Tamales de elote* (G. Shepard, Illus.). Tucson, AZ: Hispanic.

Roe, E. (1991). *Con mi hermano—With my brother.* New York: Bradbury. (5–8)

Shute, L. (1995). *Rabbit wishes.* New York: Lothrop, Lee, & Shepard.

Soto, G. (1990). *Baseball in April and other stories.* San Diego: Harcourt. (3–6)

Soto, G. (1992). *Neighborhood odes* (D. Diaz, Illus.). Sand Diego: Harcourt.

Soto, G. (1993). *Too many tamales* (E. Martinez, Illus.). New York: Putnam. (K–3)

Villaseñor, V. (1994). *Walking stars: Stories of magic and power.* Houston: Piñata.

Winter, J. (1991). *Diego.* New York: Knopf. (5–8)

Wolf, B. (1987). *In this proud land: The story of a Mexican-American family.* New York: HarperCollins (6–8)

Native American

Baylor, B. (1975). *A god on every mountain top: Stories of southwest Indian mountains.* New York: Scribner's. (3–6)

Baylor, B. (1978). *The other way to listen.* New York: Scribner's. (K–8)

Bierhorst, J. (1979). *A cry from the earth: Music of the North American Indians.* New York: Four Winds. (K–8)

Bierhorst, J. (1983). *The sacred path: Spells, prayers, and power songs of the American Indians.* New York: Four Winds. (K–8)

Bierhorst, J. (1995). *The white deer.* New York: Morrow. (2–up)

Bruchac, J. (1993). *Fox song* (P. Morin, Illus.). New York: Philomel. (K)

Bruchac, J. (1995). *Gluskabe and the four wishes* (C. Nyburg, Illus.). New York: Cobblehill.

Bruchac, J., & London, J. (1992). *Thirteen moons on turtle's back* (T. Locker, Illus.). New York: Philomel. (1–4)

Carey, V. S. (1990). *Quail song: A Pueblo Indian tale* (I. Barnett, Illus.). New York: Putnam. (K–4)

Cherry, L. (1991). *A river ran wild.* Orlando: Harcourt Brace Jovanovich. (K–8)

Cohen, C. L. (1988). *The mud pony: A Traditional Skidi Pawnee tale* (S. Begay, Illus.). New York: Scholastic. (3–7)

De Felice, C. (1990). *Weasel.* New York: Macmillan. (5–8)

Dorris, M. (1992). *Morning girl.* New York: Hyperion. (3–5)

Ekoomiak, N. (1990). *Arctic memories.* New York: Holt, Rinehart, & Winston. (4–6)

Freedman, R. (1988). *Buffalo hunt.* New York: Holiday. (3–8)

Freedman, R. (1992). *Indian Winter* (K. Bodmer, Photo.). New York: Holiday. (5–up)

Fritz, J. (1983). *The double life of Pocahontas.* New York: Putnam. (3–7)

George, J. C. (1983). *The talking earth.* New York: Harper & Row. (4–8)

Goble, P. (1988). *Iktomi and the boulder: A Plains Indian story.* New York: Orchard. (K–4)

Goble, P. (1990). *Dream wolf.* New York: Bradbury. (1–3)

Goble, P. (1992). *Crowchief.* New York: Orchard. (K–2)

Gregory, K. (1990). *The legend of Jimmy Spoon.* Orlando, FL: Harcourt Brace Jovanovich. (4–8)

Grossman, V. (1991). *Ten little rabbits.* (S. Long, Illus.). San Francisco: Chronicle. (K–2)

Hoyt-Goldsmith, D. (1991). *Pueblo storyteller* (L. Migdale, Photo.). New York: Holiday. (1–4)

Jassem, K. (1979). *Sacajawea, wilderness guide.* Mahwah, NJ: Troll. (1-4)

Kesey, K. (1991). *The sea lion* (N. Waldman, Illus.). New York: Viking. (5-8)

Larrabee, L. (1993). *Grandmother Five Baskets* (L. Sawyer, Illus.). Tucson, AZ: Harbinger. (3-8)

Larry, C. (1993). *Peboan and Seegwun.* New York: Farrar, Straus, & Giroux. (K-3)

Marrin, A. (1984). *War clouds in the west: Indians and cavalrymen, 1860-1890.* New York: Atheneum. (5-8)

Martin, R. (1992). *The rough-faced girl* (D. Shannon, Illus.). New York: Scholastic. (K-4)

Moore, R. (1990). *Maggie among the Seneca.* New York: HarperCollins. (5-6)

O'Dell, S. (1988) *Black star, bright dawn.* Boston: Houghton Mifflin. (5-8)

Paulsen, G. (1988). *Dogsong.* New York: Bradbury. (5-8)

Rodanos, K. (1992). *Dragonfly's tale.* New York: Clarion. (5-8)

Rodanos, K. (1994). *Dance of the sacred circle.* New York: Little, Brown.

Roessell, M. (1993). *Kinaalia: A Navaho girl grows up.* Minneapolis, MN: Lerner. (3-6)

Sewall, M. (1990). *People of the breaking day.* New York: Atheneum. (5-7)

Seymour, T. V. N. (1993). *The gift of changing woman.* New York: Henry Holt.

Sneve, V. (1989). *Dancing teepees: Poems of American Indian youth.* New York: Holiday. (4-8)

Sneve, V. (1994). *The Nez Perce: A first Americans book.* New York: Holiday. (2-6)

Speare, E. G. (1983). *The sign of the beaver.* Boston: Houghton Mifflin. (4-8)

Strete, D. K. (1990). *Big thunder magic* (G. Brown, Illus.). New York: Greenwillow. (K-4)

Thomson, P. (1995). *Katie Henio: Navaho sheepherder* (P. Conklin, Photo.). New York: Cobblehill.

Van Laan, N. (1993). *Buffalo dance: A Blackfoot legend* (B. Vidal, Illus.). Boston: Little, Brown. (1-8)

White Deer of Autumn. (1983). *Ceremony—In the circle of life.* Racine, WI: Raintree. (4-8)

Wisniewski, D. (1991). *Rain player.* New York: Clarion. (K-3)

Yolen, J. (1992). *Encounter* (D. Shannon, Illus.). San Diego: Harcourt Brace. (3-8)

Other Multicultural Works

Aamundsen, N. R. (1990). *Two short and one long.* Boston: Houghton Mifflin. (4-8)

Ashabranner, B. (1991). *An ancient heritage: The Arab-American minority* (P. S. Conklin, Photo.). New York: HarperCollins. (5-8)

Hamilton, V. (1988). *In the beginning: Creation stories from around the world.* Orlando, FL: Harcourt Brace Jovanovich. (4-8)

Haviland, V. (1979). *North American legends.* New York: Philomel. (4-8)

Heide, F. P., & Gilliland, J. H. (1990). *The day of Ahmed's secret* (T. Lewin, Illus.). New York: Lothrop, Lee, & Shepard. (K-3)

Langton, J. (1985). *The hedgehog boy: A Latvian folktale* (I. Plume, Illus.). New York: HarperCollins. (2-4)

Lankford, M. D. (1992). *Hopscotch around the world* (K. Milone, Illus.). New York: Morrow. (1-2)

Mayers, F. (1992). *A Russian ABC.* New York: Abrams. (K-4)

Philip, N. (1991). *Fairy tales of Eastern Europe* (L. Wilkes, Illus.). New York: Clarion. (K-8)

Reed, D. C. (1995). *The Kraken.* Honesdale, PA: Boyds Mills. (3-6)

Thematic Units

Developing a unit around a particular theme is an excellent way to allow children to delve into a specific area and share their findings and reactions with classmates. Such an activity allows every student to make a significant contribution to the group regardless of the student's reading ability or thinking skills.

The possibilities for thematic units are seemingly endless. An early-childhood-level teacher may decide to have a thematic unit on dinosaurs. The following books could be made available for students to read:

Aliki. (1981). *Digging up dinosaurs*. New York: Crowell. (1–2)
Aliki. (1988). *Dinosaur bones*. New York: Crowell. (1–2)
Arnold, C. (1989). *Dinosaur Mountain: Graveyard of the past* (R. Hewlitt, Photo.). New York: Clarion. (1–4)
Barton, B. (1989). *Dinosaurs, dinosaurs*. New York: Crowell. (K–2)
Dixon, D. (1990). *The first dinosaurs* (J. Burton, Illus.). New York: Dell/Yearling. (1–3)
Donnelly, L. (1989). *Dinosaur Beach*. New York: Scholastic. (K–2)
Gibbons, G. (1987). *Dinosaurs*. New York: Holiday. (1–3)
Gibbons, G. (1988). *Dinosaurs, dragonflies, and diamonds: All about natural history museums*. New York: Four Winds. (1–4)
Lauber, P. (1989). *The news about dinosaurs*. New York: Bradbury. (1–4)
Murphy, J. (1987). *The last dinosaur* (J. A. Weatherby, Illus.). New York: Scholastic. (2–4)
Nolan, D. (1994). *Dinosaur dream*. New York: Aladdin. (2–3)
Norman, D. (1987). *When dinosaurs ruled the earth*. Portsmouth, NH: Heinemann. (5–6)
Otto, C. (1991). *Dinosaur chase* (T. Hurd, Illus.). New York: HarperCollins. (1–3)
Pallotta, J. (1991). *The dinosaur alphabet book* (R. Masiello, Illus). Watertown, MA: Charlesbridge. (K–2)
Strickland, P. & Strickland H. (1994). *Dinosaur roar!* New York: Dutton. (K–1)
Wilhelm, H. (1988). *Tyrone the Horrible*. New York: Scholastic. (1–3)
Yolen, J. (1990). *Dinosaur dances* (B. Degen, Illus.). New York: Putnam. (1–3)
Microsoft's (1993) CD-Rom program *Dinosaurs* offers a nice complement in the form of an informational interactive computer program.

Thematic units are especially appropriate for social studies and can be based on famous adventurers, pioneer life, historical figures, historical events, and so on. Such a unit need only entail the literary element of characterization. By choosing to read about a particular time period and setting, such as the colonial period in America, including the Revolutionary War, several possibilities exist: discussing the life of the common people (farmers, fishermen, itinerant salesmen, shopkeepers, teachers, and the like), the cultural differences between the people who lived in the cities and those who lived on farms, the customs and beliefs of the period, and so on. Following is a list of books appropriate for a fifth-grade thematic unit on the colonial period in America, including books about the southeastern and southwestern parts of what is now the United States.

Famous Colonists

Bober, N. S. (1995). *Abigail Adams: Witness to a revolution*. New York: Atheneum. (6–up)
Davidson, M. (1988). *The story of Benjamin Franklin*. New York: Dell. (3–6)
Fritz, J. (1974). *Why don't you get a horse, Sam Adams?* (T. S. Hyman, Illus.). New York: Coward-McCann. (2–5)
Fritz, J. (1975). *Where was Patrick Henry on the 29th of May?* (M. Thomes, Illus.). New York: Putnam. (2–5)
Fritz, J. (1976). *Will you sign here, John Hancock?* (T. S. Hyman, Illus.). New York: Coward-McCann. (2–5)
Fritz, J. (1978). *What's the big idea, Ben Franklin?* (M. Thomes, Illus.). New York: Coward-McCann. (2–5)
Gilolin, J. C. (1992). *George Washington* (M. Dooling, Illus.). New York: Scholastic.
Monsell, H. A. (1989). *Thomas Jefferson*. New York: Aladdin. (3–6)

Siegal, B. (1989). *George and Martha Washington at home in New York* (F. Aloise, Illus.). New York: Four Winds. (2–5)

Wallner, A. (1994). *Betsy Ross.* New York: Holiday. (2–5)

Wallner, J., & Wallner, A. (1990). *A picture book of Benjamin Franklin.* New York: Holiday. (1–5)

Wallner, J., & Wallner, A. (1990). *A picture book of George Washington.* New York: Holiday. (1–5)

White, F. M. (1987). *The story of Junipero Serra: Brave Adventurer.* New York: Dell. (4–8)

Colonial Life

Anderson, J. (1984). *The first Thanksgiving* (G. Ancona, Photo.). New York: Clarion. (2–4)

Ayer, E. H. (1993). *The Anasazi.* New York: Walker. (5–8)

Blos, J. W. (1979). *A gathering of days: A New England girl's journal, 1830–32.* New York: Scribner's. (4–6)

Clapp, P. (1968). *Constance: A story of early Plymouth.* New York: Lothrop, Lee, & Shepard. (3–6)

Dalgliesh, A. (1991). *The courage of Sarah Noble* (L. Weisgard, Illus.). New York: Aladdin. (3–6)

Finkelstein, N. H. (1989). *The other 1492: Jewish settlement in the New World.* New York: Scribner's. (5–8)

Fisher, L. (1967). *The schoolmasters.* New York: Watts. (3–5)

Fisher, L. (1968). *The peddlers.* New York: Watts. (3–5)

Fisher, L. (1973). *The homemakers.* New York: Watts. (3–5)

George, J. C. (1993). *The first Thanksgiving* (T. Locker, Illus.). New York: Philomel. (1–6)

Early Colonies

Bosco, P. I. (1992). *Roanoke: The story of the lost colony.* New York: Millbrook. (4–6)

Bowen, G. (1994). *Stranded at Plimoth Plantation.* New York: HarperCollins. (3–7)

Clifford, M. L. (1993). *When the great canoes came* (J. Haynes, Illus.). New York: Pelican. (5–8)

Dorris, M. (1994). *Guests.* New York: Hyperion. (5–8)

Goor, R., & Goor, N. (1994). *Williamsburg: Cradle of the Revolution* (R. Goor, Photo.). New York: Atheneum. (3–6)

Kagan, M. (1989). *Vision in the sky: New Haven's early years.* New York: Shoe String/ Linnet. (4–8)

Wade, L. (1991). *St. Augustine: America's oldest city.* New York: Rourke. (3–5)

Revolutionary War

Avi. (1980). *Encounter at Easton.* New York: Pantheon. (5–8)

Avi. (1984). *Fighting ground.* Philadelphia: Lippincott. (5–8)

Bliven, B., Jr. (1987). *The American Revolution.* New York: Random House. (5–8)

Clapp, P. (1977). *I'm Deborah Sampson: A soldier in the War of the Revolution.* New York: Lothrop, Lee, & Shepard. (4–8)

Collier, J. L., & Collier, C. (1974). *My brother Sam is dead.* New York: Macmillan.

Collier, J. L., & Collier, C. (1983). *War comes to Willie Freeman.* New York: Dell. (5–7)

DePauw, L. G. (1994). *Founding mothers: Women of America in the Revolutionary era.* Boston: Houghton Mifflin.

Edwards, S. (1985). *George Midgett's war.* New York: Scribner's. (5–8)

Finalyson, A. (1972). *Rebecca's war.* New York: Warne. (4–8)

Forbes, E. (1943). *Johnny Tremain* (L. Ward, Illus.). Boston: Houghton Mifflin. (4–8)

Fritz, J. (1981). *Traitor: The case of Benedict Arnold.* New York: Dell.

Johnson, N. (1992). *The battle of Lexington and Concord.* New York: Four Winds. (4–8)

Knight, J. (1982). *Boston Tea Party.* Mahwah, NJ: Troll. (3–5)

Kroll, S. (1994). *By the dawn's early light: The story of the Star Spangled Banner.* New York: Scholastic. (3-8)

Reit, S. (1990). *Guns for General Washington.* San Diego: Harcourt Brace. (3-7)

Rinaldi, A. (1993). *The fifth of March: A story of the Boston massacre.* San Diego: Harcourt. (5-8)

Tunis, E. (1973). *The tavern at the ferry.* New York: Crowell. (4-7)

Turner, A. (1992). *Katie's trunk* (R. Himler, Illus.). New York: Macmillan. (2-5)

Shipbuilding and Whaling

Adkins, J. (1978). *Wooden ship.* Boston: Houghton Mifflin. (4-8)

Fisher, L. (1972). *The death of Evening Star: The story of a young whaler.* New York: Doubleday. (3-6)

Knight, J. (1982). *Salem days: Life in a colonial seaport.* Mahway, NJ: Troll. (3-5)

Monjo, F. N. (1976). *Zenas and the shaving mill.* New York: Coward-McCann. (3-6)

Patent, D. H. (1984). *Whales, giants of the deep.* New York: Holiday. (2-5)

Stein, C. (1982). *The story of New England whalers.* Chicago: Children's Press. (3-6)

Wibberly, L. (1961). *Sea captain from Salem.* New York: Farrar, Straus, & Giroux. (3-6)

Witchcraft

Aylesworth, T. (1979). *The story of witches.* New York: McGraw-Hill. (3-5)

Clapp, P. (1982). *Witches' children: A story of Salem.* New York: Lothrop, Lee, & Shepard. (4-8)

Jackson, S. (1987). *The witchcraft of Salem Village.* New York: Random House. (4-8)

Lasky, K. (1994). *Beyond the burning time.* New York: Blue Sky. (7-up)

Rinaldi, A. (1992). *A break with charity: A story about the Salem witch trials.* New York: Gulliver. (5-8)

Speare, E. G. (1971). *The witch of Blackbird Pond.* New York: Dell. (4-8)

Thematic units provide a means for having a completely integrated curriculum. Because thematic units can combine a variety of genre of children's literature such as informational books, contemporary realistic fiction, picture books, and poetry, children discover that topics can be written about in a variety of ways. By integrating the curriculum, teaching becomes more efficient and more relevant for the student.

The following "In the Classroom Mini Lessons" describe thematic units. The first thematic unit focuses on science as first graders investigate turtles. This unit, designed by Kristin Jung, a first-grade teacher, includes listening, drama, art, math, and writing activities. The second thematic unit focuses on social studies as fourth graders use a constructivism/inquiry approach to learning about the Underground Railroad. This unit was created by Lisa Vogt, a fourth grade teacher. The last example of a thematic unit likewise focuses on social studies with the Middle Ages being the primary topic. This thematic unit is appropriate for upper elementary/middle school students.

In the Classroom Mini Lesson

Thematic Unit in Science

A good science topic can evolve around the different kinds of turtles. Kristin Jung, a first-grade teacher in Claredon Hills, Illinois, designed the following thematic unit on turtles for her first-grade class. The unit includes informational books, picture books, and poetry. In addition, Kristin incorporates math activities. Students learn about the different types of turtles through the books shared in read alouds and from viewing videotapes. The students compare and contrast the various types of turtles (i.e., box, sea, and loggerhead). Students use turtle puppets in storytelling. For art projects, the students make turtles from paper plates and hatchlings from felt and rocks. Figure 4.2 presents a circular web of this study.

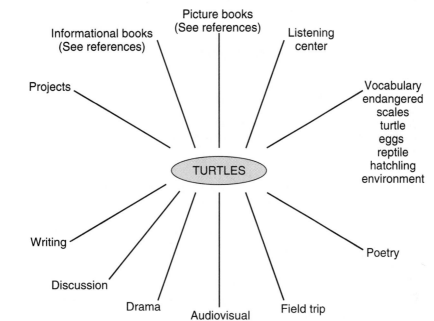

Figure 4.2

A curricular web of an integrated unit of study based on a science topic.

Listening Center

Students listen to fiction and nonfiction turtle stories, as well as watch videos/filmstrips on turtles.

Poetry and Drama

Each child makes a finger puppet and recites a turtle poem, such as the following:

The Little Turtle
by Vachel Lindsay

There was a little turtle.
He lived in a box.
He swam in a puddle.
He climbed on the rocks.
He snapped at a mosquito.
He snapped at a flea.

He snapped at a minnow.
And he snapped at me.
He caught the mosquito.
He caught the flea.
He caught the minnow.
But he didn't catch me.

Writing

Each student writes a story about the life cycle of a sea turtle and illustrates the story.

Each student writes his/her own "Franklin" story using the original stories as a framework. These stories are "published" into finished books.

The students write about the characteristic of reptiles (see example below) and draw accompanying pictures.

The children write about turtles using a framed sentence structure.

Each child writes an individual report and draws a realistic picture of the turtle he/she is researching.

Every student writes about the trip to the aquarium.

Reptiles

A reptile has _____.

A reptile is _____.

A reptile _____.

A reptile breathes with _____.

A _____ is a _____.

Art Projects

The children make turtles out of paper plates.

Each student makes a hatchling out of felt and a rock.

Each child makes a diorama of the turtle's habitat and places his/her hatchling inside the diorama.

Math

The children do a number of math worksheets related to turtles. These sheets correspond to what the students are currently learning in math.

Field Trip

The two first-grade classes go to the Shedd Aquarium. The children attend a lab where they learn about sea turtles and why they are endangered. The children also get to see a stuffed hawksbill turtle and some products that are made from sea turtles. The students look at some freshwater turtles and are able to touch the carapace and plastron. After the lab, students tour the galleries and pay special attention to the turtles. The children get to see the diver feeding the various sea creatures in the big tank. This trip is one of the culminating activities for the turtle unit.

Turtle Tea

Finished projects are presented at a "Turtle Tea," to which the children's parents are invited. After the tea, parents are invited back to the classroom to see all of the projects their children have done during the turtle unit. Cookies and juice are served in the rooms, as well.

Audiovisual Aids

What is a reptile? (1977). A National Geographic Filmstrip, National Geographic Society, Washington, DC 20036.

Chickens aren't the only ones. A Reading Rainbow Video, Great Plains National (GPN), P.O. Box 80669, Lincoln, NE 68501.

Poetry

Lindsay, V. (1920). "The little turtle." New York: Macmillan.

Silverstein, S. (1981). "Turtle." *A light in the attic.* New York: HarperCollins.

Picture Books

Bampton, B. (Illus.). (1994). *Turtle egg pop-ups*. New York: Golden Books/Western.

Berger, M. (1992). *Look out for turtles!* (M. Lloyd, Illus.). New York: HarperCollins.

Bourgeois, P. (1986). *Franklin in the dark* (B. Clark, Illus.). New York: Scholastic.

Bourgeois, P. (1989). *Hurry up, Franklin* (B. Clark, Illus.). New York: Scholastic.

Bourgeois, P. (1991). *Franklin fibs* (B. Clark, Illus.). New York: Scholastic.

Bourgeois, P. (1992). *Franklin is lost* (B. Clark, Illus.). New York: Scholastic.

Bourgeois, P. (1993). *Franklin is bossy* (B. Clark, Illus.). New York: Scholastic.

Bourgeois, P. (1994). *Franklin is messy* (B. Clark, Illus.). New York: Scholastic.

Bryan, A. (1989). *Turtle knows your name*. New York: Atheneum.

Florian, D. (1989). *Turtle Day*. New York: Crowell.

Freschet, B. (1971). *Turtle Pond* (D. Carrick, Illus.). New York: Scribner's.

George, W. (1989). *Box turtle at Long Pond* (L.B. George, Illus.). New York: Greenwillow.

Greenfield, K. (1992). *Sister Yessa's story* (C. Ewart, Illus.). New York: HarperCollins.

Leedy, L. (1993). *Tracks in the sand*. New York: Doubleday.

Selsam, M.E. (1965). *Let's get turtles*. New York: Harper & Row.

Stoddard, S. (1995). *Turtle time* (L. Munsinger, Illus.). Boston: Houghton Mifflin.

Tate, S. (1991). *Tammy Turtle: A tale of saving sea turtles* (J. Melvin, Illus.). Nags Head, NC: Nags Head Art.

Whipple, D. (1962). *The tale of a very little tortoise* (H. Williams, Illus.). New York: Warne.

Wood, D. (1992). *Old turtle* (C.K. Chee, Illus.). Duluth, MN: Pfeifer-Hamilton.

Informational Books

Ancona, G. (1987). *Turtle watch*. New York: Macmillan.

Arnold, C. (1994). *Sea turtles* (M. Peck, Illus.). New York: Scholastic.

Church, R. (1963). *Turtles*. Neptune City, NJ: T.F.H. Publications.

The Cousteau Society. (1992). *Turtles*. New York. Simon & Schuster.

Fichter, G.S. (1993). *Turtles, toads, and frogs* (B.H. Ambler, Illus.). New York: Western.

Fowler, A. (1992). *Turtles take their time*. Chicago: Children's Press.

Jahn, J. (1987). *A step by step book about turtles*. Neptune City, NJ: T.F.H. Publications.

Kaufman, E., & Kaufman, E. (1989). *Sea animals*. Los Angeles: Price Stern Sloan.

Knox, C. (Illus.). (1983). *Animal world: The turtle*. Windermere, FL: Rourke Enterprises.

Lambert, D. (1983). *Reptiles*. New York: Gloucester.

McCleery, P.R. (1988). *The turtle lady*. Austin, TX: Texas Geographic Interests.

Pallotta, J. (1989). *The yucky reptile alphabet book* (R. Masiello, Illus.). Watertown, MA: Charlesbridge.

Pope, J. (1985). *A closer look at reptiles*. New York: Gloucester.

Rudloe, J. & Rudloe, A. (1994). In a race for survival. *National Geographic, 185* (2), 95–121.

Scott, J.D. (1974). *Loggerhead turtle: Survivor from the sea* (O. Sweet, Photo.). New York: Putnam.

Stone, L.M. (1993). *Sea turtles*. Vero Beach, FL: Rourke Corp.

White, C. (1986). Freshwater turtles—Designed for survival. *National Geographic, 169* (1),40–58.

Source: Kristin Jung, first-grade teacher
Walker School
120 S. Walker Ave.
Claredon Hills, IL 60514
Reprinted by permission.

In the Classroom Mini Lesson

Theme Cycle Units

Theme cycles are units in which the students and the classroom teacher select topics of study together. According to Altwerger and Flores (1994), theme cycles allow students to be at the center of learning as they ask critical questions, engage in meaningful problem posing and problem solving, and create and recreate knowledge. Students are actively involved as they share the collective knowledge of the class, select areas of interest, seek out resources, and plan learning experiences.

Below is a theme cycle developed by Lisa Vogt and her fourth-grade class as part of a unit of study on the Civil War. The students elected to become more familiar with the Underground Railroad since some of the original stations had been located in the area near their school. Figure 4.3 presents a circular web of this study.

Altwerger, B., & Flores, B. (1994). Theme cycles: Creating communities of learners. *Primary Voices, K–6, 2,* 2–6.

Taking the Train to Freedom
Underground Railroad Study

As early as the 16th century, western European nations constructed a uniform slavery system in the Western Hemisphere. This process was composed mainly of people of African origins. Through the notorious slave trade, Africans were dispersed and forced to labor on sugar, tobacco and rice plantations throughout the Americas and Caribbean. In the 1600s and 1700s, slave labor played a vital role in the history of the British North American colonies. Beginning with Massachusetts and Virginia colonies in 1641 and 1660 respectively, slavery was legalized and regarded as essential to the colonial economy. As white colonists began to petition for freedom and human rights from the British government, this same sentiment was echoed by enslaved blacks. Those who voiced strong opposition to slavery campaigned for the destruction of the system. Although some blacks received liberation through legal suits, those who remained in bondage took considerable risks to gain freedom by escaping from their masters. This method, known as the "Underground Railroad," became a major impetus leading to the eradication of the "peculiar institution"—Slavery.

The Underground Railroad originated during the colonial era as slaves sought ways to escape the inhumane treatment of bondage. Neither "underground" nor a "railroad," this secretive system was not initially organized, but arose when escaped slaves sought refuge in unclaimed territories and newly settled colonies. With the assistance of agents such as the Quakers, free blacks and Native Americans, bondsmen were able to gain their freedom. The efforts of the "underground" promoted the enactment of local fugitive slave laws which were a response to the growing concerns of slaveholders who had lost numerous servants. But as the nation continued to struggle over the morality of slavery, the invention of the cotton gin in 1793 accorded the South justification to perpetuate slavery since it was viewed imperative to its economy.

The abolition movement of the early 1800s set its goal on exterminating slavery. To do so, abolitionists designed the "underground" into a well-organized system. Through the use of secret codes, "stations," "conductors," and "railways," runaway slaves usually travelled to their destinations by night either alone or in small groups. Guided by the North Star, their plans did not entail standard routes since it was necessary to prevent capture; thus waterways, back roads, swamps, forests, mountains, and fields were used to escape. While in flight, slaves hid in barns, caves, cellars, and even boxes or wagons and aboard ships. Food and shelter were provided at "stations" which were maintained by noted "conductors" such as William Still, Levi Coffin and Frederick Douglass. Moreover, Presbyterian, African Methodist Episcopal, African Methodist Episcopal Zion, and the United Methodist churches gave refuge to escapees. Once runaways achieved their freedom, a few like Harriet Tubman, known as a "Moses" to her people, returned to assist fellow slaves and loved ones to liberty. Single-handedly, Tubman made 19 trips to the South and led more than 300 slaves out of bondage.

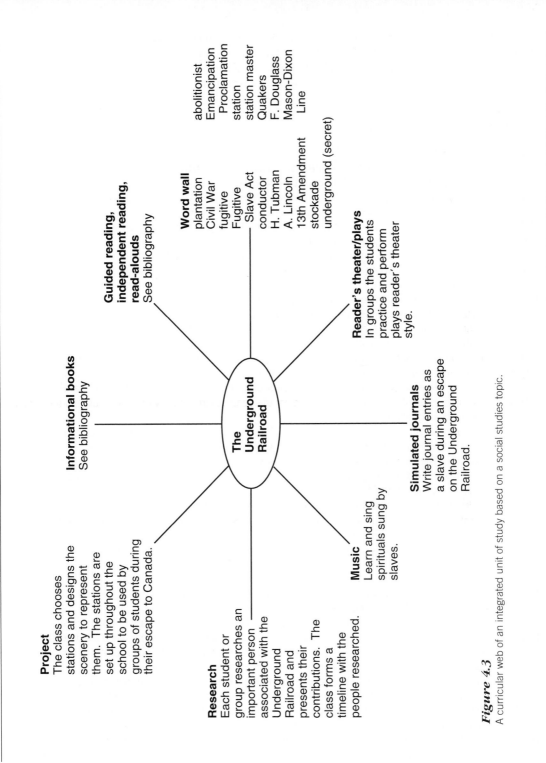

Project
The class chooses stations and designs the scenery to represent them. The stations are set up throughout the school to be used by groups of students during their escape to Canada.

Research
Each student or group researches an important person associated with the Underground Railroad and presents their contributions. The class forms a timeline with the people researched.

Informational books
See bibliography

Guided reading, independent reading, read-alouds
See bibliography

Word wall
plantation
Civil War
fugitive
Fugitive
  Slave Act
conductor
H. Tubman
A. Lincoln
13th Amendment
stockade
underground (secret)

abolitionist
Emancipation
  Proclamation
station
station master
Quakers
F. Douglass
Mason-Dixon
  Line

The Underground Railroad

Reader's theater/plays
In groups the students practice and perform plays reader's theater style.

Simulated journals
Write journal entries as a slave during an escape on the Underground Railroad.

Music
Learn and sing spirituals sung by slaves.

Figure 4.3
A curricular web of an integrated unit of study based on a social studies topic.

By the 1850s, anti-slavery sentiment had reached its peak, and the "underground" program was challenged by slaveholders through a revised Fugitive Slave Act. This law, which called for the return of runaways, jeopardized the status of freedmen, especially those who resided in northern states. Escape routes thus were no longer limited to northern midwestern regions and the federal territories of the United States. More than 100,000 American slaves sought freedom in these areas as well as in Canada, Mexico and the Caribbean. The Underground Railroad remained active until the end of the Civil War as black bondsmen continued to use the system to flee the horrors of slavery.

From National Parks Service, Taking the Train to Freedom. Copyright ©. Reprinted by permission.

Underground Railroad Chronology

1607	Jamestown, Virginia, settled by English colonists.
1619	Twenty Africans are shipped to Jamestown, Virginia, on Dutch ships.
1641	Massachusetts colony legalizes slavery.
1642	Virginia colony enacts law to fine those who harbor or assist runaway slaves.
1660	Virginia colony legalizes slavery.
1741	North Carolina colony enacts law to prosecute any person caught assisting runaways.
1775	The Pennsylvania Abolition Society is established to protect fugitives and freed blacks unlawfully held in bondage.
1776	North American colonies declare independence from Great Britain.
1777–1804	Northern states abolish slavery through state constitutions.
1787	Northwest Ordinance prevents slavery to exist in the new federal territories. Free African Society of Philadelphia, an abolitionist group, is organized by Richard Allen and Absolm Jones.
1793	Fugitive Slave Act becomes a federal law. Allows slaveowners, their agents or attorneys to seize fugitive slaves in free states and territories.
1794	Mother Bethel African Methodist Episcopal Church is established in Philadelphia, PA.
1800	Nat Turner and John Brown are born. Gabriel Prosser stages an unsuccessful slave insurrection in Henrico County, VA.
1804	Underground Railroad is "incorporated" after slaveowner, Gen. Thomas Boudes of Columbia, PA, refuses to surrender escaped slave to authorities.
1816	Seminole Wars begin in Florida as a result of many slaves taking refuge with Seminole Indians.
1818	As a response to the Fugitive Slave Act (1793), abolitionists use the "underground" to assist slaves to escape into Ohio and Canada.
1820	Missouri Compromise admits Missouri and Maine as slave and free states, respectively. The measure establishes the 36°30′ parallel of latitude as a dividing line between free and slave areas of the territories.
1821	Kentucky representatives present resolution to Congress protesting Canada's reception of fugitive slaves.
1822	Former slave Denmark Vesey performs a slave uprising in Charleston, SC.
1829	Black abolitionist, David Walker issues **David Walker's Appeal.** Afterwards, several slave revolts occurred throughout the South.
1830	Levi Coffin leaves North Carolina, settles in Indiana and continues abolitionist activities.
1831	William Lloyd Garrison prints first issues of his anti-slavery newspaper, **The Liberator.** Black entrepreneur and abolitionist Robert Forten becomes chief financial supporter of the publication. Nat Turner stages insurrection in Southampton County, VA.
1832	Louisiana presents resolution requesting Federal Government to arrange with Mexico to permit runaway slaves from Louisiana to be reclaimed when found on foreign soil.
1834	National Antislavery Society organizes Underground Railroad as a response to pro-slavery argument.
1838	Underground Railroad is "formally organized." Black abolitionist, Robert Purvis, becomes chairman of the General Vigilance Committee and "president" of the Underground Railroad.

1842	Supreme Court rules in **Prigg v. Pennsylvania** that state officials are not required to assist in the return of fugitive slaves.
1845	Frederick Douglass prints **Narrative of the Life of Frederick Douglass,** an account of his slave experience and escape to freedom.
1847	Douglass edits anti-slavery newspaper, the **North Star.**
1849	Harriet Tubman makes her escape from Maryland.
1850	Compromise of 1850 attempts to settle slavery issue. As part of the Compromise, a new Fugitive Slave Act is added to enforce the 1793 law and allows slaveholders to retrieve slaves in northern states and free territories.
1852	Harriet Beecher Stowe's **Uncle Tom's Cabin** is published as a response to the pro-slavery argument.
1857	Supreme Court declares in **Scott v. Sandford** that blacks are not U.S. citizens, and slaveholders have the right to take slaves in free areas of the country.
1859	John Brown's failed raid on federal arsenal and armory in Harper's Ferry, Virginia which was aimed at starting a general slave insurrection.
1860	Republican candidate Abraham Lincoln is elected President of the United States.
1861	Civil War begins.
1863	President Lincoln issues the Emancipation Proclamation which declares "all persons held as slaves within any state . . . be in rebellion against the United States shall be then . . . forever free."
1865	Civil War ends.
	Thirteenth Amendment is amended to the U.S. Constitution abolishing slavery permanently.

From National Parks Service, Underground Railroad Chronology. Copyright ©. Reprinted by permission.

The Underground Railroad

Nonfiction

. . . If You Traveled on the Underground Railroad by Levine—question and answer, picture book format, excellent read aloud

The Story of the Underground Railroad by Stein—picture book format, good read aloud

Allen Jay and the Underground Railroad by Brill—easy reading level, good read aloud or guided reading for less able readers, novel format

The Underground Railroad by Cosner—advanced reading level, useful for teacher information

Get on Board: The Story of the Underground Railroad by Haskins—excellent nonfiction book for read aloud or guided reading

Harriet Tubman: Call to Freedom by Carlson—read aloud or guided reading

Freedom Train: The Story of Harriet Tubman by Sterling—read aloud or guided reading

The Underground Railroad by Bial—photo essay that is appropriate for all levels of readers

Fiction

Sweet Clara and the Freedom Quilt by Hopkinson—picture book format

Aunt Harriet's Underground Railroad in the Sky by Ringgold—picture book format

Steal Away by Armstrong—novel

Freedom Crossing by Clark—novel

Underground Man by Meltzer—novel

Escape from Slavery: Five Journeys to Freedom by Rappaport—contains five short stories mentioned in many of the nonfiction books listed above

Runaway to Freedom by Smucker—novel

Running for Our Lives by Turner—novel

The People Could Fly: American Black Folktales by Hamilton—has a section entitled "Carrying the Running-Aways and Other Slave Tales of Freedom" which contains six short stories

From Sea to Shining Sea: A Treasury of American Folklore and Folk Songs compiled by Amy Cohn—has a section entitled "I've Been Working on the Railroad" which contains several folktales and songs

Vocabulary Word Wall

The students and teacher generate this list together. Here are several possibilities:

plantation
abolitionist
Civil War
Emancipation Proclamation
fugitive
Fugitive Slave Act
station, station master, conductor
Quakers

Harriet Tubman
Frederick Douglass
Abraham Lincoln
Mason-Dixon Line
Thirteenth Amendment
stockade
underground (meaning secret)

Reader's Theater

The following stories are written in play format with stage directions and can be performed as plays. The first play listed is directly related to the Underground Railroad. The second and third plays listed relate to Martin Luther King, Jr.'s birthday and the Civil Rights Movement, which we recently studied. The students choose their parts and practice before reading to the class.

"Frederick Douglass: The Douglass 'Station' of the Underground Road"
"Martin Luther King, Jr.: In the Footsteps of Dr. King"
"Rosa Parks: The Unexpected Heroine"

Simulated Journals

The students write in their journals as "slaves" telling of their attempts to escape on the Underground Railroad.

Music

During music class, the music teacher discusses the history of spirituals with the students. After the students have had time to learn the songs, all the classes are put together to perform the songs on the day of the "Escape" (see Projects). Possible songs to learn are as follows:

"Wade in the Water"
"Somebody's Knocking at Your Door"
"Who Built the Ark?"
"Swing Low, Sweet Chariot"
"Oh, Won't You Sit Down?"

Research

The students choose a person involved with the Underground Railroad and research his or her contributions and importance. This can be done individually, in pairs, or in small groups. The students present the information to the class as an "interview" with the famous person, as a news report about the person, or by dressing up as the person. The class then uses the information to form a time line sequencing the important people and their contributions.

Under Ground Railroad

It is 1837. I am a slave but a very lucky one. I know how to read and wright. It is 3:00 in the morning and I havn't got caught yet. Last time I ran away I only lasted until 1:00. My slave is very mean. We only get 10 min. to eat lunch O'h and by the way my name is Yotchy. My masters name is Mr. oops I mean Master Koncan. When we are in bed we make fun of him and we say master canon. We also make fun of our own names too because our master named us. My real name used to be Amy. We hate our names. Sometimes when we have meetings all he talks about is how lad we work never how good. I'm glad I'm free. Until morning, mabey. Mabey I can bye myself. I only need

a couple more dollars. Oh joy it is 5:00. Every one is going to get up now. Well mabey I could be lucky like Toma. She is free somewhere in Canida. Mabey I will go there. I'm going that way. Oh no its morning. I better start to run. Well here I go. Oh great there is a Slave cature. I better hide. Trouble timaw I hope he is not looking for now. I better take a run for it. One, two, three go! He hasn't seen me yet. Oh no he saw me. He's runing tord me. I better find a place to go fast. even worse he has a wagon I know I will stop & run the other way. Then it well take him longer to turn around. I hate

myself for running away. go faster you legs. aaaaaah! stay away from me. I'm abot to die! Oh so its Yotchy that ran away this time hu. Ya. I'm sorry. Yo well your.....ouch! foot is coming off.

THE END!

This is Amy's diary entry portraying herself in the role of a slave.

Projects

The students plan and design the scenery for Underground Railroad stations. Eight stations are planned and set up throughout the school hallways. Using their knowledge of the types of places used as hide-outs and stations on the Underground Railroad, the students design the scenery and signals (which indicate a safe or unsafe station). Scenery is hung throughout the school hallways and two "station masters" are assigned to each station. Two of the eight stations are deemed "unsafe." The unsafe stations rotate throughout the "escape." In groups of three or four, students are released from one end of the school and must safely travel the "Underground Railroad" to Canada (the gym) on the other end of the school. Along the way the students must stop at at least four stations. (If a group reaches Canada without four punches in their card they are considered to have starved.) If the station they choose to stop at is a safe station, their card is punched and the group continues. If they choose to stop at an unsafe station, their card is collected and they must return to the "captured slaves" room. Very few groups make it to Canada, and they must work together to look for signals and keep track of the stations passed!

Possible stations:
forest
cemetery
house/cabin
riverboat
wagon
cave
barn

Possible signals:
lanterns hung a certain way or in a certain place
quilts displayed

Bibliography

Picture Books

Bial, R. (1995). *The Underground Railroad.* Boston: Houghton Mifflin.
Hopkinson, D. (1993). *Sweet Clara and the freedom quilt* (J. Ransome, Illus.). New York: Knopf.
Levine, E. (1988). . . . *If you traveled on the Underground Railroad* (L. Johnson, Illus.). New York: Scholastic.
Ringgold, F. (1992). *Aunt Harriet's Underground Railroad in the sky* (F. Ringgold, Illus.). New York: Crown.
Stein, R.C. (1981). *The story of the Underground Railroad* (R. Canaday, Illus.). Chicago: Children's Press.

Nonfiction

Brill, M.T. (1993). *Allen Jay and the Underground Railroad* (J.L. Porter, Illus.). Minneapolis: Carolrhoda.
Cosner, S. (1991). *The Underground Railroad.* New York: Venture.
Haskins, J. (1993). *Get on board: The story of the Underground Railroad.* New York: Scholastic.

Biographies

Carlson, J. (1989). *Harriet Tubman: Call to freedom.* New York: Fawcett Columbine.
Sterling, D. (1954). *Freedom Train: The story of Harriet Tubman.* New York: Scholastic.

Fiction

Armstrong, J. (1992). *Steal away.* New York: Orchard.
Clark, M.G. (1969). *Freedom crossing* (K.B. Eanest, Illus.). New York: Funk & Wagnalls.
Meltzer, M. (1972). *Underground man.* New York: Harcourt Brace Jovanovich.
Rappaport, D. (1991). *Escape from slavery: Five journeys to freedom* (C. Lilly, Illus.). New York: HarperCollins.
Smucker, B. (1977). *Runaway to freedom* (C. Lilly, Illus.). New York: Harper & Row.
Turner, G.T. (1994). *Running for our lives* (S. Byrd, Illus.). New York: Dutton.

Folktales

Cohn, A.L. (1993). *From sea to shining sea: A treasury of American folklore and folk songs.* New York: Scholastic.
Hamilton, V. (1985). *The people could fly: American Black Folktales* (L. and D. Dillon, Illus.). New York: Knopf.

Reader's Theater Plays

Turner, G. Tilley. (1989). *Take a walk in their shoes* (E.C. Fax, Illus.). New York: Dutton.

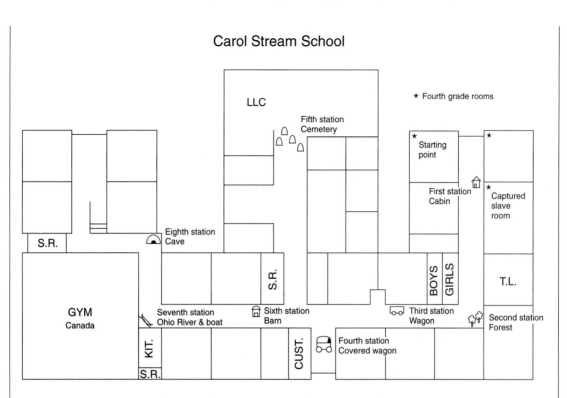

Carol Stream School

LLC

★ Fourth grade rooms

Fifth station Cemetery

★ Starting point

★

First station Cabin

★ Captured slave room

Eighth station Cave

S.R.

S.R.

BOYS GIRLS

T.L.

GYM
Canada

Seventh station Ohio River & boat

Sixth station Barn

Third station Wagon

Second station Forest

KIT.

CUST.

Fourth station Covered wagon

S.R.

Mrs. Vogt's students transformed their school into a vintage Civil War landscape, complete with Underground Railroad stations.

Songs

Crook, E., Reimer, B., & Walker, D.S. (1985). *Music.* New Jersey: Silver Burdett.

Reimer, B., & Hoffman, M.E. (1985). *Music.* New Jersey: Silver Burdett.

Staton, B., Staton, M., Davidson, M., Kaplan, P., & Snyder, S. (1991). *Music and you.* New York: Macmillan.

Map of Slave States—1860

A free map of the slave states depicting the various Underground Railroad routes to Canada, Mexico, and the Caribbean can be obtained by writing to the following address:

Underground Railroad Study Project
National Park Service
Denver Service Center—Eastern Team
P.O. Box 25287
Denver, CO 80225

or by calling (800)524–6878 and asking for the project historian, Underground Railroad.

From Lisa Vogt, Underground Railroad. Reprinted by permission.

In the Classroom Mini Lesson

Thematic Unit on the Middle Ages

*U*ntil recent years, there have been relatively few trade books available about the Middle Ages for children to read. Certainly the "age of chivalry" greatly interests children. This unit was designed for students in Grades 5 through 8.

The entire class reads E.L. Konigsburg's (1973) *Proud Taste for Scarlet and Miniver* and engages in the integrated activities as outlined in figure 4.4. At the conclusion of these activities, each student selects and reads a second novel about the Middle Ages and keeps a literature journal to record reactions and responses. Students are paired with someone who is reading the same book. They read and write in their response journals, then exchange journals to share their thoughts and reactions on the same material. They meet with their partner each day or every other day to discuss the book.

Children's Books

Bellairs, J. (1989). *The trolley to yesterday.* New York: Dial. (4–8)
> This time-warp story takes Johnny and his friend, Fergie, back to 1453 and the Byzantine Empire. The two friends arrive in Constantinople just prior to the Turkish invasion.

Cushman, K. (1994). *Catherine, called Birdy.* New York: Clarion. (6–8)
> Birdy is 14 and she faithfully keeps a diary of her experiences in England in 1290. The diary spans a one-year period during which Birdy's father attempts to marry her off for money or land. This is a Newbery Honor Book.

Cushman, K. (1995). *The midwife's apprentice.* New York: Clarion. (4–8)
> The setting is the Middle Ages where a young orphan must fend for herself until she becomes apprenticed to a midwife. The book provides very accurate descriptions of details of the period.

de Angeli, M. (1949). *The door in the wall.* New York: Doubleday. (5–8)
> This award-winning book is the story of Robin, the son of a knight, who becomes ill and loses the use of his legs. A monk takes him in and teaches him wood carving. Along the way, Robin also learns patience and strength. When the castle of Lindsay is threatened, Robin rescues the townspeople.

Konigsburg, E.L. (1973). *Proud taste for Scarlet and Miniver.* New York: Atheneum. (4–8)
> Illustrated by the author, this historical fiction novel focuses on Eleanor of Aquitaine. Proud Eleanor is waiting for her young husband, King Henry II, to join her in heaven. Henry had died before Eleanor, but had not yet been judged favorably by the angels. While she waits, Eleanor reflects upon the various events of her life. Children will find this book to be both interesting and amusing.

Osband, G., & Andrew, R. (1991). *Castles.* New York: Orchard. (K–8)
> This pop-up picture book is filled with information that will intrigue students. Early designs of castles, including how they expanded over the years, are depicted. In addition, castle life is discussed as well as the life of knights. Ten castles still in existence within a variety of European countries are portrayed and described.

Temple, F. (1994). *The Ramsay scallop.* New York: Orchard. (7–8)
> Thirteen-year-old Elenor is betrothed to Thomas—a marriage designed to join their parents estates. When they are reluctant to wed, Father Gregory sends Elenor and Thomas on a pilgrimage to Ramsey, Spain, where they receive a scallop shell. This book is targeted at the mature reader.

Winthrop, E. (1985). *The castle in the attic.* New York: Holiday. (4–7)
> William receives an old, realistic model of a castle as a gift from the housekeeper. She warns him that it is very special. This fantasy will appeal to students interested in magic and the wizards of the Middle Ages.

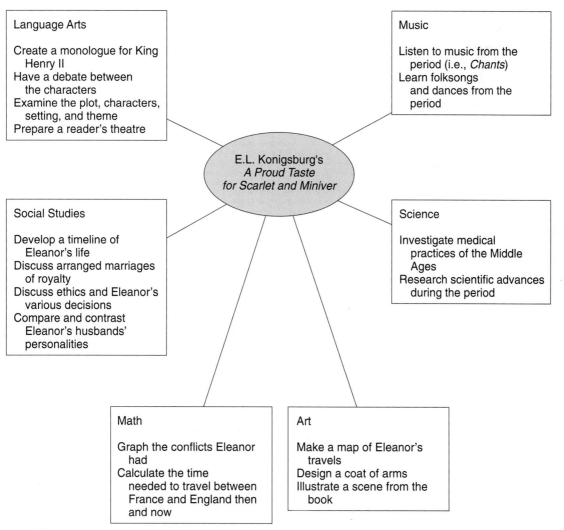

Theme: The Middle Ages

Grades 5–8

Language Arts

Create a monologue for King
  Henry II
Have a debate between
  the characters
Examine the plot, characters,
  setting, and theme
Prepare a reader's theatre

Music

Listen to music from the
  period (i.e., *Chants*)
Learn folksongs
  and dances from the
  period

E.L. Konigsburg's
*A Proud Taste
for Scarlet and Miniver*

Social Studies

Develop a timeline of
  Eleanor's life
Discuss arranged marriages
  of royalty
Discuss ethics and Eleanor's
  various decisions
Compare and contrast
  Eleanor's husbands'
  personalities

Science

Investigate medical
  practices of the Middle
  Ages
Research scientific advances
  during the period

Math

Graph the conflicts Eleanor
  had
Calculate the time
  needed to travel between
  France and England then
  and now

Art

Make a map of Eleanor's
  travels
Design a coat of arms
Illustrate a scene from the
  book

Figure 4.4
The Middle Ages is the focus of this integrated unit of instruction.

Catherine Called Birdy

by Karen Cushman

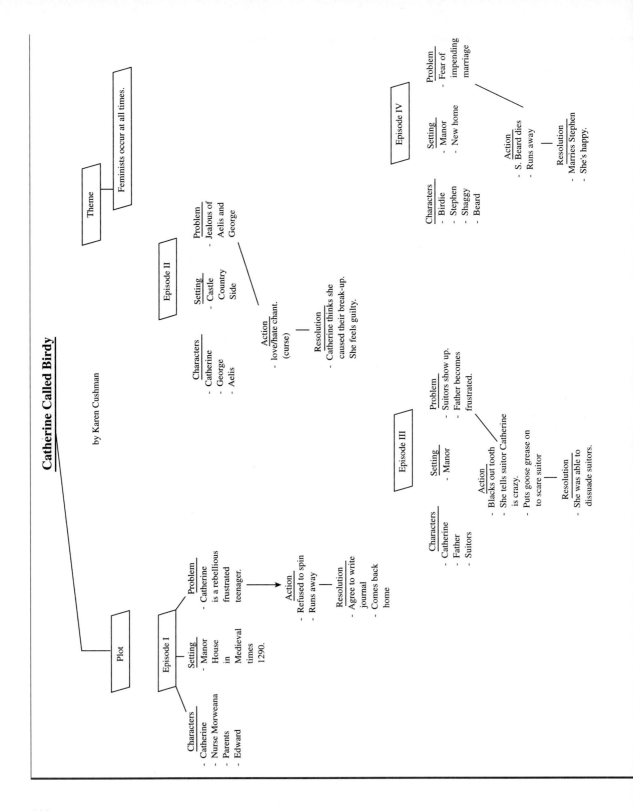

Theme

Feminists occur at all times.

Plot

Episode I

Characters
- Catherine
- Nurse Morweana
- Parents
- Edward

Setting
- Manor House in Medieval times 1290.

Problem
- Catherine is a rebellious frustrated teenager.

Action
- Refused to spin
- Runs away

Resolution
- Agree to write journal
- Comes back home

Episode II

Characters
- Catherine
- George
- Aelis

Setting
- Castle Country Side

Problem
- Jealous of Aelis and George

Action
- love/hate chant. (curse)

Resolution
- Catherine thinks she caused their break-up. She feels guilty.

Episode III

Characters
- Catherine
- Father
- Suitors

Setting
- Manor

Problem
- Suitors show up.
- Father becomes frustrated.

Action
- Blacks out tooth
- She tells suitor Catherine is crazy.
- Puts goose grease on to scare suitor

Resolution
- She was able to dissuade suitors.

Episode IV

Characters
- Birdie
- Stephen
- Shaggy
- Beard

Setting
- Manor
- New home

Problem
- Fear of impending marriage

Action
- S. Beard dies
- Runs away

Resolution
- Marries Stephen
- She's happy.

This illustration of Catherine was done by a seventh-grade student who drew the picture to accompany the preceding literary elements chart.

Figure 4.5
The literary elements of *Catherine, Called Birdy* outlined by episode by a group of middle school students.

Literature Response Journals

As more and more teachers attempt to incorporate literature into the elementary curriculum, children are increasingly being asked to respond to literature through writing and discussion. The literature response journal enables a child to write down his or her own feelings, thoughts, predictions, hunches, and reactions while reading a piece of literature. "Teaching students to respond strongly to text requires not only that they have opportunities to respond freely, but also that they be guided to a greater insight and appreciation of literary works and literature as a whole" (Wyshynski & Paulsen, 1995, p. 260). As Hancock (1992, p. 38) writes, "Although a traditional book report may reveal final interpretation of text, the literature response journal reflects the thought process on the mental journey to that final conclusion."

In the journal, a notebook kept solely for the purpose of responding to literature, the student jots down his or her notation and the page number of the book that provokes the notation. The teacher routinely reads each child's literature response journal, writing positive comments and thought-provoking, open-ended questions to the child. Only the child and the teacher share the journal.

Rather than requiring students to provide a summary and critique of what they read—as was the case with a traditional book report—the literature response journal allows students the freedom to interact with the author and/ or characters. As the children read, they gather information and make predictions that turn out to be either correct or incorrect. Then they formulate new predictions as they gain additional information in a meaning-making process. Langer (1990) refers to this as "envisionment building"; children's understanding changes and expands as they progress through a piece of literature and, after they have completed it, as they contemplate it and discuss it with others. Thus, envisionments are "a function of one's personal and cultural experiences, one's relationship to the current experience, what one knows, how one feels, and what one is after. . . . Each envisionment includes what the individual does and does not understand" (Langer, 1995, p. 9).

The following four guidelines for assisting children in environment building as they write in their literature response journals have been adapted from Langer (1990, p. 815):

1. *Initial understandings:* Begin with a question that encourages the children to respond to the story.
2. *Developing understandings:* Ask questions that help the students move beyond their initial understandings in ways that are meaningful to them. Such questions should strive to elicit deeper responses from the students, guiding them toward an exploration of motivation, cause and effect, implication, and so on.
3. *Reflecting on personal experiences:* Ask questions that help the students to relate what they are reading to their own knowledge and/or personal experiences—for example, to other books they have read or real-life experiences they have had.

4. *Elaborating and extending:* After the children have worked through their own understandings, encourage them to critique what they have read. Encourage them to analyze and evaluate it and also to compare it with other works that are similar in nature or perhaps by the same author. The students can also apply literary elements at this point.

Literature response journals are being used with preschoolers as young as age 4. The children listen to the teacher or a parent read a story and then they draw their responses (Danielson, 1992). These children will continue to include their own illustrations in their literature response journals, along with their written responses, through middle childhood.

After teachers introduce students to literature response journals, parents can become involved. Carol Fuhler (1994), a middle school teacher, invited parents of her students to keep their own literature response journals as they read the same novels as their children. Each evening the parents and their children shared their reactions with each other in the comfort of their own homes.

S u m m a r y

Children's literature should be a central part of the language arts curriculum. By sharing and discussing quality literature, children learn to appreciate and enjoy reading, essential components to becoming lifelong readers.

By understanding the literary elements of characterization, plot, setting, theme, and author's style, children discover the different components of literature and learn to appreciate more fully the value of reading books. Exposure to the various literary genre widens a child's knowledge base through vicarious experiences.

The use of thematic units in children's literature enables children to gain increased knowledge in specific topics and areas. Because children's literature offers several choices, children often are more eager and motivated to read books than textbooks in a content area.

Literature response journals help children in the meaning-making process as they relate their previous knowledge and experiences to what they are presently reading. In addition, they may use the information presented in a book to make predictions about what may take place later in the book. Finally, as they reflect on what they have read, the students may analyze and evaluate the work as they compare it with other works they have read.

Questions

1. Define the five literary elements of children's literature.
2. Why is it important for children to be exposed to a variety of genre?
3. How can children's literature add to the teaching of content-area material?
4. How does traditional literature differ from contemporary realistic fiction?

1. Select a contemporary realistic fiction book that you read as a child. Reread it and think about your reaction to it today as compared with your reaction when you first read it.
2. Select a book that has won a Newbery Medal. Read it and consider the book's literary elements as you do so.
3. Prepare a thematic unit for a particular grade level.
4. Spend a morning or afternoon in the children's section of the public library. Observe how children select books, how they interact with their parents in discussing their selections, and what kinds of questions they ask the children's librarian.

For Further Reading

Bieger, E.M. (1996). Promoting multicultural education through a literature-based approach. *The Reading Teacher, 49* (4), 308-313.

Cianciolo, P.J. (1989). No small challenge: Literature for the transitional readers. *Language Arts, 66* (1), 72-82.

Hancock, M.R. (1992). Literature response journals: Insights beyond the printed page. *Language Arts, 69* (1), 36-42.

Heald-Taylor, B. G. (1996). Three paradigms for literature instruction in grades 3 to 6. *The Reading Teacher, 49* (6), 456-467.

Trachtenburg, P., & Ferruggia, A. (1989). Big books from little voices: Reaching high risk beginning readers. *The Reading Teacher, 42*(4), 284-289.

Yokota, J. (1993). Issues in selecting multicultural children's literature. *Language Arts, 70,* 156-167.

References

Because of the large number of children's books cited in this chapter, these titles are documented in a separate subsection below.

Adams, M.J. (1990). *Beginning to read: Thinking and learning about print.* Urbana: University of Illinois, Center for the Study of Reading.

Bieger, E.M. (1996). Promoting multicultural education through a literature-based approach. *The Reading Teacher, 49* (4), 308-313.

Billig, E. (1977). Children's literature as a springboard to content areas. *The Reading Teacher, 30* (6), 855-858.

Bishop, R.S. (1992). Multicultural literature for children: Making informed choices. In V. Harris (Ed.), *Teaching multicultural literature* (pp. 37-54). Norwood: MA: Christopher Gordon.

Chomsky, C. (1972). Stages in language development and reading exposure. *Harvard Educational Review, 42*(1), 1-33.

Cullinan, B. (1987). Inviting readers to literature. In B. Cullinan (Ed.), *Children's literature in the reading program.* Newark, DE: International Reading Association.

Cullinan, B., & Galda, L. (1994). *Literature and the child* (3rd ed.). Fort Worth, TX: Harcourt Brace Jovanovich.

Danielson, K.E. (1992). Learning about early writing from response to literature. *Language Arts, 69* (4), 274-280.

Elley, W.B. (1989). Vocabulary acquisition from listening to stories. *Reading Research Quarterly, 24* (2), 174-187.

Fisher, C. (1989). The advocate's page. *New Advocate, 2*(2), xvii-xviii.

Fuhler, C. (1994). Response journals: Just one more time with feeling. *Journal of Reading, 37,* 400-408.

Hancock, M.R. (1992). Literature response journals: Insights, beyond the printed page. *Language Arts, 69* (1), 36-42.

Hildreth, G. (1991). Minority children need books, too! *Illinois Reading Council Journal, 19* (3), 11-17.

Honig, B. (1988). The California reading initiative. *The New Advocate, 1*(4), 235-240.

Huck, C. (1996). Literature-based reading programs: A retrospective. *The New Advocate, 9* (1), 23-34.

Langer, J. (1990). Understanding literature. *Language Arts, 67*(8), 812-816.

Langer, J.A. (1995). *Envisioning literature: Literary understanding and literature instruction.* New York: Teacher's College.

Microsoft. (1993). *Dinosaurs* (CD-Rom). Seattle, WA: Microsoft.

Norton, D. (1990). Teaching multicultural literature in the reading curriculum. *The Reading Teacher, 44*(1), 28-40.

Roser, N.L., Hoffman, J.V., & Farest, C. (1990). Language, literature, and at-risk children. *The Reading Teacher, 43*(8), 554-559.

Smith, F. (1992). Learning to read: The never-ending debate. *Phi Delta Kappan, 73*(6), 432-441.

Stotsky, S. (1992). Whose literature? America's! *Educational Leadership, 49* (4), 53-56.

Sutherland, Z., & Hearne, B. (1984). In search of the perfect picture book. In P. Barron & J. Burley (Eds.), *Jump over the moon.* New York: Holt, Rinehart, & Winston.

Taylor, D., & Dorsey-Gaines, C. (1988). *Growing up literate: Learning from inner-city families.* Portsmouth, NH: Heinemann.

Teale, W., & Sulzby, E. (Eds.). (1985). *Emergent literacy: Writing and reading.* Norwood, NJ: Ablex.

Wyshynski, R., & Paulsen, D. (1995). Maybe I will do something: Lessons from coyote. *Language Arts, 72*(4), 258-264.

Children's Books

Aardema, V. (1975). *Why mosquitoes buzz in people's ears* (L. Dillon & D. Dillon, Illus.). New York: Dial.

Adoff, A. (1981). *Outside inside poems.* New York: Lothrop, Lee, & Shepard.

Adoff, A. (1986). *Sports pages* (R. Kuzma, Illus.). Philadelphia: Lippincott.

Banks, L.R. (1980). *The Indian in the cupboard.* New York: Doubleday.

Beatty, P. (1981). *Lupita mañana.* New York: Morrow.

Blumberg, R. (1989). *The great American gold rush.* New York: Bradbury.

Blume, J. (1970). *Are you there God, It's me Margaret.* New York: Bradbury.

Blume, J. (1972). *Tales of a fourth grade nothing* (R. Doty, Illus.). New York: Dutton.

Blume, J. (1973). *Deenie.* New York: Bradbury.

Bober, N.S. (1995). *Abigail Adams: Witness to a revolution.* New York: Atheneum.

Brett, J. (1990). *The mitten: A Ukranian folktale.* New York: Putnam.

Brooks, B. (1984). *The moves make the man.* New York: Harper & Row.

Brooks, B. (1993). *Boys will be.* New York: Henry Holt.

Bunting, E. (1989). *The Wednesday surprise* (D. Carrick, Illus.). New York: Clarion.

Byars, B. (1980). *The night swimmers* (T. Howell, Illus.). New York: Delacorte.

Byars, B. (1981). *The Cybil war* (G. Owens, Illus.). New York: Viking.

Cameron, A. (1988). *The most beautiful place in the world* (T.B. Allen, Illus.). New York: Knopf.

Carle, E. (1969). *The very hungry caterpillar.* New York: Philomel.

Carlstrom, N.W. (1986). *Jesse Bear, what will you wear?* (B. Degan, Illus.). New York: Macmillan.

Cherry, L. (1990). *The great kapok tree.* San Diego: Gulliver/HBJ.

Cleary, B. (1968). *Ramona the pest* (L. Darling, Illus.). New York: Morrow.

Cleary, B. (1983). *Dear Mr. Henshaw* (P.O. Zelinsky, Illus.). New York: Morrow.

Cleary, B. (1988). *A girl from Yambill, a memoir.* New York: Dell.

Cleary, B. (1991). *Strider* (P.O. Zelinsky, Illus.). New York: Morrow.

Cleaver, V., & Cleaver, B. (1969). *Where the lilies bloom* (J. Spanfeller, Illus.). Philadelphia: Lippincott.

Cleaver, V., & Cleaver, B. (1971). *I would rather be a turnip.* Philadelphia: Lippincott.

Conrad, P. (1987). *Prairie songs* (D.S. Zudeck, Illus.). New York: Harper & Row.

Cowing, S. (1989). *Searches in the American desert.* New York: McElderry.

Dahl, R. (1984). *Boy: Tales of childhood.* New York: Puffin.

Delacre, L. (1989). *Arroz con leche: Popular songs and rhymes from Latin America.* New York: Scholastic.

Denim, S. (1994). *The dumb bunnies* (D. Pilkey, Illus.). New York: Blue Sky.

de Paola, T. (1975). *Strega Nona.* New York: Simon & Schuster.

de Paola, T. (Reteller). (1988). *The legend of the Indian paintbrush.* New York: Putnam.

de Paola, T. (1989). *The art lesson.* New York: Putnam.

Dewey, J. (1989). *Can you find me? A book about animal camouflage.* New York: Scholastic.

Dunphy, M. (1994). *Here is the tropical rainforest* (M. Rothman, Illus.). New York: Hyperion.

Dygard, T.J. (1978). *Winning kicker.* New York: Morrow.

Ehlert, L. (1989). *Color zoo.* New York: HarperCollins.

Ehlert, L. (1989). *Eating the alphabet.* San Diego: Harcourt

Ehlert, L. (1990). *Fish eyes: A book you can count on.* New York: HarperCollins.

Epstein, S., & Epstein, B. (1989). *Bugs for dinner? The eating habits of neighborhood creatures.* New York: Macmillan.

Fleischman, P. (1988). *Joyful noise: Poems for two voices.* New York: Harper & Row.

Fleischman, P. (1991). *The borning room.* New York: HarperCollins.

Fleischman, P. (1996). *Dateline: Troy.* New York: HarperCollins.

Fox, M. (1985). *Wilfrid Gordon McDonald Partridge* (J. Vivas, Illus.). San Diego: Harcourt.

Freedman, R. (1987). *Lincoln: A photobiography.* New York: Clarion.

Freedman, R. (1991). *The Wright brothers: How they invented the airplane* (W. & O. Wright, Photo.). New York: Holiday.

Fritz, J. (1982). *Homesick: My own story.* New York: Putnam.

George, J.C. (1959). *My side of the mountain.* New York: Dutton.

George, J.C. (1979). *River Rats, Inc.* New York: Dutton.

George, J.C. (1989). *Shark beneath the reef.* New York: Harper & Row.

George, W.T. (1989). *Box turtle at Long Pond* (L.B. George, Illus.). New York: Greenwillow.

Green, N. (1974). *The hole in the dike* (E. Carle, Illus.). New York: Crowell.

Hamilton, V. (1992). *Drylongso* (J. Pinkney, Illus.). San Diego: Harcourt Brace.

Henkes, K. (1993). *Owen.* New York: Greenwillow.

Hesse, K. (1992). *Letters from Rifka.* New York: Henry Holt.

Hoberman, M.A. (1978). *A house is a house for me* (B. Fraser, Illus.). New York: Viking.

Hoffman, M. (1991). *Amazing Grace* (C. Binch, Illus.). New York: Dial.

Holman, F. (1986). *Slake's limbo.* New York: Dell.

Huck, C. (1989). *Princess Furball* (A. Lobel, Illus.). New York: Greenwillow.

Hughes, T. (1985). *The iron giant.* New York: Harper & Row.

Jackson, E. (1994). *Cinder Edna* (K. O'Malley, Illus.). New York: Lothrop, Lee, & Shepard.

Jacobs, W.J. (1990). *Ellis Island: New hope in a new land.* New York: Macmillan/Scribner's.

Jacobs, W.J. (1991). *Mother Teresa: Helping the poor.* New York: Millbrook.

Kellogg, S. (1986). *Best friends.* New York: Dial.

Kendall, C. (1959). *The Gammage Cup* (E. Blegvad, Illus.). New York: Harcourt Brace Jovanovich.

Kennedy, X.J. (1985). *The forgetful wishing well: Poems for young children.* New York: Atheneum.

Kirk, D. (1994). *Miss Spider's tea party.* New York: Scholastic.

Kraus, R. (1971). *Leo the late bloomer.* New York: Windmill.

Lauber, P. (1990). *Seeing the Earth from Space.* New York: Orchard.

Leslie, C.W. (1991). *Nature all year long.* New York: Greenwillow.

Lester, J. (1989). *How many spots does a leopard have? And other tales* (D. Shannon, Illus.). New York: Scholastic.

Levinson, R. (1988). *Our home is the sea* (D. Luzak, Illus.). New York: Dutton.

Levy, C. (1991). *I'm going to pet a worm today and other poems* (R. Himler, Illus.). New York: McElderry.

Lewis, C.S. (1950). *The lion, the witch, and the wardrobe* (P. Baynes, Illus.). New York: Macmillan.

Lewis, J.P. (1991). *Earth verses and water rhymes* (R. Sabuda, Illus.). New York: Atheneum.

Livingston, M.C. (1984). *Sky songs.* New York: Holiday.

Livingston, M.C. (1989). *Up in the air* (L.E. Fisher, Illus.). New York: Holiday.

Lowry, L. (1989). *Number the stars.* Boston: Houghton Mifflin.

Lowry, L. (1993). *The giver.* Boston: Houghton Mifflin.

Lyon, G.E. (1992). *Who came down that road?* (P. Catalano, Illus.). New York: Orchard.

Macaulay, D. (1981). *Cathedral.* Boston: Houghton Mifflin.

Maestro, B.C. (1989). *Snow day* (G. Maestro, Illus.). New York: Scholastic.

Martin, B., Jr. (1983). *Brown bear, brown bear, what do you see?* (E. Carle, Illus.). New York: Holt, Rinehart, & Winston. (Original work published 1964).

Mayer, M. (1971). *A boy, a dog, and a frog.* New York: Dial.

McCully, E.A. (1992). *Mirette on the high wire.* New York: Putnam.

McGrath, B.B. (1994). *The M&M's counting book.* Watertown, MA: Charlesbridge.

McKissack, P. (1988). *Mirandy and Brother Wind* (J. Pinkney, Illus.). New York: Knopf.

Meltzer, M. (1990). *Brother can you spare a dime?* New York: Facts on File.

Morimoto, J. (1990). *My Hiroshima.* New York: Viking.

Murphy, J. (1993). *Across America on an immigrant train.* New York: Clarion.

Myers, W.D. (1983). *Hoops.* New York: Delacorte.

Myers, W.D. (1991). *Now is your time!: The African-American struggle for freedom.* New York: HarperCollins.

Naylor, P.R. (1991). *Shiloh.* New York: Dell.

Nelson, V.M. (1988). *Always Grandma* (K. Uhler, Illus.). New York: Putnam.

O'Dell, S. (1980). *Sarah Bishop.* Boston: Houghton Mifflin.

Osband, G. (1991). *Castles* (R. Andrew, Illus.). New York: Orchard.

Paterson, K. (1977). *Bridge to Terabithia.* New York: Harper & Row.

Paulsen, G. (1987). *Hatchet.* New York: Viking.

Paulsen, G. (1989). *The winter room.* New York: Viking.

Peck, R.N. (1972). *A day no pigs would die.* New York: Knopf.

Pilkey, D. (1990). *'Twas the night before Thanksgiving.* New York: Orchard.

Pinkney, G. (1992). *Back home* (J. Pinkney, Illus.). New York: Dial.

Prelutsky, J. (1976). *The snopp on the sidewalk and other poems.* New York: Greenwillow.

Prelutsky, J. (1984). *The new kid on the block* (J. Stevenson, Illus.). New York: Greenwillow.

Prelutsky, J. (1988). *Tyrannosaurus was a beast.* New York: Greenwillow.

Prelutsky, J. (1990). *Something big has been here* (J. Stevenson, Illus.). New York: Greenwillow.

Prelutsky, J. (1991). *Poems of A. Nonny Mouse* (H. Drescher, Illus.). New York: Dragonfly.

Rylant, C. (1993). *Missing May.* New York: Orchard.

Sanders, S.R. (1989). *Aurora means dawn.* New York: Bradbury.

San Souci, R. (1990). *The talking eggs: A folktale from the American south* (J. Pinkney, Illus.). New York: Dial.

Scieszka, J. (1989). *The true story of the three little pigs* (L. Smith, Illus.). New York: Viking.

Scieszka, J. (1992). *The stinky cheese man: And other fairly stupid tales* (L. Smith, Illus.). New York: Viking.

Scieszka, J. (1994). *The book that Jack wrote* (D. Adel, Illus.). New York: Viking.

Scieszka, J. (1995). *Math curse* (L. Smith, Illus.). New York: Viking.

Shaw, N. (1986). *Sheep in a jeep.* Boston: Houghton Mifflin.

Silverman, E. (1994). *Don't fidget a feather* (S.D. Schindler, Illus.). New York: Macmillan.

Silverstein, S. (1974). *Where the sidewalk ends.* New York: Harper & Row.

Sis, P. (1991). *Follow the dream: The story of Christopher Columbus.* New York: Knopf.

Sneve, V.D.H. (1989). *Dancing teepees: Poems of American Indian youth* (S. Gammell, Illus.). New York: Holiday.

Spinelli, J. (1990). *Maniac Magee.* New York: Little, Brown.

Spinelli, J. (1991). *There's a girl in my hammerlock.* New York: Half Moon.

Stevens, J. (1995). *Tops and bottoms.* San Diego: Harcourt Brace.

Taylor, M. (1995). *The well.* New York: Dial.

Taylor, T. (1969). *The cay.* New York: Doubleday.

Taylor, T. (1981). *The trouble with Tuck.* New York: Doubleday.

Tessendorf, K.C. (1989). *Along the road to Soweto: A racial history of South Africa.* New York: Atheneum.

Towle, W. (1993). *The real McCoy: The life of an African-American inventor* (W. Clay, Illus.). New York: Scholastic.

Van Allsburg, C. (1981). *Jumanji.* Boston: Houghton Mifflin.

Van Allsburg, C. (1985). *The polar express.* Boston: Houghton Mifflin.

Viorst, J. (1981). *If I were in charge of the world, and other worries.* New York: Atheneum.

Waber, B. (1972). *Ira sleeps over.* Boston: Houghton Mifflin.

Walton, R. (1995). *What to do when a bug climbs in your mouth and other poems to drive you buggy* (N. Carlson, Illus.). New York: Lothrop, Lee, & Shepard.

Waters, K. (1989). *Sarah Morton's day: A day in the life of a Pilgrim girl* (R. Kendall, Photo.). New York: Scholastic.

White, E.B. (1952). *Charlotte's web* (G. Williams, Illus.). New York: Harper & Row.

Whybrow, I. (1991). *Quacky, quack-quack!* (R. Ayto, Illus.). New York: Four Winds.

Winter, J. (1988). *Follow the drinking gourd.* New York: Knopf.

Wise, W. (1993). *Ten sly piranhas* (V. Chess, Illus.). New York: Dial.

Wisniewski, D. (1991). *Rain player.* New York: Clarion.

Wood, D., & Wood, A. (1984). *The little mouse, the red ripe strawberry, and the big hungry bear.* New York: Child's Play International.

Yarbrough, C. (1989). *The shimmershine queens.* New York: Putnam.

Yep, L. (1989). *The rainbow people* (D. Weisner, Illus.). New York: Harper & Row.

Yolen, J. (1991). *Wings* (D. Nolan, Illus.). Orlando, FL: Harcourt Brace Jovanovich.

Young, E. (1989). *Lon Po Po.* New York: Philomel.

Young, E. (1992). *Seven blind mice.* New York: Philomel.

Ziefert, H. (1994). *Pete's chicken* (L. Rader, Illus.). New York: Tambourine.

Oral Language: Developing the Base of Expression

© Jean-Claude Lejeune

Reading and writing float on a sea of talk.
—**James Britton**
"Writing and the Story World"

*O*n a chilly winter morning, Tyler, age 3, is talking to his mother as he is getting dressed. "Yestermorning when I got up I had pancakes for breakfast. Today I want rooster corn flakes." His mother nods affirmative, translating Tyler's "yestermorning" into yesterday morning and "rooster corn flakes" into Kellogg's corn flakes. When she touches his bare leg with her cold hands, Tyler cries out, "Hey, you're colding me!" The acquisition of language enables children to demonstrate their feelings, needs, and desires verbally and to acquire the social skills of our culture.

Although English is the primary language used in schools in the United States, 20 percent of all teachers use both English and Spanish during the school day (Lapointe, 1986). Throughout the world, English is spoken by about 750 million people, half of whom speak it as their native language. As the most widely spoken and written language, English is the first global language to exist (McCrum, Cran, & MacNeil, 1986).

This chapter discusses the history of the English language, including influences by other cultures and languages as well as American dialects. It also examines how children acquire language.

The Development of English

Like most languages, English has an oral base. English is considered a hybrid language in that it has continuously borrowed words from other languages as a result of trade, wars, and cultural revolutions. English can be broken down into three periods: Old English (600 to 1100), Middle English (1100 to 1500), and Modern English (1500 to today). Approximately one-fourth of all English words used today can be traced to Old English origins.

English is a member of the Indo-European language family, the common source of languages spoken by a third of the world's population (fig. 5.1). The Indo-European language family can be broken down into several branches. The Italic branch of the Indo-European family tree, for example, includes French, Italian, Portuguese, and Spanish. The framework for the English language was primarily created by the Celtic and Germanic branches.

The Celts were one of the earliest peoples to migrate to the British Isles. "True British" are those people who are descendants of the Celts. These include the Irish, Scots, and Welsh. When Julius Caesar arrived in the British Isles in 55 B.C., Celts met his boat. Other Roman legions followed Julius Caesar to the British Isles, but when the Roman Empire fell in A.D. 410, the legions left.

The next major invaders were the Angles, Saxons, and Jutes, those Germanic raiders who sailed from Denmark and Germany in A.D. 449. Like the American

Indo-European Family Tree

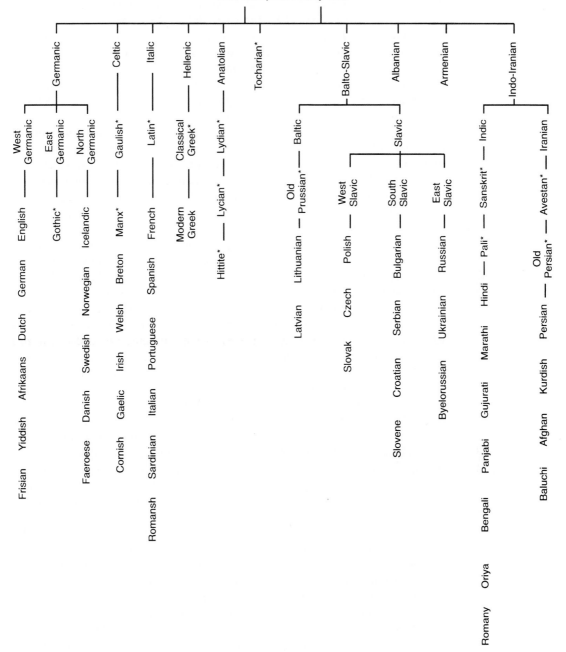

Figure 5.1

English is a member of the Indo-European language family.

From Anderson, Paul/Lapp, Diane, *Language Skills in Elementary Education,* © 1988, p. 52. Reprinted by permission of Prentice Hall, Upper Saddle River, New Jersey.

Indians in America, the Celts were driven westward by the invaders. The Angles, Saxons, and Jutes terrorized the inhabitants. "The English language arrived in Britain on the point of a sword" (McCrum, Cran, and MacNeil, 1986, p. 60).

Time passed and the Angles and Saxons became an agrarian people. Therefore, the Anglo-Saxons developed terms such as *sheep, shepherd, earth, plough, ox, swine,* and *calf.* Other familiar words, including *laughter, mirth, coat, hat, glove, man, wife, child, here, there, you, the,* and *is,* are also of Anglo-Saxon origin. Indeed, it is almost impossible to write or speak a sentence without including Anglo-Saxon words.

Since the Anglo-Saxons were largely an illiterate people, theirs was an oral culture. Relying on speech and memory, they created poems, shared stories, and sang ballads, all of which helped to perpetuate "Englisc" in "Englaland."

In A.D. 597, St. Augustine brought Christianity to England, which was predominantly pagan at the time. The building of churches and monasteries led to the improvement of education in England, for the monks taught a wide range of subjects, including arithmetic, poetry, and Latin. From Latin, English has borrowed such words as *angel, cap, beet, cheese, mass, relic, school,* and *wine.* The Anglo-Saxons contributed the words *God, heaven,* and *hell* to Christianity.

Scandinavian peoples, the Vikings, were the next to invade England. These Vikings, or Danes as the Anglo-Saxons called them, raided the British Isles in A.D. 793, plundering the gold and silver of the monasteries. Such raids continued throughout the ninth century, until the Danes were defeated by King Alfred the Great's army in A.D. 878. Unlike the Celts, whose language had little influence on English, the Danes contributed nearly a thousand words to the English language. *Hit, birth, leg, knife, sky, still, skin, steak,* and *want* are some of the most frequently used Danish terms today.

King Alfred the Great was able to unite more of England than any previous ruler. He ordered the monasteries and schools that the Danes had destroyed to be rebuilt. Most importantly, King Alfred adopted English as the official language of the land, using it to create a sense of identity for the country. As a result, books were translated into English, and King Alfred ordered a history to be written to preserve the common heritage of the English people. Therefore, King Alfred is greatly, if not solely, responsible for saving and preserving the English language.

The next major invasion came in 1066, when the Normans, under the command of William the Conqueror, landed at Hastings. The English royal family and court were destroyed in an ensuing battle, leaving the control of England to the French. Thus, French became the official language of the land and eventually French words such as *attorney, lieutenant, justice, stamp, envelope, felony, colonel, nobility,* and *sovereign* came into the English language.

When the French finally left England in 1244, a majority of the English people still spoke Anglo-Saxon, not having given in to their Norman rulers and adopted French. For example, the people of the villages and farms continued to speak of *calf, ox,* and *swine,* whereas the Normans referred to the same animals as *veal, beef,* and *pork.* Nevertheless, French words still permeate the language of the kitchen: *pâté, sauté, mutton, braise, broil, cuisine, roast, soufflé,* and *croissant.*

After the French returned to France, the English were never again successfully invaded. However, the English language was still pervious to change. Trade, wars, and the discovery of new lands provided it with new words from which to borrow. Englishman William Caxton ventured to Germany to examine the Guttenburg printing press, a remarkable machine that had movable type. So impressed was Caxton that in 1475 he produced in Bruges (in what is now Belgium) the first book printed in English. Well aware of the importance of such a printing press, entrepreneur Caxton returned to England to set up his own press in Westminster, where he printed more than a hundred books in English.

The development and use of the movable-type printing press was important because it not only increased the opportunity for the common folk to read and write but also standardized spelling. Prior to the mass production of books, people who could read and write were gentry. Words were spelled at the writer's whim, sometimes being spelled four or five different ways in a single letter.

As the English empire grew, so did the language, as sailors, soldiers, and traders encountered the peoples of other nations. From the Dutch, a great sailing people, came *yankee, yacht, keel, deck, schooner, freight, cruiser, cookie, toy,* and *tub.* The Italians provided *design, opera, cello, violin, piano, volcano, torso, cartoon, cash, carnival,* and *broccoli.*

The German language, despite being from the same branch of the Indo-European language family as English, has lent English relatively few words. Among those are *delicatessen, hamburger, frankfurter,* and *dollar.*

From Spanish come several frequently used words, including *alligator, banana, canoe, cocoa, potato, ranch, rodeo,* and *tomato.* Also from Spanish come the weather terms *hurricane* and *tornado* and the names for those infamous pesky insects *cockroach* and *mosquito.*

English has borrowed from Arabic *algebra, candy, lemon, orange, sugar,* and *magazine. Bagel, ebony, cherub,* and *sapphire* are inherited Hebrew terms. From African languages come *gorilla, jazz, chimpanzee,* and *voodoo.*

Not many words have been borrowed from Asian languages, largely because of the centuries of limited Asian contact with the Western world. From Indian come *cot, khaki, bungalow, loot,* and the sport of kings, *polo.* Malayalam gave us *teak,* a type of wood. From Chinese come *tea* and *chow mein.* Japanese has lent *bonsai, kimono, jujitsu,* and *sushi.* However, most of the Japanese terms English-speaking people use are trade names: Honda, Nissan, Sony, Yamaha, and the like.

Native Americans provided some state names, notably *Illinois* and *Indiana.* Many United States city names also derive from Native American words. For example, *Chicago* comes from a Native American word meaning "place that smells like onions." *Manhattan* translates into the "place where all got drunk." Perhaps the Indians were even prescient in the naming of Peoria, Illinois, now a city that manufactures large earth-moving equipment. *Peoria* means the "place of great beasts." *Maize, caucus, skunk, raccoon,* and *wampum* are other donated Indian terms.

In the Classroom Mini Lesson

Considering Other Languages

A delightful picture book that gets children and adults thinking about word origins and sound representations is *Who Says a Dog Goes Bow-Wow?* by Hank DeZutter (1993). This is a book that gives the English phonetic renderings of the sounds commonly known animals make as presented in different languages from throughout the world. For instance, here is a list of the sounds a rooster makes when he crows:

English—cock-a-doodle-doo
French—Coco-rico
Polish—Ku-Ku-ree-ku
Dutch—Kee-ke-le-koo
Danish—Kee-klee-ky
Spanish—Kee-kee-ree-kee
Japanese—Kokke-kokko
Chinese—Wo-wo-wo
German—Guggeru-guuhh

This book is an excellent way to introduce onomatopoeia to students.

DeZutter, H. (1993). *Who Says a Dog Goes Bow-Wow?* (S. McDonald, Illus.). New York: Delacorte.

Coinages of English Words

Some words have entered English through inventions or the use of names of individuals. The word *jeans* was coined from the Italian term *Genoa fustian,* a combination of the name of a city and a type of twilled cloth used for work clothes. Levis take their name from Levi Strauss, a San Francisco merchant during the 1849 California Gold Rush. Strauss sold jeans made of a heavy-duty denim to prospectors who preferred durable, comfortable clothing.

The word *watt,* a unit for measuring electricity, comes from the inventor James Watt. Although Watt is often incorrectly referred to as the inventor of the steam engine, he did devise an efficient steam engine. Watt is also responsible for the word *horsepower,* a unit of measurement for determining the rate of the power of engines.

The Fahrenheit and Celsius temperature scales are named after their founders. Gabriel Fahrenheit was a German physicist who supported his study by making meteorological instruments, while Anders Celsius, a Swede, was an astronomer.

The Indians of Virginia had a word meaning "one who advises or talks," *cawcaw-aasough.* John Smith, who was befriended by Pocahontas, the Indian princess, learned this term in the early 1600s and began to pronounce it as *caucus.* Approximately 150 years later, the word *caucus* became widely used to describe political meetings.

In the Classroom Mini Lesson

Foreign-Word Bingo

*A*fter talking about how our language has borrowed words from other languages, the teacher gives students a homework assignment of using a dictionary or other sources to locate two words that have been adopted into our language from another language. The following day, the students write their words on slips of paper for the bingo pot of words. Each student writes one of the words he or she has found on the chalkboard and shares its meaning with the class. The teacher then divides the class into groups of four. The members of each group write the remaining four words they found in spaces on their blank bingo cards. Order doesn't matter. The group members then select the words they wrote on the chalkboard and write them in the remaining spaces on their bingo cards. Thus, all of the group members have the same words.

After all the cards have been completed (filled in with eight words), the teacher draws a word from the bingo pot and calls it out. If members of a group have the word, they cover it with a small piece of colored paper, regardless of where it is located. As the teacher continues to call out the words from the bingo pot, the first student to cover a line of words wins.

Three groups in one class identified the following words derived from other languages:

ad lib	incognito	llama
gourmet	epaulet	fiancé
andante	pasta	taco
bronco	gorilla	patio
beret	sushi	pâté
census	rouge	quaff
persimmon	luge	suave
gesundheit	teriyaki	vindicate

Example of Foreign Word BINGO Card

B	I	N	G	O
luge	bronco	sushi	cello	taco
gourmet	incognito	fiancé	suave	zebra
persimmon	census	FREE	pâté	andante
patio	daughter	gesundheit	gorilla	piano
teriyaki	pasta	viola	yacht	llama

Some words entered the English language quite by accident. A London clerk misread the label on a consignment of cloth from Scotland, writing down *tweed* instead of *twill.* Perhaps the clerk was unable to read the handwriting on the label or was thinking of the River Tweed in Scotland, home of a large textile industry. And sometimes a product becomes identified with a brand name. The words *Coke, Kleenex, Scotch tape, Xerox,* and *Nike* are only a few examples.

English is an ever-changing language in which new words are constantly being added and some old ones are occasionally dropped.

Aspects of Language

Language, according to Noam Chomsky (Putnam, 1994–1995, p. 331) is "an essential component of the human mind, a crucial element of the human essence." The study of language is called linguistics. A linguist is a person who studies language, being predominantly interested in language as it relates to human behavior.

Linguists study language through a variety of means, including phonology, morphology, syntax, and semantics. According to Hymes (1971), the individual who knows the phonology, morphology, syntax, and semantics of a language, as well as its rules for social language use, has acquired communicative competence.

Phonology

Phonology refers to the sounds of language. A phonological system includes all of the important or most commonly used sounds, the rules for combining sounds to make words, and stress and intonation patterns.

The sounds of a language are called phonemes and are represented by symbols called graphemes. A *phoneme* is the smallest unit of speech that makes a difference in sound to a listener or a speaker of a language. For example, if you say the words *bat, cat, hat,* and *sat* aloud, you will notice that their initial phonemes, or sounds, signal different meanings. If you substitute the phoneme /d/ for /t/, the words also change in meaning; that is, the words become *bad, cad, had,* and *sad.*

English has approximately 42 phonemes. Because of dialectical differences, this number may be slightly greater or smaller, depending on the geographical area of the United States in which one lives. For example, *park* is pronounced with a distinctive /r/ sound in most of the country, while in the Boston area the /r/ sound is much softer, almost inaudible.

Since phonemes are actually sounds, they are represented by symbols called graphemes, as mentioned earlier. The *graphemes* used in English are the 26 letters of the alphabet, which are sometimes used in various combinations to represent the phonemes contained in words. For example, the sound of /f/ is written as *f* in the words *fish, football,* and *fox.* In some words the /f/ phoneme is written *ff* as in *staff* and *puff.* In still other words the /f/ phoneme is written as *gh* as in *laugh* and *tough.* The combination of *ph* represents the /f/ sound in *phenomenon, phone,* and even the word *phoneme* itself.

Morphology

The forms or structures of a language are referred to as *morphology.* A *morpheme* is the smallest unit of meaning in a language, meaning that cannot be broken down into any smaller parts. Words consist of one or more morphemes. The words *crop, galaxy,* and *neighbor* each consist of one morpheme, called a *free* morpheme because it can stand alone. Morphemes that cannot stand alone are called *bound* morphemes because they are always found attached to free morphemes. Bound morphemes are most easily identified when they are attached to the beginning or end of a word as in *happiness, freely,* and *impure.* As defined, then, the bound morphemes for these three words are *-iness, -ly,* and *im-,* respectively.

Syntax

Syntax, or the syntactic system, is the arrangement of words into meaningful phrases, clauses, and sentences; it is the grammatical rule system of a language. A knowledge of syntax allows a speaker or writer to take a basic sentence such as "The girl opens the present" and make *transformations* of it: "The girl opened the present." "Did the girl open the present?" "The girl did not open the present." "Wasn't the present opened by the girl?" This knowledge of syntax not only enables the speaker or writer to generate large numbers of new sentences but also to recognize those that are not grammatically acceptable, such as "The present opened the girl."

Semantics

The study of word meanings is known as *semantics.* Meaning is the most important thing about language (Goodman, 1986). A person's semantic development occurs at a slower pace than does his or her development of phonology, morphology, and syntax. Indeed, learning new word meanings is a lifelong process.

Children's Language Acquisition

The oldest recorded account of a study of language acquisition comes from Herodotus, a contemporary of Sophocles. Herodotus, who lived from about 484 to 425 B.C., wrote of a shepherd ordered by an Egyptian king to raise two children by caring for their needs but not speaking to them. The king wanted to prove that the children would develop the language of the Egyptians all by themselves (Gleason, 1985). The king was obviously a believer in the innatist theory of language development.

In Chomsky's (Putnam 1994–1995, p. 331) view, "a stimulating environment is required to enable natural curiosity, intelligence, and creativity to develop, and to enable . . . biological capacities to unfold." The development of speech in children is summarized in focus box 5.2. This development is the same for children throughout the world regardless of the language. French and Thai children babble between the ages of 3 and 6 months just as children who grow up in English-speaking countries do. Children who are language delayed because of mental retardation nevertheless still acquire language in the same order as children of average or above-average intelligence.

At birth, a baby is capable of producing sounds, none of which are articulate or understandable. The infant is not yet equipped to produce speech. However, within a relatively short time, the baby refines vocalization until the first word is produced.

Focus Box 5.1

Language Study

Grapheme A symbol that represents the smallest unit of sound in a language (a phoneme); in English, a letter or combination of letters of the alphabet
Morpheme The smallest unit of meaning in a language
    bound morpheme One that cannot stand alone, such as the affix *un*
    free morpheme One that can stand alone, such as the word *drink*
Phoneme The smallest unit of sound in a language—for example /p/ as in pig, in English, one of 42 units of sound
Morphology The forms or structures of a language
Phonology The sounds of a language
Semantics The meaning of words in a language
Syntax The arrangement of words in a language

Focus Box 5.2

Development of Vocalization

Crying	Birth
Cooing, crying	1–2 months
Babbling, cooing, crying	3–6 months
First words	8–14 months
First sentences (telegraphic speech)	18–24 months
Simple syntactic structures	3–4 years
Speech sounds correctly pronounced	4–8 years
Most semantic distinctions understood	9–11 years

Newborns are usually exposed to large amounts of stimulation: auditory, visual, and tactile. They quickly learn to distinguish human voices from environmental noises. By 2 weeks of age, infants can recognize their mothers' voices. Between 1 and 2 months of age, infants start producing "human" noises in the form of cooing as they make sounds that have a vowel-like *oo* quality. They use intonation. Soon they can understand some simple words and phrases.

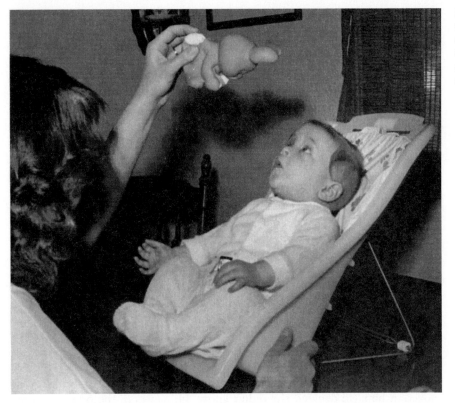

Babbling

About midway through their first year, babies begin to babble. This sign of linguistic capacity is indicated when they repeat consonant-vowel combinations such as *na-na-na* or *ga-ga-ga*. Unlike cooing, babbling tends to occur when the babies are not attempting to communicate with others; in fact, some babies actually babble more when they are alone than when people are present in the room with them (Nakazima, 1975).

During babbling, babies do not produce all possible sounds; they produce only a small subset of sounds (Oller, 1980). Indeed, sounds produced early in the babbling period are seemingly abandoned as experimentation begins with new combinations of sounds. Research by Oller and Eilers (1982) has shown that late babbling contains sounds similar to those used in producing early words, such as *da-da-da*.

Semantic Development

Young children first acquire meaning in a content-bound way, as a part of their experiences in the world that are largely related to a daily routine. Mother may say, "It's story time," but the youngster is already alerted by the picture book in Mother's hand. "It's time for you to take a bath" may not convey the message by itself; the time of day or evening and the presence of a towel, washcloth, and toys for the tub also give clues. Since the sharing of stories and baths are a regular part of the child's daily routine, the young child has mapped out language in terms of observations (McNamara, 1972).

Around their first birthday, babies produce their first word. Typically, *dada, mama, bye-bye,* or *papa* are characteristic first words; they all have two syllables that begin with a consonant and end with a vowel.

Because youngsters' first words convey much meaning for them, most first words are nouns or names: *juice, dada, doggie,* and *horsie.* Verbs such as *go* and *bye-bye,* in this case meaning to go, quickly follow. Content-laden words dominate children's vocabulary at this age, and they possess few function words such as *an, through,* and *around.*

The use of one word to convey a meaningful message is called a *holophrase.* For instance, "cookie" means "I want a cookie."

First words may be overapplied. "Doggie" may refer to a four-legged animal with a tail. The neighbor's pet cat would also qualify. Tony, age 14 months, lived next to a large cattle-feeding operation. *Cow* was one of his first words. When Tony saw a large dog or horse, he immediately identified the animal as a "cow." Later, Tony refined his definition to refer only to female cattle as "cows."

Semantic development in children is interesting, for speaking and listening abilities can vary with the same child. Gina, an 18-month-old, was playing when her uncle pointed to a clock and asked, "What's that?" Getting no response, he pointed to other objects in the room: the television set, the fireplace, and a table. Each time her uncle asked, "What's that?" Gina merely looked at him. He decided she didn't know the names of the objects. To test his theory, he tried a new line of questioning. He asked Gina: "Where's the table? Where's the clock? Where's the fireplace? Where's the television set?" Each time, Gina pointed to the correct object. Gina's listening vocabulary exceeded her speaking vocabulary. In the next few months, she began using the names of the same objects in her speaking vocabulary, as the objects became more important to her conveying of messages.

Vygotsky (1962) argued that young children initially use language only as a tool for social interaction. Later, they use language both in talking aloud during play and in verbalizing their intentions or actions.

Telegraphic Speech

After producing their first word, children rapidly develop their vocabulary, acquiring about 50 words in the next 6 months. At this time, children begin putting words together to express even more meaning than that found in a single word. In this way, children convey their thoughts, but they omit function words such as articles and prepositions. Brown and Fraser (1963) call these two-word utterances *telegraphic* because they resemble telegrams that adults would send.

The limited number of words in telegraphic speech permits children to get their message across to others very economically. For instance, Sarah, age 20 months, says, "More juice" instead of, "I want another glass of juice." The resultant message is essentially the same as the more elaborate sentence.

Focus Box 5.3
Language Development

Babble   The combination of a consonant sound and a vowel sound that is repeated, example, "da-da-da"

Holophrastic speech   A one-word utterance first used by children between the ages of 12 and 18 months to convey meaning; example, "Juice" for "I want more juice"

Telegraphic speech   Two-word utterances first used by children between 18 and 24 months of age to convey meaning; example, "Doggie allgone" for "The dog is gone"

Overgeneralization

Young children acquire the grammatical rules of English, but often they tend to *overgeneralize*. For example, a 3-year-old may refer to "mouses" and "foots" rather than mice and feet. "Comed" may be substituted for came and, similarly, "falled" for fell. Such overgeneralization indicates evidence of the creativity and productivity of the child's morphology because these forms are neither spoken by an adult nor heard by the child.

In early childhood, children tend to invent new words as part of their creativity. Clark (1981, 1982) observed children between the ages of 2 and 6 years and found that they devised or invented new words to fill gaps in their vocabularies. Clark found that if children had forgotten or did not know a noun, the likelihood of word invention increased. "Pourer" was used for *cup* and "plant-man" for *gardener* in such instances. Verbs are often invented in a similar fashion, yet the verbs tend to evolve from nouns the children know. One 4-year-old created such a verb from the noun *cracker* when she referred to putting soda crackers in her soup as "I'm cracking my soup" (Clark, 1981, p. 304).

Children often substitute words that they know for words that are unfamiliar to them. A 3-year-old was taken by her grandmother to see *The Nutcracker*. After intently watching the ballet for a period of time, the child inquired, "Is that the can opener?"

Children tend to regularize the new words they create, just as they overgeneralize words they already know. Thus, a child may refer to a person who rides a bicycle as a "bicycler," employing the frequently used *-er* adjective pattern rather than the rare, irregular *-ist* form to create the word *bicyclist* (Pease & Gleason, 1985).

Semantic development occurs at a slower rate than do phonological development and syntactic development. The grammar, or syntax, of a 5-year-old approaches that of an adult. The child can actually carry on a sensible conversation with an adult. There are only a few grammatical patterns, such as the passive voice and relative clauses, yet to be acquired at this age (Chomsky, 1969).

Focus Box 5.4
Acquisition of Consonant Sounds

Age (years)	Consonant
3½	p, m, b, w, h
4½	d, t, n, g, ng (ring), k, ch, y
5½	f
6½	l, th (voiced—this), sh, zh (azure)
7½	s, z, th (unvoiced—thick), r

From Flood and Salus, 1984, p. 26.

By age 4, a child understands all of the sounds in a language; however, the child may be 8 years old before he or she is able to produce the sounds correctly. For example, Jeff, age 3½, was going shopping with his mother and her friend Penny. While they were waiting for his mother to get ready, Penny noticed that Jeff had a wallet and some money. She asked Jeff what he planned to buy. Jeff said, "A purse." "A purse?" Penny asked. To this question, Jeff insisted, "No, I want a purse." Since the boy seemed to enjoy playing with trucks and cars, Penny was quite confused, so she changed the conversation. At the shopping mall, Penny volunteered to help Jeff with his shopping. She asked Jeff to show her what he wanted to buy, thinking perhaps a carrying case for miniature cars was what he had in mind. Jeff led her to a large display of blue, red, and white things in the department store. Penny smiled and said, "You want a Smurf!" Jeff beamed, "Yes, I want a purse." Jeff obviously could distinguish the difference between the words *Smurf* and *purse* when someone else said them, but the words sounded identical to him when he produced them.

Focus box 5.4 indicates the developmental order for the correct pronunciation of English consonants.

Children in kindergarten through third grade may not be able to articulate all of the consonants of English correctly. A second- or third-grade teacher should not be overly concerned, for example, if some students are unable to produce the /r/ sound, since it is typically the last sound to be acquired.

The Functions of Language

Halliday (1975, p. 7) describes children's language development as a process by which they progressively "learn how to mean." Thus, through interactions with others, children learn how to convey meaning through speech.

According to Halliday (1975, pp. 19–21), seven functions of language are used by children. These are listed below.

1. *Instrumental:* Children use language to satisfy personal needs and to get things done.
2. *Regulatory:* Children use language to control the behavior of others.
3. *Personal:* Children use language to tell about themselves.
4. *Interactional:* Children use language to get along with others
5. *Heuristic:* Children use language to find out about things, to learn things.
6. *Imaginative:* Children use language to pretend, to make believe.
7. *Informative:* Children use language to communicate information to others.

Children develop proficiency with language as their need to use it develops. Therefore, the interactions they have with other people, both adults and children, their own interests, and the meaning that language has for them all impact upon their language development.

Language in the Classroom

Knowing children use language both in and out of school can help teachers develop an effective language program. Kindergartners, for instance, view language as having a functional purpose. "They use language to ask, tell, report, discuss, negotiate, test, direct" (Searfoss, 1988, p. 4). Therefore, language should be used for genuine, relevant purposes in actual social contexts (Goodman, 1986; Searfoss, 1988).

Children need to interact with each other and the teacher in acquiring background knowledge and information. By creating a learning situation in which children can closely observe and examine an object, for instance, the teacher allows them to compare it to things with which they are already familiar.

Discussions should not be limited to concrete objects. Children's literature provides a variety of information. By reading to children, the teacher is providing them with an opportunity to envision a story's actions and characters in their minds.

Quality children's literature should be shared with children of all ages, from birth through elementary school. Children in kindergarten through third grade enjoy finger plays such as the "Five Little Squirrels" and "Let's Go on a Bear Hunt." They learn the parts of the body from actively participating in songs such as the "Hokey Pokey." Nursery rhymes and short poems encourage them to play with language.

Children at this level can expand their oral language skills with wordless books as they become adept at telling the story in their own words and elaborating on the illustrations they particularly enjoy. As mentioned earlier, the predictability of patterned books makes them popular with beginning readers because they "know" to a great extent what will happen on the next page.

When the teacher encourages children to retell a story that they have recently heard, they not only expand their oral language but gain a sense of

*C*hildren have the ability to use language appropriately in different settings. Klein (1977) notes four different kinds of circumstances in which major language usage differences are found. *Ceremonial settings* require formal language that may be somewhat artificial. Ceremonial settings include weddings, courtrooms, religious ceremonies, formal debates, and commencement exercises, as well as formal drama. In ceremonial settings, the events tend to convey more meaning than the words themselves. For example, the events of a wedding, including the arrival of the groom and his groomsmen, the bridesmaids, the flower girl and ring bearer, and the bride accompanied by her father are all traditional, as are the minister's words "I now pronounce you husband and wife." To a great extent, ceremonial settings are highly predictable situations.

Formal settings include those in which speeches are delivered before audiences. Such presentation usually necessitate the use of formal language. The tone may be light initially, but it soon becomes serious as the speaker attempts to make certain specific points, doing so in a preconceived sequence. Formal settings tend to produce monologues.

Informal settings differ from formal settings in that there may be more than one speaker and that the message is usually not prepared beforehand. The informal setting, since it is not preplanned, requires the participants to be active listeners because topics and purposes may change rapidly during the course of the conversation. Body language and intonation play important roles, as do the speakers' use of persuasive language, ability to describe and explain, and storytelling skills.

Intimate settings are those in which two or three people who know each other very well are engaged in a conversation. They may know each other well enough to finish each other's sentences. Gestures and intonation also play important roles, as do laughter, sighs, and groans, all of which may be as expressive as words or sentences.

Klein, M. (1977). *Talk in the language arts classroom.* Urbana, IL: National Council of Teachers of English.

story structure. Once they have attained a sense of story structure, they can concentrate on the actions within the story, making interpretations and predictions. The retelling of a story requires that thought be blended with language, resulting in the enhancement of both (Hayes, 1989). Literature response journals are also beneficial (Danielson, 1992).

The retelling of stories is valuable in that the teacher can use it for both the instruction and the assessment of oral language complexity and comprehension (Morrow, 1988). A child's retelling may provide the teacher with a more accurate measure of the child's understanding of a story than answers to questions the teacher might ask the child. However, the teacher must be cautious when evaluating students who have had little practice in retelling stories.

FOCUS BOX 5.6

Language Development of Emergent Literacy Child

Name:

Age:

Teacher:

Grade: Date:

	Always	Sometimes	Never
Has no speech defects (i.e. stuttering, articulation disorders)			
Pronounces consonant sounds correctly			
Pronounces consonant blends correctly			
Pronounces consonant digraphs correctly			
Pronounces short vowels correctly			
Pronounces long vowels correctly			
Pronounces diphthongs correctly			
Can successfully use one-word sentences			
Can successfully use two-word sentences			
Can successfully use three or more word sentences			
Can identify words that rhyme			
Can identify familiar environmental sounds			
When engaged in a conversation with adults, can understand their language and respond			
When engaged in a conversation with another child, can understand the language and respond			
Can follow oral directions			
Has a good vocabulary			
Uses a variety of sentence patterns (syntactical/ grammatical structures)			
Can be understood by adults			
Can be understood by other children			
Enjoys talking with adults			
Enjoys talking with other children			
Teacher comments:			

The teacher should tell such children beforehand that they will be asked to retell the story after it is read to them.

Language study can also take the form of word study as students discover how words came into the English language as a result of migration, trade, or wars. Students can research the names of states and their capitals or various inventions as part of a social studies lesson. Following this, the students might investigate the origins of their own last names. They can place pins in a map of the world to show where their names originated.

Children with Special Needs

The sound of human speech distinctively differs from other sounds. The human voice, even though it may not be that of a parent, is more effective in quieting a crying 2-week-old baby than other sounds, such as bells, whistles, or rattles (Wolff, 1969). Indeed, videotape analyses of day-old infants indicate that bodily movements change in direction and in rhythm to the sound of the human voice significantly more than to the sound of disconnected vowels or to tapping sounds (Condon & Sander, 1974). These early responses to speech lead to the acquisition of language in the young child.

Many children acquiring a first language progress similarly in the development of phonology, morphology, syntax, and semantics, as discussed earlier in this chapter. However, some children have problems with language acquisition. These problems may be of a physical nature, such as sensory deficits in hearing or sight, or they may be related to cognitive problems.

Dialects

A linguistic variation of the English language that is regional and differs distinctively from standard English is called a *dialect*. Three major dialects exist within the United States: Northern, Midland, and Southern. The Midland region is generally broken down into North Midland and South Midland, depending on whether major influence comes from the Northern or Southern dialect.

Each major dialect area, in turn, is divided into regional areas. For example, eastern New England has speech patterns quite different from those of the remainder of the Northern region. The Southern dialect of East Texas differs from that of Alabama and South Carolina. This holds true for the other major dialects as well.

In addition to regional dialects, there are social dialects, those speech variations correlated with social class, age, occupation, religion, and recreational preferences. Each individual's speech is a composite of regional and social dialect characteristics (Myers, 1984).

There are 26 dialects in the United States; surprisingly enough, however, they are neither as numerous nor as distinctive as dialects in other countries. For example, Great Britain, a country about the size of the state of Oregon, has a greater number of dialects than does the entire United States. In addition, the dialects of Great Britain differ more than do the American dialects.

The strongest U.S. dialects are found largely in those areas that were settled first, that is, the original 13 colonies. The advent of radio and television and increasing geographic mobility have resulted in less variation among American dialects. Broadcasting networks have become nonregional in trying to neutralize dialects. News anchor people are often the first to introduce words to the country, thereby eliminating the possibility of any dialectical differences.

Dialects differ in three possible ways: in phonology, in semantics, and in syntax. In the Midwest, the /r/ sound is pronounced clearly, as in *horse* or *earth,* and it may even intrude, as in "warsh" (wash). In eastern New England, on the other hand, the /r/ sound is often lost as in "pak" (park) or "father" (farther). In the southern states of Georgia and South Carolina, *log* rhymes with *fog* but not with *hog* or *dog,* which sound more like "hawg" and "dawg." Dropping the ends of words is a common occurrence in the Southern dialect but can also be found in the South Midland dialect. "Goin' " for *going* and "runnin' " for *running* are commonplace.

Semantic differences affect dialects too. Is it a skillet, a frying pan, or a spider? Do you get water from a tap or a faucet? Do you drink water from a water fountain, a spigot, a drinking fountain, or a bubbler? Do you eat green beans, snap beans, or string beans?

Syntactic differences among dialects are less common. In the South Midland dialect some plurals are omitted: "2 year" rather than "2 years." In the North Midland dialect, *by* is sometimes used instead of *to:* "I'm going *by* the bank and the cleaner's." Double negatives are found in the speech of some south Midland and Southern natives but also in the speech of some working-class people in other dialect regions.

A teacher should not identify any one regional dialect as superior to the others. In teaching language, a teacher should respect a child's dialect but also convey to all students the need to develop standard English for the social and working worlds.

The acquisition of standard English can be accomplished without the loss of a dialect. Both are beneficial, depending on the setting in which language is used. To avoid teaching standard English is to shackle students by limiting their future employment possibilities. For example, the child who says, "I ain't got no pin" for "I don't have a pen" will not be welcomed as an accountant, secretary, or medical doctor, if such usage continues after the child becomes an adult. The role of the teacher is to help to better the lives of students and requires that the teacher be accountable for improving language skills when necessary.

Multicultural Considerations About Language

The pluralistic nature of our society yields a large number of cultural and language variations. The classroom teacher needs to take such variations into consideration. Some children from minority groups, just as some children from the majority white culture, have language deficits. However, not all minority children have a language deficit and should not be classified as such. As Flores,

Focus Box 5.7

Spoken Languages Present in One Urban School District

*B*elow is a list of 64 first languages other than English of students in Elgin School District Unit 46, a large suburban school district of 28,000 students located just outside of Chicago. While there are large numbers of Spanish and Laotian speaking students, there are many languages, such as Gaelic and Sioux, in which there are five students or less represented.

Afrikaans (Taal)	Haitian Creole	Portuguese
Albanian	Hebrew	Punjabi
Amharic	Hindi	Romanian
Arabic	Hindustani	Russian
Armenian	Hmong	Serbian/Croatian
Assyrian	Hungarian	Sindhi
Bengali	Iroquoian	Sioux
Bisayan	Italian	Slovak
Bulgarian	Jamaican	Slovenian
Burmese	Japanese	Spanish
Chinese—Cantonese	Kannada	Swedish
Chinese—Mandarin	Khmer/Cambodian	Taiwanese
Czech	Korean	Tamil
Danish	Lao	Telugu
Dutch	Latvian	Thai
Farsi (Iranian)	Lithuanian	Tibetan
Finnish	Malayalam	Turkish
French	Marathi	Ukrainian
Gaelic	Norwegian	Urdu
German	Pilipino (Tagalog)	Vietnamese
Greek	Polish	Yugoslavian
Gujarati		

Cousin, and Díaz (1991, p. 370) note: "One of the most pervasive and pernicious myths about 'at-risk' students is that they have a language deficit. This myth is reserved not for just bilingual and non-English-speaking students. It is also commonly held about African Americans and other minorities."

The following paragraphs describe differences between Black, Spanish, Asian, and Native American influences on English.

Black English

Black English possesses many of the same characteristics as the Southern dialect; however, Black English is not tolerated as much as most geographical dialects are. African-American speakers are sometimes viewed as being socially and culturally inferior both by whites and by many educated African Americans.

Black English is highly predictable. Phonological differences include the deletion of final /t/ and /l/ sounds, as in *past* becoming "pass" and *pole* becoming "po." The /r/ sound is frequently omitted, as when *Paris* becomes "pass." As in the Southern dialect, the final consonant is often dropped as in "goin' " for *going.* The glide is deleted with long vowels and diphthongs as in "rod" for *ride* and "spall" for *spoil.* The glide is added with short vowels such as "hiyat" for *hit.* Other pronunciation differences include "aks" for *ask* and "wif" for *with.*

Syntactic differences of Black English include nonstandard verb forms *Was* for *were* and *is* for *are* are common. The variant *be* becomes a finite verb: "She *be* sick" or "He *be* mad at you." Many sentences are expressions of the future: "I'm *gonna* get you a present" or "He's goin' to do it."

Semantic differences include the words *cool* for *good* and *heavy* for *powerful.* Many African-American families do not assign nicknames to their children. For example, Edward should not be called Ed but only Edward, the name given to him at birth.

Spanish-Influenced English

With more than one-fifth of polled teachers stating that they teach in two languages, both English and Spanish (Lapointe, 1986), it is clear that many children come to school with Spanish as their native language. Children who speak Spanish as their first language have difficulty adjusting to the nine English consonants that do not exist in Spanish: *v, j, z, sh, ng, zh* as in *measure, th* voiced as in *then, th* unvoiced as in *with,* and *r* as in *rabbit.* The pronunciation of the /s/ sound in consonant clusters becomes a separate syllable as in "es-hoe" for *shoe.* There is also a tendency to substitute long vowels for short vowels and for vowel digraphs such as *caught* to be pronounced as "coat." Spanish has four consonants that do not exist in English: *r (rancho), x (examen), ñ (mañana),*

Focus Box 5.8

Consonant Phonemes Shared in English and Spanish

pat	tall	king	basket
p	**t**	**k**	**b**
puerto	todo	kilo	bebida
dish	give	family	sing
d	**g**	**f**	**s**
dar	gusto	falta	seda
yes	moon	nice	church
y	**m**	**n**	**ch**
yo	madre	nota	mucho
lady	wing		
l	**w**		
lado	Oawaca		

From Dr. Muriel Saville-Troike, *A Handbook of Bilingual Education.* Copyright © 1971. Reprinted by permission.

and *r (perro)*. Sometimes these consonants are substituted when a Spanish-speaking child becomes confused in speaking English. On the other hand, the English and Spanish languages also share some of the same consonant sounds, as indicated in focus box 5.8.

Several syntactic differences between Spanish and English can be described. The omission of verb endings among those whose first language is Spanish is very common, as in "He *run* to the store" and "She *play* a joke." Likewise, because subject pronouns do not occur in Spanish, they are sometimes eliminated in English: "She is the new girl" becomes "Is the new girl." An article in Spanish indicates both the gender and number (singular or plural) of the noun that follows it. In Spanish, inanimate objects are either masculine or feminine. In English, such objects are neuter, having no gender whatsoever.

The possessive in Spanish necessitates the use of *de (of* in English) immediately preceding the possessor, such as "el libro de Juan," meaning "Juan's book." The /s/ sound at the end of a word denotes a plural, never a possessive as it sometimes does in English.

Spanish-speaking students frequently omit contractions or use them incorrectly in English. Particularly difficult for the Spanish-speaking child to acquire are those contractions that involve a change in the vowel sound of a word. For example, if the Spanish-speaking child knows the words *does* and *not,* then *doesn't* is more easily acquired than knowing *will* and *not* and producing *won't* as the contraction.

Negation in Spanish requires that a negative be used before the verb, resulting in a double-negative construction. Thus, double negatives are commonly used by Spanish-speaking children as they acquire English: "He no have nothing." While such a construction is required in Spanish, it is not acceptable in English. Prepositions that are correctly used in the Spanish language are often—upon translation—incorrectly used according to standard English rules, such as when "*in* or *at* the table" is substituted for "*on* the table."

Semantic differences pertain to the many false cognates that exist within Spanish and English. When a word exists in two different languages and has the same meaning, it is a true cognate. For example, the word *mosquito* is a true cognate because it is a word in both English and Spanish and has the same meaning in both languages. The word for *special* in Spanish differs slightly in its spelling (*especial*) from its English counterpart, but it has the same meaning and is considered a true cognate. Because the Spanish word *pan* and the English word *pan* mean something very different, *pan* is a false cognate. Even though the Spanish word *fabrica* appears to be similar to the English word *fabric*, the two words are not true cognates because *fabrica* means factory in Spanish, and *fabric* in English refers to material.

One very costly example pertaining to a false cognate in the English and Spanish languages was an American firm's introduction of an economical car into Spanish-speaking countries several years ago. The company had sold several hundred thousand of the cars in the United States and expected the model to sell well in Mexico and Central American countries. Potential foreign buyers would look the car over and take it for a test drive, but few actually purchased the car. This lack of sales was later related to the car's name, Nova, which in Spanish means "no go."

In addition to the phonological, syntactic, and semantic differences between Spanish and English, nonverbal differences exist. In order to show respect, young children of Spanish heritage are taught to avoid looking directly into the eyes of the teacher. However, around the time of puberty, boys are encouraged to be more independent of women, and therefore they may begin to challenge the authority of female teachers or classroom aides.

Asian-Influenced English

Since the end of the Vietnam War, there has been a large influx of Southeast Asian immigrants into the United States. Initially, most of the families came from the upper-social-class structure. Many of them, especially the fathers, had been educated in English-speaking schools. Later, families from the middle and lower classes immigrated to the United States. While children of upper-class families may have been taught some English, most of the children from the middle- and lower-class Southeast Asian families had little or no familiarity with the English language.

Because of large investments by Japanese companies in American corporations and through the influence of Japanese-owned factories and businesses in the United States, children of many Japanese corporate executives have been attending public and private American schools. As noted earlier in this chapter,

English has borrowed few words from Asian languages. Thus, when beginning to learn English as a second language, Southeast Asian students are faced with a difficult task.

The languages of the Orient are tonal in quality. For example, by saying a single sound in Thai, the speaker can produce up to eight different words merely by changing intonation or pitch of voice. This tonal quality makes Asian languages difficult for English-speaking people to acquire. Nevertheless, a study by Chang and Watson (1988) reports that despite the major differences in phonemes in the Chinese and English languages, children were found to use the same cognitive activities (predicting, confirming, and integrating information) in reading Chinese materials as they use in reading English materials.

The syntax of Asian languages differs from that of English. Thai speakers talk of watching a "white and black TV" or ask for the "pepper and salt," as opposed to English speakers "black and white TV" and "salt and pepper." In giving directions, the Thai speaker says "eastnorth," not "northeast" as the English speaker does.

Asian children who attempt to acquire English as a second language are at a disadvantage because few true cognates exist in Asian languages and English. The Thai word *fit,* unlike its English counterpart, means "is the wrong size." The word *seminar* is also a false cognate for the Laotian people. In English, a seminar is a meeting of a small group of people to discuss a topic or issue; however in Laotian, a seminar is a gathering of a small group of people who have been brainwashed by the Communists. *Bun* means rice noodle in Vietnamese, unlike the bread product it represents in English.

Nonverbal communication plays a major role in the teaching of Asian children. Most early childhood teachers in the United States have their students form a circle by "holding the hands of your neighbors"; however, in most Asian cultures boys are not allowed to hold the hands of girls. In some Asian cultures, children are taught not to cross their legs because this results in their toes pointing toward the teacher. Such a position is thought to be disrespectful because the feet are considered the most unholy part of the body. Parallel to this, some Asians believe that it is a discourtesy for the teacher to touch or pat a child's head because the head is considered the most holy part of the body.

Native American Languages

There are over 40 Native American languages that are prevalent in the United States. The Cherokee language, for example, was used for sending coded messages by the Army during World War II. Native American languages differ in syntax and semantics from tribe to tribe. The sounds, or phonology, of the languages also differ.

Native American children are taught to be quiet and not to speak unnecessarily. They hold great respect for adults and will not look the teacher in the eye out of this respect. Native American children are taught to work cooperatively and may automatically help a classmate with an activity even though the activity was designed to be done individually.

In the Classroom Mini Lesson

Publishers of Bilingual Materials

*T*eachers may call or write the following publishers to obtain a catalog or brochure of the products they have to offer:

Arroyo Books
5505 N. Figueroa St.
Los Angeles, CA 90042
(213) 227–1794

Children's Press
544 N. Cumberland Avenue
Chicago, IL 60656
(800) 621–1115

Donars Spanish Books
P.O. Box 24
Loveland, CO 80539
(303) 663–2124

Hispanic Book Distributors
1665 W. Grant Road
Tucson, AZ 85745
(602) 882–9484

Ianoconi Book Imports
2220 Mariposa
San Francisco, CA 92105

Jamestown Publishers
P.O. Box 9168
Providence, RI 02940
(800) 872–7323

Los Andes Publishing Company
8303 E. Alondra Blvd.
Paramount, CA 90723

Mi Globo Publishing
Spanish Weekly Reader
15345 Midland Road
Poway, CA 92064

Modern Curriculum Press
13900 Prospect Road
Cleveland, OH 44136
(800) 321–3106

Rigby Publishing
P.O. Box 797
Crystal Lake, IL 60013
(800) 392–2179

Scholastic, Inc.
730 Broadway
New York, NY 10003
(800) 392–2179

Sundance Publishers
P.O. Box 1326
Littleton, MA 01460
(800) 727–0664

Zaner Bloser
2200 West Fifth Avenue
P.O. Box 16764
Columbus, OH 43216
(614) 487–2825

Zoo Books
3590 Kettner Blvd.
San Diego, CA 92101
(619) 299–6034

One mistake that some teachers make is to assume that the Native American tribes work in unison together. There are still bitter differences between some tribes. For instance, a Navaho child may greatly resent being seated by a Hopi child, and vice versa. In addition, the folktales of one tribe may be offensive to another tribe.

Evaluating Language Development

"Children's language processes are energized and sustained by meaningful (purposeful) use of language in varied situations. Sensible activities, and the people and things entailed in those activities, provide support for children's language learning" (Dyson, 1991, pp. 26–27).

While extensive evaluation of children's language in varied situations is not possible in the classroom, teachers can use informal means to assess language development. For example, at the beginning of the school year, a kindergarten teacher takes each student aside for a short time while the other children are busy engaging in other planned activities. The teacher shows each child a picture of a young boy playing with a collie dog and a rubber ball and asks the child to tell the story behind the picture. Some children will identify the objects in the picture. Others will give short, descriptive phrases, and still others will greatly elaborate on the scene, with long, interesting stories evolving. The teacher then notes each child's progress and develops language activities according to needs. By taping and dating the responses, the teacher can later compare the student's progress.

Another opportunity for informal assessment involves the teacher's observing a child as he or she gives directions to another student and then noting whether the directions were clear and concise. The teacher may note whether the listening student was able to work through the directions provided by the first child.

By using natural, informal assessment that is closely related to the context in which it takes place, the teacher can judge students' progress by means of a previously established set of criteria. The criteria can be shared with students so that they can judge their own progress as well (Pinnell, 1991).

Teachers can note language problems during informal and formal conversations in the classroom. Articulation, lisping, and stuttering problems are often readily noticeable. Detecting dialectical differences and incorrect usage may require more time. Barr (1990) suggests that teachers frequently keep records about a young bilingual student's talk, noting significant gains in the child's acquisition of English.

Devising a checklist for usage errors can be effective but limited to those categories included. The most obvious errors should be eliminated first. For example, if the children constantly use "ain't" and double negatives such as "He don't do nothing," it is pointless to try to make them distinguish between "shall" and "may." Begin where the children are and go from there.

Conferences between the teacher and child are a very effective way of discovering language abilities. This is particularly true if the teacher has empathy for the child and asks questions in a sensitive, supportive manner. As Barr (1990, p. 246) writes, "Sympathetic questioning and listening can enable children to share their sense of where they are doing well and where they are having problems."

S u m m a r y

The English language is the most widely spoken language in the world, and it is always changing. As it has done for centuries, English continues to borrow words from other languages. In addition, new words are created and become a part of the language and the culture.

The sounds and meanings of a language are studied in phonology and morphology. Children discover the rules governing the arrangement of words in a language, or its syntax, before they master word meanings, or semantics. Children who learn English as a second language encounter new sounds of consonants and vowels, new word meanings, and unfamiliar syntactical patterns, thereby making it a difficult task.

By incorporating language activities throughout the curriculum, teachers can guide their students' language development and expansion to increase their communicative competence.

Questions

1. How are semantics, syntax, and phonology related?
2. What is unique about your dialect?
3. Why does the English language change?
4. How does culture influence language?
5. What languages have had the most influence on English? Why?
6. How has English changed in recent years?
7. How would you encourage children to expand their language use in your classroom?

Activities

1. Make a list of five slang terms and their meanings.
2. Make a list of five terms that are unique to a particular occupation.
3. Develop an activity based on your language and cultural heritage to share with your students. (For example, you might use folktales that can be acted out.)
4. Develop methods for teaching English to non-English-speaking students.
5. Make your own list of poems and folktales from different cultures.
6. Plan a United Nation's Day in which your students are to share their cultural heritage through dress, food, song, and games.

For Further Reading

Mates, B. F., & Strommen, B. F. (1996). Why Ernie can't read: *Sesame Street* and literacy. *The Reading Teacher, 49* (4), 300–307.

McCrum, R., Cran, W., & MacNeil, R. (1986). *The story of English.* New York: Viking.

Phelan, P. (Ed.). (1989). *Talking to learn: Classroom practices in teaching English.* Urbana, IL: National Council of Teachers of English.

Putnam, L. R. (1994–1995). An interview with Noam Chomsky. *The Reading Teacher 48* (4), 328–333.

Roderick, J. (Ed.) (1991). *Context-responsive approaches to assessing children's language.* Urbana, IL: National Council of Teachers of English.

References

Barr, M. (1990). The Primary Language Record: Reflection of issues in evaluation. *Language Arts,* 67(3), 244–253.

Britton, J. (1983). Writing and the story world. In B. Kroll & G. Wells (Eds.), *Explorations in the development of writing.* New York: Wiley.

Brown, R., & Fraser, C. (1963). The acquisition of syntax. In C. N. Cofer & B. Musgrave (Eds.), *Verbal behavior and learning: Problems and processes.* New York: McGraw-Hill.

Chang, Y. L., & Watson, D. J. (1988). Adaptation of prediction strategies and materials in a Chinese/English bilingual classroom. *The Reading Teacher, 42* (1), 36–44.

Chomsky, C. S. (1969). *The acquisition of syntax in children from 5 to 10.* Cambridge, MA: MIT Press.

Clark, E. V. (1981). Lexical innovations: How children learn to create new words. In W. Deutsch (Ed.), *The child's construction of language.* London: Academic Press.

Clark, E. V. (1982). The young word maker: A case of innovations in the child's lexicon. In E. Wanner & L. R. Gleitman (Eds.) *Language acquisition: The state of the art.* New York: Cambridge University Press.

Condon, W. S., & Sander, L. W. (1974). Neonate movement is synchronized with adult speech: Interactional participation and language acquisition. *Science, 183,* 99–101.

Danielson, K. E. (1992). Learning about early writing from response to literature. *Language Arts, 69* (4), 274–280.

Dyson, A. H. (1991). Faces in the crowd: Developing profiles of language users. In J. A. Roderick (Ed.), *Context-responsive approaches to assessing children's language* (pp. 20–31). Urbana, IL: National Council of Teachers of English.

Flood, J., & Salus, P. H. (1984). *Language and the language arts.* Englewood Cliffs, NJ: Prentice-Hall.

Flores, B., Cousin, P. T., & Díaz, E. (1991). Transforming deficit myths about learning, language, and culture. *Language Arts, 68* (5), 369–379.

Gleason, J. B. (1985). Studying language development. In J. B. Gleason (Ed.), *The development of language.* Columbus, OH: Merrill.

Goodman, K. (1986). *What's whole in whole language?* Portsmouth, NH: Heinemann.

Halliday, M. A. K. (1975). *Learning how to mean: Exploration in the development of language.* London: Edward Arnold.

Hayes, D. (1989). Children as storytellers. *Reading Horizons, 29* (2), 139–146.

Hymes, D. (1971). Competence and performance in linguistic theory. In R. Huxley & E. Ingram (Eds.), *Language acquisition: Models and methods.* London: Academic Press.

Lapointe, A. (1986). The state of instruction in reading and writing in U.S. elementary schools. *Phi Delta Kappan, 68* (2), 135–138.

McCrum, R., Cran, W., & MacNeil, R. (1986). *The story of English.* New York: Viking.

McNamara, J. (1972). Cognitive basis of language learning in infants. *Psychological Review, 79* (1), 1–13.

Morrow, L. M. (1988). Retelling stories as a diagnostic tool. In S. M. Glazer, L. W. Searfoss, & L. M. Gentile (Eds.), *Reexamining reading diagnosis: New trends and procedures.* Newark, DE: International Reading Association.

Myers, D. L. (1984). *Understanding language.* Upper Montclair, NJ: Boynton/Cook.

Nakazima, S A. (1975). Phonemicization and symbolization in language development. In E. H. Lenneberg & E. Lenneberg (Eds.), *Foundations of language: Vol. 1. A multidisciplinary approach.* New York: Academic Press.

Oller, D. K. (1980). The emergence of the sounds of speech in infancy. In G. H. Yeni-Komshian, J. F. Kavanaugh, & C. A. Ferguson, (Eds.), *Child phonology: Vol. 1. Production.* New York: Academic Press.

Oller, D. K., & Eilers, R. E. (1982). Similarity of babbling in Spanish- and English-learning babies. *Journal of Child Language, 9* (3), 565–577.

Pease, D., & Gleason, J. B. (1985). Gaining meaning: Semantic development. In J. B. Gleason (Ed.), *The development of language.* Columbus, OH: Merrill.

Pinnell, G. S. (1991). Interactive assessment: Teachers and children as learners. In J. A. Roderick (Ed.), *Context-responsive approaches to assessing children's language* (pp. 79–96). Urbana, IL: National Council of Teachers of English.

Putnam, L. R. (1994–1995). An interview with Noam Chomsky. *The Reading Teacher, 48* (4), 328–333.

Saville, M. R., & Troike, R. C. (1971). *A handbook of bilingual education.* Washington, D.C.: Teachers of English to Speakers of Other Languages.

Searfoss, L. W. (1988). Winds of change in reading instruction. *Reading Instruction Journal, 31* (1), 2-6.

Vygotsky, L. W. (1962). *Thought and language.* Cambridge, MA: MIT Press.

Wolff, P. H. (1969). The natural history of crying and other vocalizations in early infancy. In Brian M. Foss (Ed.), *Determinants of infant behaviour IV. Proceedings of the fourth Tavistock Study Group on Mother-Infant Interaction.* Washington, D.C.: Tavistock Study Group.

*S*peaking: *The Oral Expression of Thoughts*

© James L. Shaffer

Language learners must invent and try out the rules of language for themselves through social interaction as they move toward control of language for meaning.

—Glenellen Pace

"When Teachers Use Literature for Literary Instruction: Ways That Constrain, Ways That Free."

V icki is crouched on the classroom floor, pretending to be a very quiet young cricket. Some of her classmates are pretending to be other insects: Jeremy is a big cricket; Cory, a locust; Paul, a praying mantis; Jennifer a worm; Susan, a spittle bug; Matthew, a cicada; Darrin, a bumblebee; Sherry, a dragonfly; Nate, a luna moth. The other students in the class are pretending to be mosquitoes. These 5- and 6-year-olds are reenacting a story their teacher just read to them, Eric Carle's (1990) *The Very Quiet Cricket.* The very quiet cricket encounters the different insects, each of which make a noise except for the beautiful luna moth. The very quiet cricket learns to appreciate silence as well as to "chirp" to another cricket. At the end of the informal drama, smiles of delight wreathe the children's faces. They have not only been involved in a drama but have discovered new knowledge about insects in a most enjoyable way.

Oral language allows for the sharing of thoughts and ideas with others. Young children who are proficient in using oral language tend to become good readers and possess a tendency to become good writers as well (Loban, 1976; Tiedt et al., 1983).

Providing children with opportunities and situations in which they are encouraged and even required to express themselves results in the expansion of their oral language. Such a fostering of conceptual development creates a language need; thus, as the complexity of children's thoughts and problem-solving abilities increases, so too does the need for language to clarify, categorize, conjecture, evaluate, interpret, synthesize, and summarize. These are all strategies for learning. Thus, thinking and language are interwoven and should be nurtured as such in teaching.

Speaking and the Other Language Arts

Children need to be free to discuss their knowledge, thoughts, and feelings with each other, for they have much to share. According to Berlin (1990, p. 159), "Language, we are now beginning to see, does not simply record our experience, it actually shapes it, structuring it in a way that determines what we see and do not see, what we know, who we are and who we are not." Cindy Shultz Rosenbloom (1991, p. 54), a kindergarten teacher in Ohio, writes: "Not only does language shape experience, but in my classroom language and literature guide the development of the curriculum."

Children enter kindergarten with knowledge gained from their own first-hand experiences and from vicarious experiences as they are read to by others. As speakers, kindergartners have engaged in both numerous and varied conversations with peers, siblings, parents, and other adults. The school curriculum, however, emphasizes the printed rather than the spoken word despite the fact that 90 percent of our language use is oral in nature (Stoodt, 1989). At this time, children are expected to be competent oral language users because they have been talking fluently for years prior to entering school. Although their speaking vocabularies are large and their formed grammatical structures are quite sophisticated, attention needs to be given to the development of the expressive, oral language skills from kindergarten through the elementary grades and beyond. Research indicates that children benefit from engagements in both informal and formal talk throughout the school day (Heath, 1983).

Speaking is important for the development of the other language arts: thinking, reading, writing, and listening. Thinking is actually enhanced by one's need to organize, conceptualize, clarify, and in some instances, simplify thoughts, feelings, and ideas as they are shared orally. Speaking facilitates reading, especially in the area of vocabulary acquisition, as children add new words to their speaking repertoires and simultaneously to their reading vocabularies. Storytelling, a form of language sharing in which children can participate and which they enjoy, provides young children with a basic grasp of the important elements of a story: plot, characters, setting (both time and place), and theme. These elements are not only present in the simple texts children complete as "beginning readers" but also in many of the materials they will encounter as "mature readers."

Oral language often supports writing, especially as young children are exposed to writing's initial stages. When undertaking a writing task, children often talk to themselves; such talk serving various functions. Some children engage in self-dialogue as they write, later using punctuation (exclamation points and underlining, for example) as graphic representations of intonation (Graves, 1983). Other children talk to themselves as they generate their writing ideas in a type of oral evaluation of the soundness of their own creative efforts. Thus, self-dialogue is used as a means of analysis of a written product (Dyson, 1981). Even as adults, people tend to read a written product aloud when the writing task is an important one.

Students at all grade levels need to engage in discussions about their individual pieces of writing. Having opportunities to talk with peers about a topic or idea prior to attempting to write a first draft enables students to refine their thoughts about the writing piece. Thus, when discussion precedes the writing event, the quality of the written product improves. This is true because the writer has probably analyzed, elaborated, questioned, and to some extent justified thoughts and ideas prior to putting them down on paper.

After students have completed a writing assignment, the teacher should set aside time for a sharing of efforts. At this point, the discussions should focus primarily on the positive aspects of each of the finished pieces; this allows all the students to benefit from one another's successes.

Finally, speaking is important to the development of listening because good speakers actually tend to be good listeners; they are genuinely interested in what others say. In addition, good speakers not only have content worthy of sharing with others but are also effective in utilizing the special oral language skills of fluency, intonation, and style. They "invite" others to listen to them by projecting an enticing message. Clearly, these skills are demonstrated by network news anchor people. Not only do they all tend to sound as though they share the same midwestern background, but all articulate clearly, delivering news stories at a steady but brisk pace free of hesitations or pauses.

Because oral language skills contribute to thinking, reading, writing, and listening, teachers need to guide children's refinement of oral material presented. This can be done through teacher modeling and the oral sharing of quality literature. It is also beneficial for teachers to ask students meaningful questions that focus on content. Clearly, children need to engage in oral language activities in order to gather and share information as well as to react to new experiences. Students need ample opportunities to engage in meaningful dialogue as part of the learning process, something that they will be required to do on a daily basis as adult members of the nation's work force.

Language Settings

Speaking is typically classified according to four types of settings: formal, informal, ceremonial, and intimate (Klein, 1977). In a formal setting, oral presentations, which include political speeches, homilies, and lectures, must be prepared in advance and presented in a serious tone.

An informal setting does not require such prior preparation of speeches or messages. Rather, the informal atmosphere is more casual and relaxed as individuals engage in conversation. Because conversations often shift from topic to topic, speakers must be alert to all the interactions within a conversation. The demands of keeping up with the discussion while preparing additional comments can make speaking in informal settings more rigorous than speaking in formal ones.

Ceremonial settings involve events of cultural importance, such as those of a legal or religious nature. Weddings, baptisms, graduations, and court trials are all examples of ceremonial settings.

In an intimate setting, people know each other very well. Speaking in this type of setting can involve two close friends, three classmates, or five teammates, all of whom are familiar with the language and behavior of the other speakers. Indeed, the way an individual pronounces a word or sighs conveys a certain meaning within an intimate setting; yet the same pronunciation or the same sigh would probably not be interpretable in any other setting. Since an intimate setting tends to be the most private of the four types, such an atmosphere is not commonplace in the elementary school classroom, although it is perhaps found within one-to-one conferences between teacher and student or in small class groups that have been established after the students have become familiar with one another.

Since students are most accustomed to and comfortable with informal language settings, it is logical to begin oral language instruction with conversations and discussions.

Conversational Skills

A good conversationalist must have oral language skills and an ability to think clearly and quickly. Interpersonal skills are also important inasmuch as conversation consists largely of personal reflections and therefore requires the sensitivity of all the participants. The participants in a conversation are collaborators; in addition to contributing thoughts, they must consider the ideas and feelings of others simultaneously. In effect, a good conversationalist is a well-rounded juggler who listens to and perceives another's input, composes an accompanying oral presentation, and adjusts to the emotional climate of the conversation itself.

The conversation process requires the following of each participant:

1. Consider what has been said and anticipate what may be exchanged later in the conversation.
2. Put thoughts and ideas together in a clear and concise manner, carefully selecting words and sentence structure before directly contributing to the conversation.
3. Detect relationships between discussed items and relate these to your own previously gained knowledge.
4. Make others in the conversation feel comfortable enough to ask questions or make comments.
5. Contribute to but do not dominate the conversation.
6. Highlight positiveness when helping to bring the conversation to a satisfactory conclusion.

Mrs. Pierce, a third-grade teacher, reviewed these seven points with her students. One student, Garth, offered his summary of the conversation process by saying, "Don't talk, unless you have something to say." His comment was immediately countered by Nathan, who said, "Everybody has something important to say." After some discussion, the class decided that the two statements were good rules that everyone should follow. On a chart at the front of the classroom, Mrs. Pierce wrote both statements as a reminder of what is considered appropriate behavior when one is engaged in conversation.

Conversation in the Classroom

Knowing what the conversation process involves is not enough for students; rather, they must be interactive participants in meaningful conversation on a daily basis so that they can develop the oral language skills deemed necessary to the good conversationalist. To this end, a teacher must plan motivating activities whereby children will discuss their thoughts, feelings, and beliefs, and are allowed to do so in an environment of trust and acceptance. As Nathan stated, everyone has something to contribute; what he failed to say, however, was that criticism must be honest and nonthreatening. By having respect for each individual's contributions to a conversation, all students feel secure with the knowledge that their own opinions and statements will not be ridiculed in any way.

In some instances, the teacher may establish students as good conversationalist role models for the class. Individuals outside the classroom setting, such as school personnel, area community leaders, or television personalities, may also serve as role models. Even characters from children's literature may be included as role models, as exemplified by Charlotte in E. B. White's (1952) *Charlotte's Web.*

Effective speaking necessitates having many varied opportunities to converse. Because such encounters must be both meaningful and purposeful, the teacher and students need to establish and meet progressive goals that can be attained through verbal interaction.

Intonation

Intonation is the stress, pitch, and juncture of spoken language. By age 2, children use intonation naturally, albeit unconsciously. When no one was paying attention to 2-year-old Richie, who had gotten his foot caught in a bucket, he called out, "Help, please!" Intonation can bring words to life with an element of excitement or create an atmosphere of death. Children need to understand how intonation can convey meaning to the listener.

Stress, also referred to as accent, is the emphasis one gives to sounds, words, or phrases as one speaks. Consider the sentence "I love hamburgers." If the sentence is read aloud three times, with the emphasis on a different word each time, the meaning changes. When one emphasizes the word *I,* the focus falls on the individual person as the one who loves hamburgers. Emphasizing *love* gives the listener the impression that the individual is deeply infatuated with hamburgers as a food. Emphasizing *hamburgers* gives the impression that burgers are one of the great delicacies of the culinary world.

Pitch, or tone, is the melodic effect of language whereby the tone of voice rises and falls. When French is spoken, one's attention is easily drawn to the beautiful, melodic sounds of the French language. Although, to the unaccustomed ear, Vietnamese appears to be a jumbled conglomeration of high- and low-pitched sounds, the Asiatic languages actually utilize tone as a way to convey different meanings of words with the same sounds. In English, pitch is used to change an ordinary statement into an exclamation or a question. Using the same sentence from above, "I love hamburgers," a speaker can change pitch at the end of the sentence to make it either an exclamation or a question.

Juncture is a pause between sounds, words, or phrases. In essence, juncture serves as punctuation for oral language. Pauses, which are made at comma, semicolon, and period stops without change in the use of stress or pitch, may also serve to distinguish points for emphasis. Examples of the emphatic use of juncture include "I planned to watch the game, [pause] but the cable went out on my television set" or "John [pause] will provide us with an explanation of the events."

This "highlighting" effect can be achieved with "I love hamburgers." By pausing after the word, the speaker clearly stresses who loves hamburgers, whereas a slight hesitation after the second word allows for full expression of the speaker's fondness for hamburgers.

FOCUS BOX 6.1
Intonation and Its Qualities

Intonation The stress, pitch, and juncture of oral language
Stress The accent or emphasis placed on a syllable, word, or phrase by pronouncing it more loudly or emphatically than other syllables, words, or phrases
Pitch Tone of voice used in speaking or singing
Juncture A pause between sounds, words, or phrases

Oral Interpretation of Poetry and Prose

Oral interpretation is the way in which poetry and prose are spoken or read aloud. The speaker or reader sets the rhythm, tempo, or cadence for the selection and by using the components of intonation—stress, pitch, and juncture—presents the poem or prose in a certain way. Oral interpretation is an enjoyable speaking activity in which every child can participate.

Because there is no single right or wrong way to interpret children's literature, oral interpretation encourages creativity and experimentation with language and its sounds. As McCauley and McCauley (1992) put it, "Children must feel free to take risks" (p. 530). Thus oral interpretation develops positive attitudes toward speaking and fosters cooperative learning.

Children who have learning disabilities or other reading problems often find a kind of refuge in oral interpretation in that it is generally a group activity. Analogous to the individual who sings off key yet feels secure in singing with the rest of the church congregation, the student who lacks fluency in oral reading can join a small group of classmates as they orally interpret children's literature and feel quite comfortable, if not competent.

The popularity of rap music has freed some children not only to participate in oral interpretation but to compose their own rap and then present it to the class. For instance, the following rap was created by a group of 9- and 10-year-old boys:

Don't Pollute the Air

We need to protect the environment
Keeping it clean just makes sense
Then the air we breathe stays clean and clear
No bad smog our lungs to fear
So don't burn trash or drive polluting cars
And at night we'll be able to see the stars
Acid rain won't kill the trees
And we'll live longer healthfully
—Max, Travis, and Tork

Choral Speaking and Reading

Choral speaking and reading are enjoyable activities for children. Choral reading itself "never fails to excite children's interest in reading regardless of their age, reading level, or level of language proficiency . . . (for) children whose first language is not English (they) are able to read choral reading selections with little difficulty" (McCauley & McCauley, 1992, p. 527).

Generally, oral interpretation in the elementary grades begins with choral speaking and reading. Mother Goose rhymes provide appropriate material for kindergartners and first graders inasmuch as young children tend to be familiar with the various verses. A Mother Goose rhyme can be introduced as an oral interpretation activity in the following manner:

1. Introduce the class to the verse of the rhyme.
2. Have the class say the verse together.
3. Have the students repeat the verse while clapping their hands to the rhythm. If drums are available, the teacher can have two students tap out the rhythm on these instruments.
4. Divide the verse into alternating sections, with a student assuming the role of the leader and the remainder of the class taking the group role. The entire class should respond at the "all" prompt.
5. Have the children suggest various ways that voices could be changed and used within the rhyme. For example, whispering the words or having the group say the words softly and the leader speak loudly might be mentioned. After each suggestion, the class could perform the verse by incorporating the changes.

As an alternative, students could be divided into two groups of equal size, with one group reciting the nursery rhyme itself and the other group softly repeating a refrain (for instance, "tick tock" for "Hickory, Dickory, Dock" or "meow, meow" for "The Three Little Kittens").

Some picture books lend themselves to choral reading. Bill Martin, Jr., and John Archambault's (1989) delightful book *Chicka Chicka Boom Boom* introduces children to the lowercase letters of the alphabet. The refrain is "Chicka chicka boom boom, will there be enough room?" Since all 26 letters of the alphabet have a role in this book, young students can recite the book together, with each member of the class taking a letter and the entire class joining in the refrain. Another example is *Pumpkin, Pumpkin* by Jeanne Titherington (1986), which is a descriptive, science-oriented story that is simplistic enough for 5- and 6-year-olds to perform as a choral reading activity. This tale centers upon the natural progression from pumpkin seed to blossom to pumpkin. *Yo! Yes?* by Chris Raschka (1993) is a superb choral reading choice for 6- and 7-year-olds. The story is about an African-American boy and a white boy who meet on the street and become friends.

Choral reading of poetry takes on new meaning for middle- and upper-grade students because they begin to acquire a true appreciation of poetry and the poets who write it. "Children usually dislike talking about poetry, often because they feel the need to construct a "right" interpretation" (McClure, 1995, p. 117). Engaging in choral reading of well-loved poems allows children the enjoyable experience of focusing on the images, rhyme, and rhythm created by the poet. For instance, children relish Jack Prelutsky's poem "A Remarkable Adventure" in *Something Big Has Been Here* (1990). In the poem, a child describes a wild and absurd adventure that happened to coincide with precisely the time he should have been doing his homework. The child elaborately explains to his teacher why he doesn't have his homework. Other humorous contemporary poetry that lends itself to choral reading or speaking can be found in three of Prelutsky's other works (1970, 1982, 1990) *Toucans Two and Other Poems, The Baby Uggs Are Hatching,* and *Beneath a Blue Umbrella* and in Shel Silverstein's (1974, 1981) *Where the Sidewalk Ends* and *A Light in the Attic.*

Older children, who are somewhat sophisticated and enjoy a wide range of choral speaking experiences, will delight in the choral readings to be found within Judith Viorst's (1981) *If I Were in Charge of the World and Other Worries: Poems for Children and Their Parents.* For poetry of a more frightening nature, Prelutsky's (1980) *The Headless Horseman Rides Tonight* contains 12 poems about giants, poltergeists, and zombies, all of which can be used for either choral reading or speaking.

Older children often relate to poetry such as the poem "Somebody Said That It Couldn't Be Done" (printed in Sloyer, 1983). Divide the class into two groups and have them present a choral reading of this anonymously written work as follows:

ALL:	Somebody Said It Couldn't Be Done
ALL:	Somebody Said It Couldn't Be Done
Group 1:	But he, with a grin replied
Group 2:	He'd never be one to say it couldn't be done— Leastways not 'til he tried.
Group 1:	So he buckled right in, with a trace of a grin;
Group 2:	By golly, he went right to it.
Group 1:	He tackled The Thing That Couldn't Be Done!
ALL:	And he couldn't do it!

Serious poetry should also be included in choral speaking as children begin to examine their own feelings and emotions. As Georgia Heard (1989, p. 14) notes, "Poems come from something deeply felt." Sometimes one child's experiences or questions will provide the opportunity for sharing poetry about real life.

Reader's Theater

Reader's theater, which is unique to choral reading and speaking techniques, allows for student portrayal of individual literary characters through oral interpretation. The written script may be based on either an entire book, such as a picture book, or an episode within a longer work, such as a novel. In essence, then, reader's theater becomes an informal reading of various dialogues woven together through narration.

Reader's theater is a formalized dramatic presentation of a piece of literature. According to Young and Ferguson (1995, p. 496), reader's theater, "a presentation of fiction, nonfiction, or poetry that is expressively and emotionally read aloud by several readers, contributes to improved reading fluency, comprehension, and confidence." Students select a script or develop their own from a piece of literature. They then rehearse and stage the presentation.

Staging a reader's theater requires that some preparations take place. Scripts need to be placed in sturdy ring binders. Each reader's lines need to be marked with a highlighter. The readers must be taught to look down at the script with their eyes, not moving their heads. In the case of a long passage that goes from one page to the next, the latter portion can be photocopied and both pages placed side by side in the binder. This prevents the reader from having to turn the page in the midst of reading (Shepard, 1994).

The readers themselves should wear smocks: simple, large rectangular pieces of cloth with holes for the head and snaps or velcro fasteners on both sides, or T-shirts that are the same color. To give an even more professional appearance, T-shirts can have the school name and "Reader's Theater Group" printed on them. Having the readers dress alike gives them a neutral appearance so that the message of the literature comes across rather than an array of different dress styles and colors. Stools are more useful than chairs and should be of varying heights to reflect the heights of different characters (for instance, a tall stool for the donkey and a short chair for the dog). In addition, stools need to be sturdy so they can be used to stand on. Some stories call for the use of a stepladder. A colored sheet attached to the chalkboard can be used as a backdrop. Other props can be used, such as a basket, plastic ivy hanging down from the ceiling to represent a beanstalk, a pot for cooking vegetables—all depending on the particular story. Since reader's theater relies heavily on mime as well as what is read, props are kept at a minimum.

The readers may stand or sit. Since children doing a reader's theater for the first time may be a bit nervous, sitting tends to lessen the anxiety level. The readers should hold their binders rather than setting them on music stands or lecterns. The binder can rest in the palm of the left hand of right-handed students and the right hand of left-handed students so that the free hand can be used for gesturing.

Students should work on focusing. The narrator will focus, or look, toward the audience while the characters look at whomever they are talking with according to the story. Other means of focus are also appropriate. The character may look off into the distance, as if out a window, while sharing his or her own thoughts. In some instances characters may talk directly to the audience.

The positions on the stage should be assigned based on the characters. Those who have similar viewpoints should be placed together. Readers with the most lines should be on the far left and far right of the cast. Rather than entering and exiting as in plays, simply stepping forward, standing, or, if seated on stools, leaning slightly forward before speaking can serve as an entrance (and reversing the action as an exit).

Reader's theater should begin with one student introducing the title and the author, and another student giving a brief introduction of the story itself. The introduction should be a hook and not give the plot, nor the ending, away. At the end of the reader's theater, the readers should become quiet so that a pause comes over the room. Then in unison, the readers close their scripts, stand, and bow to the audience.

It is best to start with commercially prepared scripts or scripts developed from picture books. Then the students can move toward making their own scripts from favorite passages.

After an appropriate story has been chosen, the material must be adapted and transposed into a script for the reader's theater. The characters' dialogue is taken directly from the story. The narrator, or storyteller, is given dialogue that consists of the story's descriptive passages. This narration provides the audience with the story's introduction, mood, theme, and conclusion. The student assigned this task must weave the tale from beginning to end with smooth transitions so that the audience can follow the story line. Sometimes characters are mentioned in descriptive passages but do not engage in the story's dialogue. In such instances, direct dialogue can be developed for the characters, who will then have formal speaking parts within the script.

The material used for reader's theater must capture children's attention. Lively and/or suspenseful plots with compelling and interesting characters allow students to readily interpret both personalities and story lines. Such materials become both enticing and exciting as a medium of experimentation within oral interpretation. Stories centered around long, drawn out narratives cause children to quickly lose their eagerness to participate. Typically, a book that lends itself to reader's theater has an abundance of dialogue interspersed with brief, descriptive paragraphs.

Generally, children can easily relate to themes deemed appropriate to reader's theater: stories of compassion, generosity, greed, and honesty. Such themes prevail with picture books, making them excellent sources of material. A few suggested picture books for young students include Arnold Lobel's (1970) *Frog and Toad Are Friends,* Steven Kellogg's (1991) *Jack and the Beanstalk,* and William Steig's (1977) *Caleb & Kate.* Students will also enjoy Charlotte Huck's (1989) *Princess Furball,* Ellen Jackson's (1994) *Cinder Edna,* Robert Munsch's (1980) *The Paper Bag Princess,* Tomie de Paola's (1982) *Strega Nona's Magic Lessons,* Vera B. William's (1983) *A Chair for My Mother,* and Loreen Leedy's (1991) *The Great Trash Bash.* Older students can write scripts from such books as *With Every Drop of Blood* (Collier & Collier, 1994), *Sarah Bishop* (O'Dell, 1980), *Number the Stars* (Lowry, 1989), and *The True Confessions of Charlotte Doyle* (Avi, 1990).

Storytelling

Storytelling is an excellent means of developing speaking skills. According to Karla Hawkins Wendelin (1991, p. 181):

Two bilingual students in Mike Ellis' sixth-grade class at May School tell stories in English and Spanish to preschoolers in the Head Start program.

Jeff Robertson photo courtesy Rochelle (IL) News-Leader

Engaging students in storytelling activities develops communication skills and encourages shared learning experiences. Telling stories enhances oral language and sharpens listening. Speaking ability is improved through attention to articulation, clarity, and volume. Poise and confidence in speaking before a group are acquired in the accepting environment of the classroom. Students experiment with various intonations and reflect a range of emotions in their voices. They are faced with the need to select just the right word to convey a thought. As they manipulate language, they also listen to, evaluate and appreciate the expression of others.

Puppets are an effective device for children to use during storytelling to develop self-confidence. By using a hand puppet, a child can tell a simple story to the class or a small group of children without feeling pressured. Children love to manipulate and play with puppets, which seem to be regarded as cousins to their beloved stuffed animals.

Puppets may be as simple as crayon faces on paper plates or as elaborate as commercially produced animals and characters. Typical favorites are hand puppets made of discarded socks or gloves. Puppets can be made for favorite books. For instance, for *The Very Hungry Caterpillar* (Carle, 1971), a caterpillar can be made from a green kneesock and two white buttons for eyes. A butterfly cut out of a small piece of yellow felt can be folded and hidden in the toe of the sock until the end of the story. The fruit, leaf, and other food mentioned in the story can be cut out of 12-inch felt squares. Each piece of food should have a slit in it so that the caterpillar can "eat" through it as it goes over the child's hand. At the end of the story, the child removes the caterpillar and pulls out the butterfly to show to the audience. An empty refrigerator or washing machine shipping box can be transformed into a puppet theater. Children can invite other classes to their performances.

Storytelling has received renewed interest in recent years, both in the classroom and in society as a whole. Storytelling abilities can benefit the development of both conversational and dramatic communication skills. Also through storytelling, children develop new awareness of meaning (Nicholson, 1992).

The storytelling process consists of six sequential stages. The first stage is the *selection of a story* that appeals to the storyteller and is appropriate for the intended audience in terms of theme and mood. The second stage is the *analysis of the story's characters and plot.* The third stage is the *experimentation with intonation and gestures* to depict the story. *Telling the story through scenes,* particularly with a set introduction and conclusion, is the fourth stage. The fifth stage is the *telling of the story in rehearsal before the actual presentation to a live audience,* the final stage. (These stages are described in further detail in focus box 6.2.)

Fables, fairy tales, folktales, and fantasies appeal to children in the primary grades. Appropriate titles include Aesop's fables; the "Jack" tales of Great Britain and Appalachia (of which "Jack and the Beanstalk" is the most famous); "The Five Chinese Brothers"; "The Princess and the Pea" and "The Ugly Duckling," both in *Hans Christian Andersen: His Classic Fairy Tales* (1974); and Laura Numeroff's (1991) *If You Give A Moose A Muffin.* Children in the intermediate grades enjoy E. J. Bird's (1990) *The Blizzard of 1896,* as well as selections from the books of Beverly Cleary, Virginia Hamilton, and Edgar Allan Poe.

Based on oral language tradition, storytelling is an excellent way to combine speaking and listening and to present lessons in music, social studies, and even science at all grade levels. American folktales are the root of the "salad bowl" culture, and their timeless characters become vivid and alive through storytelling. Popular stories for social studies include "Johnny Appleseed," "Molly Pitcher," "John Henry," "Mike Fink," "Paul Bunyan," and "Annie Oakley." Similarly, children can easily visualize the four voyages of Columbus when Jean Fritz's (1980) *Where Do You Think You're Going, Christopher Columbus?* is used as the basis for storytelling. Fritz's biographies of the founding fathers also make excellent sources for storytelling in the area of social studies instruction.

Both legends and unfamiliar cultures can be explored through the sharing of such stories as Verna Aardema's (1981) *The Riddle of the Drum: A Tale from Tizapán, Mexico;* Joseph Bruchac's (1995) *Gluskabe and the Four Wishes;* Joyce Cooper Arkhurst's (1964) *The Adventures of Spider: West African Folktales;* and Taro Yashima's (1955) *Crow Boy.* Because such tales range from simplistic to relatively complex, children with learning disabilities and those who are slow learners can just as readily find a story for storytelling as the more

Focus Box 6.2
The Storytelling Process

Stage 1   Become familiar with the story and determine its appropriateness for the intended audience.

a. Select a story that appeals to you. The story should be one that so captures your attention that you want to share it with someone else.

b. Read the story at least twice, paying particular attention to the plot. The plot should be straightforward, easy to follow, and without complexities, all of which might distract listeners. The theme should be apparent rather than hidden, and the theme and the mood of the story should be appropriate for the audience's age level.

Stage 2   Analyze characters and plot.

a. Because characters should be believable and any character differences in personalities and traits should be easy to portray, consider closely the traits and personalities of the characters. How do the characters relate to one another? What purpose does each character serve in the story? How would each character look? What type of movement and voice is appropriate for the various characters? Experiment with the development of each individual character's voice and physical appearance until you are satisfied with his or her representation.

Stage 3   Use oral interpretations and gestures in the story's presentation.

a. Read the story aloud to discover interesting phrases that must be retained for the story's complete effect. Such phrases may help the listener create visual images. For example, in "The Teeny Tiny Woman," a Brothers Grimm folktale, the phrase "teeny tiny" is used as an adjective for all the objects: teeny tiny house, teeny tiny hat, teeny tiny gate, teeny tiny bone, and so on. The repetition of "teeny tiny" makes the story "visually" dramatic for the listener.

b. Incorporate gestures that add to rather than distract from the story. For example, the portrayal of a giant requires one to stand straight and tall, keep arms out from the sides, and appear as if looking down on individuals of smaller stature. Likewise, leaning over, clasping hands together, and swinging them back and forth creates the image of an elephant walking through the jungle.

Stage 4   Note the story's sequence of events and create an established introduction and conclusion.

a. Take note of the primary scenes of the story. Don't attempt to memorize the story word-for-word; instead, rely on the highlighted scenes and settings to progress through the story.

b. Develop a set introduction and conclusion. The events in the middle of the story can be changed, but the story's beginning and ending must follow the story line.

c. Create an alluring introduction so that listeners will be compelled to follow the story throughout. Although introductions are usually brief, they establish both the setting (time and place) and the theme of a story. In the same way, folktales, which tend to begin with "Once upon a time in a forest there lived a . . . ," become quite enchanting to young children.

d. The conclusion should bring closure to the story. Detail the outcomes for all characters in such a way that listeners are not left wondering whether the story is complete.

Stage 5   Rehearse the story without an audience.

a. Using a mirror, cassette recorder, or video recorder, the storyteller should practice telling the story several times before presenting it to others. This mastery scheme requires time and several repetitions before the storyteller actually feels at ease in presenting the work to an unfamiliar audience.

Stage 6   Present the story to a live audience.

a. When sharing a story with an audience, eliminate distractions as much as possible. For example, if a storyteller stands before patterned curtains or a window facing a playground or street, the audience may have difficulty concentrating on the story. Similarly, one's dress or mannerisms can interfere with the presentation.

In the Classroom Mini Lesson

Tall Tales

*A*merica has produced several folk heroes and accompanying tall tales about them. Steven Kellogg's (1988) *Johnny Appleseed* shares the legacy of the real-life character and his work planting apple trees on the frontier. At the end of the book, Kellogg includes a mural of some of the tall tales about Johnny Appleseed. The teacher should read the book to intermediate-grade students. Afterward, the students should locate a tall tale about another American folk hero and tell it to the class.

Kellogg, S. (1988). *Johnny Appleseed.* New York: Morrow.

academically talented or gifted students. Providing children with the opportunity to experience a fascination with other cultures may help them understand and accept others' differences more easily.

Discussions as Small Group Activities

Children should learn to engage in group discussions at an early age. With kindergartners and primary-grade students, the best way to introduce discussions is for the teacher to serve as discussion guide. Until children become familiar with the discussion process, and often this is not until the third or fourth grade, they need direction and organization from the classroom teacher.

When initially arranging small discussion groups of five to seven children, the teacher should consider the interests and personalities of the individual students. The very first time such discussion groups are created, shy students should not be placed with children who like to dominate conversations. Children with attitude problems, particularly those in the upper grades, need to be assigned to groups carefully; the teacher should avoid combining students who are overly disruptive. According to Wiencek and O'Flahavan (1994, p. 491) the classroom teacher needs to "consider the social, interpretive, and reading abilities of each student, and use this information to create heterogeneous groups." They go on to say that the teacher should lead the group discussion and then coach students to lead their own discussions. In doing so, it is a good idea to have the students begin with something in common, such as a selection of quality literature. Well-developed story elements maintain students' interest, are more easily understood, and help students to make predictions and inferences, thereby facilitating student discussion. Stories from basal readers tend to be short; thus, these are particularly helpful when initiating group discussions in the classroom.

After the groups have been formed, students must be introduced to various discussion methods. Then, members of a group decide how their assignment or task will be completed; at this time, a group-appointed leader, often a more assertive student, issues individual responsibilities to each member.

In the Classroom Mini Lesson

Shadow Puppetry

Shadow puppetry is an enjoyable form of storytelling for children. By using an overhead transparency projector to create silhouettes on a screen, students can share a favorite story with an audience. To make the screen, purchase an inexpensive white window shade (the kind that rolls up). Secure the shade with weather stripping to a frame made out of 1″ by 2″ wood. Reinforce the corners of the frame with L braces screwed into the wood. Secure the screen to a table or a teacher's desk by using two C clamps.

To make the projection work, set the overhead transparency projector on a table about 12 feet in front of the screen and turn it on. Objects can be projected from both the top of the overhead projector and from immediately behind the screen. For instance, by placing a blue overhead transparency on the projector, the screen appears blue. A 3-inch cardboard cutout of a sea monster laid on top of the transparency gives the appearance of a giant sea monster in a blue ocean on the screen. If a student stands just behind the screen and pretends to be swimming, the shadow on the screen will look as though the sea monster is after the "swimmer."

Colored transparencies can create a very dramatic effect. A red transparency on the overhead projector with strips of blue and yellow transparencies overlaid on top gives the beauty of a sunrise. Similarly, keeping the blue transparency on the top and adding a green transparency on the lower portion of the projector will produce the appearance of a blue sky and green grass. One- to two-inch cutouts of covered wagons can give the impression of a wagon train moving across the prairie. Tiny toy or stuffed animals can also be placed on the transparency while larger stuffed animals can be held up by a puppeteer just behind the screen.

Other variations are suggested by David Wisniewski (1995), a puppeteer and author/illustrator of picture books. Wisniewski suggests placing a plastic vine on the bottom edge of the transparency screen and pushing it up and across the screen to give the appearance of the beanstalk growing in "Jack and the Beanstalk." At the same time, a puppeteer can stand behind the large screen and pretend to be Jack climbing the beanstalk while the narrator reads the story.

Wisniewski (1995) also suggests using lace, moving it across the overhead transparency screen as another puppeteer stands behind the large screen and jogs in place. This gives the appearance of a person running. Wax paper on the lower part of the overhead transparency screen gives the appearance of ground. By tilting the wax paper at an angle, a hill appears—good for using with a story such as *Blueberries for Sal* (McCloskey, 1948). By moving the wax paper up and down quickly, it appears that an earthquake is taking place or that a giant is walking nearby. By moving the wax paper slowly up and down, the impression is that of water and waves. By tearing the wax paper into jagged edges and overlaying them, a mountain range appears. Crinkled wax paper looks like a spider's web. When a piece of plain wax paper covers the entire transparency screen, fog appears on the large screen. A wax paper background can give the illusion of a snowy appearance for a story such as *The Polar Express* (Van Allsburg, 1985).

Figures that represent the characters of a story can be created from cardboard cutouts covered with black paper (Wisniewski, 1995). Small figures may be placed directly on the projector, whereas large figures may be held by a puppeteer behind the screen. Arms and legs can be attached to the cutouts with brass tacks, then manipulated using umbrella ribs from discarded umbrellas. Cardboard cutouts can also be attached to a puppeteer's headband with velcro. For instance, the profiles of a princess, a prince, and a frog may be attached to puppeteers' headbands for the story "The Frog Prince."

Students can have fun devising their own props and making innovations on the various stories that they elect to present. Clear transparency rolls and transparency marking pens can be used to make background scenery for a story such as *Strega Nona Meets Her Match* (dePaola, 1991) or *Sukey and the Mermaid* (San Souci, 1992). Cutting out wax paper frogs and placing them on blue overheads, in combination with cardboard profiles of other characters, can create the story *Tuesday* (Wiesner, 1991).

References

de Paola, T. (1993). *Strega Nona meets her match*. New York: G. P. Putnam's Sons.

McCloskey, R. (1948). *Blueberries for Sal*. New York: Viking.

San Souci, R. D. (1992). *Sukey and the mermaid* (B. Pinkney, Illus.). New York: Four Winds.

Van Allsburg, C. (1985). *The polar express*. Boston: Houghton Mifflin.

Wiesner, D. (1991). *Tuesday*. Boston: Clarion.

Wisniewski, D. (1995, March). *From shadow to silhouette*. Speech presented at the Northern Illinois University's Children's Literature Institute, DeKalb, IL.

In the Classroom Mini Lesson

Using Removable Sticky Notes

*P*ost It notes were originally designed by an inventor for the 3M Company. The inventor wanted something he could use to mark pages in his church hymnal. In the classroom, they make fantastic discussion markers for students that can easily be moved around without causing damage to the book. Begin by giving each student four of the small removable notes. As they read a selection, for instance a chapter in a book, have them mark the places in the text they want to discuss. You can specifically direct their reading by having them focus on major events that influenced the main character of the story, dialogue that gave clues to the main character's personality, critical points in the story where a character had to make a decision, or passages the students liked best, for instance. As they read nonfiction, students may use the removable notes to highlight important information or concepts for discussion.

Larger size removable notes can be used by students to write notes or thoughts about the story they are reading. They may react to the plot or theme of the story, or trace the change in a character's behavior, for example.

Post Its can be very helpful in collaborative reading activities. For instance, each student can be given three removable notes to mark the three most important events in the story. Then the student can join with two peers to decide as a group which events were the most important.

Although a time frame may be established for the lengthier projects of the upper grades, the first attempts at group discussion should be short, concrete, straightforward, and motivating for each student. Since discussion groups are direct, cooperative learning endeavors, tasks that are enticing will promote students' willingness to complete their portions of the assignment successfully.

Brainstorming

Brainstorming, a process used by discussion groups, occurs when all participants contribute ideas or possible resolutions to a real or proposed problem. No idea is rejected; rather, all suggestions are accepted and formally recorded in writing. Usually the time allowed for such interaction is limited, perhaps no more than five minutes. Here are some possible problems or situations that might be investigated:

If you were locked inside Walt Disney World, how would you get out without assistance?

If you won the lottery and wanted to establish a foundation for worthy children's causes, which causes would you want to include?

How many uses can you suggest for the following items: empty soda cans, railroad ties, old school buses, drinking straws, foam hamburger containers, and old sneakers?

In what ways can students be encouraged not to drop out of school?

How might you be able to get positive publicity for your school?

Why does the school need a science lab for conducting experiments?

After students have brainstormed and compiled a list of several possible solutions to an indicated problem or situation, they are ready to reach a consensus. Such problem-solving interaction involves the careful consideration and examination of all suggestions until only two or three possible solutions remain. The group must be able to justify each of these in terms of viability.

Assignments that rely on brainstorming with consensus-building outcomes are most effective when the students can directly relate to the problem or situation. Indeed, real-life dilemmas are appropriate problems for students to attempt to resolve.

Panel Discussions and Debates

After gaining experience in brainstorming and consensus building, students are ready for the more formal presentations of panel discussions and debates. In panel discussions, a group of three to five students is assigned a specific topic to be presented before a designated audience. The duty of each of the panel members is to develop an individual oral report about a particular aspect of the main topic through research and group discussion. One student assumes the responsibility of serving as the panel leader or moderator. This position requires a student not only to present the first or the last report but also to coordinate the group's work and the order of the presentations and to give the introductory and concluding statements.

For debates, each group member must be familiar with information about a relevant problem or issue in order to develop answers to questions posed by the rest of the class. A formal debate, which requires that each participant give an opening statement, allows the participants to ask each other questions. Therefore, the researching of facts and figures to be used in a response becomes especially important to the support of one's argument. Because of the level of sophistication involved, debates are not usually introduced until about the fifth grade. If they are introduced earlier, students depend on emotional pitches rather than sound, credible facts, and opinions.

Media and Oral Language

Media, including bulletin boards, dioramas, mobiles, puppetry, audiotapes, videotapes, and overhead transparencies, can be used inexpensively within the classroom. In some school districts, the sponsoring of media contests motivates children in the development of individual media presentations. These combine some oral language work, such as a play or oral report, with a media form such as a videotape or an overhead transparency. Media presentations can also be used in other ways. For example, children can illustrate a story by drawing it scene by scene; the teacher, in turn, can use a 35mm camera to make slides of the children's illustrations. If the students themselves record the dialogue and background noise, a slide/tape production can be created for less than $10. The entire class can become involved in such a project, with every student making a valuable contribution. As literature is brought to life via the video

In the Classroom Mini Lesson

Oral Language Activities

1. Have a "demonstration fair" in which every child demonstrates and explains to the class a skill or technique he or she possesses. Suggestions include making yogurt, building and riding a skateboard, or creating cartoons with video recorders.
2. Have students collect jokes and riddles to share with their classmates.
3. Have a day for book characters when each student dresses as his or her favorite character and responds to questions asked by classmates about the character.
4. Develop parallel panel discussion groups with upper-grade students who read books that have the same topic but opposite viewpoints.
5. Have students videotape their storytelling of a favorite part of a book.
6. Using a cassette recorder, have students "read" their own interpretation of a wordless picture book and share the tapes with students who share the same native language.
7. Have pairs of students design and describe a science experiment and present it to the class or videotape it.

camera, a permanent momento of the students' efforts is made, one that can be shared with other classes and with parents during an open house.

One second-grade teacher developed a black-and-white video history of dinosaurs that described how these reptiles lived, what they ate, and what they looked like. He had his students make clay replicas of the dinosaurs as well as of the flora and fauna associated with prehistoric times and assigned each student a part in the narrative. The use of black-and-white film made the presentation even more effective because the contrasts were much more striking than they would have been with color film.

The videotaping of children during both informal and formal drama exercises aids youngsters in the improvement of their verbal and body movement skills. Although there is a natural tendency toward self-consciousness initially, children become increasingly more aware of oral language habits that detract from the overall message they wish to convey. For example, Becky, a third grader, would unconsciously insert the phrase "you know" in a majority of her conversational pauses. A videotape of her portrayal of a character from a basal reader story made her recognize how distracting this phrase could be. Yet such success is most often affiliated with one's age. It is important to note that as children approach puberty, they become increasingly self-conscious; therefore, it is advantageous to familiarize students with this medium in the early elementary grades, when they are less reluctant to participate.

Since videotape cameras and VCRs are readily available in most school districts, teachers should regularly use them to enable students to perceive themselves as others see them. By becoming involved in the analysis of their own dramatic performances, students are better able to modify and adapt their role playing for better character portrayal.

Students may be asked to use the following questions during their self-evaluations:

1. Is my voice strong?
2. Do I pronounce the words carefully?
3. Do I have any distracting mannerisms, either in my oral language or my body language?
4. Do I speak clearly?
5. Do I speak at a pace that is easily understood, with few or no hesitations and pauses?
6. Do I make usage errors?

In a similar way, the recording of lessons in both audiotape and videotape forms enables the teacher to assess students' oral language usage during discussions. It can also provide a direct, effective way to evaluate student contributions in small established groups without having to monitor the group's activities personally.

Drama as Creative Play

Drama is a natural extension of creative play, in which all youngsters engage at an early age. In essence, drama is an experiment in socialization on the child's part; the child pretends or engages in "make believe" play in the simulation of real-life experiences: managing a store, attending school, protecting the community as a police officer, celebrating special events with tea parties, and the like. Unusual adventures tend to be imagined as well: rescuing survivors from a capsized ship, designing and manning a space vehicle that is going to Mars, sailing to China in search of ancient treasure, and so on. Such dramatic play permits children opportunities to deal with reality and to practice appropriate, social behavior. By providing an escape from reality, on the other hand, drama also enables children to examine and explore new behaviors and situations. Dramatic play has been found to make important contributions to children's early reading and writing development (Christie, 1990).

Children depend upon memory, imagination, observation, and interactions with others as they create new ways of behaving and communicating (Wagner, 1988). They step outside themselves and assume new roles. These roles may be ones that they have observed either firsthand, such as the role of mother or storekeeper, or through some form of media, as represented by Barbie, or Teenage Mutant Ninja Turtles, for example. Other potential roles are those created largely from imagination, such as the role of an alien from an unknown planet or a princess from an enchanted kingdom.

Through their experiences with drama, proponents of dramatics have cited the many benefits of this creative form. These include increases in critical and intuitive thinking, concentration, and reading comprehension (Gray, 1987), as well as associated improvements in vocabulary development, speech, and self-concept. Moreover, the use of drama can also personalize knowledge and yield aesthetic pleasure (Siks, 1983). A study conducted by Smilansky

(1968) found that sociodramatic play served as a means of extending the intellectual development of underprivileged children in the areas of vocabulary, speech quality, and sentence length.

In particular, drama enhances youngsters' speech because tone of voice and expression are essential components of an oral presentation. Typically, certain roles have specific, rhetorical requirements: the student who portrays Little Bear's mother in Minarik's *Little Bear* (1978) must have a soft voice to express tenderness and sensitivity, whereas, the child depicting the Big, Bad Wolf in the "Three Little Pigs" must possess a loud, booming-with-confidence voice. Audibility and clarity must be highlighted. Children need to learn to project their voices and articulate their words so that the presentation can be understood by the audience.

Burgess (1984) believes that drama has a great contribution to make to the language arts. Because of drama's needs for abstract thinking and complete cooperative interactions, Burgess supports the notion that drama aids the general development of language.

Drama as a Process

Portraying a character enables a child to internalize language and "become" that character, if only for a few minutes. As McCaslin (1984) writes, "The story one plays makes a lasting impression. Therefore, the opportunity to become well acquainted with good literature, through dramatizing it, is a major value." Through personification, drama becomes a means of deepening one's understanding of a portion of good literature.

The dramatic process requires a child to use both personal and literary experience to prepare for role playing. Like each of the characters, the plot must be thoroughly understood because it provides clarity and direction for a story or play. Haine (1985) states that through drama, the story is imagined. The student becomes engaged with it, may struggle with unfamiliar concepts or with his/her own reaction to it, and will ultimately shape it with his/her own particular interpretation. Thus, the key events, images, and themes of the story are processed as they are acted out in a drama. Focus box 6.3 describes the use of drama in the elementary grades.

Language Expansion and Extension in Drama

The dramatic medium enables children to practice and extend their language in a meaningful context. According to Heathcote (1983), drama permits many different styles and language levels to be used and examined by children. The teacher must pay close attention to language as it is used by students during dramatic play. By considering overall content, style, tone, and vocabulary, the teacher can develop appropriate language models for the students. Such models aid children in processing oral language at both the informal and formal levels of speech. As the students manipulate language, they do so consciously and unconsciously. Thus, when they are speaking, they subconsciously monitor what they say and how they say it, a form of metalinguistic awareness (Morgan & Saxon, 1988).

FOCUS BOX 6.3
Drama as a Process

*U*sing drama as a process in the elementary grades requires the following six steps:

1. Select a good story that the students will enjoy and be motivated to dramatize. The story should be one the children can relate to in terms of their own knowledge and experiences.
2. Have the students identify the story's characters and discuss ways that those characters may have appeared, talked, felt, and reacted within the story's various events. If a character has any unique characteristics, they should be noted accordingly.
3. Have the students describe the main scenes or events that occur in the story. Then have the students choose the scene or scenes they want to perform within a drama.
4. For each scene selected, have the students sequence the actions that occurred. Questions to be considered here are, "What are the essential actions of the scene"? and "What actions can be omitted without detracting from the scene's importance?"
5. Assign character roles to the students, and review the predominant characteristics of the individuals whom they are portraying.
6. Have students dramatize the scene or scenes selected by presenting their own interpretations or versions of them. They can invent their own dialogue for informal dramatics or prepare lines to read as script for formal dramatics. In addition, they may use props for greater realism.

Types of Drama

In the elementary classroom, drama is usually limited to three major types: pantomime, improvisation, and formal drama. These types are described in the rest of this chapter.

Pantomime

Pantomime relies solely on nonverbal behavior to communicate meaning. Through gestures and movements, an individual carries out a drama that symbolizes not only actions but thoughts and feelings as well. The use of such facial expressions and body movements has always been important on stage, where audiences must view and interpret the actions from afar. It is logical, then, for the gestures and actions used in pantomime to be more accentuated and detailed. For example, a person pantomiming the drinking of a cup of coffee may first go through the motions of slowly adding sugar and cream and then carefully stirring the mixture.

As children become aware that different expressions demonstrate different emotions, they learn how to make appropriate facial expressions to send a certain message to an audience. A range of emotions can be demonstrated facially, beginning with happiness, sadness, and fear and advancing to bewilderment, astonishment, apathy, empathy, and indifference. As children become more astute in observing nonverbal behavior, they are able to add body language and movements to particular facial expressions. For example, a shrug of the

shoulders can represent uncertainty, and palms open upward with arms outspread becomes an appeal for help. Such motions add to the associated facial representations.

Young children may be introduced to pantomime as an activity in which the entire class can participate. Consider having the students pretend that they are the following:

A stick floating down a quiet brook

Lambs friskily playing and jumping in the warm sunshine

Leaves gently falling to the ground in autumn

A kitten trying to find its way down a dark stairwell

An adult making a snowman after a snowstorm

After the entire class has engaged in a few pantomime activities such as these, have the children individually work on different activities. There is one difficulty in working with kindergartners and first graders on pantomime: They often get excited and announce their role while performing. For example, 6-year-old Karin burst forth in the middle of a pantomime of the "Three Billy Goats Gruff" with "I'm the troll who owns the bridge that the billy goats want to cross."

Here are some other pantomime situations that are appropriate for young children:

Taking pictures with a camcorder

Shopping for groceries

Cleaning out a closet

Raking leaves into piles and jumping in the piles

Repairing a flat tire on a bicycle

Flying a kite

Scoring a touchdown but losing a shoe in the process

Finding a winning lottery ticket

Children are very innovative and clever in creating facial expressions and actions for silent portrayals. Younger students can select events to depict from stories they have recently read, or they can attempt a pantomime of favorite characters from popular children's literature. Older students can be challenged in pantomiming individuals currently in the national and international news, including political leaders, television and movie stars, and sports figures.

Improvisation

After children feel confident in their pantomimic skills, improvisation should be introduced. Improvisational drama allows the students to now add dialogue to their dramatic skills repertoire. Although students' initial attempts at dialogue will be brief and stilted, later tries will flow more fluently, as the children become accustomed to using it. For this reason, improvisational situations should be devoid of complexity until the students are comfortable with using dialogue.

Children often wish to improvise an excerpt from a story. The emphasis here should not be on memorization of the text but on the extemporaneous use of dialogue and imagination to share a scene from the story.

Favorite characters from books are excellent sources for student improvisation. Before having the students improvise the chosen characters, ask them to consider the characters' descriptions: What type of appearance did the character present? How did the character stand and walk? How old was the character? How did the character dress? How did the character speak? What voice qualities did the character possess? What was the character doing in the scene? What kind of person was the character? Did the character possess any unique characteristics?

Some children's literature selections that offer appropriate characters for improvisation are listed below.

Early Childhood Level.
Allard, H. (1978). *Miss Nelson is missing* (J. Marshall, Illus.). New York: Scholastic.

Carrick, C., & Carrick, D. (1975). *Old Mother Witch*. New York: Clarion.

Hutchins, P. (1982). *Don't forget the bacon*. New York: Farrar, Straus & Giroux.

King-Smith, D. (1987). *Farmer Bungle forgets*. New York: Atheneum.

Lattimore, D. N. (1987). *The flame of peace: A tale of the Aztecs*. New York: Harper & Row.

Raskin, E. (1989). *Nothing ever happens on my block.* New York: Aladdin.

Stevens, B. (1990). *Handel and the famous sword swallower of Halle.* (R. T. Councell, Illus.). New York: Philomel.

Trivizas, E. (1993). *The three little wolves and the big bad pig* (H. Oxenbury, Illus.). New York: Scholastic.

Waber, B. (1975). *The house on East 88th Street.* Boston: Houghton Mifflin.

Wood, A. (1984). *The napping house* (D. Wood, Illus.). Orlando, FL: Harcourt Brace Jovanovich.

Young, E. (1992). *Seven blind mice.* New York: Philomel.

Middle Childhood Level.

Cleary, B. (1991). *Strider* (P. Zelinsky, Illus.). New York: Morrow.

Duffy, J. (1989). *The Christmas gang* (B. McClintock, Illus.). New York: Scribner's.

McCloskey, R. (1976). *Homer Price.* New York: Penguin.

Myers, W. D. (1987). *Fast Sam, cool Clyde and stuff.* New York: Puffin Viking.

Newman, R. (1984). *The case of the Baker Street irregular.* New York: Atheneum.

Pearson, K. (1990). *The sky is falling.* New York: Viking.

Peck, R. N. (1983). *Soup.* New York: Harper & Row.

Rylant, C. (1992). *Missing May.* New York: Orchard.

Spinelli, J. (1990). *Maniac Magee.* Boston: Little, Brown.

Children who are self-conscious or for whom English is a second language may be reluctant to become involved in an improvisational activity. It is important that the teacher remain patient while still encouraging them to participate. Having an entire class share folktales, with students who do not speak English as a first language contributing a folktale from their own culture, was a method Mrs. Davis used to encourage all of her fourth graders to share improvisations. Her class was entertained with the English versions of both French and Spanish folktales, along with a modified "Walt Disney" version of "Zorro" from two shy students.

Improvisation authorizes students to develop their own oral language interpretations of a story. Therefore, a Greek myth or a Norwegian folktale may easily be transformed into the local vernacular. Without the structured language restrictions of having a required text from which to speak, children are free to use and ultimately expand their speaking skills in terms of fluency, content, and vocabulary.

Props may be used in improvisation along with accompanying sounds. Props may also be used to stimulate improvisations. Students can be divided into small groups of three or four members, with each group selecting an item from a "prop box." The goal for each group is to create an improvisation about the chosen item. Suggested props include a key chain, a cane, a wallet, a computer disk, a ring, a letter in a sealed envelope, a rabbit's foot, a necklace, a flashlight, and a small wooden box.

Props could also include articles of clothing, although remnants of material can serve the same purpose very effectively. The latter offer more versatility and are likely to be machine washable and therefore inexpensive to clean. For example, a large piece of drapery material can serve as a serape for a character in a Spanish folktale, a robe for a Roman senator, or a cape for a queen. Smaller pieces of cloth can be used as belts to tie the material in place.

In the Classroom Mini Lesson
Story Drama

*W*agon Wheels, by Barbara Brenner (1984), is a short novel based on a real incident. Three young black brothers search for their father's homestead on the western plains. In trying to follow a map toward their land, the boys encounter storms, fires, and starvation. This book serves as an excellent source of story drama for second graders.

The children should develop an understanding of the period and locale described by the book. What, for example, do they know about homesteading, prairie fires, folk songs of the period, medicinal cures, folklore, and pioneer life in general? After sharing their own knowledge, they may be motivated to seek additional information from maps, pictures, and other books on the same topic.

The teacher reads the first chapter, stopping at several points so that the students can discuss the use of the book as a story drama. At the end of the first chapter, the students are asked: Who in the book would most likely tell the story of the boys' adventures? What portions of the text can be used directly in the narratives and dialogue? How should the story be told? (As elderly gentlemen looking back over their youth? As the story progresses chronologically? Via other homesteaders?)

The children are then ready to develop their own version of *Wagon Wheels*. A small portion of the first chapter can be selected for the story drama. The teacher will offer assistance in the word processing of the lines of narration and dialogue since this is one of the more time-consuming tasks and very difficult for second graders. After the lines have been selected, the students are assigned individual parts. The reading, rather than the memorizing, of lines then becomes an option for the second graders.

As an accompanying art project, the students can illustrate the various scenes to be performed, using their pictures to introduce each portion of the drama to the audience. While a few of the students prepare the stage for the next scene, 8 to 10 students can sing folk songs of the period.

Brenner, B. (1984). *Wagon Wheels.* New York: Harper & Row.

The inclusion of props in the improvisational process helps children become more aware of their creative potential and encourages them to be inventive in their thinking.

Formal Drama

Formal drama is more structured than improvisation as students either read written dialogue or recite dialogue that has been memorized for the dramatization. Some students enjoy the challenge of remembering lines; however, most children find it time-consuming and tedious, with additional pressure being placed on them. Rather than being natural in their deliveries, many children will appear to be stiff and uncomfortable. For these reasons, children should be permitted to read their characters' dialogue just as the narrator would read the narration.

When using the formal dramatic process with children in the lower grades, San Jose (1988) suggests that the story drama be emphasized. The first step in story drama is to have an opening discussion about the story. In this discussion, the students share with one another what they already know about the story's setting, characters, and theme while always seeking additional information supplied by the teacher through maps and other illustrations. Next, the teacher or a designated student reads a portion of the story aloud; this is followed by questions, which check for understanding of the characters, setting (time and place), and plot. At this point, the students are asked these questions: Who could be telling the story, and how should the story evolve? Are there direct, natural parts of the story that could serve as narratives or dialogue? Are there any actions or movements that could be pantomimed by a few of the actors? In describing the foregoing steps, San Jose (1988) recommends that children be encouraged to contribute their own ideas to activities involving role playing, interpreting characteristics, and problem solving.

Books appropriate for drama are listed below.

Early Childhood Level.

Bursik, R. (1992). *Amelia's fantastic flight.* New York: Holt.

Dooley, N. (1991). *Everybody cooks rice* (P. J. Thornton, Illus.). Minneapolis, MN: Carolrhoda.

Haley, G. (1973). *Jack Jouett's ride.* New York: Viking.

Hancock, S. (1980). *Old Blue* (E. Ingraham, Illus.). New York: Putnam.

Kellogg, S. (1989). *Yankee Doodle.* New York: Four Winds.

McSwigan, M. (1942). *Snow treasure* (M. Reardon, Illus.). New York: Dutton.

Rylant, C. (1982). *When I was young in the mountains.* New York: Dutton.

Sanders, S. R. (1989). *Aurora means dawn* (J. Kastner, Illus.). New York: Bradbury.

Sandin, J. (1981). *The long way to a new land.* New York: Harper & Row.

Turner, A. (1987). *Nettie's trip south* (R. Himler, Illus.). New York: Macmillan.

Wilder, L. (1953). *Little house in the big woods* (G. Williams, Illus.). New York: Harper & Row.

Middle Childhood Level.

Beatty, P. (1978). *Watch for me, wait for me, Eula Bee.* New York: Morrow.

Clapp, P. (1982). *Witches' children: A story of Salem.* New York: Lothrop, Lee, & Shepard.

Forbes, E. (1943). *Johnny Tremain* (L. Ward, Illus.). Boston: Houghton Mifflin.

Gross, V. T. (1991). *The day it rained forever: A story of the Johnstown Flood* (R. Himler, Illus.). New York: Viking.

Hickman, J. (1978). *Zoar Blue.* New York: Macmillan.

Hooks, W. H. (1983). *Circle of fire.* New York: Atheneum.

Keith, H. (1977). *The obstinate land.* New York: Crowell.

Lowry, L. (1989). *Number the stars.* New York: Dell.

Morpurgo, M. (1991). *Waiting for Anya.* New York: Viking.

Naylor, P. H. (1991). *Shiloh.* New York: Atheneum.

Schlee, A. (1982). *Ask me no questions.* New York: Holt, Rinehart, & Winston.

Uchida, Y. (1978). *Journey home* (C. Robinson, Illus.). New York: Atheneum.

S u m m a r y

Speaking is a vital language art inasmuch as children who are adept in the use of oral language tend to become good readers and writers. Unfortunately, many teachers fail to provide children with the opportunities they need to develop such skills. Through conversations and discussion groups, children enhance their speaking skills.

The inclusion of oral language activities such as discussions, choral reading and speaking, reader's theater, storytelling, and dramatics enables children to discover and share new information, refine oral language, and develop confidence in their ability to communicate orally. Even students with language disorders and learning disabilities can successfully participate in various speaking activities.

Questions

1. How would you introduce intonation to second graders? Sixth graders?
2. How would you select a story for use as formal drama in your classroom?
3. What elements should be part of one's conversational habits?
4. What are the three aspects of intonation and why are they effective?
5. Describe the four language settings and how you would introduce third graders to each.
6. Which of your favorite picture books would be best suited to pantomime by first or second graders? Why?
7. If your fifth-grade students have had limited experiences with speaking, what speaking activity would you introduce them to first? How would you introduce it?

Activities

1. Observe children as they engage in a conversation on the playground and then in the classroom. Record usage errors and slang. How does their language differ in the two settings?
2. Find a story that would be appropriate for storytelling. Refer to focus box 6.2 to refine your storytelling techniques and then present the story to a group of children.
3. Collect poems for choral reading and speaking activities in which the entire class could participate.
4. Develop a list of children's books with social studies and/or science themes that would be appropriate for either improvisation or formal drama.
5. Develop a media presentation for your language arts methods class in which you relate a theory to practice.
6. Collect objects for a prop box.
7. Attend a storytelling festival. Note the different delivery techniques the storytellers use: gestures, stress, pitch, juncture, props, and so on.
8. Suppose that a fourth-grade student in your class has severe language problems in terms of usage. Develop a plan to assist the student on a one-to-one basis and in small group work.

For Further Reading

Christie, J. F. (1990). Dramatic play: A context for meaningful engagement. *The Reading Teacher, 43*(8), 54.

Commeyras, M. (1994). Were Janell and Neesie in the same classroom? Children's questions as the first order of reality in storybook discussions. *Language Arts, 71*(7), 517-523.

Flynn, R. M., & Carr, G. A. (1994). Exploring classroom literature through drama: A specialist and a teacher collaborate. *Language Arts, 71*(1), 38-43.

McCauley, J. K., & McCauley, D. S. (1992). Using choral reading to promote language learning for ESL students. *The Reading Teacher, 45*(7), 526-533.

Nelson, O. (1989). Storytelling: Language experience for meaning making. *The Reading Teacher, 42*(6), 386-391.

Strickland, D. S., & Morrow, L. M. (1988). Emerging readers and writers: Reading, writing, and oral language. *The Reading Teacher, 42*(3), 240-241.

Wiencek, J., & O'Flahavan, J. F. (1994). From teacher-led to peer discussions about literature: Suggestions for making the shift. *Language Arts, 71*(7), 488-498.

References

Because of the large number of children's books cited in this chapter, these titles are documented in a separate subsection below.

Berlin, J. A. (1990). The teacher as researcher: Democracy, dialogue, and power. In D. A. Daiker & J. Morenberg (Eds.), *The writing teacher as researcher* (pp. 153-166). Portsmouth, NH: Boynton/Cook.

Burgess, T. (1984). The question of English. In T. Burgess (Ed.), *Changing English: Essays for Harold Rosen.* London: Heinemann.

Christie, J. (1990). Dramatic play: A context for meaningful engagements. *The Reading Teacher, 43*(8), 542-545.

Dyson, A. H. (1981). Oral language: The rooting system for learning to write. *Language Arts, 58* (7), 776-784.

Graves, D. (1983). *Writing: Teachers and children at work.* Portsmouth, NH: Heinemann.

Gray, M. A. (1987). A frill that works: Creative dramatics in the basal reading program. *Reading Horizons, 28* (1), 5-11.

Haine, G. (1985). In the labyrinth of the image: An archetypal approach to drama in education. *Theory into Practice, 24* (3), 187-192.

Heard, G. (1989). *For the good of the earth and sun: Teaching poetry.* Portsmouth, NH: Heinemann.

Heath, S. B. (1983). Research currents: A lot of talk about nothing. *Language Arts, 60* (8), 999-1007.

Heathcote, D. (1983). Learning, knowing, and languaging in drama. *Language Arts, 60* (6), 695-701.

Klein, M. (1977). *Talk in the language arts classroom.* Urbana, IL: National Council of Teachers of English.

Loban, W. (1976). *Language development: Kindergarten through grade twelve* (Research Report No. 18). Urbana, IL: National Council of Teachers of English.

McCaslin, N. (1984). *Creative drama in the classroom.* New York: Longman.

McCauley, J. K., & McCauley, D. S. (1992). Using choral reading to promote language learning for ESL students. *The Reading Teacher, 45* (7), 526-533.

McClure, A. A. (1995). Fostering talk about poetry. In N. L. Roser & M. G. Martinez (Eds.), *Book talk and beyond.* Newark, DE: International Reading Association.

Morgan, N., & Saxon, J. (1988). Enriching language through drama. *Language Arts, 65*(1), 34-40.

Nicholson, H. H. (1992). Stories are everywhere: Geographical understanding and children's fiction at Key Stages I & II. *Reading, 26* (1), 18-20.

Rosenbloom, C. S. (1991). From *Ox-Cart Man* to *Little House in the Big Woods:* Response to literature shapes curriculum. *Language Arts, 68* (1), 52-61.

San Jose, C. (1988). Story drama in the content areas. *Language Arts, 65*(1), 26-33.

Shepard, A. (1994). From script to stage: Tips for Readers Theatre. *The Reading Teacher, 48* (2), 184-186.

Siks, G. B. (1983). *Drama with children* (2nd ed.). New York: Harper & Row.

Sloyer, S. (1983). *Reader's theater: Story dramatization in the classroom.* Urbana, IL: National Council of Teachers of English.

Smilansky, S. (1968). *The effects of sociodramatic play on disadvantaged preschool children.* New York: Wiley.

Stoodt, B. (1989). *Teaching language arts.* New York: Harper & Row.

Tiedt, I. M., Bruemmer, S., Lane, S., Stelwagon, P., Watanabe, K., & Williams, M. (1983). *Teaching writing in K-8 classrooms.* Englewood Cliffs, NJ: Prentice-Hall.

Wagner, B. J. (1988). Research currents: Does classroom drama affect the arts of language? *Language Arts, 65*(1), 46-55.

Wendelin, K. H. (1991). Students as storytellers in the classroom. *Reading Horizons, 31*(3), 181-188.

Wiencek, J., and O'Flahavan, J. F. (1994). From teacher-led to peer discussions about literature: Suggestions for making the shift. *Language Arts, 71*(7), 488–498.

Young, T. A., & Ferguson, P. M. (1995). From Anansi to Zomo: Trickster tales in the classroom. *The Reading Teacher, 48* (6), 490–503.

Children's Books

Aardema, V. (1981). *The riddle of the drum: A tale from Tizápan, Mexico.* (T. Chen, Illus.). New York: Four Winds.

Andersen, H. C. (1974). *Hans Andersen: His classic fairy tales* (E. Haugaard, Trans.; M. Hague, Illus.). New York: Doubleday.

Arkhurst, J. C. (1964). *The adventures of Spider: West African folktales.* Boston: Little, Brown.

Avi. (1990). *The true confessions of Charlotte Doyle.* New York: Orchard.

Bird, E. J. (1990). *The blizzard of 1896.* Minneapolis, MN: Carolrhoda.

Bruchac, J. (1995). *Gluskabe and the four wishes* (C. N. Shrader, Illus.). New York: Cobblehill.

Carle, E. (1971). *The very hungry caterpillar.* New York: Crowell.

Carle, E. (1990). *The very quiet cricket.* New York: Philomel.

Collier, J. L., & Collier, C. (1994). *With every drop of blood.* New York: Delacorte.

de Paola, T. (1982). *Strega Nona's magic lessons.* San Diego, CA: Harcourt Brace Jovanovich.

Fritz, J. (1980). *Where do you think you're going, Christopher Columbus?* (M. Thomes, Illus.). New York: Putnam.

Huck, C. (1989). *Princess Furball* (A. Lobel, Illus.). New York: Greenwillow.

Jackson, E. (1994). *Cinder Edna* (K. O'Malley, Illus.). New York: Lothrop, Lee, & Shepard.

Kellogg, S. (1991). *Jack and the beanstalk.* New York: Morrow.

Leedy, L. (1991). *The great trash bash.* New York: Holiday.

Lobel, A. (1970). *Frog and toad are friends.* New York: Harper & Row.

Lowry, L. (1989). *Number the stars.* Boston: Houghton Mifflin.

Martin, B., Jr., & Archambault, J. (1989). *Chicka chicka boom boom* (L. Ehlert, Illus.). New York: Simon & Schuster.

Minarik, E. H. (1978). *Little Bear.* New York: Harper & Row.

Munsch, R. N. (1980). *The paper bag princess* (M. Martchenko, Illus.). Toronto, Canada: Annick.

Numeroff, L. (1991). *If you give a moose a muffin* (F. Bond, Illus.). New York: HarperCollins.

O'Dell, S. (1980). *Sarah Bishop.* Boston: Houghton Mifflin.

Prelutsky, J. (1970). *Toucans two and other poems* (J. Stevenson, Illus.). New York: Macmillan.

Prelutsky, J. (1980). *The headless horseman rides tonight* (A. Lobel, Illus.). New York: Greenwillow.

Prelutsky, J. (1982). *The baby uggs are hatching* (J. Stevenson, Illus.). New York: Greenwillow.

Prelutsky, J. (1990). *Beneath a blue umbrella* (G. Williams, Illus.). New York: Greenwillow.

Prelutsky, J. (1990). *Something big has been here* (J. Stevenson, Illus.). New York: Greenwillow.

Raschka, C. (1993). *Yo! Yes?.* New York: Orchard.

Silverstein, S. (1974). *Where the sidewalk ends.* New York: Harper & Row.

Silverstein, S. (1981). *A light in the attic.* New York: Harper & Row.

Steig, W. (1977). *Caleb & Kate.* New York: Farrar, Straus, & Giroux.

Titherington, J. (1986). *Pumpkin, pumpkin.* New York: Greenwillow.

Viorst, J. (1981). *If I were in charge of the world and other worries: Poems for children and their parents.* New York: Atheneum.

White, E. B. (1952). *Charlotte's web.* New York: Harper & Row.

Williams, V. B. (1983). *A chair for my mother.* New York: Morrow.

Yashima, T. (1955). *Crow boy.* New York: Viking.

Listening: A Receptive Skill

© James L. Shaffer

Listening is the language skill with which we
all begin the learning process, and which we
depend on throughout life.
—Iris M. Tiedt and Sidney W. Tiedt
Contemporary English in the Elementary School

Introduction

T he classroom was silent, save for a single voice. Lupe was sitting on a stool reading the story that she had written to the class. Her classmates sat mesmerized as she described how her family came from Mexico to live with her uncle in the United States. Some children nodded understandingly when she told them about leaving her pet dog behind with her grandmother. Her classmates laughed when she read about the car breaking down in front of an auto parts store. Her story about her journey held her classmates' interest and they listened intently. Sharing time is important as it helps to build a community of listeners in the classroom (Gallas, 1992).

This was a formal listening setting, but most listening settings are informal. According to Graves (1991), there are many "literate occasions," opportunities to listen and observe. Children must be taught how to listen and observe so that they can understand, appreciate, and evaluate the information presented to them.

Listening is one of the methods by which humans attempt to make sense of the surrounding world. By allowing us to hear and interpret environmental sounds, listening serves as an aural vehicle for comprehension development. Goss (1982a) defines listening as a process that organizes what is heard and establishes those verbal units to which meaning can be applied.

Listening is a language art that actually begins prior to birth and continues to be an important, interactive process throughout life. A fetus responds to various tones of music or to its mother's voice; within a few weeks after birth, the infant reacts to the sounds of both parents and siblings, as well as the surrounding environment. The spoken language of others is converted into meaning as the months go by, and eventually the baby distinguishes among the names for self, other individuals, and objects.

Typically, listening receives much less emphasis in the classroom than do the other language arts. As Templeton (1991, p. 133) writes, "There is little question that listening is the language art least attended to—not only in school but probably in our society as well." This is true despite the fact that research clearly indicates that listening skills can and should be taught (Jacobs, 1986; Strother, 1987). One possible explanation for the neglect of instruction in this area is that teachers generally have received little or no training in how to teach listening, and they lack the self-confidence to try (Funk & Funk, 1989). Another problem is that even experts in the field cannot agree upon a single definition of listening.

Determining whether a child has actually "listened" to an aural message is difficult. The teacher's questioning of a child may result in incorrect responses due either to the child's failure to listen or to the child's misunderstanding or misinterpretation of the question itself. Likewise, a child may give a correct response based upon previous knowledge without having listened to the presented message. As a result, the teacher may believe the child understood the question when, in fact, the child did not. Research studies conducted with first through third graders found that children will often indicate that they understand a message even though it is actually incomplete or ambiguous (Ironsmith & Whitehurst, 1978). Moreover, most children within each grade level will avoid seeking additional information by questioning the speaker when their understanding is poor or weak (Cosgrove & Patterson, 1977).

Children should be taught listening strategies explicitly, with ample opportunities to put them to use so that they eventually become automatic. This is best done when the instruction causes the children to think first about sound and then move on to the higher levels of listening awareness and ability (Templeton, 1991).

The listening process itself consists of three primary steps: (1) receiving the auditory input, (2) attending to the received auditory input, and (3) interpreting and interacting with the received auditory input. The first step involves the reception of the spoken message, for hearing the message alone does not necessarily guarantee understanding. When a listener receives a spoken message, other sounds must either be ignored or removed from the foreground. This technique, sometimes referred to as masking, allows the listener to mask or block out other sounds that are present in the surrounding environment.

The second step in the listening process, attending to the auditory input, requires the listener to concentrate on what is being presented by the speaker. Attending to this spoken message is both mentally and physically exerting, as demonstrated by the measurement of an individual's pulse rate during rest and during the attending step of the listening process. Attending while listening results in a faster pulse rate.

In the third step of the listening process, interpreting and interacting with the auditory input, the listener does not simply gather and file away information; rather, the listener takes in the spoken coded information and ultimately must classify, compare, and relate it to previous knowledge. According to Aronson (1974), this third listening step involves a rapid predict-then-confirm strategy. In the event that the listener is familiar with what the speaker is talking about, predictions can be made much more easily. Thus, at this point, on the basis of any internally developed findings, the listener may challenge the validity of, and even reject, the newly gained knowledge. Therefore, listening is described as an active, not a passive, process.

After the listener has accurately received an aural message, thinking and responding can proceed beyond the communicated event itself. According to Lundsteen (1979), the listener may respond by classifying parts of the message in terms of time, space, position, degree, and so on; ranking information according to relevance or importance; making comparisons and/or contrasts; predicting; sequencing; recognizing cause-effect relationships; using critical evaluation; appreciating the qualities of drama, tone, and rhythm; and engaging in problem solving.

This chapter describes the different purposes for listening and suggests appropriate teaching methods for successfully developing children's listening abilities and strategies.

Factors in Effective Listening

Teachers must recognize the importance of listening within the classroom. At the elementary level, especially in the lower grades, academic success is primarily related to the child's listening abilities. Generally speaking, however, students hear only 50 to 60 percent of the teacher's message to them (Blankenship, 1982; Strother, 1987). Similarly, a study conducted by Weaver (1972) rated the success of requiring students to recall information that had just been presented orally by their classroom teachers. Weaver found that students in the lower grades tended to score higher overall on the recall task than did their older, more experienced counterparts. For example, first graders were able to recall the presented instructions at a rate of 90 percent and second graders at a rate of 80 percent; however, seventh and eighth graders scored 43.7 percent, and high school students scored only 28 percent. The study's results can be explained in terms of several factors. Younger children devote more attention to their teachers than do junior and senior high school students, and for kindergartners through second graders, listening is the primary means of obtaining information because they have limited reading skills. Older students are more apt to believe that they can predict what their teachers will say. In addition, emotional concerns and problems as well as outside interests and activities serve to distract older students and to reduce listening efficiency.

Children typically enter school possessing the basic, lower-level listening skills of recall and recognition. Nevertheless, a lack of concentration due to either external or internal distractions can cause a student to respond incorrectly to a lower-level question. Although it is common for teachers to ask only lower-level questions, teachers should try to help students attain higher-level listening skills by asking them higher-level questions as well.

Focus box 7.1 presents a checklist that teachers can use to evaluate both the lower- and higher-level listening skills of elementary students. This checklist can be used at all grade levels throughout the school year to monitor students as they develop proficiency in listening. Teachers can also use it as a self-check as they talk with their students.

Teachers can incorporate several other techniques in assisting students to become better listeners. Since children must attend to the speaker in order to listen effectively, a teacher can promote this behavior by creating an atmosphere that permits students to concentrate on the listening task. Interruptions should always be kept to a minimum, and any outside noise must be reduced. Teaching in a classroom adjacent to a busy street or intersection requires more changes in one's instructional practices than does teaching in an appropriate, acoustically designed and engineered facility. Direct teacher intervention for helping students become effective listeners includes the following:

Speak with clarity.

Speak directly to the students and avoid speaking when writing on the chalkboard.

Listening Skills	Length of Message		
	Sentence	Paragraph	Short Story
Recall knowledge			
Recognize knowledge			
Follow oral directions			
Comprehend/understand			
Apply knowledge			
Summarize			
Recognize cause and effect			
Problem solve/predict			
Evaluate/judge			

Listener Distractions	Present	Not Present
Background noise		
Quiet classroom		
Low volume by speaker		
Outside problems		
Length of presentation		

Comments:

Watch the students' faces to ascertain whether or not they understand what you are saying.

Begin with an overview of the material, present it in a straightforward and logical sequence, and close with a summary.

Give clear, concise instructions and avoid ambiguity.

Encourage students to ask questions.

Stress important material through repetition.

Use visual aids such as charts, models, notes on the chalkboard, and overhead transparencies.

Funk and Funk (1989) give four suggestions for developing listening skills in the elementary classroom. First, the teacher should provide a purpose for listening. Second, a classroom atmosphere that is conducive to listening should be created. Third, the teacher should provide follow-up experiences soon after the listening activity. Fourth, the teacher should include instructional techniques that promote listening. These simple guidelines can be used to teach listening throughout the school day. According to Funk and Funk, some of the best opportunities for teaching listening occur during art, music, physical education, science, and social studies.

The Teacher as Listener

Children quickly become aware of the individual listening abilities and tolerance of their teachers and respond accordingly. The teacher who eagerly awaits student contributions finds children willing to disclose their thoughts in lively, often animated discussions, which in themselves encourage creative and divergent thinking. Such a teacher uses a particular series of open-ended questions; in this way, the teacher helps students develop necessary links between the questions, which in turn foster their skills in connecting ideas and in inferring, comparing, contrasting, and evaluating ideas. The opposing instructional style finds the teacher seeking only the correct response to a closed-ended question; therefore, the teacher is less apt to be a good listener. Through the teacher's nonverbal language, including tone of voice and facial expressions, students receive the message that "the answer" is the only acceptable response.

Teachers should conduct periodic self-checks of their own listening. For example, if teachers notice that they talk to students more often than they listen to them, teachers can take steps to modify this behavior. Teachers should conduct such self-checks because they should be "model" listeners (Leverentz & Garman, 1987), conveying empathy and sincere interest to a speaking child. Paley (1986) believes that the key to becoming a model listener is curiosity. She states that "when we are curious about a child's words and our responses to those words, the child feels respected" (p. 127).

Levels of Listening

There are four levels of listening: (1) marginal or background, (2) appreciative, (3) attentive, and (4) critical or analytical. Each level, which students use on a daily basis, is summarized in focus box 7.2.

Marginal Listening

The least demanding yet most frequent type of listening is described as *marginal* or *background listening*. Marginal listening occurs, for example, when one is able to distinguish between someone's voice and the noise from a busy street. Teachers continuously use marginal or background listening to ensure that all is going well in another part of the classroom, where too much quiet or noise could signal disruptions in learning. Yet in today's electronic world, some students find that they can study more successfully with available background

In the Classroom Mini Lesson
Background Listening

*K*indergarten and first-grade students are not always aware of background noise. To acquaint them with this phenomenon, read them Charlotte Zolotow's (1980) book *If You Listen*. Afterward, have the class recall the sounds the little girl in the story heard when she listened carefully, as her mother told her to do. Next have the class listen for sounds in the classroom, and then go outside and have them listen to and identify sounds heard on the playground. What noises can the students identify without seeing what is causing the noises? Examples include a dog barking in the distance and the siren of a police car or fire engine.

Zolotow, C. (1980). *If you listen* (M. Simont, Illus.). New York: Harper & Row.

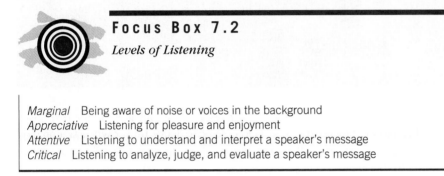

Focus Box 7.2
Levels of Listening

Marginal   Being aware of noise or voices in the background
Appreciative   Listening for pleasure and enjoyment
Attentive   Listening to understand and interpret a speaker's message
Critical   Listening to analyze, judge, and evaluate a speaker's message

noise, particularly if that noise is rock music. For such students, a quiet classroom can actually inhibit the learning process.

Appreciative Listening

Appreciative listening occurs when an individual listens to a reader, speaker, singer, or music for enjoyment. As such, it includes listening to actors in a dramatic play, a friend telling a funny story, a person describing the San Francisco earthquake and fire, a popular rock group's album, or a trite but appealing radio commercial. Whereas music classes provide students with an environment in which to learn how to appreciate various rhythms, lyrics, styles, and types of music, the development of a comparable appreciation of speaking is rarely found in the elementary classroom. However, children must witness the use of stress, pitch, and juncture by effective speakers in order to become better listeners. Likewise, they should be made aware of the tone, mood, speaker's style, and audience's influence on the listening setting. Listening to tapes of authors reading their own writings presents students with a different perspective from which to consider various works.

    To serve as effective models for speaking, teachers must develop their oral reading and storytelling expertise. In addition, they should also model

The attentive level of listening requires children to concentrate and interact with the message that is presented.

© James L. Shaffer

good listening habits for the various levels of listening. In reality, many teachers demonstrate appreciative listening quite poorly, in part because of a lack of training in this area.

Teachers tend to overlook the need for the development of appreciative listening skills, whether one is listening to the oral reading of a sentence or paragraph from a novel or to the choral reading of a short poem by students. Although most teachers stress the oral production of language, they often fail to recognize the intricacies necessary for appreciative listening within the same work. Teachers should begin to instruct kindergartners and first graders in techniques of imagery formation. For instance, teachers can assist these students in both visualizing a story's descriptive passages and orally sharing their "images" with the class. Other appreciative listening skills that teachers can help develop in younger children include identifying the rhythm of poetry as it is read, evaluating the effects of various speeds of delivery on a poem's meaning, and developing an ability to describe the tone and mood of selected pieces of writing. (These same activities could also be applied to folk songs.)

There are many benefits to appreciative listening. This level of listening allows for the sharing of quality literature with children, thereby introducing them to new concepts and experiences. When a variety of books are used, children are exposed to different literary genre that can widen their reading interests. When unfamiliar terms or unusual sentence patterns are read aloud, children are encouraged to broaden their language experiences.

In the Classroom Mini Lesson

Story Time and Story Journals

*A*ppreciative listening can be coordinated with journal writing. Since the oral sharing of books with students is an event that occurs almost daily in elementary classrooms, having students react directly to a story makes for an effective appreciative-listening activity. After selecting a book with an intriguing, fast-paced plot that is almost guaranteed to captivate and maintain a child's interest, read it to the class in a dramatic fashion. Upon completion of the story, have the students write down and illustrate their reactions to it (Farris, 1989). Although some young children may only wish to draw and others may only want to write their responses, they should be encouraged to attempt both.

An example of a story journal written after a first-grade class listened to the teacher read Mercer Mayer's (1969) *There's a Nightmare in My Closet* appears in figure 7.1. The child's journal is written in invented spelling. Here is the translated version:

My Pet Monster

My life is nice. I have a
pet you will not believe it what
it is. It is a monster. His
name is Spike. He likes
garbage. I know it is shocking
but it is not. He is my
pal. The end.

Older students tend to write more sophisticated story journal entries. Typically, these children will relate to one of the primary characters in a book by writing creative letters or descriptions from a particular character's point of view.

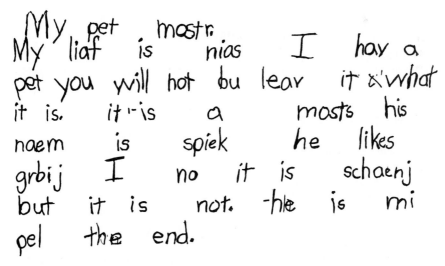

Figure 7.1
Here is a story a child wrote upon listening to a read aloud book entitled *There's a Nightmare in My Closet.*

Farris, P. J. (1989). Storytime and story journals: Linking literature with writing. *New Advocate,* 2(1), 179–185.

Mayer, M. (1969). *There's a nightmare in my closet.* New York: Dial.

Books that are appropriate for appreciative-listening story journals are listed below.

Early Childhood Level

Ballads and Folksongs

Ackerman, K. (1988). *Song and dance man* (S. Gammell, Illus.). New York: Knopf.

Allison, C. (1987). *I'll tell you a story, I'll sing you a song.* New York: Delacorte.

Growing Up

Cole, J. (1987). *Norma Jean, jumping bean.* New York: Random House.

Hoberman, M. A. (1986). *A house is a house for me.* New York: Scholastic.

Lester, H. (1994). *Three cheers for Tacky* (L. Munsinger, Illus.). Boston: Houghton Mifflin.

Russo, M. (1987). *Why do grown-ups have all the fun?* New York: Greenwillow.

Scheller, M. (1992). *My grandfather's hat* (K. Narahashi, Illus.). New York: McElderry.

Waddell, M. (1992). *Can't you sleep, Little Bear?* (B. Firth, illus.). Cambridge, MA: Candlewick.

Science

de Paola, T. (1975). *The cloud book.* New York: Holiday.

Hadithi, M. (1987). *Crafty chameleon* (A. Kennaway, Illus.). Boston: Little, Brown.

McKissack, P. (1988). *Mirandy and Brother Wind* (J. Pinkney, Illus.). New York: Knopf.

Yolen, J. (1987). *Owl moon* (J. Schoenherr, Illus.). New York: Philomel.

Social Studies

Fritz, J. (1978). *What's the big idea, Ben Franklin?* (M. Tomes, Illus.). New York: Coward-McCann.

Stevens, C. (1982). *Anna, Grandpa, and the big storm* (M. Tomes, Illus.). Boston: Houghton Mifflin.

Winter, J. (1988). *Follow the drinking gourd.* New York: Knopf.

Math

Atherlay, S. (1995). *Math in the bath* (M. Halsey, Illus.). New York: Simon & Schuster.

Jonas, A. (1995). *Splash!* New York: Greenwillow.

Pinczes, E. J. (1995). *A remainder of one* (B. MacKain, Illus.). Boston: Houghton Mifflin.

Middle Childhood Level

Ballads and Folksongs

Fox, D. (1987). *Go in and out the window: An illustrated songbook for young people.* New York: Holt, Rinehart, & Winston.

Growing Up

Avi. (1994). *The barn.* New York: Avon.

Choi, S. N. (1991). *The year of impossible goodbyes.* Boston: Houghton Mifflin.

Klein, N. (1988). *Confessions of an only child* (R. Cuffari, Illus.). New York: Knopf.

Miles, B. (1986). *Sink or swim.* New York: Knopf.

Sperry, A. (1971). *Call it courage.* New York: Macmillan.

Taylor, T. (1976). *The cay.* New York: Avon.

Science

Fields, A. (1981). *Satellites* (M. Tregenza, Illus.). New York: Franklin Watts.

Tejima. (1987). *Fox's dream.* New York: Philomel.

Williams, T. T., & Major, T. (1984). *The secret language of snow* (J. Dewey, Illus.). New York: Sierra Club/Pantheon.

Social Studies

Blos, J. W. (1979). *A gathering of days: A New England girl's journal, 1830–1832.* New York: Scribner's.

Goble, P. (1987). *Death of the iron horse.* New York: Bradbury.

Greenwood, B. (1994). *A pioneer sampler* (H. Collins, Illus.). New York: Ticknor & Fields.

Hendershot, J. (1987). *In coal country* (T. B. Allen, Illus.). New York: Knopf.

Lakin, P. (1994). *Don't forget* (T. Rand, Illus.). New York: Tambourine.

Rodanas, K. (1992). *Dragonfly's tale.* New York: Clarion.

Whelan, G. (1987). *Next spring an oriole* (P. Johnson, illus.). New York: Random House.

Math

Scieszka, J. (1995). *Math curse* (L. Smith, Illus.). New York: Viking.

Attentive Listening

The next level of listening, *attentive listening,* requires concentration and interaction on the part of the listener to ensure comprehension of the spoken message. At this level, the listener must categorize, examine, relate, question, and organize information in order to understand it and also to be able to apply it in the future. Attentive listening might involve obtaining oral directions to an unfamiliar location, watching the six o'clock news on television, getting a phone number from long distance information, or attending a lecture on water safety. Yet because a suitable strategy is required to receive a particular type of message, the listener must know a message's purpose prior to hearing it.

Once students understand the purpose for listening, they must develop a system by which to understand a spoken message thoroughly. Although it is usually impossible to recall the exact words of a message, the listener can comprehend a message by remembering its primary points. Children can be taught the attentive-listening strategies described next.

To relate a speaker's message to personal, previously gained knowledge, the listener must categorize and organize information. Prior to listening, students need to recall what they already know about the particular topic. Using familiar corresponding material as a base, students should try to correlate a speaker's points with this information. In view of the fact that one can listen at a faster rate than one can speak, time becomes available to the listener for making such correlations while at the same time attending to the message as it is delivered.

Sequencing a story's events is a common listening activity in the lower grades. In this activity, students are encouraged to visualize the major actions or scenes in their proper order. To assist students, a teacher might give each student a blank sheet of paper and direct the students to fold the sheet in half twice to make a small "book." After the students unfold the books and place them on their desks, the teacher asks the class to listen closely to and remember the four main events in a short story, which the teacher then reads aloud. After reading the story, the teacher instructs the students to illustrate the four scenes, one in each section of their books.

In the Classroom Mini Lesson
Attentive Listening

*A*fter sharing a read aloud, give each student a 3″ by 5″ colored index card with a question about the book on one side and an answer for another question on the other side. Start with one student reading the question he or she was given. The child with the card that has the answer then responds. That child then reads the question on the card he/she is holding, and so on.

In order to prepare the cards, write a question on the first index card and the answer on the next card. Set the first card aside. Then write each remaining question on a card and the answer for each on the next index card in the stack. When you reach the last card, put the answer to the last question on the first card that you set aside earlier.

This listening activity can also be used to review science concepts or a social studies chapter.

Speakers can and do provide valuable assistance for attentive listening. If a speaker prepares a listener via a cursory outline of the speaking format, the listener then has a framework for gathering information as it is delivered. This is exemplified by the speaker who announces that a lecture will contain three main highlights before identifying them. In this way, the framework or learning pegs are positioned for the listener.

InQuest, a comprehension procedure developed by Mary Shoop (1986) for use in both listening and reading, encourages students in third grade and above to mentally question an aural message while listening to it. InQuest involves the use of spontaneous drama as a means of stimulating attentive listening. Because Shoop's approach motivates students to actively monitor what they already know and do not know during listening, this form of metacognition fosters a "sensitivity to comprehension." In the InQuest procedure, the teacher reads a story, stopping at critical points. When he or she reaches one of these points, the teacher announces that a spontaneous news conference is to take place and designates one or two of the students as main characters and the remainder of the students as investigative reporters. Seeking to interpret the story's events, the investigative reporters question the main characters and then evaluate their answers. In sifting through the interview information, the investigative reporters attempt to anticipate and predict upcoming events in the story.

Students in the intermediate grades should also learn how to take notes. If students expect a message to contain three main categories, they could write an appropriate category title at the top of each of three sheets of paper or at the top of each of three columns on a single sheet. Then, while listening to the speaker's delivery, they can take brief notes in the form of phrases or single words within each category (see figure 7.2).

In the Classroom Mini Lesson
Summarizing Information

*B*oth science and social studies require students to become familiar with scientists, explorers, and their respective discoveries. One attentive-listening activity that reinforces such learning involves the use of questioning to probe for information. Because this technique utilizes the five "W" questions—who, what, when, where, and why—the activity can be successfully used with students in Grades 2 through 8.

Write the questions on an 8″ by 10″ piece of tagboard or thick cardboard and also on the chalkboard in the following order: When? Where? Who? What? Why? Because elementary students have difficulty establishing a reference point for the settings of events (both times and places), have them answer the when and where questions first; this establishes a framework for the analysis of the remaining information. Next, announce to the students that you are going to read a short paragraph and that they are to remember the information necessary to answer the five posted questions.

After dividing the class into pairs, give one pair of students the cardboard that contains the "W" questions and send them down the hallway, beyond the range of hearing the passage as it is read. Read the paragraph to the remaining students. Then have the two students in the hallway return to the room and ask the written questions of their peers. Using the information offered by their classmates, the two students are to converse and ultimately summarize the paragraph for the class. Continue with new paragraphs of information and new partners until all students have summarized a paragraph read to the remainder of the class.

The paragraph to be read may be taken directly from the students' science or social studies textbook or from any other source. The length and complexity of a paragraph should be appropriate to the students' grade level, however.

Name: Terry Smith

Famous Citizens

- Sir Walter Raleigh

- Virginia Dare - 1st white child born in U.S.

North Carolina Notes - Jeremy's oral report

History (Facts)

12th state

1st colony - Roanoke

Cherokee Indians

Southern state

1st airplane flight of Wright brothers at Kitty Hawk

Products

tar

tobaco

furniture

Figure 7.2
Terry's written notes are a summary of his classmate Jeremy's oral report on North Carolina.

In the Classroom Mini Lesson

Hunt Like an Eagle

*T*his listening activity is based upon a Native American game used to teach children hunting skills. As children played this game, the elders of the tribe watched and, based on children's performance in the game, selected those who were ready to go on a real hunt for wild game.

The role of hunter of a tribe was an honored one in that a child had to demonstrate worthiness. The elders sent out only those who were prepared to hunt because the hunter who lacked the necessary skills could become the hunted and be hurt or even killed.

Children had to learn to listen and to use their other senses as well—smell and touch. They had to think and react quickly. They had to learn to move quietly and to sit silently. The children also had to learn to observe and to develop strategies based upon what they learned in order to get their "prey."

Before this activity is begun, the class has to practice sitting silently. A hunter will have to sit for a long time before the prey comes along. In addition, the hunter needs to be constantly ready to complete the task. If the hunter is distracted by another noise, scratches his or her nose, or stretches, the deer may be alerted and dart off into the woods. The hunter then will be left with no food for dinner.

To do this activity, have the children sit on the floor cross-legged in a large circle. One child is selected to be the eagle and is blindfolded. The eagle must be honest and tell if he or she can see out the blindfold. If the eagle lies, the others playing the game will know. The elders will not choose that child to be a hunter because the child will have proven that he or she cannot be trusted.

The eagle is seated in the center of the circle with the prey (a small stuffed animal for early-childhood-level students or a keychain of keys for middle-level students). The teacher serves as the tribal elder and points to a child to be the hunter. The object is for the hunter to take the eagle's prey without being detected. The eagle catches the hunter by pointing directly at the hunter before the prey is taken away. If the hunter is caught by the eagle, the hunter goes back to the circle and a new hunter is chosen. If the hunter is successful in taking the prey and returning to the circle, that child becomes the eagle.

Critical Listening

Critical or *analytical listening* requires a listener to evaluate and judge auditory input; the listener must therefore become a reflective processor of a message. Unlike literal comprehension, which is commonly emphasized in attentive listening, reflective processing requires the development of extensive inferences, cause and effect comparisons, and evaluations and judgments of both the message and the speaker. Such involvement is much more complex than that found within the other listening levels and is more dependent on the child's higher thinking skills (Goss, 1982b).

At first glance, it might appear that adults practice critical listening more often than children do because adults make important decisions on the basis of individual analyses of oral input. Voting for a presidential candidate, buying a new car, or selecting which new movie to see depends largely on personal critical reaction to and interpretation of oral messages. However, children also use critical listening on a frequent basis. For example, when a child offers a compromise in a dispute between friends or decides to buy a toy after listening to a television advertisement, he or she is demonstrating a result of critical listening.

Because of the numerous situations and experiences that demand critical-listening skills, children must develop an ability to analyze auditory messages at an early age. Young children have been found to be easily misled and influenced by others, particularly by older individuals and commercially prepared media advertisements that prompt them to purchase (or to have their parents purchase for them) various goods or services. Research findings indicate, however, that when those problems inherent in aural messages are made more prominent and noticeable, children are better able to identify them (Pratt & Bates, 1982; Stein & Trabasso, 1982). In one study, Baker (1983) discovered that if children were told prior to their listening that the materials contained problems and, in turn, were given specific examples of those problems, then children improved in their identification of such problems overall. Thus, it is important that children be able to recognize propaganda techniques. Because there are several propaganda techniques, it is recommended that they be introduced to children a few at a time, with clear, specific examples accompanying each. Focus box 7.3 describes and provides examples of the propaganda techniques that children in the intermediate grades can be taught to recognize.

Guidelines for Developing Listening Strategies

According to Funk and Funk (1989, pp. 660–662), teachers can help students develop good listening strategies by following four steps:

1. Provide a purpose for listening: Let students know what they are to listen *for*—not just what they are to listen *to.*
2. Create an atmosphere for listening by eliminating distractions, providing interesting lead-up activities, and being flexible in arranging student seating for all listening activities.
3. Provide follow-up experiences to listening activities.
4. Use teaching strategies that promote positive listening habits in which students must listen not only to the teacher but to each other.

Brent and Anderson (1993, p. 124) believe that "the keys to meaningful listening instruction are to identify the needed skill or strategy, teach it effectively, provide supervised practice, review strategies periodically, and assist children in selecting the most appropriate strategies in a variety of situations." Brent and Anderson go on to suggest the following classroom opportunities that teachers can provide which allow students to practice effective listening:

Author's Chair. Have a student read aloud from his or her own work or a selected piece from children's literature in front of the class. The other students listen carefully and then ask the student questions about what was read.

Appeal to the elite The speaker, usually an advertiser, uses flattery to persuade the listener to do something: "Since you are obviously intelligent and money is probably no problem for you, why not take a look at this deluxe children's swing set [or European sports car or gourmet cookware or imported chocolate]." The idea behind this technique is to make listeners believe they are perceived as bright and wealthy and therefore deserve whatever the speaker is selling.

Bandwagon The speaker appeals to people's, especially children's, desire to "belong," to be part of the in-group. The aim of the speaker who says, "Everybody's wearing black sneakers this year" is to convince the listener to wear black sneakers, too.

Card stacking The speaker purposely presents only one side of an issue in an attempt to persuade listeners to share his or her specific viewpoint or opinion. Unless listeners obtain additional information on the issue, they cannot respond to the message objectively.

Glittering generality The speaker makes broad and dazzling—but unsubstantiated—claims about a product's quality or an individual's character: "Vote for John Doe because he's simply the brightest and best student you could have for class president!" The critical listener will want to know in what specific ways John Doe is the "brightest" and the "best."

Name-calling Youngsters find name-calling an easy technique to identify because it frequents both the playground and the neighborhood. As a propaganda technique, name-calling occurs when, for example, one candidate calls another candidate a name meant to be derogatory: "My opponent is nothing more than a bleeding-heart liberal."

Plain folks The plain folks technique is used most frequently by politicians in order to gain voter confidence. The speaker emphasizes that he or she is similar to the so-called common man: hardworking, apple-pie-eating, taxpaying, and quite ordinary. Former U.S. Senator Sam Ervin used this technique when he described himself as "an ol' country boy." Although he was a country boy, he also possessed a Harvard law degree obtained with honors. Likewise, former Chicago Mayor Jane Byrne would wear a fur coat in the city's annual Saint Patrick's Day parades except during election years, when she wore a less expensive cloth coat.

Rewards The inclusion of "free" prizes in boxes of cereal or offers for laundry detergent rebates can entice individuals to purchase such products. Similarly, low-interest-rate loans for cars or free merchandise for opening a long-term savings account can serve as rewards for buying large-ticket items. Yet a consumer must be wary of such gimmicks and decide whether he or she really needs or wants what must be purchased to obtain the token gift and whether that gift actually inflates the purchase price of the product.

Testimonial Having a well-known personality serve as a product spokesperson can help convince listeners that the particular item is the one to buy. If a famous athlete, film star, or musician endorses a product, fans are more likely to purchase it. Such advertisements may try to convince the listener to buy everything from articles of clothing to health insurance. Typically, the celebrity will relate to particular listeners through age similarity (for example, a retired television star advertising life insurance for the elderly) or some shared interest (for example, a professional baseball player promoting a baseball glove to sports-minded students). The listener must determine whether or not the famous individual has the qualifications to assess the product adequately before deciding to purchase it.

Transference Children and adults often confuse transference with the testimonial inasmuch as both techniques depend on famous individuals to promote products. The implication of the transfer technique is that listeners identify directly with the celebrities and their attributes. For example, a listener might believe that using the same antiperspirant that a football star is "pitching" will transform him into a big, strong, handsome athlete; likewise, the same brand of toothpaste touted by a movie superstar might be chosen by a listener because it is sure to attract the opposite sex. The fallacy, however, is that neither product will produce the desired result.

Reading Aloud to the Class. The teacher selects a variety of different materials to read to the class throughout the school year. For instance, in reading a novel to the class, the teacher may ask the students to predict what they think will happen based solely on the title of the book. Later, as they listen, students can make new predictions and validate their old ones. Students can also recall details and main events or summarize the story. In pairs, the students can take turns retelling the story.

Writing Workshop. During a writing workshop, children engage in several tasks that necessitate the use of listening skills. These include asking questions to clarify details, critiquing another student's story, and listening to other students' suggestions for improvement of a piece of writing.

Cooperative/Collaborative Groups. These group activities will not succeed without the members using good listening skills. As they begin such an activity, students need to be reminded to use encouraging and supportive comments after each group member shares information.

Reader's Theater. In reader's theater, a story or short passage from a book is converted into a script for reading aloud. Portions may be read in unison while other parts may be read individually. This requires attentive listening by all of the students.

Retelling. Students who read different books about the same topic, such as the westward movement, Native Americans, or World War II, may retell the story in small groups, thereby sharing the information they gleaned.

Brent and Anderson (1993) stress the importance of integrating listening throughout the school day and encourage the application of listening strategies in meaningful rather than isolated situations.

Instructional Approaches

The process of listening is somewhat similar to that of reading in terms of the importance of literal and inferential comprehension. Critical thinking plays a major role in both critical listening and critical reading. A study by Pearson and Fielding (1982) suggests that the instruction of children in certain reading comprehension skills will aid listening comprehension in the areas of inference and prediction formation.

Reading to young students is a common occurrence in most schools. Some teachers find it useful as a relief activity when students become distracted or "fidgety" and need a change of pace. Typically, upper-grade elementary teachers are hesitant to pursue this means with older and more sophisticated students. Yet a research study by Mendoza (1985) indicated that 74 percent of all surveyed students in the intermediate grades admitted that they enjoyed being read to by their teachers. A study of high school students by Bruckerhoff (1977) found that such reading activities at the elementary school level fostered positive attitudes toward reading. On this same line,

In the Classroom Mini Lesson

Using Nonfiction Books for Read-Alouds

Teachers reading aloud to children has been found to increase student achievement. While most teachers rely upon fantasy and realistic fiction, including historical fiction, increasingly teachers are selecting nonfiction books to share during classroom read-alouds. According to Moss (1995, p. 123), "Exposure to nonfiction read-alouds has the ever-widening effect of a pebble thrown into a pond." She offers five reasons for using nonfiction books as read-alouds. Moss also gives several suggestions for selecting and incorporating nonfiction into classroom read alouds. These are shared below.

Reasons for Reading Nonfiction to Elementary and Middle School Students (Moss, 1995, pp. 122–123)

1. Nonfiction read-alouds allow children to experience the magic of the real world.
2. Nonfiction read-alouds sensitize children to the patterns of exposition.
3. Nonfiction read-alouds provide excellent tie-ins to various curricular areas.
4. Nonfiction read-alouds can promote personal growth and move children to social response.
5. Most importantly, reading nonfiction aloud whets children's appetites for information, thus leading to silent, independent reading of this genre.

Moss (1995) suggests that in selecting a quality nonfiction book for a read-aloud, teachers need to "consider the five A's":

1. the authority of the author;
2. the accuracy of the text content;
3. the appropriateness of the book for children;
4. the literary artistry; and
5. the appearance of the book" (p. 123).

Moss, B. (1995). Using children's nonfiction tradebooks as read-alouds. *Language Arts, 72(2)*, pp. 122–126.

Boodt (1984) found that enhanced listening skills positively enhanced the reading performance of intermediate-grade remedial students. Frick (1986) believes that motivational levels are heightened when one reads to upper-grade students. She emphasizes that the teacher's personal interest and enthusiasm for reading are shared through reading aloud and these positive feelings are conveyed to student listeners. Within such an atmosphere, children want to respond to the orally presented material and, ultimately, to read it for themselves.

There have been numerous studies of children who have listened to an oral reading of a text while simultaneously reading the text themselves. Indeed, this is the way in which a large portion of the population learns to read: following along as a young child while being read to by a parent or sibling.

Good Nonfiction Books for Read-Alouds

Burleigh, R. (1991). *Flight: The journey of Charles Lindbergh* (M. Wimmer, Illus.). New York: Philomel. (1–8)
  Charles Lindbergh's preparation for and actual solo flight across the Atlantic Ocean are described as are his feelings of fright and loneliness.

Cone, M. (1992). *Come back, salmon: How a group of dedicated kids adopted Pigeon Creek and brought it back to life.* New York: Sierra Club. (2–5)
  This book has an ecological theme that will encourage students to help preserve our natural resources.

Cummings, P. (1992). *Talking with artists.* New York: Bradbury. (3–8)
  This book presents children with insights into what it is like to be an artist as provided by several different artists themselves.

Fleischman, P. (1993). *Bull Run.* New York: HarperCollins. (4–8)
  From a firsthand viewpoint, the battle of Bull Run is described. Good details and descriptions are provided.

Freedman, R. (1987). *Lincoln: A photobiography.* New York: Clarion. (3–8)
  This book won the Newbery Award. Freedman has the knack of blending historical facts with poignant photos. A teacher could use almost any of his books for nonfiction read-alouds.

Hamilton, V. (1993). *Many thousand gone: African Americans from slavery to freedom.* New York: Knopf. (3–8)
  Virginia Hamilton describes the lives of numerous African Americans, some famous, some forgotten.

Lightfoot, D. J. (1992). *Trail fever: The life of a Texas cowboy* (J. Bobbish, Illus.). (3–6)
  This book vividly describes the daily life of a cowboy during the height of the great cattle drives in the 1880s.

Murphy, J. (1995). *The Great Fire.* New York: Scholastic. (4–8)
  The 1871 Chicago fire is described based on accounts from the O'Leary family, in whose barn the fire started, and James Hildreth, a former politician who saved Chicago by blowing up parts of the city, thus preventing the fire from spreading from one set of buildings to another. Also depicted is Julia Lemo, a widow who saved her five children and her elderly parents.

Walker, S. (1994). *Volcanos!* St. Paul, MN: Carolrhoda. (2–6)
  This book is just one in a series of science books that accurately describe natural phenomena.

Walker, S. (1996). *Earthquakes!* St. Paul, MN: Carolrhoda (2–6)
  This book describes earthquakes including the recent ones in Los Angeles and San Francisco.

Such a process aids emergent literacy. In fact, if when driving in a car, a parent reads the name of a discount store aloud or repeats the message on a billboard to a child, soon the young passenger will be able to connect the aural input with the visual clues. Voila! The child is reading.

An informal study by Chomsky (1976) centering around third-grade students with reading difficulties led her to conclude that if children read along concurrently as a work is being read aloud by an adult, major improvements occur in the children's reading skills. Students in Chomsky's study were actually able to memorize picture books through repeated listening-while-reading sessions. Janiak (1983) suggests that students with reading problems engage in class choral readings, with the teacher serving as leader. Unfortunately, most current studies describe reading-while-listening activities that involve the use

Focus Box 7.4

Suggestions for a Directed Listening Activity

1. Select a text that has a clear plot and a logical, straightforward sequence.
2. Share the purpose for listening with the students.
3. Give suggestions that will aid comprehension of the material. For example, have students relate the material to previous knowledge, noting major details and the like.
4. Present the material without distractions.
5. Have students follow up their listening by sharing their understanding of the material with the class. (This also provides closure to the activity.)

of recorded readings, thereby fixing the reading rate and ignoring the children's needs to read at faster or slower rates. As might be expected, such studies have been inconclusive in terms of the value of simultaneous reading and listening (McMahon, 1983).

In addition to the approaches of reading to students and the reading-while-listening activities, two other strategies concerned with listening instruction have been developed in recent years: the directed listening activity (DLA) and the directed listening-thinking activity (DL–TA). Both the DLA and DL–TA are structured techniques used in the presentation of listening materials. The DLA is appropriate for use with individuals, small groups, or an entire class, while the DL–TA is best suited for use with groups of six to eight students.

Directed Listening Activity

The *directed listening activity* follows the traditional format of basal reader lessons; however, rather than reading, a student listens to the text as it is read. The student is required to (1) prelisten, (2) listen, and (3) follow up (Cunningham, Cunningham, & Arthur, 1981). Before the actual listening event, the student is provided with or, in some instances, must determine the purpose, establish goals, and select an appropriate listening skill. Because the DLA can be used to focus on the development of specific skills, such as determining the main idea, summarizing, understanding new vocabulary through denotation or connotation, categorizing, sequencing, evaluating, and so on, it is useful in assisting lower-achieving students and those with learning disabilities as well as children for whom English is a second language.

Teachers generally fail to delineate clearly the reasons for listening before they give students a listening assignment. Without such a base, students are unable to choose a strategic plan in accordance with the listening task. Lacking the opportunity to develop a variety of listening strategies, children will develop only one: recall of all the aural input. Obviously, such a tactic is not only ineffective and inefficient but frustrating to students. Teacher direction prior to any listening activity greatly alleviates undue tension and fosters sharpened listening skills.

A DLA permits the teacher as well as the students to focus on one or two specific listening skills at a time: recalling specific details, identifying the main idea, sequencing the events, identifying cause and effect, interpreting, synthesizing, or evaluating. In addition, vocabulary enhancement can be taught through use of the DLA, which in itself can evaluate whether students comprehend the denotative meanings of words as well as their more abstract connotative meanings.

Once goals have been established, a listener is better able to progress through the second phase of the DLA: organizing and classifying information and forming inferences about the content of a message. Finally, in the follow-up stage, the listener reacts to the aural message. Such retrospection fosters critical thinking: the ability to critique, evaluate, and judge the message.

One example of a DLA is an activity in which a teacher tells the students that they will listen to three fables and subsequently match each fable with its corresponding moral. As instructed, the students are to listen to each fable and attempt to grasp its main idea. The actual association of each fable with its correct moral constitutes the follow-up. The following "In the Classroom Mini Lesson" activity represents a DLA in which students cooperatively participate in a listening-storytelling activity.

Directed Listening-Thinking Activity

As mentioned earlier, a good listener is able to anticipate portions of an upcoming message. The same is true for the good reader who can predict what is to come next in the text. The *directed listening-thinking activity* (DL–TA) depends on children's abilities to be active, critical listeners, participants who relate to prior knowledge and experiences (Stauffer, 1975).

During a DL–TA, the teacher reads a portion of a story and then stops at a critical point in the action. At this time, the students make predictions concerning upcoming events on the basis of information obtained through listening as well as that acquired through personal knowledge and experience. Most stories contain clues that provide listeners or readers with insights as to potential outcomes. When children gain experience in recognizing and interpreting these clues, they become aware of subtleties they might otherwise miss or ignore when participating in a DLA. After the students have shared all of their predictions with each other, the teacher continues to read the text until he or she reaches another important point in the story's plot. Any students who now feel their earlier predictions were incorrect must formulate new hypotheses based on the additional information they have just been given. The variety of experiential backgrounds present in any given classroom may result in varying predictions. Then the students must defend and justify their anticipatory statements. The sharing of clues or insights gained through listening to the story can aid students in this activity.

This listening-speaking activity is appropriate for students in Grades 2 through 8. Divide the students into groups of six and give each group member one-sixth of a paper circle that is 8 inches in diameter. Next, inform the students that they are to listen carefully to a folktale as it is read aloud because each group of students must determine the six main events of the folktale. Once a group has identified the six events, have each group member illustrate one of the events on his or her sixth of the circle. (Note: The number of students per group along with the corresponding number of events may be changed, depending on class size or number of significant events in a particular folktale.)

When a group has completed its illustrations, each member describes his or her illustration of one event. Then the events are put in sequence and the story is retold. Each group's final product becomes a completed circle of six pie-shaped illustrations that tell the story in clockwise order, starting at the twelve o'clock position. When glued to bright-colored construction paper, the completed circles make an effective bulletin board display.

This activity can be extended into the writing arena by having each student write the first draft of a story and then illustrate each event in the story. By drawing the various scenes and placing them in a desired sequence, students can modify and refine a story before they begin the final writing.

Following are some suggested folktales for cooperative attentive listening:

Brothers Grimm. (1978). *The bearskinner* (F. Hoffman, Illus.). New York: Atheneum.
Brothers Grimm. (1978). *The fisherman and his wife* (E. Shub. Trans.; M. Laimgruber, Illus.). New York: Greenwillow.
Farris, P. J. (1996). *Young Mouse and Elephant: An East African Folktale* (V. Gorbachev, Illus.). Boston: Houghton Mifflin.
Galdone, P. (1968). *The horse, the fox, and the lion.* New York: Clarion.
Galdone, P. (1982). *What's in Fox's sack? An old English tale.* New York: Clarion.
Kellogg, S. (1991). *Jack and the beanstalk.* New York: Morrow.

Figure 7.3 depicts the story of *Young Mouse and Elephant: An East African Folktale* as drawn by a group of 6 third graders. The story begins as Young Mouse brags that he is the strongest animal. His grandfather then tells him that Elephant is the strongest animal. Young Mouse goes off to seek out Elephant and the adventure and fun begin.

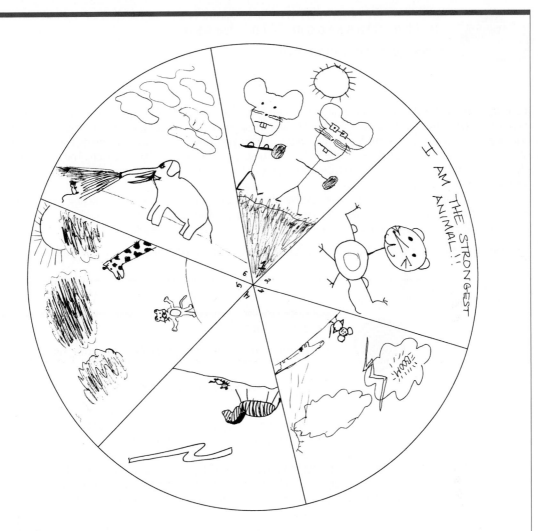

Figure 7.3
The product of a Directed Listening Activity (DLA) done by a group of six third graders after listening to *Young Mouse and Elephant: An East African Folktale.*

In the Classroom Mini Lesson

Listening in the Content Areas

Children need to be able to recognize links between history and science. To help them do this, the teacher may read Alice Fleming's (1988) *The King of Prussia and a Peanut Butter Sandwich* to students in second or third grade. Using the DL–TA approach, the teacher encourages the students to make predictions about the title of the book, namely, how the King of Prussia is connected to a peanut butter sandwich. The book tells the story of the Mennonites who were forced to leave Prussia and eventually settled in Kansas, where they introduced winter wheat from which bread is made.

After the DL–TA has concluded, the teacher places students in small groups, instructing each group to develop a story about a similar link between history and science. The teacher may provide hints as to possible topics and also give some direction as to where students can find appropriate information.

Fleming, A. (1988). *The King of Prussia and a peanut butter sandwich* (R. Himler, Illus.). New York: Scribner's.

Focus Box 7.5

Suggestions for a Directed Listening-Thinking Activity

1. Divide the class into groups of six to ten students to ensure good discussion interaction. In groups of this size, all or nearly all of the students will be able to share their predictions about the story they will hear.
2. Select a story with a clear plot and clearly delineated scenes.
3. Plan to make between two and five stops or pauses as you read the story, each immediately before you reach a critical point in the action of the story.
4. At each stop, have students summarize what has already taken place and then predict what is to occur next.
5. Accept all predictions without judgment; that is, do not classify the predictions as either right or wrong. Instead, encourage the children to defend and explain their predictions using their previously gained knowledge and experiential backgrounds.
6. Read the next portion of the story and review the predictions made earlier. Have the students confirm or deny their previously made predictions before they anticipate forthcoming events.
7. Encourage all children to join in the discussion; however, do not let the discussion become removed from the story or otherwise prolonged to the point where it diminishes the activity's stimulating nature.

S u m m a r y

Listening is an interactive process in which the listener attempts to relate previously gained knowledge to the auditory message received from the speaker. In doing this, the listener classifies, organizes, sequences, evaluates, challenges, and accepts or rejects the speaker's message.

The purposes for listening differ from situation to situation. The four levels of listening are marginal, appreciative, attentive, and critical. Marginal listening occurs when one is aware of the presence or absence of background noise, such as music piped into an elevator. Appreciative listening is the act of enjoying auditory input, whether it be music, a lecture, or a poetry reading. Attentive listening occurs when the goal is to comprehend and understand the auditory message. In critical listening, the listener attempts to comprehend the message and also to evaluate it.

The directed listening activity (DLA) and the directed listening-thinking activity (DL-TA) are methods teachers can use to help children develop their listening abilities. The DLA can be used with a single student or an entire class. The DL-TA is best suited for small groups of students.

The DLA involves prelistening, listening, and follow up. A purpose for listening is established before the activity begins. Students recall their previous knowledge about the topic and, in some cases, share that knowledge with other members of the group prior to the listening task. After the students have listened, closure is brought to the activity with a follow-up measure, such as a discussion or task based on the listening activity.

The DL-TA is designed to stimulate the use of higher-level thinking skills and to encourage divergent thinking. The teacher reads a story, stopping at pivotal points throughout. The students review what has occurred up to each point and make predictions based on clues from the story and their own experiential background as to what will occur next in the story.

For younger children, listening may be the most important language art in the learning process. As they grow older, listening seemingly diminishes in importance in the classroom. However, teachers at all grade levels must ensure that all students develop lower- and higher-level listening skills to their fullest.

Questions

1. Consider the three primary steps of the listening process in terms of the following children: (a) a fourth grader with a slight hearing loss, (b) a first grader who is learning English as a second language, and (c) a sixth grader who has recently learned that his parents are planning to divorce. How are those situations alike and how do they differ?
2. What elements are important in the teaching of critical listening?
3. How can outside factors interfere with a child's listening potential?
4. What should a teacher do to reduce distractions in the classroom and thereby improve students' listening ability?
5. Compare and contrast the four levels of listening and the role each plays in the primary grades and in the intermediate grades.

Activities

1. Observe a first-grade class and a sixth-grade class. Note the listening differences between the students in the two grades.
2. Appreciative listening receives little attention in most classrooms. Design a lesson that incorporates appreciative listening into the teaching of a subject other than language arts.
3. Record several political campaign commercials and have intermediate-grade students identify the propaganda technique(s) used in each.

4. For one entire day, note your own personal strengths and weaknesses as a listener.
5. Develop a directed-listening activity and a directed thinking-listening activity for the grade level of your choice.
6. Find five different listening activities in various professional journals (*Instructor, Learning, The Reading Teacher,* and so on). Identify which activities are most appropriate for the directed listening activity and for the directed thinking-listening activity.

For Further Reading

Brent, R., & Anderson, P. (1993). Developing children's classroom listening strategies. *The Reading Teacher, 47* (2), 122-126.

Gallas, K. (1992). When the children take the chair: A study of sharing time in a primary classroom. *Language Arts, 69* (3), 172-182.

Mandlebaum, L. H., & Wilson, R. (1989). Teaching listening skills in the special education classroom. *Academic Therapy, 24* (4), 449-459.

Moss, B. (1995). Using children's nonfiction tradebooks as read-alouds. *Language Arts, 72* (2), 122-126.

References

Aronson, D. (1974). Stimulus factors and listening strategies in auditory memory: A theoretical analysis. *Cognitive Psychology, 6* (1), 108-132.

Baker, L. (1983). *Children's effective use of multiple standards for evaluating their comprehension.* Unpublished manuscript, University of Maryland, College Park.

Blankenship, T. (1982). Is anyone listening? *Science Teacher, 49* (9), 40-41.

Boodt, G. (1984). Critical listeners become critical readers in reading class. *The Reading Teacher, 37* (4), 390-394.

Brent, R., & Anderson, P. (1993). Developing children's classroom listening strategies. *The Reading Teacher, 47* (2), 122-126.

Bruckerhoff, C. (1977). What do students say about reading instruction? *Clearing House, 51* (3), 104-107.

Chomsky, C. (1976). After decoding, what? *Language Arts, 53* (3), 288-296, 314.

Cosgrove, J. M., & Patterson, C. J. (1977). Plans and development of listener skills. *Developmental Psychology, 13* (5), 557-564.

Cunningham, J. W., Cunningham, P. M., & Arthur, S. V. (1981). *Middle and secondary school reading.* New York: Longman.

Frick, H. A. (1986). The value of sharing stories orally with middle school students. *Journal of Reading, 29* (4), 300-303.

Funk, H. D., & Funk, G. D. (1989). Guidelines for developing listening skills. *The Reading Teacher, 42* (9), 660-663.

Gallas, K. (1992). When the children take the chair: A study of sharing time in a primary classroom. *Language Arts, 69* (3), 172-182.

Goss, B. (1982a). Listening as information processing. *Communication Quarterly, 30* (4), 304-307.

Goss, B. (1982b). *Processing communication.* Belmont, CA: Wadsworth.

Graves, D. (1991). *Discover your own literacy.* Portsmouth, NH: Heinemann.

Ironsmith, M., & Whitehurst, G. J. (1978). The development of listener abilities in communication: How children deal with ambiguity. *Child Development, 49* (2), 348-352.

Jacobs, L. B. (1986). Listening—A skill we can teach. *Early years, 17* (3), 109-110.

Janiak, R. (1983). Listening/reading: An effective learning combination. *Academic Therapy, 19* (2), 205-211.

Leverentz, F., & Garman, D. (1987). What was that you said? *Instructor, 96* (8), 66-70.

Lundsteen, S. W. (1979). *Listening: Its impact at all levels on reading and the other language arts.* Urbana, IL: National Council of Teachers of English.

McMahon, M. (1983). Development of reading-while-listening skills in the primary grades. *Reading Research Quarterly, 19* (1), 38-52.

Mendoza, A. (1985). Reading to children: Their preferences. *The Reading Teacher, 38* (6), 522-527.

Moss, B. (1995). Using children's nonficton tradebooks as read-alouds. *Language Arts, 72* (2), 122-126.

Paley, V. G. (1986). On listening to what children say. *Harvard Educational Review, 56* (2), 122-131.

Pearson, P. D., & Fielding, L. (1982). Research update: Listening comprehension. *Language Arts, 59* (6), 617-629.

Pratt, M. W., & Bates, K. R. (1982). Young editors: Preschool children's evaluation and production of ambiguous messages. *Developmental Psychology, 18* (1), 30-42.

Shoop, M. (1986). InQuest: A listening and reading comprehension strategy. *The Reading Teacher, 39* (7), 670-674.

Stauffer, R. (1975). *Directing the reading-thinking process.* New York: Harper & Row.

Stein, N. L., & Trabasso, T. (1982). What's in a story? Critical issues in comprehension and instruction. In R. Glaser (Ed.), *Advances in instructional psychology* (Vol. 2). Hillsdale, NJ: Erlbaum.

Strother, D. B. (1987). Practical applications of research on listening. *Phi Delta Kappan, 68* (8), 625-628.

Templeton, S. (1991). *Teaching the integrated language arts.* Boston: Houghton Mifflin.

Weaver, C. H. (1972). *Human listening: Process and behavior.* Indianapolis: IN: Bobbs-Merrill.

Writing: A Multidimensional Process

© James L. Shaffer

The teaching of writing demands the control
of two crafts, teaching and writing.
—**Donald Graves**
Writing: Teachers & Children at Work

Introduction

*O*f all the language arts, writing is the most complex for children to learn and the most difficult for teachers to teach. As Newman (1985, p. 17) states, "Writing develops in many directions at once; it develops continually, sometimes inconspicuously, sometimes in dramatic spurts." Not only must the writer have an idea about a chosen subject, but the writing must be organized, presented with clarity, written legibly, contain correct spellings, and be free of grammatical errors. In addition, the writer must consider the readers, or audience, who will read the piece, including their interpretations and any biases that they may have.

While the student experiments with various writing experiences and techniques, the teacher must constantly evaluate student progress in the area of writing knowledge. Rather than demanding performance and ultimately confining both the writer and product, a teacher must set the classroom tone for writing. In doing so, the teacher must stress the importance of the writing process and the resulting satisfaction of sharing personal writings with peers.

But many feelings are evoked as one writes. Teachers must be aware of the hills and valleys of writing. Calkins and Harwayne (1991, p. 99) put it this way:

> Magical writing is contagious. . . . But good writing classrooms are not filled with success stories alone; they are also filled with heartache and struggle, with bravado and jealousy, with students who think they have nothing to say and with students who spend more time on their margins and handwriting than on the content of their writing.

Writing offers children ways to develop social awareness. Teachers should be "rewarded for recognizing moments when children share differing views and values with their peers through writing" (Dyson, 1994, p. 1). For young children, the classroom writing climate should be one of enthusiasm and acceptance, where correct language use and precision (correct spelling, punctuation, and grammar) take second place to reflection and expression (Walley, 1991).

Until recently, teachers taught writing as a type of command performance to be developed by students: A topic was assigned, and students wrote the corresponding stories or reports, made revisions, and turned in the final product for teacher grading of content and mechanics. By motivating, cajoling, bribing, pushing, and in some instances, threatening, teachers "taught" writing to their students. Yet under such stressful conditions, children often became apathetic toward writing; the drudgery of producing a story was second only to the painful humiliation of red notation marks used to indicate mistake after mistake, failure after failure. Macrorie (1968, p. 89) proclaimed that one of the reasons for students' lack of skills and disinterest in writing was that teachers were negatively saying, " 'Wrong! wrong! wrong' when they should have been saying, 'Right, good! Keep going!' even if they said it about only one word or one sentence in a paper."

The emphasis has shifted from product-oriented writing assignments in which little or no prior instruction was provided to process-oriented writing in which students are taught how to write. Writing is recursive and cyclical, with writers moving back and forth through a series of stages that generally include prewriting, drafting, revising, and editing (Tompkins & Hoskisson, 1994). As writers progress through a series of drafts, ideas are collected, discarded, and refined. Rather than depending upon the teacher for feedback, both positive and negative, students learn to take responsibility for their own writing (Cambourne & Turbill, 1990; Tompkins & Friend, 1988).

Initial Attempts at Writing

In a literate society, children make conscious strides toward successful reading and writing relatively early in life. Preschool-age children eagerly maneuver their pens and pencils in order to "write" on walls, magazines, tables, and other objects. Such creative marks reveal the youngsters' recognition that jottings and scrollings serve as symbols of meaning. Through these markings, a child proclaims, "Here I am world. I have something worth sharing."

Scribbling is the child's initial experimentation with writing. As the child begins to explore, some recognizable forms emerge: lines, circles, and crosses (Clay, 1987). Such shapes are eventually combined to represent familiar, tangible objects and people within the child's life: the family dog, siblings, parents, home, and so on. Yet children do learn quickly that drawing is distinguishable from writing; drawing conveys meaning through pictures, whereas writing conveys meaning through a combination of representative symbols and is therefore more adultlike in nature. Letters of the alphabet and other symbols come to represent complete words for youngsters and will often accompany the drawings of 2- and 3-year-olds. According to Harste, Woodward, and Burke (1984), when 3-year-old children are given a pen, about 75 percent of them will use the implement for writing or scribbling, while presentation of a crayon is recognized by the same age-group as a tool for drawing.

Among the first to conduct research concerning young children's early encounters with writing was Marie Clay (1975). She demonstrated that children's early writings precede any formal instruction in either reading or writing. Similarly, in a study designed to examine children's acquisition of speech sounds, Read (1971) described the key young children use to understand spelling. He discovered that young children "invented" the spelling of words, with the spellings becoming progressively more rule based and predictable.

According to Teale (1986), children as young as 2 or 3 years of age have "specific ideas about what written language is, and how the processes of reading and writing work." Indeed, some language arts authorities propose that reading and writing require either identical or analogous cognitive processes, knowledge, skills, and strategies (Aulls, 1985; Kucer, 1985; Laminack, 1990; Tierney &

Focus Box 8.1

Skills Involved in the Writing Process

1. Recollection of experiences—vicarious and real
2. Knowledge of words, sentences, paragraphs, etc.
3. Familiarity with literature of varying genres/reading and discussing skills
4. Questioning skills/research skills
5. Dictionary skills
6. Manuscript skills
7. Spelling skills

Pearson, 1983). Because reading and writing develop concurrently and are so interrelated, both should be taught in the early grades. Graves (1983) believes that teachers should provide daily writing opportunities for children as early as the first grade. Calkins (1995) extends this theory in recommending that writing be undertaken daily for one hour. However, in most elementary classrooms, 40 to 45 minutes devoted to writing each day is more realistic.

If children are going to learn writing methods, they must actively participate in writing tasks that hone their writing skills. Personal letters, thank-you notes, journals, poetry, and stories serve as appropriate subjects for classroom assignments because they allow children to practice and develop their writing techniques. Simply put, children learn to write by writing.

The Writing Process

During the past 20 years, researchers have refocused their attention on the writing process itself rather than on the writing product. The overall result has been the discovery of the writing process as an event, not an act. Writing is a process that takes place over time and which requires substantial blocks of uninterrupted time. The role of writing should be recognized as both functional and self-educative (Harste et al, 1984).

Research findings indicate that the writing process used by the professional writer is quite similar to the writing process used by the novice 6-year-old author (Murray, 1980). This four-step or four-stage process includes the sequence of prewriting, writing, rewriting, and publishing. Each of these steps is described below.

Prewriting

Prewriting includes collecting thoughts and information, experimenting with new ideas, and eventually adopting an appropriate course or map that outlines the route to be followed in a piece of writing. Murray (1980) refers to prewriting as "rehearsal." As such, it is typically short, lasting between 2 and 5 minutes (Hillocks, 1986).

As a readiness stage, prewriting involves both preparation and reflection. Connections are made through the linkage of ideas, thoughts, and newly discovered knowledge. Classification, association, analysis, and evaluation are important processes for this opening stage and further foster divergent thinking, questioning, and probing. Brainstorming, clustering, interviewing, listing, and mapping are related behaviors that assist children in discussing their ideas with each other. Smith (1982, p. 12) notes, "We do not think and then write, at least not without putting an unnecessary handicap on ourselves. We find out what we think when we write, and in the process put thinking to work—and increase its possibilities." Similarly, Abel, Hauwiller, and Vandeventer (1989) describe writing as a tool of thought, necessary for developing ideas and promoting thinking.

Motivation and stimulation are important components of the prewriting stage because it is much easier to write if one is excited about the task. Such enthusiasm is most likely to occur when the writer is permitted to undertake subjects that he or she views as relevant or even personal. The research of Donald Graves (1983) further suggests that teachers should devote more attention to the individual interests and concerns of their students, for any successful attempts at writing will more often than not revolve around those interests and concerns. Gahn (1989) asserts that what is taught in the classroom should be linked with the "real" world if writing is to be used as a tool in children's developing and retaining knowledge.

Prewriting also focuses on editing to some extent because the writer consciously adopts and rejects ideas by weighing the value of each against its negative aspects. Research indicates that by the time the prewriting stage is completed, most of the elements that the writer will include in the piece are present (Emig, 1971).

During this rehearsal or "warm-up" stage, teachers rely on activities that provide background experiences: field trips, hands-on science experiments, films, guest speakers, and so forth. In addition, teachers may focus on common personal experiences, such as a favorite tangible object, a project each student designed and completed without assistance, or a humorous incident.

Writing

The second step or stage of the writing process is *writing,* actually composing the piece. Within this stage, the writer is primarily concerned with content, while mechanics and spelling are a second priority. This writing, or drafting, is accomplished with a distinct purpose in mind and for a specified audience.

As the writer transforms thoughts and ideas into sentences, some editing automatically takes place; words, sentences, and ideas are discarded or modified. Indeed, the organization of the entire piece of writing may be altered if the writer elects to relocate whole paragraphs.

Rewriting

Rewriting is commonly referred to as editing and revising. Generally, this is the step or stage most dreaded by teachers and students, for now the piece must be polished; the writer must reread and evaluate the work in terms of both content and the conventions of language.

Focus Box 8.2

Steps in the Writing Process

1. *Prewriting* Generating and connecting ideas by means of brainstorming
2. *Writing* Developing an initial draft by putting collected thoughts on paper
3. *Rewriting* Evaluating and editing both the content and mechanics of the piece
4. *Publishing* Sharing the completed piece with others, allowing them to appreciate the work and to expand their own knowledge base.

Rewriting requires the writer to move from the role of author to that of reader. The writer therefore begins to evaluate the piece in terms of communication of the main idea, number of examples, clarity of descriptions, repetition of ideas, attractiveness of the title, length of sentences, paragraph division, and ease of reading. While the author should clean up the mechanics of grammar and spelling before sharing the finished product with the teacher, the teacher should not place too much emphasis on spelling and grammar at the expense of content (Abel & Abel, 1988).

After the writer has objectively evaluated the piece, he or she must make several decisions regarding content. The writer must consider possible adjustments in the organization of the material, the clarification of meanings, and the expansion of general ideas. Similarly, original "lead in" sentences and the conclusion may need to be reworked to make them stronger and, ultimately, more attractive to readers. At this juncture, the writer must also analyze and correct punctuation, spelling, and usage errors.

Although rewriting may occur without assistance or feedback from others, a writer may exchange drafts with a classmate or writing partner. Along the same line, writers may share and discuss their papers within small groups. When the writing is a "work in progress," that is, actively being reviewed, the pursuit of the opinions and responses of others can help the author further refine the writing.

Publishing

Although frequently overlooked by the classroom teacher, *publishing* is the final step or stage of the writing process and involves sharing a completed piece of writing with an audience, typically one's classmates. Indeed, a variety of established publishing forms exist: reading the piece aloud to a small group or the entire class; participating in individually prepared books, class books, a class literary newspaper, or a bulletin board display; recording the piece on a cassette; and so on.

Graves and Hansen (1983) believe that a special place for the sharing of writing—the "Author's Chair"—should be designated within the classroom.

I was at the beach. I was digging in the sand. Then I saw an egg. I took it home. Then it happened! It hatched! It was a dinosaur! I did not know what kind

by Devin

of dinosaur it was. I took it to the lab. And it was a baby Ankylosaurus! I took it to school one day. The kids did not like it! My Mom set him free! So

I lived a miserable life!

This "Author's Chair" serves as a formal place where a writer sits and reads a personally chosen selection to the class. The selection may be the writer's own work or that of a professional author. Once the writer has completed the reading, the listeners can react to the piece. Initial reactions *must* be positive and accepting. After this courtesy, members of the audience may ask the author more challenging questions concerning the piece.

In upper elementary and middle school classrooms, Hansen (1992) suggests that children both support and challenge, but not confront, their classmates. By doing so, the children learn about themselves and their writing as well as become better judges of their own and others' work.

Writing Considerations: Audience and Voice

Writing revolves around more than content and the conventions of language (punctuation, spelling, and usage). The writer must also be able to organize and describe ideas in such a way as to ensure clarity and the understanding of a message. In view of this, the writer must consider audience and voice.

Audience refers to those who will read (or listen to) the piece. Direct awareness of the readers' degree of knowledge and types of personal experiences can aid the writer in choosing appropriate descriptions.

Voice refers to how a piece of writing is presented, how a story is told. For example, does it reflect the writer's own experiences, views, and interests, or does it objectively describe how to do something? Voice for young children is generally expressive within written works because youngsters attempt to write in the same bouncy, rambling way in which they tell a story. In the following example of use of the expressive voice, Stacie relates a visit to a friend's house:

> Yestrday I went to Susies house and we playd
> with her new doll. She naemd it Mande but
> it looks more like a Tifene.

We now take an in-depth look at audience and voice in terms of elementary school students and their writing.

Audience

Graves (1985, p. 36) notes that "writing makes sense of things for oneself, and then for others." "Audience awareness in writing typically means being sensitive to the expectations, demands, and background of those reading the composition" (Bright, 1995, p. 71). For elementary children, four types of audiences exist: (1) self, (2) teacher, (3) known, and (4) unknown. Children's writing tends to be influenced by their sense of the audience, "the manner in which the writer expresses a relationship with the reader in respect to the writer's understanding" (Britton, Burgess, Martin, McLeod, & Rosen, 1975, pp. 65–66). According to Bright (1995, p. 12), "students' perceptions about both the value of audience and its composition undoubtedly influence the processes and products of their writing."

Self

Self, as audience, results in a very private type of writing because no one else is expected to read the message or text. The writing is done for one's own enjoyment and pleasure; therefore, diaries, journals, and personal notes exemplify writing for self. Poetry, stories, and song lyrics may also fall within this category if the writer's purpose is to compose a piece without sharing it with anyone else. It should be noted that a piece originally intended for self may later be developed for a wider audience.

Teacher

The teacher is undoubtedly the most familiar type of audience for students. Historically, the student's role has always been to undertake and complete writing tasks assigned by and for the teacher. Whether or not this is consciously understood, the teacher as audience is often brought to mind when children write. First and second graders have a strong desire to please teachers with their writing, while older children may attempt to demonstrate newly developed proficiencies. The teacher can avoid the creation of excessive student dependence by converting the classroom into a writing community. By sharing their writing with one another in pairs and in writing groups, children learn to appreciate, value, and critique one another's works. Eventually, students will learn to seek advice about their writing from one another as well as from the teacher.

Known Audience

The *known audience* is just that—a person (or people) with whom the writer is familiar. Five-year-olds are very much aware of the known audience; if a kindergartner draws a picture and is asked who the picture is for, the child will respond with the name of a person, typically "Mommy" or "Daddy."

A known audience helps the writer select and control the type of writing. In view of the writer's familiarity with the reader, a common knowledge base is available. Little or no degree of clarification is needed when a known audience is acquainted with the experience being described. The known audience may be a sibling, a good friend, or a grandparent, for example. Writing that is intended for a known audience is of a semiprivate nature, for the author will share certain thoughts and feelings with only a very restricted group of readers or perhaps only one reader.

Unknown Audience

For the fourth type of audience, the *unknown audience*, writers must create pieces along more public lines. This type of audience is usually made up of more people than any of the other types and also expects more from a piece of writing. The revising and polishing of a piece to be read by an unknown audience necessitates that a writer understand and follow the conventions of language. Thus, written communications to be shared with students in other classrooms, business letters, and thank-you notes sent to museum guides after a field trip, for example, all require careful writing and editing.

Voice

Writing usually reflects one of three primary voices: narrative, expository, and poetic. Emergent writers tend to write in the narrative as they share stories about their family, friends, and pets. Beginning writers venture further afield into expository and poetic writing as they describe how to cook a particular dish, outline the steps in making an art project, or record observations of the classroom guinea pig. Their poetry may consist of two- or three-line rhymes. As children progress in their writing skills, they include more description, better organization, improved transitions, and greater awareness of their reader audience.

Focus Box 8.3

Types of Audiences

Self: Only the writer is the audience; no one else is to read what is written. The written piece may be practical, such as a grocery list, or personal, such as a poem or a biographical statement.

Teacher: The most familiar audience for students is the classroom teacher, who not only makes the writing assignments but reads the pieces as well.

Known: A known audience is one with whom the author is familiar. This type of audience is often composed of a single friend or relative.

Unknown: An unknown audience is one that is unfamiliar to the writer. This type of audience is usually made up of several people and expects more from a piece of writing than the other types of audiences.

Narrative Writing

Narrative writing is sometimes referred to by teachers as "story writing" in which the child writes a tale. It may be an adventure, a piece of fantasy, or even a folktale. Young children do this naturally. And why not? Children, and adults alike, live in the narrative. When they talk about an event that happened to them or something they'd like to occur, they are "telling a tale." They invent characters, sometimes enhancing their own abilities so that they, themselves, are characters in their stories. Plots are mapped out and settings devised. Feelings and emotions are charged and then, ta da! A story is spun on the page.

Expository Writing

The primary goal of narrative writing is to entertain the reader. However *expository writing* takes a different route—that of informing the reader. There are three main categories of expository writing: descriptive, explanatory, and persuasive.

Descriptive writing requires that the writer point out exactly what took place without any bias. Children may write a descriptive piece that paints a portrait of their family dog or that summarizes a basketball game or video. It may describe the events that took place on a field trip or the observation of a science experiment. The key is that the writer remain objective in presenting the information.

The second category of expository writing is *explanatory* in which the writer outlines the steps or details of a process. For instance, the writing may explain how to draw a bicycle or how to make a vegetable car from an ear of corn, toothpicks, and wheels. The writer must keep in mind the sequence of events and present any directions accurately and completely.

Persuasive writing is the last category of expository writing. Persuasive writing involves presenting a want or desire and then giving ample reasons

What Is Wanted

Reason One   Reason Two   Reason Three

What Is Wanted Is Repeated

Figure 8.1
Persuasive Writing Map

why that want or desire should be fulfilled. The closing statement repeats the
request. Figure 8.1 shows a semantic map that students may use as a guide for
their persuasive writing.

Children have been found to actively explore techniques for persuading
their classmates and family members through writing. They go beyond the
models and examples provided by their teachers and develop their own persuasive writing strategies which they use within social interaction. For example, one group of six- and seven-year-olds wrote stories to persuade their
classmates to play with them (Dyson, 1994).

Poetic Voice

The *poetic voice* is the least used writing style of children. The poetic voice is
used in writing both prose and poetry that can be appreciated intrinsically.
Early-childhood-level children often believe—wrongly—that all poetry must
rhyme or follow a rhyming pattern. In fact, there are several types of poetry.
Many are discussed in the following chapter.

Prose is distinguished from poetry by its close correspondence to the patterns of everyday speech, whereas poetry is rhythmic verse. However, writers
of both poetry and prose use the poetic voice. Heard (in Calkins, 1995) lists
four characteristics of poetry:

1. Poetry uses condensed language. Every word is important.
2. Usually the language of poetry is figurative. It contains simile, metaphor,
   and imagery.
3. Poetry is rhythmical.
4. Just as the units of organization in prose are the sentence and the
   paragraph, the units of organization in poetry are the line and the stanza.

Poetry is popular provided that it comments on the aspects of life that are
meaningful to children (Huck, Hepler, & Hickman, 1987). Writing poetry often
appeals to children because it is nonthreatening. As Kormanski (1992, p. 189)
states, "Poetry is the natural language of children." Because of the relative short-
ness of poems, children can get immediate satisfaction from and responses to
their writing efforts (Kirby & Liner, 1981).

F o c u s B o x 8 . 4

Voices of Writing

Narrative: The narrative, or expressive voice, reflects the feelings and personality of the writer and includes the frequent use of the pronoun "I." The primary goal of narrative writing is to entertain the reader.

Expository: Expository writing is informational writing and can be descriptive, explanatory, or persuasive.

> *Descriptive* writing requires the writer to present only the facts and the details.
>
> *Explanatory* writing requires that the writer present the steps or details of a process.
>
> *Persuasive* writing requires that the writer try to influence the reader to accept a particular way of thinking.

Poetic: Poetic voice reflects the sensitivity, thoughts, and word selection of the writer through either poetry or prose.

The Development of Children's Writing

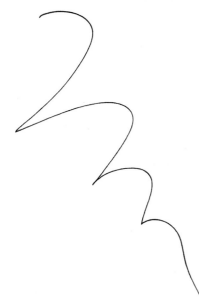

Figure 8.2
Jeff's writing of McDonald's.

Jeff, age 3½, was going shopping with his mother and her friend Jenny. While his mother was busy in a dressing room, Jeff engaged in a conversation with Jenny. "We're going shopping," Jeff said. Jenny replied, "Yes, at the shopping mall." Jeff said, "I know a great place to eat. Give me a pencil, and I'll write it down for you." Hoping to keep Jeff amused, Jenny searched through her purse and found a pen and some paper, both of which she gave to Jeff. Jeff's writing is shown in figure 8.2.

"Can you read it?" Jeff asked. "Of course," replied Jenny, somewhat surprised that she could indeed read what such a young child had written. "It says 'McDonald's.' " Jeff beamed, "Yeah, we'll eat at McDonald's. They've got good hamburgers and french fries there."

This is but one example of how children enjoy writing at an early age. Although their scribblings are often undecipherable, some of their writing can be easily recognized and understood. Consider, for example, Jenny's interpretation of Jeff's *M* (for McDonald's) when it is viewed in the context of lunch. Through the use of similar invented spellings, a young child actively engages in writing as a way to share thoughts and ideals with others. While youngsters begin by drawing, they quickly proceed to scribbling, which serves as writing's precursor.

Lots of varied opportunities for writing should be part of every elementary and middle-school classroom.
© James L. Shaffer

Kindergarten

Kindergarten children exhibit a wide range of writing abilities. Some children enter school knowing how to read and having been encouraged to write at home; others have no or only limited knowledge of sound-symbol relationships; and still others are unaware that the alphabet even exists. According to Sulzby (1992), most kindergarten children do not use conventional forms of writing. Many are still in the scribbling and drawing stage. However, by the second semester, many kindergartners do enjoy writing. This writing may consist mainly of drawings, which also convey messages, or it may be advanced to the point where an adult can actually recognize the words and read the story.

Initially, children only draw pictures of objects, never considering the use of accompanying labels. Lists are also popular with children of this age. Figure 8.3 is a list of events to take place in a neighborhood Olympics. Later, as children begin to create pictures depicting action, they use sound-symbol relationships to supply their drawings with appropriate phrases and sentences. Graves (1983) refers to such writing preceded by illustration as a "rehearsal" process inasmuch as a child is preparing for writing ventures.

Some teachers consider writing to be an unteachable skill at the kindergarten level. However, Calkins (1995) asserts that children who have a rudimentary knowledge of print tend to perceive themselves as writers. In this way, they quickly learn conventions of written language. Therefore, Calkins encourages both kindergarten and first-grade teachers to promote stimulating writing situations: for example, providing paper and envelopes for letter writing or index cards for labeling objects in the room.

Figure 8.3
Here is a list of events
to be included in a
neighborhood
Olympics as developed
by a 5½-year-old.

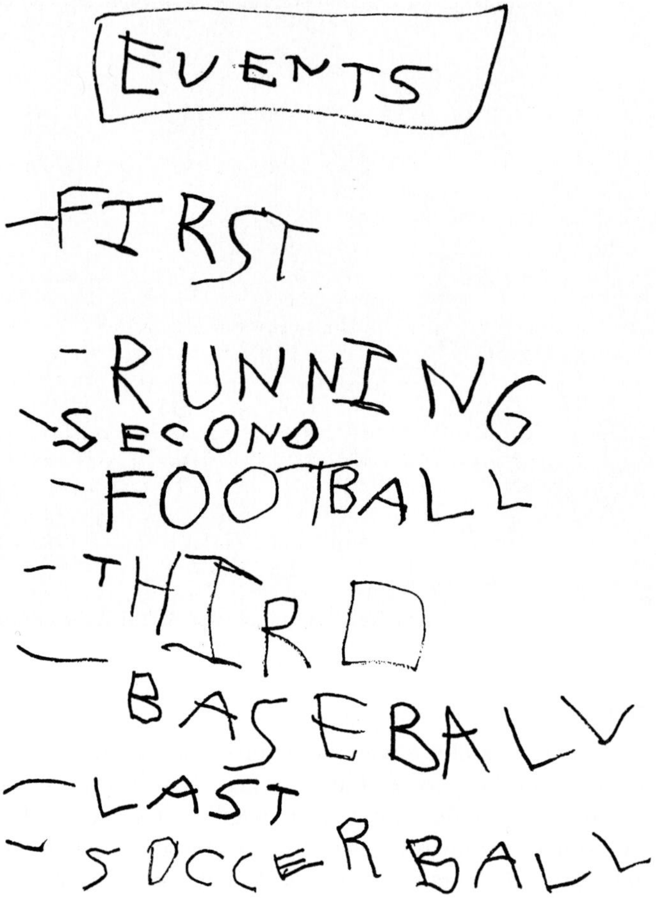

EVENTS

FIRST

RUNNING
SECOND
FOOTBALL

THIRD
BASEBALL
LAST
SOCCERBALL

First Grade

As children leave kindergarten's socialized world and enter the more academically oriented first-grade classroom, they often have a sense of "I can do it; I am a writer." At age 6, few children are reluctant to attempt anything that the teacher suggests. Along the same line, first graders rarely encounter "writer's block" because they always have something to put down on paper even when they realize that their work is to be shared with others. In living for the moment and giving little consideration to yesterday or tomorrow, first graders want to write, write, write, and write some more. Their writing projects seem to flow as if off a production line without any quality control; and as soon as one first draft is written, these youngsters are anxious to begin another. Within any single writing session, it is not unusual for an eager first grader to write three or four new stories rather than to develop and perfect the first story. First graders are persistent in getting their ideas down on paper and moving on to the other ideas that are burning in their minds.

Focus Box 8.5

Writing Development of Emergent Literacy Child

Name: Teacher:
Age: Grade: Date:

	Always	Sometimes	Never
Can differentiate between writing and drawing			
Uses pencil, marker, or pen for writing			
Writes in scribbles			
Uses letters in writing			
Uses letter strings in writing			
Uses invented spelling in writing			
Uses conventional (correct) spelling in writing			
Can print own first name			
—In all capital letters			
—Using capital and lowercase letters			
Expresses interest in writing (i.e., writes notes, keeps lists, makes cards)			
Writes from left to right			
Attempts to copy words and sentences			
Attempts to write independently			
Asks how to spell words			
Asks to dictate words/sentences/stories to someone who writes them down			
Teacher comments:			

For first-grade writers, editing is either very limited or essentially nonexistent until they recognize that polishing a piece of writing can make reading easier. Even at this point, the strong urge to begin and finish a piece within a very brief period still exists. It therefore becomes something of a momentous occasion for a child when he or she erases or crosses out a line of text for the first time. The first grader has now formally identified the piece as a draft that requires reworking to improve the text and ultimately to please the "writer."

Although first graders show growth in all the conventions of language, the most dramatic growth occurs in the area of spelling. They often will write in

In the Classroom
Supplies for Writing

Before the school year begins, the teacher can acquire writing supplies to make the writing process both organized and interesting for students. The following suggested items can help provide a variety of writing experiences:

Paper
Butcher paper
Computer paper
Drawing paper
Envelopes (small and legal size)
Graph paper
Index cards (3″ × 5″; 5″ × 7″)
Legal pads of various colors and sizes
Lined paper of various sizes and types
Newsprint
Postcards
Post-it Notes
Stationery (note cards, notepaper, and envelopes)

Writing instruments
Colored pencils
Computer and printer
Crayons
Felt-tipped pens (fine, medium, and broad tipped)
Ink pens
Markers of various colors
Pencils
Poster paints and brushes
Typewriter
Watercolor paints and brushes

Office Supplies
Brass fasteners
Clipboards
Date stamp and pad
Duct tape
Erasers (pencil and ink)
File folders (including colored folders for special projects)
Paper clips
Paper punch

Poster board
Scissors
Stapler and staples
Tagboard
Transparencies
Transparency markers
Scotch tape
Stickers (blank circles of various colors)
Vinyl adhesive letters

Reference Materials
Add It, Dip It, Fix It: A Book of Verbs (R. M. Schneider, Boston: Houghton Mifflin, 1995)
Almanac
Atlas of the world
Dictionaries
Encyclopedia (e.g., *Pocket Encyclopedia,* A. Jack, New York: Random House, 1988)
Examples of letter formats for friendly and business letters
Franklin Spelling Ace
Magazines
Thesaurus
Time to Rhyme: A Rhyming Dictionary (M. Terban, Honesdale, PA: Wordsong, 1994)

Storage Containers
Cardboard boxes to hold books to be published
Desktop In/Out boxes (editing box, publishing box)
File cabinet
Floppy disk storage box
Milk cartons (half gallon) to serve as mailboxes (one for each student and one for the teacher)
Plastic milk crates for writing folders
Shoeboxes

Focus Box 8.6

Development of Beginning Writer

Name:	Teacher:		
Age:	Grade:	Date:	
	Always	**Sometimes**	**Never**
Expresses interest in writing (i.e., writes notes, keeps lists, makes cards, writes letters, makes sports cards)			
Talks with others about own writing			
Talks with others about their writing			
Writes on lines			
Makes capital letters correctly			
Makes lowercase letters correctly			
Leaves space between words			
Leaves space between sentences			
Uses periods and question marks appropriately			
Uses commas appropriately			
Uses quotation marks for dialogue			
Teacher comments:			

capital letters or trace over and darken letters in an attempt to emphasize specific words or phrases. Punctuation marks—in particular exclamation points, question marks, and periods—are soon incorporated into their writing. The use of quotation marks is not popular at the beginning of first grade, but as the students gain exposure to dialogue in stories, they begin to incorporate quotation marks into their own writing.

Even at this young age, children notice that responsibility accompanies writing. To reinforce this sense of responsibility, the teacher can take attendance by having the children sign in each morning as they enter the classroom (Harste et al., 1984). The names of those both present and absent is an important piece of information that classroom teachers must collect every school day. After tabulating the data, the teacher forwards the information to the principal's office, which compiles all class attendance data and sends the compilation on to the central office of the school district. For first graders, then, signing in becomes both a responsibility and a morning writing ritual from the very beginning of the school year.

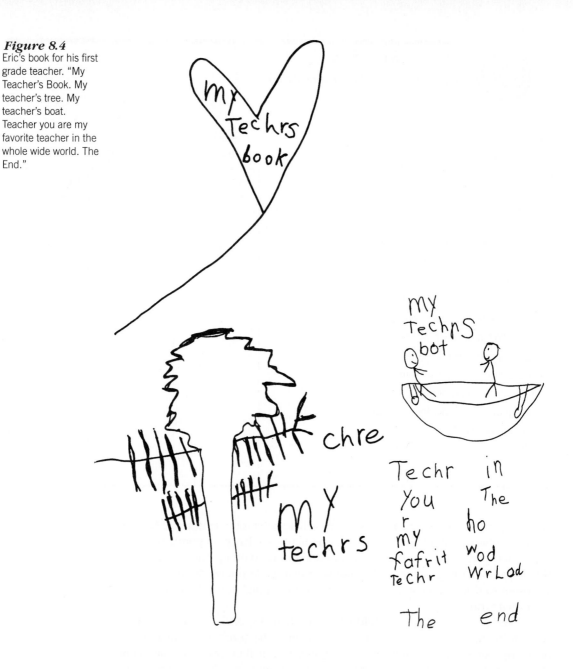

Figure 8.4
Eric's book for his first grade teacher. "My Teacher's Book. My teacher's tree. My teacher's boat. Teacher you are my favorite teacher in the whole wide world. The End."

A teacher can best distinguish and evaluate the immense changes in writing that occur during the first-grade year by dating samples of each student's work and storing the samples sequentially in writing folders (see figure 8.6). On a regular basis, the teacher should sit down with individual students to discuss and reflect on their growth and progress.

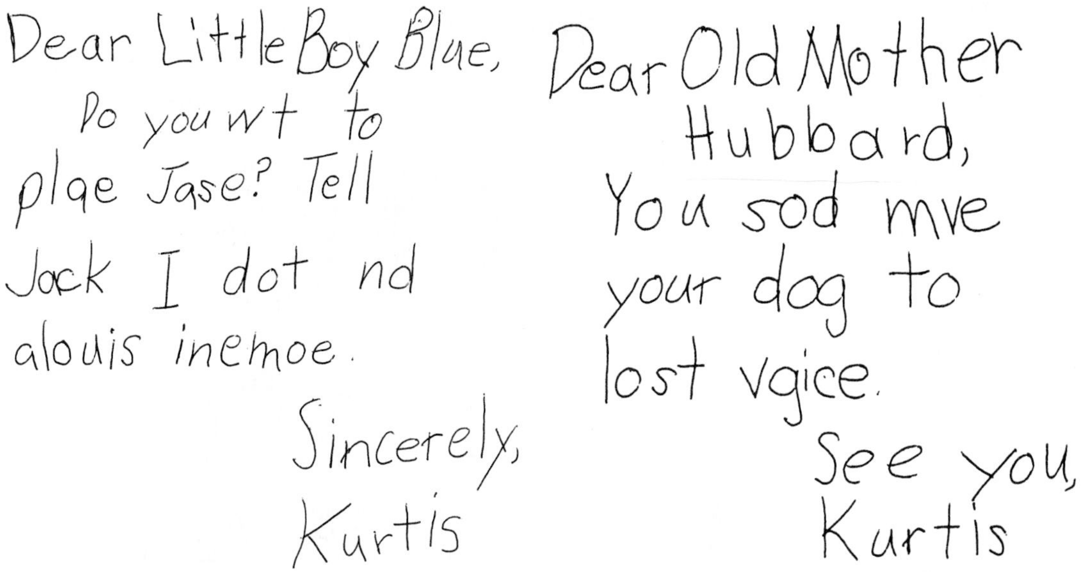

> Dear Little Boy Blue,
>   Do you wnt to
> plqe Jase? Tell
> Jack I dot nd
> alouis inemoe.
>   Sincerely,
>   Kurtis

> Dear Old Mother
>   Hubbard,
> You sod mve
> your dog to
> lost vqice.
>   See you,
>   Kurtis

```
Dear Little Boy Blue,
    Do you want to
play jazz?  Tell
Jack I don't need
an allowance anymore.
        Sincerely,
        Kurtis

        - First Grade
```

```
Dear Old Mother
        Hubbard,
You should move
your dog to
Las Vegas.
    See you,
    Kurtis
        - First Grade
```

Figure 8.5

Kurtis, a first grader, was given the assignment to write letters to nursery rhyme characters. Notice his humor as he suggests Old Mother Hubbard should move to "Lost" Vegas since she can't find a bone for her dog.

Second Grade

Writing in second-grade classrooms can be quite diversified. Some children continue to write as confidently and enthusiastically as they did in first grade, producing pages of stories that describe happenings in their lives. For other children, writing becomes a dreaded, anxious activity as they wrestle for perfection with every pencil stroke. One misspelled word in the middle of an otherwise error-free paper may cause a student to wad up and throw away the piece before he or she attempts the project again. Similarly, even a minor stray mark may result in a child's discarding the work and beginning anew.

As children leave the egocentric world of the preoperational stage and enter the stage of concrete operations, they begin to notice that some things are acceptable while others are not. First graders rarely fret over their writing because they give all their attention to enjoyment of the writing activity rather than to the audience's reaction. For second graders, on the other hand, approval and acceptance become increasingly important. For example, if the teacher praises Maria's story about her stuffed monkey, the other students may

Figure 8.6
Samples of a first
grader's writing in
September and
November.

Gignna

Grade 1
September
Sample

MiFrEGE L MiFA PAWE L
CetMiXES TEL WISh
TEJEMsEKNLeEPAK
ITSTT MS K RAWLMDA
M ESLEKGOMTHTKMSKI
MSAKLKMESEA

elect to attempt similar stories about their stuffed animals in hope that the
teacher will praise their work as well. Similarly, a sense of authorship begins to
evolve during second grade.

When second graders write about an incident, they want to include
everything: "And then" such and such occurred, "and then" such and such happened, "and then" . . . The writing is somewhat like an objective report of an
event: It contains little or no personal reflection. Every aspect of the event,
trivial or otherwise, is given equal attention, and few, if any, underlying interpretations are provided.

Children at this age frequently produce "bed-to-bed" stories, which are
narratives of the occurrences that take place from the time they awaken in the
morning until they fall asleep at night (Calkins, 1995). Even if the purpose of
the writing is to describe a child's birthday or Christmas, the opening of presents typically receives the same amount of attention as do eating breakfast and
preparing for bed.

Figure 8.6
(Continued)

11/2/

Gianna Reicha
Grade 1
November
Sample

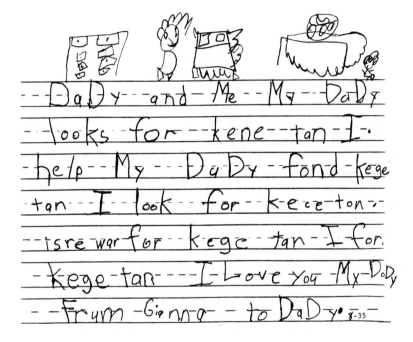

DaDy and Me My DaDy
looks for kene tan I.
help My DaDy fond kege
tan I look for kece ton.
isre wor for kege tan I for.
kege tan I Love you My DoDy
Frum Gianna to DaDy 8-35

Third Grade

Like their second-grade counterparts, third graders are still struggling to find that self-confidence they had in first grade. They have already become aware of the importance of spelling and usage, but now they are expected to write in the cursive handwriting style that they only recently learned.

In addition, third graders demonstrate an increased awareness of the influence of authorship. For example, after experimenting with two or three written drafts, third graders will produce final drafts of "books" they feel are worthy of fine leather binding and gold lettering. Likewise, after careful examination of several different books, they often will write their own dedications. Generally, a dedication is to a writer's parents, rarely to brothers and sisters. When brothers and sisters *are* included in the dedication, grandparents and all the family pets are also likely to be named. After all, since writing a book is a

In the Classroom Mini Lesson

Using Literature to Compare Human Traits

*D*on't Fidget a Feather by Erica Silverman (1994) is a delightful story of friendship, stubbornness, and love. Gander and Duck are best friends who do everything together. One day they decide to have a contest to see which of them is the best. Duck wins the swimming contest but Gander wins the flying contest. Then they decide to determine the "champion of champions" by seeing which of them doesn't "fidget a feather." Silently, Gander and Duck stand in the barnyard for hours until a Fox appears. Both fowl have a strong streak of stubbornness and neither yields as Fox tucks them into his sack and heads off to his house. When Gander is picked up by Fox to plop into his stewpot, Gander still doesn't move. But Duck can't bear to lose his friend, so he is the first to fidget; he pinches Fox and rescues Gander.

This story is a good one to share with first through third graders. They can write about how they have done a good deed for a friend or family member. Then, they can write about a time they were a bit stubborn. Kindergartners can also engage in this activity by illustrating a picture of their good deed.

Silverman, E. (1994). *Don't fidget a feather* (S. D. Schindler, Illus.). New York: Macmillan.

major effort, the family should identify with the youngster's sense of pride in publishing the piece of writing.

Of course, such a masterpiece will often describe the author in a brief section entitled "About the Author." The students will write about themselves—but use the third person—including information on their birthdays, interests, and hobbies. These students spend a great amount of time on their autobiographical statements.

Third graders continue to include every detail in their description of an incident. Considering the overall development of their oral language skills, however, this is true to form. For example, in describing a recent movie or television program, the children review every scene because they do not understand any reason for beginning a description or summary in the middle of an action. A story must start at the beginning; thus, bed-to-bed stories will continue to be produced.

Although narrative writing still predominates, third graders begin to experiment with some forms of poetry and to write informational and factual reports about science experiments and social studies topics. Children of this age are also able to create story problems as a way of better understanding mathematical concepts.

Editing is troublesome for many third graders. Some simply cannot distinguish between what is correct and what is incorrect within their writing. Therefore, editing someone else's work is an impossible task unless it is attempted as a group. Indeed, critiquing a peer's work may become synonymous with criticizing every mistake, whether it be a major error or a minor oversight. When this happens, the teacher must quickly clarify this activity's goal: to positively assist one's classmates without condemning every fault.

My Calf
by Regina Heide
4th Grade

I have a calf named Mac Kenzie. He has a black face with a sort-of white triangle on his forehead, knobby knees, short tail and he is is mostly black. My calf has a tongue like a snake. It feels like sandpaper on top.

He likes to suck your fingers. MacKenzie also likes to have one hind foot in the hay bunk and three in the straw.

When he hears me stirring milk, he holds his head up high. If you wonder what a calf's bottom chin going into his neck looks like, it is oval shaped.

The thing I like about Mac Kenzie is that he gives love to the cats.

A majority of third-grade students are adept at developing simple sentences and paragraphs. However, their stories almost universally contain a straightforward, predictable style of writing with little or no embellishment. This results in a stiff, robotlike product with relatively few mechanical errors.

Fourth Grade

Unlike third graders, fourth graders tend to project their individuality through writing. For example, a child's handwriting may evolve into an expressive message of its own when curls, loops, and hearts replace the dots over *i*'s, a common practice in this age-group. Likewise, their stories become more worldly as their experiential backgrounds expand through reading, talking, traveling, and "living" in general. Informational reporting is also used more frequently (see figures 8.7 and 8.8).

FOCUS BOX 8.7

Development of Middle Childhood Writer

Name: Age:	Teacher: Grade: Date:		
	Always	Sometimes	Never
Expresses a desire to engage in writing (i.e., is eager to join in writing activities, writes without being prompted)			
Can write in various forms —narrative —expository —persuasive —descriptive —poetic			
Can brainstorm for ideas using variety of techniques (i.e., semantic webs, questions to be answered, interviews)			
Uses resources to find information (i.e., literature, reference materials, interviews with people)			
Keeps a writing journal of ideas, vocabulary, mechanics, spelling, character traits, etc.			
Can write good first draft			
Has a good writing vocabulary			
Can sequence and organize ideas			
Can write a paragraph with a topic sentence and supporting ideas			
Is willing to edit own work			
Is wiling to have others edit work			
Can edit writing through adding, deleting, and moving text			
Can locate spelling errors			
Can correct spelling errors			
Can locate punctuation errors			
Can correct punctuation errors			
Can locate grammar errors			
Can correct grammar errors			
Is interested in listening to peers read their work			
Can accept criticism from peers			
Can accept criticism from teacher			
Can give appropriate criticism to peers			
Is proud of own writing			

	Always	Sometimes	Never
Is supportive of the writing of peers			
Can use the vocabulary of writers in discussing own or others writing			
Writes so the audience can understand			
Writes to peak audience interest			
Writes legibly			
Writes with a computer			
Keeps a writing portfolio with writing samples, writing goals, and self-critiques of work			
Teacher comments:			

Moosl Men of the Wrld

For 13 yers Men hav Bene punping iron for the USA Moosl Man cantest event. Moovestors are capeting in this avent. you will see if teh moovestors: the winr is the evilop ples. Arnold sors anger.

Robert, a fourth grader

Figure 8.8
Students often write about topics that interest them. Here, Robert writes about his hobby, weight lifting.

Muscle Men of the World

For 13 years men have been pumping iron for the USA Muscle Man contest event. Movie stars are competing in this event. You will see fifty movie stars: the winner is (the envelope please) Arnold Swartzenegger.

Robert, a fourth grader

Revising and editing are more palatable now because fourth graders want to share their work with others. Because they are more venturesome in writing, their creations become more fluent and flamboyant. Drafts become messier than they were in the primary grades as the students use erasures, eradicating marks, and arrows to refine and improve their writing.

Most fourth graders don't spend much time writing outside of school. This is true even if they enjoy writing. Thus, it is crucial that the classroom teacher provide opportunities to write, keying in on student interests.

> I Can't Whistel
>
> One day my friends asked me if I would like to be in there club. I said I would be glad to be in there club. But there were so many people in the club they decided to only let the people who could wishel in the club I had to go because I couldn't whistle.
>
> My next store neighbor said to suck something sour to pucker my mouth up I tryed some pickels but it didn't help. I thought I would never be able to wistle
>
> But that day I went to the store to get some sour cherries. They were realy sour.
>
> That night I lost a tooth. I put it under my pillow so I would get a dollar.
>
> I got into bed and had a sour cherry. I tryed to wistle. I could finaly do it. I got to be in the club after all!

Fifth and Sixth Grades

Fifth and sixth graders have diverse abilities, skills, interests, and concerns, and each of these may be reflected in their writing. Hansen (1986) believes that such variability is an asset in the teaching of writing. Students discover that everyone has personal strengths and weaknesses and that individuals must pursue those areas that highlight their own uniqueness. According to Hansen, by "celebrating, challenging, and defending" their own writing as well as that of their peers and familiar authors of children's literature, children can begin to develop pride and confidence in themselves and each other as they become "real authors."

Because fifth and sixth graders are more confident in their own writing and have had experience in deliberating their work with other students and with the classroom teacher in conferences, they tend to discuss writing problems and concerns among themselves quite freely. A type of authorship bond seems to emerge within the classroom. In an effort to rework a piece until it is in its best form, a youngster may use a different audience for each of several drafts. Moreover, writers in the intermediate grades will make insertions and deletions in their own work more readily than will younger authors. Lines with

How Monkey got its Tail

One day in the jungle there was a little monkey. Monkey was jumping from tree to tree.

Then a big leopard jumped right behind Monkey. Monkey started jumping really fast. The leopard was right behind Monkey. Then Lion roared loud. The leopard looked down and saw him. The leopard jumped down and ran away. Monkey got down from the tree and thanked Lion for saving him. From then on Monkey stayed with Lion for protection.

One day monkey was walking along and thought that Lion was behind him. A big tiger was sneaking up behind Monkey. The tiger bit Monkey's little tail. Monkey started running. The tiger was hanging on tight to Monkey's tail. The tiger let go and Monkey's tail was real long. Since then, monkeys' tails have been long.

Troy   5th grade

Figure 8.10

After studying fables, Troy wrote his own.

The Kite and the Sun

Once there was a kite who flew high in the sky. But one day he saw the sun who was the highest thing in the sky.

The kite was jealous of the sun. Each day he tried to fly higher and higher so he could be the highest in the sky.

One day the sun was no where to be seen. That made the kite happy. He thought he had finally conquered the sun. Just then the sun came out from behind a cloud. This made kite furious. He was deter-mined to be the highest.

Kite flew higher and higher and higher still. Then he got too close to sun and got burned. Kite fell down and down and could no longer fly at all.

It was then that kite realized that he should have liked himself for just what he was. And that's the way people should be.

Kristy - 6th Grade

Figure 8.11

After studying fables, Kristy wrote her own.

Writing: A Multidimensional Process

	Kindergarten-First Grade	Second Grade
Prewriting (Rehearsal)	Pretend to write Draw pictures Talk about pictures Use pictures to convey much of the meaning	Use increased oral language May talk with peers about writing
Writing (Draft)	Need variety of writing materials Need regular, set time to write Teacher-student conferences help develop ideas Skill lessons focus on basic punctuation (use of periods, capital letters, quotation marks, etc.)	Create short pieces Often include information that doesn't fit Write about start of day to end of day (bed-to-bed)
Rewriting (Revision)	Put stories in book format Share writing with others Begin rereading for content Ask editing questions	Want to change wording (cut and paste—"sloppy copy") Grow as writers

Elements the Teacher Must Provide at All Grade Levels

Modeling of the writing process Brief skill lessons One-to-one teacher-student conferences A classroom atmosphere of trust and support	Recognition of writing growth for all students A variety of writing materials Sharing of quality children's literature with the class

arrows now indicate the repositioning of entire sentences and paragraphs in initial drafts. Even when the writer is convinced that the piece is well written, he or she may still make a few changes. While mechanical skills are becoming more refined, organizational thoughts and ideas continue to be troublesome for fifth and sixth graders.

Bright (1995) found that fifth and sixth graders consider good writers to be familiar with the subjects they write about, to read a lot, to know the meanings of various words, to listen to others, and to write in a way that is interesting to others. Good writers are also hard, determined workers and write often, according to students in the study.

Seventh and Eighth Grades

Seventh and eighth graders are capable of screening information. They can research a topic and take notes. In addition, these students rely on previously

Third Grade	Fourth-Sixth Grades	Seventh-Eighth Grades
Discuss writing (ideas, etc.) Problem solve Focus on single topic	Focus on single topic Think in more abstract terms, need less concrete examples Engage in self-questioning	Think abstractly Research information Use effective organization of notes Screen information Use previous knowledge

Select personal experiences
Write sequentially
Use little reflection/thought
	Write from different points of view/voice/
	    mood
	Show audience awareness
	May begin story in middle of action
	Exhibit empathy
	Show growing awareness of elements of
	    good writing
	Can write, read, and edit
		Are more sophisticated writers
		Are sensitive to reader/audience
		Consider organization of piece

Make simple corrections only Dread revising	Self-edit Internalize mechanics Consider the reader of the piece	Present very polished final products

gained knowledge as they write. Their level of sophistication as writers sometimes surprises their teachers as these students can present very polished and well-organized final writing pieces.

The development of children's writing from kindergarten through eighth grade is summarized in focus box 8.8. Note the changes that occur in the various stages of writing.

The Teacher's Role in the Writing Process

Teachers play a significant role in helping students develop their writing skills. By providing writing models and holding conferences with children about their individual work, teachers help students understand and learn the craft of writing more thoroughly.

Increasingly, elementary students use computers for writing. Now, with the Internet, students can write to children throughout the United States, Canada, and the world.

The Teacher as a Writing Model

When teachers do not write in class, they cannot serve as models. Many classroom teachers lack the confidence to share personal writing with students because of memories of their own school years. They may readily recall their pieces of writing returned to them filled with red marks. As Smith (1981, p. 797) points out, "Children will learn what they are taught, and the teacher who perceives writing as a tedious chore with trivial applications will teach just those things." Such perceptions are unfortunate, for when teachers can share their own writing with their students, they can transform an ordinary classroom into a writing community.

The sharing of writing allows a teacher to send a message to students: Writing is a demanding but valuable skill to acquire. In referring to their own pieces of writing, teachers can be honest in conveying the personal feelings of success, frustration, and uncertainty that often accompany the writing process. As Smith (1981, p. 797) also states, teachers who write and share their compositions with their students "demonstrate what writing does, and how to do it."

Most children believe that writing develops naturally for adults. They believe that when an adult puts a pencil to paper, the words flow like water in a river until the adult decides to end the piece. Except for watching their parents write grocery lists and letters to relatives and friends, children rarely see adults actively engaged in the writing process—brainstorming, making prewriting decisions, drafting, editing, and sharing the final product.

Teachers can frequently model writing through planned activities. For example, a teacher may choose to gather primary students into a semicircle on the floor for a more relaxed writing demonstration in which he or she uses chart paper and a felt-tipped marker. In a similar fashion, intermediate-grade teachers may use an overhead projector in their writing presentations to increase eye contact between themselves and their students.

Before the teacher actually begins to write, a major classroom rule needs to be emphasized. No interruptions will be allowed during the writing period. Thus, no one is permitted to ask a question concerning the due date of a project or to whisper to classmates during the activity. All attention must be focused on the teacher's writing.

The most natural way for a teacher to begin writing is to talk about events that have actually taken place. Typically, seemingly commonplace occurrences are often intriguing to children. In choosing appropriate topics, a teacher should be certain that an event is authentic and neither spectacular nor unusual. Here are some events that almost every teacher has experienced and that children will find interesting as writing topics:

Cutting your own hair or that of a sibling when you were a child

Dressing up a pet

Following a recipe and leaving out a crucial ingredient

Learning to ride a bicycle

Venturing into the local "haunted" house with your childhood friends

Swinging for a long time during the day and then awakening in the middle of the night with the sensation that you were still swinging

Learning how to roller skate

Camping out

Reading or performing before an audience for the first time

Using certain shortcuts as a child to hasten completion of your household chores

When a teacher can demonstrate skill in writing about an everyday occurrence, children will come to realize that in having experienced similar situations, they have the potential to write. Because daily occurrences in their own lives are equally interesting, real, and relevant, students do not feel a need to write only of stabbings, shootings, or poisonings. Common happenings are just as worthy of being shared and are appreciated by audiences.

After briefly suggesting three or four possible writing topics, a teacher should select one as the writing model. By deliberating over a topic, a teacher demonstrates that beginning a piece of writing is very difficult, even for an adult. In this same way, the teacher should continue to verbalize and share thoughts while the writing is taking place. Once the draft is finished, the teacher should read the entire piece to the class. At the next writing session, the teacher should demonstrate editing techniques as the first draft is revised and the final work is produced.

While it is impossible to participate in every student writing assignment, it is critical that the teacher write about the same topics both regularly and frequently. Although there is little need for such modeling on a daily basis, a teacher can reach the same goal by working on a journal or a science essay with the students. In such an exercise, both teacher and students should write simultaneously without interruption. After all class members have completed their final drafts, the students and the teacher should share their individual works.

Conferencing with Students

The term *conferencing* evolved from secondary school and college writing courses built around the idea of a writing workshop. Murray (1968) believes that students must discuss their writings with someone if they are to learn to write. Actually, elementary teachers have been "conferencing" with their students for many years; the typical teacher walks around the classroom, responding to questions and talking at random with the students as they write.

However, Murray (1968) considers a writing conference to be more structured and formal. The typical conference between teacher and student lasts an average of 3 to 5 minutes, although a longer or shorter meeting occasionally takes place. During this time, the teacher asks the student how the work is progressing. The student, in turn, may either ask for assistance with some part of the piece or just share a favorite paragraph or sentence with the teacher. In any event, the teacher should be careful to respond initially to content rather than to mechanics. Although simple questions that encourage student reflection and thinking are preferable to those that only require a yes or no answer, the teacher must avoid overusing such questions and potentially dominating the discussion. Instead, the student should be an active participant in the conference (Mack & Farris, 1992).

It is also important that the teacher keep anecdotal records of writing conferences. These may be kept either in a notebook or on index cards and filed in the student's portfolio (Tierney, Carter, & Desai, 1991; Tompkins, 1993). Some basic conference guidelines are listed in focus box 8.9.

Conferences to Select a Writing Topic

Teachers can encourage children to think about various potential writing topics by asking questions such as these:

Tell me about your family (or friends, neighbors, pets).

What do you like?

What do you dislike?

What is your favorite sport?

What kind of hobbies do you have?

What is your favorite book?

Do you have a favorite author?

Was there something you wanted to do for a long time that you finally got to do?

What is the funniest thing that you have ever seen happen?

What is the strangest thing that you have ever seen?

Focus Box 8.9
Teacher-Student Conference Guidelines

The teacher should attempt to make the writing conference nonthreatening. For example, by sitting next to rather than across from a child, a teacher can be looked upon as a helper rather than an antagonist.

The teacher should use the child's first name.

The student and teacher should be at the same eye level when seated. Eye contact serves to highlight the teacher's support of the child's effort through nonverbal means.

The student shares the piece of writing with the teacher. The teacher should not write on the piece or take it from the student because the work belongs to the child.

The teacher should ask open-ended questions that are based on meaning and that the student can respond to freely. Even as the questions become increasingly challenging, the student still should be able to respond to them.

The teacher should give the student ample time to formulate a response to a question. Even though some questions can be answered quickly, others require more thought on the part of the youngster and a longer corresponding waiting time for the teacher. Usually, the teacher can determine whether a student needs some additional time in which to prepare a response.

The teacher should ask questions that demonstrate a natural curiosity about the work. For instance, asking, "What kind of fish did you catch?" followed by "What are some of the special things you do to catch [kind of fish]?" allows the student to describe the techniques of fishing for a particular kind of fish. The student may even begin to compare and contrast fish and the ways in which they are caught.

The teacher should never attempt to control the conference by requiring the student to change the focus of the work or to elaborate on something that is of particular interest to the teacher.

The teacher should keep the conference brief, no longer than 3 to 5 minutes.

The teacher should attempt to discuss only one or two concerns per conference. To attempt to resolve more is fruitless because the student will become confused.

The conference should end on a positive note.

Conferences While Writing Is in Progress

Here are some basic questions or comments that teachers can use during individual or small group conferences while a work is still being written:

Tell me about your work.

How is your writing coming along?

Do you have a favorite part? Read it to me.

How did you decide on your title?

Does the beginning make people want to read what you are writing?

What convinced you to write about this topic?

You seem to be very familiar with this topic. How could you find out even more about it?

What is the most exciting part of what you are writing?

In the Classroom Mini Lesson
Roulette Writing

A cooperative writing activity in which all students can take part is "roulette writing," developed by Farris (1988). For this activity, the teacher divides the class (Grades 3 and up) into groups of five students and joins one of the groups (a different group each time). The teacher becomes one of the members of the group, thereby promoting teamwork in this cooperative learning activity. Everyone is given the same topic about which to write. The topic should be an open-ended one, for example, "The Day Our School Burned Down." The teacher instructs everyone to begin writing about the topic, allows ample time for students to complete about three sentences, and then announces that the students are to finish the sentence they are working on and pass the story to the person on their right. This pattern continues until the fifth writer receives the story. The fifth, or last, writer must bring the story to a conclusion. As the papers are exchanged, the amount of time between exchanges increases so that the new writer has an opportunity to read the work of the preceding authors. An example of roulette writing is shown in figure 8.12.

Farris, P. J. (1988). Roulette writing. *The Reading Teacher, 41* (1), 91.

> It was a hot fall day. Bugs, the class troublemaker was writing a fantsy piece. He was really into it. He said something about a fire
> Suddenly I smelled smoke coming from the front of the room. A wastebasket had caught on fire.
>
> Tina screemed, "Help!" "Fire!" I RAN to my LUNCHBOX FOR MY Hi-C JUICEBOX. I ripped THE TOP OFF AND POURED IT ON THE FIRE. THE FLAMES ROSE EVEN HIGHER.
>
> Everyone started to get nervous. Next, the fire bell went off and we all started filing out.
> Well it was a happy ending: Bugs wrote this story for class, and it was so realistic that everyone sat spell bound. I never knew Bugs could write this well. Of course with Bugs around one never knew when this story could become reality.

Figure 8.12
Sample of "roulette" writing by fifth graders.

What additional details would make this part (specify the part) clearer?

Is there anything that you have repeated and you can therefore take out?

Are there any other important details that you should add?

Does the ending fit with how you want the reader to feel?

Have you run into any problems that I can help you with?

Group Conferences

Group conferences can promote the development of editing skills and provide students with associated global learning activities. Each work read during a conference usually provides some new information, insight, or knowledge for the other members of the group. For example, Mrs. Duncan's third-grade class chose pets and their care as a writing topic. Dawn decided to present facts about her older brother's pet parrot. The other third graders were amazed to learn that parrots can live to be 80 years old and that all birds ingest small bits of gravel on a daily basis. Sam, another member of the class, wrote about his brother's pet boa constrictor, which only needed to be fed every 2 or 3 weeks. The other children wrote about the daily exercise needs of dogs, the independent nature of cats, and the swimming habits of goldfish. Obviously, then, children are capable of sharing their accrued knowledge with others through group conferencing.

A group writing conference might even begin with a student reading a draft of a work in progress. As the work is being read, other group members write down any questions they may have. Upon completion of the reading, the students are allowed to make comments and to ask questions about the work in accordance with one major ground rule: The initial comments must be positive, direct, and specific. Following this criterion, one can say, "I liked what you wrote because it . . ." and then specify the reason. This eliminates the tendency to attack a writer for mistakes while allowing the writer to gain further insight into those areas that prove to be strengths or weaknesses.

Group conferencing cannot be successful unless students trust both the teacher and each other. Therefore, until a majority of students feel secure and at ease within the classroom, conferencing is best accomplished on a one-to-one basis. In undertaking this venture, a teacher must prove to be trustworthy, kind, and helpful.

S u m m a r y

The writing process is comprised of four stages: prewriting, writing, rewriting, and publishing. Rather than being a linear process, writing is recursive in nature.

The prewriting stage, also referred to as rehearsal, enables a writer to prepare for the writing task by brainstorming, gathering information, and playing with thoughts and ideas. During the writing stage, the writer put developed thoughts and ideas down on paper in the form of sentences and paragraphs. In the rewriting stage, the writer revises the draft; although limited editing and revising occur during prewriting and writing, in the rewriting stage, the writer refines, clarifies, and reorganizes ideas to a much greater extent. In the last stage, that of publishing, the writer shares what he or she has written with others.

When undertaking a writing project, the student should consider the audience, or who will read the work. For elementary children, four types of audiences exist: (1) self, (2) teacher, (3) known, and (4) unknown.

Voice is yet another aspect of the writing process. Young children naturally write in the narrative voice, but they acquire the expository and poetic voices as time passes and experiences change.

When instructing students in the writing process, the effective teacher serves as a writing model and writes on the same topics that are assigned to students. By conferring with children both individually and in groups, the teacher can gain insight into their development as writers and their understanding of the writing process. Such conferences work best if they revolve around an individual piece of writing, including its strengths and weaknesses, and if the teacher is nonjudgmental about the piece.

Questions

1. Writing is referred to as the most complex language art for children to learn and for teachers to instruct. Give rationale to support this statement.
2. Define the four types of voice and write an example of each.
3. What role does the teacher play in the development of children's writing skills?
4. In what ways can children be introduced to the different types of audiences?
5. In what ways are teacher-student conferences similar to teacher-small group conferences? How do they differ?

Activities

1. Observe a four- or five-year-old beginning writer. Compare the child's actions with those of a first or second grader.
2. Develop a list of questions for conferencing with children at a particular grade level.
3. Develop and videotape a model writing lesson. Critique the videotape prior to presenting the lesson to a group of students.
4. Conference with three children who vary from low to high in their writing abilities. Try to use many of the same questions with all three students. Compare their responses to the questions and descriptions of their works.
5. Compare and contrast the diverse writing found within second grade classrooms with the egocentric writing of first graders.

For Further Reading

Akroyd, S. (1995). Forming a reading-writing class: Connecting cultures, one pen at a time. *The Reading Teacher, 48* (7), 580-587.

Ernst, G., & Richard, K. J. (1994/1995). Reading and writing pathways to conversation in the ESL classroom. *The Reading Teacher, 48* (4), 320-327.

Hansen, J. (1992). The language of challenge: Readers and writers speak their minds. *Language Arts, 69* (2), 100-105.

Walley, C. W. (1991). Diaries, logs, and journals in the elementary classroom. *Childhood Education, 67* (3), 149-154.

References

Abel, J. P., & Abel, F. J. (1988). Writing in the mathematics classroom. *Clearing House, 62* (2), 155-158.

Abel, F. J., Hauwiller, J. G., & Vandeventer, N. (1989). Using writing to teach social studies. *Social Studies, 80* (1), 17-20.

Aulls, M. (1985). Understanding the relationship between reading and writing. *Educational Horizons, 64* (1), 39-44.

Bright, R. (1995). *Writing instruction in the intermediate grades.* Newark, DE: International Reading Association.

Britton, J., Burgess, T., Martin, N., McLeod, A., & Rosen, H. (1975). *The development of writing abilities (11-18).* London: Schools Council Publications.

Calkins, L. M. (1995). *The art of teaching writing* (2nd ed.). Portsmouth, NH: Heinemann.

Calkins, L. M., & Harwayne, S. (1991). *Living between the lines.* Portsmouth, NH: Heinemann.

Cambourne, B., & Turbill, J. (1990). Assessment in whole language classrooms: Theory into practice. *Elementary School Journal, 90* (3), 337-347.

Clay, M. (1975). *What did I write?* London: Heinemann.

Clay, M. (1987). *Writing begins at home.* Portsmouth, NH: Heinemann.

Dyson, A. H. (1994). *Negotiating a permeable curriculum: On literacy, diversity, and the interplay of children's and teachers' worlds* (NCTE Concept Papers No. 9). Urbana, IL.

Emig, J. (1971). *The composing process of twelfth graders.* Urbana, IL: National Council of Teachers of English.

Gahn, S. M. (1989). A practical guide for teaching writing in the content areas. *Journal of Reading, 32* (6), 525-531.

Graves, D. (1983). *Writing: Teachers and children at work.* Portsmouth, NH: Heinemann.

Graves, D. (1985). *Write from the start.* New York: Dutton.

Graves, D., & Hansen, J. (1983). The author's chair. *Language Arts, 60* (2), 176-183.

Hansen, J. (1986). *When writers read.* Portsmouth, NH: Heinemann.

Hansen, J. (1992). The language of challenge: Readers and writers speak their minds. *Language Arts, 69* (2), 100-105.

Harste, J. C., Woodward, V. A., & Burke, C. L. (1984). *Language stories and literacy lessons.* Portsmouth, NH: Heinemann.

Hillocks, G. (1986). *Research on written composition.* Urbana, IL: National Council of Teachers of English.

Huck, C., Hepler, S., & Hickman, J. (1987). *Children's literature in the elementary school* (4th ed.). New York: Holt, Rinehart, & Winston.

Kirby, D., & Liner, T. (1981). *Inside out.* Montclair, NJ: Boynton/Cook.

Kormanski, L. M. (1992). Using poetry in the middle grades. *Reading Horizons, 32* (3), 184-190.

Kucer, S. (1985). The making of meaning: Reading and writing as parallel processes. *Written Communication, 2* (4), 317-336.

Laminack, L. (1990). "Possibilities, Daddy, I think it says possibilities": A father's journal of the emergence of literacy. *The Reading Teacher, 43* (8), 536-541.

Mack, B., & Farris, P. (1992). Conferencing in the writing process, a primer. *Illinois Reading Council Journal, 20* (4), 17-23.

Macrorie, K. (1968). *Writing to be read.* New York: Hayden.

Murray, D. (1968). *A writer teaches writing: A practical method of teaching composition.* Boston: Houghton Mifflin.

Murray, D. (1980). How writing finds its own meaning. In T. R. Donovan & B. W. McClelland, (Eds.), *Eight approaches to teaching composition.* Urbana, IL: National Council of Teachers of English.

Newman, J. M. (1985). *Whole language: Theory in use.* Portsmouth, NH: Heinemann.

Read, C. (1971). Pre-school children's knowledge of English phonology. *Harvard Educational Review, 41* (1), 1-14.

Smith, F. (1981). Myths of writing. *Language Arts, 58* (5), 792-798.

Smith, F. (1982). *Writing and the writer.* New York: Holt, Rinehart, & Winston.

Sulzby, E. (1992). Research directions: Transitions from emergent to conventional writing. *Language Arts, 69* (3), 290-297.

Teale, W. H. (1986). The beginnings of reading and writing: Written language development during the preschool and kindergarten years. In M. R. Sampson (Ed.), *The pursuit of literacy: Early reading and writing.* Dubuque, IA: Kendall/Hunt.

Tierney, R. J., Carter, M. A., & Desai, L. E. (1991). *Portfolio assessment in the reading-writing classroom.* Norwood, MA: Christopher-Gordon.

Tierney, R., & Pearson, P. D. (1983). Toward a composing model of reading. *Language Arts, 60* (5), 568–581.

Tompkins, G. E. (1993). *Teaching writing* (2nd ed.). Columbus, OH: Merrill.

Tompkins, G. E., & Friend, M. (1988). After your students write: What's next? *Teaching Exceptional Children, 20* (4), 4-9.

Tompkins, G. E., & Hoskisson, K. (1994). *Language arts: Content and teaching strategies* (3rd ed.). Columbus, OH: Merrill.

Walley, C. W. (1991). Diaries, logs, and journals in the elementary classroom. *Childhood Education, 67* (3), 149–154.

Writing: *Personal and Practical*

© Cleo Freelance Photo

A sense of authorship comes from the struggle
to put something big and vital into print, and
from seeing one's own printed words reach the
hearts and minds of readers.
—Lucy McCormick Calkins
The Art of Teaching Writing

Introduction

W riting is a learning vehicle that enables children and adults to become more aware of personal beliefs, to nurture their techniques of evaluation and interpretation, and ultimately to formulate related decisions. According to Newman (1983, p. 860), "One develops as a writer each time one engages in the process."

Odell (1983) defines discovery as learning, and he suggests that writing can actually facilitate the learning process. Abel and Abel (1988) concur, stating that writing is a medium not only for learning but for teaching students *how* to learn. Similarly, Graves (1978) states directly that writing enhances learning. Each time children write, a period of discovery ensues; they gain new knowledge about writing, language conventions, reading, and thinking, in addition to a better understanding of themselves.

Children do not develop as writers in a linear progression, for writing is recursive. As they struggle to experiment with and incorporate new techniques into their writing repertoires, their writing can seemingly deteriorate. For every upward gain, the line reflecting their writing development may form a plateau or even turn downward.

Writing facilitates learning in two ways, according to Draper (1979). First, within the prewriting stage, a child gains control over the development of ideas. Secondly, writing requires discipline; the child must engage in the ongoing assessment of the product by responding, questioning, defining, formulating, generalizing, and theorizing. Thus, writing empowers the child during the learning process.

As children write, a natural division occurs in the type of material produced: personal and practical writing pieces. Because personal writing represents the private side of a child, feelings, beliefs, interests, desires, and innermost thoughts will be expressed and described. Practical writing, on the other hand, is used as a child plans, organizes, summarizes, expands, and elaborates upon concerns or information.

If children are to grow through their personal and practical writing, the teacher must continually evaluate their progress. Children, too, should critique their own writing development by objectively reviewing and editing their work. Such teacher evaluation and self-evaluation should also be accompanied by peer evaluation. In discussing their work with other children, youngsters not only gain the respect of their peers but can also develop a more thorough understanding of their own perspectives and interpretations.

This chapter explores personal and practical writing, tools for evaluation of student writing, and the use of word processing in the elementary classroom.

Personal Writing

Personal writing is the most common writing form children use because they often share beliefs, feelings, thoughts, or concerns that they have with others. A child's first strokes on paper signify the beginning of personal writing, for these unrefined markings are actually an extension of the child. When advancing from simple scribbling to drawing lines and circles that represent people and objects and finally to forming letters, a child continues to demonstrate that the act of "writing" remains highly personal. Indeed, as the child progresses toward adulthood, much of the writing he or she undertakes is of a personal nature.

To encourage primary-grade children to write, the teacher might share Joan Lowery Nixon's *If You Were a Writer* (1988) with them. This is a warm, humorous book that describes a mother's explanations of commonplace, everyday events of family life as she urges her daughter to search for ideas, imagine characters, and use descriptive words in her writing. In the end, the mother gives her daughter a pencil and paper and tells her to record her stories, which she can either keep to herself or share with everyone. A companion book is Martin Selway's (1992) *Don't Forget to Write*.

For children, a personal piece of writing might describe a recent family incident, the arrival of a new puppy, or a story read by the teacher. It could also include notes and letters to friends and relatives or autobiographies, poetry, and stories written for oneself or for a known audience.

The importance of personal writing to children can be seen in their strong desire to share beliefs, thoughts, and ideas with others through writing. Such high motivation provides for growth in writing skills because fluency in writing depends on the opportunity to write.

Because personal writing appears to be the primary choice, by far, of the beginning writer, the teacher must provide children with experiences that will familiarize them with the many types of personal writing, including dialogues, journals, letters, autobiographies, and poetry. Each of these types is discussed below.

Dialogues

Dialogues provide a child with an opportunity to participate in a written conversation with someone else, such as the teacher or a classmate. Unlike letter writing, dialogue writing is more informal and unstructured (Farris, 1989). A child writes a brief message of perhaps only one or two sentences, and beneath this message on the same piece of paper, the correspondent writes a response. The finished product can be likened to a two-way diary in that it is both informal and unstructured.

Introducing children to dialogue writing at the beginning of the school year encourages them to write. If the teacher serves as the correspondent, he or she may gain insights about each student from the various messages exchanged.

The use of dialogue writing can also function as a motivational technique for slow learners or children with learning disabilities. Consider Larry, a fourth grader with weak written communication skills. During the time in which his teacher, Miss Davis, read Steven Kellogg's (1971) book *Can I Keep Him?* to the

In the Classroom Mini Lesson
Pocket Books

*C*hildren like to fold paper. Just imagine how many paper airplanes have been produced by students over the years! Pocket books are one way to engage children in folding paper with a positive literary result.

Give each student four sheets of 8½″ by 11″ white or colored paper. Place the paper on the desk, positioned as if the students were going to write on it. Have them bring the bottom of the paper one-third of the way up and fold. Next, fold the sheet of paper in half lengthwise with the pockets on the outside. Do this for the other three sheets of paper, then staple the sides away from the folds together into a book.

One variation is to make angled pockets. This is done by folding the top corners into the center of the paper and then folding the paper in half as though you were going to make a paper airplane. Next, open the paper and fold it in half with the pockets on the outside. Finally, staple the open sides together to make a two pocket book.

You can add more sheets of folded paper to make a book with the number of pockets you want. Larger paper makes for larger pocket books. Tagboard covers can be decorated and stapled to ordinary white paper to give the book durability.

These pocket books can be used for a variety of purposes. For instance, after hearing *The Very Hungry Caterpillar* by Eric Carle (1970), students can label the pockets in their pocket books the days of the week. Another good book to use is *Is This a House for Hermit Crab?* by Megan McDonald (1990). The students can use tagboard or old manilla file folders and markers to make the various objects in these books.

By drawing lines on the bottom of the paper and photocopying the paper, the pockets of the book will have lines on which the students can write a story.

Older students can use the pocket books for regional studies of the states or of countries. For instance, they can draw a map of the state on the top of the page and write facts about the state on an index card that slides into the pocket.

Science concepts could be written on index cards and questions on the pockets themselves. Students can then exchange their pocket books and insert their index cards into the pockets with the matching questions.

Carle, E. (1970). *The Very Hungry Caterpillar.* New York: Philomel.
McDonald, M. (1990). *Is This a House for Hermit Crab?* (S. D. Schindler, Illus.). New York: Orchard.

class, Larry developed a dialogue with Miss Davis via a computer. Although he had access to the classroom computer during the school day, Larry arrived early every day for a week to use the computer. Each morning before class, the computer disk with Larry's dialogue would appear on Miss Davis's desk. Likewise, every afternoon, Larry would check his desk for the computer disk, which now contained Miss Davis's reply. While Kellogg's book is about a young boy's desire to acquire a pet, Larry focused his writing on his desire to obtain a sporty vehicle. A portion of Larry's written dialogue with Miss Davis follows:

Der Miss Davs,

Twoday I fnd a red crvtt car on my way to shol. It is reel cool and gos reel fast. Can I keep it?

Larry

In the Classroom Mini Lesson

Dialogue Writing with Senior Citizens

*D*ialogue writing has proved to be a successful way for children to interact with their teacher. If there is a nearby retirement home for senior citizens, students may "adopt" senior citizens for this form of interactive written communication. The students use notebooks to write dialogue about what they are learning, community events, problems with friends, and so on. The teacher collects the notebooks with the student dialogues once a week and drops them off at the retirement home on a Thursday or Friday. On the following Monday, the teacher goes to the retirement home and picks up the notebooks, which now contain the senior citizens' replies, and returns the notebooks to the students. This sort of interchange helps students with their writing and keeps senior citizens in touch with the community.

Dear Larry,

I think red Corvettes are beautiful cars. They do go very fast and look cool. But you don't have a driver's license so you could drive it. No, you can't keep the red Corvette.

Your friend,
Miss Davis

The next day the following correspondence took place:

Dear Miss Davs,

Twoday I fnd a Hrly Davisn bike. It is cool and gos faster thn a corvet. Can I keep it?

Your friend, Larry

Dear Larry,

Harley Davidson motorcycles are cool. They run in motorcycle races because they are so fast. But you need a driver's license to ride a motorcycle, and you are still too young to apply for a license. No, Larry, you can't keep the Harley Davidson.

Your friend,
Miss Davis

Journals

Like dialogue writing, journal writing is informal and often unstructured. Essentially serving as diaries, *journals* are a means by which children record events and their feelings about those events. Craig (1983) refers to journals as a spontaneous, unplanned means of understanding oneself. Along this same line, in an article entitled "Bait—We Should Abolish the Use of Personal Journals in English Classes" (Hollowell & Nelson, 1982), Nelson contends that journals serve as a means of moving from personal to public writing, thereby making journals an important part of the writing curriculum.

Figure 9.1
Journal entries of a
second grader.

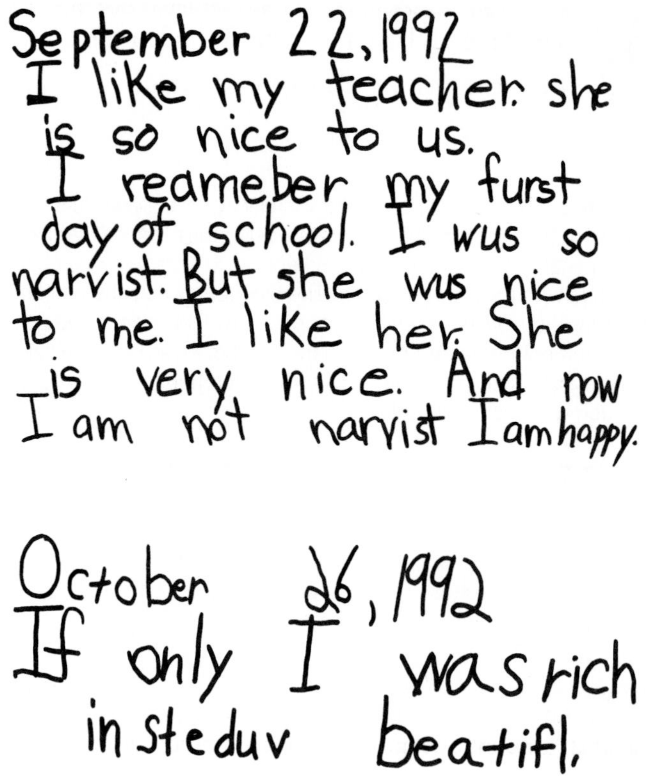

September 22, 1992
I like my teacher. she
is so nice to us.
I reameber my furst
day of school. I wus so
narvist. But she wus nice
to me. I like her. She
is very nice. And now
I am not narvist I am happy.

October 26, 1992
If only I was rich
in ste duv beatifl.

For children who have already been introduced to dialogue writing, journal writing is the next stage in a natural progression. Even though kindergartners and first graders have yet to acquire writing skills, their drawings of a day's primary events can serve as journal writing. Later, as they develop some writing talent, they can move to a combination of illustrations and words.

Initially, a thin spiral notebook makes a good, sturdy journal. Although intermediate children sometimes prefer to use two- or three-ring notebooks that allow them to insert and remove pages, such notebooks are often cumbersome and require additional storage space.

Because children in the primary grades find it a great deal easier to direct their writings to a specific audience, the teacher may ask the students to pretend that they are writing the journal for a friend outside the immediate classroom (see figure 9.1). Getting older children to write in a journal can be frustrating for a teacher at first because intermediate-grade students' seemingly enthusiastic initial attempts may yield only bland writing at best. Children at this age are suspicious of open-ended and unstructured assignments, and they simply lack experience in keeping a journal. To encourage students to take some liberties in recording life events, a teacher may share portions of another person's journal or diary with them. Beverly Cleary's (1983) *Dear Mr. Henshaw* and its 1991 sequel, *Strider*, are examples of one child's dialogue writing that evolved into journal writing. Still another introductory and motivational approach is the sharing of excerpts from the teacher's own journal with the class.

Some teachers encourage students to write in their journals on a daily basis for a short period of time, such as 5 minutes. Along with their students, these teachers write in a journal during the designated period. However, time constraints may prohibit some teachers from pursuing such a daily schedule. When this is the case, the teacher may decide that writing two or three times a week is sufficient, the journal can still function as a continuous log over some selected period of time.

At times, students may actually express a desire to write in their journals. One sixth-grade teacher, Mrs. Murphy, was asked by a student whether class members could have time to write in their journals. When Mrs. Murphy replied that journal writing was not scheduled for that day, the student exclaimed, "But I just *have to* write today!" Because she was a flexible teacher and recognized the student's distress at being unable to record her thoughts, Mrs. Murphy rearranged the day's schedule to include journal writing. Later the student shared her journal entry for that day with Mrs. Murphy; it revealed the child's concern about a serious problem she had had with one of her friends. In this instance, journal writing allowed the child to work out a potential solution to the problem.

On a regular basis, teachers should collect the journals and read the students' entries. Some teachers collect all the journals and read the entries once every week or two. Other teachers elect to collect and read a few journals each day. The latter scheme results in better time management because teachers can set aside a small amount of time each day for entry reading. This can be easily done by dividing the class into five groups corresponding to the 5 days of the school week.

Because journal writing is considered personal, a teacher must respect a student's entries and maintain confidentiality. In some instances, a child may not want the teacher to read all of the entries because some are so personal. In such specific cases, the teacher and student should establish a coding system: The student might attach a red paper clip at the beginning of a very private entry and a green paper clip at the point where the teacher may continue reading. This coding system ensures the child's freedom and privacy but keeps the journal intact.

Journal writing goes hand in hand with literature response journals. In journal writing the focus is upon the thoughts, impressions, and feelings of the child as the writer. For literature response journals, the focus is on the child as the reader and the "lived-through literary experience and experiences, thoughts, feelings, images, and associations which are evoked" (Many, 1992, p. 169).

Letters

Like journal writing, letter writing evolves from dialogue writing. Unlike dialogues and journal entries, however, letters must be structured and planned by the writer.

Letter writing is motivational in that all children are eager to receive letters in the mail. Having young children write letters is an easy way to arouse their

Figure 9.2
Writing letters allows
each student the
chance to share
experiences and
organize thoughts.

Dear Second Grade,
   One of my favorit animals
is a spider. It is a pet in
our classroom. Come visit us
Tusday and learn about spiders.
                    Your friend,
                    Aeron

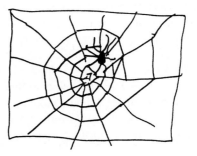

writing enthusiasm because they cannot resist the chance to communicate with those around them. This is evident in student whispering and in the passing of notes within the classroom. As children learn to share their experiences and thoughts in such notes, they are actually developing their skills in clarity as well as in organizational writing (figure 9.2). In view of this, teachers should encourage note passing by establishing a mailbox for each student. Likewise, a letter writing station can be established in the classroom and supplied with ample and appropriate writing supplies: pencils, pens, paper, and envelopes. The class may even wish to design its own stationery, with a unique logo, class motto, or marginal design. Similar group efforts, such as writing thank-you notes to room parents and invitations to other classes to share special events, not only support the development of writing skills but also function as models of appropriate social behavior.

Modeling is an appropriate approach to the teaching of letter writing. For example, a teacher can use an overhead projector while writing a friendly letter so that the class is able to observe the process. With this goal in mind, the teacher should first speculate about the letter: To whom shall it be written? What will it contain? How familiar is the audience with the planned topics? How will the contents be organized? After sharing the decision as to who will receive the letter, the teacher must express some general thoughts about the topic(s) to be covered and

Figure 9.3
A letter from a second grader to a pen pal in Mexico.

the audience's familiarity with the subject(s). As the discussion proceeds, the teacher may take notes pertaining to the topic(s) as part of the prewriting activity. At this point, the teacher is able to begin writing the initial draft of the letter.

Pen pals are very popular with children. Youngsters enjoy finding out about other children and are especially pleased to develop a writing relationship with someone of the same age or grade level (see figure 9.3). To eliminate postal expenses, a teacher who has students who want to write letters to pen pals can seek pen pals from another school in the same district. Such an arrangement can be very satisfying, particularly if the two neighboring classes can meet for a joint field trip or picnic at the end of the school year.

The U.S. Postal Service encourages writing to pen pals by suggesting how to establish a postal system within the school itself. A videotape entitled *Wee Deliver: Stamp Out Illiteracy* and an accompanying booklet explain how to set up a postal system by using different sections of the school as towns and having each classroom serve as a street. Each student is assigned his or her own street number. Students serve as the postmaster or postmistress and postal workers after applying for various jobs and successfully passing a modified version of the civil service exam (for example, being able to determine correct and incorrect addresses on envelopes). The workers change jobs each month, and every morning before school begins, the mail is delivered. More information about this program can be obtained by writing to the following address:

Stamp Out Illiteracy Program
Office of Literacy
U.S. Postal Service
470 L'Enfant Plaza SW Room 4102E
Washington, DC 20260-3110

Young pen pals from different geographical areas can help each other foster letter-writing abilities and develop social studies skills, particularly when they are in the intermediate grades. The World Pen Pals organization establishes formal networks between children of various nationalities. For further information on international pen pals, write to the following address:

World Pen Pals
1690 Como Avenue
St. Paul, MN 55108

Autobiographies

Autobiographical writing permits children to share their individual life experiences with others. Such writing helps the author gain new and often deeper perspectives on relationships and events.

An *autobiography* may describe one's entire lifetime, from birth to the present, or it may provide information only on selected portions of that lifetime, such as special events and remembrances. For children in kindergarten through the second or third grade, a modified autobiography, whereby a child may draw or write about likes and dislikes, may be more appropriate. A good book to share with children before they write such an autobiography is Susan Pearson's (1988) *My Favorite Time of Year.* Kelly, the young girl in the book, describes autumn as her favorite time of the year and then points out that each of the other seasons also holds some special joy for her and her family.

Typically, intermediate-grade children find the writing of autobiographies to be quite appealing. By this age, they have read both biographies and autobiographies about famous people, and they have also had some practice in writing "About the Author" sections, short synopses in which they describe themselves on the jacket covers of their "published books."

The teacher can also model autobiographical writing for this age-group by reading a portion of a personal, self-written statement. In addition, children's literature offers some examples of autobiographies. For instance, Jean Fritz's (1982) *Homesick,* a book to which almost every child can relate, describes the emptiness of longing for the familiar surroundings of home, family, and friends. An unusual autobiography is Eloise Greenfield and Lessie Jones Little's (1979) *Childtimes: A Three-Generation Memoir,* in which a grandmother, mother, and daughter describe the events they experienced "growing up."

Poetry

Unfortunately, teachers are less apt to share poetry, particularly their own, than narrative works with children. As a result, children often lack enthusiasm for or become indifferent to poetry. Andrews (1988) writes that sharing a variety of literature including poetry raises the level of students' language and vocabulary development. The vicarious experiences provided by and the expressive nature of poetry serve to increase students' awareness and sensitivity to the world around them. "When teachers share a variety of poems with children several times a day, children develop positive attitudes about this genre of literature" (Kormanski, 1992, p. 189). Unfortunately, "the poetry that children prefer often lacks the subtle imagery, interesting rhythms, and clever plays on words that characterize the really good examples of this genre" (McClure, 1995, p. 118). Thus, it is up to the teacher to share a variety of forms of poetry with students. Poetry should be included naturally in the classroom, both purposefully and spontaneously.

Stewig (1988) points out three misconceptions children have about poetry: (1) poetry *must* rhyme, (2) poetry must be beautiful and pretty, and (3) nothing occurs in poetry because the writing is predominately descriptive.

Students need to play with and manipulate words, combining them in new and unusual ways. Denman (1988) calls this "wordsmithing," or an awareness of the resources of language. This means that attention is given to a phrase because of its repetition of a particular sound, to the element of surprise that can be achieved by unusual combinations of words, to the power and effect of a few well-selected words, or to the insights made possible by the use of metaphor.

Poetry permits a teacher to encourage children to experiment with words as well as a wide variety of formats: lyric, narrative, limerick, rhyming, free verse, haiku, cinquain, and so on. Children almost universally prefer rhyming poetry as a style because it is the one they have encountered the most. For example, Jack Prelutsky's (1984, 1990, 1996) *The New Kid on the Block, Something Big has Been Here, Monday's Troll,* and Shel Silverstein's (1974, 1981) *Where the Sidewalk Ends* and *A Light in the Attic* typically fit into this category. However, a teacher should expose children to the other forms of poetry as well.

Children find it easiest to write about what is familiar to them. Poetry about daily life and ordinary objects provides children with an opportunity to examine and relate their own personal experiences. Collections of poetry that are appropriate for such sharing include the following:

Adoff, A. (1991). *In for winter, out for spring* (J. Pinkney, Illus.). San Diego: Harcourt Brace.

Harrison, M. (1989). *Splinters: A book of very short poems* (S. Heap, Illus.). New York: Oxford University Press.

Hopkins, L. B. (1984). *Surprises.* New York: Harper & Row.

Huang, T. (1992). *In the eyes of the cat: Japanese poetry for all seasons* (Demi, Illus.). New York: Henry Holt.

Hughes, L. (1986). *The dream keeper and other poems* (H. Sewell, Illus.). New York: Knopf.

Levy, C. (1991). *I'm going to pet a worm today and other poems* (R. Himler, Illus.). New York: McElderberry.

Merriam, E. (1986). *A sky full of poems.* New York: Dell.

Morrison, L. (1977). *The sidewalk racer and other poems of sports and motion.* New York: Lothrop, Lee, & Shepard.

Prelutsky, J. (1983). *The Random House book of poetry for children* (A. Lobel, Illus.). New York: Random House.

Shields, C. D. (1996). *Lunch money* (P. Meisel, Illus.). New York: Dutton.

Starbird, K. (1979). *The covered bridge house and other poems* (J. Arnosky, Illus.). New York: Four Winds.

Viorst, J. (1981). *If I were in charge of the world and other worries: Poems for children and their parents* (L. Cherry, Illus.). New York: Atheneum.

Poetry about various topics should also be shared with children to encourage them to write about similar topics. Holidays, humor, nature, and scary things are some of the topics to which children naturally relate. Children enjoy reading *Sweet Corn* by James Stevenson (1995) which has poems entitled "Tree House," "Cows," "Snow," "Bus Stop," and "The Dancer." Through these and similar poems, children learn that poetry can be found in common things, such as sweet corn and clotheslines.

Poetry writing should be part of writing across the curriculum. Jim Ronan, a fifth-grade teacher, includes poetry writing in his social studies units. For instance, he reads a descriptive scene from a piece of historical fiction and then has his students work in pairs or alone to write a poem about that scene.

Poetry is often about the ordinary, that is everyday things and occurrences that are taken for granted. Consider, for example, "Bug Catcher," a poem by Rick Walton (1995) in which a child attempts to catch several different insects—a ladybug, a caterpillar, a butterfly, a cricket, and a fly—but to no avail. Every child has had a similar experience and can easily relate to this poem.

Elements of Poetry

Through writing poetry, children discover the importance of word choice, as finding exactly the right word to use is more critical in poetry than in prose. Thus, students' writing and speaking vocabularies often increase as a result of incorporating more poetry into the curriculum.

Rhyme is one of the most well-known elements of poetry. A good rhyme is almost like a piece of music, but rhyme must be used appropriately. Sometimes children, and adults, overuse rhyme. Some children write lengthy rhyming poems—thoroughly enjoying the challenge of finding words that rhyme— but the rhyme is often forced and unnatural.

Alliteration is another component of poetry. Consider "Peter Piper picked a peck of pickled peppers." The constant repetition of a sound, such as [p] in this Mother Goose rhyme, is called *alliteration.* When the alliteration is the repetition of a sound within words, such as in "Fuzzy Wuzzy was a bear," it is referred to as *hidden alliteration.*

Like alliteration, onomatopoeia is based on the use of sound. For *onomatopoeia,* the poet uses words or phrases that imitate sounds. These include such words as *buzz, hiss, sigh, bang, ring, scratch, crunch,* and *tick-tock.*

Rhythm is the beat or pattern of a poem. Poems are often based on a cadence that is predictable. This is referred to as *meter.* Perfect meter is almost a singsong verse such as is found in many commercially developed greeting cards.

The poet uses the above aspects in writing but also incorporates figures of speech, including simile, metaphor, and personification. The *simile* compares one thing to another using *as* or *like.* The following phrases are similes: "big as a barn," "sweet as honey," and "crazy like a loon." A *metaphor* is used when the writer says that one thing is something else, for instance referring to bulldozers as "gigantic beasts." *Personification* assigns human qualities to non-human things, such as "the dog's eyes reflected wisdom" or "spring does her decorating rolling out emerald green carpeting with yellow daffodils and red tulips tucked along the sides of her room."

By becoming familiar with the different writing techniques that can be incorporated into writing poetry, students can hone their general writing skills, as well.

Types of Poetry

There are numerous types of poetry that children enjoy both writing and reading. Some of these are described in the paragraphs that follow.

List Poems. *List poems* offer children an introduction to poetry and free verse. These are easy to introduce to a class by using the chalkboard or an overhead projector and having the students brainstorm to generate a list about a particular topic. For instance, a first-grade class brainstormed to create the following list poem about rabbits:

Rabbits
white
furry
brown
paws
foot
hopping
hiding
tame
wild
chewing
grass
carrots
lettuce
stretching
nibble
wriggly nose
Rabbits

They then went on to write the following list poem about their classroom:

Our Classroom
books
journals
Peedee, the guinea pig
warm
yellow
loud desks
free time
lots of kids
helpers
reading buddies
library books
art projects
Mrs. Simpson
helping moms
helping dads
centers
calendar
clock
windows
trays
our best work

All responses the students offer are appropriate to include in a list poem. This helps give them confidence in writing their own list poem, regardless of their grade level.

Free Verse. Free verse does not follow any structure or rules. Thus, it is a collection of the poet's thoughts that may ramble about on the page. By being introduced to free verse, children discover that not every poem has to rhyme or follow a strict poetic structure. List poems are actually free verse.

Concrete Poetry. Concrete poetry is sometimes referred to as shape or pattern poetry. Livingston (1991) calls concrete poetry "a picture poem" since it combines both. The poem may consist of one word written over and over again in the shape of an object, for instance writing "dog" several times to outline a dog's body. Or the poem may include words that are written or drawn in an artistic manner (see figure 9.4).

Poetry Starters. Often children find it difficult to begin to write a poem. For some, the first line can seem overwhelming. For such students, a *poetry starter* can be helpful in removing that initial writer's block. Some examples of poetry starters are as follows:

Yesterday I was . . .
My pet . . .
When _____ was alive . . . (fill in the blank with a historical figure)
Can he (or she) ever play! (the student focuses on a baseball, basketball, football, or other sport star)
Don't forget _____. (fill in the blank—could be a person, place, or thing)
Green is . . . (or any color the child selects)

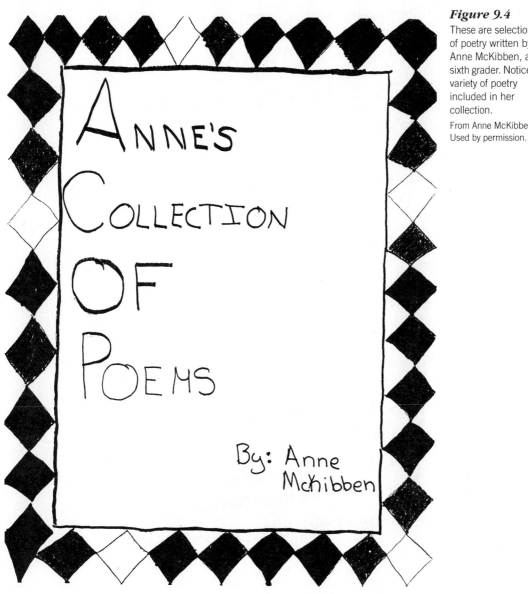

Figure 9.4
These are selections
of poetry written by
Anne McKibben, a
sixth grader. Notice the
variety of poetry
included in her
collection.

From Anne McKibben.
Used by permission.

Figure 9.4
(Continued)

If I Were In Charge Of The World

If I Were In Charge of the World
I'd end world poverty
I'd give everyone a home
I'd give everyone an education and also
Have world peace

If I Were In Charge of the World
I'd have a perfect environment
Every animal would have a home, and
I'd save all rainforests

If I Were In Charge of the World
You wouldn't have any drugs
You wouldn't have violence
You wouldn't have guns
You wouldn't have gangs
You wouldn't even have world wars.

Figure 9.4
(*Continued*)

If I Were In Charge of the World
I'd stop diseases
Let everyone have a job
And a person that forgets to make her bed
And sometimes forgets to comb her hair on her head
Would still be allowed to be
In charge of the world

anne

Figure 9.4
(Continued)

The Ocean

The Ocean Rolls and Tumbles About,
Spits and Spews as it
crashes against the Rocky Shore.

Anne

Figure 9.4
(Continued)

Nature
Quiet, Beautiful
Chirping, Swaying, Watching
Always Clean and Fresh
Soaring, Blooming, Growing
Bright, Sunny
Breathtaking

Figure 9.4
(*Continued*)

Tilton School

Terrific place to be

Laughing kids walk about
The hallways
Outstanding teachers
Numerous activities

Students are drug free

Hot test grades
Outgoing kinds
Of kids
Like this school.

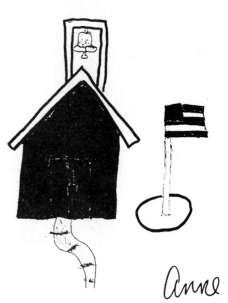

Anne

Figure 9.4
(Continued)

<u>Faraway Friends</u>

You can have a friend faraway.
But still be close in the same way.

You could read different books.
But share the same looks.

You could share the same dream.
But yours was more keen.

You could share who you like and fear.
But you don't have to be near.

Some friends come and go.
When the right one comes, you'll know.

Anne

Figure 9.4
(*Continued*)

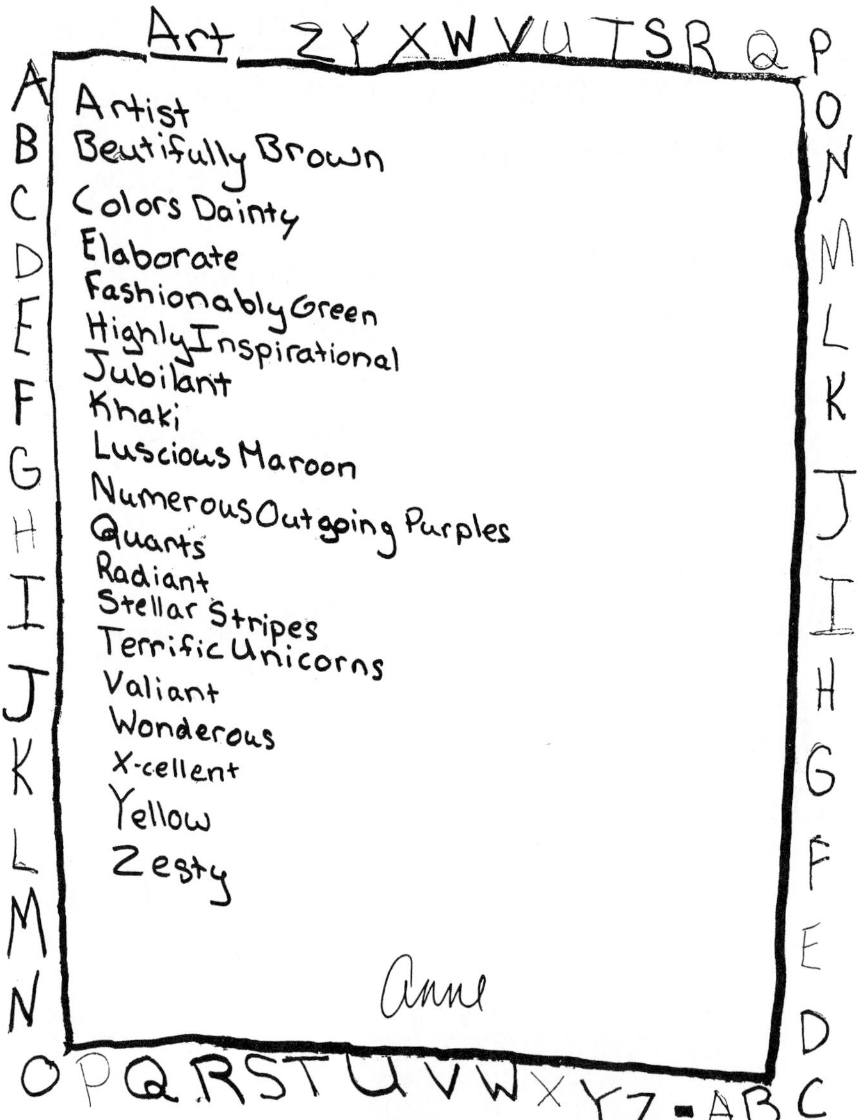

Art ZYXWVUTSRQP

A
B
C
D
E
F
G
H
I
J
K
L
M
N

Artist
Beutifully Brown
Colors Dainty
Elaborate
Fashionably Green
Highly Inspirational
Jubilant
Khaki
Luscious Maroon
Numerous Outgoing Purples
Quarts
Radiant
Stellar Stripes
Terrific Unicorns
Valiant
Wonderous
X-cellent
Yellow
Zesty

Anne

O N M L K J I H G F E D

OPQRSTUVWXYZ-ABC

Figure 9.4
(Continued)

Fifteen, Maybe Sixteen, Things To Worry About

The fan could maybe blow me away.
The heater could maybe get too hot and we could dehydrate.
The sharpener sawdust could get in my eye.
   (Ouch!)
Something could come crashing down on my head-lika plate.

The ozone layer could rapidly go away.
My pants could want to fall down during lunch.
The chalkboard could ask me a hard question.
      (maybe it won't!)
My back could become a hunch.

The teacher could maybe make all of us stay after.
I could lose my house key.
My friend could say I'm mean.

My heart could decide to quit on me.

The world could maybe fall and fall.
I could forget to make my bed.
I maybe could run out of things for me to worry about.
And then I'd have to do my homework instead.

(Ahh hhh!)

(All the things to worry about)
got to her

anne

Figure 9.4
(*Concluded*)

About The Author

Anne McKibben was born in DeKalb, Illinois. She is 12 years old and is a sixth grader at Tilton Elementary School. She likes to play tennis and basketball. She also likes to travel. She now lives in Rochelle, Illinois.

Poetry from Names or Words. Students enjoy the challenge of using a name and transforming it into a poem. They can take their first name and make it into a poem, such as the following:

JASON
Joking
Awesome
Soccer player
Only child
Neat
JASON

To begin this type of writing the teacher can either use the school's name and having the class develop a class poem, or have each student develop their own poem (see figure 9.4).

Couplets and Triplets. Couplets are two-line poems that rhyme while *triplets* are three-line poems that rhyme. These are fairly easy for students to write, even for those in the lower grades. Children enjoy them because they are pleasing to the ear (Livingston, 1991). To help students start writing these kinds of poems, the teacher may want to provide the first line of a poem and have the students complete it. Here is an example of a triplet that a fourth grader completed upon being given the first line:

The Mouse
There once was a mouse
Who lived in a house
With his little spouse.

Haiku. Haiku is a three-line poem with nature as its subject. This short, 17-syllable poem is a popular poetic form with elementary students. The first and third lines contain five syllables, and the second line seven syllables. "Haiku"

In the Classroom Mini Lesson
Poetry in the Content Areas

*P*oetry needs to be a part of the entire curriculum, including content area subjects. By reading aloud a portion from a picture book, a historical novel, or a piece of nonfiction, children can be motivated to write a poetic reflection. After the scene describing the slave auction in *Nettie's Trip South* by Ann Turner (1987) had been read to a class of seventh graders, their teacher put them into groups of three to write a poem based on what had been read to them and what they had learned about slavery through the Civil War unit they were currently studying. Below is the poem that one group of three boys wrote:

> Auction's Today
>
> Walked into town from home, with my sister
>   Hetta holt my hand and wouldn't let go.
>
> It's dusty in the pen.
>   Waiting.
> Tompkins' men pushed us up.
>   Platform's got splinters.
>   Hetta holt my hand and wouldn't let go.
>
> Tompkins yelled out, "Two youths,
>   From Will Jackson's place,
> What am I bid?"
>   Yellin' numbers and dollars.
>   Hetta holt my hand and wouldn't let go.
>
> "Boy Sold! For nine dollars."
>   Hetta holt my hand and wouldn't let go.
>
> Yellin' numbers and dollars.
>   Hetta holt my hand and wouldn't let go.
>
> "Girl Sold! For five dollars."
>   Hetta holt my hand and wouldn't let go.
>
> One of Tompkins' men took my arm.
>   Hetta holt my hand and wouldn't let go.
>
> Tompkins took Hetta's arm.
>   Hetta holt my hand and wouldn't let go.
>
> With a heave, Tompkins flung Hetta
>   off the platform.
>
> Hetta don't hold my hand no more.

Figure 9.5

This is an example of a collaborative poem composed after listening to a read aloud from *Nettie's Trip South*.

From Pamela J. Farris, "Exploring Multicultural Themes Through Picture Books" in *Middle School Journal*, January 1995. Copyright © 1995. Used by permission.

Turner, A. (1987). *Nettie's trip south* (R. Himler, Illus.). New York: Macmillan.

In the Classroom Mini Lesson

Clerihews

A type of poetry that has become popular in recent years is the *clerihew,* a four-line rhyming verse that pertains to a person. The form is as follows:

Line one: The person's name.
Line two: The last word in this line rhymes with the person's last name.
Lines three   The last words in these lines rhyme with each other.
and four:

Such poems are fun to write in pairs. For instance, pairs of students can write clerihews about their own names on the first day of school. Book characters, famous people, and historical figures are other possible subjects. Penny wrote this clerihew about television personality Oprah Winfrey:

Oprah
We love ya!
You talk and talk every day.
Where do you get those weird people anyway?

means "beginning phrase" in Japanese. The author of haiku always writes about the here and now in nature. Thus, haiku is always written in the present tense. Below is an example of haiku:

Lonely yellow leaf
Floating downward to the earth
Autumn has arrived.

Writing haiku is a real challenge, but children have, for some reason, adopted this challenge. Perhaps it is because writing haiku is like fitting together a puzzle that comes from within.

Cinquain. Cinquain is another popular poetic form with children. Like haiku, cinquain has a set structure. The five-line poem consists of two syllables in the first line, four in the second, six in the third, eight in the fourth, and two again in the fifth.

Here is a cinquain about the ocean written by a fifth grader:

Ocean

Big, deep
Expanse of blue
Home to fish, sharks, whales
Beautiful, peaceful, splashing waves
Giving.

Practical Writing

Practical writing entails using the composing process to satisfy some utilitarian need, such as knowledge acquisition, comprehension, or concept development. This type of writing can help one to understand and retain information. Elbow (1981) points out that writing down one's thoughts concerning a topic enables one to "work through" a problem by allowing for the flow of ideas. The ideas and insights thus produced are then analyzed until the individual has achieved clarity in terms of a problem's resolution. Along these same lines, practical writing can be used to evaluate one's own knowledge in that focusing on a topic and generating associated, relevant information can serve as a way of assessing what one already knows about a subject (Gaskin, 1982).

Practical writing incudes academic learning logs, informational reports, business letters, biographies, and note taking. These are discussed in the remainder of this section.

Academic Learning Logs

Academic learning logs are interpretative journals in which children explain a concept or topic through their writing. Therefore, such logs serve as records of children's understandings and, because they are written in the children's own words, can help to clarify their thoughts about a particular subject. As Boyer (1983, p. 90) writes, "clear writing leads to clear thinking; clear thinking is the basis of clear writing."

Using the academic learning log in a content area as reflective writing has proved to help students become more aware of their problem-solving methods (Brady, 1991; Hand & Treagust, 1991). Students discover which learning strategies are most effective for them.

The academic learning log can be applied to various subject areas. For example, such a log can provide explanations of scientific experiments or relay a deeper understanding of social studies concepts. Even for mathematics, such logs are beneficial in helping children gain understanding, as shown in a fourth grader's description of the steps involved in long division (see figure 9.6).

Cudd and Roberts (1989) have developed a modified academic learning log for use by primary-grade students. This version of the log is designed to enhance content area learning through writing. Cudd and Roberts use sequentially organized paragraphs so that students can easily recognize and use this type of paragraph structure in their own writing. The teacher begins instruction by modeling the writing of a simple paragraph in a series of seven steps:

1. Write a short, simple paragraph about a topic that lends itself to sequential ordering, using the sequencing terms *first, next, then,* and *finally.* Examples of topics include the development of a frog from an egg to a tadpole to a young frog to an adult frog, a bear entering and emerging from hibernation, and so on. (See the following example.)

Figure 9.6
A fourth grader's
description of steps in
long division.

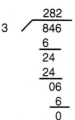

$$\begin{array}{r} 282 \\ 3 \overline{)846} \\ 6 \\ \overline{24} \\ 24 \\ \overline{06} \\ 6 \\ \overline{0} \end{array}$$

To divide in long division. First you take the 3 into the 8. It goes two times. Write the 2 above and multiply 2 times 3. Then you subtract 6 from 8 and get 2. Then you bring down the next number, a 4. You then take 3 into 24. It goes eight times. Write down 8 next to the 2 and multiply 8 times 3. You get 24. Then you subtract 24 from 24 and get 0. Bring down the 6 and divide 3 into 6. It goes two times. Write 2 next to the 8. Then subtract 6 from 6. You have nothing left. You can check the answer by multiplying 3 times 282. You get 846.

Hibernation

First, a bear eats lots of food during the summer. Next, the bear finds a cave or hollow tree to sleep in. Then the bear falls asleep for the winter. Finally, it wakes up in the spring.

2. Write the sentences on sentence strips or transparency strips.
3. Review the topic and the logical sequence of events with the entire class or group.
4. Have the children arrange the sentence strips in the correct order in a pocket chart or on the overhead if transparency strips are used.
5. Have the entire class or group read the paragraph together.
6. Have the children reorder the paragraph on their own and write it in paragraph form.
7. Have the students illustrate the details of the paragraph. (Cudd & Roberts, 1989, p. 394)

Research suggests that children recall in greater detail and completeness information that is presented with pictorial support (Marshall, 1984). Therefore, having children illustrate their paragraphs and research reports is important to the students' comprehension of the topics covered.

Biographies

Biographies require children to conduct research before they write about a person's life. Although a biography need not cover an individual's entire life span, it should describe a selected portion of it. As with autobiographies, children's literature provides a wealth of examples of biographies for students. Jean Fritz, a master biographer, combines exacting research findings with colorful language to weave stories about famous historical figures. Moreover, Fritz's intriguing book titles highlight her accurate depictions of Revolutionary War leaders. Such qualities result in books that are both appropriate for primary-grade readers and highly motivating.

Beginning any composition is a challenge for all writers; however, initiating a biographical sketch can be especially difficult for children. Because children have problems establishing a frame of reference for a setting (both time and place), their biographies often fail to describe a distinct period and locale. As a result, it is not unusual for a child's biography about a historical figure or famous athlete to begin with "Once upon a time, there was a boy [girl] named. . . ." There exist a plethora of quality biographies within literature which can serve as models for more realistic depiction of characters and setting. An example of a book in which the opening sentences entice the reader to continue reading is Jean Fritz's (1973) *And Then What Happened, Paul Revere?* In this book, Fritz opens with a description of the setting, Boston, which becomes critical in considering the Revolutionary War.

In undertaking biographical sketches, children should become aware of significant factors in an individual's life, for such factors are necessary elements for biographies. When the student biographer knows the subject's interests and values, he or she should be encouraged to include these in the biography as well.

Note Taking

Children typically find note taking difficult because they lack the ability to be selective. Generally, youngsters are unable to distinguish between important information and that of little significance. When given proper instructions, however, children can become proficient note takers at a relatively early age.

One approach to the development of note-taking skills is teacher modeling, whereby students can actually see how important information is selected. For example, with second or third graders, a teacher might choose a book about an animal to read to the class. Before proceeding with the book, however, the teacher writes four questions about the animal on the chalkboard: (1) What does it eat? (2) Where does it live? (3) What does it look like? (4) Are there any interesting facts about the animal? After sharing the book with the students, the teacher uses an overhead projector to show four boxes labeled "food," "habitat," "appearance," and "interesting facts." Next, the teacher writes information provided by the students about the animal in the appropriate box as shown in figure 9.7 (Farris, 1988). Finally, the teacher uses the information the students have provided to write a report about the animal. For each of the four areas (food, habitat, appearance, and interesting facts), the teacher uses a separate sheet of paper and leaves enough space for an illustration. Figure 9.8 shows a sample report entitled "Grizzly Bear."

Following such teacher modeling, students are better able to take notes and then write their own animal reports. Each child selects an animal book from among those the teacher checked out of the library. The students are given about two days in which to read the books. By the third day, students are taking

Kind of Animal: __ <u>GRIZZLY BEAR</u> __

Food

berries
fish
salmon
wild honey

Habitat

cave
Canada
Alaska

Appearance

thick fur
silver tips on end of fur
big claws
strong, big teeth

Interesting Facts

excellent fisherman
can walk on hind legs
hibernates during winter
can weigh over 1,000 pounds

notes about the animal's food, habitat, appearance, and other interesting facts. On the fourth day, the students begin their first drafts by writing about and illustrating the food the animal eats. On the fifth, sixth, and seventh days, the students write about and illustrate the animal's habitat, the animal's appearance, and interesting facts about the animal, respectively. On the eighth and ninth days, the students revise their entire reports. On the tenth day, the authors recopy their writing and redraw their illustrations to produce their final products for publication and sharing with classmates (Farris, 1988).

This same note-taking approach can be used with children in the intermediate grades by increasing the sophistication of the task. By selecting narrower subject areas, students can gather information that will result in more specific, well-defined research topics. For example, a unit on World War II may yield term papers with various general themes: causes of the war, political leaders, generals, famous battles, the D-Day invasion of Normandy, types of weapons, and so forth. Any chosen theme may then be divided into more specific topics. For example, given the general theme of World War II political leaders, one student may wish to focus on Adolph Hitler's youth, work, rise to power, and death. Another student may choose to do the same with Franklin Roosevelt, a third with Winston Churchill, and a fourth with Joseph Stalin.

Intermediate-grade students can use different books and periodicals as references in gathering notes for their term papers. For each piece of information used, the student must record in the body of the term paper both the name of the author(s) and the publication date of the book from which the information came. The student must also include an alphabetical list of all references at the end of the paper. Each source entry must contain the author's name, date of publication, title of book, city of publication, and name of publisher.

Children can take notes of textbook material quite easily. The headings and subheadings of most textbooks serve as summaries for chapter sections and subsections. By using these headings and subheadings as note-taking categories,

TITLE: GRIZZLY BEARS

AUTHORS: Mrs. Carpenter's Second Grade Class

ILLUSTRATOR: Mrs. Carpenter

FOOD
Grizzly bears eat fish and berries. They especially like to eat salmon. Wild honey is a special treat because grizzly bears have a sweet tooth like people do.

HABITAT
Grizzly bears live in Alaska and Canada. They live in caves to keep them warm in the winter and cool in the summer.

APPEARANCE
They have huge claws and strong teeth. Their fur is thick and has silver tips on the end each hair.

INTERESTING FACTS
Grizzly bears are large. They weigh over 1,000 pounds. They can stand on their hind feet. Grizzly bears eat a lot in the summer and fall so they can hibernate in the winter.

In the Classroom Mini Lesson

Computer Access to the Library of Congress

Teachers and students may access the Library of Congress retrieval system called LOCIS (Library of Congress Information System) by using Telnet or Internet. There are over 26 million records in 35 different online files, including files for books, audiovisuals, manuscripts, serials, maps, computer software, microforms, and music, that students may use as references for their writing.

The address for Telnet access is as follows:
locis.loc.gov
The Internet address is as follows:
K12Net

The Internet address provides an introduction to global telecommunication for teachers and students.

There is no charge for using LOCIS, but there may be fees for using the Internet. LOCIS is available Monday through Friday, 6:30 A.M. to 9:30 P.M. (Eastern Time), Saturday 8:00 A.M. to 5:00 P.M., and Sunday 1:00 P.M. to 5:00 P.M.

The Library of Congress has both a *Quick Search Guide* and a *Reference Manual* that may be purchased from the Library's Cataloging Distribution Service (202–707–6100; FAX 202–707–1334).

a student can jot down important phrases or sentences while simultaneously reading the material. Once a chapter is completed, the student can review the headings, subheadings, and notes and ultimately check for comprehension by answering any section- and chapter-end questions.

Technology and Writing

Recent advances in technology have provided students and teachers with access to a vast amount of information beyond that contained in books and periodicals on the library shelves. Some elementary schools, for example, have CD-ROM (compact disk—read only memory) and interactive video. CD-ROM is a slightly scaled down optical disk that can store a tremendous amount of information. The first type of compact disk was used to hold audio information, or music. Because the disks are touched by only a beam of light when being read, they are far more durable than traditional records. One CD-ROM disk has the capacity to store approximately 250,000 pages of text. Thus, its use permits access to a wealth of information. By having a CD-ROM disk that contains an encyclopedia, for example, and using a computer with a CD-ROM drive, a student can search and locate information in as little as 2 seconds. The use of CD-ROM and the INTERNET allows intermediate-grade students access not only to reference materials but to recently published materials as well.

Interactive video can be used at all grade levels, depending on the content and purpose of the video program. With interactive video, the teacher or a group leader may stop the video at any point to permit class discussion of the content.

```
timmy d march 2

wus a pon a tom thar wuz a

dinosr ho ludtoploa

gamz likmunoble


(Timmy D.    March 2

Once upon a time there was a

dinosaur who liked to play

games like Monopoly.)
```

Figure 9.9
A five year old's story written on a word processor.

Students are able to further develop their knowledge, experiential background, and thinking skills when such technology is appropriately included as part of language arts instruction, especially in the area of writing.

Word Processing and Writing

Writing with a word processor involves the same steps as writing with pencil and paper: prewriting, writing, rewriting, and publishing. In bypassing the "traditional" writing implements, children are freed from the problem of illegible handwriting, and some are therefore better able to concentrate on the content of the piece (see figure 9.9). When an initial draft appears clean, without distracting marks and erasures, some children are motivated to write more. Similarly, revision is easier on a word processor than on a handwritten piece of work because the word processor enables a writer to revise text by inserting, deleting, rearranging, retrieving, and replacing words and even moving entire sentences and paragraphs around.

After learning basic keyboarding skills, many children find word processing to be a quicker writing method than using pencil and paper. As implied earlier, by removing the problems of handwriting, a word processor makes writing more enjoyable for some children; because they do not need to concentrate on forming legible letters, they are more free to write their thoughts and ideas. Once primary ideas are formulated and put into the computer, an author can easily remove unnecessary details, mechanical errors, and misspellings. In addition, the final product is more polished than a handwritten piece and looks like that of the professional author.

BATTERIES

BY ASHLEY CAMMACK

TABLE OF CONTENTS

Title Page. 1
Table of Contents 2
Statement of Purpose 3
Hypothesis. 4
Research 5
Picture. 8
Materials 9
Procedure. 9
Results 10
Chart 11
Bibliography 12

STATEMENT OF PURPOSE

I wanted to learn how a battery worked, what kinds of batteries there are, and who invented the first battery.

HYPOTHESIS

I predict that the celery will create more voltage than the other vegetables.

Figure 9.10
Here is an example of an expository piece of writing done on a computer by a fifth-grade student.

KEEPS GOING AND GOING AND GOING

BATTERIES

Batteries are connected cells that store electricity. They change chemical energy into electric energy. Batteries have one or more units. The units are called electric cells. Batteries also have positive and negative charges. Batteries are used in appliances such as televisions, radios, and car engines. There are two main types of batteries, primary and secondary cell.

In a primary cell battery there are two parts. The anode, which has a negative charge, and the cathode, which has a positive charge. There are three major types of primary cell batteries, carbon-zinc oxide cell, alkaline cell, and mercury cell. The carbon-zinc oxide cell is used in flashlights and toys. The alkaline cell is like the carbon-zinc oxide cell but, the alkaline cell is used in bicycle lights and walkie-talkies not flashlights and toys. The mercury cell is used in small things such as hearing-aids and sensitive devices. Most primary cell batteries are dry cell or nonspillible.

A secondary cell battery can be recharged or used again after it has been charged. All secondary cell batteries take their own time to recharge. There are two major types of secondary batteries, lead-acid storage batteries and nickel-cadmium storage batteries. Lead-acid storage batteries are used for

powering submarines. They can be used for four years. Nickel-cadmium storage operate like a lead-acid storage. They are used in portable equipment such as drills and garden tools. They are also used in space satellites.

Solar batteries make electricity by the photoelectric conversion process. Solar batteries can be used for a very long time. They can be used to operate space equipment on a space craft.

The first battery was developed by Count Alessandro Volta in the 1790's. It was called the voltaic cell. In 1836 John F. Daniell made a more advance primary cell. Gaston Plante' made the first secondary cell battery in 1856.

There are many different kinds of Alkaline, rechargeable, and heavy-duty batteries. The cost of all the kinds vary. The costs are listed on Chart A. As the chart shows, the rechargeable batteries cost the most and the heavy-duty costs the least.

Some of the good batteries you could look for when you go to the store are Duracell, Energizer, and Sears Die hard. Duracell and Energizer are good batteries but, they cost alot. Sears Die hard is a good battery and also has a good price. One of the batteries that is not good is Rayovac.

Batteries help us in lots of ways. They are still changing to meet our needs. People will always be trying to make a better battery.

Figure 9.10
(*Continued*)

Cost	Alka line		Rechargeable		Heavy-duty	
$4.00						
$3.50						
$3.00						
$2.50						
$2.00						
$1.50						
$1.00						
$0.50						
$0.00						
	Duracell	Radio Shack	GE Charge	Millenium	Evereacy	Sears

Cost of Batteries

CHART A

MATERIALS

1 piece of celery
1 piece of a carrot
1 potato
1 lemon
1 lime
galvanometer
12" strip of copper
12" strip of nickel

PROCEDURE

Stick the copper and the nickel into a piece of food. Let the copper and the nickel sit in the piece of food for one to two minutes. Use the galvanometer find the voltage. Record the results. Repeat this two or three times. Do the same to the other foods.

0.2					
0.15					
0.1					
0.05					
0					
Volts	Lemon	Lime	Celery	Carrot	Potato

Volts created by Foods

CHART B

RESULTS

The lime created the most volts. The lemon and the carrot had the second most volts. The potato and the celery created the least volts. Chart B shows the actual volts for each vegetable. I learned that electricity travels best through some kind of liquid.

Figure 9.10
(Continued)

BIBLIOGRAPHY

Leon, de Lucenary, George, The Electricity Story, New York City, New York, Arco Publishing, 1983.

"Batteries: Disposable or Rechargeable", Consumer Reports, November 1991, pgs. 20-23.

"Battery", McGraw Hill Encyclopedia of Science and Technology, 1992 Edition, Vol. 2, pgs. 487-488.

"Battery", Microsoft Encarta, 1993, Microsoft Corporation.

"Battery", World Book Encyclopedia, 1992 Edition, Vol. 2, pgs. 168-171.

Figure 9.10
(*Concluded*)

Computers are useful in having children write, as editing and revising are easy to achieve.

Word processing programs allow for a variety of student writing interactions. For instance, children may engage in cooperative storywriting by pairing up with a classmate and actually composing a piece together at the keyboard. The pair may write notes or letters to each other, sharing a common "mailbox" or classroom bulletin board. A weekly class newspaper is yet another writing activity. By selecting an editor and a group of reporters each week, students can learn the various aspects and responsibilities of writing columns about classroom activities.

Several word processing programs have been developed for children. *Appleworks* (Apple Computer), *Bank Street Writer* (Scholastic and Broderbund), *Cut & Paste* (Electronic Arts), *Homeword* (Sierra On-Line), *Storybook Weaver Deluxe* (MECC), and *Creative Writer* (Microsoft) are but a few of the many programs on the market. In addition, a variety of accessories such as grammar and spelling checkers, thesaurus programs, and word counters are constantly being updated, and new software products are becoming available almost weekly.

Style checkers, which students can use to check for grammatical and punctuation errors, indicate awkward expressions, incorrect usages, and clichés. A few of these programs actually locate a specific error, thereby helping students identify areas in which they need further practice. Similarly, spelling checkers may be used to ensure correct spelling.

Advances in telecommunications can now enable a school in one state to communicate with a school thousands of miles away via classroom computers and the Internet. By means of such technology, information and ideas as well as school newspapers, class projects, and so on, can be exchanged quickly and efficiently.

Evaluating Student Writing

Evaluating the development of children's writing skills must be constant and ongoing. There are several different means of assessing children's writing, and they should be used in combination to give the truest picture of each child's writing development. As Valencia (1990, p. 339) writes, "No single test, single observation, or single piece of student work could possibly capture the authentic, continuous, multidimensional interactive requirement of sound assessment." Several different kinds of assessment measures, both formal and informal, are discussed here.

Portfolios

A *portfolio* is a "systematic and organized collection of evidence used by the teacher and student to monitor growth of the student's knowledge, skills, and attitudes in a specific subject area" (Varvus, 1990, p. 48). Teachers have discovered that portfolios better demonstrate a student's growth over time than do test scores.

In the elementary classroom, folders with pockets or expandable accordion files may serve as portfolios. The expandable accordion files allow for computer disks, cassette tapes, or even videotapes to be a part of the portfolio. For instance, a child may share a piece of work using the "author's chair" format and have it videotaped for future reference (Graves & Hansen, 1983). Other possibilities include audio tapes of choral reading of a poem that the students wrote together, a dramatic presentation of a play written by a group of students, or even a presentation put together by a student using a computer and hypercard technology. Portfolios allow for a wide variety of media to be used in the evaluation process, rather than only paper and pencil.

MONDAY, WE WILL FLY
TO MYRTLE BEACH,
SOUTH CAROLINA. WE WILL
HAVE A GOOD TIME
WALKING ON THE BEACH
SWIMMING IN THE
POOL, SLIDING DOWN
THE WATER SLIDE,
PICKING SHELLS, AND
PLAYING AND RUNNING
IN THE SAND.
HURRAY FOR THE
HILLCREST!

SARAH

Figure 9.11
This is Sarah's writing portfolio which includes selections from Grade 1 through Grade 7. Note the development of her writing skills.

From Sarah McKibben. Used by permission.

Sarah McKibben

I will be a mouse with a skirt. My skirt will be checkered with purple and pink. I will where a pink blouse too. My name will be Miss Mouse. I will have a ribbon on my blouse and a blet on my skirt I will be a white mouse I will look fine in my mouse sute.

Figure 9.11
(Continued)

What is black? A crack is black.
Ack! A black crack!

What is blue? A shoe is blue.
A blue shoe on Lou.

What is brown? A crown is brown
A brown crown falling down.

Sarah McKibben

THE DOG THE CAT AND THE MOUSE

One day a dog and a cat were playing outside in the yard.
It was fall and the leaves were turning bright colors.
While the dog and cat were playing in the leaves on the
ground they saw a mouse. They tried to catch the mouse.
The mouse didn't get away. They took the mouse into the
house and played with it. Then they had a snack. They
shared it with the mouse. Then they took a nap. When they
woke up, the mouse was gone. It left a thank-you note for
the cat and the dog.

The End

Figure 9.11
(Continued)

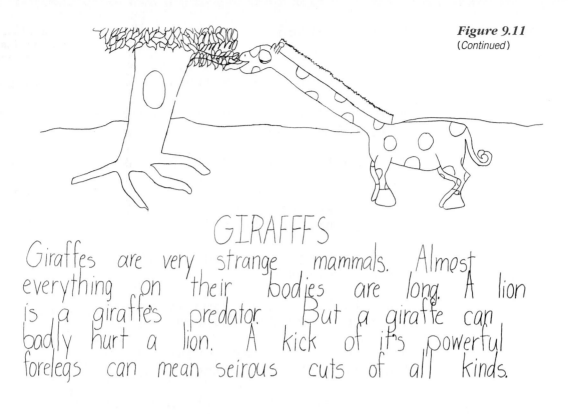

GIRAFFFS

Giraffes are very strange mammals. Almost everything on their bodies are long. A lion is a giraffe's predator. But a giraffe can badly hurt a lion. A kick of it's powerful forelegs can mean seirous cuts of all kinds.

Giraffes feed on trees leaves A giraffe's tongue is long and powerful Its tongue winds itself around a branch and pulls. It strips most of the leaves off that branch and eats them. A giraffe's neck is so long, it cannot eat grass unless it lowers its forelegs to lower itself.

Figure 9.11
(*Continued*)

Sarah McKibben

What is green? A bean is green.
A green bean that is lean.

What is blue? A shoe is blue.
A blue shoe on Lou.

What is red? A sled is red.
A red sled that fell on my head.

What is white? A kite is white.
Flying through the night.

What is black? A crack is black.
Ack! A black crack!

What is brown? A crown is brown.
A brown crown falling down.

What is tan? A can is tan.
That is as big as a man.

What is maroon? A balloon is maroon.
A great big maroon balloon.

SNOW	**ICE**
FLUFFY WHITE,	SLIPPERY, SLICK
SPARKLING ON GROUND,	SLIDING ALL AROUND
FALLING FROM THE SKY.	ICE SKATING IS FUN!
GLITTERING.	SLIP...

East: The direction in which the sun rises each morning. Lake: A body of water with land all around it.
River: A large body of water that flows through the land.
Key: A special part of a map that explains the symbols on the map. Island: A body of land that has water all around it. Continent: One of the seven large bodies of land on the earth Map: A flat drawing of the earth.

South: The direction of the South Pole. Plain: A level area of land. Mountain: Very high land. West: The direction in which the sun sets at night. Hill: A raised part of land. Ocean: A large body of salt water.

Earth: The planet on which we live. The earth is made of land and water.
Globe: A small model of the earth North: The direction of the North Pole. Model: A small-scale copy of an object.

America: The union of the fifty states.

Figure 9.11
(Continued)

Figure 9.11
(*Continued*)

Note how Wings are fastened around whole stomach and back.

Brake Speed 100

Push button many times until wings are flapping at 100 MPH

Turn Wheel to go left or right.

Push "brake" button to stop wings. Brake

Around-the-world Flight Wings

These wings can fly you around the world. All you have to do is push the little button on the side of Flight Wings until flapping lifts you off the ground and speed window says 100 M.P.H.

Figure 9.11
(Continued)

Shopper's Delight Outlet Mall

Austin, Texas

Shopper's Delight is a great place to go on rainy days or sunny days. It has everything you're looking for!! Just pick the store that you think carries your favorite brand or thing and it will be there. It has more than 100 stores!!!

Kids Are Special in the U.S.A!!!

Nashville, Tennessee

Kids are special in the U.S.A. is an all kids store. It has toys, games, and clothing for any temperature in the year! So if you are a kid, drop by sometime!!

Family Books

Portland, Maine

If you need something to do on a rainy day, come on down to Family Books. You can rent books or buy books. If you don't like the book you bought, return it 30 days from when you bought it. Family Books will either let you pick out a different book for free or give you all your money back. So get a book at Family Books!!

The Blizzard

Sarah N.

"Aauullmm......" Colleen yawned as she stretched and swung her feet out of bed.

She pulled a yellow jogging suit and flannel socks out of a drawer and sleepily trudged down the creaky stairs.

Her mother and Aunt Martha were seated at the breakfast table. They looked up from their magazines when Colleen reached the ground floor.

"You're late," Aunt Martha told her. "Its seven forty five. Get dressed and serve yourself some breakfast. Hurry or you'll be tardy for school!"

Colleen obediently changed from her sleepwear to her school clothes and tennis shoes. Then she seated herself at the breakfast table and ate a bowl of cereal.

The bitter cold Canadian wind whipped harshly at the small country cottage. Sleet pelted against the windows and banged on the roof.

Colleen quickly put on her warm winter coat, slipped her boots over her shoes, wrapped a scarf tightly around her face, and tugged on a pair of mittens.

"Be careful on your way to class. Its terrible weather out there," Mrs. Jaklinn warned.

"I will, mom," Colleen answered. "Dont worry."

Colleen arrived at school out of breath and freezing cold from the wind, but she was all right.

The morning passed slowly from subject to subject until noon when the lunch bell rang.

Colleen was the only one who lived out of the small village of Carterville except for Zachery Molston, who was home sick with the flu.

Colleen looked out the window as she went to get her coat and boots. The snow was about two feet deep and was still falling heavily!

There were many shouts as the children exited the school. A lot of them hung around and played with each other in the snow. But Colleen hurried to get on her way. She was a little worried. It was over three miles to her house, and in this weather she didn't know if she would get home in time for lunch.

She trudged through the heavy snow with great effort.

One mile from the school, Colleen reached the Nelson store. She just had to stop in to take a rest, and warm up. She found a nickel in her coat pocket and bought a cup of hot chocolate. She quickly gulped it down, and put on all of the winter gear she had taken off to get comfortable. Mr. Nelson had asked if Colleen had wanted to stay awhile, but she had insisted she had better be on her way.

The snow was being whipped around and was much deeper. It got harder and harder to walk. By the time Colleen reached the abandoned barn which was the half-way mark she could barely walk. But she plodded on. Her legs were becoming stiff and her face was numb and frost bitten. Findly she couldn't go any further. Colleen wished she had stayed at the Nelson store where it was warm and dry. There she could stay until the wind died down. Her whole body shook violently. Her head whirled and her vision was going...

The children back at the Carterville school had already begun class, but no one noticed that Colleen was missing.

About one o'clock Colleen's mother called the school to see why Colleen hadn't come home for lunch. Mrs. Archer, the secretary, had said Colleen didn't come back to school when she left for home.

Aunt Martha called the police.

Figure 9.11

(*Continued*)

They told her they would ride to the school and then to their house on horseback.

No one knew anything at the school, but when they rode further up towards the Jaklinns' house, about a mile away they found Colleen. She lay pale and unconcious in cold Canadian snow.

The police quickly unmounted and set Colleen on one of the horses rumps. They rode back to the school. Then the police called Mrs. Jaklinn and Aunt Martha to tell them what happened and to come quickly, just after they called the hospital.

First the ambulance came. It was a large horse-drawn wagon. A couple of nurses hoisted Colleen up onto the cart, and wrapped her in many blankets. Next Mrs. Jaklinn and Aunt Martha arrived on horseback. They were ordered to follow the ambulance to the hospital.

The ambulance drove up to the emergency entrance. A doctor rushed out of the building followed by two men carrying a stretcher. They laid Colleen on it and hurried away back into the hospital.

When Colleen's mother and aunt arrived, Colleen was gaining conciousness in a second floor hospital room. Four police men were there, and a doctor to make sure she recovered all right.

"Oh, Honey!" Mrs. Jaklinn cried. "I'm so relieved you're all right!" and she kissed Colleen's forehead.

"Just no school for a week, and hot tea every day for one month", the doctor said. "I'll also give you a medication."

Colleen recovered just fine. Soon she was up and healthy! But she decided from then on to ride horseback to school every winter day.

Title *The Secret Garden*

Author *Frances Burnett* Number of pages ?

Mary Lennox was a most disagreeable little girl. She was sent away to misselthwaite Manor to live with her uncle when the rest of her family died from a disease known as cholera. While Mary was exploring the area around the Manor, she came across many beautiful gardens with millions of sweet smelling flowers, tall shade trees, and lovely shrubs. All of the

gardens were surrounded by a tall stone wall and an iron gate. Eventually, she came across a gate that was locked. She did not know it at the time, but this was the Secret Garden! Will she find the key to unlock the most beautiful, unknown garden in the Manor? Read *The Secret Garden* and find out!

Sarah L. McKibben

Figure 9.11
(*Continued*)

Some teachers prefer students to have a "working" portfolio for weekly work and a "showcase" portfolio which parents view and is kept as the "official" assessment instrument (Miller, 1995). Other teachers prefer to have a single portfolio for the language arts and one for each of the content areas. Since most of the writing in science and social studies tends to be expository, one could argue for a single portfolio for each student covering all of the content areas. How it is organized is up to the individual teacher, but what is most important is that portfolios with dated work are maintained for every class member. Ideally, with some supervision by the classroom teacher, the students themselves keep track of their work, date it, and deposit it in their portfolio.

For writing, the portfolio should include a variety of samples. Narrative, expository, and poetic writing should all be represented (Tierney, Carter, & Desai, 1991). In addition, literature response journals, dialogue journals, academic learning logs, and writing about different literary components can all be a part of the student's portfolio. Notes written by the teacher during conferences should be dated and included in the portfolio as well. In addition, preliminary drafts of works can be dated, paperclipped together with the final copies, and deposited into the portfolio (Tompkins & Friend, 1988).

In order to maintain some organization within the portfolio itself, it is important to include a list of what it contains stapled directly to the inside cover of the portfolio. Following is an example of a "Portfolio Inventory Sheet" for fourth grade:

Portfolio Inventory Sheet

NAME: _____

1. Cursive Handwriting Sample: **Checklists**

    _____ Sept.   _____ Jan.   _____ Reflective Work Habits Survey

    _____ Oct.   _____ Feb.   _____ Personal Interests Survey

2. Writing Samples   _____ Books Read for Class

    _____ Narrative   _____ Books Read Independently

    _____ Expository

        _____ Descriptive

        _____ Explanatory

        _____ Persuasive

    _____ Poetic

3. Journals

    _____ Dialogue

    _____ Literature Response

4. Social Studies Informational Reports

    _____ Questioning Strategies

    _____ Research

5. Science Writing

    _____ Written "Observations"

    _____ Data Collection

Other lists and checklists may also be included, such as an attitude survey, a personal interest inventory, and a reflective work habits survey. Because reading interests influence writing, a list of books read by the child should be kept, even those books merely attempted but not completed. Children's literature selections read as part of assigned reading should also be noted. Books that have been shared in class (i.e., read by the teacher) should be kept on a separate list.

At least once a month, the student and the teacher can sit down together to review the contents of the portfolio and evaluate the student's progress. Since the student and the teacher work together in selecting the pieces of writing that are placed in the portfolio, student input is crucial (Cress & Farris, 1992). The student must formulate goals, evaluate strengths and weaknesses, and assess progress. For, as Lamme and Hysmith (1991) wrote, "If children are to become autonomous learners, they must learn to assess what they have learned and how they learn best" (p. 632). After conferencing with the teacher regarding the portfolio's contents, the student then must create new goals that are written down and stored in the portfolio until the next conference occurs.

Children should be encouraged to critique each selection when they add it to their portfolio. A 4″ by 6″ index card stapled to the top of each piece of writing can be used by the student to describe the value of the piece and indicate what writing skill was developed or enhanced. The teacher can jot down a reaction to the student's work, as well.

Responding to Children's Writing

Teachers must formally respond to children's writing efforts frequently, positively, and honestly so that students begin to recognize their individual strengths and weaknesses. In acknowledging a child's work, a teacher may want to respond either orally, as in a writing conference, or by way of a written note attached directly to the piece. When writing conferences are used, the evaluation process and response are simplified because the teacher is familiar with the piece and has observed its development throughout the writing process. Sometimes writing a note entails more time than a brief discussion with the child about the piece. Whichever method is used, the teacher must be aware that generalities do not help the child to grow as a writer; rather, direct, specific comments will guide the child in improvement and refinement of writing skills.

Positive responses should far outweigh negative comments about students' written work. If a teacher can highlight what students do correctly while pointing out two or three types of errors, children can direct their energies toward overcoming a small number of deficiencies instead of being overwhelmed by them.

Anecdotal Records and Checklists

Informal evaluation techniques can be used effectively to note children's writing progress. The teacher may jot down information on a clipboard throughout the school day, filing the information in the appropriate student's writing folder at the end of the day. Checklists noting skills mastered and new skills being attempted are also effective and require little time to manage (see figure 9.12).

Figure 9.12

Here is an example of a student's narrative writing and the accompanying teacher-student conference record.

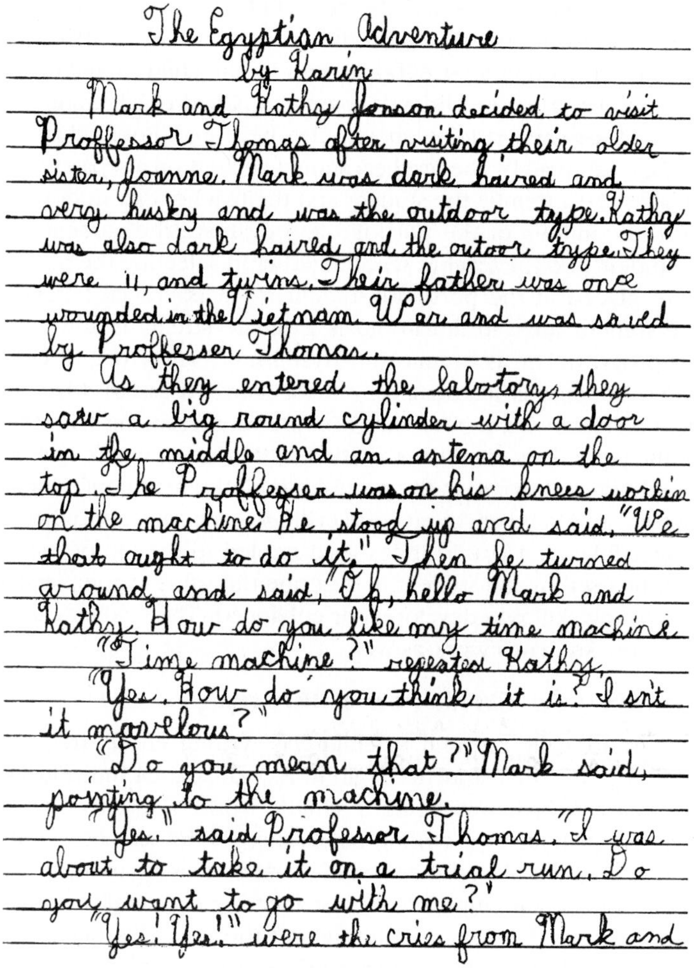

The Egyptian Adventure
by Karin

Mark and Kathy Jonson decided to visit Proffessor Thomas after visiting their older sister, Joanne. Mark was dark haired and very husky and was the outdoor type. Kathy was also dark haired and the outoor type. They were 11, and twins. Their father was once wounded in the Vietnam War and was saved by Proffesser Thomas.

As they entered the labotory, they saw a big round cylinder with a door in the middle and an antena on the top. The Proffesser was on his knees workin on the machine. He stood up and said, "We that ought to do it." Then he turned around and said, "Oh, hello Mark and Kathy. How do you like my time machine.

"Time machine?" repeated Kathy.

"Yes. How do you think it is? Isn't it marvelous?"

"Do you mean that?" Mark said, pointing to the machine.

"Yes," said Professor Thomas. "I was about to take it on a trial run. Do you want to go with me?"

"Yes! Yes!" were the cries from Mark and

Besides keeping anecdotal records and checklists, photographs of accompanying projects may also be tucked into a child's portfolio (Fueyo, 1991).

Cambourne and Turbill (1990) recommend that teachers use a hardcover, three-ring binder to hold notes from student writing conferences; four pages should be allotted for each student. Notes from both formal (for instance, a statement made by a student during a regularly planned conference) and informal (for example, a question asked by a student as the teacher moves around the room assisting students while they are writing) conferences should be placed in the notebook.

Students need to be aware of their own progress as writers. Cambourne and Turbill (1990) suggest that older students, those in the middle- and upper-elementary grades, keep their own "reflective journals." Students can use these to evaluate their own abilities in both reading and writing. When students

Figure 9.12
(*Continued*)

Kathy,

"O.K. Get in!" said the proffesser as he was stepping inside.

When Kathy and Mark got there, Professer Thomas said, "Where do you want to go?"

"Ancient Egypt!" they chorused. So the proffessor turned a dilal and they heard a great roaring sound. Next thing they knew they were on a camel headed for Cyro. Just when they were about to enter Cyro, three guards came up and one of them said, "You are strange people. We are going to take you to the Great Cleopatra." Then the other two gaur said, "Hail Cleopatra. Hail!" Then the first gaurds said, "Didn't you hear them? Hail, boy hail."

Then, Mark swiftly braugt out a little laser and turned it on. He said to the suprised gaurds, "This will hurt you if you don't let us go." While they were still suprised Mark, Kathy, and Proffessor Thomas leaped into the time machine and Went back to the twentieth century.

Writing Conference Record

Name: Karin G.   Grade: 5

Date	Title of Place	Skills Used Properly	Skill Taught	Skills to be Attained
9/14	The Egyptian Adventure	Dialogue - began new paragraph with new speaker	Write out numbers less than 25 as word	Forming complex sentences versus compound sentences -Clauses
9/17	The Greatest Band	Transitional sentences to link paragraphs	Development of relative clause	Leave out unnecessary details Stick to one story.

Temtation

The sight of that long straight stretch of hallway seems to have a dire influence on our feet. It is not we who are racing pell-mell through the hall; we are just the unwary victims of exceptionally mischievous feet. They play dual roles. Usually they play the role of our friends, walking us quietly within the buildings. But at the sight of that long corridor they turn into rogues. With a dash and a slide they sail us trough the hall. We get blamed, we face the battle, they just dangle out of sight under our desks probably planing another hectic scramble from the room, a dash down the hall, and a leap through the door. And so goes the cycle of the normal child against the abnormal feet.

WRITING FORMATIVE EVALUATION FORM

Student: David   Grade: 6

Date: 11-6   Type of Writing: Reflective

Title: Temptation (sp) = "Temtation"

Comments: Excellent vocabulary. Vivid images are created in this piece. Well organized. Parallel construction is good. Strong writing

Strengths: Vocabulary - dire, rogues, exceptionally, unwary   Well developed

Weaknesses: Spelling, Paragraphing, Run-On Sentences

Date: _____ Type of Writing: _____

Title: _____

Comments:

Strengths:

Weaknesses:

Date: _____ Type of Writing: _____

Title: _____

Comments:

Strengths:

Weaknesses:

Figure 9.13

A student's "reflective journal" entry and the teacher's feedback.

can see for themselves what they can do well and what is, to them, a good piece of writing, they become better writers (see figure 9.13). At this point, real growth and learning occur at all levels of their writing.

Children need to question their writing as part of the editing process. The following form (see focus box 9.1) is appropriate for third through eighth graders to use for self-evaluation of their writing. Such use of checklists and self-questioning are important for writing growth.

Holistic Evaluation

To determine the writing skills of two or more classes of students at a particular grade level, *holistic evaluation* can be used as a quick, effective technique. Two

Focus Box 9.1

Writing Self-Evaluation

Name: _____ Date: _____

Writing Topic: _____

Poor	Getting Better	Better	Pretty Good	Good	Great
1	2	3	4	5	6

Focus—6 Points
Did you make your idea clear to the reader?
Did you stay on the subject from the beginning to end?
Is there a topic sentence that explains what the paragraph is about?
Did you react to the idea and tell how you felt?
Is there a closing sentence or end to the idea?

Support—6 Points
Did you give enough reasons or examples to prove your idea?
Did you explain the ideas with details so the reader really understands?

Organization—6 Points
Did you plan the writing so the reader does not get mixed-up?
Are all your ideas written in the right order?

Conventions—6 Points
Did you:
   Use good english?
   Write good sentences?
   Spell all the commonly used words correctly?
   Spell the best you could on difficult words?
   Indent the beginning of the paragraph?
   Use capital letters and punctuation where they are needed?

Integration—6 Points
Is the paragraph interesting to the reader?
As a complete paragraph, will the reader feel this is well written?

Score
I received _____ out of a possible 30 points.

Developed by Dr. Elizabeth Taglieri, Teacher, May Whitney Elementary, Lake Zurich, Illinois.

or three teachers at the same grade level agree to work together to evaluate their students' writing. The teachers first decide on a topic and an appropriate writing time frame. By way of a trial session, the teachers themselves write about the topic in the specified amount of time. If they can address the topic adequately within the designated time period, they give the topic to the students. If, on the

Figure 9.14
Holistic evaluation can
be both quick and
effective.

Holistic Evaluation

		High		Average		Low
Content						
1. Quality of ideas		5	4	3	2	1
2. Organization of ideas		5	4	3	2	1
3. Word choice		5	4	3	2	1
4. Clarity		5	4	3	2	1
5. Support of ideas		5	4	3	2	1
Mechanics						
6. Capitalization		5	4	3	2	1
7. Grammar usage		5	4	3	2	1
8. Spelling		5	4	3	2	1
9. Punctuation		5	4	3	2	1
10. Handwriting		5	4	3	2	1

other hand, the topic proves to be too difficult or time-consuming, the teachers select another topic and repeat the pretesting.

All student papers are coded according to some preestablished numbering system; subsequently, 10 papers are randomly selected from the entire group. The teachers then read each of the papers and, using a 5-point rating scale such as the one suggested in figure 9.14, rate each paper according to the criteria listed.

Because a gestalt approach is used, the teacher analysis for holistic evaluation should take no more than one minute per paper. Once each of the 10 papers has been rated, the teachers compare their respective scores, which should differ by no more than 3 points for each writing sample. Any significant discrepancies pertaining to criteria should be discussed prior to the evaluation of the remaining papers.

After all the student ratings have been tabulated, an average total score can be obtained for the entire group and for each individual class. The teachers may then elect to find the average score for each of the 10 criteria. Below-average scores on any individual criterion indicate the need for additional instruction. For instance, if students in one of the classes averaged 3.7 on organization but only 2.5 on paragraph structure, the teacher would be wise to devote additional class time to paragraph structure.

To be most effective, holistic evaluation should be performed three times a year: September, January or February, and May. If the teachers remain consistent in their scoring methods, this scheme will provide them with information on how the classes are performing as a group over time, a type of summative evaluation. Whenever teachers undertake holistic evaluation, they should reread the original 10 papers and recheck the established criteria to ensure consistency in their ratings.

S u m m a r y

Writing can be personal, practical, or both. Through writing, students can enhance and develop their thinking skills. Writers can gain knowledge and understanding, as well as new insights into personal opinions, beliefs, and interests.

To evaluate student writing effectively, teachers must be both objective and compassionate. Portfolios offer an insightful approach to evaluation because they allow teachers to note growth over a period of time. Constructive criticism by both the teacher and a student's peers ought to be genuine and include positive statements about the writing. Only one or two major faults should be highlighted at a time so that young writers can focus simultaneously on correcting their errors and developing their writing skills.

Questions

1. In what ways does writing enhance a child's learning?
2. Why does personal writing tend to be more motivational than practical writing?
3. How can journal writing benefit children?
4. What are the advantages and disadvantages of using word processing with elementary-level students?
5. Why should teachers adopt an ongoing process for evaluating writing?

Activities

1. Develop a set of criteria for evaluating students' writing at a particular grade level.
2. Keep an academic learning log for one of your classes. In addition, keep a journal for jotting down thoughts about everyday occurrences. After a month has passed, reread your writing in both notebooks and make a list of observations about your learning and personal feelings that emerged from these two types of writing.
3. Prepare a poetry writing lesson in which a poem that you have written is used as an example.
4. Write a three- or four-page autobiographical sketch about an elementary school experience.
5. For 2 weeks, keep daily lists of things to do. Then determine whether you were more efficient as a result of this form of practical writing.

For Further Reading

Button, K., Johnson, M. J., & Furgerson, P. (1996). Interactive writing in a primary classroom. *The Reading Teacher, 49* (6), 446-455.

Cudd, E. T., & Roberts, L. (1989). Using writing to enhance content area learning in the primary grades. *The Reading Teacher, 42* (4), 392-405.

Kliman, M. & Kleiman, G. M. (1992). Life among the giants: Writing, mathematics, and exploring Gulliver's world. *Language Arts, 69* (2), 128-137.

McCoy, L. J., & Hammett, V. (1992). Predictable books in a middle school class writing program. *Reading Horizons, 32* (3), 230-234.

Simmons, J. (1990). Portfolios as large-scale assessment. *Language Arts, 67* (3), 262-268.

Spaulding, C. L. (1989). Understanding ownership and the unmotivated writer. *Language Arts, 66* (4), 414-422.

References

Because of the large number of children's books cited in this chapter, these titles are documented in a separate subsection below.

Abel, J. P., & Abel, F. J. (1988). Writing in the mathematics classroom. *Clearing House, 62* (4), 155-158.

Andrews, J. A. (1988). Poetry: Tool of the classroom magician. *Young Children, 43* (4), 17-24.

Boyer, E. (1983). *High school: A report of the Carnegie Foundation for the Advancement of Teaching.* New York: Harper & Row.

Brady, R. (1991). A close look at student problem solving and the teaching of mathematics: Predicaments and possibilities. *School Science and Mathematics, 91* (4), 144-151.

Cambourne, B., & Turbill, J. (1990). Assessment in whole-language classrooms: Theory into practice. *Elementary School Journal, 90* (3), 337-347.

Craig, S. T. (1983). Self-discovery through writing personal journals. *Language Arts, 60* (3), 373-379.

Cress, E. & Farris, P. J. (1992). An assessment alternative: The portfolio approach. *Florida Reading Quarterly, 284* (4), 11-15.

Cudd, E. T., & Roberts, L. (1989). Using writing to enhance content area learning in the primary grades. *The Reading Teacher, 42* (6), 392-404.

Denman, G. A. (1988). *When you've made it your own: Teaching poetry to young people.* Portsmouth, NH: Heinemann.

Draper, V. (1979). *Formative writing: Writing to assist learning in all subject areas* (Curriculum Publication No. 3). Berkeley, CA: Bay Area Writing Project.

Elbow, P. (1981). *Writing with power.* New York: Oxford University Press.

Farris, P. J. (1988). Developing research writing skills in elementary students. *Florida Reading Quarterly, 25,* 6-9.

Farris, P. J. (1989). Storytime and story journals: Linking literature and writing. *New Advocate, 2,* 179-185.

Fueyo, J. A. (1991). Reading "literate sensibilities": Resisting a verbocentric writing classroom. *Language Arts, 68* (8), 641-649.

Gaskin, I. (1982). A writing program for poor readers and writers and the rest of the class, too. *Language Arts, 59* (8), 854-861.

Graves, D. (1978). *Balance the basics: Let them write.* New York: Ford Foundation. (ERIC Document Reproduction Service No. ED 192 364)

Graves, D., & Hansen, J. (1983). The author's chair. *Language Arts, 60* (2), 176-183.

Hand, B., & Treagust, D. F. (1991). Student achievement and science curriculum development using a constructive framework. *School Science and Mathematics, 91* (4), 172-176.

Hollowell, J., & Nelson, G. L. (1982). Bait—We should abolish the use of journals in English classes. *English Journal, 71* (1), 14-17.

Kormanski, L. M. (1992). Using poetry in the intermediate grades. *Reading Horizons 32* (3), 184-190.

Lamme, L. L., & Hysmith, C. (1991). One school's adventure into portfolio assessment. *Language Arts, 68* (8), 629-639.

Livingston, M. C. (1991). *Poem-making: Ways to begin writing poetry.* New York: HarperCollins.

Many, J. E. (1992). Living through literacy experiences versus literary analysis: Examining stance in children's literature. *Reading Horizons, 32* (3), 169-183.

Marshall, N. (1984). Discourse analysis as a guide for informal assessment of comprehension. In J. Flood (Ed.), *Promoting reading comprehension.* Newark, DE: International Reading Association.

McClure, A. A. (1995). Fostering talk about poetry. In N. L. Roser & M. A. Martinez (Eds.), *Book talk and beyond,* Newark, DE: International Reading Association.

Miller, W. (1995). *Authentic assessment in reading and writing.* Englewood Cliffs, NJ: Prentice-Hall.305306

Newman, J. (1983). On becoming a writer. *Language Arts, 60* (1), 860-870.

Odell, L. (1983). Written products and the writing process. In J. Hayes, P. Roth, J. Ramsey, & R. Foulke (Eds.), *The writer's mind: Writing as a mode of thinking.* Urbana, IL: National Council of Teachers of English.

Stewig, J. W. (1988). *Children and literature.* Boston: Houghton Mifflin.

Tierney, R. J., Carter, M. A., & Desai, L. E. (1991). *Portfolio assessment in the reading-writing classroom.* Norwood, MA: Christopher-Gordon.

Tompkins, G. E., & Friend, M. (1988). After your students write: What's next? *Teaching Exceptional Children, 20,* 4-9.

Valencia, S. (1990). A portfolio approach to classroom assessment: The whys, whats, and hows. *The Reading Teacher, 43* (4), 338-340.

Varvus, L. (1990). Put portfolios to the test. *Instructor, 100* (1), 48-53.

Children's Books

Cleary, B. (1983). *Dear Mr. Henshaw.* New York: Morrow.

Cleary, B. (1991). *Strider.* New York: Morrow.

Fritz, J. (1973). *And then what happened, Paul Revere?* New York: Coward, McCann.

Fritz, J. (1982). *Homesick.* New York: Dell.

Greenfield, E., & Little, L.J. (1979). *Childtimes: A three-generation memoir.* New York: Crowell.

Kellogg, S. (1971). *Can I keep him?* New York: Dial.

Nixon, J. L. (1988). *If you were a writer* (B. Degen, Illus.). New York: Four Winds.

Pearson, S. (1988). *My favorite time of year.* New York: Harper & Row.

Prelutsky, J. (1984). *The new kid on the block* (J. Stevenson, Illus.). New York: Greenwillow.

Prelutsky, J. (1990). *Something big has been here* (J. Stevenson, Illus.). New York: Greenwillow.

Prelutsky, J. (1996). *Monday's troll* (P. Sis, Illus.). New York: Morrow.

Selway, M. (1992). *Don't forget to write.* Nashville, TN: Ideals.

Silverstein, S. (1974). *Where the sidewalk ends.* New York: HarperCollins.

Silverstein, S. (1981). *A light in the attic.* New York: HarperCollins.

Stevenson, J. (1995). *Sweet corn.* New York: Greenwillow.

Walton, R. (1995). *What to do when a bug climbs in your mouth* (N. Carlson, Illus.). New York: Lothrop, Lee, & Shepard.

Internet Sites

Indexes

These are pages that act as collections of children's resources and may be worth your first stop.

Berit's Best Sites for Children

A collection of sites organized by topic such as Animals, Sports, and Science and Math. It's part of the Theodore Tugboat Home Page.
Address: http://www.cochran.com/theosite/KSites.html

Kid List

This list of children's sites includes a search mechanism.
Address: http://www.clark.net/pub/journalism/kid.html

The Kids on the Web

In addition to an extensive list of links, this Web site features information for parents about Internet issues and kids.
Address: http://www.zen.org/~brendan/kids.html

The Ultimate Children's Internet Sites

These children's links are sorted by appropriate age groups.
Address: http://www.vividus.com/ucis.html

Fun & Games

These links point to activities appropriate for younger children.

Crayon

> The title of this site stands for CReAte Your Own Newspaper. After choosing a name for your newspaper, you can pick through a list of Web addresses with news items of interest, such as Time, USA TODAY, or the weather. When you're done, you get a page with a collection of links that you can save and load each day for news.
> Address: http://sun.bucknell.edu/~boulter/crayon/

The Asylum's Lite Brite

> Remember Lite-Brite? Now you can play online—and post your work for others to see.
> Address: http://www.galcit.caltech.edu/~ta/lb/lb.html

LEGO Information

> Not an interactive page, but if your little one is a LEGO-head you'll want to send him or her here. The pages include pictures, ideas, and activities, plus photos kids have sent in of their own LEGO creations.
> Address: http://legowww.homepages.com/

Alphabet

> Quite simply, this is a page with beginning alphabet games. A is for Apple. . . .
> Address: http://www.klsc.com/children/

Learning

Looking for help with homework? Interested in finding out about a favorite topic? These pages can give you a start.

The Homework Page

> You'll find a list of Web addresses for information likely to help you research a school project. Organized by category, there's also links to Yahoo, Galaxy, and WWW Virtual Library searches.
> Address: http://www.tpoint.net/Users/jewels/homework.html

Internet Public Library: Youth Division

> Read stories and picture books online.
> Address: http://ipl.sils.umich.edu/youth/

Children's Literature Web Guide

> Internet resources for children and young adults. Lists of links to online children's stories, songs, poetry, and folklore.
> Address: http://www.calgary.ca/~dkbrown/

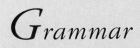

Grammar

© Michael Siluk

Grammar is at once the most controversial of
the aspects of the language arts and the least
understood.
—Barbara Stoodt
Teaching Language Arts

Introduction

*G*rammar is an integral part of language. Preschoolers use grammar without knowing, let alone understanding, the rules that accompany it, just as they run, breathe, or toss a ball without understanding the processes that make such physiological functions possible. Children in the primary grades continue to speak and write without having been formally exposed to the nuances of grammar.

Teachers must keep in mind that grammar and punctuation, like spelling, are writing conventions. They fail to enhance the meaning of the piece of writing; rather, they help the reader to better understand what the writer is saying (Graves, 1995). For instance, when a writer begins a sentence with a capital letter, practices subject-verb agreement, includes an apostrophe in a contraction such as can't, uses commas to separate a series of items, and places a period at the end of a sentence, he or she is using language conventions.

By gaining familiarity with grammar, a child discovers how to speak and write more effectively, efficiently, and precisely. The child learns to use conventions through trial and error as well as discovery until he or she can apply such conventions naturally in speaking and writing. Such knowledge results in the child's becoming a more confident speaker and writer. Experimenting with words, something preschoolers do naturally, is often curtailed during the elementary school years but resurfaces as children discover the wide variety of language possibilities. However, to understand the rules of grammar, a child must be able to think in abstract terms. Most children fail to possess this cognitive skill until age 11 or 12, or even later. Donovan (1990) believes that forcing abstract concepts on youngsters before they are ready may result in their disinterest in language study. As a result, they may be reluctant to write or engage in public speaking activities. McCraig (1977, pp. 50–51) suggests the following:

> (B)y literal count, good sixth grade writing may have more errors per word than good third grade writing. In a Piagetian sense, children do not master things for once and for all. A child who may appear to have mastered sentence sense in the fourth grade may suddenly begin making what adults call sentence errors all over again as he attempts to accommodate his knowledge of sentences to more complicated constructions.

Research findings also point out that grammar should not be taught in the artificial world of English grammar exercises but in the context of speaking and writing, which take place daily in the classroom. It is best to teach grammar or punctuation conventions in a mini lesson, one at a time, thus reducing possible confusion. Children should be informed a few days in advance of a mini lesson so they can begin practicing the convention in their own writing.

This chapter discusses the various systems of grammar and the importance of teaching grammar in a relevant manner at an appropriate time as children develop their cognitive skills. Suggestions are also made for assisting students in refining their grammar skills. Teaching the conventions of language becomes not less difficult, but more difficult as children progress through the grades, for their thought processes become increasingly more complex.

Standard and Nonstandard English

Standard English is the most widely accepted, or preferred, use of the English language. Geographical, racial, and socioeconomic distinctions do not exist in standard English; to some, this implies elitism.

In many communities, children hear nonstandard English in the home and neighborhood, while they hear standard English in the classroom and the church. According to Smith (1988a, p. 20),

> Every child learns a very specialized grammar. Children may not learn to talk the way their school teachers talk, but they do not see themselves as teachers. Children learn to talk like the people they see themselves as being. They learn to talk the way their friends talk.

In recent years, some media personalities have become more relaxed in the use of standard English—except in newscasts and documentaries, both of which are rarely viewed by children. When surrounded by adults and peers who speak nonstandard English, children often find it difficult to distinguish between what is and is not "correct."

The first researcher to distinguish social levels of language use rather than correct and incorrect uses was Fries (1964). As a result of his research, the study of the English language and how it should be taught changed to emphasize a descriptive approach rather than the prescriptive one that began in the 1700s. In describing how language is actually used, the descriptive approach fosters a more realistic view of language.

Systems of Grammar

Grammar consists of basic patterns or rules of a language. In essence, *grammar* is a theory that, when applied, explains the natural knowledge of a language that is possessed by every native speaker of the language (Dale, 1976). The rules of grammar dictate whether a group of words constitutes a viable sentence or is merely a collection of words.

Different grammatical systems have been devised to classify or categorize the workings of the English language. Traditional, structural, and transformational generative grammars have all influenced the way grammar has been taught in elementary and secondary schools in the 20th century. Using computer technology, researchers continue to search for a universal grammar that can be applied to all languages.

Traditional Grammar

During the eighteenth century, most teachers taught traditional grammar, largely because of the strong influence of Priestly and Lowth. *Traditional grammar* is Latin based; that is, its precise rules are derived from Latin, a language Priestly and Lowth considered to be perfect. As such, traditional grammar is prescriptive in nature.

From traditional grammar came the parts of speech: nouns, pronouns, verbs, adverbs, adjectives, conjunctions, prepositions, articles, and interjections. Sentences are classified as simple, compound, complex, and compound/complex. Sentence types are also defined by traditional grammar as declarative, interrogative, imperative, and exclamatory. These terms are still used today in elementary- and secondary-level English grammar textbooks.

Most of these textbooks also contain "cookbook" exercises that require the student to identify the parts of speech. The word "cookbook" is used to refer to these exercises because every exercise is based on a sentence that has been carefully crafted in terms of the rules of grammar—in effect, a recipe of sorts. A similar concept, sentence diagramming, evolved from parsing, an 18th-century method of showing the relationship of words in a sentence. Such diagramming transformed grammar from the abstract to the concrete.

Unfortunately, children perceive traditional grammar that has been taught in the form of textbook exercises as having little to do with grammar in their own writing. Meyer, Youga, and Flint-Ferguson (1990, p. 66) believe, as a result, that "traditional grammar instruction is bound to fail because it is given without any realistic context."

Structural Grammar

Unlike traditional grammar, which is prescriptive, *structural grammar* is descriptive. Propounded by Leonard Bloomfield, a prominent linguist of the early 1900s, structural grammar attempts to separate the study of syntax (structure) from the study of semantics (meaning). Rather than classifying words according to their meaning (for example, a noun is a person, place, or thing) as is done in traditional grammar, in structural grammar, words are classified according to their use or function. As a result, the term *slotting,* which refers to the "slot" or function of a word in a particular sentence, evolved. For instance, consider the following sentence:

_____ car is red with black seats.

Only a possessive noun or pronoun will correctly complete the sentence, or fill the slot. Now consider another sentence:

Tobblin is a blit.

By replacing *Tobblin* with a slot, other words may be inserted. Adjectives, adverbs, and verbs are inappropriate; only a noun or pronoun is appropriate. By replacing *blit* with a slot and inserting other words, children will eventually discover that only an adjective, or descriptive word, fits. Such experimentation with words assists students in understanding the parts of speech.

Transformational Generative Grammar

Transformational generative grammar incorporates both syntax and semantics, or surface and deep structure. Transformational generative grammar is based chiefly on the work of one man, Noam Chomsky, and his research in the late 1950s and early 1960s. Like traditional grammar, transformational generative grammar has exact, precise rules. The basic theory behind transformational generative grammar is that a kernel sentence (a simple declarative sentence) can be transformed to generate new sentences.

Chomsky's work with surface and deep structure suggests that a sentence may have an underlying meaning. For instance, consider this sentence:

Visiting relatives can be fun.

When first reading the sentence, the reader may interpret the writer's words as meaning the conversing with relatives in their homes is enjoyable. Careful analysis, however, may yield entirely different interpretations—that conversing with relatives is rarely an enjoyable experience or that relatives who appear at the writer's doorstep can be enjoyable. The actual intent of a sentence is easier to determine when it is spoken because the listener hears the speaker's intonation. A reader, however, must consider information that surrounds the sentence.

As defined by the rules of transformational generative grammar, kernel sentences can be expanded and combined. Research by Mellon (1969), Hunt and O'Donnell (1970), and O'Hare (1971) indicates that practice in combining sentences enables students to improve their own writing. Thus, rather than producing short, choppy sentences, students are able to write longer sentences that each convey more meaning.

Children are first exposed to sentence combining in kindergarten as part of classroom oral language activities. A child is told to combine two short sentences into one sentence—for instance, to combine the first two sentences below:

The bike is red.
The bike has stripes.

Combined sentence:

The red bike has stripes.

Or

The bike is red and has stripes.

As students progress through elementary school, sentence combining becomes more complex. By using examples from children's literature, students can gain insight into the effects of different sentences.

A long compound and/or complex sentence can be meaningful; a simple sentence or a short compound or complex sentence can also be powerful. Children should be encouraged to rewrite an author's original sentences, using adjectives and adverbs to expand sentences and conjunctions to combine two or more sentences.

Grammar Instruction

As mentioned earlier, children should not be expected to learn grammar by completing exercises in English grammar textbooks. Research studies conducted over the last 40 years have failed to support the benefit of such activities in developing grammatical skills. As Smith (1988b, p. 18) writes, "Punctuation, capitalization and other 'rules' of grammar are essentially circular and meaningless to anyone who cannot already do what is being 'explained'." Yet children *do* need to become familiar with grammar; they need to know what a noun, pronoun, and verb are and how to use each effectively to refine and improve their speaking and writing.

For many children—and adults—a lack of knowledge of grammar can result in personal embarrassment. For instance, after Larry Bird, the basketball superstar, graduated from Indiana State University, he confided to his mother that he had been uneasy about his lack of preparation in grammar when he entered college. "I didn't know a noun from a pronoun. I was ashamed" (Levine, 1988, p. 177).

When introducing students to grammar, teachers should remember that grammar is a convention of writing and thus a sensitive area of study. Children, like adults, are typically uneasy when placed in a position in which they lack confidence and with which they have little familiarity. It is far more effective to have students start with an analysis of sentences selected from children's literature than from their own writings, which may reflect their own shortcomings.

Grammar is best taught in short mini lessons. If students are given three to four days notice prior to a mini lesson on a particular grammar convention, they not only will have had an opportunity to experiment with that convention in their own writing, but to find examples of it in their reading of children's literature, as well. By encouraging students to bring such examples to the mini lesson, they will be more eager to engage in the mini lesson. Furthermore, the examples provided by the students will give the teacher some insight as to the level of understanding of that particular convention each child possesses.

Graves (1995, p. 41) suggests to "keep the tone of each mini lesson as one of discovery, rather than of preoccupation with accurate use of the convention."

After a mini lesson, a wall chart or handout can be made as a reference for the students. In addition, children can keep their own record of their use of writing conventions in grammar, punctuation, and spelling as follows:

Date	Convention	Writing Piece	First Time Used	Usually Accurate
9/27	+es—to make plural (tomatoes)	Joe's Lunchbox	✔	
9/27	Caps. Name of People	Joe's Lunchbox		✔
9/27	Period at end of sentence	Joe's Lunchbox		✔
9/27	subject/verb agreement— "was," "were"	Joe's Lunchbox		✔
9/29	comma in series	The Last Soccer Game	✔	

Another effective approach to the teaching of grammar includes the following five steps:

1. Introduce children to passages from children's literature.
2. Present passages from the classroom teacher's own writings.
3. Present passages from an anonymous child at the same grade level.
4. Present passages from a self-confident student in the class.
5. Present passages from all students in the class on a regular basis.

Such a succession of selections ensures that students will not lose confidence in their own abilities. Ironically, it is usually not the students but the classroom teacher who becomes the most anxious in the sharing and analyzing of one's own writing.

Teaching Punctuation

The first convention of grammar that children understand is punctuation because punctuation is noticeable in both oral and written language. For instance, in revising a piece of writing, children are able to determine where to insert a period by noticing where a pause occurs when the piece is read aloud. When a first grader is asked where a period goes, he or she will probably say, "At the end of the line." Since their sentences are usually short, a period does go at the end of the line in most of their writing.

Periods, question marks, exclamation points, apostrophes, commas, and quotation marks are the essential punctuation marks with which primary-grade students need to be familiar. Periods are used at the ends of sentences that make a statement or express a command, after abbreviations, and after initials in proper names. Question marks are used at the ends of sentences that ask a question. For the reader, a question mark signifies that the voice is to be raised for the last word. Like question marks, exclamation points signify a change of voice for the final word, in this case, for emphasis. First graders typically learn

Focus Box 10.2
Transformations of a Kernel Sentence

Sentence = Noun Phrase + Verb Phrase
Puppies bark.

Simple Transformation	Example
Negation	Puppies don't bark.
Yes/no question	Do puppies bark?
Wh-question	Why do puppies bark?
Imperative	Bark, puppies.
There	There are puppies who bark.
Passive	The cars were chased by the puppies.

readily when to use periods and question marks as stipulated here. Once they have been introduced to the exclamation point, however, many first graders demonstrate that this is the one punctuation mark for which they have been waiting; no other punctuation mark will do for their writing. Hence, some first graders' writing appears to be nothing short of a series of adamant statements, their importance dictated by exclamation points (see figure 10.1).

First graders should be introduced to the apostrophe early on because they frequently encounter it in their basal readers and library books. They need to learn that an apostrophe and the letter *s* are used to indicate possession and that apostrophes are used to indicate missing letters in contractions. Contractions are particularly difficult for students who are not native English speakers and for some students with learning disabilities. Therefore, special attention needs to be devoted to the functions of the apostrophe. Intermediate-grade students need to learn that the apostrophe can also be used to indicate the omission of a number, as in a date (the '96 Summer Olympics or the Great Depression of the '30s).

By the end of first grade, teachers should introduce the comma. This usually comes after seeing two or three pieces of writing that consist of a series of " _____ and _____ and _____ and _____ and _____ " or an entire page composed of one sentence in which "and then" is used to connect a multitude of thoughts.

Children often find the comma confusing. Even well-educated adults will debate whether a comma should be used before the word *and* when more than two items are listed in series. Unfortunately, comma use has been cyclical in terms of grammatical instruction; the comma is used either sparingly or profusely. However, students have been consistently taught to use a comma (or commas) in the following situations:

> Today I was walking to school and my cahzin and!!! my sister came with me and!!!I did a curt-weel to and I had a dress on to and thats waht I did to !!!

Figure 10.1
A second grader beginning to use exclamation points in her writing.

After the salutation of a letter:

> Dear Ron,

After the close of a letter:

> Your friend,
> Mike

To separate the name of a city from its state:

> Fort Worth, Texas

To separate the day from the year in a date:

> February 2, 1989

Primary-grade children find the foregoing rules to be clear and understandable. They also have no problems placing commas between words in a series.

To separate words in a series:

> The garden had beans, lettuce, radishes, and tomatoes.

Placing a comma before the conjunction clarifies the meaning of the sentence.

The following rules for the use of commas should be introduced to intermediate-grade students:

To set apart a direct quotation:

> "Throw me the ball," called Jenny.

Between parts of a compound sentence that are joined by a conjunction:

> The car was repaired, and they continued on their trip.

After an introductory clause:

> While the car was being fixed, they drank a can of soda.

Before and after an appositive:

> The manager, Tommy McPherson, let the customers in early.

Before and after a nonrestrictive clause:

That player, who has a bandaged left hand, is the best scorer on the team.

Quotation marks rank with exclamation points in terms of popularity among second graders. By including quotation marks in their writing, they demonstrate that they can write like adults. Upon encountering dialogue in the stories they are reading or in Big Books that they read together as a class, some first graders eagerly attempt to write their own dialogue because they insist upon having characters in their stories speak, just as the characters do in books written by professional authors. Graves (1983), in his study of beginning writers, found that a third of the first graders used quotation marks accurately. Quotation marks are used to encompass directly spoken words. For example, consider the following:

"The weatherman said to expect rain," Grandpa said as his eyes
cast about the skies, looking for clouds.

By the second or third grade, students learn that quotation marks are used around the title of a poem and that titles of books are underlined (or italicized in print).

Punctuation marks that are introduced later than those described above include the colon, semicolon, and hyphen. By the fifth grade, children typically use these punctuation marks frequently in their writing. Still, other conventions of the English language remain for students to learn.

Teaching Grammar

Upon entering school, children become aware of their own grammatical errors largely through writing. Flood and Salus (1984) advocate that children should write often in a pressureless situation, for time devoted to writing is more conducive to improvement of written language than time devoted to learning the concepts and terminology associated with grammar.

The six parts of speech with which elementary students need to become familiar are noun, pronoun, verb, adjective, adverb, and conjunction. Each of these is described in focus box 10.3. Upon entering kindergarten, children already possess and consistently use each of these parts of speech in their speaking vocabulary. In kindergarten through second grade, instruction should focus on how a word is used in a sentence. For example, descriptive words such as *huge, blue,* and *spotted,* are not initially introduced as adjectives; the precise labeling comes after students understand the concept of words that can be used to describe people, places, or things.

Ruth Heller has a delightful series of language books for children that provide examples of the parts of speech. These colorful books include *Merry-Go-Round: A Book about Nouns, A Cache of Jewels and Other Collective Nouns, Kites Sail High: A Book about Verbs,* and *Up, Up, and Away: A Book about Adverbs* (Heller, 1990, 1989, 1991a, 1991b). While kindergartners and first graders will enjoy the beautiful illustrations and prose, upper elementary and middle school students can use Heller's books as reference books for their own writing. Another helpful piece of children's literature,

Focus Box 10.3

The Parts of Speech

Noun: In traditional grammar, a noun identifies a person, a place, a thing, or an idea. A noun may be singular or plural, and it may also be possessive.

    Singular Nouns:
      Fix the *radio* in my *car*.
      He has *integrity*.
      The *pilot* headed toward *Birmingham*.

    Plural Noun:
      The blue swallow tail *butterflies* flutter among the flowers.

    Possessive Noun:
      The *bike's* fender is damaged.

Pronoun: A pronoun is a word that is used to take the place of a noun or another pronoun. Like nouns, pronouns refer to people, places, things, or ideas. Unlike nouns, pronouns change form according to their use.

    She likes to play golf.
    It is *her* game.

Verb: A verb expresses an action or links the subject of a sentence with its description. The most common linking verbs are *am, are, be, being, been, is, was,* and *were.*

    Terrance *rode* a skateboard. (Action verb)
    The house *was* once an old hotel. (Linking verb)

Adjective: An adjective is a word that modifies, or describes, a noun or pronoun.

    The *soft, white* snow fell silently.

Adverb: An adverb is a word that modifies a verb, an adjective, or another adverb. An adverb tells how, when, where, or to what extent.

    The woman worked *methodically*.
    Rags was a *very* happy dog.
    He prints *really* well.

Conjunction: A conjunction is a word that connects words or groups of words.

    The puppy *and* the older dog chased each other.
    Michael Jordan is a professional basketball player, *but* he also enjoys playing golf.

---

appropriate for kindergarten through second grade, is R. M. Schneider's (1995) *Add It, Dip It, Fix It: A Book of Verbs.* This simple alphabet book is a playful way to introduce the concept of verbs.

Substituting words to make a sentence more powerful and/or effective is good practice for children. Consider the following two sentences from *The*

In the Classroom Mini Lesson

Parts of Speech

Objective: To introduce nouns, verbs, adjectives, and adverbs to fourth graders.

Collect pictures of famous individuals with whom students can identify (for example, media, political, or sports figures). Select four of the pictures to be used for the lesson, and paste them in a single column on the left side of a sheet of paper turned sideways. Make and label four other vertical columns, one for each part of speech included in the lesson: nouns, verbs, adjectives, and adverbs. Then make four horizontal columns, separating the four pictures. On the chalkboard, write the definition and an example of each of these four parts of speech. Select one of the pictures to use in a model exercise for the class, for example, a caricature of the President of the United States or prime minister of Canada. After reviewing the definition of a noun, have the students give examples of nouns that relate to that person (president, prime minister, leader, commander-in-chief, father, husband, and so on). After completely filling the first box with nouns, follow the same procedure for verbs, adjectives, and adverbs.

After the class has completed the row for the first picture, divide the students into pairs and have them select one of the three remaining personalities and give examples of each of the parts of speech that characterize that individual. After finishing the exercise, the students should write a short story using as many of the words as possible from the lists they created.

This exercise may be modified to include only political leaders, scientists, characters from children's literature, or the like.

Trumpet of the Swan by E. B. White (1970, p. 18) which Mrs. Bridges, a fourth-grade teacher, wrote on the chalkboard to share with her students:

> When the swan had laid five eggs, she felt *satisfied*.
> She gazed at them *proudly*.

Mrs. Bridges asked her students to suggest substitute words for the word *satisfied*. The students volunteered *happy, pleased, wonderful,* and *relieved*. For *proudly*, they came up with *lovingly, peacefully,* and *happily*. Mrs. Bridges then had her students reread the current drafts of the stories they were writing to suggest words they might substitute for words they had already chosen.

Because children's literature displays a rich use of language, children should be encouraged to find and share passages that show how an author has weaved sentences together to express a certain mood or to achieve a certain tone. Then the students should examine their own stories during revision to see whether they can combine sentences or substitute words to make their stories more effective.

Grammar instruction is most effective when students are required to use inductive reasoning to discover what works and what does not. Through experimentation with language, grammatical knowledge is advanced and skills are enhanced.

Grammar for Second-Language Students

Upon their arrival in the United States or Canada, children and adults who speak a language other than English quietly observe other children and adults speaking English. This goes on for an extended length of time, usually several months, before they attempt to speak or write in English (Krashen, 1982). However, those who can read in their first language apply those same skills to "survival reading" of English words: For instance, in learning to read street signs, *st* stands for *street* and *ave* stands for *avenue*. Logos of prominent businesses and products may also be quickly learned—Walmart, McDonald's, Coke, Exxon, and Tide. The exception is when the company's name has unfamiliar letter combinations, such as *Shell* which has an *sh* beginning, a combination that is not found in Spanish.

Initially, the English used by second-language learners is quite simple and usually grammatically incorrect. Two or three word sentences are commonplace. For instance, a child may say "no book" for "I don't have a book" or "pencil" for "I need a pencil." They also overgeneralize, for instance labeling all vehicles "car" or all grown-ups at school "teacher." Second-language learners need the opportunity to use language for meaningful, functional, and genuine purposes (Urzua, 1980). For example, second-language children often learn a great deal of English from their classmates and playmates as they interact socially on the playground. This is especially important since many such children hear only their first language spoken in their homes and neighborhoods.

As second-language speakers begin to use English, they are very deliberate in their speech. They enunciate their words clearly and speak slowly. As they acquire more knowledge of syntactic structures, they become more confident and use more complex language. Focus box 10.4 is a chart of the stages of grammar acquisition of second-language learners.

In teaching the structure of the English language to second-language children, the teacher must point out the importance of noun and verb agreement and of proper placement of adjectives and adverbs. By introducing such concepts orally and having the students engage in concrete activities with language, they will more quickly learn the grammatical structures of English. One such activity is to have the students listen to directions, repeat them, and then follow them. Here are some suggestions for such directions:

Put the book under the chair.

Put the book on the chair.

Put the book beside the chair.

Pick up the chair.

Pick up the book and give it to me.

Pick up the chair and put it by the table.

Put the crayon on the desk.

Put the crayon under the chair.

Focus Box 10.4

Stages in Second-Language Acquisition

Stage 1

Yes-no answers
Positive statements
Subject pronouns (e.g., *he, she*)
Present tense/present habitual verb tense
Possessive pronouns (e.g., *my, your*)

Stage 2

Simple plurals of nouns
Affirmative sentences
Subject and object pronouns (all)
Possessive (*'s*)
Negation
Possessive pronouns (e.g., *mine*)

Stage 3

Present progressive tense (*-ing*)
Conjunctions (e.g., *and, but, or, because,
    so, as*)

Stage 4

Questions (*who? what? which? where?*)
Irregular plurals of nouns
Simple future tense (*going to*)
Prepositions

Stage 5

Future tense (*will*)
Questions (*when? how?*)
Conjunctions (e.g., *either, nor, neither,
    that, since*)

Stage 6

Regular past-tense verbs
Questions (*why?*)
Contractions (e.g., *isn't*)
Modal verbs (e.g., *can, must, do*)

Stage 7

Irregular past-tense verbs
Past-tense questions
Auxilliary verbs (*has, is*)
Passive voice

Stage 8

Conditional verbs
Imperfect verb tense
Conjunctions (e.g, *though, if, therefore*)
Subjunctive verb mood

Figure from Gonzales, Phillip C. (1981, November). Beginning English reading for ESL students. *The Reading Teacher, 35*(2), 154–162. Reprinted with permission of Phillip Gonzales and the International Reading Association. All rights reserved.

Second-language learners often engage in code-switching, or the combining of their native language and their second language (Lara, 1989). They may use English nouns but Cantonese verbs, for example.

After speaking and reading English for 1½ to 2 years, a second-language learner can carry on a conversation. But it takes several years before a second language student becomes proficient in all of the language arts—reading, writing, listening, and speaking.

The Revision Process

Understanding the various parts of speech and learning how to write better sentences are assets to a writer. However, the effective writer must also develop good proofreading and editing skills.

Proofreading

In revising a written draft, the student needs to pay close attention to both content (ideas and organization) and mechanics (grammar, usage, and spelling). A checklist for proofreading is helpful to students. For first graders, the proofreading list may be very simple:

Does the story make sense?

Have I left out anything?

Do all of the sentences begin with a capital letter?

Do all names begin with a capital letter?

Do all of the sentences end with a period or a question mark?

Are all the words spelled correctly?

For intermediate-grade students, the proofreading checklist might include the items from the earlier list written at a higher level of sophistication, along with new rules. A fourth-grade checklist, for example, might appear as follows:

Is the main idea clear?

Is the story well-organized so the reader doesn't get lost?

Have I used clear words and phrases?

Does anything take away from the story and need to be removed?

Have I used any run-on sentences?

Are all punctuation marks used correctly?

Editing

In addition to using a proofreading checklist, students need to use editing marks to assist them in revising their drafts. For the beginning writer, this may mean using a pencil to circle words that are misspelled. Focus box 10.5 contains a list of editing marks for elementary students.

Involving students in the editing process through peer editing can not only reduce the amount of teachers' paperwork but also improve children's writing. Research suggests that peer editing improves mechanics and overall writing fluency more than teacher editing alone (Weeks & White, 1982).

Peer editing provides feedback for the writer and helps the editor sharpen skills, as well. Peer editing may be done on a one-on-one basis or by editing committees assigned to critique one or more specific areas, such as mechanics or content.

The writer first edits his or her own work before exchanging it with another student or giving it to a committee. In each instance, the editor reads the paper, writes something about the paper that he or she liked, and then makes suggestions about how the writer might improve the paper. Finally, the editor provides the writer with a list of misspelled words and their correct spellings (Harp, 1988).

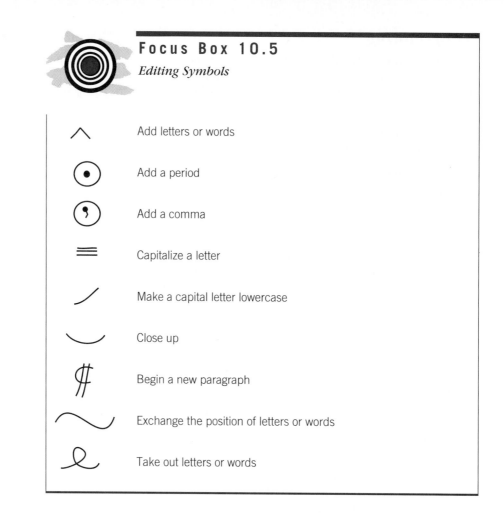

∧	Add letters or words
⊙	Add a period
(comma symbol)	Add a comma
≡	Capitalize a letter
/	Make a capital letter lowercase
‿	Close up
⌗	Begin a new paragraph
∼	Exchange the position of letters or words
(delete symbol)	Take out letters or words

S u m m a r y

To avoid the teaching of isolated pieces of information, grammar must be taught as part of the listening, speaking, reading, and writing activities that occur daily in the elementary classroom. Teachers must provide children with examples of well-constructed sentences, paragraphs, and works. By sharing specific portions of well-written children's literature, students can better understand grammar and how to improve their own writing and speaking. Thus, mini lessons can play an important role in the teaching of grammar. To be effective speakers and writers, listeners and readers, children must be fluent in their use of both oral and written language and must therefore be knowledgeable about the workings of grammar.

Questions

1. Compare and contrast traditional, structural, and transformational generative grammar.
2. What role does writing play in the learning of standard English grammar?
3. In what ways can children's literature be used to enrich students' language use?

4. Do elementary students need to know the names and definitions of the parts of speech? Why or why not?
5. How should editing be included in the writing process?

Activities

1. Observe a first- or second-grade class as students are engaged in a writing activity. What punctuation marks do they use?
2. Observe a writing lesson being taught to a group of children for whom English is a second language. What grammar problems emerge?
3. Videotape a 3-minute clip of a variety of television programs (local news, sports, home repair, and so on) and show the video to a fifth- or sixth-grade class. Have each student note obvious grammatical errors. Replay the tape, stopping it to discuss the errors as they occur.
4. Develop a lesson plan to improve fifth-grade students' ability to write complex sentences.
5. Review two English grammar series for elementary students. How is writing incorporated? In what ways are students given the opportunity to improve their grammar skills independently of "cookbook" exercises?
6. Develop and implement a lesson that includes grammar but requires knowledge in a content area, as well.

For Further Reading

Casteel, J., Roop, L., & Schiller, L. (1996). "No such thing as an expert": Learning to live with standards in the classroom. *Language Arts, 73* (1), 30–35.

Fitzgerald, J. (1988). Helping young writers to revise: A brief review for teachers. *The Reading Teacher, 42* (2), 124–129.

Graves, D. (1995). Sharing the tools of the writing trade. *Instructor, 105* (4), 38–41.

Leggo, C. (1990). Ninety-five questions for generating disputation on the power and efficacy of the pedagogical practices of writing teachers. *Language Arts, 67* (4), 399–405.

Phelan, P. (Ed.). (1989). *Talking to learn: Classroom practices in teaching English.* Urbana, IL: National Council of Teachers of English.

References

Dale, P. S. (1976). *Language development: Structure and function* (2nd ed.). New York: Holt, Rinehart, & Winston.

Donovan, J. M. (1990). Resurrect the dragon grammaticus. *English Journal, 79* (1), 62–65.

Flood, J., & Salus, P. (1984). *Language and the language arts.* Englewood Cliffs, NJ: Prentice-Hall.

Fries, C. C. (1964). *Linguistics: The study of language.* New York: Holt, Rinehart, & Winston.

Graves, D. (1983). *Writing: Teachers & children at work.* Portsmouth, NH: Heinemann.

Graves, D. (1995). Sharing the tools of the writing trade. *Instructor, 105* (4), 38–41.

Harp, B. (1988). When the principal asks? Why aren't you using peer editing? *The Reading Teacher, 41* (8), 828–830.

Heller, R. (1989). *A cache of jewels and other collective nouns.* New York: Putnam.

Heller, R. (1990). *Merry-go-round: A book about nouns.* New York: Putnam.

Heller, R. (1991a). *Kites sail high: A book about verbs.* New York: Putnam.

Heller, R. (1991b). *Up, up, & away: A book about adverbs.* New York: Putnam.

Hunt, K. W., & O'Donnell, R. C. (1970). *An elementary school curriculum to develop better writing skills.* Washington, DC: U.S. Government Printing Office.

Krashen, S. (1982). *Principles and practices of second language acquisition.* Oxford: Pergamon.

Lara, S. M. (1989). Reading placement for code-switchers. *The Reading Teacher, 42,* 278-282.

Levine, L. D. (1988). *Bird: The making of an American sports legend.* New York: McGraw-Hill.

McCraig, R. A. (1977). What research and evaluation tells us about teaching written expression in the elementary school. In C. Weaver & R. Douma (Eds.), *The language arts teacher in action* (pp. 46-56.) Urbana, IL: National Council of Teachers of English.

Mellon, J. C. (1969). *Transformational sentence combining: A method for enhancing the development of syntactic fluency in English composition* (NCTE Research Report No. 10). Urbana, IL: National Council of Teachers of English.

Meyer, J., Youga, J., & Flint-Ferguson, J. (1990). Grammar in context: Why and how. *English Journal, 79* (1), 66-70.

O'Hare, F. (1971). *Sentence combining: Improving student writing without formal grammar instruction* (NCTE Research Report No. 15). Urbana, IL: National Council of Teachers of English.

Schneider, R. M. (1995). *Add it, dip it, fix it: A book of verbs.* Boston: Houghton Mifflin.

Smith, F. (1988a). *Insult to intelligence.* Portsmouth, NH: Heinemann.

Smith, F. (1988b). *Joining the literacy club: Further essays into education.* Portsmouth, NH: Heinemann.

Weeks, J. O., & White, M. B. (1982). *Peer editing versus teacher editing: Does it make a difference?* Urbana, IL: National Council of Teachers of English. (ERIC Document Reproduction Service No. ED 224 014)

White, E. B. (1970). *The trumpet of the swan.* New York: Harper & Row.

Urzua, C. (1980). Doing what comes naturally: Recent research in second language acquisition. In G. S. Pinnell (Ed.), *Discovering language with children* (pp. 33-38). Urbana, IL: National Council of Teachers of English.

Supportive Writing Skills: Spelling and Handwriting

© James L. Shaffer

Writing is, for most, laborious and slow. The mind travels faster than the pen.
—**William Strunk, Jr. and E. B. White**
The Elements of Style, 4th edition

Introduction

W ithin society, the ability to correctly spell words identifies the educated person. Because society places such importance on accurate
spelling, some people actually form positive or negative opinions about an
individual solely on the basis of the spelling skills he or she displays in written communication.

In writing instruction, spelling is a problem for both children and teachers. As Wilde (1990, p. 276) writes, it would be ideal if learning to spell were
"analogous to learning how to speak the language" and "ultimately be as natural, unconscious, effortless, and pleasant as learning to speak." Such is usually
not the case, for although children are eager to record their thoughts on paper
as quickly as possible, they are not concerned with correct spelling until they
reach the revising stage of the writing process. In effect, proper spelling serves
as a courtesy for the writer's audience, the reader, because the correct spelling
of words eases the entire reading process. Therefore, the child as writer must
be intrinsically motivated to spell words correctly.

Another problem for both children and teachers is the fact that a number of words in the English language have been borrowed from other languages and thus have irregular spellings. In fact, over 600 different ways to
represent the 42 phonemes in English have been documented (Pitman & St.
John, 1969). Moreover, the same English words may be spelled differently by
different groups: Compare, for example, the British and Canadian spellings of
colour and *labour* with the American *color* and *labor.* Then, too, new words
are constantly being invented; some of these are based on acronyms (for
example, *scuba,* from *self-*contained *u*nderwater *b*reathing *a*pparatus), and
others develop as hybrids of consumer-oriented products (Xerox and
Polaroid, for example). Nevertheless, 86.9 percent of all the words in the
English language are phonetically rule based (Anderson & Lapp, 1988). Thus,
the relationship between a letter and the sound it represents is of a systematic nature.

In addition to phonology, one must also consider morphology, syntax,
and semantics if correct spelling is to occur. For instance, the position of a
word within a sentence may indicate the appropriate spelling. Such is the case
when choosing between *to, two,* and *too.* Emerging trends in spelling instruction suggest that expectations of perfect spelling in young children's writing
are unrealistic and inappropriate considering the developmental nature of
spelling ability (LaFramboise, 1990; Templeton, 1991a).

Stage	Characteristics	Significance	Examples
Deviant	Letters are used randomly.	Child recognizes that words are made up of letters.	RbTz for car
Prephonetic	Generally, one to three letters that represent consonant sounds are used.	Child uses some consonant sounds to spell entire words.	KR for car KT for cat
Phonetic	Letters used closely resemble sounds contained in a word.	Child adds some vowel sounds and more consonant sounds to the word.	ustuliv for used to live bot for boat
Transitional	Vowels are contained in every syllable.	Child is ready for formal instruction in spelling.	gurbul for gerbil
Correct	Spelling is generally accurate; few spelling errors are made.	Child can edit his or her own writing for spelling errors. Child continues to participate in formal spelling instruction.	

Stages of Spelling Development

Read (1971) found that preschool children tend to "invent" the spellings of words they use in their writing. He also discovered that these inventions are predictable rather than random and that consonant sounds are used quite consistently. Current research findings based on Read's work indicate that children progress through several developmental stages before they actually master the intricacies of learning to spell (Bissex, 1980; Henderson & Beers, 1980). Studies by Gentry (1981) and Henderson (1985) suggest the existence of five developmental stages: (1) deviant, (2) prephonetic, (3) phonetic, (4) transitional, and (5) standard or correct spelling. These stages are described and illustrated in focus box 11.1.

Children begin to write words in much the same way as they begin to learn to speak them; that is, they rely on experimentation (Clay, 1975). They move from invented, temporary spelling to correct spelling. Very young children draw and scribble as an attempt to represent actual writing patterns. Although children scribble for pure pleasure and enjoyment at age 2, by age 3, they begin to imitate their adult counterparts by perfecting their circular and linear drawings. From this point onward, children view writing as an entire process, not just as a combination of individual letters and words. Between the

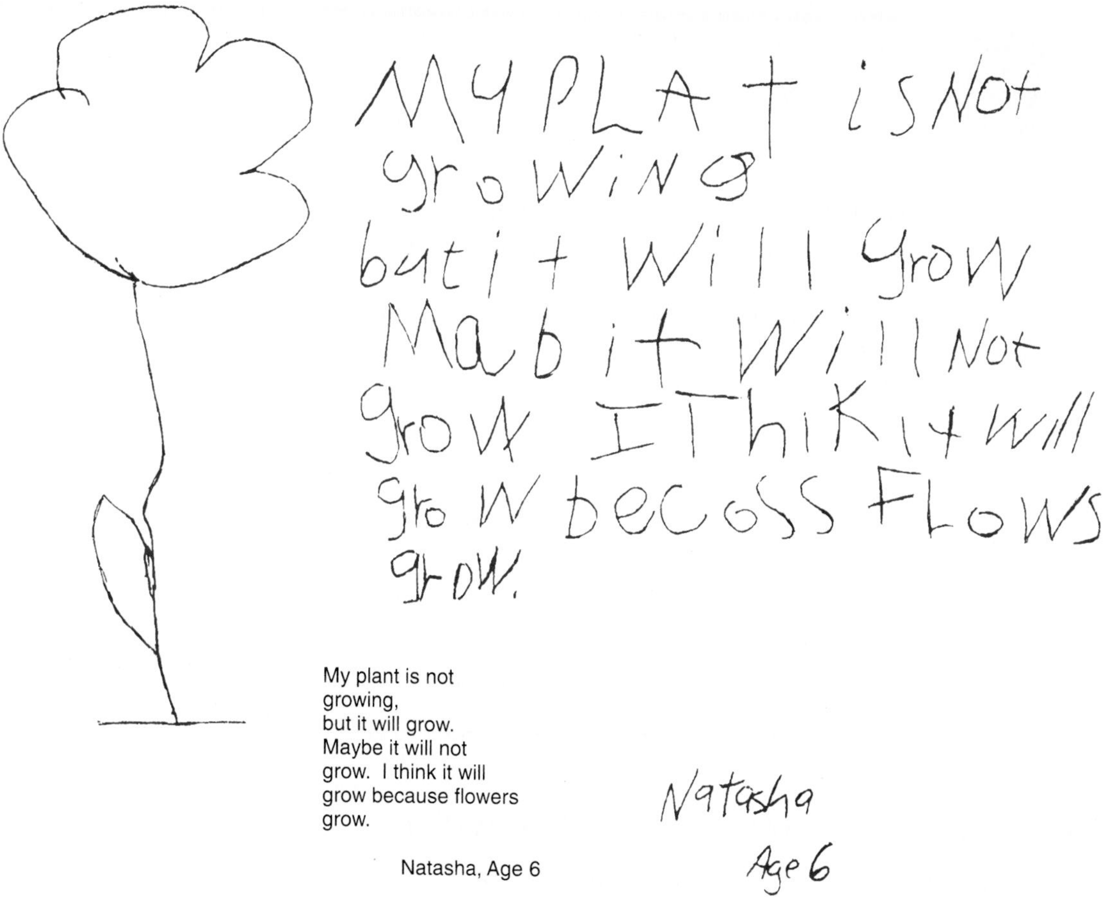

MY PLAt is Not
growing
but it Will grow
Mab it Will Not
grow I Thik it Will
gro W becoss FLoWs
grow.

My plant is not
growing,
but it will grow.
Maybe it will not
grow. I think it will
grow because flowers
grow.

Natasha, Age 6

Natasha
Age 6

Figure 11.1

Spelling samples from 6-, 7-, and 8-year-olds are represented here. Use the developmental spelling chart to classify the different stages of spelling of these three students.

ages of 3 and 5 years, children move from the imitative stage to one of creation, forming real letters to write messages for adult readers. At this time, children are not only discovering the finer features of writing but are also becoming more aware of the variations found within written language (Atkins, 1984).

Three- to five-year-olds in the *deviant stage* of spelling invent the spellings of words by developing both capital letter and numerical symbols and later grouping such symbols together in a variety of combinations. Eventually, however, only the capital letters are grouped together as children discover the concept of "word"—a combination of letters used to represent meaning. In Henderson's (1985) view, this concept serves as a major benchmark in literacy acquisition. When children can consider a word as a concrete object, they are then able to examine words systematically and to detect the spelling patterns that occur.

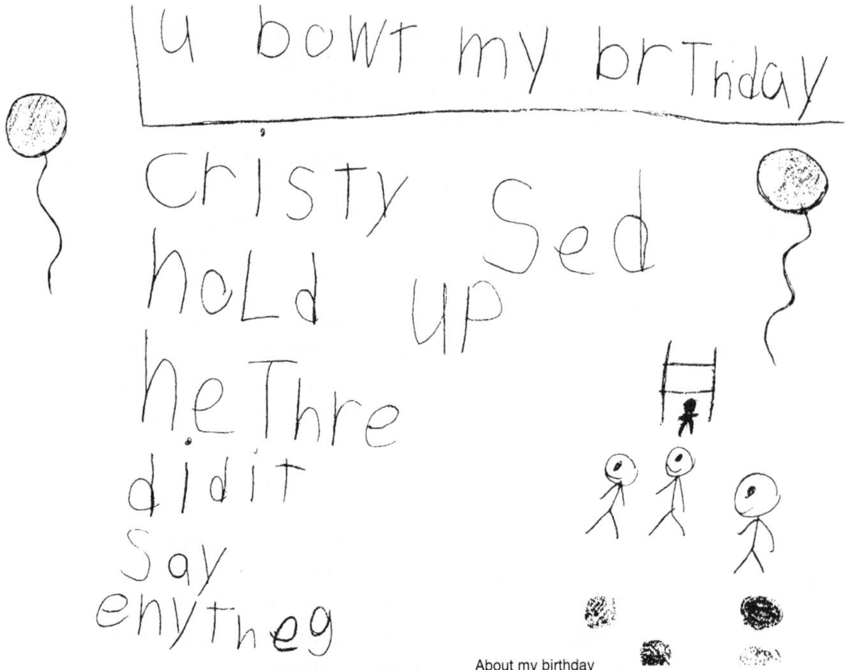

u bowt my brThday

Cristy Sed
hoLd uP
heThre
didit
Say
enytheg
Akila
Age 7

About my birthday

Christy said, "Hold up three (fingers)."
He didn't say anything.

Akila, Age 7

April 11, 1992
Dear Peter Rabbit
How are you doing
I. weh I cod see you But I
like your story and wen
I ron in a grdn I
never get my cot and hos
clt and I hope you never
get cttagen

Mike
Age 8

Dear Peter Rabbit,
   How are you doing? I wish I could see you. But I like your
story, and when I run in a garden, I never get my coat and hose
caught, and I hope you never get caught again.

Mike, Age 8

Figure 11.1
(Continued)

Initial attempts to write words at this stage result in the use of letters that are not normally found in a particular word. For instance, a child may write "TRX" to represent "Sandy," the name of the family's dog. This is in accordance with the fact that one's ability to discriminate between actual words and non-words does not usually appear until age 5 or 6 (Brownell, Drozdal, Hopmann, Pick, & Unze, 1978).

Within their own home settings, young children practice and play with graphic symbols as a way to both organize their world and express their thoughts and feelings (Piazza & Tomlinson, 1985). In Hall's (1985) view, parents should encourage their young children to use invented spellings in their writing to promote an atmosphere of acceptance for such creation; at the same time, parents should reassure the young writers that they, too, will develop the perceptual ability needed to distinguish correct from incorrect spelling.

Typically, during kindergarten or first grade, children begin to match letters with sounds. First graders should explore the left-to-right letter/sound correspondence within words as well as learn the common short vowel spellings and simple consonant blends and diagraphs (Templeton, 1991b). Since the children already understand the concept of "word" and can identify the names and shapes of most, if not all, of the letters of the alphabet, the youngsters next attempt to spell words that are used in conversations with others. Even though these children have only a limited knowledge of print, they can consider themselves to be "writers," for they quickly become attuned to the needs of their readers and the conventions of written language. Children will advance rapidly from the deviant stage to the prephonetic stage because of the confidence they possess as writers.

The *prephonetic stage* could also be referred to as the letter-name stage because children begin to display an exactness in their association of letters with the corresponding sounds of a word. In this stage, children are generally dependent upon the use of capitalized consonants: for example, Bissex's (1980) young son, in an attempt to get attention, wrote, "GNYS AT WRK" (correctly translated as "genius at work"). Furthermore, although long vowels are used with great accuracy by the letter-name speller, short vowel sounds are difficult for the child to use accurately. Typically, a child will substitute the long vowel sound that is most similar to the short vowel sound that he or she hears. This being the case, the letter *a,* as a long vowel, might be substituted for the short vowel *e* in *ten.*

During the prephonetic stage, children initially spell an entire word with only a single letter. A second letter, which they add later, usually represents the final sound of the word. Yet as children develop finer auditory discrimination, they begin to identify sounds contained within the word itself. When this happens, children are ready to enter the phonetic stage.

In the *phonetic stage,* children's spelling reflects a more perfect match between a word's letters and associated sounds (as in the writing of "klok" for *clock*). As children advance toward the transitional stage, the classroom teacher finds reading their writing relatively easy because vowels now represent each of the syllables in a word (see figure 11.2).

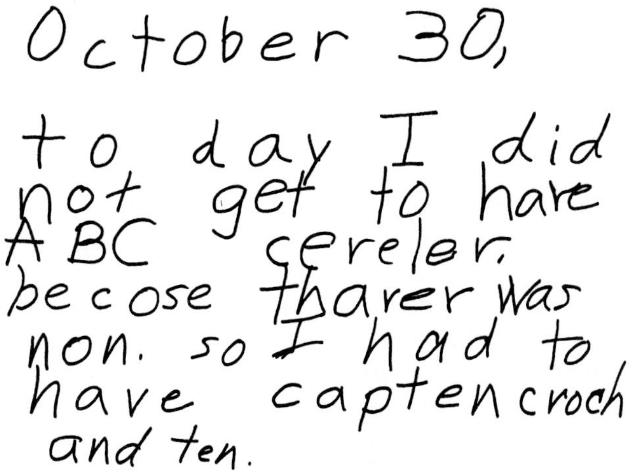

Figure 11.2
An example of writing by a student in the transitional stage. Notice that the child writes "and ten," words he knows how to spell rather than "instead," a word he uses in his oral but not written vocabulary.

During the *transitional stage,* the spelling is very close to correct and is recognizable by the reader. The student in the transitional stage is rapidly moving from temporary, invented spelling to conventional, correct spelling.

Children's progression to the *correct stage* is demonstrated through their use of common letter patterns, such as *ing, ap, et, amp, ent,* and so on. In addition, prefixes, suffixes, and root words are recognized by children in this stage. Thus, over time, children refine their spelling as they adopt spelling conventions (Wilde, 1992).

As children proceed through school, they have increasingly more experiences with both reading and writing. Such word encounters enable children to familiarize themselves with groups of words that share phonological, morphological, and syntactic features. As a result, both older children and adults learn to go beyond the use of phoneme-grapheme strategies to spell words correctly.

Henderson and Templeton (1986) observed children as they progressed through the developmental stages of spelling. The researchers concluded that the developmental theory is valid and that it provides a "rationale for the pacing and maintenance of instruction in a more detailed and clearly stated manner than has been possible before" (p. 314). Examining how children move through the stages of spelling development can therefore be helpful in terms of providing guidelines for spelling instruction.

Instruction in Spelling

The majority of students in Grades 1 through 6 learn spelling via a spelling textbook series. According to Tompkins (1993, p. 286), "children who are not yet at the correct stage of spelling development—that is, students who do not spell approximately 90 percent of spelling words correctly and whose errors are not mostly at the transitional level—do not benefit from formal spelling instruction." She suggests that such children be permitted to continue writing with invented spelling so that they will eventually learn both visual and morphological spelling strategies rather than memorize spelling words. To determine a child's readiness for spelling instruction, teachers can administer the Yopp-Singer Test of Phonemic Awareness (Yopp, 1995). This test is administered individually and is appropriate for kindergartners through second graders.

Templeton (1991b) offers a framework for spelling instruction in the elementary grades. He believes that first graders should begin their study of spelling by examining simple letter patterns in sight words (i.e., consonant–short vowel–consonant, as in *cat, did,* and *fun;* consonant–long vowel–consonant–"silent *e,*" as in *cake, bike,* and *poke;* consonant blends, as in *drip, flap,* and *slip;* and consonant digraphs, as in *phone* and *right*).

Second and third graders should acquire basic vowel patterns and simple syllable patterns. Beginning in the fourth grade, children need to compare and contrast spelling/meaning relationships in words in addition to syllable patterns. In Templeton's opinion, the examination of word meanings is important at the middle and upper childhood levels.

Bloodgood (1991) supports integrated instruction of spelling in a literature-based curriculum. Bloodgood suggests using pattern books for word study by first and second graders. For example, *Polar Bear, Polar Bear, What Do You Hear?* (Martin, 1991) provides children with repetitive use of the phrase "What do you hear?" The children can also begin to identify words that depict the names of the animals in the book.

Bloodgood (1991) believes that middle-childhood-level students (third and fourth graders) should compare different versions of folktales or fairy tales as part of word study at this level. She gives the example of *Cinderella* (Brown, 1954), *Moss Gown* (Hooks, 1987), and *Princess Furball* (Huck, 1989). Students in third grade and up could read a book in small groups. As they read, they can be given word study assignments for each chapter. For instance, a group reading a novel about the Civil War could look for words in a chapter that relate to a specific concept (i.e., the cause of the war). Another chapter may be used for the study of grammatical units (i.e., verbs that express action) or unusual vocabulary (i.e., words used during the 1860s that are not in common use today).

Graham (1983) reports that 100 words account for 50 percent of all the words children use in their writing, 1,000 words for 89 percent, and 3,000 words for 97 percent. The 100 words to which Graham refers are largely function words and verbs: *a, is, are, have, had, that, this, there, was were,* and so forth. Children tend to use such words frequently as they begin writing in sentences.

Read's (1971) discovery of invented spelling has led to the reexamination of formal spelling programs. Research conducted by Hammill, Larsen, and McNutt (1977) compared the spelling of fourth- through eighth-grade students who received formal instruction through a basal spelling textbook series with the related spelling of a similar group of students who received no formal spelling instruction. Their findings indicated that there was no significant difference between the two groups of students in terms of their spelling ability. An earlier study by Manolakes (1975) found that the average child in Grades 2 through 6 could already spell 75 percent of the words contained in a randomly chosen spelling textbook lesson before receiving any instruction for that particular word list. By the end of the eighth grade, students have often encountered a common core of 2,800 to 3,200 words in a spelling textbook series. Still, in considering grade placement and sequence, teachers should not hesitate to alter the words within particular lessons to meet student needs.

Despite the almost universal acceptance of spelling textbooks, there is a current trend to promote the integration of spelling and writing instruction. Many schools no longer use a formal spelling textbook series; instead, teachers are encouraged to forge a stronger link between writing and spelling instruction. One advocate of this approach is Hillerich (1977), who believes that the reason children learn to spell is to write. Thus, children must engage in lots of writing in order for them to not only maintain but to further develop their spelling skills. Wilde (1992) believes that children should be questioned during the writing conference as to how they know how to spell certain words and what they use to help themselves spell correctly.

Gentry and Henderson (1978) recommend that early-childhood-level teachers incorporate the following three steps in their spelling instruction:

1. Encourage writing in order that a child may actively participate in the acquisition of written language. By permitting a child to experiment with and to manipulate words, the youngster becomes directly involved with those cognitive operations which are essential to competent learning.
2. De-emphasize standard spelling for the beginning speller; in this way, children can develop their reasoning powers in order to ascertain why a particular spelling is used.
3. Respond to nonstandard spelling in an appropriate manner and provide for the smooth transition from one developmental strategy to the next.

Gable, Hendrickson, and Meeks (1988) suggest that words should be divided into three main categories: regular, predictable, and irregular. Regular words are those that follow phonetic rules, such as consonant–vowel–consonant (*fin, box,* and *bat)* and consonant–vowel–consonant–silent "e" (*fine, kite,* and *bone)*. Predictable word patterns include word families such as *ank (bank, rank, crank,* and *sank); ight (light, right, fight,* and *night);* and *end (bend, send,* and *tend)*. Irregular words are those that fail to follow phonetic rules or a set pattern, such as *penguin, their,* and *develop*. Gable et al. believe that in teaching children regular words, instruction should emphasize letter-sound correspondence within writing applications rather than memorization of the words themselves. In teaching predictable word patterns, instruction should emphasize spelling rules, rhyming words, word families, and the use of mnemonic devices. Success in the instruction of irregular words is best attained through the use of flash cards, visual memory, and multisensory approaches.

Of all the spelling study methods currently available, the most widely accepted relies on student self-discipline. In the "look, say, cover, write, and compare" approach, which has been used for generations, a student looks at a

Error Category	Example	Correct Spelling
1. Vowel omission	familis	families
2. Vowel substitution	elephunt	elephant
3. Vowel addition	develope	develop
4. Consonant omission	poses	possess
5. Consonant substitution	chrok	truck
6. Consonant addition	askt	asked
7. Letter reversal	hrap	harp

word, says and spells the word aloud softly, covers up the word, writes it on a sheet of paper, and then finally compares the original and attempted spellings. This same sequence is then repeated until the word is spelled correctly *and* the student is confident of having mastered the word. Although this study technique has proved to be quite effective, teachers must routinely reiterate the five study steps to prevent students who use it from becoming lax in its application.

Spelling Errors

Students' spelling errors should be classified as well as evaluated by the classroom teacher. Since there is more than one way to make a spelling error, an analysis of the exact nature of the mistake can aid a teacher in developing a plan for instruction (Henderson, 1985). Oftentimes, a pattern of errors seems to emerge; a child may continually delete one of a pair of consonants from a word ("tenis" for *tennis* and "batle" for *battle*). From an instructional point of view, such repetition of errors highlights the particular spelling skills a student needs to practice. Some common spelling errors are identified in focus box 11.2. These error categories can assist the classroom teacher in choosing instructional tactics.

To assess error patterns, a teacher must first acquire a sample of a student's spelling. For students in Grades 3 and above, this can easily be accomplished through the administration of either a grade-level spelling test of 25 to 50 words or a word-by-word dictation of particular sentences or paragraphs. Although student spelling errors are much more consistent across word lists (DeMaster, Crossland, & Hasselbring, 1986), sentence and paragraph writing does offer greater flexibility in spanning content area topics and materials (for example, mathematics, science, and social studies) (Gable, Hendrickson, & Meeks, 1988).

bananana na

Figure 11.3
Amber's spelling of *banana*.

Students often provide insights about their word perceptions through conversation. For example, during a writing conference with her first-grade teacher, Amber was asked whether she knew how to spell the word *banana*. She replied, "Oh, yes. I can spell banana. I just don't know when to stop" (see figure 11.3).

Good and poor spellers differ in the strategies they use to tackle difficult words. A study by Radebaugh (1985) found that good spellers thought of possible spellings syllable by syllable, while poor spellers attempted to "sound out" the word one or two sounds at a time. None of the poor spellers in Radebaugh's study reported using visual imagery when considering possible spellings of a word.

Assisting Children with Spelling

Students progress as spellers when teachers support them as readers and writers (Bartch, 1992; Scott, 1994). In particular, the teacher must help the student form links between reading and spelling. "Specific incidents in which the child focuses on the spoken and written word simultaneously may enhance the acquisition of the spellings of phonemes and of whole words" (Griffith, 1991, p. 232). Good spellers tend to be those who are wide readers and who have ample writing opportunities within which to use their spelling.

In addition, children's attitudes toward spelling are important. According to Jill Scott (1994, p. 189), a first-grade teacher, a classroom atmosphere that promotes "words and spelling as interesting and enjoyable can only be an advantage to the student. When risk taking and invented spelling are treated as natural and desirable, the students will write more and thus become more knowledgeable about words."

Scott suggests the following activities to promote spelling in early-childhood classrooms:

Teacher Modeling. The teacher demonstrates how adults determine the proper spelling of a word, for instance by pronouncing a word and then asking students to help spell it or by looking words up in a dictionary.

Labeling the Classroom. Objects and materials can be labeled using markers and tagboard. These become spelling references for young writers. Time of day can be taught this way as well; the teacher may hold up the proper sign for different activities during the day, including signs for recess, lunch, art, music, and gym, as well as time to go home.

Word Categories. Lists of words organized into categories can be hung around the room. These may include lists of words for family members, colors, animals, etc.

Pattern Charts. Charts should be displayed that demonstrate the patterns that occur in words. For example, *br* in *brick, brown,* and *bright* and *ing* in *ring, bring,* and *thing.*

Interesting Words. Bring students' attention to interesting words, such as compound words (*ladybug, fireplug,* and *gun-shy*), family words (*featherbed, featherhead, featherbrain,* and *featherweight*), and word histories (*bigwig* comes from the colonial period when the more powerful politicians wore large powdered wigs).

Word Sorts. Each student is given word cards and asked to sort them into spelling patterns. For instance, beginning spellers could be given *bin, in, tin, red, bed, fed, cat, sat,* and *bat.* Avoid using words that don't fit into the categories.

Bulletin Board Dictionary. Have the students write down words on index cards and arrange them in alphabetical order on the bulletin board. With young children, the teacher can make squares for each of the 26 letters of the alphabet. The child can then place the word in the square of the letter that starts the word.

Routman (1991) suggests the following additional ideas for improving spelling:

Spelling Big Book. The pattern and word charts can be laminated and put together in a class Big Book, which becomes a kind of class dictionary. This book can be placed near a writing center for students to use as a reference when they write.

Have-a-Go. "Have-a-go" spelling originated in Australia as children attempted to spell unknown words, or to "have a go at it." Students select three words from their writing that may be misspelled. Next the students make three attempts at spelling their words properly, each attempt resulting in a different way to spell the word until they believe they have spelled the word correctly. Each attempt is written on a "Have-a-Go Sheet" that is taken with them when they meet with the teacher for a writing conference.

The "Have-a-Go Sheet" may be modified for emergent spellers by including three different headings used to indicate how the students determined the correct spelling of a word. The headings are as follows: "My try," "Help from a friend," and "Help from the teacher or aide."

Students with Special Needs

Students with learning disabilities tend to score lower than those without such disabilities on spelling tests of both predictably and unpredictably spelled words (Carpenter & Miller, 1982). In addition, children with learning disabilities are apt to demonstrate poor visual short-term memory and often have problems with auditory and/or visual long-term memory (Wallace & McLoughlin, 1988). In order to assist such students, as well as students with other mental handicaps, spelling instructional time may be increased and additional assistance provided through peer tutoring, word lists displayed on the student's desk, increased use of the spelling words in other content areas during the week the words are being studied, and other appropriate instructional steps.

The *multisensory approach* of Grace Fernald (1943) is appropriate for use with spellers who have disabilities or those who lack confidence in their spelling ability. The teacher writes the word on a card in large letters (manuscript for first and second graders and cursive for higher grade levels). Then the teacher shows the card to the student while pronouncing the word. The student repeats the word. The teacher holds the child's hand while the child traces the letters with the index and middle fingers of the writing hand and pronounces the syllables aloud. Next, the child turns the card over and writes the word without looking at it. The child then verifies the spelling. If the word was spelled correctly, the child then writes and rechecks the word three more times. If the word was spelled incorrectly, the child repeats the finger tracing and verbalization of the word. The child may not erase any part of the word; it must be written correctly, letter by letter, or the word is considered to be incorrect. On the following day, the child is tested for the words presented the previous day.

One teacher who had several students with severe spelling problems found that this approach resulted in fewer words learned but increased correct spelling by 80 percent (Norton, 1989). The multisensory approach is time-consuming for both the teacher and the student; however, its use with students with special needs has met with much success since Fernald first developed it nearly 50 years ago.

Spelling Generalizations

The link between the sound a letter represents and its spelling is a strong one. While kindergartners and first graders tend to spell a word the way they hear it said aloud, older children and adults apply spelling generalizations to unfamiliar words. As Adams (1990, p. 103) states:

> Clearly, the connections between sound patterns and spelling patterns must enhance our ability to remember or figure out how a new word is spelled. They must enhance our ability to recognize a printed rendition of a word once having heard it. And they must enhance our ability to recognize a spoken rendition of a word once having seen it in print.

By second grade, most students have already amassed some spelling generalizations or rules, including those of capitalization, prefix and suffix addition, and phonic generalizations. Second graders usually know that the first letter of a proper name is capitalized and that the addition of an *s* changes most nouns into the plural form.

Nevertheless, formal instruction in spelling rules should begin only after a child is cognitively able to understand the generalizations being taught (Allred, 1977). Beers (1980) and Templeton (1991b) suggest that teachers should wait to introduce these rules until a child possesses a strong sight vocabulary; it is at this point that a child has a large repertoire of words within which to compare and contrast once phonics instruction is initiated. Allred's (1977) findings have yielded the following guidelines for spelling instruction:

Rather than teaching students all of the generalizations, only a few rules should be taught. Rules that have an exception should not be taught.

Only one rule should be taught at a time.

A rule should be taught when there is a direct need for it.

Rules should be taught inductively via various word examples.

Focus box 11.3 contains a list of spelling generalizations that children should know by the fourth grade. These are best learned through children's own inductive reasoning processes. For instance, if students are able to determine whether or not the suffix *-ed* is pronounced with the /d/ or /t/ sound, they should begin their inquiry by providing examples of words that actually end in *-ed*. The teacher simultaneously writes these words on an overhead transparency or the chalkboard and then asks the class to identify the words that are pronounced with the /d/ sound. At this time, students are to look for any common features among the words. The students then follow the same sequence of steps to examine the words pronounced with the /t/ sound. Such a list might include the following words:

dogged	bragged	coughed
stretched	bobbed	started
dipped	handed	pointed

Once the activity has been completed, students should have formed various conclusions. In our sample list, for example, words that end in *d, g,* and *t* are pronounced with the /d/ sound after the *-ed* suffix is added, whereas words that end in *ch, gh,* and *p* are pronounced with the /t/ sound after the suffix is added.

Dictionary Skills

Teaching children how to use a dictionary will give them a sense of writing freedom. In recent years, dictionaries written specifically for children have been greatly improved. Colorful picture dictionaries that enable young children to make picture-word associations in their quests for the correct spellings of specific words are motivational for primary-grade students. Such early experiences help students understand the importance of the dictionary as a reference tool for writing. Dictionaries are now on CD-ROMs.

Children also need to learn how to use a dictionary to discover the meanings of words, as well as their pronunciations. Proper use of a dictionary's pronunciation key will enable children to pronounce any word correctly, including placing the accent on the proper syllable of a multisyllabic word.

Besides the familiar picture dictionaries and elementary-level dictionaries, other types of dictionaries are available for use by elementary school students. Children who have difficulty with spelling or who have learning disabilities may benefit from using handheld spelling computers. With these, the child

Focus Box 11.3
Spelling Generalizations

Plurals

1. Plurals of most nouns are formed by adding an *s.*
   dog, dogs; bed, beds; car, cars
2. Plurals of nouns ending in *ch, s, sh,* or *x* are usually formed by adding *es.*
   church, churches; bus, buses; dress, dresses; brush, brushes; box, boxes
3. When a noun ends in a *y* that is preceded by a consonant, the plural is formed by changing the *y* to an *i* and adding *es.*
   fly, flies; baby, babies; candy, candies
4. Plurals of a small number of nouns are formed by changing their singular form.
   man, men; woman, women; goose, geese; mouse, mice; child, children

Possessives

5. Possessives of most singular nouns are formed by adding an apostrophe followed by an *s.*
   boy, boy's; dog, dog's
6. Possessives of most plural nouns are formed by adding an apostrophe.
   girls, girls'; ladies, ladies'
7. Possessives of a small number of plural nouns are formed by adding an apostrophe followed by an *s.*
   men, men's; children, children's

Suffixes

8. A word that ends in a "silent *e*" usually keeps the *e* when a suffix beginning with a consonant is added.
   grace, graceful; nine, ninety; hate, hateful
9. A word that ends in a "silent *e*" usually drops the *e* when a suffix beginning with a vowel is added.
   bake, baking
10. A word that ends in a single consonant preceded by a vowel usually doubles the final consonant before a suffix beginning with a vowel is added.
    tag, tagged; put, putting; big, bigger
11. A word ending in a *y* that follows a consonant usually changes the *y* to *i* before a suffix is added, unless that suffix begins with *i.*
    battery, batteries; silly, silliness

Vowels

12. An *o* at the end of a word usually represents the long /ō/ sound.
    tobacco, potato
13. When an *r* follows a vowel, the sound of the vowel is neither long nor short but is "*r*-controlled," meaning that the *r* influences the sound of the vowel that precedes it.

Capitals

14. Proper nouns begin with capital letters.
    Jim, English, Smith, New York

In the Classroom Mini Lesson

Alphabetical Order

Objective: Teaching the alphabetical order of words that begin with different letters.

The first skill required in dictionary use is alphabetical sequencing. Although children may know the "alphabet song," they may have little knowledge of the placement of letters relative to one another (for example, that *m* is the middle of the alphabet while *w* is close to the end). Certain activities can eliminate this uncertainty. With flash cards that contain words beginning with different letters, students can practice arranging words in their proper alphabetical order on their desks under the teacher's guidance. The trading of flash cards allows for repetition of the activity. Once the students have mastered this skill, they can be introduced to the alphabetizing of words beginning with the same letter; this can be followed by activities involving the alphabetizing of words that begin with the same two letters, and so on.

After learning alphabetical order, students should be instructed in the use of guide words. For example, the teacher distributes word flash cards to each student. When the teacher displays two chosen guide words, the students raise the flash cards containing the words that alphabetically come between the two guide words.

spells a word phonetically, and the computer then produces the correct spelling. However, homonyms such as *there, their,* and *they're* remain a problem because the handheld devices fail to differentiate among the meanings of such words. Most handheld computers contain up to 75,000 words.

Word processing software usually contains programs that check spelling. As with the handheld spelling computers, however, most of these programs cannot discern the proper homonym. Although such computerized devices can aid students in their spelling, students should not be allowed to become totally dependent upon them. Children still need to develop spelling skills to aid them in their writing.

Handwriting

As 4-year-old Kurtis and his mother were driving home from his child-care center, she asked him what he did at school that day.

"Oh," he answered, "We made letters."

Very slowly and deliberately he said, "We made *A.* We made *B.* We made *C.*" Then he suddenly perked up as he enthusiastically and proudly announced, "I'm a good *C*'er!"

Handwriting is the making of symbols that, when placed together, represent words. When young children first begin making letters, they find some letters easier to form than others. For instance, Kurtis found the letter *C* much easier to make than *A* or *B.* Despite the prevalence of both typed and word-processed material, handwriting is an important skill for children to master; it is used for writing drafts of compositions and letters, for taking class and source notes, and for making lists.

Focus Box 11.4
Spelling Software Programs

*S*tudents enjoy practicing their spelling with various computer software programs. Two such programs are described below.

"Super Solvers Spellbound" is a program designed by teachers and sold through The Learning Company, 6493 Kaiser Drive, Fremont, California 94555. The program is very flexible in that it comes with 1,000 different words that are sorted into several different topics, such as "planets." Teachers and/or students can add up to an additional 3,000 words. By playing three different spelling games (Word Search, Criss Cross, and Flash Card), students become engaged in a spelling bee program. The program gets more difficult as a student becomes more proficient. The sound effects are superb so that the pronunciation of the words is very clear. The program is available on CD-ROM for both IBM compatible and Macintosh computers. Suggested age levels are 7 to 12.

"Spelling Jungle" is a program created by Sierra On-Line, P.O. Box 85007, Bellevue, Washington, 98007. This program focuses on words that children often have difficulty spelling. It includes a tricky maze that even adept video game players will find challenging. The program is limited in that additional words cannot be added. It is available on CD-ROM for both Macintosh and IBM compatible computers. Suggested age levels are 7 to 10.

Both of the above programs give students suggestions for spelling rules.

When children construct words slowly and laboriously on paper, they are less effective in their overall development of compositions because they frequently lose important thoughts and ideas in the process. Thus, poor handwriting can be said to inhibit the creative, productive writer (Graves, 1978).

Young children typically initiate handwriting attempts when they are able to distinguish between pictures (or drawings) and print. For most children, this occurs at about age 4, when experiments with marking instruments and paper generally begin. Formal instruction in handwriting may profitably start either at the end of kindergarten or at the beginning of first grade. Because young children differ in their acquisition of motor skills, most teachers wait for an appropriate signal from a child before introducing handwriting. Such a signal often consists of the child's production of his or her own name. Not only does this action indicate that the child is ready to learn handwriting, but it serves to identify the point in time when a child understands that a word actually conveys meaning (Clay, 1975).

Children are introduced to the manuscript, or print, method before learning the cursive method at the end of the second or the beginning of the third grade. In the intermediate grades, handwriting receives less emphasis as part of the writing process. Because ideas flow much more quickly than does the recording of those ideas on paper, young authors often sacrifice legibility. Not until the writing of a final draft is the quality of handwriting considered a priority.

We now examine the various aspects of handwriting acquisition and instruction and offer suggestions for evaluating and improving handwriting in the various grades.

Children's Handwriting Development

By age 3, children produce drawings that are composed of the same basic lines that constitute manuscript letters: (1) vertical lines, (2) horizontal lines, and (3) circles (Harste, Woodward, & Burke, 1984). Because of such early experience, most 6- and 7-year-olds can create these vertical and horizontal lines more easily than the relatively complicated connections associated with D'Nealian manuscript or cursive handwriting. Because vertical lines are made with a straight up-and-down motion and horizontal lines by a left-to-right motion, they rely predominately on already acquired gross motor skills.

Nevertheless, preschoolers and primary-grade students need to engage in activities that will develop fine motor skills. In working with modeling clay, finger paints, beads and string, and interlocking construction toys such as Lincoln Logs, Legos, or Wee Waffle Blocks, children begin to refine the movement of their fingers and hands and thus to develop precise maneuvers required for handwriting.

Eye-hand coordination, like fine motor control, is still being developed by children in early childhood. Connecting lines and closing circles are considered difficult tasks for many of these children. Furthermore, the eye continues to develop until children reach the age of about 8. Thus, 6- to 8-year-old students either struggle in their attempts to copy assignments from the chalkboard or find such tasks impossible because they are unable to refocus their eyes from long to short distances (that is, from the chalkboard to their desks).

By the time students reach the middle childhood or intermediate level, Grades 4 through 6, they can handwrite much more quickly and reduce the size of their letters. At this time, legibility becomes a primary concern. Many students are attempting to express their own individuality, such as the way in which they dot their *i*'s and incorporate extra loops and other frills. Although teachers should permit individuality and creativity, they must not interfere with legibility; slovenly handwriting should not be accepted (Graham & Miller, 1980).

Instruction in Handwriting

Handwriting is an important tool for communicating and thus needs to be addressed instructionally. Children need to become both legible and fluent in their handwriting. Handwriting instruction may be either formal, direct instruction or incidental instruction.

> Direct instruction is more efficient while incidental instruction is more in line with the philosophy of whole language. However, without being introduced to and given instruction in the basic handwriting writing skills such as letter formation, alignment, slant, and size, children are left to discover such skills on their own. As such they develop inappropriate techniques, and legibility suffers. (Farris, 1991, pp. 313–314).

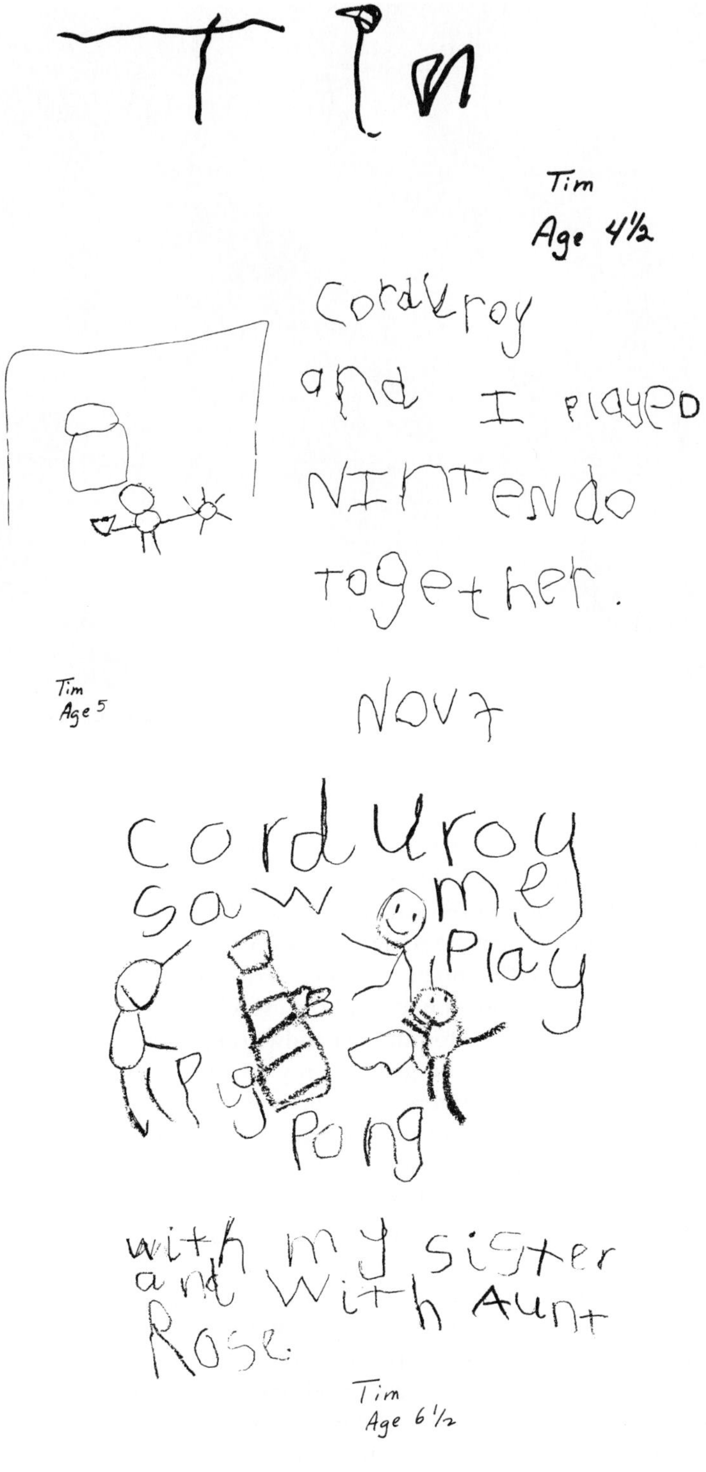

Tim
Age 4½

Corduroy
and I played
Nintendo
together.

Nov 7

Tim
Age 5

Corduroy
saw me
play
Pug Pong

with my sister
and with Aunt
Rose.

Tim
Age 6½

Figure 11.4
Tim's handwriting
development as a
preschooler and after
direct handwriting
instruction in
kindergarten and first
grade.

Experimenting with different kinds of media (felt-tip pens, colored pencils, chalk etc.) encourages children to practice writing.
© James L. Shaffer

As noted earlier, formal handwriting instruction should begin either at the end of kindergarten or at the beginning of first grade. In areas of the country where a majority of children attend preschool before entering kindergarten, such formal instruction may be undertaken even earlier. However, unless these children are able to differentiate between letter forms and to develop the motor skills needed to hold a pencil and the associated eye-hand coordination, they are simply not prepared for formal handwriting instruction.

Young children should be given plenty of opportunities to use pencils, crayons, and felt-tipped markers in their scribbling, drawing, and writing attempts before their formal introduction to handwriting (fig. 11.5). In choosing paper for such experimentation, teachers have found that blank sheets of paper are much more effective than lined sheets; the lines prove to be frustrating in that the preschooler lacks eye-hand coordination and therefore is not capable of producing letters that stay between linear boundaries. The same holds true for kindergarten children and for many beginning first graders.

Six-year-olds can more easily learn to write manuscript letters that fall between lines if the selected paper contains actual folds 1¼ inches apart. Teachers can prepare for this exercise in advance by creasing paper at the standard 1¼-inch intervals. In this way, children will rely on tactile sensation rather than sight to write the letters within the top and bottom lines.

Figure 11.5
Example of early
attempt at handwriting
by a 4½-year-old.
Notice the stiffness in
the handwriting.

If handwriting instruction is to be effective, the teacher must include four strategies in every lesson: (1) allow the students to observe the letter as it is formed, (2) describe for the students the steps needed to make the letter, (3) have the students describe the stepwise procedure as they create the letter, and (4) conclude the lesson by having the students apply the newly acquired handwriting skill in a meaningful context (such as by writing a letter to a pen pal). Because these strategies depend on the visual, auditory, and kinesthetic learning modalities, children are better able to recall proper letter formation when it is recreated in other settings. Likewise, if the letter is used in a meaningful context, teachers can actually reinforce the skill that was taught.

The classroom teacher should present new letters to beginning writers while simultaneously helping them visually identify the ways in which these letters compare or contrast with other letters of the alphabet. By asking students simple questions about letter size, shape, and required strokes, a teacher can promote a kind of visual analysis that will help the students gain insight into letter construction. The teacher should write the letter on the chalkboard using proper form and making it large enough to be visible to students in the back of the classroom without grossly misrepresenting the letter. Accordingly, capital letters should be between 3 and 4 inches in height and lowercase letters no less than 2 inches high.

As the teacher models the correct way to make the letter, a formal description of the necessary steps or movements should be included. After this, the students should use pencils and paper to form the letter at their own desks while individually describing the techniques used. Each student can then compare the letter he or she created with that produced by the teacher before the instruction is resumed. Because this process necessitates interaction, the teacher should actively circulate among the students, thereby offering both encouragement and objective criticism (Tompkins & Hoskisson, 1994).

The practicing of previously taught letters should be constantly encouraged. This can best be done by including many practical writing activities in class. Successful exercises might include writing greeting card verses for classmates or relatives, preparing and sending invitations to other classes or parents for special events, or developing posters for upcoming activities.

Writing Instruments

Years ago, people believed that children should learn to write with large, child-sized pencils. Generally, first graders would use their "fat pencils" at school and standard, adult-sized pencils at home because few of their homes possessed sharpeners large enough for the bigger pencils. We now know that although children with severe eye-hand coordination problems can benefit from writing with larger pencils, most children can use the more readily available, standard-sized pencil without difficulty. In fact, Lamme (1979) found that children may actually have better handwriting overall when they use standard pencils from the beginning.

Children should be given many opportunities to write with a variety of writing instruments, such as felt-tipped pens and markers, ink pens, and chalk. Just like adults, children will quickly find a writing implement that they prefer to use. Although felt-tipped pens are popular because their ink flows easily, the ones that release harmful odors should be avoided.

Gripping the Pencil

Children are often not taught the correct way to hold a pencil or have somehow adopted their own improper approaches to doing so, especially when they enter kindergarten never having had the opportunity to hold a writing utensil. These children are usually easy to identify because they typically curl all their fingers around the pencil in a fistlike position. As a result, it is not unusual to see a student grip a pencil in a tight, almost choking manner and in turn develop large callouses on the middle finger of the writing hand. Other children tend to point the eraser straight up into the air, and still others hold the pencil between the index and middle fingers. Despite such awkwardness, many teachers devote little attention to the manner in which students hold their pencils, even though this is crucial to the development of legible handwriting.

The proper way in which to grip a pencil can be explained methodically. A child begins by placing a sharpened pencil on a desk, with the point of the pencil pointing towards the child's midsection. If the child is right-handed, he or she then picks up the pencil with the right hand's thumb and index finger at the point where the paint and sharpened wood meet. By using the other hand, the child can gently pull the eraser end of the pencil downward so that the pencil rests on the hand between the thumb and index finger. Left-handed students follow the same procedure except that the pencil should be grasped with the thumb and index finger of the left hand about ¼ inch above the line where the paint and the sharpened wood meet. Regardless of the hand used, the grip should be somewhat loose and free of tension.

Manuscript Handwriting

Manuscript handwriting, often referred to by parents as printing, requires the use of independent strokes to form letters. There are two popular manuscript styles. The first, the *Zaner Bloser* manuscript style, emphasizes circles and lines in the forming of the 26 letters of the alphabet. In the second style, the *D'Nealian* manuscript style, letters more closely resemble cursive letters and less resemble print in books: The pencil rarely leaves the paper as circles, lines, and curves are used in D'Nealian letter construction.

Kindergartners were found to have four times more difficulty recognizing and identifying D'Nealian manuscript letters than Zaner-Bloser letters (DeWitz & Kuhl, 1994). Because of children's greater familiarity with the Zaner-Bloser letter formation, which closely resembles printed text, many schools use it instead of the newer D'Nealian style of curved manuscript letters.

In experimenting with handwriting and writing instruments, young children first produce capital manuscript letters. Once they begin to write their own pieces, they start to use the lowercase manuscript alphabet more frequently.

Because children are so eager to write and to share their recorded ideas and feelings with others, students accept manuscript handwriting lessons quite readily. Unfortunately, by the end of first grade or the beginning of second grade, this enthusiasm is offset by the fact that children have often come to accept only perfection in their work. Thus, as noted earlier, the second grader who writes several lines perfectly before making a minor error will likely wad up the paper and stomp off to the wastebasket only to return to attempt another "perfect" paper.

Some children continue to use manuscript writing throughout their school years and even beyond. Ten percent of adults print their signatures (Sedgwick, 1996). The reasons for this vary. Some students may never be introduced to cursive writing through formal instruction. This can happen, for instance, when a second grader initially attends a school district in which the transition to cursive handwriting occurs in the third grade but subsequently moves to another school district where the transition to cursive occurs in the second grade. In cases such as this, the child may attempt to make an informal, independent transition, but this may or may not prove to be successful. Thus, the child is more likely to continue to rely on the more familiar manuscript handwriting style.

Children may also come to rely solely on manuscript handwriting because they find the connecting of cursive letters to be difficult. Moreover, because some children simply write more legibly in the manuscript style, the classroom teacher may no longer insist that such students use cursive handwriting at all times. This may be the best resolution, particularly if a fifth or sixth grader is uncomfortable with cursive handwriting and this discomfort hinders composition writing. When this is the case, cursive handwriting may be required for the final draft, but the other drafts may be allowed in manuscript handwriting.

Letter Reversals

Young children frequently make letter reversals as they learn manuscript handwriting. Such reversals may involve confusing two letters, such as *b* and *d*, or actually writing a letter backwards. Furthermore, *mirror writing*, or writing entire words backwards so that when held up to a mirror, they can be read correctly, is commonplace among first graders. Some researchers believe that although all children produce such reversals, only a small number of children will continue to make these inversions over a long period of time; for those who do, instructional intervention by the teacher is necessary.

Figure 11.6

Examples of D'Nealian and Zaner Bloser manuscript and cursive handwriting styles. Compare the similarities of both D'Nealian and Zaner Bloser manuscript styles to printed text in picture books.

D'Nealian™ Manuscript Alphabet

a b c d e f g h i
j k l m n o p q r
s t u v w x y z

A B C D E F G H I
J K L M N O P Q R
S T U V W X Y Z

D'Nealian™ Cursive Alphabet

a b c d e f g h i
j k l m n o p q r
s t u v w x y z

A B C D E F G H I
J K L M N O P Q R
S T U V W X Y Z

D'Nealian™ Numbers

0 1 2 3 4 5 6 7 8 9

To help reduce the number of letter reversals, kindergarten and first-grade teachers should introduce letters that are similar in different lessons scheduled several days or even weeks apart. For example, children often confuse the letters *p* and *q;* by introducing the letter *p* first, the teacher provides students with an opportunity to acquaint themselves with this letter before they are presented with the less frequently used letter *q*.

By making sure that children know correct letter formation and use proper beginning and ending points, teachers can help students reduce letter reversals. Likewise, the use of simple mnemonic devices can also be helpful. For instance, using both hands, children can form two circles with their thumbs and index fingers. By holding the remaining fingers up and touching the thumbnails together, they can form and then visualize the letters *b* and *d,* as in *bed.* Such an activity creates a vivid impression on youngsters as they seek to recall proper techniques.

Regardless of whether the D'Nealian or Zaner Bloser handwriting approach is used, children produce reversals. (Figure 11.6 shows these two handwriting approaches.) Similarly, regardless of approach, some children were found to write the letter *s* in mirror fashion (Farris, 1994). Nevertheless, research indicates that D'Nealian-instructed students have significantly fewer reversals than students taught by the other approaches (Farris, 1994; Trap-Porter, Cooper, Hill, Swisher, & LaNunziata, 1984). On the other hand, D'Nealian-instructed students interchange letters other than those traditionally interchanged; for example, *f* and *t* are often confused by these children.

Zaner-Bloser Alphabet

Figure 11.6
(*Continued*)

Used with permission of
the publisher,
Zaner-Bloser, Inc.,
Columbus, Ohio.

Zaner-Bloser Alphabet

Cursive Handwriting

Figure 11.7
Six-year-old Penny's attempt at cursive handwriting.

Instruction in cursive handwriting differs from that of the manuscript technique, for children must be taught to read the flowing cursive style before attempting to produce letters and words in a similar fashion. Cursive writing maintains a continuous, linear motion of pencil on paper from the first to the last letter of a word. Despite this basic criterion, some children insist on stopping in the middle of a word to dot an *i* and cross a *t*.

Typically, children are expected to make the transition from manuscript to cursive handwriting during the second semester of the second grade or the first semester of the third grade. When children are older, such as beginning third or fourth grades, the transition takes place more quickly, usually within 6 to 8 weeks. Children tend to equate the mastering of cursive handwriting with being adultlike, and they are highly motivated to leave the "childish" manuscript behind in order to advance to what they perceive as the "grown-up" handwriting style. A second benefit to introducing cursive handwriting at a later age is that boys, who generally lag behind in fine motor skill development, may be more developmentally prepared to learn the new style in third grade rather than second grade.

Because children vary in the development of their handwriting skills, teachers should be aware of individual student progress in the use of manuscript handwriting. For example, Penny, a first-semester first grader, wrote her name in the kind of condensed cursive style shown in figure 11.7, an indication that she was ready for the transition to cursive. In this regard, a teacher must address the unusual advances of a certain class member so as not to hinder overall handwriting development.

As mentioned earlier, some children move from one school district to another without receiving cursive handwriting instruction. Other children will develop fine motor control later than their peers and thus will require special guidance in the acquisition of cursive skills. In either case, educators should pay particularly close attention to both student backgrounds and individual talents in evaluating students' needs for direction.

Legibility

Legibility is an important factor in both manuscript and cursive handwriting methods. Yet legibility plays a greater role in the cursive method because the connections between various letters and the letter formations themselves affect overall clarity to a greater extent.

Teachers who accept papers that are barely readable are not inspiring students to appreciate handwriting as an essential skill, and without other, more formal standards, students often lack personal goals in this regard. The teacher who feels a sense of inadequacy about his or her own handwriting may also place less emphasis on the importance of legibility for students. Therefore, it is essential that all teachers become masters of the craft.

Six letters account for 30 percent of all illegibilities in cursive handwriting: *b, i, k, p, r,* and *z.* Of these, *r* accounts for 12 percent of the overall illegibility total (Horton, 1970). Keeping this in mind, teachers must make certain that children are aware of the need for correct letter formation in their writing of these six troublesome letters.

Cursive handwriting that has a smooth beginning and ending stroke increases legibility, whereas abruptly beginning or ending the word decreases legibility. The stroke should start on the baseline and then move to begin the letter formation. Likewise, the stroke for the last letter of a word should continue with a flowing motion to the baseline. By including such strokes for each letter, legibility is increased by as much as 25 percent (Froese & Straw, 1981). This can be demonstrated by the fact that a hastily made *a* might appear as an *o* when incorrect stroking techniques are used.

Some children develop bad habits either because they have never learned correct letter formation procedures or because they have created their own shortcuts to save time. However, if such habits are quickly corrected, children are less likely to insist on using them in the future and therefore will eliminate them from any potential lifetime repertoire.

Motivating intermediate-grade children to improve their handwriting techniques can be difficult. One successful approach has been to introduce entire classes to the art of calligraphy. Simple calligraphy books can be purchased at most bookstores, and inexpensive felt-tipped pens are available in a variety of colors at most office supply stores. One or two projects using basic calligraphy skills as part of an art class can result in students' increased attention and devotion to their own handwriting.

Left-Handed Children

Hand dominance is usually established before children enter kindergarten, and sometimes by the age of 2. Still, some children enter kindergarten using both hands for coloring, drawing, and manipulating eating utensils. One kindergarten teacher, Mrs. James, expressed concern over Kyle, a student who possessed superior verbal and mathematical abilities as compared to the other students in the class. She observed Kyle in the process of coloring a picture he had drawn. He used his right hand to color from the bottom of the page to the top and his left hand to color from the top down. Mrs. James asked him to explain why he used his crayons in such a unique way. Kyle responded, " 'Cause when I color up, I like to use my right hand and when I color down, I like to use my left hand." These habits obviously made sense to him. Later on, Mrs. James had the opportunity to talk with Kyle's parents and discovered that they actually encouraged him to use both hands in hopes that such ambidextrous talent would help Kyle in athletics as he grew older.

Some children continue to use both hands for writing for a year or even longer. This is particularly true of the child who breaks his or her writing arm. In other cases, children write ambidextrously simply because they have never been forced to choose one hand over the other. Mrs. Volkman, a third-grade

In the Classroom Mini Lesson
Introducing Calligraphy

*C*alligraphy is elegant handwriting that requires much patience, time, and skill to learn. Breakthroughs in writing instruments such as felt-tipped pens have made calligraphy more accessible for intermediate-level students. Felt-tipped pens are available in several colors and are relatively inexpensive. The teacher may want to obtain a supply of such pens, calligraphy paper, and an easy-to-follow calligraphy guide and place these materials on a table where students can have access to them. Then, over a period of a few days, the teacher reads *The Strange Night Writing of Jessamine Colter,* a mystery by Cynthia DeFelice (1988). This book is about a calligrapher, or "fancy writer," who over a period of 50 years, makes posters, diplomas, birth and marriage announcements, and death notices for people in her community. As she grows older, Jessie discovers that she has the ability to foresee the future—to write about events before they occur.

After listening to the story, students are encouraged to use calligraphy to make their own posters and announcements that will predict future events. Students may wish to refer to examples of calligraphy in the DeFelice book.

DeFelice, C. C. (1988). *The strange night writing of Jessamine Colter.* New York: Macmillan.

teacher, complained about one student's illegible handwriting style. Although it was April and she had introduced the transition from manuscript to cursive handwriting at the beginning of the school year, Mrs. Volkman could barely read Terry's cursive handwriting. Upon closer observation, she noticed that Terry would begin to write with his right hand but ultimately would switch the pencil to his left hand. After witnessing this sequence several times, Mrs. Volkman asked Terry, "Why don't you write with just one hand instead of changing hands?" Terry looked up at her and responded, "When one hand gets tired, I let it rest while I write with the other one." Again, this was a perfectly logical response in view of the child's perceptions of the situation.

Wasylyk (1989) estimates that between 10 and 15 percent of students in a typical class show left-hand dominance and that the rate of incidence is increasing. These children require special instruction in the areas of pencil grip, paper position, and handwriting slant because each of these vary from those of their right-handed counterparts.

As already noted, left-handed students need to grip writing instruments about ¼ inch higher than do right-handed students. Doing this allows left-handers to avoid dragging their hand across the page, thereby smearing recently written letters, and also gives them a better overall view of what they are writing. The writing instrument should be positioned so that it points over the writer's left shoulder. As is true for right-handed students, left-handed students should keep their grip both flexible and relaxed.

Left-handed children should grip the pencil slightly higher than right-handed children.
© Jean-Claude Lejeune

The writing paper needs to be slanted to the right for left-handed students. However, each of these students must find the best location for the paper because both an individual's height and the slant of the desk necessitate some adjustment in paper position. For students in Grades 3 and up, "left-handed notebooks" are recommended; such notebooks have the spiral on the right side rather than on the left.

Grouping left-handed students together for formal handwriting instruction helps prevent the confusion that often occurs when a teacher attempts to instruct both right- and left-handed students simultaneously. In addition, teachers should provide a suitable amount of time for the completion of in-class writing assignments because left-handed students write more slowly than right-handed students when first gaining handwriting experience.

Special Problems

While some children never acquire the fine motor skills needed for legible writing, others have legibility problems caused by gripping a pencil too tightly. Teachers need to address these and other special problems through individual guidance. A lack of fine motor control may require a student to use a larger pencil. In the case of severe shaking of the hand, a teacher may have a child hold a pencil between the index and middle finger; by pointing the eraser end of the pencil toward the shoulder of the writing hand and resting the pencil on the thumb, the child achieves a more thorough command of handwriting despite the use of such an unorthodox grip. Some children simply write best by using manuscript forms.

When a child insists on gripping a pencil too tightly, the teacher can have the child use a plastic or rubber grip that slides over the pencil. The triangular-shaped grip fits comfortably in a child's hand and reduces the tension that develops between the pencil and child's fingers. Should a child continue to grip the pencil too tightly, a piece of tape wrapped around the first knuckle of the index finger may lessen the pressure of the grip. If a student clenches the pencil in a fistlike grip, holding a ball of wadded paper in the palm of the hand while writing will help to release tension (Wasylyk, 1989). It should be noted that students who produce extremely small letters are usually shy and withdrawn, whereas those who write large letters tend to be more outgoing.

Some middle-childhood-level students, particularly boys, prefer to print rather than to use cursive. Generally these children were introduced to cursive before they had sufficient fine motor skills. When a teacher notices a sudden deterioration in a child's handwriting, the teacher should be alerted to other possible changes that might be occurring within the child. The student may be physically ill or worried about family problems at home. Researchers have found that handwriting is closely linked to an individual's emotions. Because of this, some corporations have initiated a policy that requires job applicants to submit a handwriting sample for analysis.

Evaluating Handwriting

In evaluating both manuscript and cursive handwriting, the teacher should consider six primary factors: letter formation, spacing, slant, alignment, line quality, and size. Correct letter formation is, of course, extremely important, (Hackney, 1993). The teacher should evaluate this according to the handwriting method taught. The space between letters should be consistent, that is, neither too large nor too small. Likewise, the distance between words should be appropriate so that readers are readily able to identify individual words. The slant of the letters should be uniform and not overly dramatic. In general, the writing of right-handed students should slant to the right, whereas that of left-handed students should either be vertical or slant to the left.

Letters should be of even height. For example, the lowercase manuscript or cursive letters *a, c, e, g, i, j, m, n, o, p, q, r, s, u, v, w, x, y,* and *z* should all be

Focus Box 11.5
Criteria for Evaluating Handwriting

Letter formation: The shape of the letters should correspond to the handwriting method taught.
Spacing: Letters should not be cramped together or strung out across the page. Spacing should be consistent between letters and between words.
Slant: All letters should be consistent in terms of slant. That is, letters may slant slightly to the left or to the right or they may have no slant at all just as long as they all do the same thing.
Alignment: Comparable letters (for example, *a* and *c* or *h* and *l*) should be the same height.
Line quality: The writing instrument should be held correctly and in a relaxed manner. The lines should be steady and unwavering, with an even thickness.
Size: Letters should be neither too small nor too large to be read easily, and the size should be consistent.

of the same height, with *i* and *j* being dotted slightly above the other letters. Such proper alignment greatly aids readability. The size of the letters should also allow for easy reading. Students who produce microscopic-size letters should be encouraged to increase overall letter size. Students who can only fit a few words on a line because they use extremely large letters should gain practice in reducing letter size. In addition, line quality should not be too faint or too bold. Rather, lines should be of an even thickness throughout the writing.

After gaining some practical handwriting experience, children should be encouraged to evaluate their own handwriting by circling their best letters according to these six criteria. Because of its major significance, however, correct letter formation should be the first criterion they consider.

Summary

Spelling and handwriting are conventions of writing and should be taught in that context. Teachers must be aware of the 5 stages of spelling development (deviant, prephonetic, phonetic, transitional, and correct), including the characteristics of each stage. The first stages of spelling development are temporary; they last only until the student learns the conventions of writing. It is important that teachers assess students' spelling error patterns so that specific instruction can be determined and implemented for each student.

The successful acquisition of both manuscript and cursive handwriting skills is important for children because such skills provide them with the freedom to write as they wish. A lack of handwriting skills can both hinder and frustrate a child, thereby reducing writing productivity.

Manuscript handwriting, which utilizes a combination of circles and lines in the formation of letters, is usually introduced in late kindergarten or early first grade. The transition to cursive handwriting generally occurs during the second semester of second grade or the beginning of third grade. In planning instructional procedures, the teacher should consider writing grip, paper position, and the handedness of the child. The criteria for evaluating handwriting are letter formation, spacing, slant, alignment, line quality, and size.

Teachers must provide opportunities for children to write frequently if spelling and handwriting skills are to be maintained and further developed. In addition, students must realize that good spelling and handwriting help to convey the written message.

Questions

1. What are the stages of temporary or invented spelling? What are the characteristics of and instructional strategies for each stage?
2. What is the best method for studying spelling? Why don't all students succeed with this approach?
3. What are the components of a good spelling program? What can a teacher do to improve students' spelling?
4. How does manuscript handwriting differ from cursive handwriting?
5. Compare and contrast the D'Nealian and Zaner-Bloser handwriting styles.
6. What suggestions would you give to the parent of a 4-year-old who shows left-hand dominance?

Activities

1. Each content area tends to have vocabulary words that are associated with that particular area. Using an intermediate-level mathematics, science, or social studies textbook, design a spelling lesson that incorporates the use of such vocabulary.
2. Make a list of words that are difficult for you to spell. Tape the list to your refrigerator and use the "look, say, cover, write, and compare" study technique to master the spelling of the words.
3. Analyze the spelling of an elementary or middle school student. Can you detect any error patterns?
4. Compare the handwriting skills of elementary or middle school students and then ask their teacher to rate each student according to reading ability (good, average, or poor). Are the good readers necessarily better in handwriting as well?
5. Observe the body language of children as they practice handwriting. How does it compare with their body language as they write in their journals?
6. Evaluate your own handwriting according to the criteria used with children.

For Further Reading

Bartch, J. (1992). An alternative to spelling: An integrated approach. *Language Arts, 69,* 404–408.

Bloodgood, J. (1991). A new approach to spelling instruction in language arts programs. *Elementary School Journal, 92* (2), 203–211.

Farris, P. J. (1991). Handwriting instruction should not become extinct. *Language Arts, 68*(4), 312–314.

Hackney, C. (1993). *Handwriting: A way to self expression.* Columbus, OH: Zaner Bloser.

Scott, J. (1994). Spelling for readers and writers. *The Reading Teacher, 48* (2), 188–190.

Sedgwick, J. (March 18, 1996). Call the script doctor. *Newsweek,* 62.

Templeton, S. (1991). Teaching and learning the English spelling system: Reconceptualizing method and purpose. *Elementary School Journal, 92*(2), 185–201.

Wasylyk, T. M. (1989). Teaching left-handers the right stuff. *The Reading Teacher, 42*(6), 446–447.

Wilde, S. (1990). A proposal for a new spelling curriculum. *Elementary School Journal 90*(3), 275–290.

References

Adams, M. J. (1990). *Beginning to read: Thinking and learning about print.* Urbana, IL: Center for the Study of Reading.

Allred, R. A. (1977). *Spelling: The application of research findings. The curriculum series.* Washington, DC: National Education Association. (ED 135 003).

Anderson, P. S., & Lapp, D. (1988). *Language skills in elementary education* (4th ed.). New York: Macmillan.

Atkins, C. (1984). Writing: Doing something constructive. *Young Children, 40*(1), 3-7.

Bartch, J. (1992). An alternative to spelling: An integrated approach. *Language Arts, 69,* 404-408.

Beers, C. (1980). The relationship of cognitive development to spelling and reading abilities. In E. H. Henderson & J. W. Beers, *Developmental and cognitive aspects of learning to spell.* Newark, DE: International Reading Association.

Bissex, G. (1980). *GNYS AT WRK: A child learns to write and read.* Cambridge, MA: Harvard University Press.

Bloodgood, J. W. (1991). A new approach to spelling instruction in language arts programs. *Elementary School Journal, 92*(2), 203-211.

Brown, M. (1954). *Cinderella.* New York: Macmillan.

Brownell, C. A., Drozdal, J. G., Hopmann, M. R., Pick, A. D., & Unze, M. G. (1978). Young children's knowledge of word structure. *Child Development, 49*(3), 69-80.

Carpenter, D., & Miller, L. J. (1982). Spelling ability of reading disabled LD students and able readers. *Learning Disability Quarterly, 5*(2), 65-70.

Clay, M. (1975). *What did I write?* Portsmouth, NH: Heinemann.

DeMaster, V., Crossland, C., & Hasselbring, T. (1986). Consistency of learning disabled students' spelling performance. *Learning Disability Quarterly, 9*(1), 89-96.

DeWitz, P. A., & Kuhl, D. (1994, April). *The effect of handwriting style on alphabet recognition in kindergarten.* Paper presented at American Education Research Association, New Orleans, LA.

Farris, P. J. (1991). Handwriting instruction should not become extinct. *Language Arts, 68*(4), 312-314.

Farris, P. J. (1994), Learning to write the ABC's: A comparison of D'Nealian and Zaner-Bloser handwriting styles. *New Mexico Journal of Reading, 14*(2), 13-20.

Fernald, G. (1943). *Remedial techniques in basic school subjects.* New York: McGraw-Hill.

Froese, V., & Straw, S. B. (1981). *Research in the language arts.* Baltimore, MD: University Park Press.

Gable, R. A., Hendrickson, J. M., & Meeks, J. W. (1988). Assessing spelling errors of special needs students. *The Reading Teacher, 42*(2), 112-117.

Gentry, J. R. (1981). Learning to spell developmentally. *The Reading Teacher, 34*(4), 378-381.

Gentry, J. R., & Henderson, E. S. (1978). Three steps to teaching beginning readers to spell. *The Reading Teacher, 31*(6), 632-637.

Graham, S. (1983). Effective spelling program. *Elementary School Journal, 83*(5), 560-569.

Graham, S., & Miller, L. (1980). Handwriting research and practice: A unified approach. *Focus on Exceptional Children, 13*(2), 1-16.

Graves, D. (1978). Handwriting is for writing. *Language Arts, 55*(3), 393-399.

Griffith, P. (1991). Phonemic awareness helps third graders remember correct spellings. *Journal of Reading Behavior, 23,* 215-232.

Hackney, C. (1993). *Handwriting: A way to self expression.* Columbus, OH: Zaner Bloser.

Hall, S. E. (1985). Oad Mahr Gos and writing with young children. *Language Arts, 62*(3), 262.

Hammill, D. D., Larsen, S., & McNutt, G. (1977). The effects of spelling instruction: A preliminary study. *Elementary School Journal, 78*(1), 67-72.

Harste, J., Woodward, V. A., & Burk, C. (1984). *Language stories and literacy lessons.* Portsmouth, NH: Heinemann.

Henderson, E. (1985). *Teaching spelling.* Boston: Houghton Mifflin.

Henderson, E., & Beers, C. (1980). *Developmental and cognitive aspects of learning to spell.* Newark, DE: International Reading Association.

Henderson, E., & Templeton, S. (1986). A developmental perspective of formal spelling instruction through alphabet, pattern, and meaning. *Elementary School Journal, 86*(1), 305-316.

Hillerich, R. (1977). Let's teach spelling—Not phonetic misspelling. *Language Arts, 54*(3), 301-307.

Hooks, W. H. (1987). *Moss gown.* Boston: Clarion.

Horton, L. W. (1970). Illegibilities in the cursive handwriting of ninth-graders. *Elementary School Journal, 70*(8), 446-450.

Huck, C. (1989). *Princess Furball* (A. Lobel, Illus.). New York: Greenwillow.

LaFramboise, K. (1990). Journals in the classroom. *Florida Reading Quarterly, 27*(2), 27-29.

Lamme, L. (1979). Handwriting in an early childhood curriculum. *Young Children, 35*(1), 20-27.

Manolakes, G. (1975). The teaching of spelling: A pilot study. *Elementary English, 52*(2), 243-247.

Martin, B. (1991). *Polar bear, polar bear, What do you hear?* (E. Carle, Illus.). New York: Henry Holt.

Norton, D. E. (1989). *The effective teaching of language arts* (3rd ed.). Columbus, OH: Merrill.

Piazza, C., & Tomlinson, C. (1985). A concert of writers. *Language Arts, 62*(2), 150-158.

Pitman, Sir J., & St. John, J. (1969). *Alphabets and reading.* London: Pitman.

Radebaugh, M. R. (1985). Children's perceptions of their spelling strategies. *The Reading Teacher, 38*(6), 532-536.

Read, C. (1971). Preschool children's knowledge of English phonology. *Harvard Educational Review, 41*(1), 1-34.

Routman, R. (1991). *Invitations: Changing as teachers and learners.* Portsmouth, NH: Heinemann.

Scott, J. (1994). Spelling for readers and writers. *The Reading Teacher, 48*(2), 188-190.

Sedgwick, J. (1996, March 18). Call the script doctor. *Newsweek, 62.*

Templeton, S. (1991a). *Teaching the integrated language arts.* Boston: Houghton Mifflin.

Templeton, S. (1991b). Teaching and learning the English spelling system: Reconceptualizing method and purpose. *Elementary School Journal, 92*(2), 185-201.

Tompkins, G. (1993). *Teaching writing* (3rd ed.). Columbus, OH: Merrill.

Tompkins, G., & Hoskisson, K. (1994). *Language arts: Content and teaching strategies* (3rd ed.). Columbus, OH: Merrill.

Trap-Porter, J., Cooper, J., Hill, D., Swisher, J., & LaNunziata, L. (1984). D'Nealian and Zaner-Bloser manuscript alphabets and initial transition to cursive handwriting. *Journal of Educational Research, 77*(6), 343-345.

Wallace, G., & McLoughlin, J. A. (1988). *Learning disabilities: Concepts and characteristics* (3rd ed.). Columbus, OH: Merrill.

Wasylyk, T. M. (1989). Teaching left handers the write stuff. *The Reading Teacher, 42*(6), 446-447.

Wilde, S. (1990). A proposal for a new spelling curriculum. *Elementary School Journal, 90*(3), 275-290.

Wilde, S. (1992). *You kan red this!* Portsmouth, NH: Heinemann.

Yopp, H. K. (1995). A test for assessing phonemic awareness in young children. *The Reading Teacher, 49*(1), 20-29.

Reading: Interaction Between Text and Reader

IF YOU GIVE A CHILD A BOOK . . .
LITERACY LESSONS FOR TEACHERS

If you give a child a book, he's going to want to read it.

And as he reads, he's going to think about what he's reading.

And as he thinks, he's going to recall what he already knows and similar experiences he's had.

And as he thinks about those experiences, he's going to want to write.

And as he writes, he's going to want to talk to his friends and share his thoughts and ideas with them.

And as he talks with others, he's going to want to learn and discover more.

So, chances are he'll find another book to read,

And then another,

And another.

And as he reads more books, he'll discover books that make him smile, laugh, cry, angry, curious, frustrated, contented, thoughtful, happy.

And then, as time passes, he'll become a lifelong reader.

Thanks to a teacher who gave a child a book.

© Pamela J. Farris 1995

Introduction

W ith the exception of thinking, reading has received more attention over the years than any other language art. The importance of knowing how to read is immeasurable, for reading provides a means of acquiring not only information, but pleasure and enjoyment, as well. As the noted children's author, Natalie Babbitt (1987, p. 582) writes, "Honey, you know, is actually good for us nutritionally. So is peanut butter. But they taste so good that we forget about the nutrition. Reading is like that."

As children learn to read, they devour, like honey and peanut butter, book after book. And they don't realize or care that the process of reading, like honey and peanut butter, is good for them. Undoubtedly, the goal of a successful teacher should be to have every student become a "blanket reader"—a child who carefully hides under the blanket in bed, reading by flashlight a book that's just too good to put down.

Reading is more than word recognition and the gleaning of concepts, information, and ideas from text. Reading is the processing of words, concepts, information, and ideas put forth by the author as they relate to the reader's previous experiences and knowledge. Only a portion of information is included by the author of a passage; it falls upon the reader to interpret the remaining information. No written text is completely self-explanatory. When the reader interprets a text, the reader must call upon his or her store of knowledge pertaining to the topic of the text (Anderson & Armbruster, 1984). According to Palincsar, Ogle, Jones, Carr, and Ransom (1985), reading comprehension consists of three important parts: (1) an active, constructive process; (2) a thinking process before, during, and after reading; and (3) an interaction of the reader, the text, and context of the reading.

The type of reading material also influences the reading process. As Pam Bradley, a fourth-grade teacher, said in an interview, "Reading a book is different from reading a story. You have to follow one thread and remember it from day to day. You have to read books in order to know how to read books" (Whitney & Hubbard, 1986).

Research supports Bradley's statement. In comparing out-of-school activities such as watching television, participating in sports, listening to music, and reading books, researchers have found that the strongest association with reading proficiency is reading books and that a significant increase in reading achievement occurs when a child reads for at least 10 minutes a day (Anderson, Wilson, & Fielding, 1988). Other studies clearly confirm that the amount of reading children engage in affects their reading growth and fluency (Fader, 1982).

The goals in teaching reading in elementary school are first to teach students how to read and then to entice them to want to read. According to Purves (1990, p. 105), "children should be made aware from an early stage that the world of text is a rich one indeed."

To be good readers, children must have time to read, at least have temporary ownership of the material they are reading, and be allowed to respond to the material while and after reading it (Atwell, 1987). This chapter discusses various approaches to the teaching of reading in elementary school, including ways to integrate reading into the elementary curriculum.

Approaches to the Teaching of Reading

Instruction in reading may be planned or unplanned. Durkin (1990, pp. 473–474) writes that *planned* instruction occurs

> when a teacher selects materials and procedures for the purpose of attaining a prespecified goal. Instruction can also be *unplanned*, as when a teacher is wise enough to respond in helpful ways to students' questions, misinterpretations, overgeneralizations, and the like. Other things being equal, unplanned instruction has a better chance of succeeding than planned instruction because the reason that prompts it is obvious to students. That makes the instruction inherently meaningful.
>
> Based on what I know and have experienced as a classroom teacher, I am convinced that some combination of planned and unplanned instruction is essential if the reading ability of every student is to be maximally advanced.

In 1938, Louise Rosenblatt introduced the transactional theory of reading. She believed that the reader not only brings meaning to the reading act through previous experiences and other reading but that the reader's feelings add to what is taken away from the text, as well. Rosenblatt believed that people read for two purposes: for enjoyment and to get information. She called these aesthetic and efferent reading stances.

Basal readers remain the major components of most reading programs in elementary schools in the United States, despite the increasing number of followers of the transactional view of reading. Until recently, basal readers depended upon skills and subskills taught through workbook and worksheet exercises that accompanied selections, actual or condensed, from children's literature. Research findings in literacy development have led publishers to modify their basal reading series to incorporate the whole language approach and an interactive model of reading, writing, and discussing. However, workbooks and worksheets are still integral parts of basal reading programs.

In the whole language approach, children's literature is the reading material, and the classroom teacher develops planned lessons or relies on study guides for each literary selection used. This requires a typical elementary classroom library of 400 books covering a variety of genre within children's literature. Rather than directing a child to read specific selections of short or condensed stories from children's literature, as is the case in basal reading programs, the child is given more choice in the selection of reading material. As a result, a substantial portion of the responsibility for the student's learning to read fluently is shifted from the teacher to the student.

The majority of classroom teachers rely on an eclectic approach. That is, they select what they believe is the best from basal readers and from whole language, depending on the needs of their students. The basal reading program and the whole language approach are discussed in greater detail below.

Transactional View of Reading

As readers read a text they construct meaning based on their own previous experiences and background knowledge (Rosenblatt, 1938, 1978). According to the *transactional view* of reading, readers change their interpretations as they read the text. Thus, in reading, the constructed meaning is fluid and ever-changing. Langer (1990, p. 238) believes that readers start by "being out of and stepping into" their own personal "envisionment" of the text. As they move through this envisionment, they often step back and rethink or reconsider their previous understandings. They may raise questions about what they thought they knew as well as about what the text is presenting. The last stage occurs when the readers step out of this envisionment and react to the total reading experience. According to Langer, this process occurs with all types of texts, but the emphasis and reasoning processes differ depending on whether the text is informative or narrative.

Efferent and Aesthetic Reading

In 1938, Louise Rosenblatt described reading as consisting of two stances, aesthetic and efferent. Rosenblatt asserted that we read for two primary purposes: enjoyment, or *aesthetic reading,* and to be informed, or *efferent reading.* According to Cullinan and Galda (1994, p. 43), this view of creating meaning as one reads "involves connecting life and text. And the act of creating meaning while reading a story or poem is at once highly individual and intensely social. This creation, however, always begins with a reader." Thus children and adults approach the act of reading differently, depending upon their purpose for reading. Aesthetic reading enables readers to focus on the feelings, thoughts, and images evoked as they read. Associations with characters and reactions to similar events in the readers' own lives may be made. For instance, *Uncle Jed's Barbershop* (Mitchell, 1993) may remind readers of getting their own haircuts, while reading *Julius, Baby of the World* (Henkes, 1990) allows readers to explore the sibling rivalry that occurs when a new baby arrives and the strong family ties that arise when someone criticizes a family member. In contrast, the poetry in *Thirteen Moons on Turtle's Back: A Native American Year of the Moons* (Bruchac & London, 1992) may sensitize readers to the different seasons and Native Americans' appreciation and respect for nature.

In efferent reading, readers what to take away information and therefore concentrate on the "practical purpose of gaining knowledge from the text" (Cullinan & Galda, 1994, p. 43). In reading about Emperor and Adelie penguins in Helen Cowcher's *Antarctica,* readers learn how penguins survive and what frightens them, while William Jay Jacob's (1990) *Ellis Island: New Hope in a*

New Land gives readers background information on immigration in America beginning with Native Americans through the establishment of Ellis Island as an immigration center.

Aesthetic and efferent stances of reading are not at different ends of the spectrum, but rather are both often included in reading. Aesthetic reading relates to private, affective aspects of meaning—to the lived-through experience—whereas efferent reading primarily relates to public, cognitive aspects of meaning (Rosenblatt, 1991). A student studying about the war between the states may read *The Boys War: Confederate and Union Soldiers Talk about the Civil War* (Murphy, 1990). The student will not only get a better understanding of the number of young men and boys who served on both sides, but also of the roles they played as drummer boys, flag bearers, and soldiers. This represents the efferent stance of reading; however, the same student may feel a tug of emotion when considering the number of boys who died of dysentery and inadequate medical care or when reading about the bartering of tobacco for coffee and the occasional letter writing between soldiers of the two opposing sides.

Evaluation in the Transactional Reading Program

Literature circles and reading journals are important tools of evaluation in a transactional reading program. Journals may include simulated or character journals in which the reader pretends to be a favorite character and writes from that person's viewpoint, dialogue journals in which the reader writes to another student or the teacher about the book as it is read, or a literature response journal that the reader shares in a small group discussion. The teacher jots down notes about the student's journal responses and his or her contributions to group discussions. Rather than giving letter grades, a written description is given of the student's progress and growth as a reader.

Basal Reading Program

Basal readers have been extremely popular ever since the success of William McGuffey's *McGuffey's Reader,* which was handed down from sibling to sibling and parent to child beginning in the mid-1800s. A typical basal reading series includes a readiness workbook for emergent readers and a preprimer, a primer, and a first "reader" as introductory materials for beginning readers. For second and third graders, there are two readers with accompanying workbooks, while fourth through eighth graders receive one reader and a workbook. The teacher's manual that accompanies each level of reader provides a rigid format that precisely defines how the students are to be instructed. Discussion questions and follow-up activities are included so that the teacher does not need to prepare these in advance.

Basal reading programs have been criticized for their lack of flexibility. In addition, the narrative stories and informational selections may not be of interest to the students in a particular classroom. Regardless of the criticisms, however, basal reading programs remain the most popular approach to reading instruction. As recently as 1989, Shannon reported that in over 90 percent of classrooms, teachers use basal readers for reading instruction.

Children easily become engrossed in a book with a topic of which they are interested.

© James L. Shaffer

Evaluation in the Basal Reading Program

Typically, a classroom teacher administers an informal reading inventory to each student to determine his or her reading level before assigning a basal reader to the student. The informal reading inventory may be one developed by the publisher of the basal reading series used by the school district, by someone within the school district, or by the teacher. It consists of graded paragraphs and comprehension and vocabulary questions pertaining to each paragraph. As the student reads a paragraph orally, the teacher notes word recognition errors. After the student has completed the paragraph, the teacher removes the text from the student's view and asks the comprehension and vocabulary questions.

In addition to providing informal reading placement inventories, publishing companies provide unit tests for students to take after they have completed each instructional unit of the reader. Such tests are usually designed to determine the reading achievement of the student at each point in terms of skill and subskill attainment. Some school districts use the results of such tests to determine whether a student will be retained or promoted to the next grade.

Whole Language Approach

The whole language approach focuses on the reading and writing interests of the students themselves. The classroom teacher promotes the sharing of personal interests with the class—favorite books, letters handed down from one generation to the next, slides from a vacation trip, a handmade quilt completed over the summer, and the like—thereby signifying that the teacher trusts the students to such a degree that personal feelings and thoughts can be shared with them without reservation.

The whole language approach stresses independent reading and writing rather than the completion of workbook exercises and skill sheets. Independent reading and writing activities were recommended by the Commission on Reading in *Becoming a Nation of Readers* (Anderson, Hiebert, Scott, & Wilkinson, 1984). Children's literature provides a greater variety of reading materials than do basal readers. Thematic units that include literature selections related to the topic are commonplace. The whole language classroom is "littered with literacy" that makes sense and appeals to the students in the classroom (Watson & Crowley, 1988).

The whole language approach also incorporates social interaction as students discuss, plan, and evaluate together in an atmosphere of cooperative learning. Students become immersed in language learning through their own self-motivation. According to Maureen Morrissey (1988, p. 86), a third-grade teacher who teaches both English- and Spanish-speaking students:

> Students are so intimately involved in the process, they are neither aware nor concerned that I am evaluating their accomplishments or that they are involved in language learning. They are using language as a means to an end, and I am getting a true picture of their abilities at work.

The whole language approach is informal but requires that the classroom teacher be observant and in tune with student needs and interests. Purves (1990, p. 107) recommends that teachers "explore with the students what they do and do not know when they begin to read and write, and how they might go about supplying the missing knowledge."

Holdaway (1986, p. 42) agrees, stating, "The teacher of reading is a skilled attendant to the natural language processing abilities of children. Many of these processes lie beyond complete understanding or control but are nevertheless guaranteed by the amazing learning potential of the young human brain." Thus, decision making and evaluation are ongoing processes, and the teacher must be constantly alert for "teachable moments."

Many teachers feel uncomfortable with the whole language approach, which in its purist form is the direct opposite of the basal reader philosophy. The whole language approach has been criticized as being a "warm and fuzzy" approach to reading rather than one that truly challenges students. A second criticism is that some of the tenets of the whole language approach are in conflict with effective teaching, according to research findings that strongly support direct instruction (Klesius, 1988). Whole language advocates vigorously dispute such criticism (Church, 1994); however, because of this controversy, many teachers are apt to incorporate whole language activities while adhering to a basal reading program.

Because the whole language approach offers flexibility, it is the reading/ writing program selected for use in most bilingual classrooms. Students with learning disabilities and special education students who have been frustrated with skill-driven instruction utilizing phonics and/or basal reader programs have been found to flourish within the whole language approach (Brazee & Haynes, 1988).

Evaluation in the Whole Language Approach

Evaluation of student reading achievement in a whole language program is not based solely on formal tests or standardized measurements. Such measures lend themselves more readily to a scope and sequence skills orientation. Yet most states mandate formal evaluation of reading competence at specified grade levels. Without standardized reading achievement tests, teachers and school administrators often have difficulty convincing parents—who themselves were taught according to the isolated skills approach—that their child is performing at an appropriate level.

If students in a whole language program are to be evaluated with standardized reading achievement tests, the classroom teacher can instruct the students so they will become "test wise." According to Weaver (1988, p. 270), "Children who are immersed in purposeful reading and writing experiences with sensible materials in a supportive environment do at least as well as students who drill on minute, abstract skills in the limited context of a worksheet."

The evaluation of reading progress in a whole language program relies on a combination of techniques, including teacher observation and analysis of records kept over a period of time. Teachers should be concerned with children's interests, level of functioning, and literacy development as evidenced through student evaluation and classroom activities (Harp, 1988). According to Routman (1991, p. 305) evaluation should include five components that occur interactively, "That is, the observation, activity, test, or task must be relevant, authentic, and part of the teaching-learning process by informing the learner and furthering instruction."

The teacher must observe the student working individually, in small groups, and in whole class activities to determine the child's ability to use language, solve problems, and work cooperatively with peers. The teacher must also interact with the student through conferences, questioning, and written dialogues to assess the student's knowledge level and approaches to problem solving. Finally, the teacher must analyze the student's oral and written reactions to written material, both published books and the student's own pieces, to evaluate the student's knowledge of language and its use (Goodman, 1988).

By means of checklists, anecdotal records, journals, and portfolios, the classroom teacher can monitor the learning and development of each student. A monthly review of each student's reading growth, such as a comparison of anecdotal records and checklists over several weeks time, helps the teacher determine the types of experiences and activities that have been successful and unsuccessful for each child. The addition of journals enables teachers to reflect on their own teaching as well as the learning of each student.

The whole language teacher should also encourage students to evaluate themselves. By keeping lists such as "Books I Have Read" and "Things I Can Do

A working father may fit in reading a storybook to his child before heading to the kitchen to prepare dinner, doing chores, or running errands.

in Writing" and dating such lists to indicate progress, students can self-monitor their efforts. By determining what they already know and do not know, they can direct their learning to new and unfamiliar areas. Thus, students take control of their own learning.

Instructional Practices for Emergent and Beginning Readers

The rudimentary beginnings of reading are exhibited in attentiveness to a story as it is read and recognition of a sign advertising a favorite fast-food restaurant. This section examines emergent reading more closely and describes instructional practices for use with beginning readers.

Emergent Reading

As soon as a baby is brought home from the hospital, he or she is surrounded by stimulating materials: toys, household objects, television, and so on. Even the essentials needed to care for the baby are put in colorful, inviting packages, such as disposable diapers that feature tiny illustrations on their waistbands. As the child grows older, training pants and underwear featuring the antics of favorite cartoon characters may be worn. And videos are available for children as young as 18 months. An abundance of printed materials is also available to stimulate children, including children's books, children's magazines (as well as those for grown-ups), and colorful advertisements and brochures.

Growing up in such an environment, a child's literacy development begins early, as exemplified by the 3-year-old who recognizes brands of cereal, soup, and toothpaste during the weekly grocery shopping excursion with Mom. This early literacy acquisition is emphasized in a story shared by Yetta Goodman at an international symposium focusing on preschoolers. Goodman said that in a study of over 5,000 4-year-olds, it had been impossible to find an American child who could not read the word "McDonald's" (Smith, 1986).

A study of early readers conducted by Durkin (1966, 1972) indicated that the children did not learn to read by themselves, but that they learned in a developmental and natural way. Durkin found that early readers had four things in common: (1) their parents conversed with them, (2) the children asked many questions, (3) the parents responded to the children's questions, and (4) the children frequently asked, "What is that word?" Durkin's research has been supported by findings by Heath (1983), Lartz and Mason (1988), Snow (1983), and Taylor (1983), which show that a child's awareness of and desire to demonstrate literacy result from meaningful communication in regard to literacy. Putting notes on the refrigerator, writing a thank-you note to Aunt Mary for a birthday present, dropping a postcard to a friend who has moved away, and reading bedtime stories are all informal activities in which a parent can assist the youngster in acquiring literacy.

According to Holdaway (1979), parents do not typically read to their children out of a sense of duty or to ensure that their child has an educational advantage; they do so for the satisfaction and enjoyment that their child gets from the situation. Holdaway states that during such informal reading time,

> the parent makes no demands on the child, but is deeply gratified by the lively responses and questions that normally arise. It provides a stimulus for satisfying interaction between parent and child, different, richer, and more wide-ranging than the mundane interactions of running the house (p. 39).

Being read to can have a major effect on children's attitudes toward reading (Lartz & Mason, 1988). A study of four preschoolers who were read to on a regular basis found that they associated the sharing of books with a positive, secure, and enjoyable environment (Doake, 1981). Indeed, the warm and comfortable sense of sharing while reading to his children led one father to say, "You don't even have to listen to the words; it's that kind of rapport" (Teale, 1984, p. 72).

Writing also plays a significant role in early reading (Calkins & Harwayne, 1991). According to Clay (1982, p. 208), writing is a "synthetic experience where letters are built into words which make up sentences. . . . [Thus] when a child writes she has to know the sound-symbol relationship inherent in reading." Through writing, children learn to organize and discover the features of written language.

Clay (1982) further explains that when children share their own stories with their classmates, a framework and purpose for writing evolve. Research indicates that children who write before they enter school are more apt to be better readers (Clark, 1976; Durkin, 1966). Other research studies (Bissex, 1980; Heath, 1983; Schickedanz & Sullivan, 1984) show that the beginning of writing is contemporaneous with the emergence of reading.

The increasing number of working women has changed the role of kindergarten as a transition or socialization process between home and school. Today youngsters attend day care, nursery schools, and/or preschools; this results in their being socialized prior to entering kindergarten. In some communities, the language arts curriculum has been changed to include reading instruction that in the 1950s and 1960s was reserved for the first grade. Some research studies indicate that formal, structured "reading readiness" programs are beneficial; other studies indicate that informal, well-developed programs are just as effective for the emergent reader (Bissex, 1980; Durkin, 1974–1975; Edwards, 1991; Meyer, Gersten, & Gutkin, 1983).

Children who enter school with a familiarity of books and how they should be handled have been observed to possess the following reading behaviors: (1) identification of letters, (2) identification of words, (3) retelling of a story, (4) indication of where to begin reading on a page, and (5) awareness of the direction of print, left to right (Wiseman & Robeck, 1983).

Evaluating Emergent Reading

Children enter school having encountered different experiences, each developing at his or her own pace; it is therefore important for kindergarten and first-grade teachers to determine the degree of emergence of reading so that they can plan instruction accordingly. Unfortunately, one study of kindergarten programs revealed a heavy reliance on developmental and academic tests, with little evidence that the tests were used to determine the suitability of the instructional programs for the children. Rather, in most schools the children were expected to adjust to the program instead of an adjustment of the program to meet the students' needs (Durkin, 1987).

The following simple checklist for emergent reading can be used soon after the start of the school year:

Checklist for Emergent Reading

	Yes	No
1. Can the child listen attentively to a 5-minute story?		
2. Can the child play/work independently for short periods of time?		
3. Is the child interested in books?		
4. Does the child ask for word meanings?		
5. Can the child tell a story without confusing the order of events?		
6. Does the child recognize that letters make up words?		
7. Does the child attempt to write?		
8. Does the child draw pictures to illustrate an idea?		
9. Can the child remember the main parts of a story?		
10. Does the child enter into group and/or class discussions freely?		
11. Can the child identify the letters of the alphabet?		
12. Does the child know directionality of books (left to right, top to bottom)?		

A Closer Look

Our Own Stories
On Baseball Cards and Literacy Acquisition
Pamela J. Farris

The spring before entering kindergarten, my son signed up to play T-ball, his first formal experience with a team sport. Kurtis was the youngest player on the team, and he dutifully attended practices, eagerly taking his turn at bat and not so eagerly attempting to catch the soft rubber ball. When the team's yellow and black "Pirate" shirts were handed out, with their accompanying yellow baseball caps with a black *P* insignia, Kurtis couldn't wait to get home, try them on, and see himself in the mirror.

Late afternoons that summer were spent at the diamond amidst other families of T-ball players. Conditions were idyllic. No one kept score. Every player got a turn at bat every inning. An out usually meant tears as the player rushed to a parent for a hug and consolation. No one struck out because strikeouts weren't part of the rules. No overly aggressive play was allowed and good plays received cheers from both teams' fans. Games concluded with the opposing players giving each other high fives along with a sincere "Good game." T-ball offered Kurtis the best of what sports have to offer.

After each game, the Pirates would gather around for a snack. During this period, the players socialized, talking about things that were important to them—the worm that the left fielder had found while standing in the outfield, a scraped knee or elbow, or weekly reports of scores on a variety of video games. Then one day, a player shared his baseball cards with the team.

Kurtis was taken in by the baseball cards, those colorful miniature information data banks that have been around for over a century. As the various noteworthy players and their teams were handed around to be duly admired, Kurtis became hooked. He had to have his own baseball cards.

A new hobby takes form

On a trip to the local discount retailer with his dad, Kurtis selected his first packet of baseball cards. It didn't matter that he couldn't read any of the information or recognize any of the team logos; he was immeasurably content just to possess them. He would fan them out over the carpet before carefully examining each card.

As a mother, I felt this was a phase boys went through. As a professor of language arts and children's literature, I wasn't overly pleased that he was devoting hours to his baseball cards when he had literally hundreds of picture books in the house that had more substantial quality and content to peruse. I believe he should be pouring over Eric Carle's, Mem Fox's and Steven Kellogg's work rather than Steve Avery's, Barry Larkin's, and Ryne Sandberg's statistics.

Kurtis began to identify the teams by their logos. The Cubs, his father's favorite team, and the Reds, my favorite team, were learned first, along with the Pirates of course. The next team he learned, perhaps because of seeing them so frequently on television, was the Braves, which became his favorite team. At first he referred to the New York Yankees as the New York Lincolns. After a couple of futile attempts to correct him, both his father and I gave up. If Kurtis wanted to refer to the Yankees as the Lincolns, that was fine. We knew what he meant.

As the season progressed, Kurtis's card collection grew from a few cards wrapped with a rubber band to a pile of cards in a small shoebox to finally filling a paper grocery sack. As the number of cards increased so did Kurtis's obsession with them. He wanted to know the names of all the teams and all the players. He invented games with them, playing his own modified version of T-ball in which everyone got to bat and no one kept score.

By late summer, Kurtis was collecting football and basketball cards as well. Every day he stacked and restacked his cards. He continued to seek out information. "What does this say?" "How do you spell Cowboys?"— or Reds or Bulls.

Kurtis's literacy strategies expand

Kurtis added writing to his daily review of his cards. By now he had created several new games. Each day would find him carefully copying the names of the teams and creating scoreboards for imaginary games. Kurtis would design a football field complete with the logo of the home team on the 50-yard line and the names of the teams printed in block letters in their respective end zones. He made lists of baseball and basketball teams and their opponents along with their scores, which he invented.

Before long Kurtis decided that the cards could be put in a variety of categories besides teams. He moved his collection to the basement family room, where he had plenty of space to sort out his new categories. Animals, birds, cowboys, and space were some of the new groupings Kurtis developed. For example, among his animal teams were the Chicago Bulls, Detroit Lions, Chicago Bears, Florida Marlins, Miami Dolphins, and Minnesota Timberwolves. There were always leftover teams that Kurtis couldn't find a category to designate. Kurtis referred to the Indiana Pacers as the "P-balls"—their logo being a *P* with a basketball in the center of the loop. The P-balls cards were always set aside along with the Green Bay Packers and Milwaukee Brewers—teams that Kurtis couldn't regroup into his categorical system.

There were also teams with unfamiliar names. He would ask either his dad or me, "What's a Padre?" or "What's a Dodger?" or "What's a Knick?" and we would diligently provide an explanation.

The more Kurtis categorized the teams, the more groupings he made. He moved to grouping by initial sounds—M for Mariners, Marlins, and Mets; R for Reds, Rockies, and Rangers. Then he began to question initial sounds and initial letters. "Why do the Giants and Jets start with different letters?" and "How come Expos doesn't start with X?"

The teams helped Kurtis to discover different parts of the United States and Canada as he located the different home cities of the teams on a map. He learned that some teams were named after cities—Boston Red Sox, Cleveland Indians, Philadelphia Phillies, San Francisco Giants—while others were named after states— California Angels, Colorado Rockies, Minnesota Twins, Texas Rangers.

With football cards, Kurtis discovered something new about the data offered—the linemen were "huge guys." He would sort out all the linemen and play a card game that he invented, a kind of variation of Old Maid and Euchre. Each player was dealt a stack of cards. Then one player would place a card on the table. The other player had to put a card down with a player who weighed more than the first player's card. If the players were the same weight, the taller (that is, bigger) player won. Prior to this, Kurtis could recognize numbers up to 100 and didn't really understand feet and inches in terms of height. Now he could accurately identify any three-digit number and had a better grasp of height as measured in feet.

As Kurtis's familiarity with the teams increased, he would walk past a game on television and note which teams were playing and tell us which players' cards he had from the two teams. He could draw all of the team logos and noted the different fonts used in their lettering. For instance, the Spurs, Kurtis pointed out to me, have a real spur in their name.

Literacy lessons

Kurtis's love of sports cards taught me some valuable lessons. Although we had read him quality children's literature every day since birth, he needed other literary genre. Informational print on the sport cards was very important to him. The cards represented real people that he could occasionally see on television. The weights and heights represented real pounds and real inches of real human beings. The team logos were also important. Kurtis noticed them on the baseball caps, shirts, and jackets that he saw people wearing in the grocery store, the park, and the shopping mall.

Enthusiasm for and interest in the textual material overcame Kurtis's initial lack of experience and ability with the topic. He repeatedly and doggedly pursued literacy, determined to understand the cards that meant so much to him. Kurtis helped me realize that the reader's enthusiasm and interest are really far more important than the material itself.

Maybe the biggest lesson I learned was that sports cards and a child's imagination can be combined to foster literacy development. Categorization, recognizing words, learning to spell, and the identification of numbers are all important in literacy acquisition.

Spring has arrived and Kurtis is eager for the T-ball season to begin. As for me, I'm heading to the store to purchase some more baseball cards for Kurtis.

Farris teaches language arts and children's literature at Northern Illinois University, DeKalb, Illinois, USA.

On Baseball Cards and Literary Acquisition, Pamela J. Farris, *The Reading Teacher*, April 1995. Reprinted with permission of the author and the International Reading Association.

These 12 items reflect the essentials for learning to read. "Yes" answers to 9 of the questions suggest that the child is an emergent reader and should be given opportunities to engage in simple reading activities. For instance, the teacher needs to share pattern books with the child so that after listening to the text a few times, the child will be able to join in the rereading of the book. Other activities include listening to a cassette recording of a picture book and following along with the text, learning simple songs and poetry, learning finger plays and rhymes, and using writing instruments.

Children who fail to meet this informal cutoff need to be given lots of opportunities to develop oral language skills; to be read quality literature, especially predictable literature that allows the child to anticipate upcoming events; and to use crayons and pencils freely for drawing and writing.

One out of every 600 children enters kindergarten knowing how to read (Lapp & Flood, 1983). For such a child, pattern books soon become too predictable and easy to read. More challenging material must be provided for the child at this point. Concept picture books such as *The Last Dinosaur* by Jim Murphy (1987), which describes the habits of these extinct creatures, often enthrall such a child. Narratives also delight early readers; the unforgettable *Frog and Toad Are Friends* (Lobel, 1970) series of books is a popular example.

Instruction for Children as They Begin to Read

As children leave the emergent reading stage and enter the beginning reading stage, they are enthusiastic about reading and eager to stretch their world through encounters with printed text. The following methods of teaching the beginning reader may be used alone or with a basal reader or whole language program.

Shared Book Experiences

Kindergarten and first graders in the emergent reading stage and the beginning reading stage benefit from the experience of sharing books. "Shared reading is one way of immersing students in rich, literary-level language without worrying about grade level or reading performance. For young children who have had limited exposure to the language of storybooks, shared reading and discussion of stories provide a framework for literature and language" (Routman, 1991, p. 33). The teacher devotes a half-hour each day to sharing simple stories that the children easily understand and enjoy. This is in addition to the amount of time set aside for reading instruction either with a basal reader or a whole language program. Each month 20 to 30 books are shared, including three or four *Big Books,* popular books that have been enlarged by the publisher so that children can easily read the print from 12 to 15 feet away as they sit in a semi-circle around the teacher.

Holdaway (1979) believes that a shared reading experience should meet three criteria: (1) the books read should be ones children love to hear; (2) children need to see the print themselves; and (3) the teacher must display genuine enjoyment in reading the books aloud.

Adams (1990, p. 69) refers to the sharing of Big Books as the "classroom version of bedtime stories, and like bedtime stories, they are meant to be read over

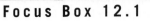

Focus Box 12.1

Shared Book Experiences (Kindergarten through Grade 3)

Students engage in shared book experiences as they become involved in reading a *Big Book,* one that has large enough print so that everyone in the class can see the words. The procedure summarized below was developed in New Zealand by Don Holdaway (1979).

Steps in the Shared Book Experience

1. The teacher introduces the book to the students. (This introduction typically occurs on Monday and the book is used daily for the remainder of the week.)
2. The teacher asks students to predict what the book will be about.
3. The teacher reads the book to the students. The book is usually placed on an easel or held so that the students can see the words and illustrations. The teacher also points to the words as they are read.
4. The teacher may stop periodically to encourage students to tell what they think will happen next in the story.
5. The teacher rereads the book, encouraging the students to read along with him or her.
6. On subsequent readings, a student may read a page individually or join with another student in reading a portion of the book aloud.
7. All members of the class read the book together every day for a week.

and over, as often as they are enchanting." A typical half-hour shared book activity includes the singing of a simple song or choral speaking of a simple poem or rhyme. This is followed by the introduction of a Big Book that the teacher reads, using a pointer so that the children are aware of exactly where the teacher is as the story is being read. The teacher then rereads the story and encourages the children to join in. The teacher may select a small group to act out the story as it is read for a third time. The activity usually ends with the teacher reading a new book or perhaps rereading a class favorite (Holdaway, 1979).

The shared book activity may begin the first day of kindergarten and continue through third grade. It is appropriate for use with either a literature-based whole language program or a developmental, basal reading program.

A beginning reader reads with oral fluency after having been read a story several times and modeling the classroom teacher's reading. In Routman's (1988) view, such fluency transforms the child into a reader because the child reads with emotion, inflections, and enjoyment, and the emphasis is on reading for meaning. According to Clay (1991a, p. 264), "A child who already enjoys shared reading can be encouraged to become more independent as a reader if new stories are introduced before he tries to read them for himself. A good introduction makes the new text more accessible to the reader."

The classroom teacher is a major influence on children's reading according to research by Anderson, Wilson, and Fielding (1988). This is an important finding for every teacher, at every grade level. For example, when children enter kindergarten, it falls upon the teacher to provide a literacy-rich environment with ample opportunities for all students to engage in meaningful conversations about reading and writing. Because not every 5-year-old has had an abundance of literary experiences—being read to, having books to browse through, talking about stories—the teacher must share quality literature informally in the classroom so that students will be motivated to engage in discussion and eager to explore books on their own. The shared book activity provides the teacher with a positive instructional opportunity.

Language Experience Approach

The *language experience approach* (LEA) is sometimes viewed as a precursor to the whole language approach. Emphasizing the relationships between thought, oral language, and written language, the LEA builds on a child's interests and oral language. As mentioned earlier, 5- and 6-year-olds are eager to share thoughts, ideas, and feelings with others. The language experience approach capitalizes on this personal and, to some extent, social need by having children share their own thoughts and experiences through both verbal and written interchanges. A prominent advocate of the language experience approach, Allen (1976) stresses the need for reading materials that grow out of children's oral expressions rather than published materials.

A language experience lesson is comprised of the following five steps:

1. Discuss a shared experience with the class: what may happen, what they may see or feel, what preparations they must make, and so forth.
2. Have the shared experience with the students (for example, cooking breakfast or visiting a museum or zoo).
3. Discuss what took place during the activity.
4. Have the students write about the experience.
5. Have the students share what they wrote with the class.

For the child who lacks the skills needed to write, the teacher or an aide should write down exactly what the child says during the language experience so that he or she can make the sound-print connections. This enables the child to read a piece correctly in his or her own words.

When firsthand experiences are not possible, the teacher must rely on vicarious experiences. For example, a poem and a book about kangaroos, a video about how sheep are raised in New Zealand, a filmstrip about pioneers traveling on flatboats down the Ohio River, and a film about making kites are all vehicles for sharing and can enrich children's experiences and knowledge without requiring them to leave the classroom. Although vicarious experiences may be effective, firsthand experiences, such as seeing a sheep sheared or making a kite from plastic garbage bags and bamboo strips, followed by writing about such activities will usually be more vividly recalled by children and for a longer period of time.

As part of the language experience approach, each student creates a dictionary for reading and writing called a *word bank*. Using 3″ by 5″ index cards, the student creates word categories according to how the words are used: words for people, words for colors, action words, and the like. The student may cut out a picture from a magazine or draw an appropriate illustration so that each word will be recognized. After attaching a picture and writing the word, the student places the card in a plastic card file, a mobile container that he or she may carry around the classroom or take home to write about personal experiences involving family or friends.

Shared Story Reading

Shared story reading evolved out of cross-age tutoring. In *shared story reading*, students at different grade levels are paired up as partners. Once a week, time is set aside during the school day for shared story reading in which the older child reads a book to the younger child and the younger child reads a book to the older child. Both students select books they believe their partner will enjoy; both practice reading their selections aloud before the sharing time. This type of sharing increases children's familiarity with children's literature and builds self-confidence. The social interaction is an added plus (Newman, 1984).

When simple pattern books are used, even the beginning reader who only recognizes a few words can participate in this activity. When wordless picture books are used, the beginning reader can describe the actions that occur in the illustrations.

Phonics Instruction

Phonics instruction involves teaching relationships between letters and the sounds they represent. Once children are able to identify the letters of the alphabet, the teacher can introduce rhyming words and words that have the same beginning or ending consonant sound. Some phonics programs require students to know 25 to 30 sight words, or words they recognize when seen in isolation, such as on a piece of tagboard or the chalkboard. At that point, words with the same beginning consonant sound are introduced. Later, short and long vowel sounds and then consonant blends are introduced as part of the instruction. The introduction of each sound and accompanying letter should begin with several examples of words with which the students are familiar. Proper names should be avoided because of their wide variation in terms of both spelling and pronunciation.

Phonics instruction should begin early and accompany meaningful text. After reviewing, evaluating, and integrating several research studies, Adams (1990, p. 578) came to the following conclusions about how children learn to read:

> The vast majority of the studies indicated that approaches [that include] intensive, explicit phonics instruction resulted in comprehension skills that are at least comparable to, and word recognition and spelling skills that are significantly better than those that do not. . . . Approaches in which systematic code instruction is included along with meaningful connected reading result in superior reading achievement overall.

"Many of the activities of the early elementary classrooms already incorporate elements that heighten phonemic awareness" (Griffith & Olson, 1992, p. 520). However, upon completion of the second grade, a child need not receive phonics instruction unless a specific need for such instruction has been diagnosed (Anderson et al., 1984).

Phonics has developed a negative connotation largely because many teachers believe that phonics instruction consists of having children complete workbook pages. In actuality, every student learns about letter-sound correspondences, or phonics, as part of learning to read, regardless of the type of reading instruction they receive—including whole language (Stahl, 1992). "There is substantial evidence that phonemic awareness is strongly related to success in reading and spelling acquisition" (Yopp, 1995, p. 21). Phonics involves not only learning about letter-sound relationships, but learning about words, as well. It has been suggested that children go through three stages in learning about words. Initially they learn about words in whole units, such as when a child can identify a Burger King or Wal-Mart sign. This is the *logographic stage.* The next stage for the emergent reader is the *alphabetic stage* in which children use individual letters and sounds to identify words, such as "luv" for *love* or "tu" for *to.* The third stage is the *orthographic stage,* within which children see patterns in words, or word families, and use these patterns to identify words without attempting to sound them out. For instance, a child who knows the words *boy* and *toy* can then pronounce *joy.* In this last stage, children develop the ability to recognize words automatically without pausing to think about how they are constructed or spelled (Frith, 1985).

In regard to teaching phonics, Stahl (1992, p. 620) points out that "letter-sound instruction makes no sense to a child who does not have an overall conception of what reading is about." Stahl suggests the following nine guidelines for exemplary phonics instruction:

1. Build on the child's concepts about word formation (i.e., the arrangement of letters in predictable patterns).
2. Build on a foundation of the child's phonemic awareness.
3. Be clear and direct.
4. Integrate phonics instruction into the total reading program.
5. Focus on reading words rather than learning phonics rules.
6. Include instruction of *onsets,* the part of the syllable before the vowel, and *rimes,* the part of the syllable from the vowel onward. For instance, in the word *meat, m* is the onset and *eat* is the rime. If the child knows the *eat* rime, the child can then transfer that knowledge to *wheat* and *feat* in decoding those words.
7. Include practice with invented spelling.
8. Develop independent word recognition strategies, focusing instruction on the internal structure of words or word patterns.
9. Develop automatic word recognition skills so that the students can focus on comprehension of the text and not the words themselves.

The Yopp-Singer Test of Phoneme Segmentation (Yopp, 1995) measures a child's ability to separately articulate—in order—the sounds of a spoken word. For instance, for the word *sat*, the child should respond with the following: /s/-/a/-/t/. Students who answer most of the items correctly are considered phonemically aware. On the other hand, students who answer with random sounds (e.g., /b/-/d/ for *cat*) lack phonemic awareness. If a student spells the word rather than presenting the individual sounds, the teacher can determine the degree of letter-sound correspondence for the given word.

Yopp-Singer Test of Phoneme Segmentation

Student's name _____   Date _____

Score (number correct) _____

Directions: Today we're going to play a word game. I'm going to say a word and I want you to break the word apart. You are going to tell me each sound in the word in order. For example, if I say "old," you should say /o/-/l/-/d/." (*Administrator: Be sure to say the sounds, not the letters, in the word.*) Let's try a few together.

Practice items: (Assist the child in segmenting these items as necessary.)   ride,   go,   man

Test items: (*Circle those items that the student correctly segments; incorrect responses may be recorded on the blank line following the item.*)

1. dog _____		12. lay _____
2. keep _____		13. race _____
3. fine _____		14. zoo _____
4. no _____		15. three _____
5. she _____		16. job _____
6. wave _____		17. in _____
7. grew _____		18. ice _____
8. that _____		19. at _____
9. red _____		20. top _____
10. me _____		21. by _____
11. sat _____		22. do _____

The author, Hallie Kay Yopp, California State University, Fullerton, grants permission for this test to be reproduced. The author acknowledges the contribution of the late Harry Singer to the development of this test.

Test from Yopp, Hallie Kay. (1995, September). A test for assessing phonemic awareness in young children. *The Reading Teacher, 49* (1), 20–29. Reprinted with permission of Hallie K. Yopp and the International Reading Association. All rights reserved.

Focus Box 12.2
Common Rimes

Rime	Word That Uses the Rime	Rime	Word That Uses the Rime
-ack	back, sack, track	-ick	brick, sick, trick
-ail	sail, mail, nail	-ide	hide, ride, side
-ain	pain, rain, train	-ight	bright, fright, night
-ake	cake, make, snake	-ill	fill, hill, pill
-ale	pale, sale, whale	-in	chin, twin, win
-ame	came, game, name	-ine	fine, nine, shine
-an	can, man, ran	-ing	king, sing, thing
-ank	bank, drank, thank	-ink	pink, sink, think
-ap	cap, map, trap	-ip	lip, ship, sip
-ash	cash, mash, trash	-ir	fir, sir, stir
-at	cat, hat, that	-ock	block, lock, sock
-ate	hate, late, plate	-oke	joke, poke, woke
-aw	jaw, paw, saw	-op	hop, mop, shop
-ay	day, play, say	-ore	more, shore, store
-eat	beat, seat, wheat	-uck	duck, luck, truck
-ell	bell, sell, shell	-ug	bug, hug, rug
-est	best, chest, west	-ump	bump, jump, lump
-ice	mice, rice, twice	-unk	bunk, junk, sunk

A balanced or combined approach to reading includes the strengths of a whole language, literature-based program with those of a phonics program. Thus, the skills of reading in context are included along with decoding, or phonics, skills (Adams, 1990). Trachtenburg (1990) uses a three-step combined approach with kindergarten through second-grade students. The steps are whole-part-whole as follows:

1. Whole: The students read, comprehend, and enjoy an entire quality literature selection.
2. Part: The teacher provides instruction in a high-utility phonic element by drawing from the preceding literature selection.
3. Whole: The students apply the new phonic skill when reading and enjoying another quality literature selection.

As Adams (1990, p. 17) notes in her findings, "Perhaps the single most striking characteristic of skillful readers is the speed and effortlessness with which they can breeze through text. In particular they appear to recognize whole words at a glance, gleaning their appropriate meaning at once." This level of skill is the goal of teachers in the instruction of phonics and comprehension.

Oral activities such as songs, games, and riddles can draw children's attention to the basic elements of language—phonemes and graphemes. Such activities should supplement rather than replace children's interactions with relevant and meaningful language, both oral and written (Yopp, 1992). By combining phonics with a whole language approach, that is, with the use of quality literature as the primary reading material, teachers can apply the best of both instructional approaches.

Instructional Methods for Primary and Middle Childhood Readers

For children who possess more than beginning reading skills, there are other instructional methods from which the teacher may select according to the appropriateness of the learning situation. Effective teachers of reading plan, implement, monitor, and evaluate each lesson or instructional activity. Some teachers keep tally sheets for every lesson, noting which portions of the lesson were successful and possible ways to improve on the lesson when working with other children.

Teachers should be strategists in reading instruction and teach their students to be strategic readers using the following methods:

1. Provide *assistance* during reading instead of suggesting a reading procedure or assessing the child's progress.
2. Help a student to know how he or she knows.
3. Make conscious connections to previous and future learning.
4. Emphasize the context in which new skills will be applied.
5. Make invisible cognitive skills tangible.
6. Respond to student confusion with advice about how to think strategically (Paris, 1985).

In guiding children to become strategic readers, the teacher must be familiar with a variety of instructional techniques. Questioning, graphic organizers, Book Clubs, the directed reading activity (DRA), and the directed reading-thinking activity (DR-TA) are techniques that have proved effective with elementary-level students.

Graphic Organizers

Graphic organizers, sometimes referred to as semantic webs, are helpful for organizing information so that students better understand the textual material they have read. By using these visual guides, students can predict what will occur next, make comparisons, and recognize cause-and-effect relationships.

On pages 384–389 are examples of graphic organizers that can be used individually or in groups to help students process what they have read. These organizers can be used with a variety of reading genre.

Consonants

1. A consonant cluster consists of two (or three) consonants that appear together and are blended when pronounced.

*bl*ip	*br*at	*cl*ip	*cr*ow
*dr*ag	*fl*og	*fr*ame	*gl*ow
*pl*ane	*pr*ide	*sc*oop	*sk*ip
*sl*ate	*sm*ut	*str*eam	*st*amp
*sw*im	*tr*im	be*nt*	coa*st*
gra*sp*	me*lt*	bo*ld*	ma*sk*

2. A consonant digraph consists of two consonants that appear together and result in one consonant sound when pronounced.

*ch*ip	*ch*ur*ch*	*th*igh
*th*ey	*wh*ip	si*ng*

Vowels

1. A vowel is short if it is in a closed syllable (a syllable that ends in a consonant).

   dĭg, crăb, rĭp, făst, jŭmp

2. A vowel is long if it is the last vowel in an open syllable (a syllable that ends in a vowel).

   trēē, crādle

3. A vowel digraph consists of two vowels that together represent one vowel sound.

   tr*ai*n   br*ea*d   c*ou*gh

4. A vowel diphthong consists of one of the following four vowel combinations: oi, oy, ou, ow.

   s*oi*l   pl*oy*   h*ou*se   t*ow*el

5. When e appears at the end of a one-syllable word, the first vowel in the word is usually long.

   cāpe, fāde, rōbe, drāpe, pīne

Focus Box 12.3

(Continued)

Syllabication

1. A syllable must have a vowel sound.

   tan, med/i/um, flex/i/ble

2. A final *e* in a word is usually silent.

   mane, fine, dance

3. An open syllable is a syllable that ends with a vowel other than a "silent *e*."

   o/bey, a/dore

4. A closed syllable is a syllable that ends with a consonant.

   um/pire, ba/*boon*

5. When a consonant appears between two vowels, the word is divided between the first vowel and the consonant.

   a/far   i/deal

6. When two consonants appear between two vowels, the word is divided between the consonants.

   ham/mer   fis/cal

7. When a word ends with a consonant and the letters *le,* the word is divided immediately before the consonant preceding *le.*

   ca/ble   dou/ble

8. A compound word is divided between the two words.

   fire/arm   base/ball   flash/light

Questioning

Teachers must not only ask effective questions but model such behavior so that students can develop a questioning technique that they can use independently. The quality of students' answers and the degree to which students actively participate in the discussion are influenced by the quality of the questions the teacher asks (Norton, 1985). The type and quality of the text material used also influence the quality of student responses. For example, a simple, straightforward text might not provide the teacher with sufficient material to develop higher-order questions, whereas a good realistic fiction book may provide such material (Monson, 1992).

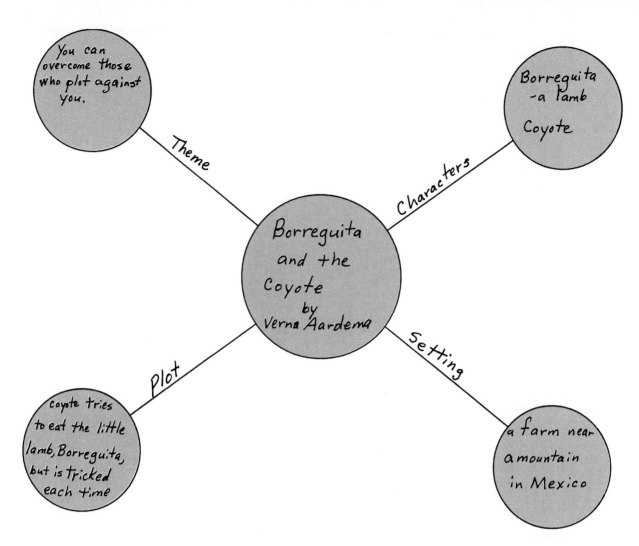

Figure 12.1

The Spoke Wheel. The spoke wheel is used to summarize what is known about one thing or character. The spokes serve as primary headings or categories.

Aardema, Verna. (1991). *Borreguita and the Coyote* (Petra Matthews, Illus.). New York: Alfred K. Knopf.

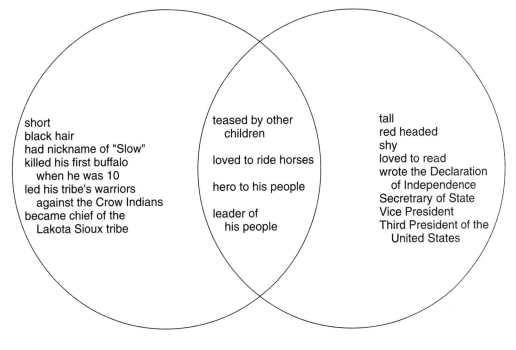

Figure 12.2

Venn Diagram. Two intersecting circles are used to include information about how two things or characters differ and how they are alike. A comparison of Sitting Bull and Thomas Jefferson.

Bruchac, Joseph. (1994). *A Boy Called Slow: The True Story of Sitting Bull* (Rocco Baviera, Illus.). New York: Philomel.
Giblin, James Cross. (1994). *Thomas Jefferson* (Michael Dooling, Illus.). New York: Scholastic.

Teachers can help students develop their cognitive skills by asking them questions designed for different levels of thinking. Literal, inferential, critical, and creative questions should all be asked with equal frequency. It is best, however, to begin with literal, or knowledge-level, questions in order to build the students' self-confidence.

Literal questions are based on facts that students can readily recall or locate in a specific passage. Such questions typically refer to main ideas, story details, and sequences of events.

Inferential questions require students to be familiar with the text at the literal level but also to think beyond the printed word. By using previously gained knowledge along with information acquired from the text, students are able to make inferences. Comparing and contrasting, drawing conclusions, formulating generalizations, recognizing relationships, and predicting outcomes are all types of inferential thinking.

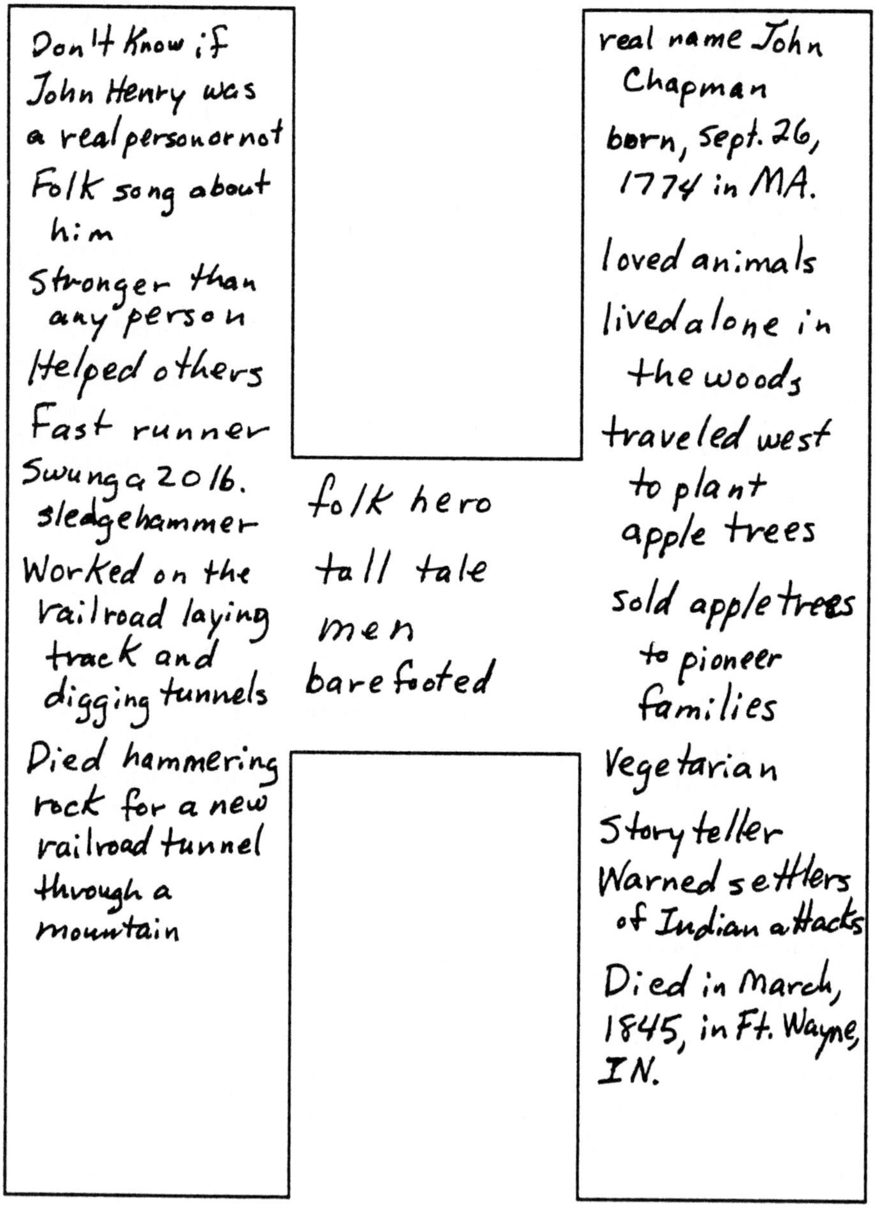

Don't know if
John Henry was
a real person or not
Folk song about
him
Stronger than
any person
Helped others
Fast runner
Swung a 20 lb.
sledgehammer
Worked on the
railroad laying
track and
digging tunnels
Died hammering
rock for a new
railroad tunnel
through a
mountain

folk hero
tall tale
men
barefooted

real name John
Chapman
born, sept. 26,
1774 in MA.

loved animals
lived alone in
the woods
traveled west
to plant
apple trees
sold apple trees
to pioneer
families
Vegetarian
Storyteller
Warned settlers
of Indian attacks
Died in March,
1845, in Ft. Wayne,
IN.

Figure 12.3
The Big H. The big H works the same way as the Venn Diagram.
Kellogg, Steven. (1988). *Johnny Appleseed* New York: Morrow.
Lester, Julius. (1994). *John Henry* (Jerry Pinkney, Illus.). New York: Scholastic.

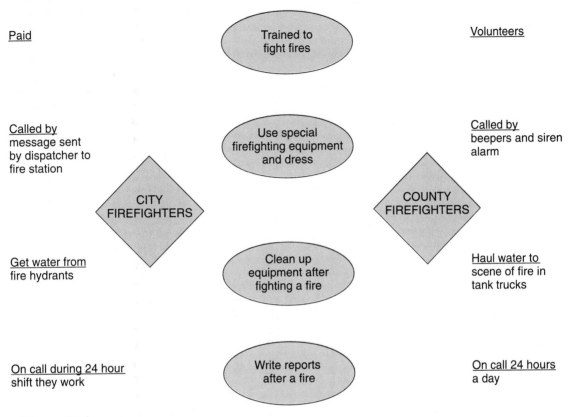

Paid

Trained to
fight fires

Volunteers

Called by
message sent
by dispatcher to
fire station

Use special
firefighting equipment
and dress

Called by
beepers and siren
alarm

CITY
FIREFIGHTERS

COUNTY
FIREFIGHTERS

Get water from
fire hydrants

Clean up
equipment after
fighting a fire

Haul water to
scene of fire in
tank trucks

On call during 24 hour
shift they work

Write reports
after a fire

On call 24 hours
a day

Figure 12.4

The Double Diamond. The double diamond allows students to not only compare how two things are alike but also how they differ. Unlike the Venn Diagram and the big H, the information can be presented in a more organized, easier to read format.

Gibbons, Gail. (1984). *Fire! Fire! Fire!* New York: Harper and Row.

Critical thinking requires students to make judgments. Unless students can effectively think at the literal and inferential levels, their critical thinking ability will be quite limited. In thinking critically, students must objectively view the material and withhold final judgment until they have evaluated enough information to form that judgment.

Teachers often ignore creative thinking in their haste to ask literal, inferential, and critical thinking questions. Yet creative thinking allows students to view a situation, idea, or character in a new or unique way. It also encourages appreciation of the material, which stimulates further reading in an area. Creative thinking is more personalized than other types of thinking in that it prompts students to respond in a manner that reveals their own feelings, thoughts, and beliefs about what they have read.

The Barn - Avi

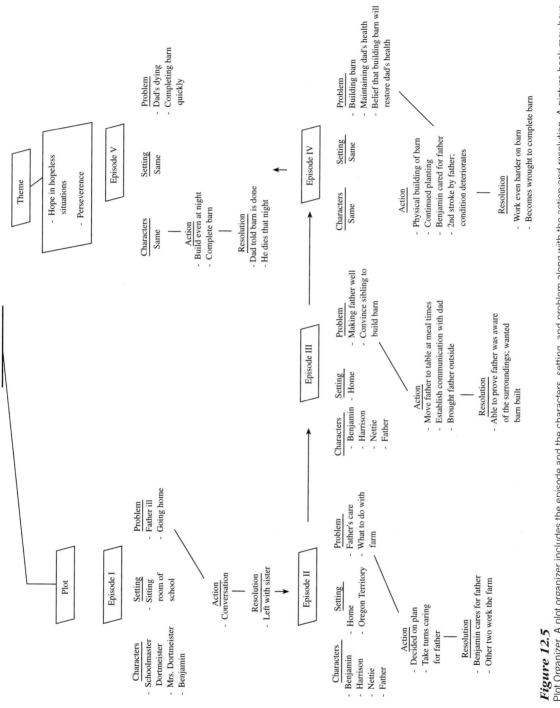

Figure 12.5

Plot Organizer. A plot organizer includes the episode and the characters, setting, and problem along with the action and resolution. A picture book may have only one episode while a novel may have several episodes.

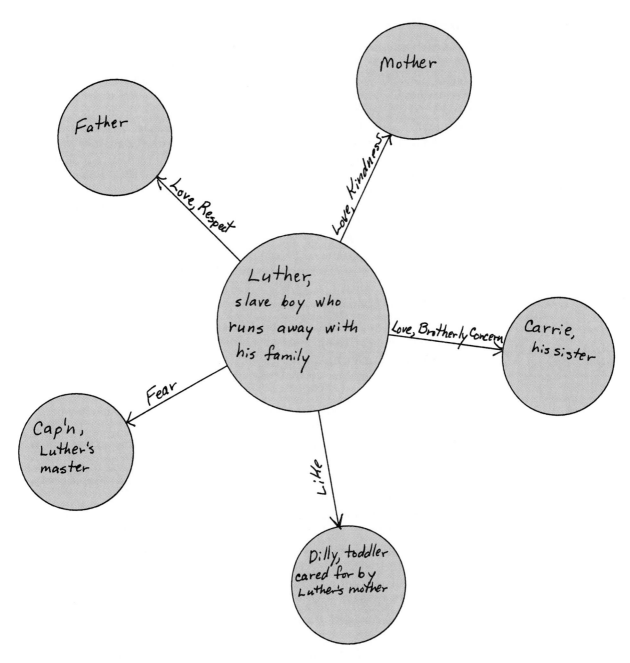

Figure 12.6

A Character Web. A character web can take different formats. It may be a circle, representing the main character, and have several surrounding circles, each representing another character. The student writes in the names of the characters with an arrow from the main character and the way that character feels or acts toward each of the other characters.

Turner, Glennette Tilley. (1994). *Running for Our Lives* (Samuel Byrd, Illus.). New York: Holiday House.

Book Clubs

Reading, writing, student-led discussion groups, and whole-class discussions are included in the *Book Club,* a literature-based reading program. Originated by Taffy Raphael and Susan McMahon (1994), the Book Club requires that the teacher locate good literature with an identifiable theme, such as the Revolutionary War, westward expansion, famous inventors, or the Great Depression. The teacher then discusses with the class the differences between talking about books in a group discussion/conversation and answering questions about books. Next, the students are given guidelines for using reading logs as they read the books. Finally, the teacher and the class discuss what makes good speakers and good listeners, making a wall chart of characteristics of each.

As students read their books, they keep a vocabulary sheet that has the title of the book and the student's name on the top. The sheet is divided into four columns: date, word, page number, and meaning of the word. As the students read, they record the vocabulary information. After reading the book or an assigned portion, such as two or three chapters in a novel, the students write in their reading logs. Below are some possible reading log entries (Raphael and McMahon, 1994):

Character Map. The student thinks about a character that he or she liked or didn't like and makes a map of the character. The map shows what the character looked like, things the character did, what was interesting about the character, how the character interacted with other characters, etc.

Wonderful Words. New, unusual, or descriptive words are jotted down. These are words that the student may want to use in his or her own writing. The student also writes a short explanation of why the word was chosen.

Pictures. The student draws a picture depicting a scene and writes a brief reason for including the picture.

Book/Chapter Critique. The student writes what he or she thinks is good or could be improved about the book or a chapter of the book.

Sequences. The student keeps a sequence of events chart, adding to the chart as he or she reads the book. For each event listed, the student writes a brief reason for why it was included.

Special Story Part. The student writes down a phrase or sentence that begins a special part of the book, as well as the page number on which it appears.

Author's Crafts. The student writes down special words, descriptive or funny phrases, dialogue examples, etc., that make the book appealing to the reader.

Me and the Book. The student relates an event or character in the book to his or her own life.

The students then form their Book Clubs and discuss what they have read. When initiating Book Clubs, the teacher offers guidelines and models how discussion groups work. Students are encouraged to prepare a couple of questions in advance to bring with them to their Book Club. The teacher floats from Book Club to Book Club and notes the progress and problems that arise. The teacher doesn't interrupt the groups unless an unusual circumstance arises or the students ask for clarification or assistance with a problem. Later the teacher uses the information gathered from his or her own observations of the Book Clubs to use in entire class instruction.

In addition to the reading log, the students keep "What I Learned" sheets in which they briefly summarize, in one to three sentences, what they learned from each book they read within the thematic unit. These sheets are used as part of the assessment of the student's work.

Directed Reading Activity

The *directed reading activity* (DRA) has been a part of basal reading programs for decades. It consists of six steps:

1. Establish a purpose for reading.
2. Develop background information.
3. Introduce new vocabulary.
4. Provide students with questions to serve as reading guides.
5. Read the passage silently or aloud.
6. Ask follow-up questions.

In establishing a purpose for reading, the teacher's role is that of a promoter and motivator, often bringing in related materials and items for the students.

Directed Reading-Thinking Activity

The *directed reading-thinking activity* (DR-TA), developed by Stauffer in 1969, engages students in the reading process by having them make predictions as they read. The teacher breaks the text into appropriate sections or stopping points, where the students discuss the text. The students are given more control of the discussion in the DR-TA than in the DRA. In making a prediction about what will happen in upcoming text, a student relies on two sources of information: (1) personal knowledge and (2) the text material.

The DR-TA begins with the teacher outlining the purpose for reading and the students analyzing the title of the material to be read. The text may be a narrative, such as a story from a basal reader or a chapter in a fiction book, or descriptive writing, such as that found in a science or social studies textbook. The students discuss what they already know from previous experiences and from the title itself, then they make predictions about what will happen in the text. After the students resume reading, the teacher has the students stop at a predetermined point, and the students confirm or reject their predictions and form new hypotheses based on the newly acquired information. The process is one of formulating questions, testing those questions for affirmation or denial, and generating new questions based on the information gathered (Moore, Readence, & Rickelman, 1982).

In the Classroom Mini Lesson

WEATHER
A Theme Cycle

Informational Books
See the bibliography.

Read Alouds
Where the River Begins by Thomas Locker—picture book
The Night of the Twisters by Ivy Ruckman—novel
Many of the informational books are suitable for read alouds, too.

Choral Reading
Tornado! by Arnold Adoff—poems
Weather by Lee Bennett Hopkins—poems

Interview
The class will interview a meteorologist from the National Weather Service in Joliet.

Word Wall
Both the students and the teacher contribute to the word wall. Some possibilities are as follows:

weather vane	water cycle	Celsius
thermometer	condensation	predict
anemometer	evaporation	cold front
rain/snow gauge	precipitation	warm front
hygrometer	accumulation	humidity
barometer	high pressure	meteorologist
psychrometer	low pressure	frigid
wind sock	Fahrenheit	wind chill factor

Charts and Maps
Using outline maps of the United States, the students will take turns recording the progress of cold and warm fronts as they move across the United States. Newspapers provide these maps in their daily weather sections. Each day's map will be compared to the previous maps and used to predict and discuss weather changes.

Project
In small groups the students will assemble and use a weather instrument such as a barometer, weather vane, snow/rain gauge, anemometer, hygrometer, or psychrometer.

Learning Log
Twice a day for the duration of the theme cycle all students will record in their learning logs the findings of the instruments they assembled (see Project) along with the findings of the "real" instruments within the classroom and outside the school. The students will also note the current weather and cloud conditions and make predictions as to any weather changes they believe will occur and why. The learning logs are also used to reflect upon other scientific information learned throughout the unit.

Computers/Technology
Each day one group of students will prepare a weather report using the *Weatherschool* program on the computer. Using daily weather information, the group will present the weather using the visuals provided by the computer.

Research
Each student or pair of students will choose a weather-related question to research. The research will be compiled to form a class report explaining why and how different types of weather occur and how weather can be helpful or harmful. Some possible questions are as follows:

How do oceans affect weather?
What is the water cycle?
What part does evaporation (or condensation, precipitation, or accumulation) play in the water cycle?
What is a tornado?
What is a hurricane?
What causes lightning and/or thunder?
What does low pressure (or high pressure) mean?
How does a low (or high) pressure system affect the weather?
How is wind formed?

Art

The students will design and make wind socks. They will write a description of how the wind sock works in their learning log.

Bibliography

Informational Books

Barrett, N. (1989). *Picture library: Hurricanes and tornadoes.* New York: Watts.
Bartlett, M. F. (1973). *Where does all the rain go?* (P. Collins, Illus.). New York: Coward, McCann, & Geoghegan.
Bramwell, M. (1994). *Earth science library: Weather* (C. Forsey, Illus.). New York: Watts.
Branley, F. M. (1983). *Rain & hail* (H. Barton, Illus.). New York: HarperCollins.
Branley, F. M. (1985). *Flash, crash, rumble, and roll* (B. & E. Emberley, Illus.). New York: HarperCollins.
Branley, F. M. (1987). *It's raining cats and dogs* (T. Kelley, Illus.). Boston: Houghton Mifflin.
Branley, F. M. (1988). *Tornado alert* (G. Maestro, Illus.). New York: Crowell.
Cole, J. (1986). *The magic school bus at the waterworks* (B. Degen, Illus.). New York: Scholastic.
Compton, G. (1981). *What does a meteorologist do?* New York: Dodd, Mead.
Cooper, J. (1992). *Wind: Science secrets.* Vero Beach, FL: Rourke.
de Paola, T. (1975). *The cloud book.* New York: Holiday.
DeWitt, L. (1991). *What will the weather be?* (C. Croll, Illus.). New York: HarperCollins.
Fradin, D. B. (1982). *Disaster! Tornadoes.* Chicago: Childrens Press.
Gibbons, G. (1987). *Weather forecasting* (G. Gibbons, Illus.). New York: Four Winds.
Gibbons, G. (1990). *Weather words and what they mean* (G. Gibbons, Illus.). New York: Holiday.
Lambert, D. (1990). *Our planet: Weather* (M. Camm, Illus.). New Mahwah, NJ: Troll.
Martin, C. (1987). *I can be a weather forecaster.* Chicago: Childrens Press.
Parker, S. (1990). *Fun with science: Weather* (K. K. Chen & P. Bull, Illus.). New York: Warwick.
Simon, S. (1989). *Storms.* New York: Scholastic.
Steele, P. (1991). *Weather watch: Snow causes and effects.* New York: Watts.
Ward, A. (1992). *Project science: Sky and weather* (A. Pang & R. Turvey, Illus.). New York: Watts.
Webster, V. (1982). *A new true book: Weather experiments.* Chicago: Childrens Press.

Fiction

Adoff, A. (1977). *Tornado! Poems* (R. Himler, Illus.). New York: Delacorte.
Hopkins, L. B. (1994). *Weather* (M. Hall, Illus.). New York: HarperCollins.
Locker, T. (1984). *Where the river begins* (T. Locker, Illus.). New York: Penguin.
Ruckman I. (1984). *Night of the twisters.* New York: HarperCollins.

Teacher Resources

Williams, J. (1992). *The weather book: An easy-to-understand guide to the U.S.A.'s weather.* New York: Random House.
Yaros, R. A. (1991). *Weatherschool.* Chesterfield, MO: Yaros Communications.

Videodisc

Windows on science—Earth science: Vol. 2 [Videodisc]. (1988). Warren, NJ: Optical Data Corp.
This videodisc demonstrates various natural phenomena, including an actual tornado as it moves towards a town. The video was taken by a television news crew from a helicopter.

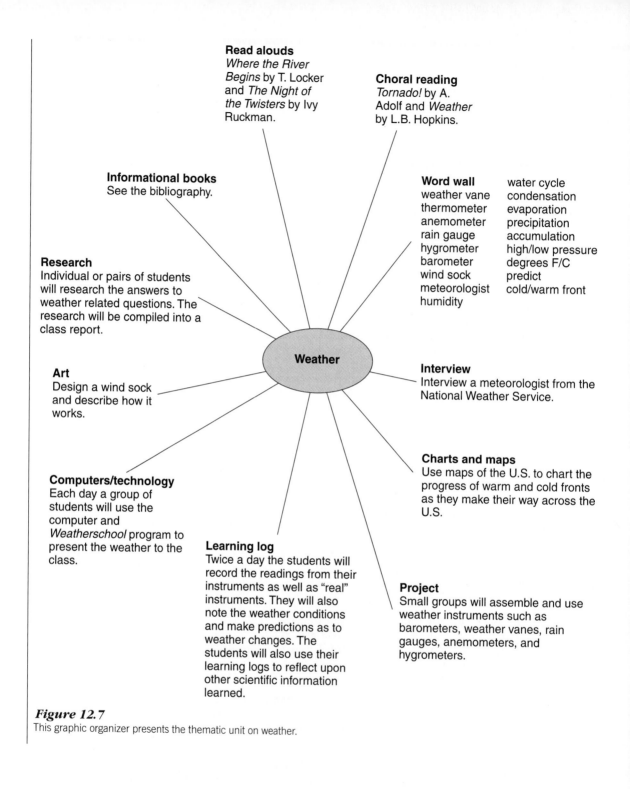

Read alouds
Where the River Begins by T. Locker and *The Night of the Twisters* by Ivy Ruckman.

Choral reading
Tornado! by A. Adolf and *Weather* by L.B. Hopkins.

Informational books
See the bibliography.

Word wall
weather vane water cycle
thermometer condensation
anemometer evaporation
rain gauge precipitation
hygrometer accumulation
barometer high/low pressure
wind sock degrees F/C
meteorologist predict
humidity cold/warm front

Research
Individual or pairs of students will research the answers to weather related questions. The research will be compiled into a class report.

Weather

Art
Design a wind sock and describe how it works.

Interview
Interview a meteorologist from the National Weather Service.

Computers/technology
Each day a group of students will use the computer and *Weatherschool* program to present the weather to the class.

Charts and maps
Use maps of the U.S. to chart the progress of warm and cold fronts as they make their way across the U.S.

Learning log
Twice a day the students will record the readings from their instruments as well as "real" instruments. They will also note the weather conditions and make predictions as to weather changes. The students will also use their learning logs to reflect upon other scientific information learned.

Project
Small groups will assemble and use weather instruments such as barometers, weather vanes, rain gauges, anemometers, and hygrometers.

Figure 12.7
This graphic organizer presents the thematic unit on weather.

FRONTS

BY: ANNE
McKIBBEN

Fronts

Some fronts cause dangerous storms and may cause serious damage to property. What are fronts? What are the different kinds of fronts? How do they affect weather? Fronts help you plan your everyday activities.

A front is the interface between air masses at different temperatures. When cold air and warm air meet they form a front. The air masses can make two kinds of fronts which are cold fronts and warm fronts. In a cold front, the edge of the mass of cold air moves under the warm air. Then the warm air is pushed upward while the cold air moves down to ground level. In a warm front, the edge of the air moving toward the cold air goes over the cold air that is moving away. The warm air takes the place of the cold air at ground level.

Most of the changes in the weather happen along fronts. The moving of the fronts depend on the shape of the pressure systems. Cyclones push fronts along at twenty to

Figure 12.8
Here is a report by Anne on "Fronts" that she researched as part of the weather unit.

From Anne McKibben. Used by permission.

thirty miles per hour. An anticyclone is where the air mass moves in the opposite direction of a cyclone and rotates around the center of high barometric pressure. Anticyclones go into an area after a front has passed.

Cold fronts cause quick changes in weather. The kinds of changes rely alot on the amount of moisture that is being replaced. If the air is dry, it may cause the weather to be partly cloudy but no rainfall. If the air is humid, then the weather could be cloudy and maybe bring rain or snow. The precipitation caused by most cold fronts are pretty heavy but doesn't last long. Cold fronts also could bring strong winds. When cold fronts pass, most of them bring a fast drop in temperature, quickly clearing skies, and a drop in humidity.

Warm fronts make a slower change in the weather than cold fronts do. The changes rely mostly on the humidity of the oncoming warm air. If the air is dry, thin clouds could form and little or no precipitation would fall. If the air is humid, the sky will turn gray. Light steady rain or snow could fall for a couple

of days. Sometimes fog may come. Most warm fronts have light winds. When warm fronts pass, they bring a quick rise in temperature, clearing skies, and a rise in humidity.

Cold fronts travel twice as fast as warm fronts do. So when a cold front meets a warm front, it forms an occluded front: cold front occlusions and warm front occlusions. In a cold front occlusion, the air behind the front is cooler than the air in front of the warm front. A cold front occlusion is like a cold front and has similar weather conditions. In a warm front occlusion, the air in the back of the cold front is warmer than the air ahead of it. A warm front occlusion is like a warm front and has similar weather conditions. But occluded fronts cause less violent weather than warm and cold fronts.

Another kind of front starts when a cold air and warm air mass meet, but they move very little. This kind is called a stationary front. It may stay in one area for a couple of days. The weather of a stationary front is usually moderate.

Fronts can be dangerous. They also affect the weather and people. Fronts have alot to do with our lives and what we do during the day.

Bibliography

The World Book Encyclopedia
Volume 21 W·X·Y·Z
Copywrited by World Book Inc.
1990

The World Book Encyclopedia
Volume 21 W·X·Y·Z
Copywrited by World Book Inc.
1983

Figure 12.8
(Continued)

From Lisa Vogt, Weather: A Theme Cycle. Reprinted by permission.

Content Area Reading

Increasingly, children's literature is being used to teach content areas such as science, social studies, and even math. Such literature can be used to introduce students to different viewpoints. For instance, "Selected picture books can offer older students new insights into historical perspectives" (Farris & Fuhler, 1994, p. 383). While stories in basal readers are predominately realistic fiction or narratives, content area textbooks contain predominately nonfiction or expository material. Students need to develop different strategies for reading expository prose than for narration because each content area makes use of specific vocabulary and concepts. For instance, Saul (1992, p. 1) writes, "Science books may help children realize the pleasures, potential, and limits of science. The best of these do far more than inform; they give voice to the beauty, the intricacy, and the connectedness of physical existence." This section describes instructional approaches designed to assist students in content area reading.

Study Skills

Students need to develop their own reading strategies and to become less dependent upon the teacher for establishing purposes for reading. Thus, students must become adept at formulating questions and making predictions about the text without teacher or classmate assistance.

To learn to generate questions independently, students must practice this skill with their classmates. For instance, the teacher may ask the class what questions they have about the Underground Railroad and write those questions on an overhead transparency. After viewing these questions, students will begin suggesting additional questions about the same topic. It is probably best to demonstrate such question generation in both science and social studies rather than to assume that students will be able to formulate good questions in both areas since different reading strategies exist for science and social studies.

SQ3R

One strategy for prereading is the SQ3R process developed by Robinson (1983). *SQ3R* consists of five steps: survey, question, read, recite, and review. The student surveys the passage to be read by reading the headings, highlighted items, italicized words and phrases, questions at the end of the sections and chapter, and the introductory and concluding paragraphs. The student formulates questions based on the headings and then reads the passage to find the answers to the questions. Next, the student recites what was read. In the last step, review, the student looks back over the text as well as any notes jotted down while reading and determines the author's major points. The SQ3R process must be practiced on a regular basis if students are to use it effectively.

Response

Another study strategy is the Response approach created by Jacobson (1989). Like SQ3R, *Response* encourages students to generate questions about the text, but unlike SQ3R, Response requires students to categorize their questions. For

In the Classroom Mini Lesson

Geography Themes and Children's Literature

*T*eachers can use selections of children's literature based on the five themes of geography to help students better understand and enjoy geography. The five themes are location, place, human and environment interactions, movement, and regions. Below are some trade books associated with each theme.

Location and Place

Bisel, S. C. (1991). *The secrets of Vesuvius*. New York: Scholastic. (4–7)

> This is a fictional account, as told by a slave girl, of the eruption of Mount Vesuvius in 79A.D. The nearby city of Herculaneum, Italy, was buried under several layers of lava. Students can locate Mount Vesuvius on a map and discuss how the volcano's eruption changed the lives of the people of Herculaneum.

Place

Frasier, D. (1991). *On the day you were born*. San Diego: Harcourt Brace. (K–3)

> This picture book presents several geographical concepts, including tides, gravity, and the rotation of the earth, as events that took place around the world on the day a baby is born. Students can talk about time zones and the rotation of the earth.

Human and Environment Interactions

Brown, R. (1991). *The world that Jack built*. New York: Dutton, (K–8)

> This book follows the familiar format of the cumulative tale "The House that Jack Built." The book begins with a lush, green valley and moves to a neighboring, dirty valley that has become polluted because of the factory that Jack built. Teachers of all grade levels find this book appropriate for stimulating discussion about environmental issues.

Murphy, J. (1995). *The great fire*. New York: Scholastic. (5–8)

> This book describes how weather and nature played a role in the destruction of Chicago during the 1871 fire.

Movement

Russell, N. (1991). *The stream*. New York: Penguin. (K–5)

> This book portrays the water cycle as rain falls in the mountains and then travels down a stream and eventually into the ocean. Condensation and evaporation are explained. While it appears to be a science book, the book offers a good geography lesson in that many geographical terms are introduced (e.g., source, mouth, and tributary). In addition, as the water flows from the stream to the river and on to the ocean, the author describes how it affects the people along the way.

Regions

One author who has devoted much of her work to regional themes is Diane Siebert. In eloquent prose accompanied by the beautiful paintings by Wendell Minor, Siebert describes the geographical and social aspects of a region, such as the Midwest in *Heartland* (Siebert, 1987). Below are three of her picture books.

Siebert, D. (1987). *Heartland* (W. Minor, Illus.). New York: Crowell. (K–8)
Siebert, D. (1989). *Mojave* (W. Minor, Illus.). New York: Crowell. (K–8)
Siebert, D. (1991). *Sierra* (W. Minor, Illus.). New York: Crowell. (K–8)

> After reading the three books to younger students, the teacher can have them compare and contrast the differences between the landscapes. Older students can do the same, as well as discuss how the different regions influence the lives of the people living within each region.

Figure 12.9

The Response form.

Response

Name: **Date:**

Reading assignment:

Important points: *As you read, list essential information and state important ideas; cite page numbers.*

Questions: *As you read, note questions that occur to you. Cite page numbers of their source. Some questions will be ideas for discussion. For others, you will want an immediate answer; star* these.*

New terms/concepts/vocabulary/names: *List words, phrases, technical terms, names of people, basic ideas which are new to you. Cite page numbers. Star* items you would like to have defined or explained.*

The response technique, originated by Jeanne M. Jacobson, is described in the winter '89 issue of *Reading Horizons.*

this reason, it is most appropriate for students in Grades 4 through 6. A Response form is shown in figure 12.9.

The Response form is an interactive device in that the student is given the opportunity to ask questions and to request immediate responses to those questions. After completing the Response form, the student gives it to the teacher, who notes the questions, names, vocabulary, concepts, and the like that have asterisks (*) next to them. The teacher then "responds" to those items, either in class discussion or in writing. By having the students record the page numbers that accompany the questions, names, and so on, the teacher can go directly to the appropriate section, thereby making the process more efficient.

In the Classroom Mini Lesson

Comparing Different Versions of Folktales

$\mathcal{M}$any folktales have been written and rewritten in several versions. Children may find one version of a folktale in their basal reader and another version of the same folktale in their school library. Analyzing how the versions are similar and how they differ can result in an excellent discussion about what makes a good folktale.

Among the folktales that are available in several versions are *The Little Red Hen, The Three Billy Goats Gruff, Chicken Little, Snow White and the Seven Dwarfs, Beauty and the Beast, Little Red Riding Hood, The Three Little Pigs, The Gingerbread Man, The Fisherman's Wife,* and the *Anasi* tales. The teacher should bring to class as many versions of the same folktale as possible and encourage the students to do likewise.

The teacher divides the class into groups of three or four students and gives each group two versions of the same folktale to compare and contrast. The children should compare the literary elements of character, plot, setting (time and place), theme, and author's style. They should also note the differences in language use (words, phrases, and so on) that enrich the two versions of the folktale.

Children can create their own charts to compare the differences between the two versions. The individual literary elements and the different uses of language can serve as the headings for such charts. Here is an example of a comparison chart for "The Three Little Pigs."

Title	Characters	Setting	Problem	Resolution
The Three Little Pigs	3 pigs wolf	Country	Wolf blows down houses of pigs.	Pigs are safe in brick house. When wolf tries to climb down chimney, he burns his tail and leaves.
The True Story of the Three Little Pigs	3 pigs wolf	Country	Wolf's cold makes him sneeze causing him to blow down the pigs' houses. Then he eats the pigs.	Wolf is arrested for murdering the three little pigs.
The Three Little Wolves and the Big Bad Pig	3 wolves big bad pig	Country	Big bad pig destroys homes of wolves.	Big bad pig becomes friend of three wolves.

References

Scieszka, J. (1989). *The true story of the three little pigs* (L. Smith, Illus.). New York: Viking.

Trivizas, E. (1993). *The three little wolves and the big bad pig* (H. Oxenbury, Illus.). New York: Scholastic.

Reciprocal Teaching

Reciprocal teaching may be used with intermediate and middle school students and older students with learning disabilities. It requires students to use four strategies in summarizing content area material. First, the student reads the passage and then summarizes it in one sentence. Second, the student asks one or two high-level questions about the material read. Third, the student clarifies any difficult portions of the passage. Fourth, the student predicts what will occur in the next paragraph or portion of the text to be read.

Reciprocal teaching places less emphasis on teacher explanation and focuses more on the teacher and student collaborating in an attempt to bring meaning to the text. "At the heart of reciprocal teaching is a dialogue about the meaning of the text" (Palincsar & Brown, 1989, p. 33). In essence, reciprocal teaching is a type of individual DR-TA in that the student must use previously gained knowledge along with information gathered from the passage being read to formulate questions and to make feasible predictions. Research findings support the use of such strategies with low-ability intermediate-grade students and seventh and eighth graders with learning disabilities (Palincsar & Brown, 1985). It is essential that the classroom teacher model reciprocal teaching and then encourage students with a great deal of positive feedback as they implement the strategies in their reading of content area materials.

Instructional Approaches for High-Risk, Bilingual, and Special Needs Students

High-risk students are students who may graduate or drop out of school without having attained sufficient skills to function successfully in society. Typically, such students come from low socioeconomic backgrounds, are low achievers, have poor attendance records, and demonstrate behavior problems. Bilingual students are children for whom English is a second language. Special needs students are children with a disability or handicap and are often mainstreamed in inclusion programs.

High-Risk Students

Children from low socioeconomic backgrounds have been studied extensively in terms of reading achievement (Adams, 1990). As Allington (1991, p. 237) writes, "It is the children of poverty who are most likely to have literacy-learning difficulties." Programs for high-risk students have been available for many years. Among them are Head Start, a program designed for deprived pre-schoolers, and Chapter I, a remedial reading, writing, and mathematics program for elementary and secondary students. These programs were heavily funded by the federal government in the 1960s, but receive less attention in the 1990s.

Some states have adopted their own programs, such as Indiana's Operation Prime Time and Texas, which encourage school districts to have smaller classes for first, second, and third graders. The Indiana and Texas programs are not directed solely at the high-risk population but includes regular students as well.

Slavin and Madden (1989) found that effective programs for high-risk students all had a comprehensive approach. According to Slavin and Madden, an overall school plan for these students should include (1) a statement that the school is responsible for ensuring that every student succeeds, (2) recognition that a successful program requires substantial fiscal and personnel resources, (3) an emphasis on prevention rather than remediation, (4) an emphasis on classroom change that includes follow-up programs, and (5) reliance on remedial programs as a final resort.

Another program to aid beginning readers is Reading Recovery, a program for first graders in Ohio that focuses on intensive reading instruction provided by a specially trained teacher. Research on the long-term effects of the Reading Recovery program suggests that students in the program read at levels substantially higher than those students who received no assistance. Although the gains diminished over a 2-year period, they remained significant even though the Reading Recovery students received no assistance after first grade (DeFord, Pinnell, Lyons, & Young, 1987).

Reading Recovery is one whole language approach to working with high-risk students; other ways of developing reading strategies with such students include the language experience approach and literature-based instruction. In the language experience approach, described earlier in this chapter, the child dictates a story to the teacher or an aide, who writes it down exactly as the child tells it. The teacher or aide reads the story back to the child, and the child then reads it aloud. This occurs until the child literally memorizes the story and the words. The child will write several stories in this fashion. Then the teacher introduces the child to pattern books, which are also read repeatedly to and with the child until they are memorized.

The literature-based approach with high-risk students provides a wide variety of options (Indrisano & Paratore, 1992). For the beginning reader, pattern books are often used. For the student who has some reading proficiency, literature response journals can be used. In these, a student shares his or her reactions with the teacher, who writes comments and questions back to the child on a daily basis. The literature-based approach is good for pairing up students with similar interests. For example, two or three students at different reading levels who are interested in basketball may each read a book selected from a *text set,* a set of books on the same theme (basketball in this case). The students meet daily to discuss their books. Thus, the low-ability student has the opportunity to share a similar interest and discuss it with students who have greater reading ability.

Another whole language technique includes pairing a high-risk student with a student of higher reading ability and having them read a book or short story to each other. The students take turns reading the sentences. This enables the lower-ability reader to hear an average or good reader read aloud (modeling of good oral reading). It also forces the low-ability reader to keep up and not "lose his or her place."

Bilingual Students

Bilingual students are often considered to be high-risk candidates. When a bilingual student in a regular classroom has difficulty with reading or writing, he or she should be given tests to determine whether the problem in learning is due

Focus Box 12.4

Reading Recovery

*R*eading Recovery began in New Zealand as a means of helping young children who failed to respond to literacy instruction during their first year of schooling. Created by Marie Clay (1996), Reading Recovery is an intensive, individualized instructional program. A regular classroom teacher who is specially trained in the Reading Recovery methodology devotes part of the school day to working with Reading Recovery students on a one-to-one basis.

Reading Recovery teachers assist low-achieving 6- and 7-year-old students to reach average or close to average classroom achievement levels. The materials used are simple: a magnetic chalkboard, magnetic letters, felt-tipped pens, simple storybooks, and exercise books. Lesson plans are created daily, not a week in advance as for a typical class.

Record keeping for each child includes notes on the lesson plans used, records and graphs on reading accuracy, vocabulary charts, and a record of books selected by the teacher for the child to read. A child may be in the program for 12 to 16 weeks or longer if necessary.

In an attempt to explain why Reading Recovery programs work while traditional remedial reading programs fail, Spiegel (1995) offers the following 15 reasons:

1. Intervention must take place early.
2. Reading instruction should focus on the comprehension of connected text, not the fragmented study of isolated skills.
3. Children should spend time reading rather than completing worksheets.
4. Both the teacher and the child should be aware of the goals of instruction.
5. Children must have the opportunity to learn.
6. Children should be given materials to read that are appropriate for their reading level.
7. Children should be taught reading strategies and how to transfer those strategies to new situations.
8. Writing should be an integral part of a beginning reading program.
9. A beginning reading program should include phonemic awareness as part of the curriculum.
10. The intervention program should be congruent with the classroom reading program.
11. Direct instruction should be part of the program.
12. Instruction in special reading programs should be individualized.
13. Children's attempts to make meaning of text should be monitored and reinforced.
14. Children most at risk should be taught by the best teachers.
15. Children who have fallen behind need a program that accelerates their progress.

Clay, M. M. (1991). Why is an inservice programme for Reading Recovery teachers necessary? *Reading Horizons, 31*(5), 355–372.

Spiegel, D. L. (1995). A comparison of traditional remedial programs and Reading Recovery: Guidelines for success for all programs. *The Reading Teacher, 49*(2), 86–96.

to second-language acquisition or to a learning disorder in the child's native, or first, language. If a child has a learning or language disorder within his or her native language, instruction should not continue in a second language.

Special Needs Students

Students with special needs may have an emotional handicap, a learning disability, a hearing or visual impairment, some other physical impairment, a speech or language problem, or be mentally retarded. Most of these students read below the average reading level of their peer group, and they typically lack practice in reading because they are poor readers. They need positive experiences with reading—and many of them. Using children's literature with such students is helpful because literature shapes events into some kind of meaning. According to Bruner (1990), literature is the driving force in language learning.

Students with learning disabilities (LD students) may have difficulty remembering what they have seemingly already learned. This can be discouraging, both for the student and the classroom teacher. Success with LD students typically occurs when a reading program is individually tailored for each child and an underlying support system to develop the child's self-concept is in place. Such a program meets with less resistance by LD children.

An essential ingredient for working with any student with a special need is to provide many opportunities for small and large group involvement in which the child contributes in a positive way to the learning environment and is not considered an outcast within his or her own classroom.

Computers and Reading

Computers are finding their way into more and more classrooms. While early software programs for children emphasized "drill and practice" exercises, such as IBM's "Writing to Read," current software is more challenging for students. Students can send each other messages across the room or by using a telephone modem and the Internet, across the country and throughout the world.

Students in the intermediate grades can use a computer to engage in such sophisticated techniques as "hypertext" and "hypermedia" to read the latest edition of an encyclopedia or to read about earthquakes before seeing actual film footage of the 1995 Kobe, Japan earthquake. Hardware interfacing also allows a student to produce a written biographical report on Martin Luther King, Jr., with short inserts of actual television footage of King's "I Have a Dream" speech and civil rights marches of the 1960s or a science report about the 1992 Hurricane Andrew in Florida, including film footage of the damage that occurred to farms, ranches, businesses, and homes. Even though the equipment necessary to do these things is still relatively expensive, advances in technology continue to bring down costs so that eventually every school may be able to afford interactive video equipment.

Evaluating Reading

The evaluation of student reading should be a continuous process. Every day a teacher observes a new skill being acquired by a student and discovers that a skill thought to have been mastered by another student has yet to be acquired. By using both formal and informal measures, the classroom teacher can effectively gauge the reading ability of all students in the class.

Formal Evaluation Measures

Formal evaluation measures include standardized tests and the tests that accompany basal reader series, such as unit tests. Many formal measures are either norm referenced or criterion referenced. A *norm-referenced test* compares a student's test results with those of other students who have previously taken the same test. A *criterion-referenced test* compares the student's test result with a set performance, or criterion. For example, standardized achievement tests are norm-referenced tests, whereas a written examination for a driver's license is a criterion-referenced test.

Norm-referenced tests are useful to the classroom teacher in terms of reading evaluation. By administering a norm-referenced standardized achievement test each year and comparing the results with those of the previous year, teachers can evaluate their students' progress. Furthermore, when the scores of all students in a school or a school district are compiled together according to grade level, the overall effectiveness of the school's or district's reading program can be measured.

Criterion-referenced tests are frequently used to determine whether or not students have mastered specific skills. For instance, a criterion-referenced test may contain 10 items pertaining to syllabication rules; if a student successfully completes 8 of those items, that student is considered competent in syllabication.

Criterion-referenced tests are also useful in working with high-risk students. For example, a teacher may construct a criterion-referenced test to measure a specific behavior. The student is evaluated on his or her own work, and the results are not compared with those of other students.

Reading Readiness Tests

Typically, formal reading readiness tests are administered to young children before they enter elementary school. Such tests include subtests to evaluate the emergent literacy skills of young children in such areas as auditory discrimination, letter identification, letter-sound association, letter copying, and the following of directions. In selecting a readiness test, a teacher must be careful to choose one that can effectively identify language-delayed, high-risk children.

Diagnostic Tests

As students progress through elementary school, formal diagnostic tests may be administered to determine individual skill competency. Such tests are usually given when a child has difficulty with a particular reading skill, such as the ability to recognize consonant or vowel sounds, consonant blends and diphthongs, the ability to sequence events, or the ability to comprehend what is read. Diagnostic tests are administered individually and require careful scoring and interpretation of the results.

A proliferation of commercial reading tests has resulted in the "overtesting" of students. One superintendent complained that some teachers in his district were administering unit reading tests before the students had even completed the unit being evaluated. When the students scored poorly, one teacher told his class, "That's okay. We haven't covered the material so I didn't expect you to do well on the test." Obviously, such misuse of tests should be avoided.

Informal Evaluation Measures

Many teachers believe that to make reading instruction more effective, they should find out all they can about their students: their interests, attitudes, preferences, and abilities. Such teachers have students keep lists of things they like and don't like, of what they would like to do during their free time, of what their hobbies are, and so forth. In addition, the students keep lists of the books they have read as well as those they would like to read, and these teachers routinely peruse the students' lists in an attempt to keep up with their current interests and reading activities.

Other teachers prefer to informally measure student attitudes and interests in reading by means of inventories or checklists. Still other teachers arrange time for informal *reading interviews,* audiotaped interviews within which the student shares a "special" passage from a favorite book. The teacher then questions the student about the book and other reading interests.

Anecdotal Records

Anecdotal records are notations made by the classroom teacher about a student after observing the student. Routman (1991, p. 309) defines anecdotal records as being

> "dated, informal observational notations that describe language development as well as social development in terms of the learner's attitudes, strengths, weaknesses, needs, progress, learning styles, skills, strategies used, or anything else that seems significant at the time of the observation. These records are usually brief comments that are very specific to what the child is doing and needs to be doing. They provide documented, accumulated information over time and offer an expanded view of the student's development of literacy."

Anecdotal records can be about a variety of things. For instance, they can be about "written products or can include information about both process and product" (Rhodes & Nathenson-Mejia, 1992, p. 502). Rhodes and Nathenson-Mejia further state that "taken regularly, anecdotal notes become not only a vehicle for planning instruction and documenting progress, but also a story about an individual" (p. 503).

Unlike checklists, anecdotal records are time consuming for the classroom teacher. However, the records can provide valuable information, particularly when viewed with other evaluation measures. Anecdotal records are especially important for providing the teacher with insightful information during student-teacher and parent-teacher conferences.

In the Classroom Mini Lesson

The Reading Portfolio and its Assessment

A reading portfolio should contain a running list of the books a child has read, including the date on which each book was finished, and a running list of books the child would like to read. Vocabulary words can also be maintained and dated in a list kept in the portfolio.

During the primary grades (beginning in January with first graders), a record should be kept of the number of words each child can read from a simple children's book in one minute's time. The record should be updated three times a year. The children's book should be one that no student can finish, and the same book should be used for the entire class so that the teacher can gauge the progress of all the students (Pils, 1991).

Tierney, Carter, and Desai (1991) suggest that a portfolio should show the breadth of different reading experiences (reading stories; reading poetry, songs, and other material; and reading across content areas while working on projects). In addition, they suggest that the portfolio should contain a record of how reading and writing are used in combination, that is, to solve problems, communicate with others, make new connections and discoveries, and pursue projects both in and out of school.

The teacher should review and evaluate the portfolio periodically, at least once a month. This assessment should indicate types of reading and writing selections and their content. For instance, how does the child analyze literary elements in his or her literature response journal over a period of time? Does one author (or topic) seem to captivate the student's reading interests? After evaluating the portfolio, the teacher should have a conference with the student to discuss the portfolio, including how the student is progressing and what the student's current reading interests are compared to what they were at the beginning of the school year. The student should feel free to examine his or her strengths and weaknesses in a candid manner during the conference. Some teachers exchange portfolios of four different ability students (Gillespie, et al., 1996) (one superstar, one average, one struggling, and one puzzling or inconsistent). This aids in keeping their judgments reliable and valid.

The reading portfolio can be assessed in combination with the writing portfolio. In fact, it is to the advantage of the teacher and the students to do so because students' interests and patterns evolve from both their reading and writing.

Gillespie, C. S., Ford, K. L., Gillespie, R. D., & Leavell, A. G. (1996). Portfolio assessment: Some questions, some answers, some recommendations. *Journal of Adolescent and Adult Literacy, 39* (6), 480–491.

Pils, L. J. (1991). Soon anofe you tout me: Evaluation in a first-grade whole language classroom. *The Reading Teacher, 45* (1), 46–50.

Tierney, R. J., Carter, M. A., & Desai, L. E. (1991). *Portfolio assessment in the reading-writing classroom.* Needham, MA: Christopher-Gordon.

S u m m a r y

Until recently, reading was the primary focus of language arts instruction. Today two prominent instructional approaches prevail: the basal reader approach and the whole language (literature-based) approach. Basal reading programs are moving toward the whole language approach, which incorporates reading, writing, and discussion of the text. In a summary of research studies, Adams (1990) suggests that phonics instruction should be added to the basal reader or whole language approach for young children who are beginning to learn how to read.

The reading field has witnessed recent interest in the area of emergent literacy as researchers seek to examine how children acquire literacy. Along with this has come a renewed interest in sharing books with preschoolers and extending this practice into the primary and intermediate grades.

A variety of reading methodologies exist for both beginning and experienced readers. Moreover, several study techniques are available for reading in the content areas. Finally, there are a number of formal and informal methods for evaluating children's reading progress.

Questions

1. Compare the whole language or literature-based reading approach with the basal reader approach. What are the advantages and disadvantages of each?
2. What are the characteristics of a child in the emergent reading stage?
3. How does the shared book activity compare with your own experiences of having the teacher read to you during "story time"?
4. Compare and contrast the different study skill techniques. Suggest a strength and a weakness of each.

Activities

1. Observe four children of different ages varying between age 4 and age 9 while they are reading. Make a chart to indicate when children possess the specific reading skills (for example, left-to-right directionality, top-to-bottom directionality, and use of picture clues).
2. Find a book that would be appropriate for a directed reading-thinking activity. Attempt a DR-TA with a group of six to eight elementary students who are reading at that instructional level.
3. Help a kindergartner or first grader write a language experience story.
4. Adopt one of the study skill techniques described in this chapter for one of your own classes. Use it for at least a month and then compare your performance on tests or quizzes with your earlier scores.

For Further Reading

Church, S. (1994). Is whole language really warm and fuzzy? *The Reading Teacher, 47*(5), 362–371.

Farris, P. J., & Fuhler, C. J. (1994). Developing social studies concepts through picture books. *The Reading Teacher, 47*(5), 380–387.

Gambrell, L. B., Palmer, B. M., Codling, R. M., & Mazzoni, S. A. (1996). Assessing motivation to read. *The Reading Teacher, 49*(7), 518–533.

Gray, M. J. (1988). The reading process for the beginning reader. *Reading Horizons, 29*(1), 22–34.

Griffith, P. L., & Olson, M. (1992). Phonemic awareness helps beginning readers break the code. *The Reading Teacher, 45*(7), 516–525.

Mates, B. F., & Strommen, L. (1996). Why Ernie can't read: Sesame Street and literacy. *The Reading Teacher, 49* (4), 300–306.

Stewart, R. A., Paradis, E. E., Ross, B. D., & Lewis, M. J. (1996). Student voices: What works in literature-based developmental reading. *Journal of Adolescent and Adult Literacy, 39* (6), 468–479.

Unwin, C. G. (1995). Elizabeth's story: The potential of home-based literacy instruction. *The Reading Teacher, 48* (7), 552–557.

References

Because of the large number of children's books cited in this chapter, these titles are documented in a separate subsection below.

Adams, M. J. (1990). *Beginning to read: Thinking and learning about print.* Urbana, IL: Center for the Study of Reading.

Allen, R. V. (1976). *Language experiences in communication.* Boston: Houghton Mifflin.

Allington, R. L. (1991). Children who find learning to read difficult: School responses to diversity. In E. H. Hiebert (Ed.), *Literacy for a diverse society: Perspectives, practices, and policies.* New York: Teachers College Press.

Anderson, R. C., Hiebert, E. H., Scott, J. A., & Wilkinson, I. A. G. (1984). *Becoming a nation of readers: The report of the Commission on Reading.* Washington, DC: National Institute of Reading.

Anderson, R. C., Wilson, P. T., & Fielding, L. G. (1988). Growth in reading and how children spend their time outside of school. *Reading Research Quarterly, 23,* 285–303.

Anderson, T. H., & Armbruster, B. (1984). Content area textbooks. In R. C. Anderson, J. Osborn, & R. J. Tierney (Eds.), *Learning to read in American schools.* Hillsdale, NJ: Erlbaum.

Atwell, N. (1987). *In the middle.* Portsmouth, NH: Heinemann.

Babbitt, N. (1987). Boston Globe Award speech. *The Horn Book, 63,* 582–585.

Bissex, G. (1980). *GNYS AT WORK: A child learns to read and write.* Cambridge, MA: Harvard University Press.

Brazee, P., & Haynes, S. W. (1988). Special education and whole language: From an evaluator's viewpoint. In K. Goodman, Y. Goodman, & W. Hood (Eds.), *The whole language evaluation book.* Portsmouth, NH: Heinemann.

Bruner, J. (1990). *Acts of meaning.* Cambridge, MA: Harvard University Press.

Calkins, L. M., & Harwayne, S. (1991). *Living between the lines.* Portsmouth, NH: Heinemann.

Church, S. (1994). Is whole language really warm and fuzzy? *The Reading Teacher, 47* (5), 362–371.

Clark, M. (1976). *Young fluent readers: What can they teach us?* Portsmouth, NH: Heinemann.

Clay, M. M. (1982). *Observing young readers: Selected papers.* London: Heinemann.

Clay, M. M. (1991a). Introducing a new storybook to young readers. *The Reading Teacher, 45* (4), 264–273.

Cullinan, B. E., & Galda, L. (1994). *Literature and the child* (3rd ed.). Fort Worth: Harcourt Brace.

DeFord, D. E., Pinnell, G. S., Lyons, C. A., & Young, P. (1987). *Ohio's Reading Recovery Program: Vol. 3. Report of the follow-up studies.* Columbus: Ohio State University.

Doake, D. (1981). *Book experience and emergent reading in preschool children.* Unpublished doctoral dissertation, University of Alberta, Alberta, Canada.

Durkin, D. (1966). *Children who read early: Two longitudinal studies.* New York: Columbia Teachers College Press.

Durkin, D. (1972). *Teaching young children to read.* Boston: Houghton Mifflin.

Durkin, D. (1974-1975). A six-year study of children who learned to read in school at the age of four. *The Reading Teacher, 10*(1-5), 9-61.

Durkin, D. (1987). Testing in the kindergarten. *The Reading Teacher, 37,* 766-770.

Durkin, D. (1990). Dolores Durkin speaks on instruction. *The Reading Teacher, 43*(7), 472-477.

Edwards, P. A. (1991). Fostering early literacy through parent coaching. In E. H. Hiebert (Ed.), *Literacy for a diverse society: Perspectives, practices, and policies.* New York: Teachers College Press.

Fader, D. (1982). *The new hooked on books.* New York: Berkley.

Farris, P. J., & Fuhler, C. J. (1994). Developing social studies concepts through picture books. *The Reading Teacher, 47*(5), 380-387.

Frith, U. (1985). Beneath the surface of developmental dyslexia. In K. E. Patterson, K. C. Marshall, & M. Coltheart (Eds.), *Surface dyslexia: Neuropsychological and cognitive studies of phonological reading.* Hillsdale, NJ: Erlbaum.

Goodman, Y. (1988). Evaluation of students: Evaluation of teachers. In K. Goodman, Y. Goodman, & W. Hood (Eds.), *The whole language evaluation book.* Portsmouth, NH: Heinemann.

Griffith, P. L., & Olson, M. (1992). Phonemic awareness helps beginning readers break the code. *The Reading Teacher, 45*(7), 516-525.

Harp, B. (1988). When you do whole language instruction, how do you keep track of reading and writing skills? *The Reading Teacher, 42,* 160-161.

Heath, S. B. (1983). *Ways with words: Language, life, and work in communities and classrooms.* Cambridge, England: Cambridge University Press.

Holdaway, D. (1979). *The foundations of literacy.* Sydney, Australia: Ashton Scholastic.

Holdaway, D. (1986). Guiding a natural process. In D. R. Tovey & J. E. Kerber (Eds.), *Roles in literacy learning: A new perspective.* Newark, DE: International Reading Association.

Indrisano, R., & Paratore, J. R. (1992). Using literature with readers at risk. In B. E. Cullinan (Ed.), *Invitation to read: More children's literature in the reading program.* Newark, DE: International Reading Association.

Jacobson, J. M. (1989). RESPONSE: An interactive study technique. *Reading Horizons, 29,* 86-92.

Klesius, J. (1988). What is whole language? *Florida Reading Quarterly, 25*(2), 17-23.

Langer, J. A. (1990). The process of understanding: Reading for literary and informative purposes. *Research in the Teaching of English, 24,* 229-260.

Lapp, D., & Flood, J. (1983). *Teaching reading to every child* (2nd ed.). New York: Macmillan.

Lartz, M. N. & Mason, J. M. (1988). Jamie: One child's journey from oral to written language. *Early Childhood Research Quarterly, 3,* 193-208.

Meyer, L. A., Gersten, R. M., & Gutkin, J. (1983). Direct instruction: A Project Follow Through success story. *Elementary School Journal, 84*(2), 241-252.

Monson, D. L. (1992). Realistic fiction and the real world. In B. Cullinan (Ed.), *Invitation to read: More children's literature in the reading program.* Newark, DE: International Reading Association.

Moore, D. W., Readence, J. E., & Rickelman, R. J. (1982). *Prereading activities for content reading and learning.* Newark, DE: International Reading Association.

Morrissey, M. (1988). When "shut up" is a sign of growth. In K. Goodman, Y. Goodman, & W. Hood (Eds.), *The whole language evaluation book.* Portsmouth, NH: Heinemann.

Newman, J. M. (1984). Using children's books to teach reading. In J. M. Newman (Ed.), *Whole language: Theory in use.* Portsmouth, NH: Heinemann.

Norton, D. E. (1985). *The effective teaching of language arts* (2nd ed.). Columbus, OH: Merrill.

Palincsar, A. S., & Brown, A. L. (1985). Reciprocal teaching: Activities to promote "reading" in your mind. In T. L. Harris & E. J. Cooper (Eds.), *Reading, thinking, and concept development* (pp. 147-158). New York: College Board Publications.

Palincsar, A. S., & Brown, A. L. (1989). Instruction for self-regulated learning. In L. B. Resnick & L. E. Klopfer (Eds.), *Toward the thinking curriculum: Current cognitive research*. Washington, DC: Association for Supervision and Curriculum Development.

Palincsar, A. S., Ogle, D. S., Jones, B. F., Carr, E. G., & Ransom, K. (1985). *Facilitators' manual for teaching reading as thinking*. Washington, DC: Association for Supervision and Curriculum Development.

Paris, S. G. (1985). Using classroom dialogues and guided practice to teach comprehension strategies. In T. L. Harris & E. J. Cooper (Eds.), *Reading, thinking, and concept development* (pp. 133-146). New York: College Board Publications.

Purves, A. C. (1990). *The scribal society*. New York: Longman.

Raphael, T. E., & McMahon, S. I. (1994). Book Club: An alternative framework for reading instruction. *The Reading Teacher, 48*(2), 102-117.

Rhodes, L. K., & Nathenson-Mejia, S. (1992). Anecdotal records: A powerful tool for ongoing literacy assessment. *The Reading Teacher, 45*(7), 502-511.

Robinson, H. A. (1983). *Teaching reading, writing, and study strategies: The content areas* (3rd ed.). Boston: Allyn & Bacon.

Rosenblatt, L. (1938). *Literature as exploration*. New York: Noble & Noble.

Rosenblatt, L. (1978). *The reader, the text, the poem: The transactional theory of the literary work*. Carbondale, IL: Southern Illinois University.

Rosenblatt, L. (1991). Literature—S.O.S.! *Language Arts, 68,* 444-448.

Routman, R. (1988). *Transitions: From literature to literacy*. Portsmouth, NH: Heinemann.

Routman, R. (1991). *Invitations: Changing as teachers and learners, K-12.* Portsmouth, NH: Heinemann.

Saul, W. (1992). Introduction. In W. Saul & S. A. Jagusch (Eds.), *Vital connections: Children, science, and adults*. Portsmouth, NH: Heinemann.

Schickedanz, J., & Sullivan, M. (1984). Mom, what does U-F-F spell? *Language Arts, 61*(1), 7-17.

Shannon, P. (1989). *Broken promises*. Granby, MA: Bergin & Gavey.

Slavin, R. E., & Madden, N. A. (1989). What works for students at risk: A research synthesis. *Educational Leadership, 46*(5), 4-13.

Smith, F. (1986). *Insult to intelligence: The bureaucratic invasion of our classrooms*. Portsmouth, NH: Heinemann.

Snow, C. E. (1983). Literacy and language: Relationships during the pre-school years. *Harvard Educational Review, 53*(2), 165-189.

Stahl, S. A. (1992). Saying the "p" word: Nine guidelines for exemplary phonics instruction. *The Reading Teacher, 45*(8), 618-625.

Stauffer, R. G. (1969). *Directing reading maturity as a cognitive process*. New York: Harper & Row.

Taylor, D. (1983). *Family literacy*. Portsmouth, NH: Heinemann.

Teale, W. H. (1984). Reading to young children: Its significance for literacy development. In H. Goelman, A. Olberg, & F. Smith (Eds.), *Awakening to literacy*. Portsmouth, NH: Heinemann.

Trachtenburg, P. (1990). Using children's literature to enhance phonics instruction. *The Reading Teacher, 43*(9), 648-654.

Watson, D., & Crowley, P. (1988). How can we implement a whole-language approach? In C. Weaver (Ed.), *Reading process and practice* (pp. 232-279). Portsmouth, NH: Heinemann.

Weaver, C. (Ed.). (1988). *Reading process and practice*. Portsmouth, NH: Heinemann.

Whitney, J., & Hubbard, R. (1986). *Time and choice: Key elements for process teaching* (Videotape). Portsmouth, NH: Heinemann.

Wiseman, D. E., & Robeck, C. P. (1983). The written language behavior of two socio-economic groups of preschool children. *Reading Psychology, 4*(2), 349-363.

Yarington, D. (1978). *The great American reading machine.* Rochelle Park, NJ: Hayden.

Yopp, H. K. (1992). Developing phonemic awareness in young children. *The Reading Teacher, 45*(9), 696-703.

Yopp, H. K. (1995). A test for assessing phonemic awareness in young children. *The Reading Teacher, 49*(1), 20-29.

Children's Books

Bruchac, J., & London, L. (1992). *Thirteen moons on turtle's back: A Native American year of the moons* (T. Locker, Illus.). New York: Philomel.

Cowcher, H. (1990). *Antarctica.* New York: Farrar, Straus, & Giroux.

Henkes, K. (1990). *Julius, baby of the world.* New York: Greenwillow.

Jacob, W. J. (1990). *Ellis Island: New hope in a new land.* New York: Macmillan/ Scribner's.

Lobel, A. (1970). *Frog and Toad are friends.* New York: Harper & Row.

Mitchell, M. K. (1993). *Uncle Jed's barbershop* (J. Ransome, Illus.). New York: Scholastic.

Murphy, J. (1987). *The last dinosaur.* New York: Scholastic.

Murphy, J. (1990). *The Boys War: Confederate and Union soldiers talk about the Civil War.* Boston: Houghton Mifflin.

Murphy, J. (1995). *The great fire.* New York: Scholastic.

*E*xtending *the Language Arts Curriculum*

© James L. Shaffer

From the standpoint of the child, the great waste in school comes from his inability to utilize the experience he gets outside of school in any complete and free way.
—**John Dewey**
School and Society

E lementary school is an extension of the local community. Just as the super-market, park, and library should be familiar territories, children need to feel comfortable in the classroom if they are to enjoy the learning experience. This is not possible if the school fails to include the community as a whole, thereby suggesting that learning occurs only in the school setting and is not applicable outside it. Learning is a social phenomenon that takes place everywhere, whether it be in a classroom, an airport, a supermarket, or the neighborhood McDonald's. In promoting such learning, the teacher plays a vital role (Ford, 1992).

Because learning is a social phenomenon, children learn from those around them: parents, siblings, peers, teachers, and other adults. As Smith (1989) notes, children in the company of music lovers learn about music; those who join gangs learn the nuances of gang activities and rules. The classroom teacher must incorporate into the school community the community at large, and even the world.

This chapter discusses ways to extend the school community to the larger community and beyond. Parental involvement, senior citizen participation as classroom volunteers, and school-school and school-business partnerships are examined in terms of language arts instruction.

Family Literacy

Involving parents in the teaching of language arts through family literacy programs has long been promoted by educators. The acquisition of literacy begins in the home; therefore, it is logical to promote activities in which parents can contribute to their child's literacy development. Indeed, a strict, linear approach to the teaching of literacy can reduce children's opportunities for literacy learning in their own homes in that their parents are alienated and thus made to feel inadequate about their own literacy knowledge and abilities (Heath, 1980).

Feelings of inadequacy can extend to children as they examine their own abilities. Consider, for example, homogeneous ability grouping for reading instruction. Research indicates that such grouping results in the overrepresentation of students from working-class, poor, and minority families in the lower-ability reading group, and the overrepresentation of students from middle- and upper-class families in the higher-ability group (Cummins, 1986; Fraatz, 1987; Routman, 1991). Instruction differs between the high and low groups, with more time devoted to silent reading in the higher groups. Moreover, the teacher asks more higher-level questions and interrupts students less to correct oral reading errors in the higher groups. Thus, children in the lower groups are not provided with the same opportunities for learning to read. Indeed, increased interruptions have been found to inhibit the development of

Students should be encouraged to learn from all family members. This student, for her report on Women's History Month, interviewed her grandmother about the hardships she encountered during World War II, including rationing, clothing shortages, and war bond drives.

students' self-correction strategies (McNaughton, 1981), as well as to impair their ability to answer questions (Wilson, 1988). Obviously, there is a need for teachers to reexamine the logic of this instructional practice if the goal is to help students become literate.

Students provide the strongest link between the school and the home. They must be respected, and they must clearly recognize that they are respected. Otherwise, they and their parents will have little regard for learning, and that feeling will eventually permeate the community.

A study of parental involvement in schools suggests that without such involvement, overall student achievement will not improve (Henderson, 1988). Typically, parents are most willing to assist their children during the primary grades. However, parental involvement at the intermediate, junior, and senior high levels has also been shown to increase student achievement.

Teachers need to try to involve all parents in the schools. Henderson (1988) found in her review of the research that it is minority children from low-income families who benefit the most when their parents are involved in the schools. Henderson also discovered that parents do not have to be well educated for student achievement to improve. Teachers may find that such parents possess feelings of inadequacy. For instance, a parent who was a high school dropout may associate school with failure but still want his or her child to graduate.

Some parents may find it difficult to get to the school—baby-sitters cost money, bosses don't always allow time off during working hours, transportation is not always readily available, and so on. And gone are the days when

Teachers need to provide parents with suggestions for encouraging student interests. For instance, this child's teacher suggested this pop-up book to encourage the child's interest in knighthood.

mothers stayed at home with their children, and families consisted of two parents living under the same roof. Nevertheless, the classroom teacher must reach out to parents so that students are given ample opportunities to become literate. It is up to the individual teacher to find creative ways of involving parents in the learning process. The need to reach the caretaker-parent is critical and more difficult today than at any other time in the history of American education. Following are some suggestions for assisting and encouraging parents to take a greater role in their children's literacy acquisition.

Because parents do not always have the financial resources to subscribe to a variety of magazines, a classroom teacher may recycle current issues of magazines by sending them home with a student for a specified period of time. Students can take turns taking the recent magazine issues home. Older issues can be sent home separately. A helpful "magazine pack" might include special-interest magazines to help various family members—for example, magazines with recipes, consumer reports, auto repair tips for parents and older siblings, and those with games and activities for children—as well as a newsmagazine. Fridays are good days to send home such magazine packs because most families have more time to spend reading together on weekends.

Another possibility is to arrange for class subscriptions to a local or nearby large-city newspaper. To increase subscriptions, many newspapers offer low- or no-rate subscriptions for students for a short period of time. Through a class's subscription to such newspapers, students can use the newspapers both at school and at home. In addition, the students' families can read the newspapers. Parents can encourage their children to read the grocery ads and cut out coupons, a practical, real-life literacy activity that also saves the family money.

Andrea L. Burkhart (1995) designed a family projects curriculum for her class. This enabled her students to work with their parents on a variety of different activities, such as tracing family roots and sharing an object that represented the family, such as food, music, dance, literature, or clothing. December was designated "biography month" when the students interviewed a family member and wrote a biography about that person. Other monthly features included weather, plants, measurement, poetry, and simple machines.

Teachers should keep parents informed of what is occurring in the classroom and what their children are currently studying. Mrs. Markgraft did this by having her students take turns working in pairs as classroom reporters and newspaper editors. The students wrote brief paragraphs to describe each day's activities, Monday through Friday, and edited and revised their "articles" for the "final edition." On the following Monday, copies were sent home for the parents to read (see figure 13.1).

Parents should also be included in as many on-site, school-related activities as possible. Research indicates participants in family literacy programs have significant reading and writing gains (Philliber, et al., 1996). For example, Mrs. Kilgard, a first-grade teacher in Texas, has several students whose parents are migrant workers. During the time that there is no field work because of the climate, she arranges activities for her students that include their parents. Early in February, for instance, her students write and mail invitations to their parents, inviting them to an afternoon tea. Mrs. Kilgard's students politely greet their parents at the classroom door, serve tea and cookies, and read the books they have written. Each child wears a large yellow button that says, in both English and Spanish, "Ask me for my autograph; I'm an author." The next day, the students again write short notes to their parents, this time thanking them for attending the tea.

Activities such as those just described promote parental involvement in literacy in a special, yet nonthreatening way. In general, parents are proud of their children and want to do more to help them but often do not know how or do not believe they have the time or the means to do so.

Classroom Volunteers

Opening the classroom to volunteers from the community is important, but such assistance is becoming more difficult to obtain. Because of the increasing number of working mothers and single-parent families, parent volunteers are becoming fewer in number. Senior citizens, however, make up a steadily increasing population of potential volunteers. The involvement of senior citizens in the classroom can serve a dual purpose by providing assistance for students and fulfilling the need of senior citizens to keep active and involved.

Many senior citizens are very active in volunteer work in the community and with their social and travel activities. Some enjoy physical activities, such as golf and tennis. A book for children to read is *Supergrandpa,* a picture book by David M. Schwartz (1991), which tells the true story of Gustaf Hakansson. A 66-year-old grandfather from Sweden, Hakansson wanted to enter a 1,000 mile

Figure 13.1
Here is a weekly class newspaper. Each day, two students are assigned to write, edit, and produce completed articles for the newspaper.

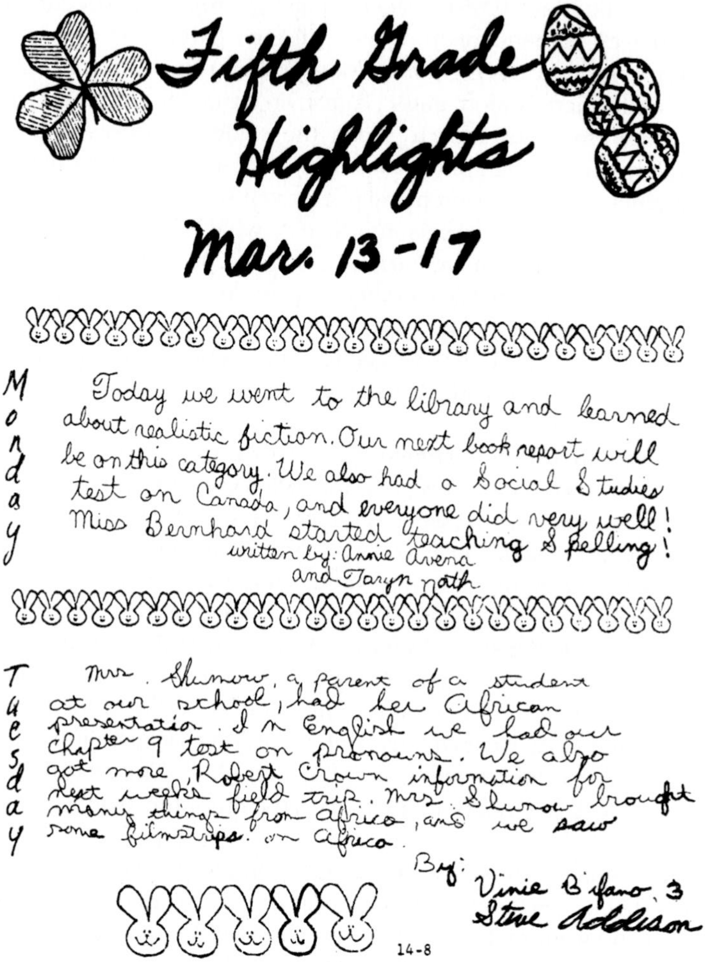

Fifth Grade Highlights

Mar. 13-17

Monday

Today we went to the library and learned about realistic fiction. Our next book report will be on this category. We also had a Social Studies test on Canada, and everyone did very well! Miss Bernhard started teaching Spelling!

written by: Annie Avena and Taryn Nath

Tuesday

Mrs. Shumow, a parent of a student at our school, had her African presentation. In English we had our Chapter 9 test on pronouns. We also got more Robert Crown information for next week's field trip. Mrs. Shumow brought many things from Africa, and we saw some filmstrips on Africa.

By: Vinie Bifano, Steve Addison

14-8

bike race. Because of his age, the judges refused to let him enter. Hakansson rode the 1,000 miles anyway and was the first to cross the finish line. He rode longer hours than his competitors, often riding during the night. This book is good to share with all elementary level children before having them interact with senior citizens, as they will gain a different perspective of older individuals.

Involving senior citizens in the classroom usually results in an enriched curriculum because as adults, they are able to share lifetime experiences as well as their skills. Storytelling, for instance, is a natural way in which senior citizens can describe local historical events that have occurred over the years. They can share old photographs of area landmarks and old newspaper clippings that the students can analyze and compare in terms of community growth or decline. Many senior citizens are involved in "Generation to Generation," in which they correspond with students via the Internet or through American Online. The students and seniors write stories together as well as share historical and other information.

Figure 13.1
(Continued)

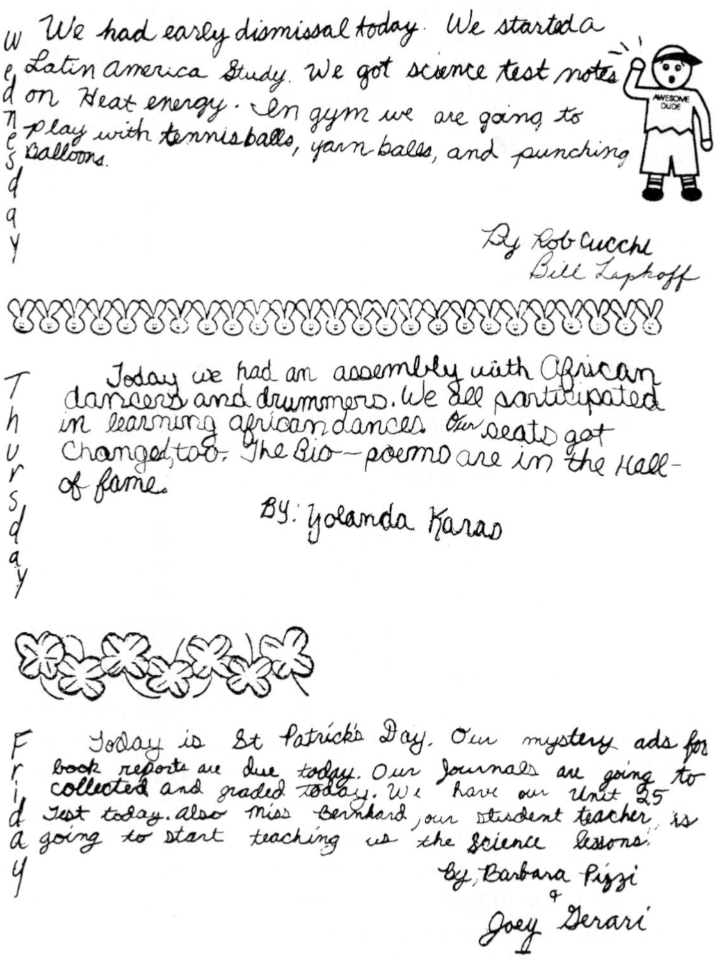

Wednesday

We had early dismissal today. We started a Latin America Study. We got science test notes on Heat energy. In gym we are going to play with tennisballs, yarn balls, and punching balloons.

By Rob Cucchi
Bill Lipkoff

Thursday

Today we had an assembly with African dancers and drummers. We all participated in learning african dances. Our seats got changed, too. The Bio—poems are in the Hall of fame.

By: Yolanda Karas

Friday

Today is St Patrick's Day. Our mystery ads for book reports are due today. Our Journals are going to collected and graded today. We have our Unit 25 Test today. also miss Bernhard, our student teacher, is going to start teaching us the Science lessons.

by, Barbara Pizzi
&
Joey Gerari

Since only 6 percent of people age 65 and older are in nursing homes (Hedberg, 1989), senior citizens are a viable classroom resource to tap. Many are active and involved in local community activities such as singing in church choirs, bowling in leagues, working as hospital volunteers, and the like. After retiring from one career, many individuals begin a new career because increased leisure time has allowed them to develop new interests and hobbies. Such individuals are excellent candidates for inclusion in school activities.

One fourth-grade class invited senior citizens from a nearby retirement center to participate in an activity each month of the school year. The monthly activities included the following:

September: Watermelon festival to celebrate the opening of school. Students were paired with senior citizens, and each pair made a time capsule from an empty paper towel roll to open at the end of the school year.

October:	A harvest festival for which some of the senior citizens taught the class how to square dance. Activities included a taffy pull, bobbing for apples, a three-legged race (student and senior citizen pairs), and other games from the 1800s.
November:	The class prepared a Thanksgiving Day feast for the senior citizens.
December:	The class performed their version of Dickens' *A Christmas Carol* and gave the retirement center a framed print purchased with funds from a bake sale.
January and February:	Pen pal months. Since most of the senior citizens were vacationing in a warmer climate, the students and senior citizens exchanged letters.
March:	Kite building and flying contest.
April:	Favorite book character day. Each person dressed up as his or her favorite character from a children's book.
May:	Spring planting of flower beds and a flowering crab tree purchased by the class for the school. Students volunteered to give up recess for a day to clean up trash and litter on the school playground before the spring planting day.
June:	The senior citizens hosted a picnic for the students at the retirement center. Students were allowed to fish in the center's pond and play games in the morning. The afternoon was devoted to skits and storytelling by both students and senior citizens.

There are other ways to involve senior citizens. Since there are many senior citizen travel groups, teachers may contact the local senior citizens club or a travel agency and arrange to have the senior citizens serve as pen pals during one of their upcoming trips. Even if a trip is no more than a one-day shopping expedition to San Francisco from Los Angeles, receiving a picture postcard of the Golden Gate Bridge or Fisherman's Wharf in San Francisco with a brief note scribbled on the back can mean a great deal to a child who has never been outside Los Angeles. On longer trips, the tourists may keep a travel log, writing down events as they occur to send to their student pen pals on a regular basis.

Inviting guest speakers is still another way to link the classroom with the community. Because today's children are predicted to change jobs at least eight times during their lives, it is important that they discover what careers are currently available. Having people from a wide variety of career areas share some of their work experiences adds to a child's knowledge base. Rather than setting aside one day as "Career Day" and bringing in 20 people to speak, it is far more effective to invite one person at a time to speak to the class. This frees the speaker from having to compete for the audience's attention and allows the students to study one career at a time and to formulate questions for the speaker before the presentation.

Asking people who live near the school to speak to the class is relevant to students because those individuals are a part of the community, and children see many of them in the neighborhood, in local stores, and at church. Involving such people promotes a sense of belonging for children, and thereby strengthens the community. When inviting local people into the classroom, the teacher should spend some time helping them to decide on an appropriate speaking topic. For example, if the teacher can suggest one of the skills that an individual uses daily in his or her work and that the students will be able to understand and appreciate, both the students and the guest speaker will benefit. Skills that local merchants must possess include the following:

Banker:	determining a client's credit standing; explaining the different types of accounts
Beautician:	determining appropriate hair styles; pleasing hard-to-please customers
Gas Station Owner:	handling flammable materials; locating engine problems; giving directions to strangers
Grocery Store Manager:	displaying merchandise; estimating costs; handling perishables
Hardware Store Manager:	understanding customers' problems in order to sell them the right parts; predicting seasonal sales

A local naturalist with the U.S. Department of the Interior was a guest of Mr. Bauman's fourth-grade class. The class had been studying the flora and fauna of the area, and the naturalist explained the effects of the Ice Age and glacial movement in geological terms, showing slides to demonstrate his points. A few days after the naturalist's presentation, one student made a flora and fauna web for the book *Sarah, Plain and Tall* by Patricia MacLachlan (1985) (see figure 13.2).

The World

Students have access to events that are occurring around the world at a moment's notice via telecommunication satellites. Because such information is so readily available, children should be encouraged to discover more about widely reported locations. For example, Alaska was often in the news during 1989. In January and February, the state experienced the coldest temperatures on record: as low as –60° F. During that period, Mr. Sable, a fifth-grade teacher, used the opportunity to have students read books, magazines, and newspaper articles about the country's largest state. Most of the students were unaware that fishing and tourism are major industries in Alaska. Other students, curious about how the cold affects daily routines, sought out information on the temperatures at which oil and tires freeze.

Later that spring, the massive oil spill, off the Alaskan coastline after an oil tanker ran aground, was given massive media attention for several weeks. Because of their earlier studies of the state, the students developed empathy for the people of Alaska and their environment. A group of five students did a report on the effects of an oil spill on the environment and, by using motor oil, feathers, and a piece of an old fur coat, demonstrated how difficult it is to remove oil from birds and mammals. Another group of students wrote letters to their congressmen urging stricter laws to protect the environment from such disasters. Still another group wrote to the state's department of natural resources for information about the severity of the oil spill's impact on fish hatcheries and the future of salmon and wildlife in the area.

Mr. Sable effectively capitalized on his students' natural interests as he taught reading, writing, speaking, and listening, as well as math, science, and social studies. Undoubtedly, the activities in which Mr. Sable's students took part

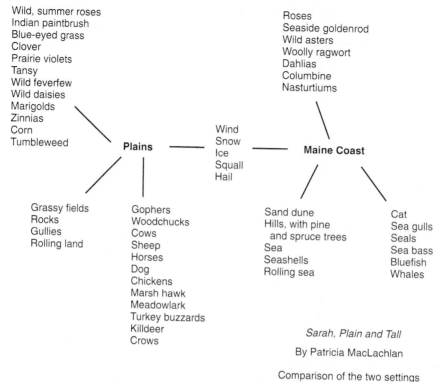

Wild, summer roses
Indian paintbrush
Blue-eyed grass
Clover
Prairie violets
Tansy
Wild feverfew
Wild daisies
Marigolds
Zinnias
Corn
Tumbleweed

Roses
Seaside goldenrod
Wild asters
Woolly ragwort
Dahlias
Columbine
Nasturtiums

Plains

Wind
Snow
Ice
Squall
Hail

Maine Coast

Grassy fields
Rocks
Gullies
Rolling land

Gophers
Woodchucks
Cows
Sheep
Horses
Dog
Chickens
Marsh hawk
Meadowlark
Turkey buzzards
Killdeer
Crows

Sand dune
Hills, with pine
  and spruce trees
Sea
Seashells
Rolling sea

Cat
Sea gulls
Seals
Sea bass
Bluefish
Whales

Sarah, Plain and Tall

By Patricia MacLachlan

Comparison of the two settings
(vegetation, animals, geology, weather)

Figure 13.2
A web comparing the flora and fauna of the Maine coast with those of the prairie.

will make them more sensitive to the state and people of Alaska than the assigned reading of a chapter about Alaska in a social studies textbook would have.

Happenings throughout the world can similarly be used to stimulate students' learning. When Mr. Boatswain's students wanted to find out more about UNESCO, the United Nations children's relief organization, he arranged to have an overseas conference phone call with one of the organization's directors. The students were required to prepare their questions in advance, and each student was permitted to ask one question. All of the questions were written on the chalkboard before the conference call. Months after the phone call, the students were still interested in UNESCO's programs, so they held a bake sale and donated the proceeds to UNESCO.

Arranging to have teleconferences with classes in other states two or three times a year can foster cooperative learning. Common interests can be pursued by sending letters, poetry, reports, riddles, jokes, and stories back and forth via computers and traditional mail. Such activities expand students' worlds by widening the scope of their interests and their goals.

In the Classroom Mini Lesson

Bringing Community History into the Classroom

*B*arbara Cooney's (1988) *Island Boy* tells the story of Matthias, who was born on Tibbetts Island off the coast of Maine. As a boy, Matthias became a cabin boy on his uncle's schooner, the "Six Brothers," and years later he became the captain of the ship. However, he couldn't forget the island, and he returned there to live and raise a family. As Matthias grew older, he shared the stories of the island with his grandson, who also loved Tibbetts Island. The book ends with Matthias's drowning in rough seas. The theme of the book is repeated throughout: "It is good to see the world beyond the bay, then you will know where your heart lies."

      After reading the book to the class, have a member of the local historical society visit the class to tell about two of the community's early founders. Students can then write a "fictionalized" biography about one of the two and his or her life in the area.

Cooney, B. (1988). *Island boy.* New York: Viking.

S u m m a r y

Through a variety of means, students can discover how the language arts are a major part of everyday life. By interacting with classroom guests and volunteers, children learn from the experiences of adults. By helping to keep students abreast of events occurring in their communities and throughout the United States and the world, the teacher encourages their sensitivity to other cultures and countries. As a result, students are more likely to become active citizens and lifelong learners—a worthy goal for a language arts program.

Questions

1. Why do elementary students need to be aware of the world outside their classroom?
2. In what ways can teachers involve parents in classroom activities?
3. The school dropout rate is high among minority children. What can be done to reduce this trend? How are the language arts involved?
4. How can a community's involvement in the activities of a class benefit student's language arts skills?

Activities

1. Develop a unit that incorporates the teaching of the language arts and involves individuals, businesses, or groups from outside the school setting.
2. Write to a relative in a distant state or foreign country and ask the relative to give you the name and address of the principal of the elementary school in his or her neighborhood. After you receive the information, write a letter to the principal to arrange a pen pal program for your students.
3. Make a list of potential guest speakers who could provide insight into their fields of work.
4. Brainstorm for ways in which students can interact with local businesses in your area.

Akroyd, S. (1995) Forming a parent reading-writing class: Connecting cultures, one pen at a time. *The Reading Teacher, 48*(7), 580-587.

Burkhart, A. L. (1995). Breaking the parental barrier. *The Reading Teacher, 48*(7), 634-635.

Edwards, P. A. (1991). Fostering early literacy through parent coaching. In E. H. Hiebert (Ed.), *Literacy for a diverse society: Perspectives, practices, and policies.* New York: Teachers College Press.

Ford, M. P. (1992). A single rose: Remembrances of a good teacher. *The Reading Teacher, 45*(7), 512-513.

Fowler, R. C., & Corley, K. K. (1996). Linking families, building community. *Educational Leadership, 53*(7), 24-26.

Fredericks, A. D., & Rasinski, T. V. (1990). Whole language and parents: Natural partners. *The Reading Teacher, 43*(9), 692-694.

Klobukowski, P. (1996). Parents, buddy journals, and reader response. *The Reading Teacher, 49*(4), 349-350.

References

Burkhart, A. L. (1995). Breaking the parental barrier. *The Reading Teacher, 48*(7), 634-635.

Cummins, J. (1986). Empowering minority students: A framework for intervention. *Harvard Educational Review, 56*(1), 18-36.

Ford, M. P. (1992). A single rose: Remembrances of a good teacher. *The Reading Teacher, 45*(7), 512-513.

Fraatz, J. M. B. (1987). *The politics of reading: Power, opportunity, and the prospects for change in America's public schools.* New York: Teachers College Press.

Heath, S. B. (1980). The functions and uses of literacy. *Journal of Communications 30,* 123-133.

Hedberg, A. (1989). The crisis that lurks. *Money, 18*(10), 148-157.

Henderson, A. (1988). Parents are a school's best friend. *Phi Delta Kappan, 70*(1), 148-153.

MacLachlan, P. (1985). *Sarah, plain and tall.* New York: Harper & Row.

McNaughton, S. (1981). The influence of immediate teacher correction on self-corrections and proficient oral reading. *Journal of Reading Behavior, 13*(1), 367-371.

Philliber, W. W., Spillman, R. E., & King, R. E. (1996). Consequences of family literacy for adults and children: Some preliminary findings. *Journal of Adolescent and Adult Literacy, 39*(7), 558-565.

Routman, R. (1991). *Invitations: Changing as teachers and learners, K-12.* Portsmouth, NH: Heinemann.

Schwartz, D. M. (1991). *Supergrandpa* (B. Dodson, Illus.) New York: Lothrop, Lee, & Shepard.

Smith, F. (1989). Overselling literacy. *Phi Delta Kappan, 70*(5), 353-359.

Wilson, P. T. (1988). *Let's think about reading and reading instruction: A primer for tutors and teachers.* Dubuque, IA: Kendall/Hunt.

Appendix

Books for the Teacher's Library

Atwell, N. (1987). *In the middle.* Portsmouth, NH: Heinemann.
Considered a classic, this book outlines how to teach reading and writing at the intermediate/middle-school level. Teachers of all grades will find something of interest in this book.

Calkins, L. & Harwayne, S. (1991). *Living between the lines.* Portsmouth, NH: Heinemann.
This book describes the reading-writing connection from the authors' observations of and participation in elementary classrooms. The focus is on teaching reading and writing with a process emphasis.

Cullinan, B. E. (Ed.). (1987). *Children's literature in the reading program.* Newark, DE: International Reading Association.
This book has sold more copies than any other IRA publication. It describes various ways of incorporating children's literature across the curriculum.

Cullinan, B. E. (Ed.). (1992). *Invitation to read: More children's literature in the reading program.* Newark, DE: International Reading Association.
A superb sequel to her 1987 edited book, this follow-up features chapters by Tomie de Paola and Bill Martin, Jr.

Cullinan, B., & Galda, L. (1994). *Literature and the child* (4th ed.). Orlando, FL: Harcourt Brace Jovanovich.
An excellent overview of children's literature, this book contains numerous resources.

Daniels, H. (1994). *Literature circles: Voice and choice in the student-centered classroom.* York, ME: Stenhouse.
Literature circles at all grade levels are explored in this book.

Gill, K. (Ed.). (1993). *Process and portfolios in writing instruction.* Urbana, IL: National Council of Teachers of English.
This is a short but thorough handbook of how to incorporate portfolios into the curriculum.

Graves, D. H. (1994). *A fresh look at writing.* Portsmouth, NH: Heinemann.
This is an updated version of his classic book, *Writing: Teachers & Children at Work.* Many good suggestions for supporting and assessing children's writing are included in this book.

Hennings, D. G. (1992). *Beyond the read aloud: Learning to read through listening to and reflecting on literature.* Bloomington, IN: Phi Delta Kappa.
This book describes how to organize and conduct read alouds, as well as follow-up activities.

Hiebert, E. H. (1991). *Literacy for a diverse society: Perspectives, practices, and policies.* New York: Teachers College Press.
This book deals with multicultural issues involved in literacy acquisition.

Kruse, G. M., Horning, K. T., Lindgren, M. V., & Odahowski, K. (1991). *Multicultural literature for children and young adults.* **Madison, WI: Cooperative Children's Book Center, University of Wisconsin.**
This is a selected listing of books from 1980 to 1990 written by and about minorities.

Laughlin, M. K., & Street, T. P. (1992). *Literature-based art and music: Children's books and activities to enrich the K–5 curriculum.* **Phoenix, AZ: Oryx.**
Several trade books along with accompanying activities are provided. This is an especially good book for the elementary teacher who teaches in a district that doesn't employ art or music teachers.

McClure, A. A., & Kristo, J. V. (Eds.). (1994). *Inviting children's responses to literature: Guides to 57 notables.* **Urbana, IL: National Council of Teachers of English.**
This is a terrific resource book that briefly describes 57 notable trade books and how to incorporate them into the classroom.

Norton, D. (1995). *Through the eyes of a child* (4th ed.). **Columbus, OH: Merrill.**
This book contains full-color illustrations taken from children's books. It is a superb resource of children's literature.

Roser, N. L., & Martinez, M. G. (Eds.). (1995). *Book talk and beyond: Children and teachers respond to literature.* **Newark, DE: International Reading Association.**
This collection of writings is divided into four sections: getting ready for story talk, the tools of story talk, guiding book talk, and other responses to literature.

Routman, R. (1991). *Invitations.* **Portsmouth, NH: Heinemann.**
An extension of Routman's earlier book, *Transitions,* this book describes how to adopt the whole language approach in kindergarten through 12th grade.

Silvey, A. (1995). *Children's Books and Their Creators.* **Boston: Houghton Mifflin.**
This reference book covers the books children are reading now. In autobiographical sketches, 75 contemporary writers and illustrators comment on the meaning of their works for children and themselves. This is a good library reference addition.

Tierney, R. J., Carter, M. A., & Desai, L. E. (1991). *Portfolio assessment in the reading/writing classroom.* **Norwood, MA: Christopher-Gordon.**
This book was written after 2 years of classroom experimentation with portfolio assessment. It provides a comprehensive overview of why and how to use portfolios.

Tompkins, G. (1994). *Teaching writing* (2nd ed.). **Columbus, OH: Merrill.**
Probably the best book currently available on the teaching of writing, it offers a wealth of practical ideas and suggestions, all based upon sound theory and research.

Vopat, J. (1994). *The parent project: A workshop approach to parent involvement.* **York, ME: Stenhouse.**
Designed for teachers who want to encourage parents to become more involved in school activities, this book provides lots of specific ideas and suggestions.

Professional Journals

Book Links

American Library Association
50 E. Huron Street
Chicago, IL 60611

An excellent source of information about new books, the columns within this journal focus on the use of children's literature with students and provide background information about authors and books.

Journal of Adolescent and Adult Literacy

International Reading Association
800 Barksdale Road, P.O. Box 8139
Newark, DE 19714-8139

This journal is appropriate for teachers in the intermediate grades and above.

Language Arts

National Council of Teachers of English
1111 Kenyon Road
Urbana, IL 61801

This journal covers the language arts from preschool through Grade 6. Each issue contains a column on current research in the language arts plus a list of children's books.

The New Advocate

Christopher-Gordon Publishers
480 Washington Street
Norwood, MA 02062

This quarterly journal provides in-depth information about children's literature, including articles and book reviews.

Reading Horizons

Reading Center and Clinic
Western Michigan University
Kalamazoo, MI 49008

Published five times a year, this outstanding journal contains a bevy of articles that link theory and practice and is very reasonably priced.

The Reading Teacher

International Reading Association
800 Barksdale Road, P.O. Box 8139
Newark, DE 19714-8139

This is an old standard for elementary teachers. It includes articles on the elements of language, sections on children's literature, and practical classroom ideas.

WEB (Wonderfully Exciting Books)

Martha L. King Center for Language and Literacy
The Ohio State University
Columbus, OH 43210

This journal reviews recently published children's books and their role in the classroom.

Caldecott Medal and Honor Books
(1996–1970)

1996: *Officer Buckle and Gloria* by Peggy Rathmann
Honor Books: *Alphabet City* by Stephen Johnson; *Zin! Zin! Zin!: A Violin* by Lloyd Moss, illustrated by Marjorie Priceman; *The Faithful Friend* by Robert San Souci, illustrated by Brian Pinkney; *Tops and Bottoms* by Janet Stevens

1995: *Smoky Night* by Eve Bunting, illustrated by David Diaz
Honor Books: *Swamp Angel* by Anne Issacs, illustrated by Paul O. Zelinsky; *John Henry* by Julius Lester, illustrated by Jerry Pinkney; *Time Flies* by Eric Rohmann

1994: *Grandfather's Journey* by Allen Say
Honor Books: *Peppe the Lamplighter* by Elisa Barton, illustrated by Ted Lewin; *In the Small, Small Pond* by Denise Fleming; *Owen* by Kevin Henkes; *Raven: A Trickster Tale from the Pacific Northwest* by Gerald McDermott; *Yo! Yes?* by Chris Raschka

1993: *Mirette on the Highwire* by Emily Arnold McCully
Honor Books: *Seven Blind Mice* by Ed Young; *The Stinky Cheese Man & Other Fairly Stupid Tales* by Jon Scieszka, illustrated by Lane Smith; *Working Cotton* by Sherley Anne Williams, illustrated by Carole Byard

1992: *Tuesday* by David Wiesner
Honor Book; *Tar Bleach* by Faith Ringgold

1991: *Black and White* by David Macaulay
Honor Books: *Puss in Boots* by Fred Marcellino; *"More, More, More," Said the Baby: Three Love Stories* by Vera B. Williams

1990: *Lon Po Po: A Red-Riding Hood Story from China* translated by Ed Young
Honor Books: *Bill Peet, an Autobiography* by Bill Peet; *Color Zoo* by Lois Ehlert; *Hershel and the Hanukkah Goblins* by Eric Kimmel, illustrated by Trina Schart Hyman; *The Talking Eggs* by Robert D. San Souci, illustrated by Jerry Pinkney

1989: *Song and Dance Man* by Karen Ackerman, illustrated by Stephen Gammell
Honor Books: *The Boy of the Three-Year Nap* by Dianne Snyder, illustrated by Allen Say; *Free Fall* by David Wiesner; *Goldilocks* retold and illustrated by James Marshall; *Mirandy and Brother Wind* by Patricia C. McKissack, illustrated by Jerry Pinkney

1988: *Owl Moon* by Jane Yolen, illustrated by John Schoenherr
Honor Book: *Mufaro's Beautiful Daughters: An African Tale* by John Steptoe

1987: *Hey, Al* by Arthur Yorinks, illustrated by Richard Egielski
Honor Books: *Alphabatics* by Susie MacDonald; *Rumpelstiltskin* retold and illustrated by Paul O. Zelinsky; *The Village of Round and Square Houses* by Ann Grifalconi

1986: *The Polar Express* by Chris Van Allsburg
Honor Books: *King Bidgood's in the Bathtub* by Audrey Wood, illustrated by Don Wood; *The Relatives Came* by Cynthia Rylant, illustrated by Richard Egielski

1985: *St. George and the Dragon* retold by Margaret Hodges, illustrated by Trina Schart Hyman
Honor Book: *Hansel and Gretel* retold by Rika Lesser, illustrated by Paul O. Zelinsky

1984: *The Glorious Flight: Across the Channel with Louis Bleriot* by Alice and Martin Provensen
Honor Books: *Ten, Nine, Eight* by Molly Bang; *Little Red Riding Hood* retold and illustrated by Trina Schart Hyman

1983: *Shadow* by Blaise Cendrars, illustrated by Marcia Brown
Honor Books: *When I Was Young in the Mountains* by Cynthia Rylant, illustrated by Diane Goode; *Chair for My Mother* by Vera B. Williams

1982: *Jumanji* by Chris Van Allsburg
Honor Books: *A Visit to William Blake's Inn: Poems for Innocent and Experienced Travelers* by Nancy Willard, illustrated by Alice and Martin Provensen; *Where the Buffaloes Begin* by Olaf Baker, illustrated by Stephen Gammell; *On Market Street* by Arnold Lobel, illustrated by Anita Lobel; *Outside Over There* by Maurice Sendak

1981: *Fables* by Arnold Lobel
Honor Books: *The Bremen-Town Musicians* by Ilse Plume; *The Grey Lady and the Strawberry Snatcher* by Molly Bang; *Mice Twice* by Joseph Low; *Truck* by Donald Crews

1980: *Ox-Cart Man* by Donald Hall, illustrated by Barbara Cooney
Honor Books: *Ben's Trumpet* by Rachel Isadora; *The Treasure* by Uri Shulevitz; *The Garden of Abdul Gasazi* by Chris Van Allsburg

1979: *The Girl Who Loved Wild Horses* by Paul Goble
Honor Books: *Freight Train* by Donald Crews; *The Way to Start A Day* by Byrd Baylor, illustrated by Peter Parnall

1978: *Noah's Ark* by Peter Spier
Honor Books: *Castle* by David Macaulay; *It Could Always Be Worse* retold and illustrated by Margot Zemach

1977: *Ashanti to Zulu: African Traditions* by Margaret Musgrove, illustrated by Leo and Diane Dillon
Honor Books: *The Amazing Bone* by William Steig; *The Contest* retold and illustrated by Nony Hogrogrian; *Fish for Supper* by M.B. Goffstein; *The Golem: A Jewish Legend* by Beverly Brodsky McDermott; *Hawk, I'm Your Brother* by Byrd Baylor, illustrated by Peter Parnall

1976: *Why Mosquitoes Buzz in People's Ears* retold by Verna Aardema, illustrated by Leo and Diane Dillon
Honor Books: *The Desert Is Theirs* by Byrd Baylor, illustrated by Peter Parnall; *Strega Nona* retold and illustrated by Tomie de Paola

1975: *Arrow to the Sun* adapted and illustrated by Gerald McDermott
Honor Book: *Jambo Mean Hello: A Swahili Alphabet Book* by Muriel Feelings, illustrated by Tom Feelings

1974: *Duffy and the Devil* by Harve Zemach, illustrated by Margot Zemach
Honor Books: *Three Jovial Huntsmen* by Susan Jeffers; *Cathedral: The Story of Its Construction* by David Macaulay

1973: *The Funny Little Woman* retold by Arlene Mosel, illustrated by Blair Lent
Honor Books: *Anansi the Spider: A Tale from the Ashanti* adapted and illustrated by Gerald McDermott; *Hosie's Alphabet* by Hosea Tobias and Lisa Baskin, illustrated by Leonard Baskin; *Snow White and the Seven Dwarfs* translated by Randall Jarrell, illustrated by Nancy Ekholm Burkert; *When Clay Sings* by Byrd Baylor, illustrated by Tom Bahti

1972: *One Fine Day* by Nonny Hogrogian
Honor Books: *If All the Seas Were One Sea* by Janina Domanska; *Moja Means One: Swahili Counting Book* by Muriel Feelings, illustrated by Tom Feelings; *Hildilid's Night* by Cheli Duran Ryan, illustrated by Arnold Lobel

1971: *A Story: An African Tale* by Gary E. Haley
Honor Books: *The Angry Moon* by William Sleator, illustrated by Blair Lent; *Frog and Toad are Friends* by Arnold Lobel; *In the Night Kitchen* by Maurice Sendak

1970: *Sylvester and the Magic Pebble* by William Steig
Honor Books: *Goggles!* by Ezra Jack Keats; *Alexander and the Wind-Up Mouse* by Leo Lionni; *Pop Corn and Ma Goodness* by Edna Mitchell, illustrated by Robert Andrew Parker; *Thy Friend, Obadiah* by Brinton Turkle; *The Judge: An Untrue Tale* by Have Zemach, illustrated by Margot Zemac

Newbery Medal and Honor Books (1996–1970)

1996: *The Midwife's Apprentice* by Karen Cushman
Honor Books: *What Jamie Saw* by Carolyn Coleman; *The Watsons Go to Birmingham, 1963* by Christopher Paul Curtis; *Yolanda's Genius* by Carol Fenner; *The Great Fire* by Jim Murphy

1995: *Walk Two Moons* by Sharon Creech
Honor Books: *Catherine, Called Birdy* by Karen Cushman; *The Ear, the Eye, and the Arm* by Nancy Farmer

1994: *The Giver* by Lois Lowry
Honor Books: *Crazy Lady* by Jane Leslie Conly; *Eleanor Roosevelt: A Life of Discovery* by Russell Freeman; *Dragon's Gate* by Laurence Yep

1993: *Missing May* by Cynthia Rylant
Honor Books: *What Hearts* by Bruce Brooks; *The Dark-thirty: Southern Tales of the Supernatural* by Patricia C. McKissack; *Somewhere in the Darkness* by Walter Dean Myers

1992: *Shiloh* by Phyllis Reynolds Naylor
Honor Books: *Nothing But the Truth* by Avi; *The Wright Brothers: How They Invented the Airplane* by Russell Freedman

1991: *Maniac Magee* by Jerry Spinelli
Honor Book: *The True Confessions of Charlotte Doyle* by Avi

1990: *Number the Stars* by Lois Lowry
Honor Books: *Afternoon of the Elves* by Janet Taylor Lisle; *Shabanu, Daughter of the Wind* by Susan Fisher Staples; *The Winter Room* by Gary Paulsen

1989: *Joyful Noise: Poems for Two Voices* by Paul Fleischman
Honor Books: *In the Beginning: Creation Stories from around the World* by Virginia Hamilton; *Scorpions* by Walter Dean Myers

1988: *Lincoln: A Photobiography* by Russell Freedman
Honor Books: *After the Rain* by Norma Fox Mazer; *Hatchet* by Gary Paulsen

1987: *The Whipping Boy* by Sid Fleischman
Honor Books: *A Fine White Dust* by Cynthia Rylant; *On My Honor* by Marion Dane Bauer; *Volcano: The Eruption and Healing of Mount St Helens* by Patricia Lauber

1986: *Sarah, Plain and Tall* by Patricia MacLachlan
Honor Books: *Commodore Perry in the Land of the Shogun* by Rhoda Blumberg; *Dogsong* by Gary Paulsen

1985: *The Hero and the Crown* by Robin McKinley
Honor Books: *Like Jake and Me* by Mavis Jukes; *The Moves Make the Man* by Bruce Brooks; *One-Eyed Cat* by Paula Fox

1984: *Dear Mr. Henshaw* by Beverly Cleary
Honor Books: *The Sign of the Beaver* by Elizabeth George Speare; *A Solitary Blue* by Cynthia Voigt; *The Wish Giver* by Bill Brittain

1983: *Dicey's Song* by Cynthia Voigt
Honor Books: *Blue Sword* by Robin McKinley; *Dr. Desoto* by William Steig; *Graven Images* by Paul Fleischman; *Homesick: My Own Story* by Jean Fritz; *Sweet Whisper, Brother Rush* by Virginia Hamilton

1982: *A Visit to William Blake's Inn: Poems for Innocent and Experienced Travelers* by Nancy Willard
Honor Books: *Ramona Quimby, Age 8* by Beverly Cleary; *Upon the Head of the Goat: A Childhood in Hungary, 1939-1944* by Aranka Siegal

1981: *Jacob Have I Loved* by Katherine Paterson
Honor Books: *The Fledgling* by Jane Langton; *A Ring of Endless Light* by Madeleine L'Engle

1980: *A Gathering of Days: A New England Girl's Journal 1830-32* by Joan Blos

1979: *The Westing Game* by Ellen Raskin
Honor Book: *The Great Gilly Hopkins* by Katherine Paterson

1978: *Bridge to Terabithia* by Katherine Paterson
Honor Books: *Ramona and Her Father* by Beverly Cleary; *Anpao: An American Indian Odyssey* by Jamake Highwater

1977: *Roll of Thunder, Hear My Cry* by Mildred D. Taylor
Honor Books: *Abel's Island* by William Steig; *A String in the Harp* by Nancy Bond

1976: *The Grey King* by Susan Cooper
Honor Books: *The Hundred Penny Box* by Sharon Bell Mathis; *Dragonwings* by Laurence Yep

1975: *M. C. Higgins, the Great* by Virginia Hamilton
Honor Books: *Figgs & Phantoms* by Ellen Raskin; *My Brother Sam Is Dead* by James Lincoln Collier and Christopher Collier; *The Perilous Gard* by Elizabeth Marie Pope; *Philip Hall Likes Me. I Reckon Maybe* by Bette Greene

1974: *The Slave Dancer* by Paula Fox
Honor Book: *The Dark is Rising* by Susan Cooper

1973: *Julie of the Wolves* by Jean Craighead George
Honor Books: *Frog and Toad Together* by Arnold Lobel; *The Upstairs Room* by Johanna Reiss; *The Witches of Worm* by Zilpha Keatley Snyder

1972: *Mrs. Frisby and the Rats of NIMH* by Robert C. O'Brien
Honor Books: *Incident at Hawk's Hill* by Alan W. Eckert; *The Planet of Junior Brown* by Virginia Hamilton; *The Tombs of Atuan* by Ursula K. Le Guin; *Annie and the Old One* by Miska Miles; *The Headless Cupid* by Zilpha Keatley Snyder

1971: *Summer of the Swans* by Betsy Byars
Honor Books: *Kneeknock Rise* by Natalie Babbitt; *Enchantress from the Stars* by Sylvia Louis Engdahl; *Sing Down the Moon* by Scott O'Dell

1970: *Sounder* by William H. Armstrong
Honor Books: *Our Eddie* by Sulamith Ish-Kishor; *The Many Ways of Seeing: An Introduction to the Pleasures of Art* by Janet Gaylord Moore; *Journey Outside* by Mary Q. Steele

Multicultural Literature for Children

African-American

Adoff, A. (1973). *The poetry of Black America: Anthology of the 20th century.* New York: Harper & Row. (K–8)

Adoff, A. (1973). *Black is brown is tan.* New York: Harper & Row. (K–8)

Arkhurst, J. C. (1964). *The adventures of spider: West African folktales.* Boston: Little, Brown. (K–2)

Arkhurst, J. C. (1986). *Lion and the ostrich chicks.* New York: Atheneum. (3–5)

Bryan, A. (1991). *All night, all day: A child's first book of African-American spirituals.* New York: Macmillan/Atheneum. (3–8)

Burchard, P. (1995). *Charlotte Forten: A black teacher in the Civil War.* New York: Crown. (4–7)

Collier, J., & Collier, C. (1981) *Jump ship to freedom.* New York: Delacorte. (5–8)

Cox, C. (1993). *The forgotten heroes: The story of the Buffalo Soldiers.* New York: Scholastic. (5–8)

Farris, P. J. (1996). *Young mouse and elephant: An East African folktale* (V. Gorbachev, Illus.). Boston: Houghton Mifflin. (K–3)

Golenbeck, P. (1990). *Teammates* (P. Bacon, Illus.). Orlando, FL: Gulliver. (3–8)

Hamilton, V. (1974). *Paul Robeson: The life and times of a free black man.* New York: Harper & Row. (5–8)

Hamilton, V. (1985). *The people could fly: American black folktales.* (L. Dillon & D. Dillon, Illus.) New York: Knopf. (3–8)

Hamilton, V. (1991). *The all Jahdu storybook* (B. Moser, Illus.). San Diego: Harcourt Brace. (3–8)

Hamilton, V. (1992). *Drylongso* (J. Pinkney, Illus.). San Diego: Harcourt Brace. (3–6)

Hansen, J. (1986). *Which way freedom?* New York: Walker. (5–8)

Harris, J. C. (1986). *Jump! The adventures of Brer Rabbit.* Orlando, FL: Harcourt Brace Jovanovich. (K–8)

Haskins, J. (1977). *The life and death of Martin Luther King, Jr.* New York: Lothrop, Lee, & Shepard. (4–8)

Haskins, J. (1993). *Get on board: The story of the Underground Railroad.* New York: Scholastic. (5–8)

Hoffman, M. (1991). *Amazing Grace* (C. Birch, Illus.). New York: Dial. (K–3)

Hopkinson, D. (1993). *Sweet Clara and the freedom quilt* (J. Ransome, Illus.). New York: Knopf. (2–5)

Hoyt-Goldsmith, D. (1993). *Celebrating Kwanzaa* (L. Midgale, Illus.). New York: Holiday. (K–8)

Hurmence, B. (1982). *A girl called boy.* Boston: Houghton Mifflin. (4–6)

Isadora, R. (1991). *At the crossroads.* New York: Greenwillow. (3–5)

Kimmel, E. A. (1994). *Anansi and the talking melon* (J. Stevens, Illus.). New York: Holiday. (K-3)

Knutson, B. (1990). *How the guinea fowl got her spots: A Swahili tale of friendship.* New York: Carolrhoda. (K-2)

Lawrence, J. (1993). *The great migration: An American story.* New York: HarperCollins. (3-6)

McKillack, P. (1986). *Jesse Jackson.* New York: Scholastic. (4-6)

Meltzer, M. (1984). *Black Americans: A history in their own words.* New York: HarperCollins/Crowell. (4-8)

Mettger, Z. (1994). *Till victory is won: Black soldiers in the Civil War.* New York: Lodestar. (5-9)

Mollel, T. M. (1995). *Big boy* (E. B. Lewis, Illus.). New York: Clarion (K-3)

Myers, W. D. (1988). *Scorpions.* New York: Harper & Row. (5-8)

Myers, W. D. (1991). *Now is your time!: The African American struggle for freedom.* New York: HarperCollins. (4-8)

Petry, A. (1955). *Harriet Tubman: Conductor on the Underground Railroad.* New York: Crowell. (4-6)

Pinkney, A. D. (1993). *Seven candles for Kwanzaa* (B. Pinkney, Illus.). New York: Dial. (K-up)

Ringgold, F. (1991). *Tar beach.* New York: Crown (1-3)

Ringgold, F. (1992). *Aunt Harriet's Underground Railroad in the sky.* New York: Crown. (1-4)

Yates, E. (1950). *Amos Fortune, free man.* New York: Dutton. (4-6)

Asian-African

Cassedy, S. & Suetake, K. (Trans.). (1992). *Red dragonfly on my shoulder* (M. Bang, Illus.). New York: HarperCollins. (K-3)

Choi, N. S. (1991). *Year of impossible goodbyes.* Boston: Houghton Mifflin. (4-8)

Clark, A. N. (1978). *To stand against the wind.* New York: Viking. (4-8)

Coerr, E. (1993). *Sadako* (E. Young, Illus.). New York: Putnam. (3-8)

Compton, P. A. (1991). *The terrible eek* (S. Hamanaka, Illus.). New York: Simon & Schuster. (1-3)

Conger, D. (1987). *Many lands, many stories: Asian folktales for children.* New York: Tuttle. (3-5)

Dunn, M., & Ardath, M. (1983). *The absolutely perfect horse.* New York: Harper & Row. (3-6)

Hamanaka, S. (1990). *The journey: Japanese Americans, racism, and renewal.* New York: Orchard. (4-7)

Haugaard, E. C. (1995). *The revenge of the forty-seven samurai.* Boston: Houghton Mifflin. (6-8)

Hong, L. T. (1991). *How the ox star fell from heaven.* New York: Albert Whitman. (4-6)

Johnson, R. (1992). *Kenji and the magic geese* (J. Tseng & M. Tseng, Illus.). New York: Simon & Schuster. (K-2)

Lord, B. B. (1984). *In the year of the boar and Jackie Robinson.* New York: Harper & Row. (4-6)

Morris, W. (1992). *The future of Yen-Tzu* (F. Henstra, Illus.). New York: Atheneum. (1-4)

Nhuong, H. Q. (1982). *The land I lost: Adventures of a boy in Vietnam.* New York: Harper & Row. (4-8)

Say, A. (1990). *El chino.* Boston: Houghton Mifflin. (4-8)

Say, A. (1993). *Grandfather's journey.* Boston: Houghton Mifflin. (K-3)

Shea, P. D. (1995). *The whispering cloth* (A. Riggio & Y. Yang, Illus.) Honesdale, PA: Boyds Mills. (K-2)

Siberell, A. (1990). *A journey to Paradise.* New York: Henry Holt. (4-6)

Surat, M. M. (1983). *Angel child, dragon child.* Racine, WI: Carnival/Raintree. (3-5)

Uchida, Y. (1993). *The bracelet* (J. Yardley, Illus.). New York: Philomel. (K-2)

Wallace, I. (1984). *Chin Chiang and the dragon's dance.* New York: Atheneum. (3-7)

Yacowitz, C. (1992). *The jade stone*. (J. H. Chen, Illus.). New York: Holiday. (1–3)

Yee, P. (1990). *Tales from gold mountain: Stories of the Chinese in the new world* (N. Ng Illus.). New York: Harper & Row. (4–8)

Yee, P. (1991). *Roses sing on new snow* (H. Chan, Illus.). New York: Macmillan. (3–6)

Yep, L. (1989). *The rainbow people* (D. Wiesner, Illus.). New York: HarperCollins. (4–8)

Yep, L. (1993). *Dragon's gate*. New York: HarperCollins. (5–8)

Native American

Baylor, B. (1975). *A god on every mountain top: Stories of southwest Indian mountains*. New York: Scribner's. (3–6)

Baylor, B. (1978). *The other way to listen*. New York: Scribner's. (K–8)

Bierhorst, J. (1979). *A cry from the earth: Music of the North American Indians*. New York: Four Winds. (K–8)

Bierhorst, J. (1983). *The sacred path: Spells, prayers, and power songs of the American Indians*. New York: Four Winds. (K–8)

Bierhorst, J. (1995). *The white deer*. New York: Morrow. (2-up)

Bruchac, J. (1993). *Fox song* (P. Morin, Illus.). New York: Philomel.

Bruchac, J. (1995). *Gluskabe and the four wishes* (C. Nyburg, Illus.). New York: Cobblehill.

Bruchac, J., & London, J. (1992). *Thirteen moons on turtle's back* (T. Locker, Illus.). New York: Philomel. (1–4)

Carey, V. S. (1990). *Quail song: A Pueblo Indian tale* (I. Barnett, Illus.). New York: Putnam. (K–4)

Cherry, L. (1991). *A river ran wild*. Orlando: Harcourt Brace Jovanovich. (K–8)

Cohen, C. L. (1988). *The mud pony: A traditional Skidi Pawnee tale* (S. Begay, Illus.). New York: Scholastic. (3–7)

De Felice, C. (1990). *Weasel*. New York: MacMillan. (5–8)

Dorris, M. (1992). *Morning girl*. New York: Hyperion. (3–5)

Ekoomiak, N. (1990). *Artic memories*. New York: Holt, Rinehart, & Winston. (4–6)

Freedman, R. (1988). *Buffalo hunt*. New York: Holiday (3–8)

Freedman, R. (1992). *Indian winter* (K. Bodmer, Photo.). New York: Holiday. (5–8)

Fritz, J. (1983). *The double life of Pocahontas*. New York: Putnam. (3–7)

George, J. C. (1983). *The talking earth*. New York: Harper & Row. (4–8)

Goble, P. (1988). *Iktomi and the boulder: A Plains Indian story*. New York: Orchard. (K–4)

Goble, P. (1990). *Dream wolf*. New York: Bradbury. (1–3)

Goble, P. (1992). *Crowchief*. New York: Orchard. (K–2)

Gregory, K. (1990). *The legend of Jimmy Spoon*. Orlando, FL: Harcourt Brace Jovanovich. (4–8)

Grossman, V. (1991). *Ten little rabbits* (S. Long, Illus.). San Francisco: Chronicle. (K–2)

Hoyt-Goldsmith, D. (1991). *Pueblo storyteller* (L. Migdale, Photo.). New York: Holiday. (1–4)

Jassem, K. (1979). *Sacajawea, wilderness guide*. Mahwah, NJ: Troll. (1–4)

Kesey, K. (1991). *The sea lion* (N. Waldman, Illus.). New York: Viking. (5–8)

Larrabee, L. (1993). *Grandmother Five Baskets* (L. Sawyer, Illus.). Tucson, AZ: Harbinger. (3–8)

Larry, C. (1993). *Peboan and Seegwun*. New York: Farrar, Straus, & Girou. (K–3)

Marrin A. (1984). *War clouds in the west: Indians and cavalrymen, 1860-1890*. New York: Atheneum. (5–8)

Martin, R. (1992). *The rough-face girl* (D. Shannon, Illus.). New York: Scholastic. (K–4)

Moore, R. (1990). *Maggie among the Seneca*. New York: HarperCollins (5–6)

O'Dell, S. (1988). *Black star, bright dawn*. Boston: Houghton Mifflin. (5–8)

Paulsen, G. (1988). *Dogsong*. New York: Bradbury. (5–8)

Rodanos, K. (1992). *Dragonfly's tale*. New York: Clarion. (5–8)

Rodanos, K. (1994). *Dance of the sacred circle*. New York: Little, Brown. (5–8)

Roessell, M. (1993). *Kinaalia: A Navaho girl grows up.* Minneapolis MN: Lerner. (3-6)

Sewall, M. (1990). *People of the breaking day.* New York: Atheneum. (5-7)

Seymour, T. V. N. (1993). *The gift of changing woman.* New York: Henry Holt. (4-6)

Sneve, V. (1989). *Dancing teepees: Poems of American Indian youth.* New York: Holiday (4-8)

Sneve, V. (1994). *The Nez Perce: A first Americans book.* New York: Holiday. (2-6)

Speare, E. G. (1983). *The sign of the beaver.* Boston: Houghton Mifflin. (4-8)

Strete, D. K. (1990). *Big thunder magic* (G. Brown, Illus.). New York: Greenwillow. (K-4)

Thomson, P. (1995). *Katie Henio: Navaho sheepherder* (P. Conklin, Photo.). New York: Cobblehill.

Van Laan, N. (1993). *Buffalo dance: A Blackfoot legend* (B. Vidal, Illus.). Boston: Little, Brown. (1-8)

White Deer of Autumn. (1983). *Ceremony—In the circle of life.* Racine, WI: Raintree. (4-8)

Wisniewski, D. (1991). *Rain player.* New York: Clarion. (K-3)

Yolen, J. (1992). *Encounter* (D. Shannon, Illus.). San Diego: Harcourt Brace. (3-8)

Other Multicultural Works

Aamundsen, N. R. (1990). *Two short and one long.* Boston: Houghton Mifflin. (4-8)

Ashabranner, B. (1991). *An ancient heritage: The Arab-American minority* (P. S. Conklin, Photo.). New York: HarperCollins. (5-8)

Hamilton, V. (1988). *In the beginning: Creation stories from around the world.* Orlando, FL: Harcourt Brace Jovanovich. (4-8)

Haviland, V. (1979). *North American legends.* New York: Philomel. (4-8)

Heide, F. P., & Gilliland, J. H. (1990). *The day of Ahmed's secret* (T. Lewin, Illus.). New York: Lothrop, Lee, & Shepard. (K-3)

Langton, J. (1985). *The hedgehog boy: A Latvian folktale* (I. Plume, Illus.). New York: HarperCollins. (2-4)

Lankford, M. D. (1992). *Hopscotch around the world* (K. Milone, Illus.). New York: Morrow. (1-2)

Mayers, F. (1992). *A Russian ABC.* New York: Abrams. (K-4)

Philip, N. (1991). *Fairy tales of Eastern Europe* (L. Wilkes, Illus.). New York: Clarion. (K-8)

Reed, D. C. (1995). *The Kraken.* Honesdale, PA: Boyds Mills. (3-6)

Hispanic

Aardema, V. (1991). *Borreguita and the coyote: Tale from Ayutia, Mexico.* New York: Knopf. (K-3)

Ancona, G. (1994). *The piñata maker/El piñatero.* San Diego, Harcourt. (K-8)

Anzaldua, G. (1993). *Friends from the other side/Amigos del otro lado.* Chicago: Children's Book Press. (1-7)

Bunting, E. (1990). *The wall* (R. Himler, Illus.). New York: Clarion. (3-8)

Cisñeros, S. (1994). *Hairs/Pelitos.* New York: Apple Soup/Knopf. (K-3)

Clark, A. N. (1980). *Secret of the Andes.* New York: Viking. (4-8)

De Gerez, T. (1981). *My song is a piece of jade: Poems of ancient Mexico in English and Spanish.* Boston: Little, Brown. (3-8)

de Paola, T. (1980). *The lady of Guadalupe.* New York: Holiday. (3-6)

Dorros, A. (1991). *Abuela.* New York: Dutton. (4-8)

Ets, M. H., & Labastide, A. (1959). *Nine days to Christmas: A story of Mexico.* New York: Viking. (4-8)

Mohr, N. (1993). *All for the better: The story of El Barrio.* Dallas: Steck-Vaughn. (2-5)

Mora, P. (1995). *The desert is my mother/El desierto es mi madre* (D. Leshon, Illus.). Houston: Piñata.

O'Dell, S. (1981). *Carlota.* Boston: Houghton Mifflin. (5-8)

Palacios, A. (1993). *!Viva Mexico!: The story of Benito Juarez and Cinco de Mayo.* Cleveland, OH: Modern Curriculum Press. (2-5)

Pitre, F. (1993). *Juan Bobo and the pig: A Puerto Rican folktale* (C. Hale, Illus.). New York: Lodestar.

Rodriguez, G. M. (1994). *Green corn tamales/Tamales de elote* (G. Shepard, Illus.). Tucson, AZ: Hispanic.

Roe, E. (1991). *Con mi hermano—With my brother.* New York: Bradbury. (5–8)

Shute, L. (1995). *Rabbit wishes.* New York: Lothrop, Lee, & Shepard.

Soto, G. (1990). *Baseball in April and other stories.* San Diego: Harcourt. (3–6)

Soto, G. (1992). *Neighborhood odes* (D. Diaz, Illus.). Sand Diego: Harcourt.

Soto, G. (1993). *Too many tamales* (E. Martinez, Illus.). New York: Putnam. (K–3)

Villaseñor, V. (1994). *Walking stars: Stories of magic and power.* New York: Piñata. (4–8)

Winter, J. (1991). *Diego.* New York: Knopf. (5–8)

Wolf, B. (1987). *In this proud land: The story of a Mexican-American family.* New York: HarperCollins. (6–8)

Trucker Buddy Program

The Trucker Buddy Program is designed to enhance children's writing and geography skills. A trucker is assigned a class in September. Throughout the year, the trucker and the class exchange postcards and letters. The class plots out the trucker's travels on a map in the classroom.

Trucker Buddy Program

- The program is underwritten by Kenworth Truck Company in Washington and Chevron Oil Lubricant Division.
- It was the idea of 26-year-old truck driver Gary D. King who wanted to share his travel experiences with children.
- Since it began in November, 1992, it has grown to include 10,000 drivers and teachers to serve children in every state.
- For more information on the program, call (800) MY-BUDDY or write: Trucker Buddy, P.O. Box 7788, Madison, WI 53707-7788.

Source: Trucker Buddy International, Inc.

Subject Index

A

Aardema, V., 78
Abel, F.J., 218, 248, 252, 305
Abel, J.P., 217, 218, 248, 252, 305
Acquisition of Syntax in Children from 5 to 10, The, 152
Acts of Meaning, 409
Adams, M., 26
Adams, M.J., 41, 74, 120, 339, 374, 377, 380, 401, 408, 409
Advance organizers, 50, 51, 51-52, 70
Akroyd, S., 248, 424
Allen, R.V., 25, 41, 376, 409
Allington, R.L., 401, 409
Allred, R.A., 339
Ames, C., 55, 71
Anderson, P.S., 328
Anderson, R.C., 25, 41, 45, 71, 362, 367, 376, 378, 409
Anderson, T.H., 362, 409
Andrews, J.A., 261, 305
Anecdotal records, 32
Armbruster, B., 362, 409
Art of Teaching Writing, The, 249
Assessment, 32-35, 288
    anecdotal records, 299-302
    checklists, 299-302
    holistic evaluation, 302-304
    See also Anecdotal records
    See also Checklists
    See also Portfolios
    See also Rubric
    See also Standardized achievement tests
Atkins, C., 330
Attention deficit hyperactivity disorder (ADHD), 40
Atwell, N., 363, 409
Auditory discrimination, 29
Augustine, D.K., 55, 71
Aulls, M., 215, 248
Ausubel, D., 51, 71
Awakening to Literacy, 411

B

Babbitt, N., 362, 409
Babbling, 135
Balance the Basics: Let them Write, 306
Banks, J., 36
Banks, J.A., 41
Banks, L.R., 76
Barr, M., 150, 151
Bartch, J., 337
Basal reader, 26
Basal Reading Program, 365, 375
Beatty, P., 79
Becoming a Nation of Readers: The Report of the Commission on Reading, 25, 41, 71, 367, 409
Beecher, H.W., 24
Beers, C., 329, 339
Beginning to Read: Thinking and Learning about Print, 26, 41, 120, 409
Behaviorally challenged, 38
Bell-Gredler, M.E., 48, 71
Berlin, J.A., 156, 183
Bieger, E.M., 94, 120
Big Books, 374
Bilingual, 27, 367
Bilingual students, 402
Billig, E., 88, 120
Bird: The Making of an American Sports Legend, 326
Bishop, R.S., 94, 120
Bissex, G., 329, 332, 370, 409
Black English, 144
Bloodgood, J.W., 334
Bloom, B., 67, 70, 71
Book Talk and Beyond, 183, 306
Boyer, E., 277, 305
Brady, R., 277, 306
Brainstorming, 171
Brazee, P., 368, 409
Bright, R., 220, 240

Britton, J., 151, 220, 249
Broken Promises, 411
Brown, A.L., 401, 411
Brown, R., 136, 152
Brownell, C.A., 332
Bruemmer, S., 156, 183
Bruner, J., 404, 409
Bunting, E., 80
Burgess, T., 175, 183, 220, 249
Burke, C., 41, 58, 71, 344
Burke, C.L., 215-216, 229, 249
Burkhart, A.L., 417, 424
Button, K., 305

C

Calkins, L., 6, 20
Calkins, L.M., 214, 216, 223, 225, 232, 249, 370, 409
Callahan, R.C., 8, 20
Cambourne, B., 215, 249, 300, 306
Carpenter, D., 338
Carr, E.G., 50, 71, 362, 411
Carr, G.A., 182
Carter, M.A., 244, 250, 298, 306
Casteel, J., 325
Chang, Y.L., 152
Changing English: Essays for Harold Rosen, 183
Checklists, 32
Cherry, L., 79
Child Phonology: Vol. 1. Production, 152
Child's Construction of Language, The, 152
Children and Literature, 306
Children Who Read Early: Two Longitudinal Studies, 409
Children's Effective Use of Multiple Standards for Evaluating Their Comprehension, 210
Children's literature, 75
    author's style, 75
    autobiography, 83, 88-89
    biography, 83, 88-89

characterization, 75-76
contemporary realistic
    fiction, 83
historical fiction, 83, 88
illustrations, 75, 82
multicultural, 94-99
picture book, 83, 85
plot, 75, 78-80
setting, 75, 80
style, 81-82
theme, 75, 80-81
traditional literature, 83, 85
See also Genre
See also Poetry
*Children's Literature in the
    Elementary School*, 249
Chomsky, C. S., 74, 120, 152
Chomsky, N., 132, 133, 137
Choral reading, 162-163
Choral speaking, 162
Christie, J., 174, 183
Christie, J. F., 182
Church, S., 367, 408, 409
Cianciolo, P. J., 120
Clark, E. V., 137, 152
Clark, M., 370, 409
Classroom management, 3, 10-15
    organization, 3
Clay, 329
Clay, M., 215, 249, 329, 343, 370,
    375
Cochran-Smith, M., 31, 41
Codling, R. M., 408
Cofer, C. N., 152
Coltheart, M., 410
Commeyras, M., 182
*Composing Process of Twelfth
    Graders, The*, 249
Computers, 5, 404
    See also Internet
Concept development, 47
Condon, W. S., 152
Conrad, P., 80
Constructivism, 26, 52
    See also Inquiry
*Context-Responsive Approaches to
    Assessing Children's
    Language*, 151, 152
Cooper, E. J., 411
Cooper, J., 350
Cooperative learning, 50, 51, 52,
    53, 70
Cooperative learning, 72
Corley, K. K., 424
Cousin, P. T., 152

Craig, S. T., 255, 306
Cran, W., 126, 151, 152
*Creating classrooms for authors:
    The reading-writing
    connection*, 71
*Creative Drama in the
    Classroom*, 183
Cress, E., 299, 306
Critical thinking, 4
Crossland, C., 336
Crowley, P., 367, 411
Cudd, E. T., 277, 278, 305, 306
Cullinan, B. E., 74, 94, 120, 364,
    409, 410
Cummins, J., 414, 424

D

Daiker, D. A., 183
Dale, P. S., 325
Daniels, H., 58, 63, 71
Danielson, K. E., 31, 41, 42, 120,
    140, 152
DeFord, D. E., 402, 409
DeMaster, V., 336
Denman, G. A., 261, 306
Derry, S. J., 50, 71
Desai, L. E., 244, 250, 298, 306
*Determinants of Infant
    Behaviour IV. Proceedings
    of the fourth Tavistock
    Study Group on Mother-
    Infant Interaction*, 153
Deutsch, W., 152
*The Development of Writing
    Abilities (11-18)*, 249
*Development of Language,
    The*, 152
DeWitz, P. A., 349
Dialects, 142
Díaz, E., 152
Dictionary skills, 340
Dinosaurs, 121
*Directing Reading Maturity as a
    Cognitive Process*, 411
*Directing the Reading-Thinking
    Process*, 211
Direct instruction, 23, 30
*Discovering Language with
    Children*, 326
Discover Your Own Literacy, 210
Discussion groups, 181 .
Discussions, 139, 169, 172
    panel, 172
    See also Debates
Disorder, 403

D'Nealian, 350
Doake, D., 370, 409
Doctorow, M., 72
Donovan, J. M., 310, 325
Donovan, T. R., 249
Dorsey-Gaines, C., 85, 94, 121
Douma, R., 326
Drama, 58, 174, 176, 178, 180
    formal, 176, 180
    improvisation, 176, 178
    pantomime, 176
Draper, V., 252, 306
Dreher, M. A., 20
Drozdal, J. G., 332
Duffy, G., 9, 20, 26, 42
Dunphy, M., 79
Durkin, D., 363, 370, 409
Dygard, T., 79
Dyson, A. H., 150, 152, 157, 183,
    214, 223, 249

E

Early childhood, 25
Early childhood education, 12
    See also preschool,
        kindergarten
Edwards, P. A., 410, 424
Effective teaching, 18-19
*Effective Teaching of Language
    Arts, The*, 410
*Eight Approaches to Teaching
    Composition*, 249
Eilers, R. E., 135, 152
Elbow, P., 277, 306
*Elementary School Curriculum to
    Develop Better Writing
    Skills, An*, 325
*Elementary Spelling Book,
    The*, 24
    See also "Blue Back Speller"
Elley, W. B., 74, 120
Emergent literacy, 22-23, 30, 141
    See also Language Development
Emig, J., 217, 249
English, development of, 126
*Envisioning literature: Literary
    understanding and
    literature instruction*, 121
Ernst, G., 248
Experiential backgrounds, 27
*Explorations in the Development
    of Writing*, 151

F

Facilitators' Manual for Teaching Reading as Thinking, 411
Fader, D., 362, 410
Family Literacy, 411
Family literacy, 414
Farest, C., 85, 94, 121
Farnan, N., 20
Farris, P.J., 23, 42, 244, 246, 249, 253, 279, 280, 299, 306, 344, 350, 397, 408, 410
Ferguson, P.M., 164
Fernald, G., 339
Ferruggia, A., 120
Fielding, L.G., 362, 376, 409
Fisher, C., 27, 42, 75, 120
Fitzgerald, J., 325
Flint-Ferguson, J., 312, 326
Flood, J., 54, 71, 152, 306, 318, 325, 374, 410
Flores, B., 152
Flynn, R.M., 182
Ford, M., 27, 42
Ford, M.P., 414, 424
Formative Writing: Writing to Assist Learning in all Subject Areas, 306
For the Good of the Earth and Sun: Teaching Poetry, 183
Foss, B.M., 153
Foulke, R., 306
Foundations of Language: Vol. 1. A Multidisciplinary Approach, 152
Foundations of Literacy, The, 410
Fowler, R.C., 424
Fox, M., 76
Foxfire, 58
Fraatz, J.M.B., 414, 424
Fraser, C., 136, 152
Fredericks, A.D., 424
Friend, M., 215, 250, 298, 307
Fries, C.C., 311, 325
Frith, U., 378, 410
Fueyo, J.A., 306
Fuhler, C.J., 26, 42, 120, 397, 408, 410
Furgerson, P., 305

G

Gable, R.A., 335-336
Gahn, S.M., 217, 249
Galda, L., 94, 120, 364, 409
Gambrell, L.B., 408

Gardner, H., 45, 48-50, 71
Gaskin, I., 277, 306
Gavan, E.M., 58, 71
Genre, 83, 93
Gentile, L.M., 152
Gentry, J.B., 329
Gentry, R., 335
George, J.C., 79
Gersten, R.M., 410
Gibson, H., 8, 20
Gifted student, 40
Gilmore, J., 7, 20
Gingerbread Boy, The, 78
Glazer, S.M., 152
Gleason, G.B., 133
Gleason, J.B., 137, 152
Gleitman, L.R., 152
GNYS AT WORK: A Child Learns to Read and Write, 409
Goelman, H., 411
Gollnick, D.M., 42
Goodlad, J., 70, 71
Goodman, K., 6, 20, 23, 42, 139, 152, 409, 410
Goodman, Y., 368, 409, 410
Graham, S., 334
Grammar, 27, 214, 310, 311, 314, 321
    instruction, 314-320
    punctuation, 315-318
    second language students, 321
    structural, 311-312
    systems of, 311
    traditional, 311-312
    transformational generative, 311-313
    See also Second language students
    See also Usage
Grant, C., 36, 42
Grapheme, 132
Graves, D., 29, 42, 157, 183, 216, 217, 218, 220, 225, 249, 252, 288, 306, 310, 315, 318, 325, 343
Gray, M.A., 174, 183
Gray, M.J., 408
Great American Reading Machine, The, 412
Green, N., 79
Griffith, P., 337
Griffith, P.L., 378, 408, 410
Growing up Literate: Learning from Inner-City Families, 94, 121

Gruber, K.D., 55, 71
Gursky, D., 50, 71
Gutkin, J., 410

H

Hackney, C., 356
Haine, G., 175, 183
Hall, S.E., 332
Halliday, M.A.K., 138-139, 152
Hammett, V., 305
Hammill, D.D., 334
Hancock, M.R., 120
Hand, B., 277, 306
Handbook of Bilingual Education, A, 153
Handwriting, 27, 38, 342-357
    cursive, 352
    development, 344
    D'Nealian, 348
    eye-hand coordination, 344
    instruction, 344-356
    left-handed children, 353
    legibility, 352
    legible, 344
    letter reversals, 349
    manuscript, 348
    mirror writing, 349
    pencil grip, 348
    writing instruments, 348
    Zaner Bloser, 348
Hansen, J., 218, 219, 238, 248, 249, 288, 306
Hanson, L.R., 55, 71
Harder, R.J., 8, 20
Harp, B., 325, 368, 410
Harris, T.L., 411
Harste, J.C., 58, 71, 215-216, 229, 249, 344
Harwayne, J., 370
Harwayne, S., 6, 20, 214, 249, 409
Hasselbring, T., 336
Hauwiller, J.G., 217, 248
Hayes, D., 140, 152
Hayes, J., 306
Haynes, S.W., 368, 409
Heald-Taylor, B.G., 120
Heard, G., 163, 183
Hearne, B., 83, 121
Heath, S.B., 157, 183, 370, 410, 414, 424
Heathcote, D., 175, 183
Hedberg, A., 419, 424
Henderson, A., 415, 424
Henderson, E., 329, 333, 335, 336
Hendrickson, J.M., 335-336

Henkes, K., 79
Hennings, D. G., 27, 29, 42
Henny Penny, 78
Hepler, S., 223, 249
Hickman, J., 223, 249
Hiebert, E. H., 25, 45, 71, 367, 378, 409, 424
High School: A Report of the Carnegie Foundation for the Advancement of Teaching, 305
Hildreth, G., 94, 121
Hill, D., 350
Hillerich, R., 335
Hillocks, G., 216, 249
Hoffman, J. V., 85, 94, 121
Hoffman, M., 79
Holdaway, D., 367, 370, 374-375, 410
Hollowell, J., 255, 306
Holman, F., 79
Holt, J., 70
Honig, B., 75, 121
Hood, W., 409, 410
Hopmann, M. R., 332
Hornbooks, 24
Horton, L. W., 353
Hoskisson, K., 215, 250, 347
House That Jack Built, The, 78
Hubbard, R., 362, 412
Huck, C., 75, 121, 223, 249
Hunt, K. W., 313, 325
Hymes, D., 152
Hysmith, C., 299, 306

I

Individualized instruction, 25
Indo-European language, 126
Indrisano, R., 402, 410
Inquiry, 52
  See also constructivism
Inside Out, 249
Instruction
  Student-centered, 52
  See also Advance organizers
  See also constructivism
  See also cooperative learning
  See also Inquiry
  See also Nondirective
Instructional methods, 9
Insult to Intelligence: The Bureaucratic Invasion of Our Classroom, 326, 411
Integrated curriculum, 25, 48
Interdisciplinary approach, 32

See also Integrated instruction
Internet, 5
  See also Computers
In the Middle, 409
Intonation, 160
  juncture, 160
  pitch, 160
  stress, 160
Invented spelling, 29
Invitations: Changing as Teachers and Learners, K-12, 411, 424
Invitation to Read: More Children's Literature in the Reading Program, 410

J

Jacobsen, L., 9, 20
Jacobson, J. M., 397, 410
Jagusch, S. A., 411
Jensen, J. M., 50, 71
Johnson, D. W., 53-54, 71
Johnson, M. J., 305
Johnson, R. T., 53-54, 71
Johnson, T. D., 23, 42
Joining the Literacy Club: Further Essays into Education, 20, 326
Jones, B. F., 50, 71, 362, 411
Journals, 365
Joyce, B., 51, 52, 72
Jump over the moon, 121

K

Kaczmarski, D., 23, 42
Kauchak, D. P., 8, 20
Keogh, A. J., 8, 20
Kindergarten, 7
King, R. E., 424
Kirby, D., 223, 249
Kitagawa, M., 72
Kleiman, G. M., 305
Klein, M., 140, 158, 183
Klesius, J., 367, 410
Kliman, M., 305
Klobukowski, P., 424
Klopfer, L. E., 48, 72, 411
Kormanski, L. M., 223, 249, 261, 306
Krashen, S., 321, 326
Kroll, B., 151
Kroll, M., 58, 65, 72
Kucer, S., 215, 249
Kuhl, D., 349

L

LaFramboise, K., 328
Laminack, L., 215, 249
Lamme, L. L., 299, 306, 348
Lane, S., 156, 183
Langer, J. A., 121, 364, 410
Language, 138, 140, 158
  functions of, 138-139
  settings, 140, 158
Language Acquisition: The State of the Art, 152
Language and the Language Arts, 152, 325
Language arts, 3
Language Arts: Content and Teaching Strategies, 250
Language Arts Teacher in Action, The, 326
Language delayed, 27
Language development, 133-138, 141, 150
  assessment, 150
  checklist, 141
  special needs children, 142
  See also Drama
  See also Special needs children
Language Development: Kindergarten Through Grade Twelve, 183
Language Development: Structure and Function, 325
Language Experience Approach, 25, 376
Language Experiences in Communication, 41, 409
LaNunziata, L., 350
Lapointe, A., 126, 152
Lapp, D., 328, 374, 410
Lara, S. M., 322, 326
Larsen, S., 334
Lartz, M. N., 370, 410
Learning, 403
Learning and Instruction: Theory into Practice, 71
Learning disabled students, 27, 38, 404
Learning How to Mean: Exploration in the Development of Language, 152
Learning theory, 3, 9, 46-50
  behaviorism, 46
  cognitive development, 46
  information processing, 47

information-processing theory, 47
Innatism, 46
See also concept development
See also constructivism
See also multiple intelligences
See also schemata
Learning together and alone Cooperative, competitive, and individualistic learning, 71
Learning to Read in American Schools, 409
Leggo, C., 325
Lesson plans, 5, 51
Let's Think About Reading and Reading Instruction: A Primer for Tutors and Teachers, 424
Letters from Rifka, 76-77
Levine, L. D., 326
Lewis, A. C., 9, 20
Lewis, M. J., 409
Liner, T., 223, 249
Linguistics, 132
Linguistics: The Study of Language, 325
Lipman, M., 71
Listening, 22, 25, 27, 29-30, 38, 45, 157, 158, 186
  appreciative, 190-192
  attentive, 190, 195-196
  critical/analytical, 190, 198-199
  directed listening activity, 204-205
  directed listening-thinking activity, 204-205
  factors in effective assessment, 188-189
  INQuest, 196
  marginal, 190
  propaganda techniques, 200
Listening: Its Impact at all Levels on Reading and the Other Language Arts, 211
Literacy for a Diverse Society: Perspectives, Practices, and Policies, 72, 409, 424
Literary web, 84
Literature and the Child, 120, 409
Literature as Exploration, 411
Literature-Based Approach, 402
Literature-Based Whole Language Approach, 375
Literature circles, 58, 60-66, 365

Literature Circles: Practical Ideas and Strategies for Responding to Literature, 72
Literature Circles: Voices and Choice in the Student-Centered Classroom, 71
Literature Response journals, 402
Living Between the Lines, 249, 409
Livingston, M. C., 264, 306
Loban, W., 156, 183
Louis, D. R., 23, 42
Lowry, L., 76
Lyon, G. L., 80
Lyons, C. A., 402, 409

M

Mack, B., 244, 249
MacNeil, R., 126, 151, 152
Macrorie, K., 214, 249
Madden, L., 71
Madden, N. A., 401, 411
Madigan, D., 41
Mahler, W. R., 32, 42
Making of a Reader, The, 41
Manolakes, G., 334
Many, J. E., 257, 306
Marks, C., 72
Marshall, K. C., 410
Marshall, N., 278, 306
Martin, N., 220, 249
Martinez, M. A., 306
Martinez, M. G., 183
Mason, J. M., 370, 410
Mates, B. F., 151, 409
Mathematics, 3
Mazzoni, S. A., 408
McCaslin, N., 175, 183
McCauley, D. S., 161-166, 182, 183
McCauley, J. K., 161-162, 182, 183
McClelland, B. W., 249
McClure, A. A., 163, 183, 261, 306
McCoy, L. J., 305
McCraig, R. A., 310, 326
McCrum, R., 126, 151, 152
McCully, E. A., 76
McGuffey, W. H., 24
McGuffey's Eclectic Readers, 24, 365
McLeod, A., 220, 249
McLoughlin, J. A., 338
McMahon, S., 390
McMahon, S. I., 411

McNamara, J., 136, 152
McNaughton, S., 415, 424
McNutt, G., 334
Media, 172
Meeks, J. W., 335-336
Mellon, J. C., 313, 326
Meloth, M. S., 54, 72
Mendoza, A., 201, 211
Mentally challenged, 27, 38
Metacognition, 50
Meyer, J., 312, 326
Meyer, L. A., 410
Microsoft, 121
Middle and Secondary School Reading, 210
Miller, L. J., 338
Models of Teaching, 72
Monson, D., 383
Monson, D. L., 410
Moore, D. W., 391, 410
Morenberg, J., 183
Morgan, N., 175, 183
Morpheme, 132
Morphology, 132-133, 142
Morrissey, M., 367, 410
Morrow, L. M., 140, 152, 182
Multicultural, 3, 35-38
  See also Cultural
  See also Ethnic
Multicultural education, 55, 94, 143, 367, 402
  languages, 126-131
  language variations, 143-144
  See also Ethnic
Multicultural literature, 94
Multiple Intelligences, 71
Multiple intelligences, 48, 71
  See also Learning theory
Murphy, D. A., 50, 71
Murray, D., 216, 244, 249
Musgrave, B., 152
Myers, D. L., 142, 152
Myers, W. D., 79

N

Nakazima, S. A., 135, 152
Nathenson-Mejia, S., 406, 411
Negotiating a Permeable Curriculum: On Literacy, Diversity, and the Interplay of Children's and Teachers' Worlds, 249
Nelson, G. L., 255, 306
Nelson, O., 182
New England Primer, The, 24

New Hooked on Books, The, 410
Newman, J. M., 214, 249, 252, 306, 377, 410
Nicholson, H. H., 183
Nondirective instruction, 50, 51, 52
Nondirective teaching, 52, 70
Non-English-speaking, 40
Nonstandard English, 311
Norton, D., 94, 121, 383
Norton, D. E., 339, 410

O

Observing Young Readers: Selected Papers, 409
Odell, L., 252, 306
O'Dell, S., 79
O'Donnell, R. C., 313, 325
O'Flahavan, J. F., 169, 182
Ogle, D. S., 50, 71, 362, 411
O'Hare, F., 313, 326
Ohio's Reading Recovery Program: Vol. 3. Report of the Follow-up Studies, 409
Ohlhausen, M., 27, 42
Olberg, A., 411
Oller, D. K., 135, 152
Olson, M., 378, 408, 410
Oral language, 24, 25, 27, 156, 172, 182
See also Language development
Orlich, D. C., 8, 20
Osborn, J., 409
Ouchi, W., 55, 72
Overgeneralization, 137

P

Padak, N., 36, 42
Palincsar, A. S., 50, 71, 362, 401, 411
Palmer, B. M., 408
Paradis, E. E., 409
Paratore, J. R., 402, 410
Parental involvement, 414
Paris, S. G., 381, 411
Paulsen, D., 121
Paziotopoulos, A., 58, 65, 72
Pearson, P. D., 216, 250
Pease, D., 137, 152
Peck, R. N., 80
Peer Editing Versus Teacher Editing: Does it Make a Difference?, 326
Pendergrass, R. A., 8, 20
Phelan, P., 151, 325

Philliber, W. W., 424
Phoneme, 132
Phonemic awareness, 379
Phonics, 26
Phonics instruction, 377–379
    guidelines for exemplary, 378
Phonology, 132, 142, 143
Physically challenged, 38
Piazza, C., 332
Pick, A. D., 332
Pilkey, D., 79
Pinnell, G. S., 150, 152, 326, 402, 409
Pitman, Sir J., 328
Place Called School, A, 71
Pocket books, 254
Poem-Making: Ways to Begin Writing Poetry, 306
Poetry, 24, 90–93, 223, 261
    anthologies, 92
    biographical, 28
    cinquain, 276
    concrete, 264
    couplet, 274
    elements of, 262–263
    free verse, 264
    haiku, 274
    list poems, 263
    names, 274
    starters, 264
    triplet, 274
    types of, 263–276
Politics of Reading: Power, Opportunity, and the Prospects for Change in America's Public Schools, The, 424
Portfolio, 35, 288
    example of, 288–299
Portfolio Assessment in the Reading-Writing Classroom, 250, 306
Prairie Songs, 80
Praise, 39
Prereading Activities for Content Reading and Learning, 410
Preschool, 7
Primary Language Record, The, 151
Principles and Practices of Second Language Acquisition, 326
Problem-solving skills, 4
Processing Communication, 210
Promoting Reading Comprehension, 306

Psychology of Meaningful Verbal Learning, The, 71
Punctuation, 214, 220
Puppets, 166
Pursuit of Literacy: Early Reading and Writing, The, 249
Purves, A. C., 363, 367, 411
Putnam, L. R., 132, 133, 151, 152
Pygmalion in the classroom, 20

Q

Questioning strategies, 18, 67
Questions
    critical thinking, 387
    inferential, 387
    literal, 387

R

Radebaugh, M. R., 337
Ramey, E. K., 32, 42
Ramsey, J., 306
Rangel, L., 55, 72
Ransom, K., 362, 411
Raphael, T., 390
Raphael, T. E., 411
Rasinski, J., 36
Rasinski, T., 42
Rasinski, T. V., 424
Read, C., 215, 249, 329, 334
Read aloud, 25, 64
Readence, J. E., 391, 410
Reader, the Text, the Poem: The Transactional Theory of the Literary Work, The, 411
Reader's theater, 163–165
Reading, 3, 22, 24–26, 27, 29, 30, 38, 45, 158, 216, 362
    "look-say" method, 24
    aesthetic, 364
    anecdotal records, 406
    approaches, 363
    assessment, 404
    beginning readers, 369
    bilingual students, 402
    Book Club, 390–391
    Book Clubs, 381
    checklist for emergent reading, 371
    checklists, 406
    computers, 404
    content area, 397
    criterion-referenced test, 405
    cross-age tutoring, 377
    diagnostic tests, 405
    directed reading activity, 391

directed reading activity (DRA), 381
directed reading-thinking activity, 391
directed reading-thinking activity (DR-TA), 381
efferent, 364
emergent readers, 369
evaluating emergent reading, 371
evaluating, 404
evaluation, 365, 366
formal evaluation measures, 405
graphic organizers, 381
high-risk students, 401
informal evaluation measures, 406
instruction, 374
instructional approaches, 401
instructional methods for primary and middle childhood readers, 381
inventories, 406
language experience approach, 376
literary experiences, 376
norm-referenced test, 405
parents and, 30
phonetics approach, 24
phonics, 377-379
questioning, 383
reading interviews, 406
Reading readiness tests, 405
reading recovery, 402
reciprocal teaching, 400
response, 397
shared story, 377
sight words, 24
SQ3R, 397
student attitudes, 406
study skills, 397
transactional view of, 364
See also Phonics instruction
Reading groups, 25
Reading Process and Practice, 411
Reading, Thinking, and Concept Development, 411
Reexamining Reading Diagnosis: New Trends and Procedures, 152
Research on Written Composition, 249
Resnick, L. B., 48, 72, 411

Retention, 7
Rhodes, L. K., 406, 411
Richard, K. J., 248
Rickelman, R. J., 391, 410
Riley, R. W., 8, 20
Robeck, C. P., 412
Roberts, L., 277, 278, 305, 306
Robinson, H. A., 397, 411
Roderick, J., 151
Roderick, J. A., 152
Roderick, J. B., 152
Rolheiser-Bennett, C., 52, 72
Roop, L., 325
Rosen, H., 220, 249
Rosenblatt, L., 363, 364-365, 411
Rosenbloom, C. S., 156, 183
Rosenthal, I., 9, 20
Rosenthal, R., 9, 20
Roser, N. L., 50, 71, 85, 94, 121, 183, 306
Ross, B. D., 409
Roth, P., 306
Routman, R., 338, 368, 374-375, 406, 411, 414, 424
Rubric, 32, 33-34

S

Salus, P., 318, 325
Salus, P. H., 152
Sampson, M. R., 249
Sander, L. W., 152
Sanders, S. R., 80
San Jose, C., 183
Saul, W., 397, 411
Saville, M. R., 153
Saxon, J., 175, 183
Schemata, 47
Schickedanz, J., 370, 411
Schiller, L., 325
School Science and Mathematics, 306
Science, 3
Scott, J., 65, 71, 72, 337
Scott, J. A., 25, 41, 45, 71, 367, 378, 409
Scribal Society, The, 411
Searfoss, L., 23, 42
Searfoss, L. W., 139, 152, 153
Second language learners, 145-149
Second-language students, 321
Sedgwick, J., 349
Semantics, 132-133, 135, 137, 142, 143

Sentence Combining: Improving Student Writing Without Formal Grammar Instruction, 326
Setting, 80
Shadow puppetry, 170
Shakespeare, W., 24
Shannon, P., 26, 42, 365, 411
Sharan, S., 55, 72
Sharan, Y., 55, 72
Shared book experiences, 374
Shared Story Reading, 377
Sharer, P. L., 41
Shepard, A., 164, 183
Shepard, L. A., 71
Short, K., 58, 71
Short, K. G., 41
Showers, B., 52, 72
Siks, G. B., 174, 183
Simmons, J., 305
Slavin, R. E., 53-54, 55, 72, 401, 411
Sleeter, C., 36
Sleeter, C. E., 42
Sloyer, S., 163, 183
Smilansky, S., 174-175, 183
Smith, E. M., 41
Smith, F., 4, 9, 20, 27, 31, 42, 74, 121, 217, 242, 249, 311, 314, 326, 370, 411, 414, 424
Snow, C. E., 370, 411
Social studies, 3
Sometimes a shining moment: The Foxfire experience, 58, 72
Spanish, 145
Spaulding, C. L., 305
Speaking, 22, 25, 27, 29, 38, 45, 157, 181
Special needs, 36
 See also Hearing impaired
 See also Learning disabled
 See also Mentally challenged
 See also Physically challenged
 See also Visually impaired
Special needs children, 142
Special needs students, 38, 404
Spelling, 24, 27, 29, 38, 214, 215, 220, 227, 328-342
 errors, 336
 generalizations, 339
 instruction, 333-336, 337
 invented, 215, 329-332
 temporary, 215, 329-332
 See also Phonics
Spelling development, 329-332

deviant, 329
phonetic, 329
prephonetic, 329
standard or correct, 329
transitional, 329
Spiegel, D. L., 42
Spillman, R. E., 424
Stahl, S., 378
Stahl, S. A., 411
Standard English, 311
Standardized achievement
    tests, 35
Stauffer, R., 391
Stauffer, R. G., 411
Stelwagon, P., 156, 183
Stewart, R. A., 409
Stewig, J. W., 261, 306
St. John, J., 328
Stoodt, B., 157, 183
Story of English, The, 151
Storytelling, 58, 165-169
    process of, 168
Stotsky, S., 94, 121
*Strategic Teaching: Cognitive
    Instruction in the Content
    Areas*, 71
Strickland, D., 20, 22, 26, 42
Strickland, D. S., 182
Strommen, B. F., 151
Strommen, L., 409
Sullivan, M., 370, 411
Sulzby, E., 85, 121, 225, 249
*Surface Dyslexia:
    Neuropsychological and
    Cognitive Studies of
    Phonological Reading*, 410
Sutherland, Z., 83, 121
Swisher, J., 350
Syntax, 132-133, 142, 143

T

Talbot, B., 20
*Talking to Learn: Classroom
    Practices in Teaching
    English*, 151, 325
*Talk in the Language Arts
    Classroom*, 140
*Taxonomy of Education
    Objectives*, 71
Taylor, D., 31, 42, 85, 94, 121, 370,
    411
Teaching, 3, 8-12
Teaching methods, 3
Teaching models, 50
    See also Advanced organizers

See also Constructivism
See also Cooperative learning
See also Inquiry
See also Nondirective
    instruction
*Teaching Reading to Every
    Child*, 410
*Teaching Reading, Writing, and
    Study Strategies: The
    Content Areas*, 411
*Teaching Strategies: A Guide to
    Better Instruction*, 20
*Teaching the Integrated Language
    Arts*, 211
Teaching Writing, 250
*Teaching Writing in K-8
    Classrooms*, 183
*Teaching Writing: Balancing
    Process and Product*, 72
*Teaching Young Children to
    Read*, 409
Teale, W. H., 85, 121, 215, 249,
    370, 411
Telegraphic speech, 136
Templeton, S., 23, 42, 328, 332,
    333, 334, 339
Terry, A., 27, 42
Thematic units, 6, 99-117
    See also Integrated curriculum
*Theory Z: How American Business
    Can Meet the Japanese
    Challenge*, 72
Thought and Language, 153
Tiedt, I. M., 156, 183
Tierney, R. J., 215, 244, 250, 298,
    306, 409
*Time and Choice: Key Elements
    for Process Teaching*, 412
Tomlinson, C., 332
Tompkins, G. E., 45, 72, 215, 244,
    250, 298, 307, 333, 347
*Toward the Thinking Curriculum:
    Current Cognitive
    Research*, 72, 411
Trachtenburg, P., 120, 380, 411
*Transformational Sentence
    Combining: A Method for
    Enhancing the
    Development of Syntactic
    Fluency in English
    Composition*, 326
*Transitions: From Literature to
    Literacy*, 411
Trap-Porter, J., 350
Treagust, D. F., 277, 306

Trelease, J., 23, 42
Troike, R. C., 153
Turbill, J., 215, 249, 300, 306
*'Twas the Night Before
    Thanksgiving*, 79

U

U.S. Department of Education, 26
U.S. Postal Service, 259
Understanding Language, 152
UNESCO, 422
*Unschooled Mind: How Children
    Think and How Schools
    Should Teach, The*, 71
Unwin, C. G., 409
Unze, M. G., 332
Uphoff, J. K., 7, 20
Urzua, C., 321, 326
Usage, 220
    See also Grammar

V

Valencia, S., 288, 307
Vandeventer, N., 217, 248
Varvus, L., 288, 307
*Verbal Behavior and Learning:
    Problems and
    Processes*, 152
Videotaping, 173
*Vital Connections: Children,
    Science, and Adults*, 411
Vocabulary, 27, 29, 57
    development, 27
Vygotsky, L. W., 136, 153

W

Waber, B., 79
Wagner, B. J., 174, 183
Walker-Dalhouse, D., 35, 42
Wallace, G., 338
Walley, C. W., 214, 248, 250
Wanner, E., 152
Wasylyk, T. M., 354, 356
Watanabe, K., 156, 183
Watson, D. J., 55, 72, 152, 367, 411
*Ways with Words: Language, Life,
    and Work in Communities
    and Classrooms*, 410
Weaver, C., 326, 368, 411
Webster, N., 24
*Wee Deliver: Stamp Out
    Illiteracy*, 259
Weeks, J. O., 326
Weil, M., 51, 72
Wells, G., 50-51, 72, 151

Wendelin, K. H., 165, 183
What Did I Write?, 249
What's Whole in Whole Language?, 20, 152
When Writers Read, 249
When You've Made it Your Own Teaching Poetry to Young People, 306
White, E. B., 80, 160
White, M. B., 326
Whitin, D. J., 31, 42
Whitin, P. E., 31, 42
Whitney, J., 362, 412
Whole language, 27, 30
   See also constructivism
   See also inquiry
Whole language approach, 26, 366
   evaluation, 368
Whole Language Evaluation Book, The, 409, 410
Whole Language: Theory in Use, 249, 410
Wiencek, J., 169, 182
Wigginton, E., 58, 72
Wilde, S., 328, 333, 335
Wilkinson, I. A. G., 25, 41, 45, 71, 378, 409
Wilkinson, J. A. G., 367
Williams, M., 156, 183
Wilson, P. T., 362, 376, 409, 415, 424
Winter, J., 80
Wiseman, D. E., 412
Wittrock, M. C., 72
Wolff, P. H., 153
Woodward, V. A., 215–216, 229, 249, 344
World Pen Pals, 260
Write from the Start, 249
Writer's Mind: Writing as a Mode of Thinking, The, 306
Writer Teaches Writing: A Practical Method of Teaching Composition, A, 249

Writing, 22, 24, 25, 27, 29, 30, 38, 45, 58, 158, 214–304, 322, 328, 370
   academic learning logs, 277
   anecdotal records, 299–302
   assessment, 228, 236–237
   assessment of, 288
   audience, 220–221
   autobiography, 260
   biography, 278
   checklists, 299–302
   conferences, 244–247, 300
   conventions of, 310
   descriptive, 222–224
   development of, 224–241
   dialogue, 253–255
   diary, 255
   drafting, 215
   editing, 215, 217, 323
   explanatory, 222–224
   expository writing, 222–224
   holistic evaluation, 302–304
   Internet, 282
   journal, 255, 257
   letter, 257–260
   narrative, 222–224
   note taking, 279
   parents, 30
   personal, 252–253
   persuasive, 222–224
   poetic, 223–224
   poetry, 261–276
   portfolio, 288
   practical, 252, 277
   prewriting, 215, 216–217, 240, 247
   process, 216
   product, 216
   proofreading, 323
   publishing, 216, 247
   rehearsal, 216
   research, 278
   revising, 215, 217, 322
   rewriting, 216–217, 240, 247
   stages of, 216

   teacher's role in, 241–247
   technology, 282
   topics, 243–244
   voice, 220–221
   word processing, 283–288
   writing, 240, 247
   writing stage, 216–217
   See also Grammar
   See also Assessment
   See also Emergent literacy
   See also Poetry
   See also Portfolios
   See also Punctuation
   See also Spelling
Writing and the Writer, 249
Writing Begins at Home, 249
Writing Instruction in the Intermediate Grades, 249
Writing Teacher as Researcher, The, 183
Writing: Teachers and Children at Work, 183, 249, 325
Writing to be Read, 249
Writing with Power, 306
Wyshynski, R., 121

Y

Yarington, D., 412
Yokota, J., 120
Yopp, H. K., 334, 378–379, 412
Yopp-Singer Test of Phoneme Segmentation, 379
Yopp-Singer Test of Phonemic Awareness, 334
Youga, J., 312, 326
Young Fluent Readers: What Can They Teach Us?, 409
Young, P., 402, 409
Young, T. A., 164

Z

Zaner Bloser, 350

Children's Literature and Author Index

A

Aardema, V., 121, 167, 184
Abigail Adams: Witness to a Revolution, 81, 121
Across America on an Immigrant Train, 90, 123
Add It, Dip It, Fix It: A Book of Verbs, 319, 326
Adoff, A., 91, 92, 121, 261
Adventures of Spider: West African Folktales, The, 167, 184
Aesop, 86
Alexander, L., 61, 72
Along the Road to Soweto: A Racial History of South Africa, 90, 124
Always Grandma, 87, 123
Amazing Grace, 79, 122
Amber on the Mountain, 69
Amelia Bedelia, 16
Andersen, H. C., 184
Anderson, P., 199, 201, 210
Andrew, R., 114
And Then What Happened, Paul Revere?, 279, 307
Annie Oakley, 167
Antarctica, 364, 412
Archambault, J., 162
Are You There God, It's Me Margaret, 86, 121
Arkhurst, J. C., 167, 184
Armstrong, W., 56, 72
Aronson, D., 187, 210
Around the world in 100 years: From Henry the Navigator to Magellan, 91
Arroz con leche: Popular songs and rhymes from Latin America, 122
Arthur, S. V., 210
Art Lesson, The, 89, 122
Aunt Martha and the golden coin, 39

Aurora means dawn, 80, 123
Avi, 61, 72, 165, 184

B

Baby Uggs Are Hatching, The, 163, 184
Back Home, 88, 123
Baker, L., 199, 210
Banks, L. R., 121
Banks, R., 86
Barn, The, 61, 72
Bates, K. R., 199, 211
Be a Perfect Person in Just Three Days!, 58, 72
Beatty, P., 121
Beauty and the Beast, 85
Bellairs, J., 114
Beneath a Blue Umbrella, 163, 184
Best friends, 76, 79, 122
biography, 88–89
Bird, E. J., 167, 184
Bishop, R. S., 95
Blankenship, T., 188, 210
Blizzard of 1896, The, 167, 184
Blueberries for Sal, 170
Blumberg, R., 90, 121
Blume, J., 86, 121
Bober, N. S., 81, 121
Boodt, G., 202, 210
Book that Jack Wrote, The, 123
Borning Room, The, 88, 122
Bound for Oregon, 91
Box Turtle at Long Pond, 85, 122
Boy, a Dog, and a Frog, A, 84, 123
Boys War: Confederate and Union Soldiers Talk About the Civil War, The, 365, 412
Boys Will Be, 89, 121
Boy: Tales of Childhood, 89, 122
Branley, F., 47, 72
Brenner, B., 180
Brent, R., 199, 201, 210
Brett, J., 82, 121
Bridge to Terabithia, 76, 123

Bridwell, N., 6, 20
Brittain, B., 68
Brooks, B., 79, 89, 121
Brother Can You Spare a Dime?, 81, 123
Brown Bear, Brown Bear, What Do You See?, 74, 75, 82, 123
Brown, M., 334
Bruchac, J., 167, 184, 364, 412
Bruckerhoff, C., 201, 210
Bugs for Dinner? The Eating Habits of Neighborhood Creatures, 89, 122
Bunting, E., 121
Byars, B., 86, 121

C

Cache of Jewels and Other Collective Nouns, A, 318, 325
Caleb & Kate, 165, 184
Cameron, A., 87, 121
Can I Keep Him?, 253, 307
Can You Find Me? A Book About Animal Camouflage, 84, 122
Carle, E., 16, 82, 121, 156, 166, 184, 254
Carlstrom, N. W., 81
Castle in the Attic, The, 114
Castles, 89, 114, 123
Cathedral, 85, 123
Catherine, Called Birdy, 114
Cay, The, 87, 124
Chair for My Mother, A, 165, 184
Charlotte's Web, 16, 77, 80, 124, 160, 184
Cherry, L., 61, 72, 86, 121
Chicka Chicka Boom Boom, 162, 184
Childtimes: A Three-Generation Memoir, 260
Chomsky, C., 203, 210
Cinder Edna, 85, 122, 165, 184
Cinderella, 65, 334

Cleary, B., 86, 87, 89, 121, 256, 307
Cleaver, B., 86, 122
Cleaver, V., 86, 122
Clifford, the Big Red Dog, 6, 20
Cohen, B., 68
Collier, C., 165, 184
Collier, J. L., 165, 184
Color Zoo, 82, 122
Complete Works of Peter Rabbit, The, 72
Compton, P. A., 69
Conrad, P., 122
Cosgrove, J. M., 187, 210
Covered Bridge House and Other Poems, The, 262
Cowcher, H., 364, 412
Cowing, S., 89, 122
Crossing, The, 12, 20
Crow Boy, 167, 184
Cunningham, J. W., 68, 210
Cunningham, P. M., 210
Cushman, K., 31, 41, 114
Cybil War, The, 86, 121

D

Dahl, R., 89, 122
Dancing Teepees: Poems of American Indian Youth, 93
Day No Pigs Would Die, A, 80, 123
de Angeli, M., 114
Dear Mr. Henshaw, 87, 121, 256, 307
Deenie, 86, 121
Delacre, L., 122
Denim, S., 85, 122
de Paola, T., 82, 86, 89, 122, 165, 170, 184
Dewey, J., 84, 122
DeZutter, H., 130
Don't Fidget a Feather, 82, 123, 234
Don't Forget to Write, 253, 307
Door in the Wall, The, 114
Dragon's gate, 39
Dream Keeper and Other Poems, The, 261
Drylongso, 88, 122
Dumb Bunnies, The, 85, 122
Dunphy, M., 122
Dygard, T. J., 122

E

Earth Verses and Water Rhymes, 93, 123
Eating the Alphabet, 82, 122
Ehlert, L., 82, 122
Ellis Island: New Hope in a New Land, 81, 122, 364, 412
Epstein, B., 89, 122
Epstein, S., 89, 122

F

Farris, P. J., 206
Fielding, L., 201, 211
Fish Eyes: A Book You Can Count On, 82, 122
Five Chinese Brothers, The, 167
Five Little Squirrels, 139
Flash, Crash, Rumble, and Roll, 47, 72
Fleischman, P., 88, 93, 122
Fleming, A., 208
Fleming, D., 61, 72
Flip Flop Girl, 61, 72
Follow the Dream: The Story of Christopher Columbus, 88, 124
Follow the drinking gourd, 124
Forgetful Wishing Well: Poems for Young Children, The, 92, 122
Fortune-Tellers, The, 61, 72
Fox, M., 61, 72, 122
Freedman, R., 81, 84, 122
Frick, H. A., 210
Fritz, J., 89, 91, 122, 167, 184, 260, 278–279, 307
Frog and Toad Are Friends, 165, 184, 374, 412
Fuhler, C. J., 119
Funk, G. D., 186, 190, 199, 210
Funk, H. D., 186, 190, 199, 210

G

Galda, L., 95
Gallas, K., 186, 210
Gammage Cup, The, 86, 122
Garman, D., 190, 210
Garth Pig Steals the Show, 77
George, C., 87
George, J. C., 122
George, W. T., 85, 122
Gibbons, G., 61, 72
Girl from Yamhill, a Memoir, A, 89, 121

Giver, The, 61, 72, 86, 123
Gluskabe and the Four Wishes, 167, 184
Goble, P., 69
Goss, B., 186, 198, 210
Grandfather's Journey, 61, 72
Graves, D., 186, 210
Great American Gold Rush, The, 90, 121
Great Fire, The, 412
Great Kapok Tree, The, 61, 72, 86, 121
Great Trash Bash, The, 165, 184
Green, N., 122
Greenfield, E., 260, 307

H

Hamilton, V., 88, 122
Hancock, M. R., 118
Hans Christian Andersen: His Classic Fairy Tales, 167, 184
Harrison, M., 261
Hatchet, 80, 81, 87, 123
Headless Horseman Rides Tonight, The, 163, 184
Heller, R., 318, 325
Henkes, K., 122, 364, 412
Here is the tropical rainforest, 122
Hesse, K., 122
Hickory, Dickory, Dock, 162
Hill, E., 68
Historical fiction, 88
Hoberman, M. A., 57, 83, 122
Hoffman, M., 122
Hokey Pokey, 139
Hole in the Dike, The, 122
Holman, F., 122
Homesick, 260, 307
Homesick: My Own Story, 89, 122
Hooks, W. H., 334
Hoops, 123
Hopkins, L. B., 261
House Is a House for Me, A, 57, 83, 122
House that Jack Built, The, 85
How Many Spots Does a Leopard Have? And Other Tales, 123
Huang, T., 261
Huck, C., 85–86, 122, 165, 184, 334
Hughes, L., 261
Hughes, T., 86, 122

I

If I Were in Charge of the World and Other Worries: Poems for Children and Their Parents, 91, 124, 163, 184, 262
If You Give A Moose A Muffin, 167, 184
If You Listen, 191
If You Were a Writer, 253, 307
Iktomi and the Boulder, 69
I'm Going to Pet a Worm Today and Other Poems, 92, 123, 261
Indian in the Cupboard, The, 86, 121
In for Winter, Out for Spring, 261
In the Eyes of the Cat: Japanese Poetry for All Seasons, 261
In the Small, Small Pond, 61, 72
Ira Sleeps Over, 79, 124
Iron Giant, The, 86, 122
Ironsmith, M., 187, 210
Is This a House for Hermit Crab?, 254
I Would Rather Be a Turnip, 86, 122

J

Jack and the Beanstalk, 165, 167, 184
Jackson, E., 122, 165, 184
Jackson, J., 85
Jacob, W. J., 364, 412
Jacobs, L. B., 186, 210
Jacobs, W. J., 81, 122
Janiak, R., 203, 210
Jesse Bear, What Will You Wear?, 81, 121
John Henry, 167
Johnny Appleseed, 16, 167, 169
Johnston, T., 69
Joyful Noise: Poems for Two Voices, 93, 122
Julius, Baby of the World, 364, 412
Jumanji, 86, 124

K

Kellogg, S., 16, 122, 165, 169, 184, 253, 307
Kendall, C., 86, 122
Kennedy, X. J., 92, 122

King of Prussia and a Peanut Butter Sandwich, The, 208
Kirk, D., 122
Kites Sail High: A Book about Verbs, 318, 325
Koala Lou, 61, 72
Konigsburg, E. L., 114
Kraus, R., 74, 122

L

Langer, J. A., 118
Last Dinosaur, The, 374, 412
Lauber, P., 89, 122
Leedy, L., 165, 184
Legend of the Indian Paintbrush, The, 82, 86, 122
Leo the Late Bloomer, 74, 122
Leslie, C. W., 89, 123
Lester, H., 61, 72
Lester, J., 123
Let's Go on a Bear Hunt, 139
Letters from Rifka, 122
Leverentz, F., 190, 210
Levinson, R., 87, 123
Levy, C., 92, 123, 261
Lewis, C. S., 86, 123
Lewis, J. P., 93, 123
Light in the Attic, A, 163, 184, 261, 307
Lincoln: A Photobiography, 84, 122
Lion and the Mouse, The, 86
Lionni, L., 60
Lion, the Witch, and the Wardrobe, The, 86, 123
Little, L. J., 260, 307
Little Bear, 175, 184
Little House, 47
Little House on the Prairie, 75
Little Mouse, the Red Ripe Strawberry, and the Big Hungry Bear, The, 85, 124
Little Red Riding Hood, 85
Livingston, M. C., 93, 123
Lobel, A., 165, 184, 374, 412
Lon Po Po, 82, 124
London, L., 364, 412
Lowell, S., 77
Lowry, L., 61, 72, 86, 123, 165, 184
Lunch Money, 262
Lundsteen, S. W., 187, 211
Lupita mañana, 121
Lyon, G. E., 123

M

M&M's Counting Book, The, 90, 123
Macaulay, D., 85, 123
MacLachlan, P., 47, 72, 421, 424
Maestro, B. C., 84, 123
Mandlebaum, L. H., 210
Manes, M., 58
Manes, S., 72
Maniac Magee, 61, 72, 87, 124
Martin, A. M., 69
Martin, B., 334
Martin, B., Jr., 74, 82, 123, 162, 184
Math Curse, 82, 123
Mayer, M., 84, 123, 193-194
McCloskey, R., 170
McCully, E. A., 123
McDonald, M., 254
McGrath, B. B., 90, 123
McKissack, P., 82, 123
McMahon, M., 204, 211
McPhail, D., 77
Meltzer, M., 123
Merriam, E., 261
Merry-Go-Round: A Book about Nouns, 318, 325
Midwife's Apprentice, The, 31, 41, 114
Mike Fink, 167
Minarik, E. H., 175, 184
Mirandy and Brother Wind, 82, 123
Mirette on the high wire, 123
Missing May, 80, 123
Miss Spider's Tea Party, 85, 122
Mitchell, M. K., 364, 412
Mitten: A Ukranian Folktale, The, 82, 121
Molly Pitcher, 167
Monday's Troll, 307
Morimoto, J., 84, 123
Morrison, L., 262
Moss, B., 210, 211
Moss Gown, 334
Most Beautiful Place in the World, The, 87, 121
Mother Goose Rhymes, 162
Mother Teresa: Helping the Poor, 81, 122
Moves Make the Man, The, 121
Mr. Blue Jeans: A story about Levi Straus, 39
Munsch, R., 165

Munsch, R. N., 184
Murphy, J., 90, 123, 365, 374, 412
Myers, W. D., 90, 123
My Favorite Time of Year, 260, 307
My Hiroshima, 84, 123
My Side of the Mountain, 87, 122

N

Nature All Year Long, 89, 123
Naylor, P. R., 87, 123
Nelson, V. M., 87, 123
Nettie's Trip South, 275
New Kid on the Block, The, 91, 123, 261, 307
Nightmare in My Closet, There's a, 193–194
Night Swimmers, The, 86, 121
Nixon, J. L., 253, 307
Now is Your Time!: The African-American Struggle for Freedom, 90, 123
Number the Stars, 123, 165, 184
Numeroff, L., 167, 184

O

Oaf, 68
O'Dell, S., 68, 123, 165, 184
Off the Map: The Journals of Lewis and Clark, 91
Osband, G., 89, 114, 123
Our Home Is the Sea, 87, 123
Outside Inside Poems, 92, 121
Owen, 122
Owl Moon, 61, 72

P

Paley, V. G., 190, 211
Paper Bag Princess, The, 165, 184
Parish, P., 16
Paterson, K., 61, 72, 123
Patterson, C. J., 187, 210
Paul Bunyan, 167
Paulsen, D., 118
Paulsen, G., 12, 20, 80, 81, 87, 123
Pearson, P. D., 201, 211
Pearson, S., 260, 307
Peck, R. N., 123
Peter Rabbit, 68
Pete's Chicken, 85, 124
Pfister, M., 69
Pig in the Pond, The, 77
Pigs Aplenty, Pigs Galore!, 77
Pigsty, 77
Pilkey, D., 123

Pink and Say, 61–62, 72
Pinkney, G., 88, 123
Poems of A. Nonny Mouse, 91, 123
Polacco, P., 61, 72
Polar Bear, Polar Bear, What Do You Hear?, 334
Polar Express, The, 86, 124, 170
Potter, B., 72
Prairie Songs, 122
Pratt, M. W., 199, 211
Prelutsky, J., 91, 93, 123, 163, 184, 261, 262, 307
Princess and the Pea, The, 85, 167
Princess Furball, 85–86, 122, 165, 184, 334
Principal from the Black Lagoon, The, 31, 42
Proud taste for Scarlet and Miniver, 114
Pumpkin, Pumpkin, 162, 184

Q

Quacky, Quack-Quack!, 81, 124

R

Rainbow Fish, The, 69
Rainbow People, The, 86, 124
Rain Player, 85, 124
Ramona the Pest, 86, 121
Ramsay Scallop, The, 114
Random House Book of Poetry for Children, The, 262
Raschka, C., 162, 184
Raynor, M., 77
Reading, 202
Real McCoy: The Life of an African-American Inventor, The, 89, 124
Riddle of the Drum: A Tale from Tizapán, Mexico, The, 167, 184
River Rats, Inc., 87, 122
R, my name is Rosie, 68
Rodriguez, A., 39
Roop, C., 91
Roop, P., 91
Rylant, C., 76, 80, 123

S

Sanders, S. R., 123
San Souci, R., 82, 123
San Souci, R. D., 170
Sarah Bishop, 123, 165, 184

Sarah Morton's Day: A Day in the Life of a Pilgrim Girl, 88, 124
Sarah, Plain and Tall, 47, 72, 421, 424
Say, A., 61, 72
Schneider, R. M., 319, 326
Schwartz, D. M., 417, 424
Scieszka, J., 67, 77, 82, 123
Searches in the American Desert, 89–90, 122
Seeing the Earth from Space, 89, 122
Selway, M., 253, 307
Seven Blind Mice, 82, 124
Shark Beneath the Reef, 122
Shaw, N., 81, 123
Sheep in a Jeep, 81, 123
Shields, C. D., 262
Shiloh, 87, 123
Shimmershine Queen, The, 81, 124
Shoop, M., 196, 211
Sidewalk Racer and Other Poems of Sports and Motion, The, 262
Sign of the Beaver, The, 68
Silverman, E., 82, 123, 234
Silverstein, S., 60, 91, 124, 163, 184, 261, 307
Sing Down the Moon, 68
Sis, P., 88, 124
Sky Full of Poems, A, 261
Sky Songs, 93, 123
Slake's limbo, 122
Smith, L., 82
Sneve, V. D. H., 93, 124
Snopp on the Sidewalk and Other Poems, The, 91, 123
Snow Day, 84, 123
Something Big Has Been Here, 91, 123, 163, 184, 261, 307
Sounder, 56–57, 72
Speare, E. G., 68
Spinelli, J., 61, 72, 87, 124
Splinters: A Book of Very Short Poems, 261
Sports Pages, 91, 121
Spot's First Walk, 68
Starbird, K., 262
Stauffer, R., 211
Steig, W., 165, 184
Stein, N. L., 199, 211
Stevens, J., 85, 124
Stevenson, J., 262, 307

Stinky Cheese Man: And Other Fairly Stupid Tales, The, 82, 123
Stowe, H. B., 56, 72
St. Patrick's Day, 61, 72
Strega Nona, 82, 122
Strega Nona Meets Her Match, 170
Strega Nona's Magic Lessons, 165, 184
Strider, 87, 121, 256, 307
Strother, D. B., 186, 188, 211
Sukey and the Mermaid, 170
Supergrandpa, 417, 424
Surprises, 261
Sweet Corn, 262, 307
Swimmy, 60
Szilagyi, M., 47, 72

T

Tales of a Fourth Grade Nothing, 86, 121
Talking Eggs: A Folktale from the American South, The, 123
Talking Egg, The, 82
Taylor, M., 124
Taylor, T., 87, 124
Teague, M., 77
Temple, F., 114
Templeton, S., 186-187, 211
Ten Kids, No Pets, 69
Ten Sly Piranhas, 90, 124
Terrible Eek, The, 69
Tessendorf, K. C., 90, 124
Thaler, M., 31, 42
There's a Girl in My Hammerlock, 124
Thirteen Moons on Turtle's Back: A Native American Year of the Moons, 364, 412
Three Billy Goats Gruff, The, 85
Three Cheers for Tacky, 61, 72
Three Little Javelinas, The, 77
Three Little Kittens, The, 162
Three Little Wolves and the Big Bad Pig, The, 77
Thunderstorm, 47, 72
Titherington, J., 162, 184
Tops and Bottoms, 85, 124
Toucans Two and Other Poems, 163, 184
Towle, W., 89, 124

Trabasso, T., 199, 211
Trivizas, E., 77
Trolley to Yesterday, The, 114
Trouble with Tuck, The, 87, 124
True Confessions of Charlotte Doyle, The, 165, 184
True Story of the Three Little Pigs, The, 67, 77, 82, 123
Trumpet of the Swan, The, 320, 326
Tuesday, 86, 170
Turner, A., 275
'Twas the Night Before Thanksgiving, 123
Tyrannosaurus Was a Beast, 93, 123

U

Ugly Duckling, The, 167
Uncle Jed's Barbershop, 364, 412
Uncle Tom's Cabin, 56, 72
Up in the Air, 93, 123
Up, Up, & Away: A Book about Adverbs, 318, 325

V

Van Allsburg, C., 86, 124, 170
Van Leeuwen, J., 91
Very Hungry Caterpillar, The, 16, 82, 121, 166, 184, 254
Very Quiet Cricket, The, 156, 184
Viorst, J., 91, 124, 163, 184, 262

W

Waber, B., 124
Waddell, M., 77
Wagon Wheels, 180
Walton, R., 93, 124, 262, 307
Waters, K., 88, 124
Weaver, C. H., 188, 211
Wednesday Surprise, The, 121
Weidt, M. N., 39
Well, The, 124
What to Do When a Bug Climbs into Your Mouth, 93, 124, 307
When I Was Young in the Mountains, 76
Where Do You Think You're Going, Christopher Columbus?, 167, 184

Where the Lilies Bloom, 86, 122
Where the Sidewalk Ends, 60, 91, 124, 163, 184, 261, 307
White, E. B., 16, 77, 124, 184, 320, 326
Whitehurst, G. J., 187, 210
Who came down that road?, 123
Who Says a Dog Goes Bow-Wow?, 130
Whybrow, I., 81, 124
Why Mosquitoes Buzz in People's Ears, 121
Wiesner, D., 170
Wilder, L. I., 47, 75
Wilfrid Gordon McDonald Partridge, 122
William, V., 165
Williams, V. B., 184
Wilson, R., 210
Wings, 86, 124
Winning Kicker, 122
Winter, J., 124
Winter Room, The, 87, 123
Winthrop, E., 114
Wise, W., 90, 124
Wish Giver, The, 68
Wisniewski, D., 85, 124, 170
With Every Drop of Blood, 165, 184
Wood, A., 85, 124
Wood, D., 85, 124
Wright Brothers: How They Invented the Airplane, The, 81, 122
Wyshynski, R., 118

Y

Yarbrough, C., 81, 124
Yashima, T., 167, 184
Yep, L., 39, 86, 124
Yolen, J., 61, 72, 86, 124
Young Mouse and Elephant: An East African Folktale, 206
Young, E., 82, 124
Yo! Yes?, 162, 184

Z

Ziefert, H., 85, 124
Zolotow, C., 191
Zorro, 179